WILLIAM JAFFE'S
ESSAYS ON WALRAS

In this book Dr. Walker brings together Dr. William Jaffé's essays on the important and interesting work of Léon Walras, the founder of general equilibrium analysis. The essays were selected on the basis of their importance to the Walrasian literature, in that they provide information on Walras's intellectual biography with which we would otherwise be unfamiliar or they make a contribution to the interpretation and analysis of his ideas. The essays reveal the range of Jaffé's scholarship and the thoroughness of his examination of Walras's theoretical and applied economics.

One of Jaffé's main interests was to explain the genesis of Walras's work, which he did by examining Walras's biography. The biographical materials presented in the essays deal with the social and economic milieu in which Walras lived and worked, his father's influence on him, and his intellectual history. Using a wide variety of sources, Jaffé pieced together an account of these matters in the belief that biography is essential for understanding the origins and development of a scientist's work. Jaffé also dealt with many special topics in Walras's economics, including his theory of individual demand, his theory of capital formation, his theory of *tâtonnement,* and his exposition of equilibrium conditions in a system of interrelated markets. Jaffé corrected what he regarded as errors of interpretation of Walras by other writers, evaluated Walras's contributions, and indicated his significance for modern economics. The essays are informative, illuminating, and–as a result of Jaffé's scholarly and literary craftsmanship–aesthetically satisfying.

WILLIAM JAFFE'S
ESSAYS ON WALRAS

Edited by
DONALD A. WALKER
Department of Economics
Indiana University of Pennsylvania

CAMBRIDGE UNIVERSITY PRESS

Cambridge
London   New York   New Rochelle
Melbourne   Sydney

Published by the Press Syndicate of the University of Cambridge
The Pitt Building, Trumpington Street, Cambridge CB2 1RP
32 East 57th Street, New York, NY 10022, USA
296 Beaconsfield Parade, Middle Park, Melbourne 3206, Australia

First published 1983

Printed in the United States of America

Library of Congress Cataloging in Publication Data
Jaffé, William.
William Jaffé's Essays on Walras.
Includes bibliographical references and index.
1. Walras, Léon, 1834–1910 – Addresses, essays,
lectures. 2. Economists – Switzerland – Biography –
Addresses, essays, lectures. I. Walker, Donald A.
(Donald Anthony), 1934– . II. Title.
III. Title: Essays on Walras.
HB118.W34J33   1983   330'.092'4   [B]   82–22001
ISBN 0 521 25142 7

To William and Pippin Jaffé

CONTENTS

Preface   *page ix*
Acknowledgments   *xiii*

Introduction   1

PART I. WALRAS'S BIOGRAPHY

1 Unpublished papers and letters of Léon Walras (1935)   17
2 Léon Walras, an economic adviser *manqué* (1975)   36

PART II. THE GENESIS AND DEVELOPMENT OF WALRAS'S IDEAS

3 A. N. Isnard, progenitor of the Walrasian general
   equilibrium model (1969)   55
4 The birth of Léon Walras's *Eléments* (1977)   78
5 A centenarian on a bicentenarian: Léon Walras's *Eléments*
   on Adam Smith's *Wealth of Nations* (1977)   93
6 Léon Walras and his relations with American economists
   (1960)   108

PART III. THE SCOPE OF WALRAS'S WORK

7 Léon Walras and his conception of economics (1956)   121
8 Léon Walras (1968)   131

PART IV. SPECIAL TOPICS IN WALRAS'S ECONOMICS

9 Léon Walras' theory of capital accumulation (1942)   139
10 Walras's theory of capital formation in the framework of his
   theory of general equilibrium (1953)   151
11 New light on an old quarrel: Barone's unpublished review
   of Wicksteed's "Essay on the coordination of the laws of
   distribution" and related documents (1964)   176
12 The Walras-Poincaré correspondence on the cardinal
   measurability of utility (1977)   213
13 Walras' theory of *tâtonnement:* a critique of recent
   interpretations (1967)   221
14 Another look at Léon Walras's theory of *tâtonnement* (1981)   244

PART V. WALRAS'S PLACE IN THE HISTORY OF ECONOMIC THOUGHT

15   Reflections on the importance of Léon Walras (1971)   269
16   Léon Walras's role in the "marginal revolution" of the
      1870s (1972)   288
17   Menger, Jevons and Walras de-homogenized (1976)   311
18   The normative bias of the Walrasian model: Walras versus
      Gossen (1977)   326
19   Walras's economics as others see it (1980)   343

Index   *371*

PREFACE

In July of 1979, I wrote to Professor Jaffé, whom I had known for many years, and suggested to him that the time had come for him to put together a collection of his essays on Walras. My reasoning was based on several considerations. There is, and will continue to be, a deep interest in Walras's work; Jaffé was the foremost authority on that work; and there consequently has been, and will continue to be, a deep interest in Jaffé's essays. The essays are individually of great value, displaying soundness of scholarship, perceptiveness of interpretation, wisdom in evaluation, and scrupulousness in bibliographical accuracy; and, taken as a collection, they form a well-rounded body of Walrasiana. Some of them were published in sources that are not easily accessible, three of them (Chapters 6, 7, and 10 in this book) were written in French, and one of them (Chapter 11) consists largely of quotations in French.

Jaffé responded to my letter by confessing that he had had the same thought and that he was gratified that my suggestion encouraged him in the belief that he was not merely becoming subject to "senile megalomania" in contemplating such a collection. He went further, and asked me if I would undertake the task of editing the volume. I responded that I would be honored to do so. Jaffé became ill shortly after I began the project, and when he died I temporarily abandoned it. I did not abandon my friend, however, for during the subsequent year I reflected and wrote extensively on his life and work.[1] Nor did I forget the project that Jaffé and I had conceived together, and on which we had already expended a considerable amount of thought and energy. Therefore, as soon as the status of his estate had been clarified and I was empowered as his literary executor, I determined that I would complete the work of putting together the volume of collected essays.

My objective was to accomplish six tasks. First, I decided which publications should be presented in the volume. The criterion for inclusion was that the publication must be important in the literature of Walrasian scholarship, either because it informs us of details of Walras's intellectual biography with which we would otherwise be unfamiliar or because of its interpretive and analytical value. In truth, the business of

[1] See the references listed in the Introduction and also Donald A. Walker, "William Jaffé, Historian of Economic Thought, 1898–1980," *American Economic Review, 71,* December 1981, 1012–19.

selecting materials for inclusion was easy, because all of Jaffé's essays on Walras satisfied one or the other of the foregoing criteria, and the minor pieces, such as reviews, notes, and transcriptions of comments at conferences, automatically excluded themselves. The result is that this volume is a comprehensive collection of Jaffé's essays on Walras.[2] Second, I put the essays into various groups in order to bring out their significance as contributions to various topics in the study of Walras. The groups reveal the range of Jaffé's scholarship on Walras's work, including as they do an examination of all its major aspects; the essays within any group show how thoroughly Jaffé covered each aspect. Third, I undertook some purely editorial tasks. I did not find it necessary or desirable to litter the essays – essays that are well-proportioned and intellectually and aesthetically complete – with comments of my own. Jaffé was a master at explaining himself, at cross-referencing his own publications, and at citing the work of others that was relevant to his interests, and his essays do not need my assistance in those regards. I did, however, eliminate many of their repetitions, a procedure that carries out Jaffé's wishes. I also made many small changes in such respects as the style of presentation of references and the placement of quotation marks. Fourth, I translated the three articles that Jaffé wrote in French. I owe to the promptings of Dr. Colin Day, editorial director of the American branch of the Cambridge University Press, the fortunate circumstance that I translated those articles while Jaffé was alive, and that I was therefore able to obtain his advice on the translations and his approval of the versions that appear in the present volume. In the case of "Walras's Theory of Capital Formation in the Framework of His Theory of General Equilibrium" (Chapter 10), the translation is especially interesting in that it incorporates corrections of the extensive typographical errors in the equations and text of the original French article, corrections made by Jaffé in an offprint of the article that he gave to me. Fifth, I translated the French quotations that constitute almost three-quarters of Jaffé's original version of "New Light on an Old Quarrel" (Chapter 11), in the certainty that my professional colleagues will find the material of deep interest. Sixth, I tried in the Introduction to provide a guide to the reader of the essays, striving to give an overview of the scope of Jaffé's writings, to explain the issues that were of concern to him, and to show the contributions of individual essays to the part of Walras's work with which they deal.

[2] An essay that has not been included is the one that I entitled "The Antecedents and Early Life of Léon Walras" which will be published in *History of Political Economy, 16*, Spring 1984. I prepared that essay from the drafts and notes written by Jaffé as the basis for a projected biography of Walras, which was to have been entitled *The Life and Writings of Léon Walras*. I decided not to include the essay because it does not deal with Léon Walras, but with his family history and with the writings of his father, Auguste Walras,

I want to thank Dr. Day for his initial receptiveness to the idea of this project and for his subsequent editorial advice and assistance. I am also grateful to the Social Sciences and Humanities Research Council of Canada for a grant that supported the preparation of this volume and that made possible my trips to Jaffé's home to discuss the project with him and subsequently to locate his notes and offprints of several of his articles. I deeply appreciate the help in obtaining the grant that was given by Dr. Graeme McKechnie of the Department of Economics at York University. Finally, I want to express my gratitude to my friend Pippin Jaffé, whose home has always been open to me.

DONALD A. WALKER
Indiana, Pennsylvania
January 1983

ACKNOWLEDGMENTS

The editor and the Cambridge University Press wish to thank the publishers of the following essays for permission to reprint them in this volume.

Chapter 1. "Unpublished Papers and Letters of Léon Walras," *Journal of Political Economy*, *43*, April 1935, 187–207. Reprinted by permission of The University of Chicago Press. Copyright 1935 by The : University of Chicago.

Chapter 3. "A. N. Isnard, Progenitor of the Walrasian General Equilibrium Model," *History of Political Economy*, *1*, Spring 1969, 19–43. Reprinted by permission of Duke University Press. Copyright 1969, Duke University Press (Durham, N.C.).

Chapter 4. "The Birth of Léon Walras's *Eléments*," *History of Political Economy*, *9*, Summer 1977, 198–214. Reprinted by permission of Duke University Press. Copyright 1977, Duke University Press (Durham, N.C.).

Chapter 5. "A Centenarian on a Bicentenarian: Léon Walras's *Eléments* on Adam Smith's *Wealth of Nations*," *Canadian Journal of Economics*, *10*, February 1977, 19–33. Reprinted by permission of the *Canadian Journal of Economics* and The Canadian Economics Association.

Chapter 6. "Léon Walras et ses rapports avec les économistes américains," *Revue économique et sociale*, *18*, April 1960, 133–40. Reprinted by permission of the Société d'Etudes Economiques et Sociales, Lausanne, Switzerland.

Chapter 7. "Léon Walras et sa conception de l'économie politique," *Annales juridiques, politiques, économiques et sociales*, la Faculté de Droit d'Alger, Librairie Ferraris, 1956, 207–21. Slightly abridged.

Chapter 8. "Léon Walras." Reprinted with permission of the publisher from the *International Encyclopedia of the Social Sciences*, edited by David L. Sills. New York, Macmillan Co. and The Free Press, vol. 16, pp. 447–53. Copyright 1968 by Crowell Collier and Macmillan, Inc. Abridged by permission of the copyright holders.

Chapter 9. "Léon Walras' Theory of Capital Accumulation," in *Studies in Mathematical Economics and Econometrics*, edited by Oscar Lange et al. Chicago, University of Chicago Press, 1942, pp. 37–48. Reprinted by permission of The University of Chicago Press. Copyright 1942 by The University of Chicago.

Chapter 10. "La théorie de la capitalisation chez Walras dans le cadre de sa théorie de l'équilibre général," *Economie appliquée, 6,* April-September 1953, 289–317. Reprinted by permission of the Institut de Sciences Mathématiques et Economiques Appliquées, 11 rue Pierre et Marie Curie, 75005 Paris, France.

Chapter 11. "New Light on an Old Quarrel. Barone's Unpublished Review of Wicksteed's 'Essay on the Coordination of the Laws of Distribution' and Related Documents," *Cahiers Vilfredo Pareto, 3,* 1964, 61–102. Reprinted by permission of Librairie Droz, S.A., Geneva.

Chapter 12. "The Walras-Poincaré Correspondence on the Cardinal Measurability of Utility." *Canadian Journal of Economics, 10,* May 1977, 300–7. Reprinted by permission of the *Canadian Journal of Economics* and The Canadian Economics Association.

Chapter 13. "Walras' Theory of *Tâtonnement:* A Critique of Recent Interpretations," *Journal of Political Economy, 75,* February 1967, 1–19. Reprinted by permission of The University of Chicago Press. Copyright 1967 by The University of Chicago.

Chapter 14. "Another Look at Léon Walras's Theory of *Tâtonnement,*" *History of Political Economy, 13,* Summer 1981, 313–36. Reprinted by permission of Duke University Press. Copyright 1981, Duke University Press (Durham, N.C.).

Chapter 15. "Reflections on the Importance of Léon Walras," in P. Hennipman Festschrift, *Schaarste en Welvaart,* edited by A. Heertje et al., Amsterdam, Stenfert Kroese, 1971, pp. 87–107. Reprinted by permission of H. E. Stenfert Kroese, B.V. Slightly abridged by permission.

Chapter 16. "Léon Walras's Role in the 'Marginal Revolution' of the 1870s," *History of Political Economy, 4,* Fall 1972, 379–405. Reprinted by permission of Duke University Press. Copyright 1972, Duke University Press (Durham, N.C.).

Chapter 17. "Menger, Jevons and Walras De-homogenized," *Economic Inquiry, 14,* December 1976, 511–24. Reprinted by permission of the Western Economic Association.

Chapter 18. "The Normative Bias of the Walrasian Model: Walras versus Gossen," *Quarterly Journal of Economics, 91,* August 1977, 371–87. Copyright 1977 by the President and Fellows of Harvard College. Reprinted by permission of John Wiley and Sons, Inc.

Chapter 19. "Walras's Economics as Others See It," *Journal of Economic Literature, 18,* June 1980, 528–49. Reprinted by permission of the American Economic Association.

INTRODUCTION

At the time that Jaffé started his career, Walras's work was familiar on a somewhat superficial level to Swedish and Italian economists, either directly or through the work of Wicksell, Cassel, Pareto, and Barone, but most European economists did not study his contributions to economics, and even the French neglected him. For example, in the authoritative survey of the history of economic thought by Charles Gide and Charles Rist published in France in successive editions from 1909 to 1947, there is no chapter on Walras, despite the fact that both authors knew him personally.[1] He is mentioned occasionally in the book, primarily in footnotes, and a few of his theoretical ideas are surveyed briefly, but there is no real exposition or analysis of his economic theories. In the early 1920s, when Jaffé was studying for his doctorate in economics at the University of Paris, he never heard Walras's name mentioned in his classes. Similarly, outside the Continent, Walras was almost totally ignored. To the majority of English-speaking economists, he was not only unknown but – because his work was in French and because he emphasized the mathematical method – unknowable. Insofar as his general equilibrium approach began to be incorporated into British and American economics, it was not the result of direct reference to his work by most economists, but a consequence of a study of the Walrasian economics of such writers as H. L. Moore, Irving Fisher, Henry Schultz, and J. R. Hicks.

It was Jaffé who changed this situation. He translated Walras's principal work in economics, the *Eléments d'économie politique pure*,[2] thus making Walras's theoretical ideas accessible to the English-speaking reader. He edited Walras's professional correspondence, furnishing a sourcebook on the evolution of Walras's ideas and on their relation to the development of neoclassical economics generally.[3] Jaffé also examined,

---

[1] Charles Gide and Charles Rist, *Histoire des doctrines économiques depuis les physiocrates jusqu'à nos jours*, Larose and Tenin, Paris, 1909; Charles Gide and Charles Rist, *A History of Economic Doctrines*, 2d English ed., Heath, New York, n.d. (probably 1948), 503–5.
[2] Léon Walras, *Elements of Pure Economics*, trans. William Jaffé, Irwin, Homewood, Ill., 1954.
[3] William Jaffé, ed., *Correspondence of Léon Walras and Related Papers*, North-Holland, Amsterdam, 1965.

interpreted, and evaluated Walras's work in the essays presented in this volume. Written over the years from 1934 to 1980, the essays are Jaffé's original contribution to Walrasian scholarship, for they are his own writings on Walras, as distinct from his efforts as editor or translator.

The first group of essays reflects Jaffé's belief that biography is important for the study of the history of economic thought.[4] "The view I take of my subject, which is the history of a branch of intellectual discourse known as economics," he wrote in 1979,

is that it is an account of successive achievements by individuals, each endowed with an individuality of his own. To fully understand the import of the contributions of distinctive individuals, it does not suffice to assess each new theoretical construct as if it were a product of a disembodied spirit. The great innovations that have effectively given a new direction to the way in which we see the world around us are always to some extent expressions and reflections of the personal traits and the private experiences of their respective innovators.[5]

When Jaffé referred to a writer's traits and experiences, he did not mean such matters as the details of the writer's domestic life, but his intellectual characteristics and experiences, including his perception of the social and economic conditions and problems of his time. These, Jaffé maintained, are the elements of biography that affect a writer's selection of theoretical problems and his method of handling them.

There were three major respects in which Jaffé thought that biography is valuable for the history of science. First, he adopted the controversial position that knowledge of the intellectual characteristics of a scientist is necessary to understand the meaning of his work.[6] He also believed, with good reason, that biography helps to explain the genesis of ideas. "The genesis of an 'original' analytical contribution is idiosyncratic and . . . this genesis cannot be adequately understood without reference to the peculiarities of mind of the originator of the novelty. . . . Such is the justification of my call to historians of economics, as to historians of any other science, to study in detail and in depth, wherever the materials permit, the process of scientific creation which is *au fond* a process of poetic imagination."[7] To achieve an understanding of the

---

[4] For a full account of Jaffé's views on biography and on the study of the history of economic thought see my papers "Biography and the Study of the History of Economic Thought" and "William Jaffé, *Officier de liaison intellectuel,*" in *The Craft of the Historian of Economic Thought,* vol. 1 of *Research in the History of Economic Thought and Methodology,* ed. Warren J. Samuels, published for the History of Economics Society, JAI Press, Greenwich, Conn., forthcoming.

[5] William Jaffé, "Requested Self-Presentation as Newly Inducted Fellow of the Royal Society of Canada," in Royal Society of Canada, *Newsletter, 2,* Sept. 1979, 14–15.

[6] William Jaffé, "Biography and Economic Analysis," *Western Economic Journal, 3,* Summer 1965, 223–32.

[7] William Jaffé, "Notes on George Stigler's Paper, 'The Scientific Uses of Scientific Biography, with Special Reference to J. S. Mill,' " unpub. ms., May 24, 1973, pp. 3–4.

genesis of economic ideas was one of Jaffé's principal objectives. Finally, without refuting the contention that a writer's biography has little or no relation to the interpretation or evaluation of his ideas by his contemporaries, Jaffé maintained that biography illuminates the process of acceptance of a theory.[8]

Jaffé put his ideas on the importance of biography into practice, beginning with the task of establishing the facts of Walras's personal and professional life, as is shown by the first group of essays (Chapters 1 and 2 in this book, and passim in Jaffé's essays). Relying on the vast correspondence between Walras and his relatives, friends, and fellow economists, as well as on information obtained directly from his daughter, from official archives, and from his autobiography, Jaffé traced Walras's activities as a young man in France. During this period, bearded and with long hair, Walras wrote romantic novels, and then became successively a journalist and a director of a credit union. Patiently and meticulously, Jaffé pieced together the story of Walras's growing interest in economics, his unsuccessful attempts to get an academic appointment in France, his success in that regard in Switzerland, his efforts to serve as an adviser to government on various economic issues, and his life in Lausanne.

In a second group of essays (Chapters 3, 4, 5 and 6) Jaffé applied to the case of Walras his view that biography helps to explain the genesis of ideas, investigating the relation of Walras's intellectual experience and social and economic environment to the origins and development of his work. Walras was greatly stimulated and influenced, Jaffé discovered, by the form and method of analysis used by Louis Poinsot in his *Eléments de statique,* in which appears a general theory of the equilibrium and movement of systems with reference to the physical universe, showing the mutual dependency of its parts. Another important influence was Antoine Augustin Cournot, from whom Walras learned that calculus could be applied to the analysis of economic phenomena. According to Jaffé, however, the most important progenitor of Walras's specific economic theories was Achylle-Nicholas Isnard. In his *Traité de richesses,* published in 1781, Isnard developed a theory of exchange, a theory of production, and the technique of using a *numéraire* commodity, each of which, Jaffé maintained, served as a starting point and model for Walras's work. Samuel von Pufendorf, Grotius, and Walras's father were the progenitors of Léon Walras's philosophical views, imbuing him with a conviction of the reality of natural law and the desirability of

[8] William Jaffé, "Biography, A Genetic Ingredient of Economic Analysis. Answer to a Challenge," mimeo., delivered at the Allied Social Science Association meetings under the joint auspices of the American Economic Association and the History of Economics Society, San Francisco, December 30, 1974, p. 29.

adhering to it. Similarly, Descartes and Newton contributed to Walras's methodological and scientific outlook, and left their mark upon the particular form in which he conceived of economic behavior and in which he chose to express it. Continuing to investigate the genesis of Walras's ideas, Jaffé examined the birth of the *Eléments* in an essay devoted to that specific subject (Chapter 4). Relying principally upon Walras's letters and papers, Jaffé explored the circumstances surrounding the writing of the book, and traced the influences – such as the comments of J. L. F. Bertrand, Ladislaus von Bortkiewicz, and Eugene von Böhm-Bawerk - that led to its modification in the last four editions.

The relation of other economists to Walras's intellectual biography was revealed by Jaffé in two major essays (Chapters 1, 6). Jaffé's investigation of this matter has two dimensions. There is the lighter side of the sociology of neoclassical economics – the personalities of the leading players, their clashes of will and temperament, their striving for recognition of priority in an exciting period of discovery, their use of positions of power and prestige in the profession, and their occasional pettiness, including notably Walras's. On the other hand, there is the story of scientific progress made through the refinement of their ideas in their correspondence. Jaffé's essays explore the scrutiny by first-class minds of many of the important problems of neoclassical economics, such as the theory of demand, the dynamic processes by which markets move to equilibrium, the theory of production, and the theory of capital. The materials for the study of these matters are extensive, because Walras's desire to persuade others to accept his ideas led him to engage in a vast correspondence for a period of over 40 years with such scholars as Cournot, Jevons, Edgeworth, Marshall, Menger, Pareto, and Barone. In the case of the Italians especially, Walras and his correspondents developed their ideas and reached agreement on a number of issues. Americans, including Irving Fisher, H. L. Moore, Francis Walker, and J. L. Laughlin, were also among his correspondents and the recipients of copies of his articles and books. Walras's relationships with the English began badly, with the shock of recognition that Jevons had preceded him in the investigation of marginal utility and the equation of exchange, and subsequently did not improve. In the course of correspondence with Edgeworth over the role of the entrepreneur and the theory of capital, Walras came to feel that Edgeworth, whom he called a past master of mathematical charlatanism, was obtusely unwilling to try to understand him. The relationship deteriorated further when Walras became convinced that the English economists were so insular and egotistical that they would not give fair consideration to his ideas, and then disintegrated when he decided that Marshall was refusing to recognize his priority of discovery in certain areas and that Wicksteed and Jevons had plagiarized his work.

A third subject that engaged Jaffé's attention was the general form and content of Walras's work, which he surveyed and reflected upon with the objective of providing a framework within which its particular parts can be fitted into place and interpreted in the light of their relation to Walras's whole system of ideas. Jaffé showed (Chapter 7) that Walras divided his work into three parts in accordance with the philosophical position that it is important to identify what is *true* – which led him to contribute to economic theory; what is *useful* – which stimulated him to investigate problems in applied economics; and what is *just* – which motivated his concern with "social economics." Walras's economic theory, contained primarily in the *Eléments*, was principally an analysis of the equilibrium of a multimarket economic system, using the assumptions of pure competition and static certainty. His applied economics, to which he devoted his attention in the articles collected in the *Etudes d'économie politique appliquée*,[9] was concerned with the development of policies based upon theory, on the assumption that the goals are given. His social economics, exemplified by the essays in his *Etudes d'économie sociale*,[10] was a normative branch of study, dealing with the formation of desirable goals. Going beyond the scope of modern welfare economics, Walras's social economics did not merely work out the welfare consequences of trying to achieve different objectives but also evaluated the objectives themselves and formulated new goals. In this connection, as Jaffé pointed out, Walras produced many special studies, treating subjects such as communism, individualism, socialism, liberalism, and utilitarianism. Most notably, Walras formulated the view that the state should nationalize all land and lease it to private parties, financing itself exclusively through those means rather than through taxation, which he regarded as unjust. So convinced was Walras of the value of this proposal that in his old age he suggested that it made him a worthy candidate for a Nobel Prize.

The fourth group of essays consists of Jaffé's work on various special topics in Walrasian theory: the demand for consumption goods, the theory of marginal productivity, the theory of capital formation, and the theory of *tâtonnement*. The importance of Walras's treatment of demand, both within his system of ideas and for economic science generally, was emphasized by Jaffé in several essays which also deal with other topics (Chapters 4, 16, 17). Rather than being relegated to a single chapter of the *Eléments*, the theory of demand occurs again and again throughout

[9] Léon Walras, *Etudes d'économie politique appliquée*, F. Rouge, Lausanne, 1898.
[10] Léon Walras, *Etudes d'économie sociale*, F. Rouge, Lausanne, 1896.

Walras's various models, because he used it primarily to examine the conditions of equilibrium of economic participants, rather than to deal with various alternative subjective conditions of a consumer or with the properties of consumer demand functions. Consequently, the conditions established in his theory of demand are an integral part of the theories of exchange, of production and consumption, of capital formation, and of money.

Jaffé also explored the question of who deserves credit for the derivation of the demand function from preferences, income, and price conditions. Some years ago I argued that credit for the derivation, although not for the initial formulation of the problem, should go to Antoine Paul Piccard, who solved the problem at Walras's request in 1872.[11] I think that Jaffé was somewhat nettled by the suggestion that Walras should be deprived of his right of priority, and he initially developed a contrary position (Chapter 16). After further consideration, however, in two other articles that dealt with Walras's theory of demand (Chapters 4, 17), Jaffé came to accept the account that I had originally urged, for the reason that the letter which Piccard wrote to Walras containing the derivation of the demand function is an incontrovertible fact.[12]

Was that derivation methodologically and mathematically acceptable? This was a question that troubled Walras intermittently until, as Jaffé showed (Chapter 12), his correspondence in 1901 with Henri Poincaré settled the matter. Walras had been attacked many times by scholars of a literary persuasion for his use of mathematics in connection with economics in general and with demand theory in particular. They had variously argued that economics is an ethical discipline which has no room for quantitative relationships, that the data of economics are too complex to be handled in mathematical formulas, and that mathematics cannot correctly represent human behavior because it cannot grasp the intangible qualities of motivation. What perturbed Walras in 1901, however, was that he was charged with having undertaken a methodologically indefensible procedure by a professional mathematician, someone who, Walras felt, should have known better. Walras turned to Poincaré as the final judge, asking whether it is legitimate to use mathematics to derive a demand function from a utility function. The result, Jaffé revealed, was an extremely interesting exchange of letters in which Poincaré reassured Walras and discoursed knowledgeably upon methodologically appropriate procedures for deriving demand functions.

---

[11] Donald A. Walker, "Léon Walras in the Light of His Correspondence and Related Papers," *Journal of Political Economy*, *78*, July–Aug. 1970, 685–701.
[12] Jaffé, *Correspondence of Léon Walras*, vol. 1, pp. 308–11.

Walras's theory of marginal productivity was the topic of a special study undertaken by Jaffé (Chapter 11) in which he performed the remarkable feat of disentangling the origins of the mathematical treatment of marginal productivity theory. Those origins had been the subject of much controversy, with claims and counterclaims as to rights of priority having been made by the English, the Italians, and by followers of Walras on his behalf. Jaffé's essay, drawing as it does upon a wide range of materials written at different times by different individuals, is a masterpiece of historical research, illuminated by the qualities of precision, attention to detail, and understanding of the economic issues involved that distinguish his work. Had it not been for Jaffé's patient research into the rich store of papers and correspondence of Walras that he found at the University of Lausanne, and had it not been for the existence among them of a translation by Walras of Barone's review of Wicksteed's *An Essay on the Coordination of the Laws of Distribution,* the origins of the mathematical theory of marginal productivity might never have been uncovered. Jaffé demonstrated that Walras independently verged upon the completion of a marginal productivity theory, and that he would have had the answer in 1877 had he been able to understand the mathematical formulation provided to him in that year by Hermann Amstein, seventeen years before Wicksteed's book, and long before any work on the matter by Pareto and Barone. Jaffé established the contributions made by Pareto and Barone to the development of Walras's ideas, and revealed that Barone deserves the major part of the credit for the first mathematical formulation of the theory of marginal productivity. Both Barone and Pareto, however, acknowledged Walras as the principal source of their inspiration on the topic.

A third special topic that Jaffé treated was Walras's theory of capital formation. By reason of its complexity, obscurity, and multiplicity of revisions, this subject exercised all Jaffé's exegetical and analytical skills. In Jaffé's first article on the topic (Chapter 9), he started with an exposition of the equation system that Walras used to demonstrate the conditions of equilibrium in production, which was the beginning point for his theory of capital formation. Jaffé then went on to discuss Walras's explanation of why capital accumulation occurs, and to show how he introduced saving and investment. Jaffé granted that Walras's theory explains the pricing of existing capital goods, but argued that Walras faced an impossible task in trying to treat the accumulation of new capital goods within a static framework. His attempt led, Jaffé believed, to incompleteness and hence indeterminacy in the theory.

Walras was dissatisfied with his theory of capital and consequently revised it periodically, and Jaffé, in turn, was dissatisfied for many years with his interpretation of it, and revised it several times. Jaffé's second study of the topic was a long and careful treatment of the theory of capital formation within the framework of Walras's general equilibrium theory (Chapter 10). In this essay, Jaffé no longer referred to capital accumulation, but rather to capital formation, a difference in emphasis that was to lead to a fundamental reevaluation of Walras's theory. Jaffé's main objective in the essay, however, was to show the way that the theory fitted into the succession of models that Walras constructed, that is, the succession which began with the theory of exchange, then took up production and consumption, and then, as a third stage, considered the question of capital formation. Jaffé related the theory to the general equilibrium framework that Walras developed and showed that Walras believed that the real market system solves his equations of capital formation and credit and thus tends to move into general equilibrium.

As the years passed, Jaffé came to believe with increasing conviction that, rather than a theory of capital accumulation, Walras had a theory of capital formation, by which Jaffé meant a theory in which decisions to save and invest occur but in which the quantities of capital goods do not actually change. Jaffé expressed that view in a review of Morishima's book on Walras's economics[13] and then developed it still further in his penultimate article (Chapter 19). If net investment were to occur continually in Walras's system, then the capital stock, which is one of the parameters in his static theory, would continuously change in an ongoing dynamic system. The result would be that the equilibrium path of that system would not be described by Walras's equations. Jaffé argued persuasively, however, that Walras did not permit the quantity of capital goods to vary, and thus maintained intact his static general equilibrium model. The view that the quantity of capital goods does not actually vary in Walras's mathematical model is correct.[14] He made some remarks about the dynamics of economic growth when the quantities of capital goods and population change, but those changes were not made an endogenous part of an equation system expressing a model of general equilibrium.[15] Walras's theory defines an equilibrium that is determined ex ante by reference to notional excess demands. Accordingly he was concerned in his mathematical model with equilibrium decisions to save and invest, but not with the real ongoing consequences of those decisions. On the other hand, Jaffé went too far in maintaining that any change in the quantity of capital goods would destroy the static founda-

[13] William Jaffé, Review of *Walras' Economics; A Pure Theory of Capital and Money,* by Michio Morishima, 1977, *Economic Journal, 88,* Sept. 1978, 574–76.

[14] See Donald A. Walker, Review of *Walras' Economics; A Pure Theory of Capital and Money,* by Michio Morishima, 1977, *History of Political Economy, 12,* Spring 1980, 131–5.

[15] Léon Walras, *Eléments d'économie politique pure,* édition définitive, R. Pichon et R. Durand-Auzias, Paris, 1926, section VII; Walras, *Elements of Pure Economics,* part VII.

tions of Walras's model. Walras's system can accommodate a one-time change in the capital stock, namely, a change that does not induce subsequent similar changes. Such a parametric variation can be introduced and its consequences determined by comparative static analysis.

Walras's theory of *tâtonnement* was another topic that held Jaffé's interest for decades. His first interpretation of it was published in 1954 in the notes to his translation of the *Eléments,* but thirteen years later he presented a restatement of the subject (Chapter 13). The issue at that time was whether Walras had established that the real system of markets arrives by a process of trial and error at the set of prices and quantities that are the solutions to his general equilibrium system of equations. The *tâtonnement* process, Jaffé argued, was an attempt to describe how this occurs. Jaffé's opinion was that in his theory of exchange, Walras failed to show that the *tâtonnement* process reaches the same solution as the market, because of his neglect of disequilibrium transactions. Jaffé believed that in his example of a particular exchange market Walras had allowed trading at disequilibrium prices but was unaware of the significance of such trading. Disequilibrium transactions would change the distribution of assets before equilibrium is reached, thus altering the excess demand curves of traders and therefore changing the equilibrium itself to one that differs from the solutions to Walras's equations.

In Walras's theory of production, in contrast, Jaffé maintained that Walras recognized that the production and acquisition of disequilibrium quantities would change the distribution of asset values and hence the equilibrium position. As a consequence, Walras devised a theory of *tâtonnement* in production that depends on the use by producers of tickets on which they write down the quantities that they would like to produce at each quoted price. Without explaining the mechanism in detail, Walras stated that proposed selling prices would be varied until they are equal to the average cost of production in each firm, whereupon actual production of the equilibrium quantities would occur. Prices are also cried in the markets for the services of the factors of production, whose owners use tickets to indicate their offers, and prices are changed until excess demands are equal to zero. Walras's treatment of these matters, Jaffé demonstrated by an exhaustive examination, is incompletely specified, vague, and slipshod. Although Walras recognized that disequilibrium production had to be excluded from his model in order for the initial solution prices and quantities to be equilibrium values, by making that exclusion he described an equilibrating process that is unrealistic. Jaffé concluded that Walras failed in his attempt to show that the real market system solves his equations by the *tâtonnement* process.

In 1970 I wrote to Jaffé about his view that Walras had assumed that disequilibrium transactions occur in his example of a real exchange market but was unaware of the effects of such transactions. In opposition to that view, I argued that Walras knew that disequilibrium transactions would make it impossible in most cases to predict equilibrium prices with the use of the excess demand functions based on the initial endowment of assets, and that as a result he explicitly stated in his example of a particular market that disequilibrium transactions were not allowed, and made that assumption throughout his theory of exchange. Walras wrote that if the supply and demand quantities are unequal, "l'échange doit être suspendu" and another price is tried. He clearly indicated that exchange takes place only when the *tâtonnement* equilibrium price has been found.[16]

In his last article (Chapter 14), Jaffé took account of my argument and set forth his views on Walras's *tâtonnement* process as they had evolved over the preceding thirteen years. Jaffé began this essay by correcting his error in having stated that Walras had allowed disequilibrium transactions but failed to recognize their consequences, and conceded that in fact Walras had excluded them from his model of exchange. Jaffé did not conclude, however, that Walras was therefore realistic in regard to the *tâtonnement* process. By the time this essay was published (1981), Jaffé had developed a new view of *tâtonnement,* a view best discussed by contrasting it with the received interpretation.

As it had developed by the late 1970s, the standard interpretation of Walras's *tâtonnement* process was that it involves a central price-setter who cries prices at which traders report excess demand quantities. Through a temporal sequence of prices that are adjusted by the price-setter according to the rule that the change in the price has the same sign as the market excess demand quantity in any particular market, the equilibrium vector of prices at which all markets would simultaneously be in equilibrium is eventually found. It is declared to be the vector of prices at which actual transactions, flows of consumption and production, and decisions to save and invest can occur.

Using all the evidence in Walras's writings, Jaffé evaluated that interpretation and tried to reconstruct the *tâtonnement* process as Walras actually saw it. This was a complicated task, because Walras described the process somewhat differently in his theories of exchange, of production, and of capital formation, and because his ideas about the process altered over the years and were differently represented in the successive editions of his *Eléments.* By the time of the fourth edition, Jaffé main-

---

[16] Walras, *Eléments d'économie politique pure,* p. 46; Walras, *Elements of Pure Economics,* p. 85.

tained, Walras had abandoned the attempt to show that his *tâtonnement* theory was a description of how either actual or hypothetical markets move to equilibrium. Walras was not concerned, he argued, with a temporal sequence of price adjustments. There is no central price-setter or auctioneer in Walras's models, and no reference to the quotation of a series of possible prices. In Walras's final version of the *tâtonnement* process, according to Jaffé, the market system simultaneously reaches equilibrium, whereas the process of trial-and-error to solve general equilibrium equations is a convenience of analytical exposition. Walras described trial-and-error *tâtonnement* as the groping of a mathematical economist who makes successive adjustments in his equation system, obtaining first a solution to one set of equations representing one market, and then examining the consequences upon other equation sets representing other markets. The trial-and-error process is therefore one in which by iteration the theoretician comes progressively closer to and ultimately finds the general equilibrium solution to the equations on the piece of paper on which he is making his calculations.

As in his earlier essay on *tâtonnement* (Chapter 13), Jaffé used his own interpretation as a vantage point from which to criticize what he regarded as misconceptions of Walras's theory. The received interpretation of the *tâtonnement* process, Jaffé argued, is a sophistication of modern mathematical economists, who read into Walras's work what they deem to be logically necessary, but what is often not actually there. It is a myth, perpetuated and elaborated by writers such as Edgeworth, Lange, Patinkin, and Morishima, to suppose that Walras in his discussion of *tâtonnement* was presenting a theory of the dynamic path of the market system. Jaffé also deplored the tendency of modern mathematical economists to find fault with Walras for having dealt incompletely or ineptly with certain problems that emerge in modern general equilibrium models, but that never occurred to Walras.

The essays that have been gathered together in the final group in this volume represent Jaffé's efforts to determine and evaluate Walras's place in the history of economic thought. In addition to the many places in Jaffé's work where he touched upon the importance of Walras in relation to the development of neoclassical economics, Jaffé also devoted two entire essays specifically to that matter. In one of these (Chapter 16) he tried to assess the role that Walras played in the marginal revolution of the 1870s. For this purpose he examined Walras's development of the principle of marginal utility and the uses that he made of it in his *Principe d'une théorie mathématique de l'échange,* which predated his 1874 *Eléments,* and in the *Eléments* itself. Briefly, Walras formulated the law of diminishing marginal utility and utilized it in the statement of the conditions of equilibrium of traders and consumers. In following this procedure, Walras manifested his interest in developing the relationship between marginal utility and the formation of equilibrium prices, rather than concentrating, as did most of his predecessors and many of his contemporaries, upon the production of income and its distribution. He thereby laid the foundations for the study of the allocation of resources and of exchange. Walras's role in the marginal revolution, Jaffé concluded, was to utilize the principle of marginal utility and the equilibrium conditions involving it as a "power-generating engine to activate the market mechanism."

Jaffé delineated even more clearly Walras's relationship to his contemporaries by examining the received doctrine that Walras, Jevons, and Menger were all very similar in their work on marginal utility and demand (Chapter 17). Jaffé was concerned to show that those writers differed in their treatment of the theory of demand and in other respects also, rather than being three independent discoverers of the same principle. Walras, unlike Jevons, was not interested in a theory of individual consumption, and he did not devote himself to an analysis of the many features of individual demand. Walras used the principle of marginal utility to connect preference conditions and market equilibrium conditions, concentrating upon the equation of exchange. Menger, preoccupied with institutional and disequilibrium economics, did not even try to explain prices. Jaffé therefore allotted to Walras, rather than to Jevons or Menger, the credit for having set economics out upon the path that led to the development of modern theory.

Jaffé also passed judgment upon Walras's work in several respects. Most notably, he squarely faced the central question of the value of Walras's general equilibrium theory (Chapters 7, 15). As has already been seen, Jaffé did not feel that Walras's *tâtonnement* process was realistic. Rather than being a description of how markets behave on the way to equilibrium, his theory was a statement of multimarket static equilibrium conditions. As such, Jaffé observed, it cannot be applied directly to the formation of policies for our economy. A second major criticism that Jaffé leveled at Walras's theory was that its static nature and confinement to pure competition rendered it useless for analyzing the development and behavior of imperfectly competitive market structures. In particular, Jaffé felt that the incapacity of Walras's theory to deal with oligopoly was a serious deficiency. On the other hand, Jaffé contended, the theory also made some major contributions to economic science. His claims for Walras's theory were not all convincing, however. For example, he was surely wrong to assert that it does not depend upon a particular set of institutional characteristics and therefore can be used to analyze any type of an economy in which there are competitive market processes. It is wholly dependent upon the existence of the institutions that result in purely competitive markets. Furthermore, Jaffé himself had made clear that the theory is not suitable for analyzing the dynamics of market behavior. Jaffé was perfectly accurate, nevertheless, to have recognized Walras as the progenitor of modern general equilibrium analysis, the creator of the foundations upon which later economists were to build.

In the last decade of his life Jaffé developed a new evaluation of Walras's contribution to economics (Chapters 18, 19). He became convinced that Walras was not concerned with constructing a realistic description of the market system but with framing an ideal system that has normative significance. According to Jaffé, Walras wanted to show that an economic system could be devised that would lead to the maximization of social welfare and would secure distributive and commutative justice. Jaffé maintained that Walras was prevented from presenting his theory explicitly as a normative scheme because he feared that the censors of the Third Empire would regard it as an indictment of the existing social order and as a visionary proposal to reorganize the economy along lines that would be prejudicial to the interests of the ruling class. Jaffé argued that by neglecting the normative intent of Walras's theory, its critics have failed to understand its fundamental character. They have consequently supposed that it was attempting to achieve certain objectives that were no part of Walras's plan, and have therefore criticized it for the wrong reasons.

When Jaffé referred to "the normative bias" of Walras's general equilibrium theory, he implied that its structure and conclusions are distorted by normative conceptions. The theory is better characterized, however, as a description of the conditions prevailing in the general equilibrium of interrelated purely competitive markets. Of course, Walras used the theory as a foundation for policies that he believed should be adopted to establish the conditions of pure competition, but he did not adopt the assumptions of the theory because he thought they would result in a utopian scheme. Walras believed that his analysis of pure competition was positive. All that he needed to do, Walras wrote, was to assume pure competition as a hypothesis, regardless of whether or not it actually existed. He studied the consequences of the hypothesis, and determined that they result in the attainment of a relative maximum of social utility. He then made the normative judgment that those consequences are good, and therefore argued that competition becomes a rule that should be applied to agriculture, industry, commerce, and banking. "Thus, the conclusion of pure science carries us to the threshhold of applied science."[17]

In summary, when we look over the sweep of Jaffé's work on Walras, we can see that he made enormous progress in establishing the facts of Walras's intellectual life and explaining the character and meaning of his work. Jaffé himself would have been the last to say that he had definitively settled all the questions with which he dealt, because he was vividly aware that each generation finds new things of interest in the work of its predecessors and reads the past in the light of new knowledge. As Jaffé emphasized in his essay published in 1971 (Chapter 15),

In taking seriously so childish and otiose a question as, 'Is Walras important?', it is not the answer that matters, but the search for an answer. In the course of speculating on the importance or unimportance of Léon Walras or any other figure in the history of economics, we are led to examine 'with greater clearness and fulness' the meaning and significance of that economist's contribution to our science.

There will always be room for alternative interpretations of the issues that Jaffé discussed, but there will never be a more scrupulous, diligent, and intellectually honest attempt to explain the genesis and meaning of Walras's conceptions than the body of scholarship that Jaffé created.

[17] Walras, *Eléments d'économie politique pure*, p. 232; Walras, *Elements of Pure Economics*, p. 256. I have given a detailed evaluation of Jaffé's thesis in my paper "Was Walras's Theory of General Equilibrium a Normative Scheme?" delivered at the annual meeting of the History of Economics Society, Duke University, May 24, 1982.

PART I

WALRAS'S BIOGRAPHY

1

UNPUBLISHED PAPERS AND LETTERS OF LÉON WALRAS[1]

Je ne suis pas un économiste. Je suis un architecte. Mais je sais mieux l'économie politique que les économistes.

—LÉON WALRAS.

INTRODUCTION

The unpublished papers and letters of Léon Walras constitute a mass of documents of great scientific importance and of deep human interest. Not only do they shed light on the inner workings of his mind as he developed his system of general economic equilibrium, but they also reveal the intimate personal trials and tribulations of a pioneer scholar hewing out new paths despite the "scoffs and scorns and contumelious taunts" of his contemporaries. They frequently illuminate obscure passages of his published works; and, incidentally, they discover to us traits of character and developments of thought of his correspondents.

The original unpublished documents to which I refer are located mainly in the University of Lausanne, which serves as a depositary for them. Some few of these papers and letters have found their way to the University of Lyons, but these belong to the earlier and less interesting years of Walras' life. After Walras' death the bulk of this scientific correspondence was painstakingly copied by his daughter, Mlle Aline Walras, from almost illegible rough drafts; and these copies were handed over to Professor Etienne Antonelli for eventual publication.[2]

[1] Paper read before the Econometric Society in joint session with the American Economic Association and the American Statistical Association, as part of the Walras centennial program, Chicago, December 28, 1934.

[2] It was thanks to the courtesy and generosity of Mlle Aline Walras and of Professor Etienne Antonelli that I was first permitted to consult Mlle Walras' copies in Paris. For a long time I could not discover where the originals were. Finally, last summer (1934), I traced them to the Salle des Commissions at the Palais de Rumine of the University of Lausanne, where they lay neglected in neat bundles gathering upon them the dust of passing decades. The chancellor was good enough to allow me access to these papers. I was, however, requested not to publish my collection of these documents, since prior rights of publication belong to others. I wish to take this occasion to express my gratitude also to the Social Science Research Council and to Northwestern University, without whose material assistance in the form of grants-in-aid my pursuit of these papers would have been impossible.

17

Among the papers I have seen and copied is Léon Walras' complete autobiography, only part of which was published in 1908.[3] This autobiography was composed mainly at the instance of one of our pioneer mathematical economists, Professor Henry Ludwell Moore, who on May 30, 1904, wrote to Walras as follows:

> You yourself have realized how essential it is for the progress of the social sciences that the man should be known as well as his work, and you have, consequently, told the world what little it knows about Gossen. The memoirs of Jevons exist, and as you know, I have discovered the Souvenirs of Cournot. We must have the autobiography of Walras.

In the Walras centennial year it is eminently appropriate to recount the story of his life. And since it was a life wholly devoted to science, we shall have occasion, in the course of these biographical remarks, to refer to the scientific and philosophical adventures described in his letters and personal notes.

1834–70

Léon Walras was born in Evreux, a provincial town of Normandy, on December 16, 1834. He received the ordinary primary and secondary education of a French boy of his class. He studied both literature and mathematics. At the age of nineteen he attempted to enter the École Polytechnique, but failed in the competitive entrance examination for want of sufficient training in mathematics. He resolved to try again the following year, in the meantime reading a great deal of mathematics which he had hitherto neglected. Among the books he then studied was one published in 1838 by his father's classmate, Augustin Cournot: *Recherches sur les principes mathématiques de la théorie des richesses.* Though he read, marked, learned, and inwardly digested this great book, he again failed in his attempt to enter the École Polytechnique and sought refuge in the École des Mines. But mining engineering did not interest him. He took to writing novels. His principal novel, *Francis Sauveur,*[4] published in 1858, throws some light on what manner of man he was.

[3] "Leone Walras—autobiografia," edited by M. Pantaleoni, in *Giornale degli economisti,* 2d ser., XXXVII (December, 1908), 603–10. Some of Walras' correspondence has been published as well, viz: "Lettres inédites de et à Walras" (letters between Léon Walras and his father) in *La Révolution de 1848, Bulletin de la Société d'Histoire de la Révolution de 1848* (Paris: Cornély), IX (1912–13), 179–98, 286–309, 367–82, 427–46; X (1913–14), 138–56, 231–53, 327–43, 405–31; XI (1914), 508–25; the correspondence between Léon Walras and Henri Laurent, "De l'unité de valeur" in the *Revue d'économie politique,* 48ᵉ année, No. 4, pp. 1146–78, edited by Etienne Antonelli; and "Léon Walras et sa corréspondance avec Augustin Cournot et Stanley Jevons avec une note d'Etienne Antonelli," *Econometrica,* III, No. 1 (January, 1935), 119–27.

[4] Another of Léon Walras' literary products belonging to the same epoch was "La lettre" published in the *Revue française,* 5ième année, tome XVI (1859).

We see him in 1858, as a young man of twenty-four, bitterly disillusioned by the results of the Revolution of 1848, which at first seemed to hold out so many promises to the ardent and generous youth of the time. Though disappointed, he could never completely abandon his pursuit of a social idea. In 1858 he stood at the fork of the roads: Should he pursue a scientific career and demonstrate the logical validity of his ideal, or should he pursue a literary career and write social novels? He was troubled by a sense of the futility of idealism in a world so grossly and so iniquitously selfish. One of his characters in *Francis Sauveur,* forced into a conventional position, cries out: "Since the world has won a victory over me, I am going to retire to a place of solitude where the world cannot reach me and where I can remain faithful to my dream."[5] It was in order to remain faithful to his dream that Léon Walras later in life did retire into an ivory tower of pure science, though opportunities for a political career had been open to him.

Walras, however, often fretted in the ivory tower where his ideal could only be realized in the abstract. From time to time he would indulge himself in an escapade. This impatience explains certain lapses from the logical rigor which generally characterizes his work. For example, the logically untenable conclusion that collective satisfaction is maximized under perfect competition assuming the absence of class pricing can only be understood in the light of the psychological history of the author.[6] Walras' fervent pleas for the nationalization of the soil[7] and for a monetary system based on gold coupled with a compensating silver token currency[8] are also manifestations of this indomitable spirit of youth which never left him to his dying day.

It was on a summer evening in 1858 that Léon Walras decided once for all that the path he would follow was to be the scientific path. The circumstances of his decision were dramatic. He was walking with his father along one of the mountain streams that grace the south of France. The elder Walras was endeavoring to persuade his son that there would always be enough *littérateurs* in the world, but what was needed was a social scientist. In his autobiography written nearly half a century later

---

[5] *Op. cit.,* p. 225.

[6] Léon Walras, *Éléments d'économie politique pure* (édition définitive; Paris, 1926) (hereafter referred to as *Éléments*), p. 99. See also Knut Wicksell's *Lectures on Political Economy,* I (London, 1934), 73 ff., for a discussion of this point.

[7] E.g., "Théorie mathématique du prix des terres et de leur rachat par l'état," read before the Société Vaudoise des Sciences Naturelles at Lausanne in 1880; first published in the *Théorie mathématique de la richesse sociale* (Lausanne, 1883), pp. 177–253, and again in the *Études d'économie sociale* (Paris, 1896), pp. 267–350.

[8] E.g., "Monnaie d'or avec billon d'argent régulateur," first published in the *Revue de droit international,* December 1, 1884, pp. 3–16, and again in the *Études d'économie politique appliquée* (Paris, 1898), pp. 3–19.

Léon Walras related that, as they passed a small country villa called "Les Roseaux," he promised to abandon literature and to dedicate his life to the continuation of his father's work. Thus the die was cast.

So phenomenal an accomplishment as the creation of the Walrasian system of general equilibrium can only be explained by the fact that this work was the fruit of two generations of continuous scientific industry. While John Stuart Mill represents in some respects the attitude of revolt of the son against the father, Léon Walras, scion of a *petit bourgeois* family *"très honorable, très catholique, très royaliste"* [9] represents the spirit of veneration of the son for the father. In describing to Professor Moore the genesis of his system Léon Walras wrote on January 2, 1906: "To my father I owe the economic definitions which are the basis of my system, and to Cournot I owe the mathematical language which is most apt for formulating this system. . . ."

To be sure, he took over bodily from his father's *De la nature de la richesse* (Paris, 1831), his peculiar and useful distinction between capital and income, the former referring to all social wealth that may be used more than once, and the latter referring to those items of wealth which are used up as soon as they are used at all.[10] Moreover, many of Léon Walras' categories and definitions of factors of production were copied almost verbatim from his father's later book, *Théorie de la richesse sociale,* published in 1849. For example, both father and son rejected the current land-labor-and-capital classification, adopting instead land-services the source of which is land, labor-services the source of which is personal faculties, and capital-services the source of which is capital in the narrow sense of artificial or produced capital goods.[11] Certainly, the more refined definitions borrowed from his father enabled Léon Walras to develop a theory of production of remarkable clarity and logical consistency within the limits of the problem he set for himself. Would that his filial piety had stopped there! For not only did he appropriate some of his father's excellent definitions, but unfortunately he also remained faithful to much of his father's antiquated terminology. Thus, while he endowed his father's vague expression "extensive utility" with the mathematically precise meaning of the length of the intercept of a collective demand curve on the quantity axis, and the expression "intensity of utility" with the equally precise meaning of the slope of the demand curve, his use of the word "utility" in this connection is,

[9] L. Walras, "Un initiateur en économie politique, A. A. Walras," published in *La revue du mois,* August 10, 1908, and cited by L. Modeste Leroy, *Auguste Walras* (Paris, 1923), p. 1.
[10] Auguste Walras, *op. cit.,* p. 40. Cf. *Éléments,* p. 177.
[11] Auguste Walras, *Théorie de la richesse sociale* (1849), pp. 71–72. Cf. *Éléments,* pp. 176–77.

however, confusing, for by his own subsequent use of the term, he properly restricted it to the realm of individual psychological reactions to goods.[12] Malthus was better advised when he called this same relation of quantity to price "intensity of demand."[13] A most annoying piece of outworn terminology, again taken from his father, is his use of the word *"profits"* in one connection to designate capital-services while he uses the same word in another connection to describe the entrepreneur's gain when price exceeds cost.[14] Still another example is the word *"numéraire"* used by Auguste Walras as a synonym for money of account, but given a subtly different connotation by Léon Walras, who means by it a standard commodity the value of a unit of which may serve as a standard of value.[15] That he meant definitely to depart from his father's use of the term is clear from a letter written on September 14, 1894, to Enrico Barone apropos of the latter's article "Sulla Consumer's Rent," which appeared in the *Giornale degli economisti* in 1894. Walras said: " . . . the word numéraire is not exactly rendered by your 'moneta ideale.' What is needed is a special word to express a special idea, namely, that of a commodity in terms of a unit of which prices are expressed." Most unfortunate of all in the inherited galaxy of terms is the ambiguous *"rareté,"* which the elder Walras described as a ratio between the amount of wants for a good and the amount of the good available for the satisfaction of these wants.[16] Out of this nebulous concept Walras developed the precise concept of a derivative of utility with respect to quantity,[17] but he did not, alas, discard his father's term or free himself from his father's pursuit of a cause of value.[18]

For better or for worse, Auguste Walras' work was the starting-point of his son's theoretical constructions. What influenced the son even more than these definitions was his father's suggestion, originally made as far back as 1831, that economics is a mathematical science.[19]

It was not sufficient for Léon Walras to entertain the noble ambition of creating a new mathematical science of economics. He needed

---

[12] Auguste Walras, *De la nature de la richesse* (1831), p. 150. Cf. *Éléments*, pp. 72–74.

[13] T. R. Malthus, *Principles of Political Economy* (2d ed.; London, 1836), pp. 65–66 n.

[14] *Théorie de la richesse sociale*, pp. 71–72. Cf. *Éléments*, pp. 181 and 204.

[15] "Ces réflexions [i.e., those A. Walras had just quoted from Germain Garnier's *Histoire de la monnaie* (1819), I, 77] . . . expriment très-bien la différence qui existe . . . entre deux choses essentiellement distinctes, la *monnaie réelle* et la *monnaie de compte*, ou, si l'on aime mieux, la *monnaie* proprement dite et le *numéraire* . . . ." (A. Walras, *De la nature de la richesse*, p. 297). Cf. *Éléments*, p. 150. In fact, both father and son, each in his own way, used the word *numéraire* in a peculiarly strict sense, for ordinarily the word in French has the same loose and ambiguous connotation as the English word "currency." See Michel Chevalier's article on "Monnaie" in Coquelin and Guillaumin's *Dictionnaire de l'économie politique* (2d ed.; Paris, 1863), II, 201.

[16] *De la nature de la richesse*, pp. 279–80.   [17] *Eléments*, p. 76.

[18] *Ibid.*, Lesson 10.   [19] *De la nature de la richesse*, pp. 278 ff.

material means, and these means were sadly lacking. There was no money in the family. As for an academic chair in France, this was impossible, for he stood outside the charmed circle of those who were content to sing unmitigated praises of the existing social order. The official French economists of that epoch formed a closed corporation made up of worthy individuals who were interested in economics as a branch of politics and not as a branch of science. Since this same group also controlled the economic journals, Walras soon found himself excluded from this avenue of expression as well. The only thing left for him to do was to take whatever jobs he could find and devote his spare moments to writing essays on the application of mathematics to economics.

Among his early unpublished papers which I found at the University of Lausanne were two closely written manuscripts both entitled "Application des mathématiques à l'économie politique," one of eight pages, called *première tentative,* dated 1860 and the other of forty-seven pages, called *deuxième tentative,* dated 1869–70. They were pathetic efforts, giving not the slightest inkling of what was presently to follow when a real opportunity finally fell to his lot. The best he could do in his effort of 1869–70 was to translate into the most jejune mathematical symbols his father's absurd definition of *"rareté."* He attempted to prove that the proposition that price varies directly with demand and inversely with supply was not devoid of meaning, as Cournot had thought. There was no trace at all of the concept of a functional relationship between utility and quantity.

The reason for this early scientific barrenness is perfectly apparent from his letters and autobiography. He was completely absorbed by the struggle to make a living for his family, and he was eaten by the canker of bitter disappointment. During the period from 1858, when at the age of twenty-four he took the vow before his father to consecrate himself to economics, until 1870, when he finally did obtain a chair, he was driven continuously from pillar to post and sorely tried. He started out as a journalist but was soon discharged for the independence of his opinions. He worked for a while at the secretariat of the Chemin de fer du Nord. Then he became a managing director of the Caisse d'escompte des Associations populaires, until the bank failed.[20] And finally he was a corresponding secretary for a large private banking establishment in Paris. In the end, when he received his call from the University of

---

[20] Failure resulted largely because the borrowing co-operatives refused to follow Léon Walras' counsels not to sell below current market prices and not to pay more than current wages.

Lausanne, he had to ask the *recteur* for an advance on his salary to meet his traveling cost. He did not have enough money to transport his family to Lausanne until a later date.

And yet the experience of those twelve years had an important bearing on his intellectual development as an economist. It gave him firsthand contact with concrete economic reality. This practical background is reflected in Lesson 19 of his *Éléments,* which deals with the relationship between accounting and economics, and also in Lessons 33 and 34, which give a lucid description of the process of issuing fiduciary paper and of establishing international exchange rates.

Though he could not elaborate any detailed theorems at that time, he could and did reflect upon the general philosophic structure of his system. In fact, this was adumbrated very early, as is evident from a letter written December 23, 1862, to M. du Mesnil Marigny proposing literary collaboration. Thus, at the age of twenty-eight he had a complete presentiment of his life work as consisting, in the first place, of the creation of a pure science of economics dealing with the logically inevitable consequences of perfect competition; in the second place, of the creation of an applied science of economics dealing with the theory of the choice of a most efficient and most useful economic organization from the point of view of the production of social wealth; and in the third place, of the creation of a science of social economics designed to examine a given economic structure, its distribution of wealth, and its methods of taxation, from the point of view of social justice. As is seen from the very titles of his three main works, he never swerved from his original plan. The first book of the Walrasian trilogy, written after 1870, his *Éléments d'économie politique pure,*[21] represents a system of necessary economic relationships; the second, *Études d'économie sociale* (1896), is concerned with such problems of social ethics as communism, individualism, private property, nationalization of land, and public finance; while the third book, *Études d'économie politique appliquée* (1898), discusses practical issues like bimetallism versus monometallism, monopoly versus free competition, free trade, the rôle of banking and credit, and the uses and abuses of stock-market speculation.

Walras' interest in taxation as an instrument of social justice led him to participate in an international taxation congress held at Lausanne in

[21] There were, in all, five editions of the *Eléments d'économie politique pure ou théorie de la richesse sociale:* 1874–77, 1st edition (2 vols.); 1889, 2d edition (1 vol.); 1896, 3d edition (1 vol.); 1900, 4th edition (1 vol.); and 1926, definitive edition (1 vol.). The last was a posthumous edition embodying revisions made by Léon Walras up to 1902. The most extensive changes were introduced into the second and fourth editions, but the modifications found in the other editions are not without importance. A translation of the definitive edition of the *Éléments* with variorum notes is in preparation by the author.

1860.[22] He made so excellent an impression that ten years later, when a chair in political economy was established at the University of Lausanne, Léon Walras was appointed on a trial one-year contract. He held the chair until he retired for reasons of ill health in 1892, and was succeeded by his disciple, Vilfredo Pareto.

1870–92

Léon Walras opened his first lecture, which he delivered on December 16, 1870, as follows:

The Rector's kind words of introduction add to the emotion that I feel. For fifteen years I have been fervently hoping for the day when I might come into a chair in economics and devote every moment of my life to science and the communication of my ideas to young and open minds.

This day ought to have been the happiest of my life; and indeed it would have been, were it not for the cruel circumstances that becloud it, and were it not for the anguish I suffer when I view the uncertain destiny of my country and my own precarious fate. Those who have assumed responsibility in France for the national defense are, as you know, calling to the colors, as soon as they can find sufficient arms and munitions, all physically eligible men from twenty to forty— young men, bachelors, married men, and fathers. I belong to the last class; and when my turn comes, I hold myself ready to go. If we must lose all, at least let us do as our ancestors have done and preserve our honor.

Thus perhaps in a few days I may have to leave this chair which I today occupy for the first time. If such be the case, remember me with sympathy and kindness. I shall carry with me the remembrance of your cordial welcome. Meanwhile, whatever the future may have in store for us, let us settle down to work as if nothing might interrupt us, as if we were sure to remain together— you, as my first students, to remain, I hope, my lasting friends, and I with a firm resolve conscientiously to inculcate in you a knowledge and love of the principles of economics and of social ethics, which principles may guarantee the increase of wealth and the triumph of justice in a world that we now view with horror, a world today abandoned to the mercy of iniquitous and devastating ambitions.[23]

Professor Léon Walras did settle down to work immediately. His autobiography describes his first step in the development of his pure theory as follows:

I had been working steadily with the idea of creating a mathematical economics ever since 1860. . . . The only serious attempt along these lines that

[22] Léon Walras, *Théorie critique de l'impôt précédée de souvenirs du Congrès de Lausanne* (Paris, 1861), and *De l'impôt dans le Canton de Vaud, mémoire auquel un quatrième accessit a été décerné ensuite du concours ouvert par le Conseil d'Etat du Canton de Vaud sur les questions relatives à l'impôt* (Lausanne, 1864).
[23] Quoted in a letter to Bory-Hollard dated December 16, 1870.

was known to me was that of Cournot. I soon perceived, however, that Cournot's demand curve, which depicted the quantity demanded as a function of price, was rigorously accurate only in the case of a market confined to two commodities. Where more than two commodities are involved in the exchange process, this demand curve is merely an approximation. Restricting my attention, therefore, to the case of two commodities, I rationally derived from the demand curve of each commodity the supply curve of the other and demonstrated how current equilibrium results from the intersection of the supply and demand curves. Then I proceeded to derive the demand curve itself from the quantities possessed by each individual in the market and from each individual's utility curves for the two commodities considered. Thus I obtained the *intensity of the last want satisfied,* or the *rareté* [marginal degree of utility] as a function of the *quantity consumed.* These are the primary data from which price may be rationally deduced, and they constitute the very keystone of mathematical economics.

I repeat, this was no more than the first step in the development of the Walrasian system of general equilibrium, and while it was essential, it did not constitute the whole of Léon Walras' contribution to theory, as many historians of economic thought who are incapable of following him any further are wont to repeat *ad nauseandum.* If this were all he had done, he would have been simply a co-discoverer of marginal or final degree of utility, unfortunately born too late, since Gossen, Jevons, and Carl Menger had preceded him. And, perhaps, too there would have been some slight justification on the part of the author of a recent book on the development of economics in not mentioning Léon Walras even in a footnote.[24] But the Walrasian system has vast dimensions. To give some idea of its comprehensiveness, which is so little known, it may be well briefly to summarize a few outline features of the system. Léon Walras assumes perfect competition and uniformity of prices in all parts of the market; and then he demonstrates mathematically that general equilibrium in such a market requires that the following five conditions be simultaneously satisfied: (1) Each individual, characterized by certain utility curves for each good and service in the market, must have attained maximum possible satisfaction through exchange. This condition is realized when for each individual prices are proportional to the marginal degrees of utility. (2) The supply of each commodity or service must equal the demand for it. (3) The price of each product must equal its cost of production. (4) The rate of net yield on capital investments must be equal for all capital goods, due allowance being made for differences in rates of depreciation and differences in risk. (5) The quantity of money in circulation must be such that the price of the money commodity is the same in monetary uses as it is in the arts. This

[24] William A. Scott, *The Development of Economics* (New York, 1933). Cournot is not mentioned either, which leaves Walras in good company.

last condition, which involves the theory of the demand for cash balances, is particularly important because Walras integrated his pure theory of money with the rest of his economic theory instead of allowing it to remain something apart from the whole.[25]

One day, as he reflected on his general system, he scribbled in an undated notebook which I found at Lausanne: "I am not an economist. I am an architect, but I know economics better than economists do."

Léon Walras was, of course, very proud of his first step, the rational derivation of the demand curve from utility and quantity data. He thought at first that no one had had this idea before. It was quite a blow to him when he received a letter early in May, 1874, from M. d'Aulnis de Bourouill, then a student at Leyden, telling him how much he liked Walras' theory of exchange and how similar it was to a theory he had read in W. Stanley Jevons' *Theory of Political Economy*. Walras, on verifying this, immediately wrote to Jevons, conceding Jevons' priority. Walras later published some of this correspondence;[26] but in a letter dated July 29, 1874, which was not published, he said:

> I make no pretense of being above human frailty. I confess to you frankly that I was at first quite upset by the loss of my priority as the inventor of the equation which is so fundamental to the mathematical theory of exchange and of social wealth. . . . . When there is nothing else left to do but yield, one might as well do so with good grace.

The fact is, as letters written to others show, he continued to bear the same sort of grudge against Jevons as Marshall bore, until the discovery of Gossen's book by Professor Adamson in 1878 made all feeling of jealousy ridiculous. In any case, toward the end of the letter I have just quoted Walras wrote:

> I have made some points, which, I believe, will remain my own—for example, the theorem of general equilibrium and the laws of the emergence and variation of equilibrium prices. And there are many other things besides! Thus I find some consolation for my self-esteem.

Walras was always rather touchy about matters pertaining to his self-esteem. Years later, in 1889, writing to Pantaleoni,[27] he expressed his resentment at the tenor of Jevons' Preface to his second edition. He was particularly annoyed by the sentence reading: "The working out of a complete system based on these lines must be a matter of time and labour, and I know not when, if ever, I shall be able to attempt it."

---

[25] In addition to a theory of the *determination* of general equilibrium, Walras presents a theory of the *emergence* of equilibrium.

[26] *Théorie mathématique de la richesse sociale* (1883), pp. 26–31. See also *Letters and Journal of W. Stanley Jevons,* edited by his wife (London, 1886), pp. 302–6.

[27] Letter dated August 17, 1889.

Walras felt that he had been slighted, for he thought Jevons should have known perfectly well when he wrote this that "the working out of a complete system" had been accomplished by Léon Walras. But this, in Walras' mind, was of a piece with other actions by English economists, for example, Marshall's device of printing his theorems "for private circulation," thus preserving his rights to priority without publishing anything, and allowing himself leisure for further research. Edgeworth's impishness—and it must be admitted he could be impish—irritated Walras more than anything else. Albion was ever perfidious—in French eyes.

The years immediately following the first appearance of his *Éléments d'économie politique pure* in 1874 were particularly rich in scientific correspondence. I pass over the exchange of letters between Walras and Cournot at this time, since Professor Antonelli has already published some of these letters in *Econometrica*. I shall, however, quote at some length a letter addressed to a German, Herr Edward Pfeiffer, on April 2, 1874, because in this letter Walras defines his position with reference to mathematical economics. After dividing economic problems into three categories—those of the pure-science variety, those of the applied-science variety, and those of the practical variety—Walras goes on to say:

Now the application of mathematics to economics is a very different thing in the first two categories from what it is in the third. In the first category the use of the language, method, and principles of mathematics has no other object than to make our analyses more rigorously accurate and more comprehensive than ordinary logic can do. It also helps us to reach more rational conclusions. In pure theory, therefore, our formulas not only may be abstract, but should be so, in order that they may be general and permanent in their validity. Our curves and functions ought to be applicable to any commodity which may be exchanged. It is only when we are concerned with problems of the third category, i.e., of practical economics, that our formulas ought to have concrete significance and our formulas or curves ought to have numerical coefficients.

This leaves to the application of mathematics the whole field of pure and applied economics. Here we can use mathematics without falling into the errors to which the historical school objects. These objections are really directed against numerical applications. This is a fact which very few understand, because few people know what mathematics really is and how it is applied in the natural sciences, for example, by a Newton to the theory of astronomical movements, and by a Fourier to the theory of heat. Most economists have no conception of the calculus and know only the four rules of arithmetic. In their eyes the application of mathematics to economics consists of an operation which necessarily resolves itself into the addition, subtraction, multiplication, and division of concrete numbers. They are mistaken. The application of mathematics to economics consists in discussing and reasoning about *utility, quantity, effective demand, effective supply, price,* etc., which are *magnitudes . . . ,* in setting these magnitudes as functions of one another and in making use of a knowledge of the general properties of these functions in a study of economic phenomena.

. . . .

The application of mathematics to practical economics is quite another thing. In the place of general and abstract formulas, one can, within certain limits and under given conditions, substitute special determinate formulas and obtain a price by calculation instead of waiting for the market to discover these prices. . . . . It is the business of good statisticians to tell us how, in a given country, an increase in the price of a given commodity influences the consumption of that commodity. It is incontestable that such data—true under certain conditions— will not be true when these conditions change. But is it not equally true that the statistics of births and deaths vary? And yet they do not vary so much but that such vital statistics are useful in the life insurance business. Are price data sufficiently regular to permit us to calculate approximately the effects of the demonetization of a metal or the effects of an excise tax or a protective tariff? Can they enable us to foresee and perhaps conjure economic crises? I have not studied this matter sufficiently to say. In any case, I consider it possible, up to a certain point and within certain limits, to replace empirical trial and error methods by rational practices in the administration of public and private business. Not only do I esteem with Descartes that only that which is evident can be considered as true, but I esteem further that only that can be regarded as impossible which is evidently absurd.

. . . .

For a long time German economics has accumulated facts derived from observation, and in doing that the Germans are right. But they fail to subject these facts to a rational theory—and in that they are wrong. We ought to fight against anti-scientific prejudice. When the Hegelian idealism, which attempted to create a physical and social universe by a priori methods, was at its height, it was appropriate for a reaction to take place in favor of experience. Today empiricism has gone too far; and the time has come for a vindication of the rights of reason and for a conciliation of the two great methods: the experimental and the rational. For my part, my most deeply felt desire is to see this beautiful scientific and philosophical synthesis accomplished and to share in this accomplishment.[28]

Walras dealt with the relation of economics to statistics also in two letters to Bortkiewicz. In the first, dated January 9, 1891, he wrote:

Now that you are teaching statistics, I trust that you will not abandon your study of economics. The two are intimately related. For example, how can one establish price statistics without a scientific knowledge of the elements of price determination and of price variation? It is impossible. For want of such knowledge, price statistics is still in a rudimentary state.

[28] The substance of this letter was later expanded and incorporated in an article entitled "Un nuovo ramo della matematica, dell'applicazione delle matematiche all'economia politica," which appeared in the *Giornale degli economisti* for April, 1876 (III, No. 1, 1–40).

In the second, dated July 30, 1899, Walras added:

> Statistics is a science upon which economics can shed much light, and I hope that you will find occasion to make use of the knowledge you have acquired of the new science of economic equilibrium.

Walras was at this time carrying on a considerable amount of epistolary propaganda in favor of the application of mathematics to economics. Among the most interesting replies is that of Carl Menger. In two letters to Walras—one dated June 28, 1883, and the other, a lengthy one, dated February, 1884—Menger insisted that what the economist is after is not only the quantitative relationships *(Grössenverhältnisse)* but also the essence *(das Wesen)* of economic phenomena. "How can we," he asks, "attain to a knowledge of this essence, for example, the essence of value, the essence of land rent, the essence of entrepreneur's profit, the essence of the division of labor, the essence of bimetallism, etc., by mathematics?" In so far as mathematics was useful at all, he maintained that it was only a tool, a *"Hilfswissenschaft."* [29] *Quis negavit?*

But Walras, for all his championship of the use of mathematics, was, by his own confession, not a mathematician properly speaking. The result was that he was attacked on both sides. He was accused of burdening his presentations with unnecessary mathematical paraphernalia incomprehensible to the layman. We find an indirect reply to this accusation in a letter Léon Walras addressed to W. Stanley Jevons, dated September 24, 1874:[30]

> I have been asked on several occasions to lecture and to contribute articles on the very delicate and complex question of money. I have always replied that it was impossible for me to do so, that the theory of money which I have developed in my published course could no more be popularized than Newton's binomial theorem in algebra and that, in order to understand my "Lesson" 25 on money, it is necessary first to study the preceding twenty-four "lessons." No one is satisfied with this reply, and I continue to receive requests. If I simply had to popularize economics, I should do as popularizers of astronomy do. I should

[29] Dr. von Hayek has recently observed in *Economica* for November 1934 (N.S., No. 4, pp. 396–97), that, so far as he was aware, Menger "has nowhere commented on the value of mathematics as a tool of economic analysis." It would seem that Menger's prudent abstention from publishing what he had developed on the subject in his correspondence with Walras and also the foregoing reference to "the essence of value" as having an existence apart from *"Grössenverhältnisse"* hardly support Dr. von Hayek's surmise that "there is no reason to assume that he [Menger] lacked either the technical equipment or the inclination [to use mathematics]." Certainly, Carl Menger's brother's and son's interest in mathematics is totally irrelevant.

[30] This was written in response to a letter sent to Walras by Jevons on September 13, 1874, announcing that the latter was engaged upon a book on money "of a semipopular character." This was Jevons' *Money and the Mechanism of Exchange,* which first appeared in 1875.

skip the proofs and say that they had been given by competent men, and simply enunciate clear and exact conclusions. But that is not what people want nowadays—they want us to present one of the most complicated of sciences as an easy science. They want us to give them the whole of celestial mechanics using only elementary arithmetic. If we do not consent to do this, we are enemies of democracy, devoid of philanthropic and humanitarian sentiments.

To those who, like Perozzo, suggested more elaborate mathematical formulations of theory, Walras replied, in a letter dated February 14, 1890:

> I have been particularly impressed by one thing, and that is that economists who are mediocre mathematicians, like Jevons, have produced excellent economic theory, whereas some mathematicians who have an inadequate knowledge of economics, like Edgeworth, Auspitz and Lieben, talk a lot of nonsense *(disent beaucoup de bêtises)*.

When, however, errors of a mathematical nature were pointed out to him by Bortkiewicz and D'Ocagne, the latter a mathematician and engineer, he adopted a truly humble attitude. Though Bortkiewicz was only a young student in 1888, Walras wrote to him in a letter dated May 19, 1888:

> As I am not a professional mathematician and have no one near me, like yourself, who is a mathematician and who will take pains to examine my theories, I must resign myself to discovering in my work, in all probability, other errors of the kind to which you have just called my attention.

To D'Ocagne he replied, in a letter dated May 10, 1891:

> I learned the calculus all by myself, and I probably made a poor choice among the methods by which one acquires a good foundation in the subject. Moreover, I consider my work both from the economic and the mathematical points of view simply an incomplete sketch. I hope that in the near future it will be superseded by other work more complete and better done.

Walras soon woke up to the futility of methodological controversies, and after a while refused to be drawn into them. His correspondence attains a higher order of interest when he endeavors to dispel obscurities that baffled his readers or when he defines certain irreconcilable differences with his contemporaries. It would exceed the scope of this paper and it would require very lengthy mathematical developments to present these important matters with any fulness. I shall confine myself, therefore, to brief indications of some of the major issues in pure theory raised in these letters. I must perforce leave aside also any consideration of Walras' voluminous correspondence dealing with monetary questions.

The exchange of letters between Walras and Alfred Marshall in the early eighties contains no capital points of theory. It is curious to note, however, the manner in which Marshall insists that he had lectured on what he originally called the "terminal-value-in-use" before Jevons' *Theory of Political Economy* was published.[31] Marshall claimed also that he had anticipated Walras' doctrine of unstable equilibrium.[32]

The correspondence with Wicksteed is much more illuminating, for it deals, in part, with the delicate problem of the empirical groping of the market toward equilibrium. Wicksteed pointed out,[33] and Walras admitted,[34] that when the price of any one commodity rises or falls, thus bringing the supply and demand for that commodity nearer to equilibrium, the effects of this change on other prices and the subsequent repercussions on the price of the principal commodity in question need not necessarily result in a closer approach to equality between demand and supply than existed at the start. It becomes a matter of greater or lesser probability.

This is, of course, not the same thing as, but is definitely related to, another difficulty which Edgeworth raised, not in his correspondence, but in his published work, namely, that Walras' description of the process by which prices emerge in the market is the description of *a* path, not of *the* path, to equilibrium.[35] In his correspondence Edgeworth argued another point. He was and remained, even after repeated explanations by Walras, mystified by the Walrasian theorem of maximum satisfaction as it related to capital goods.[36] Nor has any satisfactory solution yet been found for the problem of the imputation of marginal degrees of utility to fixed capital goods whose services yield no direct utility. Walras evolved a theory of imputation which was ingenious enough but which was based on the assumption that the services of new capital goods are proportional to the quantity of these goods and that consequently the same quantity symbol may be used for both.[37] Edgeworth could not swallow this assumption, because of the existence of old

[31] " . . . I cannot be said to have accepted the Jevons doctrine of 'final utility.' For I had taught it publicly in lectures at Cambridge before his book appeared. I had indeed used another name, viz.: 'terminal-value-in-use.' But, following the lead of Cournot, I had anticipated all the central points of Jevons' book and had in many respects gone beyond him. I was in no hurry to publish, because I wished to work out my doctrines on their practical side. Latterly I have been hindered by illness. . . ." (letter dated November 1, 1883, from Alfred Marshall to Léon Walras). It may be noted at this point that Jevons never used the term "final utility," only "final degree of utility."

[32] *Ibid.*

[33] Letter from Philip H. Wicksteed to Léon Walras, dated December 1, 1884.

[34] Letter to Wicksteed, dated December 14, 1884.

[35] F. Y. Edgeworth, *Papers Relating to Political Economy* (London, 1925), II, pp. 311–12.

[36] Letters from Walras to Edgeworth dated March 22, April 4, April 15, May 3, May 9, 1889, and from Edgeworth to Walras dated March 19, March 29, April 12, and May 9 of the same year.

[37] Lesson 26 of the *Éléments* (definitive edition).

durable capital goods whose services are not consistently proportional to the quantity of these goods.[38]

Another interesting point raised in the correspondence of this period is Walras' controversy with Böhm-Bawerk concerning the theory of interest. As a matter of fact, Walras shifted his position on interest when he came to prepare the fourth edition of his *Éléments* between 1896 and 1900. In the first three editions his equation of demand for savings is simply given as an empirical datum; but he adds that this equation could, if necessary, have been derived from the difference between present utility and future utility. In the fourth edition this passage was suppressed.[39] Walras imagines, instead, a new commodity which he calls perpetual net income, the price of which is the reciprocal of the rate of interest. Thus he deduces the rate of interest from the price of rights to perpetual net income, and this price is determined like all other prices in his total equilibrium scheme. The symmetry of his original system remains intact. He avoids, furthermore, injecting a new element, time preference. Not that he denies the existence of time preference. In a letter to Böhm-Bawerk dated May 5, 1889, he writes:

> You deduce the rate of interest from the difference in value between present and future goods. For my part, I think the difference in value between present and future goods cannot be directly determined, for this difference can only be deduced from the rate of interest which is determined directly by the ratio of the total net yield from new capitals to the volume of savings.

The delay in introducing this change and other changes, which his correspondence shows he had worked out earlier, into his successive

[38] "As I had anticipated, the import of the new theory is to apply statements which had been already proved for one sort of market—that of services and products—to another sort of market, that of capital: in your sense of that term, a sense which had not escaped so diligent a student of your book as I am. To use the old metaphor of the goose with the golden eggs—you before showed that in the egg market, price is determined by 'rareté,' and that maximum utility (in a certain sense which you have carefully defined) is realized. You now prove the same propositions for the goose market. Sometimes as I understand, you make abstraction of the *food* required by the goose in order to keep her in (good [? illegible]) condition; and sometimes you make allowances for her support and risk of her flying away, when you use your π's instead of your p's. Your use of both sets of coefficients on p. 305 [of ed. 2] has a little puzzled me.

"The only other difficulty which I continue to feel in the exposition which you give in the added chapter is at the third page where you speak of certain increments being *at the same time* of the nature of capital and 'services'; for so I interpret your statement and the correlated symbolism. Your system of differentials involves a relation between the goose market and the egg market which I have failed to grasp. Take a simple extreme case of a quite indestructible capital such as I had in view when instancing silver plate. The amount of *service*, i.e., use of plate (supposing, as happens, that plate may be lent to grace an entertainment) demanded by a person, and the amount of plate or a *possession* forever demanded by the same person are not to be bracketed as the formula suggests" (letter from Edgeworth to Walras dated April 12, 1889).

[39] Compare pages 270–71 of the third edition of the *Éléments* with page 250 of the fourth edition or the definitive edition.

editions is symptomatic of the increasing difficulties under which he was laboring. Personal tragedies began to beset him from the time of the publication of his first edition. His daughter wrote to me recently apropos of a photograph of Walras dated 1878:

> This photograph always brings to my mind sad memories. My poor mother was very ill at that time. Her illness lasted three years, and her death in 1879 was for her a merciful release. The expense was so great that my father's annual salary of 4,000 francs could not cover it. He gave an extra course at Neuchâtel; he gave private lessons and even wrote literary columns over the pseudonym Paul which were published every fortnight in the *Gazette de Lausanne.*

Léon Walras' nervous system broke down under the strain. Time and again we read in his letters of the eighties and nineties, "J'ai la tête très fatiguée." Curiously enough, he was suffering from the same sort of malady with which Jevons had been afflicted. In 1892, he took a year's leave of absence in the hope of recovering sufficient strength to carry on his teaching with his accustomed conscientiousness. But he soon saw that it was hopeless and resigned definitively.

1892–1910

Walras' retirement from his teaching post was by no means a retirement from scientific activity. As is well known, many of his publications and important revisions of the *Éléments* belong to this period. What is less well known is the extent of his correspondence in the nineties. His rich scientific correspondence with his successor Pareto, with Enrico Barone, and with Irving Fisher, belongs to this period. In the last decade of his life he wrote touching letters to Henry Ludwell Moore, whom he looked upon as a spiritual child to whom he might well intrust the task of carrying on his work. In this his hope was not in vain. In general he found great satisfaction in the recognition he received in America. Walras always took great pride in the fact that the American Economic Association had elected him an honorary member in 1892. Though, in the last decade of his life, honors were heaped upon him in Switzerland and abroad, and he had the consolation of seeing his theories gaining a firm foothold in Switzerland, Italy, Holland, Belgium, and the United States, he was bitterly disappointed by the coldness and hostility with which they were received in his own country, France.[40]

I can here do no more than briefly indicate one or two of the principal scientific questions discussed in the letters of the last period of Walras'

[40] There were no Walras centennial meetings in France in the year 1934.

life. Walras always showed himself highly appreciative of Irving Fisher's criticisms published in 1892 as an introductory note to his translation of Walras' *Geometrical Theory of the Determination of Prices*.[41] Walras maintained, however, that there was no foundation to Fisher's charge that he had neglected the element of time in his price analysis and had failed to consider production as a flow. His answer to this charge was first written on a manuscript note I found among his papers, and then printed, without mentioning Professor Fisher, on page 336 of the *Économie politique appliquée*. This note insists that it was only in the statical development of his theory that the time element and the flow concept do not appear. In the dynamical development, presented in Lesson 20 of the *Éléments*, the productive process is studied in motion and products are considered as flowing at a definite rate through time. Walras, however, admitted that Fisher was right in saying he had omitted to discuss the utility of any good as a function of the quantities of other goods and that he had left out of account the "permanent" profits of enterprise, i.e., the profits resulting from the fact that only marginal cost price equals selling price at equilibrium.[42] But Walras added that he had not overlooked these matters in his own notes and had later purposely left them out of his *Éléments* for the sake of simplicity. It was, according to Walras, a task for future generations of economists to rectify and add certain details to his system. He had fulfilled the task of giving to the world his system as a whole in the simplest form.

In 1902, when Walras brought to his printer the last revisions for the definitive edition of his *Éléments*, he was sixty-eight years old, weary with toil, and surfeited with controversies.[43] At times he would write to his intimate friends that he hoped he had sufficient philosophical self-

[41] *Annals of the American Academy of Political and Social Science*, III (1892), 45–64.
[42] Letter to Irving Fisher, dated July 28, 1892.
[43] As early as 1891, in a letter dated February 27, Walras had written to Bortkiewicz: "I have no more strength left, and the time has come for me to cede my place to others. But I shall wait, if necessary, until I find men who know that the secret of science is to keep the general case to the fore and to relegate particular cases and exceptions to the background. Fundamentally, that is the crux of my quarrel with Edgeworth. Take the question of the emergence of equilibrium through the groping of the market. I consider the quasi-universal case of free competition in exchange, the one that John Stuart Mill describes, which consists in raising prices when demand exceeds supply and in lowering prices when supply exceeds demand; and I demonstrate that this process results in equilibrium when supply and demand are equal. Upon which, my critics hurl at my head the English public security market, the English labor market, the English auction, the Dutch auction, etc., etc. When I treat the question of personal services [labor], my formulas include first the case of *unskilled labor*, which is characteristic of the labor of those who have never been apprenticed, then the case of *skilled labor*, which is characteristic of the labor of those who have served their apprenticeship, and finally the case of labor characterized by the individual workman's personal qualities. All this is nothing. The case which ought to have first consideration is the case of an individual who has served two or three apprenticeships and who passes two or three times a day from one kind of

restraint to give up his work in economics soon and to spend the rest of his days fishing and pottering about with painting and numismatics. But he could not really stop. His last writings were an article called "Économique et mécanique," published in 1909,[44] and a newspaper article entitled "Doctrines économiques," which appeared in the *Gazette de Lausanne* the day after he died: Professor Rist tells the story that during the last year of Walras' life a delegation of foreign economists came to Clarens, a small town near Lausanne to which Walras had retired in 1901, to pay their respects to the master. They had to inquire their way to his modest flat. A townsman, who had not at first caught the name, replied: "Ah, you mean the old professor who is continually reading his own books and looking for his mistakes." He remained a scholar and a scientist to the end. He died on January 5, 1910, only six months after the University of Lausanne had celebrated the jubilee of his service to economics.

In the nature of things, no autobiography has ever been finished. And yet, among Walras' notes I found these words, scribbled in pencil on a piece of blue paper with a parenthetical notation "end of autobiography":

The only immortality left for us to hope for is that of our own work. We must labor and enjoy the success of our labor by anticipation. This is the secret of morality and the secret of happiness.

work to another [cf. Edgeworth's *Papers,* II, 318–19], just as, for Auspitz and Lieben, the essential case is that of two commodities which complement each other. Well, these gentlemen would do better to work out these cases (which are not difficult, once the method has been found) instead of arguing about them in an attempt to prove that the general case 'does not belong to the sphere of science.' I do not claim to have created a finished science of pure economics by myself; all I claim is that I have sketched its broad outlines. . . . . ."

[44] *Bulletin de la Société Vaudoise des Sciences Naturelles,* XLV, No. 166 (April, 1909), 1–15.

2

LEON WALRAS, AN ECONOMIC ADVISER
MANQUE[1]

There were several episodes in Léon Walras's life in which he appeared as an economic adviser to governments, sometimes at the behest of public authorities, but for the most part uninvited.[2] There is, however, no case on record where he had any success or was taken seriously. Walras's ineptitude in his approach to officialdom, which manifested itself in his very first attempt to influence public policy, illustrates the difficulty that was to thwart his later attempts and, not surprisingly, doomed them all to failure. It is with this first attempt that I propose to concern myself in this paper, not only because of its interest as an anecdote, but also because of the light it sheds on Walras's social philosophy and his sense of reality.

Early in 1860, when Léon Walras was a struggling young journalist in Paris and had not yet found himself as the economic theorist he was destined to become, the Council of State of the Vaud Canton in Switzerland announced a prize of 1,200 francs for the best essay on the question, "Within the present social order, what system of taxation would achieve the most equitable possible distribution of the burden on taxpayers or taxable commodities?"[3] Confident in the economic and social philosophy he had imbibed from his father, Auguste Walras, who was an economist in his own right, Léon Walras answered the challenge. He submitted a memoir which, though it did not win the coveted prize, was published by the Vaud Council in 500 copies primarily for local distribution[4] and was awarded a fourth honourable mention with a consolation prize of 300 francs. Besides submitting the memoir, Léon

Editor's note: This chapter orginally appeared as "Léon Walras, an Economic Adviser *Manqué*," *Economic Journal, 85,* December 1975, 810–23.
    [1] Earlier versions of this paper were presented at the Sixth International Congress on Economic History held in Copenhagen, 19–23 August 1974, and at economic seminars in Keio University (Tokyo), 5 November 1974, and Simon Fraser University (Canada), 14 November 1974. I am grateful for the comments and suggestions made on these occasions. Research support from the Canada Council is gratefully acknowledged.
    [2] For Léon Walras's own account of several of these episodes, see references in footnote 1, p. 817, and footnotes 1–4, p. 822 below. Hereinafter Léon Walras is referred to as L.W.
    [3] Jaffé (1965), vol. I, p. 51, letter 26; my translation.
    [4] Walras (1861*b*). See also Jaffé (1965), vol. I, pp. 98–9, letter 64, and p. 103, letter 68.

Walras managed to get himself invited to read a paper at the International Congress on Taxation held in July of the same year, 1860.[5]

The reception of these two performances, which overlapped in content, was curiously mixed. They were greeted with both ridicule and respect. It is difficult not to sympathise with those who described Léon Walras as a tiresome upstart after he insisted on taking up a large part of two sessions of the Congress in reading an interminable manuscript.[6] Nevertherless, the *Gazette Vaudoise* acclaimed him as "the most substantial and the most erudite of all the speakers." It was even hinted that the Vaud Council of State contemplated calling him to a professorial chair in economics.[7]

Exactly! What else but a professorship would a young man (not yet turned 26 at the time) be good for, who, as the *Gazette Vaudoise* observed, was "wholly devoted to science for science's sake without admixture of any other preoccupation" and who could imperturbably inflict a ponderous lecture upon a distinguished and restless audience? Moreover, with an air of professorial superiority designed to put to shame the rambling debates and improvised recommendations of mere practitioners and publicists, he asked in the deliberative sessions that the following four summary propositions be put to a vote:

"I. If it is proposed to reduce the diverse imposts to a single tax in strict conformity with the requirements of political economy and justice, then the establishment of a single tax on rent follows logically.

"II. The reduction to a single tax on rent would be entirely feasible and would be more beneficial than harmful to agriculture.

"III. It would, [however], be tantamount to an outright confiscation of land by the State, and would therefore be an iniquitous act of spoliation in flagrant contravention of the interests and rights of landowners.

"IV. The problem of a single tax is insoluble."[8]

No wonder this paradoxical set of propositions won very few adherents among the down-to-earth economists voting at Congress.[9] Surely Léon Walras here betrayed an approach to practical problems that would hardly recommend him as an official economic adviser.

The counsel of despair which Walras offered the Congress found no

[5] Jaffé (1965), vol. I, pp. 63–6, letters 35–7. The paper was published as a book [Walras (1861*a*)] the following year.
[6] *Ibid.* vol. I, pp. 71–2, letter 43, n. 5.
[7] *Gazette Vaudoise*, 1 August 1860, unsigned article.
[8] Walras (1861*a*), pp. xxviii–xxix; reprinted in Walras (1896/1936), p. 395 of the 1936 ed. only. My translation.
[9] *Ibid.* p. 31; reprinted in Walras (1896/1936), p. 397 of the 1936 ed. only. Cf. Jaffé (1965), vol. I, p. 75, letter 47, n. 2.

place, however, in the essay he submitted in competition for the Vaud prize. There he declared his conviction that *at the scientific level* absolute logical rigour in the derivation of conclusions from premises must be the rule, while *at the applied level,* or, as the case may be, at the political level, compromises have to be made in the name of expediency, but always in the direction of the ideal goal previously established with scientific rigour.[10] He then examined each of the items of the then current Vaud tax system, reclassified them according as they did or did not conform in their incidence and their effects to his ideal goal, and recommended that the items that did conform be increased and the others decreased or eliminated. The upshot was a recommendation of a threefold increase in the land tax—and this despite proposition III of his resolution which denounced the absorption of other taxes by a single tax on rent as a flagrant and iniquitous spoliation of landowners!

As Polonius remarked on Hamlet's strange utterances, "Though this be madness, yet there is method in't." Indeed the Walrases, father and son, were nothing if not methodical. And just as Hamlet felt constrained to dress reason in apparent incoherencies, so did Léon Walras in the early 1860s. In a reminiscent mood, Walras wrote more than forty years later, "In those days, one was hauled into the police court and put in prison for merely inquiring into the existing institutions of property. That was precisely the fate of Vacherot.[11] But my father had made me promise not to take this risk, though I for my part should have considered myself honoured by it. This explains why I did no more than hint at the theory of the collective ownership of land, without enlarging upon it in my ... *Théorie critique de l'impôt* (1861). On learning of the opening of a *concours* on taxation at Lausanne, I saw an opportunity to expatiate on my doctrine. . . ."[12] It was too dangerous in the France of Napoleon III to suggest a course of action that an intolerant government was likely to regard as subversive. In Switzerland, however, which lay outside the jurisdiction of the French imperial magistracy, Léon Walras nevertheless

[10] In L.W.'s words: "Il ne faut pas oublier que les conclusions de la science pure ont un caractère éminemment abstrait et idéal, qu'elles peuvent et doivent être critiquées au nom de la raison, de la vérité, de la justice absolue (Walras, 1861 *b,* p. 64)." "Il est une chose que j'ai déjà dite et que je ne saurais trop répéter, c'est que les conclusions de la théorie ne préjugent rien d'absolu au sujet de l'application pratique où peuvent intervenir bien des compromis et des tempéraments" (*ibid.* p. 77).
[11] The allusion to Vacherot is doubly significant, for not only was the philosopher Etienne Vacherot (1809–97) a prominent victim of intellectual intolerance in the reign of Napoleon III, he was also a direct source and inspiration of several ideas underlying Walras's philosophy of taxation. See Vacherot (1860), pp. v–viii and 383–6, for an account of his persecution.
[12] My translation from an unpublished letter addressed to Charles Rist, dated "7bre o6," but marked "n'a jamais été envoyée." The existence of this letter was not discovered until 1966, when it was found along with other papers of L.W., in a forgotten cupboard of the Bibliothèque cantonale et universitaire de Lausanne.

ventured cautiously, ever so cautiously, to unveil the social philosophy in which his apparently paradoxical views on taxation were rooted.

The caution with which Léon Walras addressed the Swiss was not born of fear for his person; it was born of fear for society. Coming as he did from a French provincial petit-bourgeois family that had remained quietly royalist through the Revolution of 1789 he held revolutionary convulsions in abhorrence. Hence he prefaced his declaration of social philosophy in his memoir very much as Plato prefaced his ruminations on the theory of feminism and the community of women and children in the *Republic*. He insisted on the abstract and purely ideal character of his philosophy, the realisation of which, he recognised, would have to be tempered by practical considerations and exigencies.[13]

The ideal he had in mind was an ideal of absolute social justice subject to presumed ineluctable laws of social forces imposed by the very nature of society and revealed by the science of political economy. Nature having endowed every person with reason and free will to be exercised in the pursuit of happiness as far as his native capacities allow, each individual is entitled by natural law to whatever position in society, wealth, honours, etc., his industry, savings, intelligence, foresight and moral character make it possible for him to achieve. Since nature decreed an unequal distribution of innate endowments, inequality of positions inevitably follows. Provided that the conditions under which unequal positions are attained are the same for all, inequality of positions must always be deemed just from the standpoint of natural law. Justice requires also that no individual be allowed to subject another to his will or to infringe upon the rights of others in their pursuit of unequal positions. Auguste Walras's maxim, *égalité de conditions, inégalité de positions,* epitomised for Léon Walras the whole principle of social justice.[14] It also expressed for Léon Walras the essence of the principle of individualism which should preside over the distribution of wealth among individuals. No philosophy of taxation based on equity may contravene it.

Individualism, however, was not enough for Léon Walras. In fact, he vehemently rejected absolute unfettered individualism as a guide to

[13] "Je demande que, pour le moment, mes idées soient examinées, discutées et jugées . . . indépendamment de toute considération pratique: ainsi seulement je n'aurai point à me repentir de les avoir exprimées" [Walras (1861b), p. 64]. See above n. 3, p. 811.

[14] Excellent accounts of the Walrasian social philosophy are found in Bompaire (1931), pp. 432–544; Gide and Rist (1948), pp. 597–600; Boson (1951), *passim,* especially pp. 43–5, 205–12; and Hutchison (1953), pp. 210–15. The principal primary sources for Auguste Walras's social philosophy are his MSS published posthumously in Leroy (1923), and the letters of Auguste Walras to his son in [A. Walras] (1912–14). For L.W.'s social philosophy, see Walras (1860); Walras (1861b), pp. 64–79; Walras (1896/1936), pp. 147–71, 175–202, 438–41 (461–4 of 1936 edition); and Walras (1898/1936), pp. 449–62, 485–95.

public policy because, as he saw it, individuals are members of society by virtue, not of a social contract, but of their essential social nature. Moreover, the inherent right of individuals to a fair and full realisation of their separate moral personalities cannot have any existence apart from society.[15] Equality of conditions and respect by each individual for the rights of others can only be assured by society organised for the purpose as a State. Individuals intent on their private strivings cannot be entrusted with this task.

But where and how can the State obtain the means to fulfil this essential function? The usual answer is by taxation. In that case, the only debatable issues are whether taxation should be multiple or single; whether taxes should be "direct" (i.e. levied on persons) or "indirect" (i.e. levied on commodities); whether, if levied on persons, they should be calculated on the basis of the taxpayer's income or his property; whether the taxes, however levied, should be proportional or progressive. Léon Walras would have none of this: he rejected the whole taxation solution out of principle and consequently considered the subsidiary issues misplaced in the context of social justice. At best, he would allow the subsidiary issues to be examined from the standpoint of mitigating the evils of an inherently unjust system. Justice demands that an alternative be found to taxation as a source of public finance.[16]

The characteristically Walrasian thesis, first enunciated by Auguste Walras, was that the problem of taxation and the problem of property are one and the same.[17] As soon as it is postulated that any incursion whatsoever upon an individual's income derived from his person or his property is unjust, then the question arises, what property is properly his? It goes without saying that, slavery excluded, property in his person, let us say his human capital, is properly his. It must also be granted that the individual's property in his artificial capital, which is the more or less lasting fruit of his labour, care and foresight, is also properly his. There remains, then, the question of the right of an individual to own what is not the fruit of his labour, care and foresight,

---

[15] This idea, which is found repeatedly in L.W.'s writings, was clearly set forth in Walras (1861b), pp. 6–7.

[16] A similar view was expressed quite recently by Professor Harry Johnson, who also stressed the "dilemma" inherent in "our antiquated way of financing governmental activity" and proposed an alternative to taxation, albeit different from L.W.'s. Professor Johnson suggested that "one way of moving in [the] direction [of giving the government a direct participation in the income of the economy, rather than a tax claim on it] would be to accumulate the proceeds of inheritance taxes in the form of a government portfolio of ordinary shares and industrial bonds, instead of spending them as current income" [Johnson (1962), p. 194]. L.W. would probably have rejected this alternative because it would make the State a capitalist performing investment functions he would reserve for individuals.

[17] L.W., echoing his father's views, declared, " . . . il est certain qu'il y a une intime connexité, mieux encore, une identité absolue entre les deux problèmes de la propriété et de l'impôt" [Walras (1861b), p. 10].

namely land, which was given by nature to all mankind. Land, the Walrases argued, belongs to society and, by its nature and origin, constitutes the legitimate property of none other than the State.[18]

In this way, the Walrases were convinced that their philosophy of individualism and the State killed two birds with one stone. It not only dispelled the antithesis between individualism and collectivism by reconciliation, but also resolved the problems of taxation by elimination. Once the State comes into possession of its own natural property, it can obtain the revenue it needs[19] by leasing the land to individuals under the usual contracts negotiated in a free market. The Walrases were opposed to any direct exploitation of the land by the State, because that would grossly distort the operation of the principle of individualism, which, they insisted, should remain intact.

This is the principle which Léon Walras sketched in §§I and IV of the memoir he submitted to the authorities of the Vaud Canton. He had enough realistic sense to know that anything approaching an immediate realisation of this ideal would entail the outright confiscation of all existing private property rights in land, with attendant grave injustices to current landowners, who, after all, were neither legally nor morally responsible for the system by which they profited. He therefore suggested palliatives and a course of action that would eventually bring about the consummation of the ideal, slowly and gradually and without harsh or unjust side-effects.[20]

---

[18] "*La Terre appartient à l'Etat,* le sol cultivable forme la propriété commune de tous les citoyens. Le revenu du sol ou le *fermage* constitue le *revenue public. Le Travail appartient à l'individu,* en d'autres termes, l'individu s'appartient à lui-même. Chaque citoyen a, pour vivre, sa force industrielle, son aptitude laborieuse, sa capacité physique, intellectuelle et morale. L'exercice quotidien de nos facultés personnelles et le *salaire* qui en resulte, voilà notre *revenu privé,* notre fortune personnelle. A cela il faut ajouter les *profits* [in the sense of income] *de nos capitaux artificiels.* Et, en effet, le capital est le fruit du travail et de l'économie, c'est du travail accumulé; le capital ne se forme que par le travail et par l'épargne, c'est le produit d'un bon calcul et d'une sage modération. A ce titre il appartient très légitimement à celui qui l'a créé par son travail, et qui, non content de le créer par son travail, a plus fait encore en le conservant par sa prudence et par sa tempérance" [from A.Walras's suppressed chapter VIII of his *Théorie de la richesse sociale,* published in Leroy (1923), pp. 127–8].

[19] L.W. maintained that in ordinary circumstances the needs of the State should be tailored to its resources. See Walras (1896), "Le problème fiscal."

[20] L.W. made every effort to reassure his Swiss readers that he had no thought of violating existing property rights of landowners, despite his low opinion of their social and economic role. "Quant aux propriétaires fonciers qui ne sont pas travailleurs et qui sont oisifs, je ne dirais pas que leur position peut paraître moins intéressante et qu'on peut être tenté d'aller contre leurs droits. Non, l'on a dû remarquer que, durant le cours de ce mémoire, il n'a jamais été fait appel à de semblables idées. Le droit est sacré partout et toujours; . . ." [Walras (1861*b*), p. 97]. In his Vaud memoir, the way L.W. proposed to avoid infringing on the vested rights of landlords was to restrict increases in land taxes to the absorption of *new* windfall increases in land-rents, thus making the State a virtual co-proprietor of the land. Later, inspired by James Mill and M. H. Gossen, he devised an elaborate, mathematically formulated scheme for repurchasing land, thus making the State its sole proprietor [Walras (1881/3, 1896/1936)].

Though Walras acknowledged a family resemblance between his
proposed tax policy and that of Quesnay, he denied that they were really
the same thing.[21] Indeed, he disowned the Physiocratic idea of a single
tax on land rent because he had no more faith than his father in the
Physiocratic doctrine that taxes of every variety fall ultimately on
landowners.[22] He insisted that the Physiocratic proposal of a reduction of
all taxes to a single tax on land rent would, in final analysis, add to the
burden placed on land by transferring to it taxes whose ultimate
incidence, according to Walras, had previously fallen elsewhere. His
objection was that this would effectively entail a wholesale and indis-
criminate confiscation of whatever portion of the land is represented by
the capitalised value of the additional tax.[23] Léon Walras was opposed to
confiscatory measures, however unjustly private property rights in land
may have been established in the beginning. Both Walrases wanted only
to put a stop to *further* usurpations of land, which they saw as an ongoing
process that manifests itself in the increase in land values as rents rise
and the interest rate falls in a progressive society.[24]

On closer examination it is seen that Léon Walras's recommendation
to the Vaud government of a tripling of the land tax[25] had nothing
paradoxical about it; nor was it inconsistent with his economic analysis
and social philosophy. Reckoned as a tax on ground rent, the proposal
was not as drastic as it looked. The tax that Walras wanted tripled was a
land tax of only one quarter of 1% of the assessed land values and one
tenth of 1% on the value of the buildings, these being the rates
stipulated in the Vaud cantonal budget of 1859. In that budget the land
tax constituted about 24% of the estimated total cantonal tax revenue.
Walras was careful to point out that a tripling of this proportion would
not result in a threefold increase of the current burden on the landowner,
since he advocated, at the same time, that the increase in the land tax be

---

[21] Walras (1861a), pp. xxix–xxx. The same passage is found reproduced *verbatim* on
pages 395–6 of L.W's revised version of his "Souvenirs du Congrès de Lausanne"
published in Walras (1896/1936), pp. 377–400 of the 1936 edition only.

[22] Auguste Walras had written: "Sans doute, les Physiocrates se trompaient grossière-
ment en croyant que tous les impôts tombaient, en definitive, sur les propriétaires
fonciers ou sur le produit net. Il n'est que trop vrai que la plus grande partie des impôts
tombe sur les travailleurs" ("La vérité sociale," Leroy (1923), pp. 178–9).

[23] On this point, both Walrases acknowledged their indebtedness to de Tracy (1823/
1817/1970) and quoted liberally from him. See chapter xii, especially pages 206–9, of the
English version of de Tracy's treatise.

[24] In Auguste Walras's words, "La propriété individuelle, appliquée au sol, constitue
une usurpation croissante et continue du domaine public et du revenu qui en provient.
Au fur et à mesure que la valeur du sol et le montant du fermage s'élèvent, dans une
société progressive, l'Etat est incessamment dépouillé de son revenu" [from A. Walras's
suppressed chapter viii of his *Théorie de la richesse sociale,* published in Leroy (1923), p.
128].

[25] Walras (1861b), pp. 87–9.

accompanied by the complete elimination of the tax on transfers of real property, which constituted 22% of the estimated cantonal tax revenue and, in the final analysis, had always fallen on the landowners with the same quasi-confiscatory effect as the land tax.

Landowners would be treated gently enough under Walras's proposal, for they would not be deprived of anything more than the unearned increment in land values which had accrued to them during the previous sixty years for no other reason than that the assessed values had not kept pace with increases in actual land values in that period of exceptional economic growth. From the standpoint of equity, the proposed threefold increase in the land tax would, therefore, be no more than just. From the standpoint of economic analysis, Walras argued that far from being harmful, the increase in the land tax would very likely have a stimulating effect on economic activity because it was designed to replace other taxes with which capital and labour had been hitherto burdened.[26] Unlike artificial capital which is produced and maintained only to the extent that capitalists consider the net return adequate after taxes, raw land given by nature would remain available as an instrument of production in exactly the same quantity after the increase in the land tax as before. Moreover, the exploitation of the land and the demand for its products would be improved as the return on the artificial capital applied to it was freed from tax deductions and as labour was relieved of indirect taxes on the agricultural products it consumed.

While both Walrases held that considerations of justice should take precedence over considerations of plenty,[27] they were far from ignoring the latter. In fact, they held that there was not and could not be any essential contradiction between economic laws which the scientist discovers in his study of the spontaneous operation of a competitive market economy and the principle of justice which the philosopher discovers in his study of the conscience of man. The two are on different planes—one natural, i.e. governed by the intractable laws of nature, and the other

[26] August Walras had summarised the argument with disarming finality: "Supprimez les impôts, et vous verrez l'industrie et le commerce prendre un nouvel essor. Ceci est trop élémentaire pour avoir besoin de démonstration" ["La vérité sociale," Leroy (1923), p. 162].

[27] L.W. made the point explicitly in a letter dated 6 September 1870: "... c'est peu que la richesse sociale soit produite abondamment, si elle n'est équitablement répartie entre tous les membres de la société" [Jaffé (1965), vol. I, p. 209, letter 148]. His father had written in 1849, "Si l'*économie politique* a ses principes, le *droit naturel* a les siens qui ne le cèdent à aucun autre en importance et en dignité. . . . Tout ce qu'on peut dire en faveur de l'*économie politique*, c'est qu'elle a le droit d'apporter ses lumières, de faire intervenir ses principes. . . . Ce qu'on peut imposer au *droit naturel*, c'est l'obligation de consulter l'*economie politique*, et de légitimer les résultats de ses recherches par le contrôle des vérités que peut lui fournier la science de la richesse" [A. Walras (1849), pp. 102–3]. Cf. Walras (1860).

moral, i.e. governed by the tractable conscience of man. Natural alienation and acquisition take place in market exchange wherever society is organised on the basis of the division of labour; anything else, like taxation, is contrived, and being contrived must necessarily be brought to the test of justice. At the same time, in order to determine whether or not any contrived scheme of alienation or acquisition conforms to a given moral principle, it is necessary to follow through the working of the scheme to its ultimate economic effects on persons and classes of persons.

It is precisely at this juncture that Léon Walras introduced into his memoir bits and pieces of economic analysis and tried his hand at tracing the incidence of various types of taxes. In later years he recognised the crudity of this first analytical performance,[28] but he remained faithful throughout his life to the social philosophy he had expounded in the early 1860s. The same philosophical position gave direction not only to his policy prescriptions for taxation, but also to his subsequent proposals regarding monetary management, monopolies, wages, speculation and foreign trade. Indeed, none of his policy pronouncements could be appreciated without reference to Walras's whole philosophical system and, in later years, to his general equilibrium theory as well. It is little wonder that the public authorities to whom Walras profferred advice were impatient when he insisted on boring them with lengthy disquisitions on his pet social philosophy and arduous expositions of his mathematico-economic model, as a prelude to his specific proposals.[29] After all, what the authorities wanted was succinct guidance for day-to-day accommodation to transient circumstance, and this Léon Walras was congenitally incapable of furnishing.

This is not to say that Walras was so blinded by the glitter of his philosophy or the radiance of his economic theory as to be incapable of tackling practical questions realistically. In fact, in one of his essays in applied economics, he warned economists against being fooled by their own abstractions.[30] Quite early in his career, when he was still at the journalistic stage, Léon Walras evinced a pragmatic sense which might well have recommended him to governments as an official adviser. This

[28] L.W.'s candid confession of analytical errors in his early writings on taxation is found in his introduction to the revised version of his "Souvenirs du Congrès de Lausanne" published in the 1936 edition only of his *Etudes d'économie sociale* [Walras (1896/1936), pp. 377–8]. He there referred to the final lesson (lesson 42) of his *Eléments d'économie politique pure* for his definitive analysis of taxation and its incidence.

[29] For a dramatic display of such impatience when L.W. presented oral testimony before a Swiss federal commission on banknote legislation, see Jaffé (1965): vol. II, pp. 359–62, letter 925, n. 12. So far as I know, L.W. was never invited again to give expert testimony in Switzerland.

[30] "Mais l'économiste ne doit pas être la dupe de ses abstractions" [Walras (1897/1898/1936), p. 275 of the *Etudes d'économie politique appliquée*].

was in 1861, when the financial world was in a state of crisis occasioned by violent fluctuations in the price of cotton in the United States. The question was then whether the Bank of France should raise the discount rate or suspend convertibility of banknotes to stem the outflow of specie which was taking place at an alarming rate. Walras favoured the former alternative, though he recognised the disadvantages of a rising discount rate for the domestic economy of France. He argued that the discount rate would rise in any case as it became necessary to regulate the issue of inconvertible banknotes and that, furthermore, under inconvertibility, coins in circulation would be melted down and exported along with bullion, thus increasing the domestic price of bullion and exposing France to the grave dangers of a fiduciary currency. Though, in theory, he thought that only the Scots system of 100% specie reserve requirements against banknotes for issues exceeding a legally defined maximum was 'scientifically' justifiable, he was not so doctrinaire as to be blind to the historical relativity of his ideal system.[31]

Better still as an example of Walras's sense of reality was the position he took at this time in a controversy with a rival journalist who had urged that an international monetary conference be called to impose orderly discount and note issue practices on the banks of the United States. Walras protested that the scheme, besides being impracticable, was misdirected. He contended that American financial crises were part and parcel of the inevitable growing pains of the rapidly expanding economy of the new world, that the rash banking practices of the United States had contributed prodigiously to the development of its capital, and that the rest of the world would profit in the end by submitting to the effects of American crises even at the cost of rising discount rates at home. Eventually America would mature and then adopt more prudent banking policies of its own accord. France, in the meantime, might learn from American experience what fructifying benefits could be derived from greater freedom in banking and modify its own rigid, ultra-prudent, authoritarian practices imposed by the Bank of France.[32]

Walras, however, did not persist in cultivating an interest in day-to-day practical issues, though he would return to them from time to time. He was always reaching for higher things in a manner that disqualified him as a professional guide to governments trying to find their way through the maze of pressing workaday problems. And yet he remained in two minds about it.

At times he appeared consecrated to pure theory exclusively and would explain his occasional lapses from virtue by a desire to attract attention to his theoretical work, with policy proposals as bait. Writing

[31] Jaffé (1965), vol. I, p. 95, letter 61, n. 4.   [32] *Ibid.* vol. I, pp. 91–4, letter 61.

to one of his correspondents in 1881, when he was professor at the Académie de Lausanne, he confessed, "If I were my own master, I should gladly confine myself entirely to pure theoretical analysis. But I cannot do this, because I am obligated to give a complete course [comprising applied economics and normative economics ("économie sociale") in addition to pure economics]. Those who have a taste for pure theory are rare, especially in our day. Generally, all the reader looks for in pure theory are the [practical] results. You, however, are among the few capable of disinterested, scientific speculation, and you can appreciate for its own sake a rigorous mathematical theory of price determination under a regime of absolutely free competition. You will see that [pure] theory will command attention and be taken seriously only when it is perceived that among the things to which it leads are the theories of increasing land-rents in a progressive society which lie at the bottom of any proposal for the repurchase of land by the State."[33]

At other times Léon Walras appeared to be primarily interested in curing the world's ills and setting it on the high-road to justice and prosperity. When in that mood, he regarded pure theory less as an end in itself than as an instrument, a compass, to help in the search for rational direction in the pursuit of progress. It was with this object in view that he entered upon a serious study of economics in the first place. Just before that he had published a novel, *Francis Sauveur,* with a Preface, dated March 1858, which was, in fact, his manifesto of social justice. In it he denounced the society of his day as "an iniquitous association" in which "the mass of workers are wretched proletaires living side by side with a set of idlers who are the fortune-favoured owners of the land on which we were born."[34] But now, Walras went on to say, after the Revolution of 1848 which had introduced universal suffrage,[35] his

[33] *Ibid.* vol. I, p. 711, letter 519; my translation. Great as Léon Walras was as a pure theorist he was a poor prophet. He is celebrated today not for his policy recommendations but for his pure theory. For the most part, Walras's policy excursions are either ignored or deprecated [e.g. Stigler (1941), p. 229; Schumpeter (1954), pp. 827–8; Schumpeter (1951), pp. 76–7 for an expression of his earlier opinion; De Rosa (1960), vol. 3, p. 121 for Pareto's condemnation]. In the few non-contagious cases where commentators make Walras's policy outlook an object of sympathetic interest, his pure theory is denounced as a regrettable excrescence [Oulès (1948), pp. 269, 271, and Oulès (1950)].

[34] Walras (1858), p. ix. L.W. did not use the term *prolétaires* in the modern socialist sense of propertyless wage-earners exploited by capitalists but in quite a different sense defined by his father in harmony with his conception of a socially inherent class struggle, the only true one he insisted, between the landed and the landless, the latter being all "prolétaires," whether they be workers or capitalists. See A. Walras's suppressed chapter VIII of his *Théorie de la richesse sociale* published in Leroy (1923), p. 128; Walras (1858), p. xi, and Walras (1861b), p. 75.

[35] With the passage of time, L.W.'s unbounded faith in the blessings of universal suffrage (male, of course!) faded. On the first page of the Preface of his own copy of *Francis Sauveur* [Walras (1859)], now preserved in the Fonds Walras of the Bibliothèque cantonale et universitaire de Lausanne, is found an undated marginal annotation in his

generation could recreate society without recourse to fratricidal violence. Industrial progress contained within itself the seeds of a new moral order. Provided that the State did its part in establishing equality of conditions, the new industrial order could be relied upon to insure that all unequal positions were in proportion to the market values of the individual contributions to society rendered by its members.[36] It was with the object of giving scientific substance to this ideal that in the summer of 1858, when *Francis Sauveur* was still fresh off the press, Léon Walras declared his intention to abandon literature and become an economist[37] like his father, to whom he now owed his profession as well as his social ideal.

Unfortunately the Walrasian social philosophy was fast becoming obsolete by the time Léon Walras entered the scene as a policy advocate. Auguste Walras had acquired his passion for the conciliation of opposites from the philosophers in vogue during the French Restoration. At the political level, after the return of the Bourbons to the throne of France, the *Doctrinaire* philosophers of the Restoration proclaimed that only by reconciling the principles of 1789 with legitimism could internal peace be maintained.[38] At the social level after the advent of the industrial era attended by mounting clamours against property, Auguste Walras maintained that only by reconciling individualism with collectivism would it be possible to avert the added danger of internal dissension proceeding now, not from past political conflict, but from new social tensions.

In the 1840s August Walras was as aware as Karl Marx that "a spectre [was] haunting Europe – the spectre of communism." Like Karl Marx, Auguste Walras felt that the spectre was too genuine a manifesta-

own hand, reading: " . . . mon opinion sur le suffrage universel s'est modifiée ensuite de la distinction que je suis arrivé à faire entre la théorie ou science sociale et la pratique ou politique. Je crois toujours que le suffrage universel est une vérité scientifique en ce sens qu'il se place dans l'idéal social à la condition d'être organisé rationnellement; mais je crois aussi que son avènement prématuré et son fonctionnement sous une forme grossière et brutale ont été un malheur *politique* dont la démocratie française pourrait bien ne pas se relever."

[36] In a letter to L.W. dated 1 April 1860, Auguste Walras explained the idea as follows: "Les Saint-Simoniens ont proclamé la maxime: *à chacun suivant sa capacité, à chaque capacité suivant ses oeuvres;* mais cette maxime est toujours restée assez vague et assez peu précise. Qui jugera de la capacité? qui jugera de la valeur des œuvres? Il n'y a ni père suprême, ni collège du premier degré qui puisse suffire à cette tâche. Il vaut mieux s'en rapporter à l'opinion publique et à la libre concurrence.

"Je conviens, il est vrai, que cette maxime consacre la distinction que je fais entre la justice commutative et la justice distributive, et qu'elle semble réserver le domaine de l'égalité et celui de l'inégalité. Mais tout cela n'est pas très clair, et je préfère de beaucoup ma formule: égalité des conditions, inégalité des positions" [A. Walras (1912–14), 9 (53), p. 377].

[37] Jaffé (1965), vol. I, p. 2 (L.W.'s "Notice autobiographique").

[38] Cf. *Cambridge Modern History* (1907), vol. x, chapter II, "The Doctrinaires."

tion of protest against flagrant social injustices to want it dispelled.[39] Again, like Karl Marx, whom we may be sure he had never heard of, Auguste Walras sought to give rational direction to the spectre which hovered aimlessly over the industrial scene in wild and terrifying convolutions of utopian inspiration. For both Auguste Walras and Karl Marx the new direction was to be found in sound political economy, the political economy bequeathed by the Physiocrats and Adam Smith which needed only to be reinterpreted, corrected, amended and adapted to the new conditions of the nineteenth century.[40] From here on, however, all resemblance between Auguste Walras and Karl Marx ceases. Karl Marx founded his socialism on the Hegelian historical dialectic. Though there were intimations of historical relativism in the Walrasian doctrine, since both Auguste and Léon Walras agreed that their theories of value and price were relevant only to the particular stage in economic history in which developed markets had made their appearance,[41] yet it never occurred to either of the Walrases to inquire, as Marx did, whether there were any immanent laws governing the succession of stages. The only laws Auguste Walras appealed to, in support of his directions to the spectre, were the supposedly perennial static laws embodied in traditional natural law philosophy. Léon Walras, who never departed one iota from his father's philosophical creed, was inevitably handicapped in urging upon public authorities measures that were inseparable from a philosophy which just at that time was being displaced by positivism and historicism in the natural and social sciences.

Léon Walras had no illusions. He knew perfectly well that he was swimming against the tide. Nowhere is this more evident that in his remarks on fiscal policy. In the papers he presented at Lausanne he confined his attention to the receipts aspects of public finance, leaving the expenditure aspect to one side. He did, however, hint that government expenditures too should be tailored on the pattern of the maxim, "Equality of conditions, inequality of positions." What this meant for him specifically, he revealed much later, in 1896, in a two-part article

[39] A. Walras, "La vérité sociale," published in Leroy (1923): pp. 181–2. Writing under the inspiration of his father, L.W. declared in 1860, "Le socialisme contemporain a eu sa raison d'être dans le malaise d'une société en voie d'organisation, mais encore éloignée du terme de ses efforts" [Walras (1860), p. lix)].
[40] "Prenez les théories socialistes...; et je me fait fort de vous démontrer que l'exagération et le vice de tous ces systèmes reposent également sur la nature fausse ou incomplète de la richesse sociale ou de la valeur d'échange.... Et il est incontestable que les erreurs de Proudhon proviennent exclusivement de ce qu'il a pris l'économie politique telle que l'ont laissée Adam Smith et J. B. Say, et qu'il n'a pas corrigé l'erreur de ces grands maîtres sur cette notion fondamentale" [A. Walras, "petit manuscrit," Jaffé (1965), vol. I, pp. 41–3, letter 16, n. 14, where "le petit manuscrit" was mistakenly attributed to L.W.].
[41] Cf. Walras (1898/1936), pp. 468–9.

entitled "Le problème fiscal," which first appeared in the *Revue socialiste,* of all places![42] There it is clear that the reconciliation of individualism with collectivism meant for him that fiscal policy should serve no other purpose than to establish and preserve "equality of conditions." Léon Walras deduced from this that once land was nationalised, once taxation was eliminated, once all impediments to free trade in international commerce were removed, once natural monopolies were brought under the control of the State, once money was stabilised in value, and once labour was assisted not only in adapting itself to free competition in the labour market but also in becoming co-proprietors of capital through individual saving and co-operative investment, then indeed the goal of fiscal policy should be limited to financing only those public services which confer equal benefits upon all citizens. Such public services are, for example, national defence, police protection, the administration of justice, elementary education and the maintenance of only those public works which are designed to serve all in equal measure. He denounced as morally and economically pernicious any use of fiscal policy to attenuate "inequality of positions." He included among the fiscal measures he condemned all government expenditures (in contradistinc-tion to private or co-operative expenditures) on such services as social medicine, unemployment insurance, old-age insurance, accident insur-ance and public works undertaken to create employment. To be sure, these public services hardly existed in 1896, but Walras foresaw with dread that they were perilously imminent unless society mended its ways and espoused his social philosophy.[43]

This is not to say that Léon Walras was an advocate of *laisser-faire* liberalism.[44] On the contrary, he strongly believed in State intervention, but only to the degree that it was necessary to assure "equality of conditions" and to insure "inequality of positions" properly arrived at. Upon the effective realisation of the social ideal as Léon Walras envis-aged it, each individual would be held wholly responsible for his own welfare and that of his family. Then those who found themselves at the lowest end of the scale of "inequality of positions" would, in general, have only themselves to blame.[45] Léon Walras thought it the duty of the State to refrain from using fiscal policy to alleviate the retributive consequences of incompetence or fecklessness, for that would be in contravention of natural law. Of course, there is a place for charity, both

[42] Walras (1896 and 1896/1936).

[43] *Ibid.* p. 397 (p. 437 of the 1896 ed. of the *Etudes d'économie sociale;* p. 460 of the 1936 ed.).

[44] This point is all too frequently overlooked. See Jaffé (1965), vol. I, p. 746, letter 548; vol. II, p. 478, letter 1042, and vol. III, p. 168, letter 1499.

[45] Walras (1896), pp. 397–8 (pp. 437–8 of the 1896 ed. of the *Etudes d'économie sociale,* pp. 460–1 of the 1936 ed.).

public and private, but only where the object is a victim of pure mischance. But as charity, by definition, is always voluntary, its recipients can claim no established right to it.

Obviously, the Walrasian social philosophy was in essence a philosophy of individualism; and yet Auguste Walras called it "socialism" and Léon Walras went so far as to call it "scientific socialism."[46] Joseph Schumpeter thought that Léon Walras "is best described as a semi-socialist."[47] But, in the light of his social philosophy, we may well ask whether Léon Walras was a socialist at all, even a sixty-fourth of a socialist, a hemisemidemi-socialist? In his own day, however, it was sufficient for him to parade a social philosphy that would assign any direct economic function at all to the State to qualify him, in the eyes of the authorities, as a socialist and consequently disqualify him from exerting an effective influence on statesmanship.

All of Léon Walras's attempts to play a public role met with polite rebuffs: when he offered his services in 1879 to Jules Ferry, Minister of Public Instruction in France, to help him reform the French university system;[48] when he indicated to Louis Ruchonnet, an influential member of the Swiss Federal Council, that he would like to be appointed a representative of Switzerland to the International Monetary Conference of 1881;[49] and when in 1884 he asked Jules Ferry, now French Minister of Foreign Affairs, to let him represent France at the International Monetary Conference of that year.[50] The rebuffs were polite, because both Jules Ferry and Louis Ruchonnet were his personal friends. In the end, he resigned himself to renouncing his long cherished hope that a day would come when, through the good offices of Louis Ruchonnet, he might be made an official delegate of Switzerland and succeed in bringing his symmetallic scheme for monetary reform to the attention of public authorities of the entire world.[51]

Ruminating upon his failures, Léon Walras concluded that, after all, the right place for an academic economist was in his study. He professed that it was always with the greatest reluctance that he ever entertained the idea of taking part in public affairs, and then only under special circumstances.[52] He found comfort in appealing to the principle of a strict division of labour between contemplative theorists and the active

[46] In 1877, writing from the Académie de Lausanne, L.W. introduced himself in the following terms to the philosopher Paul Janet of the Sorbonne who had claimed acquaintance with Auguste Walras's work: "Votre sympathie ne se refroidira-t-elle pas, Monsieur, en recontrant un socialiste là où vous ne croyiez trouver qu'un savant? Mais, croyez, je vous prie, que le fils et l'élève d'un agrégé de philosophie [Auguste Walras] ne peut professer qu'un socialisme très scientifique" [Jaffé (1965), vol. I, p. 525, letter 369].
[47] Schumpeter (1954), p. 888.   [48] Jaffé (1965), vol. I, pp. 592–5, letter 429.
[49] Ibid. vol. I, pp. 692–3, letter 503.   [50] Ibid. vol. II, p. II, letter 610.
[51] Ibid. vol. II, pp. 77–8, letter 680.   [52] Ibid. vol. II, p. 30, letter 632.

practitioners.[53] The practitioner, though he may look for guidance from the theorist, often finds that facts move so much faster than theory that he is obliged to improvise when under pressure to make decisions which cannot be postponed. The academic theorist, on the other hand, whose function it is to formulate and to propagate guiding conceptual principles, cannot perform his proper task unless he is free to ignore the immediate exigencies with which the practitioner must cope. Never once suspecting that he lacked the required aptitudes of a practitioner or politician, he persuaded himself that he had deliberately chosen to be an ivory tower scientist, specialising in pure and applied *theory*, because the supply of politicians attracted by the prospect of glittering rewards is always abundant, while there are never enough theorists willing to shut themselves up in their studies and remain content with the modest recompense and obscurity which is their lot.[54]

Perhaps this was simply making a virtue of necessity. Or was it wisdom in a deeper sense? That is a question which every academic economist aspiring to the rank of official adviser might well ask himself, especially if E. H. Phelps Brown is right in his observation on "the smallness of the number of contributions that the most conspicuous developments of economics in the last quarter of a century have made to the most pressing problems of the times."[55]

[53] *Ibid.* vol. I, p. 583, letter 418, n. 2.
[54] Walras (1898/1936), p. 456.   [55] Phelps Brown (1972), p. 1.

REFERENCES

Bompaire, F. (1931). *Du principe de liberté économique dans l'œuvre de Cournot et dans celle de l'Ecole de Lausanne (Walras, Pareto)*. Paris: Sirey.

Boson, M. (1951). *Léon Walras, fondateur de la politique économique scientifique*. Paris: Librairie Générale de Droit et de Jurisprudence.

De Rosa, G., ed. (1960). *Vilfredo Pareto, Lettere a Maffeo Pantaleoni*, 3 vols. Rome: Banca Nazionale del Lavoro.

Destutt [de] Tracy, A. (1970). *Traité d'économie politique*, Paris: Bouguet et Lévi, 1823. Previously published in English translation, *A Treatise on Political Economy*, 1817. Photographically reproduced in Reprints of Economic Classics Series. New York: Augustus M. Kelley.

Gide, C. and Rist, C. (1948). *A History of Economic Doctrines from the Time of the Physiocrats to the Present Day*, 2nd English ed., trans. R. A. Richards. New York: Heath.

Hutchison, T. W. (1953). *A Review of Economic Doctrines 1870–1929*. Oxford: Clarendon Press.

Jaffé, W., ed. (1965). *Correspondence of Léon Walras and Related Papers*, 3 vols. Amsterdam: North Holland (for Royal Netherlands Academy of Sciences and Letters).

Johnson, H. G. (1962). *Money, Trade and Economic Growth*. Cambridge, Mass.: Harvard University Press.

Leroy, L. Modeste (1923). *Auguste Walras, économiste, sa vie, son œuvre*. Paris. Librairie Générale de Droit et de Jurisprudence.

Oulès, F. (1948). "Discours." *Revue économique et sociale*, vol. 6, no. 4 (October), pp. 269–81.

   (1950). "Les insuffisances théoriques fondamentales de la doctrine économique de la première école de Lausanne." *Metroeconomica* 2, nos. 1 and 3 (April and December), pp. 20–34, 134–71.

Phelps Brown, E. H. (1972). "The underdevelopment of economics." *Economic Journal*, vol. 82, no. 325 (March), pp. 1–10.

Schumpeter, J. A. (1951). *Ten Great Economists from Marx to Keynes*. New York: Oxford University Press.

   (1954). *History of Economic Analysis*. New York: Oxford University Press.

Stigler, G. J. (1941). *Production and Distribution Theories*. New York: Macmillan.

Vacherot, E. (1960). *La Démocratie*, 2nd ed. Brussels: Lacroix, van Meenen and Co.

Walras, A. (1849). *Théorie de la richesse sociale ou résumé des principes fondamentaux de l'économie politique*. Paris: Guillaumin.

   (1912–14). "Lettres inédites de et à Léon Walras." *La Révolution de 1848, Bulletin de la Société de la Révolution de 1848*, vol. 9 nos. 51–4, pp. 179–89, 286–309, 367–82, 427–46; vol. 10 nos. 56–7 (1913), pp. 138–56, 231–53; vol. 11 nos. 58–60 (1913–14), pp. 327–43, 405–31, 508–25.

Walras, L. (1858). *Francis Sauveur*. Paris: E. Dentu.

Walras, L. (1860). *L'Economie politique et la justice. Examen critique et réfutation des doctrines économiques de M.P.-J. Proudhon*. Paris: Guillaumin.

Walras, L. (1861a). *Théorie critique de l'impôt, précedée de Souvenirs du Congrès de Lausanne*. Paris: Guillaumin.

Walras, L. (1861b). *De l'impôt dans le Canton de Vaud. Memoire auquel un quatrième accessit a été décerné ensuite du concours ouvert par le Conseil d'Etat de Vaud sur les questions relatives de l'impôt*. Lausanne: Imprimerie de Louis Vincent.

Walras, L. (1881). "Théorie mathématique du prix des terres et de leur rachat par l'Etat." *Bulletin de la société Vaudoise des Sciences Naturelles*, vol. 17, no. 85 (June), 2nd series, pp. 189-284. Republished in L. Walras, *Théorie mathématique de la richesse sociale*. Lausanne: Corbaz, 1883, pp. 177–253; and in L. Walras (1896/1936), pp. 267–350.

Walras, L. (1896). "Le problème fiscal." *Revue socialiste, syndicaliste et cooperative*, vol. 24, nos. 142-3 (October and November), pp. 386–400, 537–51. Republished in L. Walras (1896/1936), pp. 422–62 of the 1896 edition, pp. 445–85 of the 1936 edition.

Walras, L. (1896). *Etudes d'économie sociale (Théorie de la répartition de la richesse sociale)*, 1st ed. Lausanne: Rouge, 2nd ed., Lausanne: Rouge, 1936, and Paris: Pichon and Durand-Auzias, 1936, edited by G. Leduc.

Walras, L. (1897). "L'économie appliquée et la défense des salaires." *Revue d'économie politique*, vol. 11, no. 10 (December), pp. 1018-36. Republished in Walras (1898/1936); pp. 265–85.

Walras, L. (1898). *Etudes d'économie politique appliquée (Théorie de la production de la richesse sociale)*, 1st ed., Lausanne: Rouge; 2nd ed., Lausanne: Rouge, 1936, and Paris: Pichon and Durand-Auzias, 1936, edited by G. Leduc.

PART II

THE GENESIS AND DEVELOPMENT OF WALRAS'S IDEAS

3

A. N. ISNARD, PROGENITOR OF THE WALRASIAN GENERAL EQUILIBRIUM MODEL

To the best of my knowledge, the first allusion to Achylle-Nicolas Isnard (1749–1803) as a precursor of Léon Walras (1834–1910) is found in a little-known French doctoral thesis published in Poitiers in 1909, *Les théories économiques d'Achylle-Nicolas Isnard* by Louis Renevier. Renevier wrote the thesis under the direction of Professor Auguste Dubois, a competent historian of economic doctrines, but not of mathematical economics. So far as one can see, Renevier's sole reason for linking Isnard's name with that of Walras[1] was that both employed mathematics in their economic reasoning. By the same token, Renevier considered Isnard an "ancestor" not only of Léon Walras, but of Jevons as well! The thesis, however, passes very lightly over Isnard's contribution to mathematical economics, simply quoting a brief passage[2] from Isnard's theory of exchange. The few deprecatory comments Renevier thought fit to add serve only to reveal his complete lack of comprehension of the passage quoted. This is not to say that Renevier's thesis is without value. It contains, besides the only published biography of Isnard, a reasonably good summary of the non-analytical side of his thought, which was cast in the mold of the Physiocratic philosophy, although Isnard vehemently rejected Quesnay's doctrine that the soil alone produces a *produit net*. It is surprising that Isnard's name is nowhere mentioned, unless I have overlooked it, in any work on Physiocracy, its opponents, or its dissidents.[3] But this is beside my present purpose, which is to define in terms of documentary evidence the relation of Léon Walras's theory of general equilibrium to Isnard's analytical contribution.

Renevier's thesis was certainly not known to Schumpeter nor could it have been that study which inspired him to refer repeatedly to Isnard as

[1] Louis Renevier, *Les théories économiques d'Achylle-Nicolas Isnard d'après son ouvrage "Le Traité des richesses"* (Poitiers, 1909), p. 25.

[2] Ibid., pp. 25–27.

[3] E. Castelot in his article on Isnard in *Palgrave's Dictionary of Political Economy*, 2 (London, 1923): 460, and Joseph A. Schumpeter, *History of Economic Analysis* (New York, 1954), p. 217, n. 3, do refer to Isnard's opposition to some of the Physiocratic doctrines, but Schumpeter dismisses Isnard's argument as "conventional."

"a precursor of Léon Walras."[4] In fact, Schumpeter himself tells us that he first learned of Isnard's *Traité des richesses* (1781) from its inclusion in Jevon's list of mathematical writings;[5] and he adds, as if to explain why he had not encountered any reference to the treatise elsewhere, "I have found no traces of its influence."

It is this last remark of Schumpeter's that I contest. I believe I have evidence enough to indicate that Isnard was not merely "a precursor of Léon Walras," but actually a direct progenitor of the Walrasian general equilibrium model.

If Schumpeter overlooked the possibility of a direct influence of Isnard on Walras, it may be, I dare say, because Rheginos D. Theocharis' *Early Developments in Mathematical Economics* (1961),[6] with its superlative summary of the whole of Isnard's mathematico-economic contributions, had not yet appeared. I suspect that Schumpeter contented himself with a single passage from the *Traité des richesses,* the one quoted by Renevier and again quoted with more pertinent comments by Jacques Moret (1915).[7] While this passage deals only with the theory of exchange, it is developed in a manner so clearly foreshadowing the structural features of the Walrasian multiequational model that it would have been sufficient, even without considering Isnard's mathematical treatment of production, capital, and money,[8] to merit unstinted praise from Schumpeter, who was always ready to give high marks to a theory that approached in any way the ideal set by Walras. For all his praise, Schumpeter gave no inkling of the content or extent of Isnard's analytical achievement.

The trouble was, as Schumpeter observed, that "Isnard's historic performance . . . is embedded in a conventional argument against

---

[4] Joseph A. Schumpeter, *History,* p. 307, n. 14. Some aspects of the parallelism between Isnard's and Walras's theory of exchange have also been noticed in Léon Walras, *Elements of Pure Economics,* trans. William Jaffé (London, 1954), p. 499, Translator's Note 6 to Lesson 5, where relevant passages from Isnard are quoted.

[5] Schumpeter, *History,* pp. 217, 242, 307.

[6] Rheginos D. Theocharis, *Early Developments in Mathematical Economics* (London, 1961), pp. 65–71. On pp. 103–5 of the same book and in his article, "Joseph Lang and Macroeconomics," *Economica* 25, no. 100 (Nov. 1958): 319–25, Theocharis demonstrated quite conclusively that Joseph Lang, whose *Grundlinien der politischen Arithmetik* was published in 1811, "must have known Isnard's work for his influence is obvious." Lang is not mentioned in Schumpeter's *History.*

[7] Jacques Moret, *L'emploi des mathématiques en économie politique* (Paris, 1915), pp. 66–69.

[8] Achylle-Nicolas Isnard, *Traité des richesses,* 2 vols. (London and Lausanne, 1781). In vol. 1, the mathematical treatment of the theory of exchange without money is found on pp. 16–21; that of the theory of exchange with the intervention of money, on pp. 21–22; that of the quantity theory of money, on pp. 25–26; that of the theory of capital and interest on pp. 30–34 and 48–50; that of the theory of production on pp. 34–44; and that of the theory of foreign exchange on pp. 289–97. In vol. 2, there is only one mathematical passage, found on pp. 4–5, dealing with problems of taxation, but of interest also from the point of view of production theory. The object of this passage, as the subsequent pages show, is to refute the Physiocratic doctrine of a single-tax on the net product of the land.

physiocrat doctrines."[9] Indeed, Isnard's scattered algebraic and arithmetic arguments are embedded in the running lines of text and nowhere stand out typographically. They are buried in some 25 pages out of a total of 665 pages of otherwise tedious, prolix, and turgid prose that make up the two volumes. If one managed to locate a copy of the rare *Traité des richesses* and simply turned over the pages, it would be only too easy to miss the algebraic interludes. We are, therefore, all the more grateful to Theocharis (1961) for locating for us nearly all the relevant pages of the book, summarizing and elucidating the mathematical arguments, and commenting upon their significance—with only one error, so far as I can see. That error consisted in a misinterpretation of Isnard's algebraic analysis of foreign exchange.[10]

Theocharis can hardly be blamed for this error, since Isnard's algebra is as turgid as his prose. As Castelot (1923) points out, Isnard "does not venture farther than equations of the first degree and simple problems in the rule of three"; and paradoxical as it may seem, this renders his argument all the more difficult to follow. Moreover, Isnard's mathematics lacks the saving grace of employing symbols with the minimum of ambiguity possible. The symbols are not always defined; and on consecutive pages the same letter symbol may change its meaning without warning.[11] As if this were not enough, Isnard's idiosyncratic economic vocabulary is bewildering. Of course, economic terminology had not been standardized to the extent it is today, but surely had Isnard turned to Turgot, whose choice of terms leaves little to be desired, he would have been more sensitive to the need for using words in a more commonly understood sense. For example, on p. 30 of Volume I, we encounter the term "richesses foncières", which normally stands for landed wealth; but everything in the immediate context, in both the verbal and algebraic discussion, shows unmistakably that Isnard meant by "richesses foncières" not landed wealth but produced capital. Though reading Isnard is exceedingly arduous, it is possible, with an effort, to read *out of* Isnard a perfectly coherent analytical argument without reading anything *into* it.

Once the analytical argument has been dug out of the *Traité des richesses* and deciphered, a remarkable number of striking adumbrations of the structural aspects of the Walrasian general equilibrium model

[9] Schumpeter, *History*, p. 217, n. 3.   [10] Theocharis, *Early Developments*, p. 70.

[11] E.g., Isnard, *Traité*, 1:18. The symbol M sometimes denotes the physical measure of a unit of a given commodity and sometimes the abstract (absolute) value of a unit of the same commodity. On p. 20, in one place, M apparently stands for the name of the commodity. The first paragraph of a second section on p. 21 in vol. 1 is particularly disconcerting, for unless one pays meticulous attention to the particular connotation of the symbols, the mathematical argument appears to be an empty tautology, which, in fact, it is not.

appear. Not one parallelism, but many, are revealed in this way. If we take into account, furthermore, that Léon Walras knew Isnard's *Traité des richesses* early in his career as an analytical economist and had the book in his private library, then the hypothesis of a direct influence immediately suggests itself.

We are thus faced with a problem of historiography. Is the evidence I have adequate to sustain the hypothesis that Walras was directly influenced by Isnard in constructing his general equilibrium model? The evidence, it will be seen, is not complete, but is it sufficient for my purpose? Since it is impossible, in any case, to recover the past "wie es eigentlich gewesen war," we must content ourselves with trying to represent the past "wie es höchst wahrscheinlich gewesen war." I am trying to establish my point on the plane of historical inference rather than the plane of historical conjecture. Far too often in histories of economics, allegations of filiation of ideas are founded on alluring, gratuitous guesswork instead of carefully sifted documentary evidence.

Before producing the exhibits I intend to use as evidence in an attempt to prove my point beyond reasonable doubt, I should like to identify my star witness, Isnard, who was unknown even to the most canny of historical sleuths, Joseph Schumpeter. He could not even discover the dates of birth and death of the man.[12] The whole range of biographical dictionaries are of no avail, for all they tell of Isnard, besides naming his major publications, is that he was born in Paris, was an engineer by profession, was a member of the Tribunate under Napoleon's Consulate, and died in "1802 or 1803." This is precious little. Renevier's thesis, however, does give us a very satisfactory sketch of Isnard's career,[13] for which Renevier obtained his material from a dossier in the Archives Nationales.[14]

Achylle-Nicolas Isnard, as his name was spelled in the eighteenth century, was born in Paris in 1749, on February 25, it seems. Of his family nothing is recorded except that he had a devoted brother, J. L. Isnard, who became a lawyer and judge. At the age of seventeen, Achylle-Nicolas entered the Ecole des Ponts et Chaussées (School of Civil Engineering); and after successfully completing his studies, started his career in the public employ, first as an apprentice engineer, and then, in 1776, as assistant engineer at Arbois, in the Generality of Besançon. It was while he was at Arbois, proving his worth in his profession, that in addition to writing a report on the construction of

---

[12] Schumpeter, *History*, p. 217, n. 3.   [13] Renevier, *Théories économiques*, pp. 5–23.
[14] Ibid., p. 2: "Nous avons eu la bonne fortune de trouver aux Archives Nationales le dossier d'Isnard, comme ingénieur des Ponts et Chaussées, ce qui nous a permis de faire de lui une biographie aussi complète que possible."

roads and navigable canals, he published anonymously at the age of 32, his remarkable two-volume *Traité des richesses.*

Modest and aloof in his bearing, he was too proud to entangle himself in the usual intrigues so necessary in any epoch for advancement; and he was too short-tempered to conceal his contempt for his ignorant and pretentious hierarchical superiors. These traits of character nearly lead to his undoing, and would indeed have done so if his more tactful brother had not interceded for him from time to time in high places. As it was, his career suffered: for a long time he was refused posts of responsibility and was subjected to frequent transfers of locality, always in a subordinate capacity. After fifteen years of service, his emoluments were still in the 1200 to 1500 francs per annum bracket, too little for the support of a family of three children. At one point, in the late 1780's, he was assigned to Evreux, the birthplace of Léon Walras.[15] The shifts and vicissitudes of Isnard's professional life were never happy, even after the Revolution when he was promoted to the rank of Chief Engineer and given an important post at Le Havre—still with another engineer above him. From Le Havre he was sent to Carcassonne, at long last with full responsibility. Hardly had he begun there, when his wife, whom he had left at Le Havre, died. At this juncture, he abandoned government service and lived in straitened circumstances with his three motherless children. In 1798 he was recalled by Napoleon, who thought of sending him on the expedition to Egypt. For some unknown reason, Isnard was left behind. What made it all the more difficult for Isnard was that he was obliged to take an oath of allegiance to the Republic, though he was a fervent royalist and had publicly declared himself such in his *Observations sur le principe qui a produit les révolutions de France, de Genève et d'Amérique au XVIIIe siècle,* published in Evreux in 1789. On January 3, 1800, he was made a member of the Tribunate and took a notable part in its deliberations on public finance and on the conscription laws under the Consulate. When his term as member of the Tribunate ended, he resumed his engineering career at Lyons, but soon fell victim to the same malady that had carried away his wife. He died on February 25, 1803, at the age of fifty-four, leaving his three children penniless in the care of his faithful brother.

That engineering had not absorbed all of his attention is seen in five publications he left on questions of public interest. In addition to the

[15] It is not at all unlikely that Isnard, besides leaving traces of his engineering prowess on the improved internal waterways in the region of Evreux, may also have left there some copies of his *Traité des richesses.* Perhaps it was in this way that a copy found its way into the Walras library, for Léon Walras's father, Auguste Walras (1801–1866), was principal of the Collège d'Evreux at the time of Léon's birth in 1834 and was passionately interested in economics.

Traité and the *Observations* already mentioned, these works include a *Catéchisme social ou Instructions élémentaires sur la morale sociale à l'usage de la jeunesse* (Paris, 1784); *Les devoirs de la 2e Législature ou des Législatures en France,* 4 vols. (Paris, 1791); and *Considérations théoriques sur les Caisses d'amortissement de la dette publique* (Paris 1801).[16]

In attempting to establish the probability of a direct filiation of ideas from Isnard to Léon Walras, we must first have proof that Léon Walras was acquainted with Isnard's work. While this is not a sufficient condition, it is certainly a necessary one. Fortunately, there is incontrovertible evidence that Léon Walras had the book in his private library and had some knowledge of its contents. From this evidence, we learn, moreover, that it was not "by a lucky chance," as Schumpeter surmised,[17] that Isnard's *Traité des richesses* found its way into Jevons's "List of Mathematico-Economic Books, Memoirs and Other Published Writings" which was appended to the second edition of the *Theory of Political Economy* (1879), but through Léon Walras's intervention. On July 9, 1878, Jevons wrote to Walras, enclosing three copies of an offprint of his preliminary "Bibliography of the Mathematical Theory of Political Economy," which he had just had published, unsigned, in the *Journal of the Statistical Society* (June 1878). Jevons asked Walras to assist him "not only by naming any omitted works known to [Walras], but also by procuring the republication of the list in the *Journal des Economistes* . . . ."[18] Walras replied on July 13, 1878, that among the items he was adding to Jevons's original list were some that he owned himself, among them a "two volume *Traité des richesses,* in 8°, published in London and Lausanne in 1781, in which," the letter ran, "the ratios of value between commodities exchanged are expressed altogether correctly in algebraic language and which should, I think, be placed at the head of the list."[19] The letter went on to say that the book was anonymous, "but it is known that the author was a French engineer, Isnard, who was a member of the Tribunate and died in 1802 or 1803." When he published Jevons's list in the *Journal des économistes* in Decem-

---

[16] See Renevier, *Théories économiques,* pp. v–vi, for a bibliography of Isnard's writings, reports, and addresses.

[17] Schumpeter, *History,* p. 217, n. 3.

[18] William Jaffé, ed., *Correspondence of Léon Walras and Related Papers,* 3 vols. (Amsterdam, 1965), 1: 568–69, Letter 409. This is not to say that Walras was the first economist to call attention to the existence of Isnard's *Traité des richesses.* The book is listed by J. R. McCulloch, *The Literature of Political Economy: A Classified Catalogue* (London, 1845), pp. 20–21, with a summary of its contents, but not mentioning the mathematical parts. Also at the end of J. A. Blanqui's brief article on Isnard in the Coquelin and Guillaumin *Dictionnaire de l'économie politique* (1854), 1: 971, the *Traité* is mentioned, again without any allusion to the mathematical analysis.

[19] Jaffé, *Correspondence of Walras,* 1: 570–72, Letter 410.

ber 1878, he added twenty-seven items, and in an introductory paragraph singled out Isnard's *Traité* for special mention:

On my own account, I have inserted at the head of the list the work of Isnard,
published in 1781. In the early pages of this book, ratios of values are correctly
stated in algebraic symbols as equal to the inverse ratios of the quantities of
commodities exchanged. The equation of exchange, though by no means fully
or deeply considered by the author, remains, nevertheless, the starting point of
the scientific theory of social wealth. Despite its inadequacies, this equation is
enough to effect, within certain limits, the transformation of theoretical political
economy into a mathematical science.[20]

Having stumbled upon this impressive tribute to Isnard in Walras's
obscure bibliographical article, I expected to find it echoed in other
writings of Léon Walras. I must report, however, that, so far as I could
see, Isnard is not mentioned anywhere else in Walras's published work. I
have fared no better in my search through Walras's extant unpublished
manuscripts, including his worksheets.[21] In Walras's correspondence, his
letter to Jevons of July 13, 1878, appears to be the only one in which
Isnard's name is found. I looked especially throughout the manuscripts
of Walras's earliest attempts at mathematical economics,[22] one dated
1860 and the other 1869–1870. In the latter Walras first broached the
idea of ratios of (absolute) values in relation to ratios of quantities
exchanged, without, however, once mentioning Isnard or the *Traité des
richesses*. Again in Walras's notes for a series of lectures he gave at
Geneva in 1872 under the title, "Système des phénomènes économiques,"[23] he produced an equation analogous to Isnard's without alluding
to Isnard or the *Traité*. When, finally, Walras published the same
equation in the first instalment of the first edition of the *Eléments
d'économic politique pure* toward the end of July 1874,[24] Isnard's name did
not appear in that connection or indeed anywhere in the *Eléments*. All
this bodes ill for my hypothesis that the *Traité des richesses* exerted a
formative influence on Walras, but I don't think the hypothesis need be
abandoned for that reason.

We must bear in mind that Walras was exceedingly niggardly in his

[20] Leon Walras, "Bibliographie des ouvrages relatifs à l'application des mathématiques à l'économie politique," *Journal des économistes*, 4th ser., 4, no. 12 (Dec. 1878): 470.
[21] For a list of the repositories of the Walras mss., see Jaffé, *Correspondence of Walras*,
1: xii.
[22] These lecture notes, which were prepared toward the end of 1871, are summarized
in ibid., 1: 293–96, n. 2 to Letter 198.
[23] The contents of these mss. are summarized in ibid., 1: 216–21, n. 33 to Letter 148.
[24] Léon Walras, *Eléments d'économie politique pure*, 1st ed., 2 vols. (Lausanne and Paris,
1874–77), 1: 53: *"Les prix, ou les rapports des valeurs sont éguax aux rapports inverses des quantités
de marchandise échangées."*

acknowledgement of indebtedness to others[25] except in the case of his father. When he deigned to cite predecessors or contemporaries it was usually to refute them. Hence his failure to mention Isnard in connection with his own work is not surprising, though it is disconcerting, since it leaves us without any straightforward evidence of indebtedness of Walras to Isnard. Though we are obliged to fall back on derivative evidence, we have so much that its cumulative effect is to create a strong presumption of direct filiation.

The equation which Léon Walras touted as constituting the turning point in the transformation of theoretical economics into a mathematical science was undoubtedly Isnard's

$$aM = bM', \tag{1.1}$$

from which Isnard established the proportionality

$$M : M' : : \frac{1}{a} : \frac{1}{b} , \tag{1.2}$$

where, in the assumed two-commodity model without money, M denoted the (absolute) value of commodity M; M' the (absolute) value of the other commodity M'; a the quantity exchanged of commodity M; and b the quantity exchanged of commodity M'.[26] Isnard defined the quantity a exchanged as the excess supply ("le superflu") in the hands of owners of M and wanted by owners of M'; and the quantity b as the excess supply of M' in the hands of its owners and wanted by owners of M. In Isnard's model, the aggregate quantities exchanged (a and b in the two-commodity case; a, b, c, d . . . in the multicommodity case) are constants, predetermined by considerations of utility behind the scenes, as it were. The part played by utility is alluded to in the text, but does not appear explicitly in Isnard's equations.[27]

The fact that a and b, though determined outside the model, are assumed to be fixed within the model is a matter of crucial importance. Since Isnard defines a and b as the quantities of M and M' freely bartered without, apparently, leaving any unsatisfied demand on either

[25] Cf. Jaffé, *Correspondence of Walras,* 1: 309, n. 4 to Letter 211.

[26] Isnard, *Traité,* 1:18.

[27] As Isnard stated it, "En parlant des richesses, on ne prend guère le mot valeur dans un sens absolu. Le mot qui exprime proprement la signification absolue qu'on pourroit lui donner est utilité." Isnard, *Traité,* 1:17, n. *a.* Walras later expressed the same idea, substituting, however, his mathematically precise concept of *rareté* for the vague notion of utility: "la valeur est une chose essentiellement relative. Sans doute derrière la valeur relative il y a quelque chose d'absolu, savoir les intensités des derniers besoins satisfaits, ou les raretés." Walras, p. 147 and §146 in the definitive edition (Paris, 1926) of the *Eléments.* Again in the 4th edition of the *Eléments* (Lausanne and Paris, 1900), Walras added a footnote, reading, "The distinction between value in exchange, which is *relative* and *objective,* and *rareté,* which is *absolute* and *subjective,* is a rigorous expression of the difference between *value in exchange* and *value in use.*" Walras, *Elements of Pure Economics,* p. 178, n. 1.

side of the exchange, they must be equilibrium quantities, and the ratios of the absolute values M/M' and its reciprocal which satisfy equation (1.2) are, in a sense, equilibrium relative values. This amounts to saying that Isnard, in effect, first postulated equilibrium amounts exchanged and then proceeded to show how the corresponding relative values are determined.

As has already been intimated above, Isnard's equation (1.1) finds its exact counterpart in Walras—in his unpublished essay in mathematical economics of 1869–1870; in his Geneva lecture notes prepared in 1871 for 1872; and, for the first time in print, in 1874 in the first edition of the *Eléments d'économie politique pure* ($44 in all editions). In all three, he wrote

$$mv_a = nv_b, \tag{2.1}$$

where v_a is the (absolute) value in exchange of a unit of commodity (A); v_b the (absolute) value in exchange of a unit of commodity (B); and m the number of units of (A) exchanged for n units of (B).

This is not to say that I suspect Walras of simply copying Isnard, changing only the notation. Far from it. If he used Isnard's *Traité des richesses* at all, as I contend he did, he used it as a starting point for constructing a model which was distinctly his own. For example, in the same $44 of the *Eléments,* Walras converted the relation expressed in the above equation (2.1) into an algebraic definition of relative price:

$$\frac{v_b}{v_a} = \frac{m}{n} = p_{b,a}, \tag{2.2}$$

where $p_{b,a}$ is the price per unit of (B) in terms of (A). This certainly constitutes a significant improvement on Isnard. Moreover, as we read further on in the *Eléments,* beyond the introduction of the utility maximization theorem, we discover in $97 of the first edition[28] that

$$p_{b,a} = \frac{v_b}{v_a} = \frac{r_{b,1}}{r_{a,1}} = \frac{r_{b,2}}{r_{a,2}} = \frac{r_{b,3}}{r_{a,3}} = \cdots, \tag{2.3}$$

where the r's stand for the *raretés* (i.e., marginal degrees of utility) of the commodities designated by the letter subscripts, the numerical subscripts designating the several individuals in the economy. This represents a tremendous advance over Isnard, who had done no more than to hint at the role of utility in the determination of ratios of value. In fact, it turns out that Walras's v's, his (absolute) values, are only vestigial components of the model, inherited certainly from his father and, as I think likely, from Isnard as well. Surely all Walras's semantic rigmarole

[28] Cf. ibid. $100 and p. 572, Collation Note (c) to Lesson 10.

about value in Parts I and II of the *Eléments* is mercifully absent from the rest of the book, and if excised, would never be missed. Pareto, in his *Manuel,* rightly condemned it as metaphysical nonsense.[29]

Of course, the underlying resemblance between the Walrasian equation (2.1) and Isnard's equation (1.1) could be dismissed as a banal coincidence. The annals of the history of science are replete with well-authenticated instances of independent rediscoveries. The evidence is clear, for example, that Walras introduced his mathematical concept of *rareté,* which is virtually the same as Jevons's earlier concept of "final degree of utility," quite independently of Jevons, before he had read anything of Jevons's theoretical work.[30] It is, however, more difficult to attribute the same independence to Walras with respect to Isnard when we see how closely the further elaboration of Walras's theory of exchange follows the Isnard pattern.

As is well known, Walras built up his theory of exchange by first constructing a two-commodity model and then expanding it to accommodate any number of commodities.[31] The example for such an expository sequence had been set by Isnard in 1781.[32] In passing from the two-commodity case to the multicommodity case, Isnard moreover provided a precedent for solving the problem of the determination of ratios of values by formulating a multiequation system; and he took great pains to see that the number of independent equations equals the number of unknowns, as, indeed, Walras did after him in solving for equilibrium relative prices. Since Isnard's multiequational system was seemingly overdetermined, he implicitly eliminated one equation which could be derived from the rest, thus foreshadowing Walras's explicit elimination of a redundant equation from his system of supply and demand equations. That is not all. Isnard also reduced the number of unknowns by employing the device of an arbitrary standard commodity, exactly as Walras did by designating one of the commodities as the *numéraire.* Thus nearly the whole formal apparatus of Walras's theory of exchange, apart from the utility maximization engine, was ready at hand in Isnard's *Traité des richesses* for Walras to use. The concentrated accumulation of resemblances within the theory of exchange alone makes it very hard to believe that Walras constructed his model without direct inspiration from Isnard.

[29] Vilfredo Pareto, *Manuel d'économie politique, traduit sur l'édition italienne par Alfred Bonnet* (Paris, 1909), pp. 242–46.

[30] Jaffé, *Correspondence of Walras,* 1: Letter 275.

[31] Walras, *Elements of Pure Economics,* pts. 2 and 3 ("Section II" and "Section III" in all editions of the *Eléments*).

[32] Isnard, *Traité,* 1: 18–21.

This deserves looking into in some detail. Isnard expanded his model[33] by assuming three commodities M, M', and M'' and designated the respective absolute values of these commodities by the same symbols. He denoted the total quantities of M, M', and M'' available for exchange (and effectively exchanged) by a, b, and c respectively, which, like the a and b in the two-commodity case, he regarded as exogenously determined constants. Since the a units of M are exchanged in part for M' and in part for M'', a fraction m of a is exchanged for M' and a fraction n of a is exchanged for M'', such that $m + n = 1$ or $ma + na = a$. Similarly the b units of M' are divided between a fraction p of b exchanged for M and a fraction q of b exchanged for M'', such that $p + q = 1$ or $pb + qb = b$; and the c units of M'' are divided between a fraction r of c exchanged for M and a fraction s of c exchanged for M', such that $r + s = 1$ or $rc + sc = c$. The equality between the sum of each pair of these fractions and unity is equivalent to a postulate, presupposing that all three markets are cleared. Accordingly, Isnard set forth the following equations:

$$
\begin{aligned}
aM &= pbM' + rcM'' \\
bM' &= maM + scM'' \\
cM'' &= qbM' + naM,
\end{aligned}
\qquad (3.1)
$$

each of which is analogous to equation (1.1) and equates values; for the M, M', M'' in the equations denote the (absolute) values of the respective commodities.[34] From these equations Isnard derived the continued proportion

$$
M : M' : M'' :: \frac{r + p - rp}{a} : \frac{s + m - sm}{b} : \frac{n + q - nq}{c}
\qquad (3.2)
$$

The first thing to be noted about system (3.1) is that, under the postulated conditions, and only under those conditions, any one of the three equations can be derived from the other two, so that the system

[33] Ibid., pp. 19–20.

[34] For a mathematical exegesis and analysis of Isnard's equations (3.1), see, besides Theocharis, *Early Developments*, p. 68, n. 2, Helmut Reichhardt, *Augustin A. Cournot, sein Beitrag zur exakten Wirtschaftswissenschaft* (Tübingen, 1954), pp. 71–75; Ross M. Robertson, "Mathematical Economics Before Cournot," *Journal of Political Economy* 57, no. 6 (Dec. 1949): 531–33, where excellent English translations of significant passages from Isnard's theory of exchange are found; and G. H. Bousquet, "Histoire de l'économie mathématique jusqu'à Cournot," *Metroeconomica* 10, no. 3 (Dec. 1958): 125–27. Bousquet's explanation is unfortunately marred by a misinterpretation of Isnard's symbols M, M', and M'' in the equations.

can be reduced to two independent equations. For example, adding Isnard's second and third equation, we obtain

$$bM' + cM'' = maM + scM'' + qbM' + naM ;$$

and then, collecting terms,

$$(m + n) aM = (1 - q) bM' + (1 - s) cM'',$$

whence, by virtue of the postulated relations $m + n = 1$, $p + q = 1$, and $r + s = 1$, we derive

$$aM = pbM' + rcM'' ,$$

which is precisely the first equation of system (3.1).

The significance of this reduction lies in the fact that there are only two unknowns to be determined—not M, M', and M'', which, being imponderable (absolute) values, are indeterminate, but any two independent ratios of these values, say M/M' and M'/M'', which, being equal to ratios of quantities interchanged, are quantifiable.

The equality between the ratio of any pair of (absolute) values and the corresponding pair of quantities interchanged is seen most clearly in the derivation of Isnard's continued proportion (3.2).[35] Eliminating cM'' between the first and second equations of system (3.1), we have

$$bM' = maM + s\left(\frac{aM - pbM'}{r}\right) ,$$

or, after clearing fractions and collecting terms,

$$(rma + sa)M = (rb + spb)M',$$

whence

$$\frac{M}{M'} = \frac{b(r + sp)}{a(rm + s)} . \tag{3.3}$$

In like manner, eliminating aM between the same first and second equations of system (3.1), we have

$$bM' = m (pbM' + rcM'') + scM'',$$

or, after collecting terms,

$$(b - pbm)M' = (rcm + sc)M'',$$

[35] The derivation presented here follows closely to that of Theocharis, *Early Developments*, p. 68, n. 2.

whence

$$\frac{M'}{M''} = \frac{c(rm + s)}{b(1 - pm)}. \tag{3.4}$$

To convert (3.3) and (3.4) into Isnard's continued proportion (3.2), it is only necessary to multiply the numerators and denominators of the right-hand sides of these equations by appropriate factors in order to derive a mean proportional. Multiplying the right-hand side of (3.3) by c/c and the right-hand side of (3.4) by a/a, we obtain

$$\frac{M}{M'} = \frac{bc(r + sp)}{ac(rm + s)}$$

and

$$\frac{M'}{M''} = \frac{ac(rm + s)}{ab(1 - pm)},$$

which permits us to write

$$M : M' : M'' :: bc(r + sp) : ac(rm + s) : ab(1 - pm).$$

Dividing each of the quantities on the right-hand side of the continued proportion by abc, we get

$$M : M' : M'' :: \frac{r + sp}{a} : \frac{s + mr}{b} : \frac{1 - mp}{c},$$

and substituting, again from the postulated relations, $s = 1 - r$ in the first right-hand-side quantity, $r = 1 - s$ in the second, and $m = 1 - n$, $p = 1 - q$ in the third, we obtain Isnard's solution (3.2) given above.

From this it is clear that (3.3) and (3.4) are implicit in (3.2), which serves to determine Isnard's ratios of any two pairs of values.

On the face of it, except for its presentation in multiequational form, system (3.2) may appear remote from anything we find in Walras. This is not so. Leçons 19, 20 and 21 of the first edition of the *Eléments* (corresponding roughly to Leçons 11 and 12 of the subsequent editions) contain a host of analytical components reminiscent of Isnard. These Leçons in particular bear, as I see it, the sharp imprint of Isnard's influence. The very complexity of the argument and the efforts Walras made to overcome this complexity in the successive editions[36] of the *Eléments* are indicative, I should say, of the difficulties he encountered in

[36] Cf. Walras, *Elements of Pure Economics*, pp. 573-76, Collation Notes to Lessons 11 and 12.

Table 1. *Notational equivalents*

Isnard		Walras
Commodities denominated M, M', M"	⇌	Commodities denominated (A), (B), (C)
M ≡ (absolute) value of M	⇌	v_a ≡ (absolute) value of (A)
M' ≡ (absolute) value of M'	⇌	v_b ≡ (absolute) value of (B)
M'' ≡ (absolute) value of M"	⇌	v_c ≡ (absolute) value of (C)
a ≡ total quantity exchanged of M	⇌	D_a ≡ market demand for (A)
b ≡ total quantity exchanged of M'	⇌	D_b ≡ market demand for (B)
c ≡ total quantity exchanged of M"	⇌	D_c ≡ market demand for (C)
ma ≡ quantity of M exchanged for M'	⇌	$D_{a,b}$ ≡ quantity of (A) exchanged for (B)
na ≡ quantity of M exchanged for M"	⇌	$D_{a,c}$ ≡ quantity of (A) exchanged for (C)
pb ≡ quantity of M' exchanged for M	⇌	$D_{b,a}$ ≡ quantity of (B) exchanged for (A)
qb ≡ quantity of M' exchanged for M"	⇌	$D_{b,c}$ ≡ quantity of (B) exchanged for (C)
rc ≡ quantity of M" exchanged for M	⇌	$D_{c,a}$ ≡ quantity of (C) exchanged for (A)
sc ≡ quantity of M" exchanged for M'	⇌	$D_{c,b}$ ≡ quantity of (C) exchanged for (B)

adapting Isnard's model to his own purposes. To bring out the structural resemblances, I have drawn up a table of notational equivalents (Table 1).

With these definitions of the symbols in mind, let us examine the following system of Walras's equations (abbreviated here to take no more than three commodities into account), as it first appears in §115 of the second edition of the *Eléments* (§116 in the definitive edition):

$$
\begin{aligned}
D_{a,b} + D_{a,c} &= D_{b,a}\, p_{b,a} + D_{c,a}\, p_{c,a} \\
D_{b,a} + D_{b,c} &= D_{a,b}\, p_{a,b} + D_{c,b}\, p_{c,b} \\
D_{c,a} + D_{c,b} &= D_{a,c}\, p_{a,c} + D_{b,c}\, p_{b,c} \; ,
\end{aligned}
\tag{3.5}
$$

where p_{ij} (i and $j = a \ldots c; j \neq i$) is the price of commodity i in terms of commodity j. Though there are four relative prices in system (3.5), they can be reduced to two by virtue of the following relations emerging, in equilibrium, from arbitrage operations:

$$
p_{a,b} = \frac{1}{p_{b,a}}
$$

$$
p_{a,c} = \frac{1}{p_{c,a}}
$$

$$
p_{c,b} = \frac{p_{c,a}}{p_{b,a}}
$$

$$
p_{b,c} = \frac{p_{b,a}}{p_{c,a}} ,
$$

from which we may substitute into equation (3.5), to read

$$
\begin{aligned}
D_{a,b} + D_{a,c} &= D_{b,a}p_{b,a} + D_{c,a}p_{c,a} \\
D_{b,a} + D_{b,c} &= D_{a,b}\frac{1}{p_{b,a}} + D_{c,b}\frac{p_{c,a}}{p_{b,a}} \\
D_{c,a} + D_{c,b} &= D_{a,c}\frac{1}{p_{c,a}} + D_{b,c}\frac{p_{b,a}}{p_{c,a}}.
\end{aligned}
\tag{3.6}
$$

This system corresponds exactly to the final set of equations in §115 of the second edition (§116 of the definitive edition of the *Eléments*). Unless (3.6) contained a redundant equation, it would be overdetermined in solving for the $p_{b,a}$ and $p_{c,a}$, which would clear the separate markets for all possible pairs of commodities once the conditions of arbitrage equilibrium have been satisfied. It is easy to show, as Walras indicated (§116 of the definitive edition) that (3.6) does contain a redundant equation, simply by clearing the second and third equations of fractions, giving

$$
\begin{aligned}
D_{b,a}p_{b,a} + D_{b,c}p_{b,a} &= D_{a,b} + D_{c,b}p_{c,a} \\
D_{c,a}p_{c,a} + D_{c,b}p_{c,a} &= D_{a,c} + D_{b,c}p_{b,a},
\end{aligned}
$$

and then adding these two equations and canceling identical terms on both sides of the sum, yielding

$$
D_{b,a}p_{b,a} + D_{c,a}p_{c,a} = D_{a,b} + D_{a,c},
$$

which is precisely the first equation in (3.6) with the sides reversed.[37] The reduction in the number of equations to equal the number of unknowns is similar in every respect to the reduction which we have already seen is implicit in the Isnard solution.

Though Isnard did not write the quantities interchanged as functions of the relative values, it is clear that the relative values he derived from (3.1) involve equilibrium prices, albeit of a peculiar sort. To show this, let us start by dividing each of the equations in (3.1) by M, and then convert the resulting ratios of (absolute) values into relative prices in the manner of Walras. Thus letting

$$
\frac{M'}{M} = p_{m',m} \quad \text{and} \quad \frac{M''}{M} = p_{m'',m},
$$

where $p_{m',m}$ and $p_{m'',m}$ are respectively the prices of M' and M'' in terms of M, we obtain in place of (3.1):

$$
\begin{aligned}
a &= pb\, p_{m',m} + rc\, p_{m'',m} \\
bp_{m',m} &= ma + sc\, p_{m'',m} \\
cp_{m'',m} &= qb\, p_{m',m} + na
\end{aligned}
$$

[37] Ibid., pp. 515-16, Translator's Note (8) to Lesson 11.

Adding these three equations and collecting terms, we have

$$[a - (ma + na)] + [b - (pb + qb)]p_{m\,',m} + [c - (rc + sc)] \cdot p_{m\,'',m} = 0.$$

Since, as has been seen, Isnard postulated

$$ma + na = a$$
$$pb + qb = b$$
$$rc + sc = c,$$

which is tantamount to postulating that the sum of the quantities effectively demanded of each of the three commodities (the left-hand side of each of the equations) is equal to the total fixed quantity effectively offered of each of the commodities (the right-hand side of the equations), it follows that the prices $p_{m\,',m}$, and $p_{m\,'',m}$ are not equilibrium prices in the Walrasian sense, but are derived from a given set of market equilibrium conditions prescribed to begin with.

The extraordinary parallelism between Walras and Isnard in the theory of exchange does not end here. Walras and Isnard demonstrated in much the same fashion how the designation of one of the commodities as the *numéraire* makes the reduction in the number of relative values (Isnard) or relative prices (Walras). As Isnard stated it,

If there are several goods, M, M', M'', M''', etc., whose values are known and which are in the ratio of a to b to c to d to e, we can compare all the goods to one of them; thus we have $M : M'$ ::a:b; $M : M''$ ::a:c; $M : M'''$ ::a:d; $M : M''''$ ::a:e, etc.. The value of M', M'', M''', M'''' will then be $\frac{bM}{a}, \frac{cM}{a}, \frac{dM}{a}, \frac{eM}{a}$, etc....[38]

Walras went about it more elaborately. In §106 of the first edition of the *Eléments* (§109 of the definitive edition), he virtually formed a matrix of all possible relative prices and pointed out that there are $n(n-1)$ such prices for n commodities. He might have obtained this result by utilizing the general formula for the number of *permutations* of n dissimilar objects taken r at a time, viz.,

$$n(n - 1)(n - 2) \cdots (n - r + 1),$$

using $r = 2$ for relative prices. Then in §123 of the first edition of the *Eléments* (§115 of the definitive edition) Walras announced that this number could be halved by virtue of the relation $p_{j,i} = 1/p_{i,j}$ (here i and j $= 1 \ldots n$; $i \neq j$). Since the order of subscripts is immaterial in this case, the problem in combinatorial analysis becomes one of determining the number of *combinations* of n dissimilar objects taken r at a time, for which the general formula is

$$\frac{n(n - 1)(n - 2) \cdots (n - r + 1)}{r!},$$

[38] Isnard, *Traité*, 1:21. Ross M. Robertson's translation, slightly altered ("Mathematical Economics Before Cournot," p. 533).

so that for $r = 2$, we obtain $n(n - 1)/2$. Finally, with the designation of the one of the commodities as the *numéraire*, Walras indicated in §143 of the first edition of the *Eléments* (§145 of the definitive edition) that the number of relative prices could be still further reduced to $n - 1$. He might have obtained this result rigorously from another general formula in combinatorial analysis, according to which the number of *specific combinations* of n dissimilar objects taken r at a time with one specified object always included is equal to

$$\frac{(n - 1)(n - 2) \cdots (n - r + 1)}{(r - 1)!}.$$

In the case where $r = 2$, this number reduces to $n - 1$, which is precisely the number of relative prices to be determined by the $n - 1$ independent equations in Walras's system.

It was not by any appeal to elegant elementary propositions of combinatorial analysis that Walras arrived at the conclusion he enunciated in §143 of the first edition of the *Eléments* (§145 of the definitive edition):

> The theorem of general equilibrium in the market may be stated in the following terms: *When the market is in a state of equilibrium, the $n(n - 1)$ prices, which govern the exchange between all possible pairs drawn from n commodities are implicitly determined by the n—1 prices which govern the exchange between any n—1 of these commodities and the nth.*[39]

Nor did Walras content himself with a simple algebraic example, as Isnard had done. He appealed rather to the processes of the market and insisted upon describing in detail how arbitrage operations between freely communicating markets culminate in a consistent set of relative prices, such that

$$p_{k,j} = \frac{p_{k,i}}{p_{j,i}} \quad (i, j, \text{ and } k = 1 \ldots n; \ i \neq j \neq k).$$

However much Walras may have been influenced by Isnard, he was no slavish imitator. Between Isnard's (3.1) and Walras's (3.5) there is a fundamental difference in conception. For Isnard, the total amounts of each commodity exchanged are given and fixed, and the fractions of these amounts interchanged between commodities are parameters. In Isnard's words,

> It is easy to account for variations in values by variations in offers; one can see how, proceeding from the supposition that m equals n, p equals q, and r equals s, to the supposition that the quantities n, q, and s equal zero, how, I say, between the extreme suppositions, progressive changes in the offers have an influence on all the values; to do this it is only necessary to make different suppositions in

---

[39] Walras, *Elements of Pure Economics,* p. 185.

numbers in place of the algebraic quantities we have just used, *supposing always, as we have done up to now, that the quantities [exchanged] of merchandise remain constant.*[40]

I have inserted the word "exchanged" in brackets in order to make clear that in Isnard's model it is the quantities exchanged and not the total existing quantities of the several commodities (to which Isnard never referred), that are held constant. In Walras, on the other hand, it is the total *existing* quantities that are held constant in the theory of exchange, the quantities exchanged being functions of the relative prices. In Isnard's model, there is no place for reserve demand; while in Walras's model reserve demand is a variable to be determined like all other quantities demanded (or offered) as functions of the prices.

This is no small matter. Actually, for Walras, *both* the quantities demanded (or offered) *and* the prices are variables to be determined simultaneously by his comprehensive general equilibrium system of equations. None of them is a constant or a parameter. For Isnard, who allows his ratios of value to change only with a shift in the parametric proportions of the fixed quantity exchanged of each commodity for each of the other commodities, this implies that he considered price a function of the quantities interchanged. Walras, on the other hand, consistently and explicitly expressed the quantities interchanged as a function of the price vector, e.g.,

$$D_{b,a} = F_{b,a} (p_{b,a}, p_{c,a}, p_{d,a} \cdots)$$

(§105 of the first edition of the *Eléments*; §108 of the definitive edition).

This is as far as we need go, so far as the theory of exchange is concerned, in establishing the presumption of direct influence of Isnard on Walras. A similarly detailed comparison of Isnard's contributions to the theories of production, capital and money, which I must forgo on the present occasion, would undoubtedly reinforce this presumption when it is seen how many elements of these theories Walras shared with Isnard.

The very manner in which Isnard passed from his theory of exchange to his theory of production[41] immediately suggests Walras's passage, at a later date, from the one theory to the other.[42] What had been regarded up to this point simply as commodities are now to be viewed as products, the prices of which are determined, on the one hand, by competition among demanders, and on the other hand, by costs of

[40] Isnard, *Traité*, 1:21. Robertson's translation, altered only by the addition of italics and the insertions of "exchanged" ("Mathematical Economics Before Cournot," p. 533).
[41] Isnard, *Traité*, 1:27–30.
[42] Walras, *Eléments* (1877), Leçons 35–38, corresponding to Leçons 17–18 in the definitive edition of the *Elémentes*.

production, which constitute, as Isnard saw it, a floor for the prices. Isnard implicitly set the example for Walras to follow by defining costs of production in terms of the unit prices of inputs multiplied by corresponding fixed coefficients of production.[43] Some of the inputs, according to Isnard, are themselves outputs which can be used alternatively for consumption or for production.[44] The prices of inputs, he insisted, are determined like all other prices.

The foreshadowings of Walras in Isnard's theory of production are, to a certain degree, formal as well as conceptual. His algebraic model[45] was constructed of elements which are readily translated into elements found in Walras's more comprehensive theory. Isnard's model was more restricted because it was designed to demonstrate the double proposition that, contrary to the doctrine of the Physiocrats, industry as well as agriculture may normally yield a surplus over and above the costs of production, and that, again contrary to the Physiocratic doctrine, this surplus may normally accrue not only to owners of land but also to owners of whatever productive resources command a high price for their services because of their scarcity.[46] Even labor may earn a surplus which is reckoned as anything above subsistence wages.

To prove his central proposition, Isnard assumed two products, M and M', and then specified the following technical production conditions:

$$10M + 10M' \text{ produce } 40M$$
$$5M + 10M' \text{ produce } 60M'.$$

Expressing their exchange values in terms of M'', he first let the price of $M = M''$ and the price of $M' = 2M''$. The surpluses in terms of M'' are then

$$40M'' - (10M'' + 20M'') = 10M''$$

for producers of M; and

$$120M'' - (5M'' + 20M'') = 95M''$$

for producers of M'. To show the effect of a change in prices on the surpluses and their distribution, Isnard next assumed the price of M' to be $3M''$, while holding the price of M at M'' as before. The surpluses,

[43] Ibid., §§246-47, corresponding to §§203-4 in the definitive edition.

[44] If Isnard may be considered a precursor of modern linear programing (Theocharis, *Early Developments,* p. 67, n. 1), it is at least equally justifiable to consider him a precursor of Piero Sraffia's theory of *Production of Commodities by Means of Commodities* (Cambridge, 1960).

[45] Isnard, *Traité,* 1: 34-37.   [46] Ibid., p. 39.

under these new market conditions, the technical conditions of production remaining the same, become

$$40M'' - (10M'' + 30M''') = 0$$

for producers of M; and

$$180M'' - (5M'' + 30M''') = 145M''$$

for producers of M'. In general, the technical production conditions can be written in the form

	M	M'
M	$a_{m,m}$	$a_{m,m'}$
M'	$a_{m',m}$	$a_{m',m'}$

where $a_{i,j}$ is the amount of input i entering into the production of one unit of j; or, in terms of Isnard's numerical example,

	M	M'
M	1/4	1/12
M'	1/4	1/6

With the unit price of M in terms of M'' designated as $p_{m,m''}$ and that of M' as $p_{m',m''}$, for m, the unit costs of production can be written

$$a_{m,m}p_{m,m''} + a_{m',m}p_{m',m''},$$

for M; and

$$a_{m,m'}p_{m,m''} + a_{m',m'}p_{m',m''},$$

for M'. It is seen that, while there is no exact counterpart of Isnard's production equations in Walras, who designed his theory of production for a different purpose, Isnard's formulation contained implicitly Walras's fixed coefficients of production as well as his cost of production equations. Walras, moreover, included within his model the production of products by means of products in §§248 and 275 of the first edition of the *Elémentes* (§§205 and 238 of the definitive edition).

In his analytical discussion of capital and interest,[47] Isnard calculated the rate of return on capital as a net rate, which he arrived at after first

[47] Ibid., p. 30-34, 48-50.

deducting depreciation and upkeep from the gross return on capital, leaving a net return which he called "perpétuel"—exactly as Walras did after him.[48] Moreover, Isnard used a general average rate of net return to determine the market prices of capital goods by capitalizing the net income at the average rate. Perhaps the most remarkable trail that Isnard blazed in advance of Léon Walras's construction of an elaborate mathematical highway was that which led to the theory of the allocation of capital resources among various employments. Isnard's argument ran as follows:

Capitals are distributed among different employments in agriculture, industry, and commerce in such a way that the ratios of their values to receipts from the sale of their products less the costs of upkeep, repair, and replacement—that is, the ratios of [invested] funds to [net] returns—are everywhere the same in all enterprises. This uniformity is achieved and equilibrium establishes itself because funds flow toward and abound in places where the yield [*intérêt*] is highest and because like things have one and the same value. When things have a higher price in one place than in another, they rush there and equilibrium is reestablished. Let F be the value of the funds employed in agriculture and F' that of the funds employed in industry; let B be the payments for the value of the products of agriculture less the cost of upkeep, repairs and replacement and B' the payments for the products of industry less the same costs, then the ratio of F to F' must be equal to the ratio of B to B' for the ratio of F to B to be equal to the ratio of F' to B' or for the rate of interest [in the sense of rate of capitalization] to be everywhere the same. This uniformity [in the rate of capitalization] is realized not only between agriculture and industry in general, but also among individual enterprises.[49]

Walras wrote virtually the same thing in §286 of the first edition of the *Eléments* (cf. §249 of the definitive edition), where he laid out, as a condition of competitive equilibrium in capital formation, a set of l equations "*expressing the uniformity of the rate of net income* for all capital goods proper," the only difference being that Walras inverted Isnard's ratios in order to give a common rate of net income. All this, as well as Isnard's clearly drawn distinction between return on capital and money interest, is echoed by Walras, who gave greater precision to these concepts in working out his theory of the determination of the prices of capital goods.

In his treatment of money, Isnard strikingly anticipated Walras's idiosyncratic use of the term *numéraire,* not in the ordinary sense of hard cash or specie, nor in the sense of an abstract unit of account, but rather

[48] Walras, *Eléments* (1877), Leçons 45-48. Cf., Walras, *Elements of Pure Economics,* Lessons 23-25.

[49] Isnard, *Traité,* 1:49-50.

to designate a concrete standard commodity in terms of which the relative values of all other commodities can be expressed.[50] Whether consciously or not, Walras certainly followed Isnard in drawing the distinction between the *numéraire* function of money and its function as a "pledge" (Isnard) or as a medium of exchange (Walras). Moreover, they both perceived that these functions could be performed by separate commodities, though usually they were performed by one and the same commodity, money. The resemblances between Isnard and Walras are so close both in the terminology and in the analytical employment of the concept that it places a great strain on one's imagination to suppose that Walras arrived at his idea of *numéraire* wholly independently of Isnard. On the other hand, Isnard's qualified quantity theory of money[51] was so sketchy that it probably exerted no influence at all on Walras.

Lastly, I should like to refer to Isnard's lengthy and involved analysis of foreign exchange,[52] not because of any similarities with anything found in Walras on the subject, but because it really considers in anticipation Ricardo's problem of the relationship of fluctuations in the exchange rate of a currency other than gold on the bullion price of gold, rather than the problem of "rates of exchange of two countries with bimetallistic systems," as Theocharis supposed.[53]

If, as the evidence accumulates, one has the impression that Walras worked out the mathematical framework of his general equilibrium theory with Isnard's *Traité des richesses* at his elbow, and, as I have

[50] Ibid., p. 21-23. Isnard entitled the second section of his second chapter, "Du rapport des marchandises à l'une d'elles, ou de l'usage de la monnoie," and went on to say: "la mesure d'une des marchandises peut servir de mesure commune à toutes les autres, et . . . .on peut toujours rapporter à cette marchandise les valeurs de toutes les autres.—Si cette marchandise a beaucoup de valeur sous peu de volume, il s'ensuit encore qu'elle pourra servir de gage commode de toutes les autres. Les marchandises qui servent ainsi de mesures communes et de gages sont appellées monnoies.—Le prix des marchandises exprimé en argent peut être considéré comme une manière de compter, pour laquelle on prend un objet de comparaison. Le prix exprimé en livres, sols, et deniers, auroit pu être exprimé en toute autre mesure, ou même en nombres abstraits et en fractions. L'argent considéré comme *numéraire* est donc en effet de convention; mais si on le considère comme monncie, on ne peut dire que c'est par convention qu'il a une valeur en servant de gage. Il est naturel que les mesures des marchandises qui servent de monnoie servent en même temps de *numéraire* . . ." [italics added]. Cf., Walras, *Elements of Pure Economics*, §§68,115, 145-50; and Lesson 30, for Walras's discussion of *numéraire* and its relation to money. Léon Walras's father, Auguste Walras, had also distinguished between the *numéraire* function of money and its function as a medium of exchange. Auguste Walras, *De la nature de la richesse et de l'origine de la valeur* (Paris and Evreux, 1831), pp. 290-98; in the reedition, ed. Gaston Leduc (Paris, 1938), pp. 275-80. But unlike Isnard before him and Léon Walras after him, he considered *numéraire* purely and simply as an abstract unit of account, which may or may not coincide with "la monnaie réelle," depending on circumstances extraneous to its *numéraire* function. At no point did Auguste Walras even hint that *numéraire* as such could be conceived as a *concrete* commodity. This Isnard did; and Isnard even alluded to the choice of a *numéraire* commodity as arbitrary, subject to analytical convenience—in anticipation of Léon Walras.

[51] Isnard, *Traité*, 1:25-26.   [52] Ibid., pp. 289-97.
[53] Theocharis, *Early Developments*, p. 70.

indicated in another place,[54] with Louis Poinsot's *Eléments de statique* at his bedside, not to speak of the very substantial assistance he received from his colleagues at Lausanne, Paul Piccard[55] and Hermann Amstein,[56] this does not detract one jot or tittle from the originality of Walras's achievement.[57] Theoretical discoveries are never made wholly of brand-new pieces. They consist generally of novel and illuminating rearrangements of preexisting elements taken not only from the science for which the discovery is destined, but from other sciences as well. It was not the object of this paper, however, to evaluate the originality or the significance of Walras's work. All that has been intended here is to offer an example of the sort of problems one encounters in attempting to trace the filiation of ideas in the history of economics. Coping with such problems is part of the task of intellectual history, one of the objects of which is to draw from *demonstrable* connections in the sequence of novelties what conclusions one can regarding the nature of scientific progress.[58]

[54] Jaffé, *Correspondence of Walras* 3: 148-49, Letter 1483 and n. 7 to that letter.

[55] Ibid., 1:308-11, n.7 to letter 211.

[56] Ibid., 1:516-20 and nn. 1-5 to Letter 364; 688-89, Letter 500; 789-90, Letter 590; 793, Letter 594; 2:269-71, Letters 850-51.

[57] At the Nottingham Conference on the History of Economic Thought referred to in footnote 58, a discussant raised the question whether Léon Walras's substantial indebtedness to Isnard's work did not detract at least a "tittle" from the "originality" of Walras's achievement. Perhaps, but the answer depends upon what is meant by "originality" in any scientific discovery, which, however "revolutionary" it may be, must always contain elements of continuity with the past, or else it would be totally incomprehensible. Considered in proper perspective, *scientia* (like *natura*) *non facit saltum,* in the sense that discontinuities in science, like discontinuties in nature, if they exist, are not amenable to rational analysis. To probe this question further is beyond the scope of the present paper.

Professor William J. Baumol, who very kindly offered to read the typescript of this article, wrote to me, "I am still not convinced that we can rule out some degree of coincidence plus subconscious imitation." He suggested also that "it might have been desirable for you to discuss a bit more explicitly some alternatives to your hypothesis." Similar criticisms were made by participants in the Nottingham Conference. It was certainly not my intention to rule out the possibility of "some degree of coincidence plus subconscious imitation" or any other possibility. Either the documentary evidence I have produced sustains my hypothesis of direct and conscious influence or it does not. If it does not, there is no limit to the number of conjectures one might make to explain the multiplicity of parallelisms between Walras and Isnard, and there would be little point in discussing them in the absence of additional documentary evidence in favor of one or more alternative hypotheses.

[58] Work for this article was supported by the National Science Foundation under Grants GS-1516 and GS-1997 to Northwestern University. A first draft of the article was presented as a paper at a Symposium on the History of Economic Thought at Duke University, December 6-7, 1968; and an emended and expanded draft was read at the Conference on the History of Economic Thought held at the University of Nottingham, January 3-5, 1969. I am indebted to discussants on these two occasions for valuable suggestions, and to Mr. Adolf Vandendorpe of Boston College and my students, Messrs., Stephen B. Cohen, John L. Eatwell, and W. David Montgomery, for helpful comments on the mathematical problems encountered in the early stages of this research during my visiting professorship at Harvard in 1967-1968. Professor Robert W. Clower and Stanley Reiter came to my aid *in extremis* with suggestions for the clarification of the analytical argument which I was glad to follow.

4

THE BIRTH OF LEON WALRAS'S *ELEMENTS*

The publication dates 1874–77 of the first edition of Léon Walras's *Eléments d'économie politique pure* make this, its centenary, a fitting season of commemorating its birth. Whether one is inclined to applaud or to berate the memorialized book, its author must be credited with having earned the title of a "classical author," at least in the sense that Alfred Marshall defined the term:

> I do not myself hold a classical author to be one who more than others had said things which are true, as they stand. I don't feel bound to agree with him on many points, even on any point. But he is not for me classical unless either by the form or the matter of his words or deeds he has stated or indicated architectonic ideas in thought or sentiment, which are in some degree his own, and which, once created, can never die but are existing yeast ceaselessly working in the Cosmos.[1]

If the advent of Walras's *Eléments* can lay claim to more than anecdotal interest, it is because it represented from its first appearance a theoretical innovation which, as time went on, imparted a new direction to economic thinking. It taught economists to discern in the hubbub of countless markets the semblance of a coherent pattern of interdependencies amenable to rational comprehension and rigorous analysis. To be sure, adumbrations of the same pattern had already appeared in earlier literature and were known to Walras. He did not even invent the techniques he employed, but took them ready-made as he found them. What remains, however, "in some degree his own" is the "architectonic" plan Walras drew up to give unified structure and form to the preexisting intuitions and scattered components located in the storehouses of the Physiocrats, the great classical writers, and their more perspicacious predecessors and critics. No one has better characterized the true nature of Walras's original accomplishment than Walras himself when he jotted down on a scrap of paper which I found in his archives: "Je ne suis pas un économiste. Je suis un architecte. Mais je sais mieux l'économie politique que les économistes. (I am not an economist. I am

This is a revised version of a lecture delivered at Keio University in Tokyo, November 1, 1974. Research support by the Canada Council is gratefully acknowledged.
 [1] Pigou 1925, p. 374, Marshall to Bonar, 27 Sept. 1898.

an architect. But I know political economy better than economists do.)"[2] And Vilfredo Pareto was among the first to appreciate the essential significance of Walras's contribution for the future of economics when he wrote in 1898: "It is to Léon Walras that we are indebted for the general representation of economic equilibrium in equations. The discovery of this highly generalized formulation marks the beginning of a very important epoch for the development of new theories."[3]

The centenary of so important a "classic" as Léon Walras's *Eléments* provides a suitable occasion for inquiring into the circumstances under which the book came into being. Though there is no surviving parent or witness to give firsthand testimony of its delivery into the world, there are records of the event which turn out to be of instructive interest. It is with these records that I shall be concerned in this article.

As every author knows, books, like babies, are born in travail, but the attendant circumstances are different. The record of the exact date of birth of a baby may be lost—such is the case of Adam Smith, for example—but we may be sure that there was a day of birth. We cannot be so sure that there was a day of the first appearance of a finished book, notwithstanding the practice of some publishers to announce in advance, for trade purposes, a precise date of publication. Usually the day can only be guessed at. Piero Sraffa gives his reasons for supposing that the day of publiction of the first edition of Ricardo's *Principles* was the 19th day of April 1817.[4] Neil de Marchi gives the day of publication of John Stuart Mill's *Principles* as the 25th of April 1848, without, however, indicating the source of this information.[5] Is it possible to fix with precision the day of birth of Walras's *Elements?*

The question is not easy to answer and is further complicated by the fact that the book came out in two instalments, three years apart. Circumstantial evidence points to the 27th of July 1874, as the day on which the first instalment made its initial appearance. On that day, Léon Walras wrote from Lausanne to Mlle Guillaumin, the well-known Paris publisher and bookseller of economic treatises, "My book has just come off the press; and my [Lausanne] publisher will send you a certain number of copies."[6] Similar evidence points to the 6th of September 1877 as the day of publication of the second instalment, for on that day Walras wrote to his Dutch correspondent, d'Aulnis de Bourouill, "I take pleasure in sending you the last part of my *Eléments d'économie politique pure* which has just been published."[7] I call these two successive publica-

---

[2] Preserved in the *Fonds Walras* at Lausanne.
[3] Pareto 1898, p. 100 of the 1966 reprint of the article; my translation.
[4] Sraffa 1951, p. xix.   [5] de Marchi 1974, 119.
[6] Jaffé, 1965, 1, 410, Letter 284; my translation of all extracts from the *Correspondence of Léon Walras and Related Papers* cited in the text of this article.
[7] Ibid., I, 540, Letter 382.

tions instalments rather than first and second volumes, since Walras himself regarded the 1874 book as only a half volume, the second half being initially withheld until the sales of the first half proved sufficient to justify the additional expense of printing the rest.[8] Certainly the bulk of the whole first edition, 404 consecutively numbered pages of text in all, was not enough to warrant a two-volume work.

Such, then, are the dates of parturition, as nearly as can be determined. Can anything be said of its period of gestation? Fortunately we have some clues. Walras first conceived the idea of writing a comprehensive treatise at least as far back as December 23, 1862, when he made an extraordinary proposal to Jules du Mesnil Marigny,[9] a well known economist in his day and a pioneer in mathematical economics. At the time of the proposal Walras was a struggling young journalist twenty-eight years of age and du Mesnil Marigny an established writer and wealthy man, fifty-two years old. Walras nevertheless suggested that they enter into a compact to produce either a comprehensive treatise of four volumes or a modest Outline ("Esquisse") to bear both their names as joint authors, but with Walras doing all the writing and with du Mesnil Marigny paying all the bills, allotting Walras a stipend besides. Du Mesnil Marigny naturally declined this incredibly presumptuous proposal. As there was nothing in the scheme of 1862 foreshadowing the great theoretical system of the *Eléments,* the gestation period proper cannot be said to have begun then. It began rather in 1869-70, when Walras made what he called his second attempt (*"tentative"*) to formulate economics mathematically after a first attempt in 1860 which proved abortive.[10] Though Walras, quite sensibly, never saw fit to publish either of these attempts, the second is of particular interest because the manuscript reveals, in embryo, several important features of the future *Eléments,* at least so far as the theory of the market mechanism is concerned. The embryo is even more clearly discernible in a letter of September 6, 1870, which he addressed to the Swiss statesman Louis Ruchonnet to offer himself as a candidate for the chair in political economy at Lausanne. In that letter, he referred to his unpublished notes for a projected treatise and presented an outline which anticipated in large part the table of contents of the *Eléments.*[11]

The period of gestation thus begun was attended by several exciting incidents, one of which, in particular proved to be of crucial importance in the development of Walras's theory of general equilibrium. Though

---

[8] Mlle Guillaumin, having better business sense, warned Léon Walras (hereafter referred to in these notes as L.W.) that bringing out his books in instalments was bad for sales, Jaffé 1965, I, 416, Letter 288.
[9] Ibid., I, 117–25, Letter 81.   [10] Ibid., I, 216–21, Letter 148, n. (33).
[11] Ibid., I, 204–12, Letter 148; cf. pp. 306–7, Letter 210, Enclosure, and p. 424,

the embryo of the *Eléments* was, *grosso modo,* morphologically defined in 1870, physiologically it was still incomplete.[12] What was lacking was, so to speak, a heart which would automatically energize the system and give it life. There was no sign of such an organ until late in 1872, when Walras's colleague, Paul Piccard, helped him solve the long nagging problem of getting away from empirical demand curves of the sort he had inherited from Cournot.[13] Once Piccard had showed Walras how to apply the calculus technique of maximization to the problem of deriving demand curves rationally from utility functions, everything fell into place and Walras's system was made viable.

Another incident was the knowledge first conveyed to Walras by d'Aulnis de Bourouill on May 4, 1874, that Jevons had already published a final utility theory remarkably similar to the theory of *rareté* which Walras had enunciated in his initial analytical paper, "Principe d'une théorie mathématique de l'échange," in the April 1874 issue of the *Journal des Economistes.*[14] This explains why Walras hastened his pace and insisted that his Lausanne publisher, Corbaz et Cie., bring out the first half of his volume containing his new found theory of exchange as quickly as possible, without waiting to print the second half. Walras grew frightened lest the rest of his discoveries should be made by others and published before his own, thus depriving him of all honors of priority.[15]

Though Walras had asserted that the second instalment of the *Eléments* was ready for the press when he announced the publication of the first instalment, the process of gestation nevertheless went on in the interval between the two stages of parturition. Driven compulsively to seek perfection in his work, Walras ceaselessly corrected, amended and

Letter 295, n. (3). See n. 12 below.

[12] Jaffé 1972, pp. 387–98 (pp. 121–32 in Black 1973). Writing to Mlle Guillaumin on 5 Sept. 1872, L.W. described the first part of his proposed treatise, which he prematurely thought complete and ready for publication at the time, as follows: "J'ai d'abord défini avec beaucoup plus de rigueur qu'on ne l'a fait jusqu'ici le mécanisme du marché et de la concurrence. Supposant alors ces mécanismes en fonction dans des conditions de l'abstraction scientifique, j'ai élaboré toute une théorie mathématique de l'échange de 2 marchandises (A) et (B); puis de 3 marchandises (A), (B) et (C); puis de m marchandises (A), (B), (C), (D)... entre elles sur le marché. J'ai aussi donné un sens et une formulation nette et précise à la loi de l'offre et de la demande...." (Jaffé 1965, I, 298–99, Letter 202). Not the slightest hint of a marginal utility theory! Obviously Paul Piccard, about whom more anon, had not yet come into the picture.

[13] Jaffé 1965, I, 308–11, Letter 211, n. (4).

[14] Ibid., I, 388, Letter 267. For an account of L.W.'s "Principe d'une thórie mathématique de l'échange" and a comparison of L.W.'s theory with that of Jevons, see Jaffé 1972, 380–87 (pp. 114–21 in Black 1973).

[15] Among Léon Walras's occasional jottings preserved in the Lyons Collection (described in Jaffé 1965, I, xii), there is an undated jotting which reads, "Je disais il y a quelque temps à M. Charles Secrétan [a professor of philosophy at Lausanne] que j'avais connu deux périodes, une pendant laquelle j'étais un fou, et une pendant laquelle tout le monde avait trouvé la chose avant moi...."

emended his manuscripts up to the very moment they passed to the printer's hands, and even after that, as he confessed, he made substantial changes in the proofs.[16] It is not surprising, therefore, to find evidence of two episodes between 1874 and 1877, one of which is interesting because it left an identifiable trace on the second instalment, while the other is interesting precisely because it did not leave any such trace. Had Léon Walras's competence in mathematics been adequate to the task, the second episode would have enabled Walras to introduce into the *Eléments* as early as 1877 a momentous technical innovation which did not take firm root in the literature of mathematical economics until the following century.

The effect attributable to the first of these episodes is seen in the 61st "Leçon" of the first edition, corresponding, without change, to §382–387 of the definitive edition. The "Leçon" in question, entitled, "Du monopole. Prix multiple," starts out as a straightforward account of Dupuit's theory of price discrimination and then suddenly, without warning, though not without rhyme or reason, veers to a caustic criticism of Dupuit's theory of "consumers' surplus" as it is now called. Walras's criticism of Dupuit's unconditional identification of the utility curve with the demand curve—worse still, with the market demand curve, a fact that Walras overlooked—was valid enough and justified his insistence on the difference between his own utility theory and that of Dupuit.[17] Nevertheless, the vehemence and acerbity of Walras's disagreement with Dupuit, and, more importantly the context in which it is located in the *Eléments*—far removed from the first instalment where his own theory of *rareté* (marginal utility) and his critical analysis of rival theories of value are found[18]—may strike the reader as startling.

The only explanation I can offer for this anomaly is that Walras was provoked to insert his attack on Dupuit in the gestation period from 1874 to 1877 by a claim made *after* the publication of the first instalment that it was Dupuit and not Walras, nor Jevons either, who first discovered the modern utility theory of value. The claim was published in a letter to the Editor of *Le Temps* on November 10, 1874 to protest against an article which had appeared in the same newspaper on October 14, 1874 attributing to Jevons and Walras a theory that the letter writer insisted properly belonged to Dupuit.[19] Before he learned of Gossen, nothing infuriated Walras more than a challenge to Jevons's and his

---

[16] Jaffé 1965, I, 439, Letter 308.

[17] Actually, as late as January 1872, virtually on the eve of Paul Piccard's redeeming intervention, L.W. himself described the relation between his "price curve" and utility along very much the same lines that he later denounced as Dupuit's flagrant error. See Jaffé 1965, I, 294, Letter 198, n. (2), outline of fifth lecture planned for Geneva.

[18] Walras 1874, Leçons 14–18 and 27 of the first edition, corresponding to Leçons 8–10 and 16 of the subsequent editions (§§157–161 in the definitive edition).

[19] Jaffé 1965, I, 456, Letter 320.

own rights to priority in the discovery of a rigorous marginal utility theory. His private letters written at that time bristle with indignant denials of the claim made for Dupuit.[20] This is what leads me to surmise that Walras's criticism of Dupuit was meant as an indirect contradiction of the challenge to his priority and was introduced into the *Eléments* between 1874 and 1877 as a coda to the theory of price discrimination at the point where Dupuit's name had to be mentioned.

The occasion of the second episode was Walras's dissatisfaction with his own theory of production while it was still in embryo. Troubled by his unrealistic assumption of fixed coefficients of production, he appealed for help from the mathematician Hermann Amstein, who like Paul Piccard, was a colleague of his at Lausanne. In a letter dated January 6, 1877 (exactly nine months before the second instalment containing the theory of production was published), Amstein demonstrated to Walras in terms worthy of a Samuelson how the Lagrangean multiplier technique could be used to solve the problem.[21] Amstein's mathematics, alas, baffled Walras, who then contented himself, *faute de mieux*, with the following limp explanation as it appeared in the 41st Leçon of the first edition of the *Eléments:*

We are evidently assuming that the coefficients a_i, a_p, a_k, ... b_i, b_p, b_k ... c_i, c_p, c_k ... d_i, d_p, d_k are determined *a priori*. In reality they are not so determined, for in the production of a good, it is possible to use more (or less) of one productive service, say land-services, provided that correspondingly less (or more) of other productive services, say labor- or capital-services, are used. The respective quantities of each of the productive services which thus enter into the making of a single unit of each of the products can only be determined by the condition of minimum cost of production after the prices of the productive services have been determined. It would be easy *(sic)* to express this condition by a system of as many equations as there are coefficients of production to be determined; but as this system would be, in a way *(sic)*, independent of the other systems we are primarily concerned with, we shall disregard it for greater simplicity and suppose that the above coefficients figure among the data rather than the unknowns of the problem.[22]

How uncomfortable Walras was with this assumption is seen further on in the second instalment of the first edition, in the 51st Leçon, where, in his discussion of economic growth and technological progress, he reverted to the theme of variable vs. constant coefficients of production.

[20] Ibid., I,, 471, Letter 327; and p. 477, Letter 330.
[21] Ibid., I, 516–21, Letter 364. See also Jaffé 1964, pp. 94–97, reprinted with an English translation of Amstein's letter in Baumol and Goldfeld 1968, pp. 310–12. Baumol and Goldfeld (p. 189) also note that "one of the first uses of Lagrange [indeterminate] multipliers" is found in Edgeworth 1881, p. 27, four years after the date of Amstein's letter, which was, of course, then still unpublished.
[22] Walras 1877, §247 in the second instalment of the first edition of the *Eléments*; my translation. For changes in the subsequent editions, see p. 582 of the English translation, Collation Note [f] to Lesson 20.

In this connection he adumbrated something that suggests, but fell short of, a marginal productivity theory.[23] Walras, nevertheless, posed the problem in 1877; and that, as we know, is half of science. How the other half found its way into later editions of the *Eléments*, I have recounted and documented elsewhere.[24] Here we are concerned with the first edition only and how it took form.

Books, again like babies, at any rate modern babies, cost money to be born. Usually, however, this is not the concern of the author, but of the publisher. In that respect the Lausanne publisher of the first edition of the *Eléments*, L. Corbaz et Cie., can only be regarded as a publisher by courtesy. Louis Corbaz was a commercial printer and stationer. The real publisher was Léon Walras himself, with Corbaz et Cie. intervening as banker and business agent. Walras took upon himself a large part of the commercial risk, paying, in the end, the printing expenses, the binding expenses, the cost of the plates, the shipping costs, the postage, the insurance, etc. himself. This is evident from a jumble of bills, receipts, cryptic private accounts and copies of correspondence with his titular publishers, which are now in my possession.[25] It transpires from this confusion of business papers, so far as I have been able to decipher and interpret them, that not only the first edition of the *Eléments*, but also the subsequent editions, as well as the *Théorie mathématique de la richesse sociale* (1883), the *Théorie de la monnaie* (1886), the *Etudes d'économie sociale* (1896) and the *Etudes économie politique appliquée* (1898) were all published under similar conditions—unbelievably onerous to the author. The co-publishers named on the title page of the first edition, Guillaumin et Cie. of Paris and H. Georg of Basel, acted merely as booksellers, who had agreed to take a certain number of copies on consignment, stipulating a 50 percent profit margin and the right to return remainders eventually to Léon Walras. Who sought out and initiated negotiations with booksellers? Who paid for the distribution of review copies? It was always Léon Walras.[26]

Despite his tireless activity as virtual publisher of his own works, despite the effort and money he expended on advertising his books, Léon Walras was a dismal failure from the financial point of view. Had he set himself up as a commercial enterprise, he would quickly have

[23] Ibid., §§306–307 in the second instalment of the first edition of the *Eléments*, corresponding to §§324–325 of the definitive edition. See pp. 604–6 of the English translation for Collation Notes to Lesson 36 of the definitive edition indicating changes made in the successive editions.

[24] Jaffé 1964.

[25] Generously passed on to me by Professor Gaston Leduc who had inherited the documents from L.W.'s daughter, Aline Walras. See Jaffé 1965, I, xii.

[26] Ibid., I, 299, Letter 202; p. 301, Letter 205; pp. 410–11, Letter 284; p. 416, Letter 288; and pp. 726–27, Letter 534.

been declared bankrupt and that would have been the end of it. The reason for the miserable showing was quite simple: his product did not sell.[27] Take the first edition of the *Eléments* alone: it appears from a summary statement of disbursements and receipts established for the seventeen year period from 1874 to 1891, that all Corbaz et Cie. owed him on the two instalments of that edition was 400 francs 25 centimes. This was the amount due to him after he had himself purchased 212 copies of the first instalment and 210 copies of the second instalment for his own use and distribution to economists all over the world gratis. The Department of Public Instruction of the Vaud Canton had also purchased 100 copies of each instalment at the reduced price of 2 fr. 50 per copy, the list price being 3 fr. 75 per copy.[28] As nearly as I can figure it out, over the same seventeen year period no more than 500 copies of the first instalment and little over 350 copies of the second instalment were sold in normal course. In 1891, when Walras came to close his accounts with his "publisher" of the first edition of the *Eléments* and several other publications (including the *Théorie mathématique de la richesse sociale* of 1883), *he* owed Corbaz et Cie. 1,803 fr. 13 net.

Léon Walras was indeed, an eleemosynary publisher. Not that he had a vast fortune. On the contrary, for most of his life he was in straitened circumstances. Until his mother died and left him a modest inheritance, he carried on his private publishing business by borrowing money from devoted friends. His passion lay in spreading the gospel of social justice and mathematical economics. To satisfy this passion he went to extraordinary lengths. In 1902, the year in which Walras, then sixty-eight years old, decided to retire from the fray, he perceived that he had inherited in all 101,500 francs and only had 25,500 francs to leave to his heirs.[29] The difference was eaten up mainly by his publications, not only his books, but his articles as well, for these articles were more often than not published in journals so obscure[30] that the only way he could bring them to the attention of economists was to go to the expense of having offprints printed and posting them to his correspondents everywhere. Walras impoverished himself in the fond hope of establishing himself in the memory of future generations as an apostle of "scientific" economics.

The difficulties under which Léon Walras produced the first edition of his *Eléments* were, indeed, formidable. And wonderful as the product was, even in the first edition, it was not delivered into an expectant world. The world Walras was particularly interested in impressing was

[27] It took from 1874 to 1886 for the few hundred copies constituting the first edition to be exhausted (Jaffé 1965, II, 149–50, Letter 740).
[28] Ibid., I, 315–18, Letters 215–16.   [29] Ibid., III, 181–82, Letter 1508, n. (2).
[30] E.g. the *Bulletin de la Société Vaudoise des Sciences Naturelles*.

that of his native land, France. But in France, hardly any serious notice at all was taken of Walras's work.

When the initial instalment of the first edition appeared, the *Journal des Economistes,* which was the only prominent economic journal in France at the time, accorded it nothing more than a listing in the advertisement of new publications of Guillaumin et Cie.[31] No book review of the first edition of the *Eléments* ever found a place in that journal. One reason for this was that it was not a simple matter in those days to find anyone competent and willing enough to review a book as difficult and as scientifically disinterested in tone as the *Eléments.*[32] Even so, a less prominent French journal, *L'Economiste Français,* managed to ferret out a certain Charles Letort who took some account of Walras's first instalment in an otherwise undistinguished article, "De l'application des mathématiques á l'étude de l'économie politique," which was published October 31, 1874.[33] All Letort had to say was that Jevons's *Theory of Political Economy* and Walras's book were simply the latest manifestations of a trend hitherto represented by such writers as Canard, Dupuit, von Thünen and especially Cournot, a trend which, in the reviewer's opinion, was of doubtful value because economic and psychological phenomena were too complex and too fluid to be forced into a rigid structure of mathematical formulas.

In response to Léon Walras's personal solicitation, he obtained a formal review of the first instalment in *La Critique Philosophique, Politique, Scientifique, Littéraire* of March 25, 1875, by no less a figure than the philosopher Charles Bernard Renouvier.[34] Though Renouvier had had an early training in mathematics at the Ecole Polytechnique, he confined his criticism to the philosophical implications of Walras's pure economics and criticized Walras's restriction of the application of moral principles to the theory of property and taxation. Renouvier insisted that questions of justice also arise in the determination of wages, interest, and rent. Walras replied that his pure theory, which confined itself to investigating the "natural" and inevitable consequences of pure competition, was not the place to raise moral issues.[35] The answer was, in my opinion, superficial. I hope to show in another paper that moral considerations did enter quite consciously and deliberately into Walras's choice of a perfect-competition model for his economic analysis.

Apart from the advertisement in the *Journal des Economistes,* Letort's insipid pronouncement in *L'Economiste Français,* and Renouvier's philosophical discussion in *La Critique Philosophique,* the only other published comment in France on Walras's first instalment was the article already

---

[31] Jaffé 1965, I, 424, Letter 295.
[32] Ibid., I, 437, Letter 306.   [33] Ibid., I, 458, Letter 320, n. (18).
[34] Ibid., I, 448–49, Letter 316, n. (4).   [35] Ibid., I, 542, Letter 385.

alluded to in connection with Dupuit, a "Causerie scientifique," which appeared in *Le Temps* on October 14, 1874. It was an unsigned article, written by a mining engineer and journalist, Auguste Langel; but the substance of the article was inspired by Walras himself in a letter to Langel asking for the review.[36] Walras admitted in a letter he wrote to Jevons on November 29th of the same year that the article was of little import, apart from the publicity it afforded.[37]

Before leaving the scene of the French reaction to Walras's first edition of the *Eléments,* I should also mention the answer Joseph Bertrand made to Walras's complaint that Cournot's, Jevons's, and his own work had been neglected in France.[38] Bertrand, who was one of the foremost mathematicians of that epoch, published in the *Journals des Savants* of September 1883 a joint review of Cournot's *Recherches sur les principes mathématiques de la richesse sociale* (1838) and Walras's *Théorie mathématique de la richesse sociale,* the latter having appeared in 1883 as a retrospective collection of papers resuming and sometimes extending the mathematical substance of the first edition of the *Eléments.* Bertrand began with a defense of the neglect of Cournot. He insisted that Cournot's *Recherches* deserved to be neglected because of its want of realism and because its algebraic argument was faulty and led to erroneous conclusions on such questions as the incidence of a tax on monopoly price, the determinacy of duopoly price, and the effects of free trade in international commerce. Bertrand, however, was less severe in his criticism of Walras's theories, which he conceded were interesting. Nevertheless he took issue with Walras's theory of *tâtonnement.* Bertrand, finding that transactions at nonequilibrium prices undoubtedly take place in the real world, concluded that final prices are indeterminate. Bertrand also objected to Walras's theorem of proportionality of marginal utilities to prices at equilibrium, because the theorem was inapplicable to the commercial transactions where merchants are primarily interested in maximizing money profits, not utility. These were substantial criticisms that Walras, to the end of his working days, tried desperately to answer.[39] On the subject of *tâtonnement,* he evaded the issue, to begin with by assuming in the theory of exchange that markets were institutionally so organized as to preclude transactions at nonequilibrium prices; and later by introducing into the fourth edition of

[36] Ibid., I, pp. 433–34, Letter 302; and p. 446, Letter 313, n. (2).
[37] Ibid., I, 456, Letter 320. [38] Ibid., I, 790–91, Letter 590, n. (3).
[39] Ibid., II, 630, Letter 1200, Enclosure, Part II. Referring to himself in the third person, L.W. wrote in an unpublished, undated note: "M. Joseph Bertrand dans son article du *Journal des Savants* (7bre 1883) a objecté que le problème ainsi posé n'était pas déterminé. Mais M. Walras dans sa notice sur Gossen insérée au *Journal des Économistes* (avril 1885) a soutenu à juste titre qu'il l'était du moment où l'échange était suspendu en cas d'inégalité de l'offre et de la demande, hypothèse qu'aucun esprit scientifique n'hésitera à concéder au théoricien."

the *Eléments* in 1900 his imaginary device of provisional contracts (he called them "bons," i.e. tickets) which were not to become binding until all prices, in production and capital formation as well as exchange, had been so adjusted that equilibrium was achieved everywhere in the economy.[40] This was hardly a proper response to Bertrand's call for realism.

In other countries Walras had better luck. His persistent epistolary prodding yielded results in the form of published and private comments that were not only more numerous than those elicited in France, but also more constructive. Their principal importance lies in the effect they had on the later editions of the *Eléments*. To obtain such results Walras kept pumping his correspondents far and wide for the names of economists anywhere in the world to whom to send copies of his publications for critical evaluation.

Though I could not find more than two formal book-reviews of Walras's first edition of the *Eléments* in non-French journals, this was no index of the serious attention given to Walras's work outside his native country. The two reviews, moreover, one in the Danish *Nationaløkonomisk Tiddskrift* in 1875 by Aleksis Petersen[41] and the other in the *Deutsche Allgemeine Polytechnische Zeitung* for December 9, 1876,[42] were, as it turned out, of no interest apart from calling attention to Walras's *Eléments*. From Walras's standpoint, the great event was the publication in 1878 of an Italian translation of four of his mathematico-economic papers in the volume of the *Biblioteca dell'economista* devoted to the quantitative method in the social sciences.[43] The editor of this volume, Gerolamo Boccardo, explained that these papers of Walras would have to do in lieu of the *Eléments* because the second instalment had not appeared early enough for inclusion in the volume.[44] The Italians at that time held Walras in very high regard, but, apart from G. B. Antonelli, showed limited critical understanding of his work until Pareto appeared on the scene.

Little need be said here of the notice taken of the *Eléments* by W. Stanley Jevons: first, in his paper, "The Progress of the Mathematical Theory of Political Economy, with an Explanation of the Principles of the Theory," which he read before the Manchester Statistical Society on November 11, 1874, and which was reported in the *Manchester Examiner* the following day;[45] and secondly, in the "Preface to the Second Edition"

[40] Walras 1900, p. viii of the "Préface" to the fourth edition (p. 37 in the English translation); and §§207–208 and §251. See also the English translation, pp. 528–29, Translator's Note [6] to Lesson 20; pp. 582–83, Collation Note [h] to Lesson 20; and p. 590, Collation Note [f] to Lesson 24. cf. Jaffé 1967.
[41] Jaffé 1965, I, 480, Letter 332, n. (2). [42] Ibid., I, 515, Letter 363.
[43] Ibid., I, 472–73, Letter 327, n. (8).
[44] Ibid., I, 465, Letter 324; and p. 470, Letter 327.
[45] Ibid., I, 457, Letter 320, n. (2).

of Jevons's *Theory of Political Economy* published in 1879. Jevons, who was the first to bring Walras's *Eléments* to the attention of English econo-mists, always bestowed high praise on Walras's contribution, stressing, however, little else than Walras's independent discovery of the marginal utility theory of value as a confirmation of his own discovery. Walras, on his side, felt aggrieved because Jevons looked to the future for a full-blown new design of economic theory to replace the old classical structure. Walras was sure that he had already created such a design in the *Eléments*.[46]

Far more interesting were the three constructive criticisms proferred, one by a distinguished German economist, Wilhelm Lexis; another by a young Russian student, Ladeslaus von Bortkiewicz, who was destined to become a statistician and economist of world renown, and the third by the already renowned Austrian economist, Eugen von Böhm-Bawerk. In the *Jahrbücher für Nationalökonomie und Statistik* of 1881 Lexis reviewed a recently published German translation of Walras's same four analytical papers that Boccardo had translated for the *Biblioteca dell'economista*.[47] Lexis made four points which would have been equally pertinent to the *Eléments:* (1) that Walras's assumption of perfect competition and uni-form market prices neglected too many features of the real world to serve as a guide to policy; (2) that there was no justification for assuming (as Walras did also in the first edition of the *Eléments*) that the marginal utility (*rareté*) curves were linear; (3) that Walras's equational systems might not have any real positive solutions or indeed any solution at all; and (4) that the principle of maximum satisfaction was not applicable to the offer function of labor in an industrialized economy because the wage earner, for want of needed complementary capital equipment in his possession, could not make use of any reservation demand for his services. Turning now to Bortkiewicz, we find his criticisms in his remarkable exchange of letters with the master. In 1887, when the correspondence began, Bortkiewicz was only nineteen years old, too young to aspire to publishing commentaries on Walras. Employing a tactful blend of diffidence and intellectual firmness, Bortkiewicz called Walras's attention to two defects in his exposition of utility theory. One defect lay in Walras's original construction and explanation of the marginal utility graph in Figure 3 of the first instalment of the *Eléments*;[48] the other lay in his mathematical demonstration of the theorem of maximum satisfaction from which the second-order condition was miss-ing.[49] When we come to Böhm-Bawerk, we see that though in his

[46] Ibid., I, 623, Letter 448; p. 628, Letter 453, n. (3); II 210–11, Letter 799; p. 224, Letter 812; and p. 244, Letter 828.
[47] Ibid., I, 394, Letter 272, n. (2); and pp. 746–47, Letter 548, n. (2).
[48] Ibid., II, 233–34, Letter 820.   [49] Ibid., II, 248, Letter 831.

Grundzüge der Theorie des wirtschaftlichen Güterwerts of 1886 he had paid public tribute to Walras as a co-founder of the modern theory of value,[50] in his private correspondence with Walras a year later he challenged the Walrasian proposition that at equilibrium the prices of commodities are exactly proportional to their respective marginal utilities for all traders in the market.[51] This would hold, Böhm-Bawerk argued, in the exceptional case of continuous utility functions, but in the more general case of discontinuous utility functions, prices might well change without traders necessarily changing their purchases and sales.

In the measure that he was able to cope with them, Walras profited by these criticisms. Already in the *Théorie mathématique de la richesse sociale* of 1883, we see his linear marginal utility curves of the first edition of the *Eléments* replaced by nonlinear curves.[52] This, I suspect, was in response to Lexis's criticism of 1881. Unquestionably it was Böhm-Bawerk's doubts about the general validity of Walras's conclusions drawn from the assumption of continuous marginal utility curves that led Walras to tack on to the 8th "Leçon" in the second edition of the *Eléments* (1889) his well-known discussion reconciling his theorem of proportionality with discontinuous marginal utility curves.[53] The part Bortkiewicz's observations played in the confection of the second edition is seen in the distinct improvement in the construction and mathematical interpretation of marginal utility curves where Walras adopted Bortkiewicz's suggestions almost to the letter.[54] For reasons difficult to determine, Walras did not, however, introduce the second-order condition of a maximum into his theorem of maximum satisfaction until the fourth edition (1900), then following, despite the delay, Bortkiewicz's directions of 1888 exactly.[55]

I surmise that this delay, like the need Walras had for Piccard's technical aid in deriving demand functions from utility functions or like his failure to profit by Amstein's version of a marginal productivity theory, was due to Walras's inadequacy as a mathematician. He had mathematical vision, but little systematic training in the subject. Lacking technical competence in mathematics Walras could make nothing of Lexis's acute observation that the Walrasian system of equations might not have any solution at all. Walras remained convinced to the end of his days that equality between the number of unknowns and the number of independent equations was sufficient to guarantee the required solu-

[50] Ibid., II, 153, Letter 743, n. (4).   [51] Ibid., II, 181–83, Letter 770 and n. (8).
[52] Walras 1883, Plate 1, Fig. 3, following p. 31.
[53] Walras 1889, §§82–83 of the second edition, corresponding to §§83–84 of the definitive edition.
[54] Ibid., §74 of the second and subsequent editions. Cf. English translation of the *Eléments*, pp. 567–68, Collation Note [b] to Lesson 8.
[55] Ibid., §82 of the fourth and definitive editions. Cf. English translation, pp. 570–71, Collation Note [m] to Lesson 8.

tions. We must remember, however, that it was not until well on in the twentieth century that Abraham Wald, at Karl Schlesinger's instigation, broached the problem of existence theorems,[56] so that only now do we know how to demonstrate unequivocally that, provided appropriate inequalities are stipulated, the general equilibrium system does have a meaningful solution.

There were other criticisms of Walras's *Eléments* outside France before the first edition was superseded by subsequent editions. Some of these criticisms were pertinent, like that of the mathematician and astronomer George H. Darwin (son of Charles Darwin) who found fault with Walras's notation,[57] or that of the German philosopher and psychologist Wilhelm Wundt who laid bare the restrictive and highly abstract character of the Walrasian theory by listing in admirable detail the purely abstract assumptions on which the theory rested;[58] while others were irrelevant, like that of the German economist Wilhelm Launhardt who grossly mistook the scope and meaning of Walras's theorem of maximum social satisfaction.[59]

Thus, once born, the *Eléments* grew up and matured through four subsequent editions under the watchful tutelage of its author and the critical gaze of its contemporaries. To the last, however, it retained the salient distinguishing feature of the first edition, the general equilibrium structure. It is this feature as imprinted by Walras which, more than anything else in the *Eléments,* has made it, down to our own day, the object of a host of commentaries, modernizations, emendations, criticisms and at times outright condemnations. It has by no means been relegated to the museum of antiquities of interest solely to palaeographers. It lives among us. For some, as for the late Joseph Schumpeter and for Kenneth Arrow, Sir John Hicks, Paul Samuelson, and Takuma Yasui, the *doyen* of Japanese orthodox economists,[60] it is a fundamental source of inspiration and still serves as a prototype of modern economic theory; for others, as for the Cambridge School of economists,[61] for Professor Michio Morishima[62] and for Jànos Kornai,[63] it is at best an unfortunate anachronism and at worst a diabolical influence that has led modern economics woefully astray. The plain fact is that Walras's *Eléments,* one hundred years after its birth, indeed by virtue of the very controversy that it continues to arouse, has remained as "existing yeast ceaselessly working in the Cosmos."

[56] Karl Menger, "Austrian Marginalism and Mathematical Economics" in Hicks and Weber 1973, pp. 47–48.   [57] Jaffe 1965, I, 475, Letter 328, n. (4).
[58] Ibid., II, 234–35, Letter 820; and p. 243, Letter 827. Cf. Wundt 1895, II, 509.
[59] Launhardt 1885, pp. 29–30.
[60] Matsuura 1972, pp. 541–42 (pp. 275–76 in Black 1973).
[61] Robinson and Eatwell 1973, pp. 37–44.
[62] Morishima 1964, passim.   [63] Kornai 1971, pp. 348–49.

REFERENCES

Baumol, W. J., and S. M. Goldfeld, eds. *Precursors in Mathematical Economics: An Anthology.* L.S.E. Series of Reprints of Scarce Works on Political Economy, No. 19. London, 1968.

Black, R. D. Collison, A. W. Coats, and Craufurd D. W. Goodwin, ed. *The Marginal Revolution in Economics, Interpretation and Evaluation.* Durham, N. C. 1973.

de Marchi, N. B. "The Success of Mill's *Principles.*" *History of Political Economy* 6 (1974): 119–57.

Edgeworth, F. Y. *Mathematical Psychics.* London, 1881. L.S.E. Series of Reprints of Scarce Tracts in Economics and Political Science, No. 10. London, 1932.

Hicks, J. R., and W. Weber, eds. *Carl Menger and The Austrian School of Economics.* Oxford, 1973.

Jaffé, W. "New Light on an Old Quarrel." *Cahiers Vilfredo Pareto,* 1964, no. 3, pp. 61-102.

Jaffé, W. ed. *Correspondence of Léon Walras and Related Papers.* 3 vols. Amsterdam, 1965.

Jaffé, W. "Walras's Theory of *Tâtonnement:* A Critique of Recent Interpretations." *Journal of Political Economy* 75 (1967): 1–19.

Jaffé, W. "Léon Walras's Role in the 'Marginal Revolution' of the 1870s." *History of Political Economy* 4 (1972): 379–405 (pp. 113–39 in Black 1973).

Kornai, J. *Anti-equilibrium. On Economic Systems and the Tasks of Research.* Amsterdam and New York, 1971.

Launhardt, W. *Mathematische Begründung der Volkswirtschaftslehre.* Leipzig, 1885.

Matsuura, T. "Marginalism in Japan." *History of Political Economy,* 4 (1972): 533–50 (pp. 267–84 in Black 1973).

Morishima, M. *Equilibrium, Stability and Growth, A Multi-Sectoral Analysis.* Oxford, 1964.

Pareto, V. "De l'économie mathématique." *Zeitschrift für Sozialwissenschaft* (1898): 320–21. Reprinted in vol. 9 *(Marxisme et économie pure)* of Vilfredo Pareto's *Œuvres complètes,* ed. G. Busino, Geneva, 1966, pp. 100–101.

Pigou, A. C., ed. *Memorials of Alfred Marshall.* London, 1925.

Robinson, J., and J. Eatwell. *An Introduction to Modern Economics.* London, 1973.

Sraffa, P., ed. *The Works and Correspondence of David Ricardo,* vol. i, *On the Principles of Political Economy and Taxation.* Cambridge, 1951.

Walras, L. *Eléments d'économie politique pure ou Théorie de la richesse sociale.* 1st ed. (in two instalments), Lausanne: Corbaz; Paris: Guillaumin; Basel: Georg, 1874–77; 2d ed., Lausanne: Rouge; Paris: Guillaumin; Leipzig: Duncker and Humblot, 1889; 3d ed., Lausanne: Rouge; Paris: Guillaumin; Leipzig: Duncker and Humblot, 1896; 4th ed., Lausanne: Rouge; Paris: Pichon, 1900; definitive ed. (published posthumously), Paris: Pichon and Durand-Auzias; Lausanne: Rouge, 1926. Reprinted Paris: Pichon and Durand-Auzias, 1952. English translation by William Jaffé, *Elements of Pure Economics.* London: Allen and Unwin, 1954; and in Reprints of Economic Classics, New York: Augustus Kelley, 1969.

Walras, L. *Théorie mathématique de la richesse sociale.* Lausanne: Corbaz; Paris, Guillaumin; Rome: Loescher; Leipzig: Duncker and Humblot, 1883.

Wundt, W. *Logik,* 2d ed., Stuttgart: F. Enke, 1893–1895.

A CENTENARIAN ON A BICENTENARIAN:
LEON WALRAS'S *ELEMENTS* ON
ADAM SMITH'S *WEALTH OF NATIONS*

This year (1976), with the celebration of centenaries all the rage, the two hundredth anniversary of the *Wealth of Nations* is being grandly commemorated, as it deserves to be, all over the world. Occasionally it is remembered, here and there, that this year may also be considered the centenary of another outstanding event in the history of economics, the appearance of the first edition of Léon Walras's *Eléments d'économie politique pure* in 1874–77, just about one hundred years ago. If the *Wealth of Nations* seems to be taking precedence of the *Eléments* in the frequency and in the pomp and circumstance of their respective centenary observances, it is indicative of one of two things. Either we have here an instance of falsification of Newton's famous inverse square law of diminishing attraction with distance, since the greater distance from us of the *Wealth of Nations* apparently lends greater attraction to our view of the work; or the Scots know better than the French how to honour their intellectual forebears.

We may think of Walras's *Eléments* as a sprightly centenarian, still hobbling about and insinuating itself into all sorts of current economic literature where it persists in playing a living role, much to the dismay of the Marshallians and still more to the dismay of the classical neo-Marxists of Cambridge, England. The *Wealth of Nations,* on the other hand, has meanwhile been relegated to the role of a venerated dead ancestor, whose memory is saluted on successive centenaries out of respect, but whose words no longer enter as an active ingredient in present-day theoretical discourse. For historians of economics, however, the *Wealth of Nations* continues to be an object of sympathetic critical appreciation which has been nowhere better expressed than by Vincent

This is a slightly revised version of the paper I presented at the Tenth Annual Meeting of the Canadian Economic Association, Laval University, Quebec City, 1 June 1976. I am indebted for editorial guidance to two constant friends, Professor Samuel Hollander of the University of Toronto and Professor John Buttrick of York University, who, in all fairness, must be absolved from blame for the contents of the paper. The research was supported by a Killam Senior Research Scholarship of the Canada Council, for which I am most thankful.

Bladen in his recent book, *From Adam Smith to Maynard Keynes: the heritage of political economy*. It has remained, above all, an inexhaustible source of material for exegetic commentary, which has been nowhere better conducted than by Samuel Hollander in his recent book, *The Economics of Adam Smith*.

It is precisely in Professor Hollander's masterly treatise that we see most clearly the link between the Walrasian and the Smithian theoretical systems. To reveal this link was indeed Professor Hollander's purpose, for he tells us explicitly:

We adopt the position that the use of modern analytical tools, concepts, and procedures may be of considerable aid in an analysis of the work of an early writer, *provided that he was operating within the general frame of reference for which these devices are appropriate.* In particular, we believe that there is justification for the utilization of the current state of knowledge regarding the general equilibrium process in a study of the economics of Adam Smith insofar as he adopted the position that the price mechanism can be relied upon to clear product and factor markets. [Hollander, 1973, 13]

And Professor Hollander quotes with approval Lord Robbins's earlier remark that 'from the point of view of theoretical Economics, the central achievement of [Adam Smith's *Wealth of Nations*] was his demonstration of the mode in which the division of labour tended to be kept in equilibrium by the mechanism of relative prices – a demonstration which . . . is in harmony with the most refined apparatus of the modern School of Lausanne.'[1]

For our present purpose, it does not matter whether we adopt the Robbins–Hollander view of the *Wealth of Nations* as an adumbration of modern general equilibrium theory, or whether we see in it a growth-cum-welfare model to which the allocation principle is subsidiary, or whether we regard the *Wealth of Nations* as an elaborate analytical plea for freedom from mercantilist-inspired state intervention, or whether we see in Adam Smith's great work the harbinger of a theory of capitalistic exploitation because of the emphasis he placed on 'the relations of production' (to use a Marxist phrase) in his analysis of market relations – the important thing is that from whatever perspective we may be inclined to view *Wealth of Nations* we are bound to confront Adam Smith's pioneer analysis of the mechanism which holds the market system in general equilibrium. If this seems obvious to all historians of

[1] Hollander (1973, 19–20), quoted from Robbins (1932, 68–9). Before Lord Robbins, Jacob Viner had observed in 1927 in his justly famous lecture, 'Adam Smith and laissez faire': 'There is much weight of authority and of evidence . . . that Smith's major claim to originality, in English thought at least, was his detailed and elaborate application to the wilderness of economic phenomena of the unifying concept of a co-ordinated and mutually interdependent system of cause and effect relationships which philosophers and theologians had already applied to the world in general' (reprinted in Viner, 1958, 213).

economics nowadays, whatever their school, surely one would think it must have been evident to Léon Walras, the celebrated founder of the modern full-fledged version of general equilibrium economics. Strange to relate, it was not so. In what follows, I propose to offer an explanation for the failure on the part of Walras to recognize in the *Wealth of Nations* the presence of rudiments of his own great theory.

Let us first see what Walras's *Eléments,* now centenarian, had to say about Adam Smith's *Wealth of Nations,* now bicentenarian. The *Eléments* began, promisingly enough, with a tribute to Adam Smith, whom Walras credited with having achieved 'remarkable success' in establishing political economy as an autonomous branch of social science in 1776.[2] Having said this, Walras proceeded immediately to undo the praise by taking issue with what he thought was Adam Smith's too narrow conception of the scope of this autonomous branch of study.[3] To prove his point Walras quoted a passage from the Introduction to Book IV of the *Wealth of Nations,* where Adam Smith announced the topic of that particular Book as follows: 'Political œconomy, considered as a branch of the science of a statesman or legislator, proposes two distinct objects: first, to provide a plentiful revenue or subsistence for the people, or more properly to enable them to provide such a revenue or subsistence for themselves; and secondly, to supply the state or commonwealth with a revenue sufficient for the public services. It proposes to enrich both the people and the sovereign.'[4]

In total disregard of Adam Smith's qualifying phrase, 'considered as a branch of the science of a statesman or legislator,' Walras took this passage to represent a definition of economics in general instead of a characterization of *political* economy in the narrow sense which Adam Smith clearly intended. This characterization was all the more appropriate at the opening of Book IV because Adam Smith was just then embarking upon a particular discussion of various types of government policies in relation to trade and industry. Walras did not see that elsewhere Adam Smith ascribed a wider scope to economics in general-toward the end of Book IV where he defined appositionally 'what is *properly* called Political Economy' as a study of *'the nature and causes of the wealth of nations,'* and nothing else (Smith, 1776/1937, 643, italics mine).

Adam Smith meant by political economy in the large,[5] in contradis-

---

[2] Walras (1874–77/...), §3 in all eds. of the *Eléments.*
[3] Ibid., §§4–5 in all eds.
[4] Smith (1776/1937, 397). Here as elsewhere the pages referred to in the *Wealth of Nations* are those of the Modern Library edition.
[5] We must not allow ourselves to be misled by the ambiguity of Adam Smith's use of the term 'political economy.' The short and simple term 'economics' to designate our subject in the large was not brought into current use until 1879 when Alfred and Mary Paley Marshall introduced it in their *Economics of Industry* (2).

tinction to 'political œconomy as a branch of the science of a statesman or legislator,' precisely what Léon Walras meant by it. Adam Smith's inquiry into 'the nature and causes of the wealth of nations' is no different, in essence, from Walras's 'théorie de la richesse sociale,' which is the subtitle of his *Eléments d'économie politique pure.* Yet Walras, who looked no further than the introduction to Book IV of the *Wealth of Nations,* and who did not even look into that properly, condemned Adam Smith's 'definition' as excessively narrow, because it confined the scope of the subject to its applied component and ignored all the rest.

For Walras, economics, considered as a whole, is made up of three components: the pure science component, the applied science component and the normative component. Had Walras penetrated more deeply into the *Wealth of Nations,* he could hardly have avoided perceiving that Adam Smith's *Inquiry* encompassed within its rich texture the other aspects of economics which together with the applied science aspect constituted the whole science of economics as Walras saw it. If there were no core of pure theory to the *Wealth of Nations,* the latter-day commentators quoted above could not have discerned foreshadowings, however imperfect, of general equilibrium models of the Lausanne School type in Adam Smith's analysis of the emergence of equilibrium from the spontaneous operations of free markets. If there were no normative content, in Walras's sense, to the *Wealth of Nations,* Adam Smith could not have denounced 'violations of natural liberty' as 'unjust,' as, in fact, he did (Smith, 1776/1937, 141, 497). Of course, the particular aspect of applied economics, which Walras mistakenly thought made up the totality of Adam Smith's conception of the scope of economics, is the special subject matter of Book IV of the *Wealth of Nations.* There Adam Smith developed the very same theme that Walras did in his *Etudes d'économie politique appliquée,* to which, significantly, he gave the subtitle, *Théorie de la production de la richesse sociale.* The central problem of both Adam Smith's Book IV and Léon Walras's 'economie politique appliquée' was to determine what government policies best promote the production of wealth.

How little Walras understood, or even tried to understand, the *Wealth of Nations* is next seen in his treatment of Adam Smith's theory of value in Lesson 27 of the first edition of the *Eléments,* which later became Lesson 16 of the definitive edition.[6] In all the editions, this Lesson is entitled 'Exposition and refutation of Adam Smith's and J.B. Say's doctrines of the origin of value in exchange'; and in all editions the subhead of this Lesson summarizing Walras's argument reads, so far as Adam Smith is concerned, 'Adam Smith's *labour theory:* this doctrine

[6] Walras (1874–77/ . . .), §§155–156 (§§157–158 of definitive ed.).

merely declares that labour alone has value, but since it does not explain why labour has value, it leaves unexplained whence things in general derive their value.' The text that follows starts with the quotation of Adam Smith's well-known second paragraph from chapter v of Book I, which begins, 'The real price of everything, what every thing really costs to the man who wants to acquire it, is the toil and trouble of acquiring it,' and contains also the sentence 'Labour was the first price, the original purchase-money that was paid for all things' (Smith, 1776/ 1937, 30–1). Walras understood this passage to say that 'all things which have value and are exchangeable are labour in one form or another, so that labour alone constitutes the whole of social wealth.' Then, after brushing aside, as 'peu philosophique' (insufficiently philosophical), the subsidiary objection that there are things not produced by labour which also have value in exchange, Walras mounted the main attack. The argument which he thought clinching ran:

Whether labour is all or part of social wealth is beside the point. In either case why is labour worth anything? Why is it exchangeable? That is the question before us. Adam Smith neither asked nor answered it. Surely, if labour has value and is exchangeable, it is because it is both useful and limited in quantity, that is to say because it is scarce. Value therefore comes from scarcity. If there are things other than labour which are scarce, they, like labour, will also have value and be exchangeable. So the theory which traces the origin of value to labour is a theory that is completely devoid of meaning rather than too narrow, entirely gratuitous rather than merely deficient.[7]

Thus at one fell syllogistic stroke, Walras imagined he had demolished Adam Smith's theory of value forever, leaving nothing more to be said. It turns out, however, that Walras's argument, which he presumably meant to be truly 'philosophique,' was flagrantly sophistical. What Walras destroyed so effectively was not Adam Smith's theory of value at all, but a caricature of that theory. Where did Adam Smith declare, as Walras alleged, that labour alone has value? Neither I nor anyone else I know of has ever found such an assertion in the *Wealth of Nations* or in any other writing of Adam Smith for that matter. Germain Garnier's French translation of *Wealth of Nations* from which Walras took his quotation did not contain any such misconstruction of the original.[8] Labour may well have been for Adam Smith the source of value, the

[7] Walras (1874–77/ . . .), §156 (§158 of the definitive ed.).

[8] The French translation of the *Wealth of Nations* (*Recherches sur la nature et les causes de la richesse des nations*) which was considered standard in the nineteenth century was that of Germain Garnier. The first edition of this translation, which appeared in 1805, was followed through the century by a series of revised editions, annotated and amplified by a succession of editors. The best known was the Guillaumin edition, published in 2 vols in 1843–4.

substance of value, or the measure of value, but was never represented as the only thing which has value in exchange.

This is not to say that Walras's criticism was devoid of any semblance of validity. Insofar as Adam Smith used his labour theory (be it a labour-cost or labour-command theory) to define an ultimate source of value, whatever that may mean, Walras's argument against it was logically impeccable, even if he was wrong in attributing to Adam Smith the notion that 'labour alone has value.' Though a phrase here and a phrase there in the *Wealth of Nations* may betray a fleeting interest in the ultimate source of value, that was clearly not Adam Smith's major concern. In his chapter v of Book i, devoted to the distinction between 'real and nominal price,' he was primarily interested in value not from the standpoint of evaluation but from two other standpoints, in fact the same two standpoints that Karl Marx subsequently adopted. The two functions that the labour theory of value performed for Adam Smith were, in essence, the same as those Michio Morishima tells us it performed for Marx: '(1) to explain the equilibrium prices (or the exchange values) of commodities, around which actual prices fluctuate over time, and (2) to provide aggregators, or weights of aggregation, in terms of which a large number of industries . . . are aggregated' (Morishima, 1973, 10). Though the principle of aggregation was the same, Karl Marx and Adam Smith nevertheless differed in the uses to which they put their respective aggregates: Karl Marx used his to analyse the relations in the economy between the 'department' producing capital goods taken in the aggregate and the 'department' producing consumers' goods, again taken in the aggregate; Adam Smith on the other hand wanted to measure, or at least to estimate, the progress of 'opulence,' i.e. the movement in the aggregate output of the nation over time and under various systems of government policy (cf. Robertson and Taylor, 1957, 195–7).

If Léon Walras had taken the pains to unravel Adam Smith's theory of value in the light of the purpose or purposes it was designed to serve, I don't see how he could have concluded that the theory was irredeemably specious. Instead of saying that the theory was entirely gratuitous rather than merely deficient, he might have put it the other way around, and said that the theory was merely deficient rather than wholly gratuitous. The latter is certainly the judgment of several of our contemporary scholars who have examined the theory. Professor Bladen, who places Adam Smith's theory of value in the context of the problem of measuring *changes* in real price over time, calls the theory 'debatable,' but not one that it is legitimate to regard as nonsense (Bladen, 1974, 24; cf. Bladen, 1975). Joseph Schumpeter, whom no one would accuse of being

excessively partial to Adam Smith and who found no better place for
Adam Smith than in a chapter on 'Consultant administrators and
pamphleteers,' nevertheless opposed no 'logical objection' to Adam
Smith's choice of labour as *numéraire* for making intertemporal and
interlocal comparisons of value in exchange (1954, 188). Yet Léon
Walras thought the labour theory deserved nothing better than cavalier
dismissal.

This is not an appropriate occasion, nor am I qualified, to puzzle out
what Adam Smith really meant by his bewildering variety of pronouncements on value. As Jacob Viner once observed: 'Smith can be
quoted in support of all of the following propositions: that labour is the
sole regulator of exchange value; that labour has, among the elements
entering into production, a peculiar and perhaps even an exclusive
value-creating power; that the relative values of different commodities
are, or should be, proportional to their labour-time costs; that all
incomes are extracted from the product of labour' (1968, 327). No
wonder, then, that the *Wealth of Nations* is so often read, as Marcel Proust
tell us novels are read, allowing the reader to find his own innermost
preoccupations mirrored in the book. Nor is it any wonder that the
Wealth of Nations is susceptible of as many interpretations as there are
commentators, whose preoccupations range from those of Ronald Meek
or Maurice Dobb at one end of the ideological spectrum to those of
Friedrich Hayek at the other end (Hayek, 1976).

What can we say was Léon Walras's preoccupation that led him to
condemn Adam Smith's theory of value out of hand as a logical
absurdity? It turns out that the cavilling interpretation of the theory we
find in the *Éléments* was not Léon Walras's, but that of his father,
Auguste Walras. Léon Walras did little more than repeat in summary
what his father had written before him in chapter XII of *De la nature de la
richesse et de l'origine de la valeur,* published in 1831.[9] The little more that
Léon Walras added was unfortunate, for Auguste Walras had made a
better job at it.

Auguste Walras perceived more clearly than his son that Adam Smith
had been principally concerned with the measure of value and had
considered only peripherally and inferentially its origin. To illustrate the
weakness of Adam Smith's implicit understanding of the origin of value
he cited the very same passage from the *Wealth of Nations* that Léon
Walras used as the basis for his argument. Auguste Walras, on his side,
reproached Adam Smith not only for implying in this passage that all
exchangeable goods are produced in one way or another by labour, but
also and more importantly for failing even to inquire why labour has

[9] Auguste Walras (1831 [167–72]/1938 [188–91]).

value. The question of the ultimate source of value in some absolute, rather than relative, sense loomed large in Auguste Walras's mind because of his point of departure when he turned from philosophy and law to economics (Walras, 1908, 171-2). His interest in economics was first aroused when he attempted to clarify the concept of property in order to meet the challenge of the socialists of his day who were denouncing the institution of property with more vehemence than understanding. Seeking guidance from economics and not finding it there, he came to the conclusion that both property and value in exchange have a common origin in the limitation in quantity of certain objects of desire. If all desirable things were not scarce, there would be no property, nor would there be value in exchange. The source of value, irrespective of its measure, was then for Auguste Walras, not Adam Smith's labour, but scarcity.

There is no need to retell here the well-known tale how Léon Walras metamorphosed his father's nebulous notion of scarcity into an analytical precision tool which he still called 'rareté,'[10] but which we usually call marginal utility[11]; nor need we repeat how Léon Walras used the tool as a unifying and organizing principle to endow his general equilibrium model with over-all consistency. It suffices to note that, though it was altogether irrelevant to the construction of his general equilibrium model, he attributed to his new 'rareté' the same capacity to generate absolute value his father had attributed to the old 'rareté.'[12] This he did in deference to his father's central proposition that 'la rareté est la cause de la valeur,' a proposition which, to say the least, had nothing to do with Léon Walras's multi-equational system of general equilibrium. Nevertheless, he seized upon it as the ultimate standard of a correct theory of value, thus permitting him to reject Adam Smith's theory as he did all other theories that did not conform to the standard.

It is a great pity that Léon Walras foreclosed in this way all true communication with his great predecessor. In fact, outside of Walras's misbegotten criticism of Smith's alleged 'definition' of economics and his peremptory attack on Smith's theory of value, there is no mention of Adam Smith's name in the *Éléments*. Indeed, it is doubtful that Walras ever read the *Wealth of Nations* attentively, even in the Garnier translation. Not only in the *Éléments,* but on the rare occasions that he cited Adam Smith elsewhere, the quotations appear to be, if not second-hand, at least drawn from references already made by others.[13] In this and

[10] Jaffé (1972 [387-9]/1973 [121-3]).

[11] Walras (1874-77/ . . .) English transl., 506-7, Translator's Note 9 to Lesson 8.

[12] Ibid., §98 (§101 of definitive ed.). Cf. English transl., 512-13, Translator's Note 3 to Lesson 10.

[13] This is the case, for example, with one of the quotations from Adam Smith in Walras (1880 [1898/1936, 370]). The passage quoted from Book II, chapt. II of the *Wealth of Nations* (304-5) had appeared (in a different French translation) in Say (1819) 1, 446-7.

other ways, Léon Walras's occasional excursions into the history of economics show him up as an execrable historian. His only interest was either to bolster his own theoretical contributions by invoking the posthumous support of respected forerunners, or else to berate as fatal flaws anything he found in the writings of others that did not accord with his own ideas.[14]

Had Léon Walras been a better historian, had he read the entire *Wealth of Nations* with care, and, above all, had he contemplated the *Wealth of Nations* in the light of Adam Smith's other writings which were available to him, he might have found that he had much more in common with the reputed founder of his science than he suspected. Other writings of Adam Smith were, in fact, available to him, as is clear from the existence in his day of French translations not only of *The Theory of Moral Sentiments,* but also of *The Essays on Philosophical Subjects,* the latter of which contained Adam Smith's all-important 'Principles which Lead and Direct Philosophical Inquiries, Illustrated by the History of Astronomy.'[15]

If Walras had read the 'History of Astronomy' in the original English (which he was perfectly capable of doing) or in translation, he could hardly have failed to inquire into its relation to the *Wealth of Nations,* which he might then have found was methodologically as much inspired by Newtonian celestial mechanics as his own *Eléments d'économie politique pure.* The *Wealth of Nations* alone could have told Walras as much, for in Article 2nd of chapter I in Book V, Adam Smith distinctly drew an analogy between the sciences which account for 'the great phenomena of nature, the revolutions of the heavenly bodies, eclipses, comets; thunder, lightning and other extraordinary meteors' on the one hand, and moral philosophy, which we would to-day classify as social or behavioural science, on the other. According to Adam Smith, after natural philosophy had set the example of 'a systematical arrangement of different observations connected by a few common principles,' then 'something of the same kind was attempted in morals' (Smith, 1776/1937, 723–4).

Certainly the attempt was made in Adam Smith's *Theory of Moral Sentiments,* where 'sympathy' in the etymological sense served as the common principle regulating the conduct of individuals in such a manner as to create a harmonious human society. And in the *Wealth of Nations* it was the joint principle of an alleged primordial 'propensity to

[14] E.g. Lessons 16 and 37–39 of the definitive edition of Walras (1874–77/...).
[15] Adam Smith's *Théories des sentiments moraux* 2d ed. (Paris: Barrois, 1830) translated by the Marquis de Condorcet in 1798 is generally considered the best of the early French translations of *The Theory of Moral Sentiments.* Adam Smith's posthumously published *Essays on Philosophical Subjects,* ed. Joseph Black and James Hutton (London: Cadell and Davies; Edinburgh: Creech, 1795), was translated as *Essais philosophiques* by P. Prevost (Paris: Agasse, 1797). The 'History of Astronomy,' first published in the *Essays on Philosophical Subjects,* has recently been reprinted in Lindgren (1967, 30–109).

truck, barter and exchange' and a universal 'desire of bettering our
condition,' which, working in tandem, bound together the operations of
innumerable markets in such a way as to promote the orderly progress
of 'opulence.' In each of these systems the connecting principles played
the same role as Newton's principle of universal gravitation; and, as
may be surmised from Adam Smith's 'History of Astronomy,' they were
probably intended to do so in much the same mechanical fashion.

Walras, having also been guided by the precedent of Newtonian
celestial mechanics, used his 'rareté' as the connecting common principle in the construction of his general equilibrium model. One of Léon
Walras's last publications, 'Economique et mécanique' (1909), published the year before he died, was a reaffirmation of his reliance on the
pattern of Newtonian mechanics to inform his conception of catallactic
mechanics. From the age of nineteen on, when Walras first read Louis
Poinsot's *Eléments de statique,* he had sought to create a theory of
economics with the same formal properties that characterized celestial
mechanics.[16] A hundred years or so before Walras, when Adam Smith
was still at the threshold of his intellectual career, he too had imprinted
upon him for life the Newtonian ideal of science founded on chains of
reasoning deducible from mechanistic laws. It appears from Adam
Smith's 'Letter to the Authors of the *Edinburgh Review,*' dated July 1755,
that in his case it was d'Alembert who pointed the way by his articles in
Diderot's *Encyclopédie* on the rise, progress, and affinities of the various
sciences (Lindgren, 1967, 18; cf. Scott, 1937, 53). We now have Herbert
F. Thomson's article (1965) on 'Adam Smith's philosophy of science' to
demonstrate how Adam Smith pursued the Newtonian ideal of science
both in the *Theory of Moral Sentiments* and in the *Wealth of Nations.*

In their analytical mode of thinking, Adam Smith and Walras were,
at bottom, Cartesians. One being the child and the other the grandchild
of the Enlightenment, they both employed in their economic reasoning
the method that Descartes was the first to define and that served the
physical sciences so spectacularly during the Enlightenment. How far
Adam Smith was Cartesian has been very well shown in a recent book
on *Philosophy and Economics* by Piero V. Mini, a book which, though
uneven in other respects, is excellent for its discussion of the Cartesian
inspiration of the *Wealth of Nations* (Mini, 1974, chap. 4). It should be
noted that Adam Smith's repudiation of the *substance* of Descartes'
theories of vortices, and so on, did not prevent him from holding the *form*
of Descartes' analysis in the highest regard. In his *Lectures on Rhetoric and
Belles Lettres* Adam Smith declared that Descartes was in reality the first
'in Natural Philosophy, or any science of that sort' to attempt a method

---

[16] Jaffé (1965, III,148–50, Letter 1483, esp. n. 7).

of laying down 'certain principles, primary or proved, in the beginning, from whence we account for the several phenomena, connecting all together by the same chain.' Though Adam Smith took Descartes' application of the method to be, to say the least, 'dubious,' he thought the method itself 'most philosophical' since it was the very same method that Newton employed (quoted by Thomson, 1965, 214–15).

Léon Walras proved to be more wholeheartedly Cartesian. We know from his 'Notice autobiographique' and from his letters that he studied Descartes, Newton, and Lagrange at an early age.[17] Toward the end of his life, he was delighted to read in an article, 'Les mathématiques dans les sciences sociales,' by Vito Volterra, that the new mathematical economics, which Walras, among others, was instrumental in creating, belonged methodologically to the same class of scientific achievements as those of Descartes in geometry, of Lagrange in mechanics, of Maxwell in physics, and of Helmholtz in physiology.[18]

This is not all that Walras might have discovered he had in common with Adam Smith. Though more than a century apart in the years of their birth, though they were brought up in quite different lands and different social and cultural settings, nevertheless, in their early, most impressionable years they had imbibed the same philosophy of natural law. While the particular streams from which each of them drew this philosophy were wide apart, the separte streams had their source in the writings of Grotius and Pufendorf. It is well known that between the ages of fourteen and seventeen, Adam Smith studied these two great exponents of natural law in Francis Hutcheson's class at Glasgow College, where an edition of Pufendorf's *De officio hominis et civis* annotated by Francis Hutcheson's teacher, Gershom Carmichael, was used as a text (Taylor, 1965, 25–8). Walras, on his side, absorbed this same philosophy from his father, Auguste Walras, who had studied a textbook presentation of Pufendorf in the *Elémens du droit naturel* by a Swiss publicist, Jean Jacques Burlamaqui. Besides, Burlamaqui was cited by both Auguste Walras and Léon Walras as an anticipator of the scarcity theory of value.[19]

Moreover, had Walras been so inclined, he might have learned from the *Theory of Moral Sentiments* that he and Adam Smith were kindred souls in their philosophical contempt for those advances in modern technology which corrupt and contaminate our private lives. In one of those striking figures of speech which adorn Adam Smith's writings, he conjured up

[17] Jaffé (1965, I, 2; III, 149, Letter 1483, and 252–3, Letter 1576).
[18] Ibid. (III, 296, Letter 1618, n. 2). Vito Volterra's article appeared in *La revue du mois,* 10 Jan. 1906, 1, 1–21.
[19] Burlamaqui (1821). See also Auguste Walras (1831/1938, chap. 15) and Léon Walras (1874–77/..., §159) (§161 of definitive ed.).

the vision of 'enormous and operose machines contrived to produce a few trifling conveniences to the body, consisting of springs the most nice and delicate, which must be kept in order with the most anxious attention, and which in spite of all our care are ready every moment to burst into pieces, and to crush in their ruins their unfortunate possessor'[20] — a perfect premonition, if there ever was one, of the modern automobile. Had Walras known this passage, it would have warmed his heart. In 1909 when the rector of the University of Lausanne, who knew Walras's eccentricities well, offered to take Walras to his Jubilee ceremony in an automobile, he added, 'if you are not afraid of this sort of conveyance.'[21] Before that, writing to his friend Georges Renard in 1896, Walras described with horror the new electric tramway in Lausanne, with its ugly overhead trolley wires and screeching wheels, and then exclaimed: 'We have too much chemical and mechanical progress and not enough political and economic progress. We are going to the devil by electric tramway!'[22] Walras longed for the peace and quiet he knew in his childhood in Evreux, Normandy, in the prerailway days. In 1892 he wrote to another friend, Gustave Maugin, 'For my part, I prefer the simpler life that France led around 1847, before the advent of railways.'[23]

Actually, Walras and Adam Smith were very much of the same temper in their attitude to life and the world. Léon Walras was born in the apartment of the principal of the Collège d'Evreux, where his father, besides being principal, taught rhetoric and philosophy. Adam Smith came from a family of higher civil servants with connections in the professions and in the Aberdeen universities (Scott, 1937, 395–408). Both Adam Smith and Léon Walras were university professors for whom, whatever their particular occupation was at any moment of their careers, intellectual life was all. I venture to say that this circumstance is reflected in their respective economic theories, each in its own way. Adam Smith belonged to an ancient line, now nearly, if not wholly, extinct, of philosophers who turned their attention to economics— primarily, so it seems to me, to discover a way to make the world safe for philosophy. If Aristotle concerned himself with justice in exchange, it was because without such justice, intellectual and social merit, which he measured not in physical or market valued productivity but in virtue, would not receive the material support it deserved.

Adam Smith, who perceived more clearly than Aristotle the dependence of the cultivation of philosophy on the material conditions of society, urged the suppression of all impediments to the natural growth

---

[20] Smith (1759/1797), I, 462 [8th ed.]).   [21] Jaffé (1965, III, 416, Letter 1750).
[22] Ibid. (II, 690–1, Letter 1256).   [23] Ibid. (II, 493, Letter 1057).

of the wealth of nations. Though he was keenly aware of the existence of flagrant injustices in the distribution of wealth and income in 'civilized societies,' though he attributed the glaring disparities not only to 'violence,' as Boisguilbert and Cantillon had done before him, but also to what he called, in an unforgettable phrase, 'the more orderly oppression of law' (Scott, 1937, 327), he nevertheless refrained from suggesting any remedy for these acknowledged injustices. Why is that so? I should say that it was because, in his eyes, the inequitable distribution of wealth and income possessed the saving grace of creating and preserving the 'distinction of ranks,' without which there would be no class possessing sufficiently 'liberal fortunes' to permit its members to pursue 'study for its own sake, as an original pleasure or good in itself, without regarding its tendency to procure the means of other pleasures' (Lindgren, 1967, 47–50). As Adam Smith meant his philosophers' paradise for this side of eternity, he had to take into account the world here below. His economics, then, consisted of a systematic analysis of the workings of human society, such as he knew it and such as he conceived it to have evolved in the course of history. It was an analysis directed primarily to an understanding of the growth of the opulence within a society humanely organized for the cultivation of philosophy.

Walras, without being anything like the complete philosopher we find in Adam Smith, was none the less a devotee of natural law philosophy and designed his general equilibrium model as an analytical expression of ethical ideals derived from that philosophy. Though the *Eléments* appears on the surface as a completely *wert-frei* synoptic view of the interdependent operations of an economic system under a hypothetical regime of perfect competition, it can be shown that the model is through and through informed and animated by Walras's moral convictions.[24] His latent purpose in contriving his general equilibrium model was not to describe or analyse the workings of the economic system as it existed, nor was it primarily to portray the purely economic relations within a network of markets under the assumption of a theoretically perfect regime of free competition. It was rather to demonstrate the possibility of formulating axiomatically a rationally consistent economic system that would satisfy the demands of social justice without overstepping the bounds imposed by the natural exigencies of the real world.

Why did Léon Walras stubbornly refuse to open his eyes to so many resemblances between himself and Adam Smith? The only explanation I can offer lies in his fanatical anglophobia, an anglophobia which in the

[24] From his very first book on economics, *L'économie politique et la justice* (1860), to his last public utterance on the occasion on his Jubilee in 1909, Walras's predominant preoccupation was with the problem of social justice, (see my article, Jaffé (1977) and cf. Jaffé, 1965, *I*, 208–12, Letter 148).

nineteenth century made no distinction between the Scots and the English. This is not surprising when we remember that Léon Walras's father was a lad in Montpellier during the Napoleonic Wars and that thenceforth for the whole Walras family everything across the Channel betokened 'perfidious Albion.'

Lest it be imagined that I am inventing this explanation out of whole cloth or exaggerating, let me cite in the original two typical expressions of Léon Walras's deep-seated feelings against the English. In 1881 he wrote to a Dutch correspondent, d'Aulnis de Bourouill, 'Quant à vous, ami des Anglais, je vous souhaite bien du plaisir avec eux, mais mon expérience ne leur est pas favorable. Leur philosophie est nulle; leur science étroite et bornée; et [leur] point de vue égoïste et mesquin.'[25] Ten years later, writing to the Russian economist Bortkiewicz, he declared, 'les Anglais sont d'autant plus gracieux qu'on est plus ferme avec eux. On peut, jusqu'à un certain point, leur appliquer notre ancien proverbe français: "Oignez vilain, il vous poindra, Poignez vilain, il vous oindra."'[26]

If there is a lesson to be learned from this sad story of Walras's failure to appreciate Adam Smith, it is that science and scholarship suffer grievously when national, sectarian, and ideological animosities are allowed to invade their realm.

REFERENCES

Bladen, V. (1974) *From Adam Smith to Maynard Keynes: the heritage of political economy* (Toronto: University of Toronto Press).

Bladen, V. (1975) 'Command over labour: a study in misinterpretation.' *Canadian Journal of Economics*, 8, 504–19.

Burlamaqui, J.J. (1821) *Elémens du droit naturel.* Nouvelle édn (Paris: Delestre-Boulage).

Hayek, F.A. (1976) 'Adam Smith's foresight: open society and disorder.' *Globe and Mail* (Toronto, March 23).

Hollander, S. (1973) *The Economics of Adam Smith* (Toronto: University of Toronto Press).

Jaffé, W., ed. (1965) *Correspondence of Léon Walras and Related Papers* 3 vols (Amsterdam: North Holland, for the Royal Netherlands Academy of Sciences and Letters).

Jaffé, W. (1972) 'Léon Walras's role in the marginal revolution of the 1870s., *History of Political Economy* 4, 379–405; Republished in Black et al., eds. *The Marginal Revolution in Economics* (Durham, North Carolina: Duke University Press).

Jaffé, W. (1977) 'The normative bias of the Walrasian mode: Walras vs Gossen.' *Quarterly Journal of Economics* 91, 371–87.

[25] Jaffé (1965, i, 704, Letter 513).
[26] Jaffé (1965, ii, 428, Letter 996).

Lindgren, J.R., ed. (1967) *The Early Writings of Adam Smith* (NY: A.M. Kelley).
Marshall, A. and M.P. Marshall (1879) *The Economics of Industry* (London: Macmillan).
Mini, P.V. (1974) *Philosophy and Economics* (Gainesville: University of Florida Press).
Morishima, M. (1973) *Marx's Economics, A dual theory of value and growth* (Cambridge: University Press).
Robbins, L. (1932) *An Essay on the Nature and Significance of Economic Science* (London: Macmillan).
Robertson, H.M. and W.L. Taylor (1957) 'Adam Smith's approach to the theory of value.' *Economic Journal* 67, 181–98.
Say, J.B. (1819) *Traité d'économie politique* 4th ed., 2 vols (Paris: Deterville).
Schumpeter, J.A. (1954) *History of Economic Analysis* (New York: Oxford University Press).
Scott, W.R. (1937) *Adam Smith as Student and Professor* (Glasgow: Jackson, Son and Co).
Smith, A. (1759/1797) *The Theory of Moral Sentiments* (London: Millar; 8th ed., 2 vols; London: Cadell and Davies).
Smith A. (1776/1937) *An Inquiry into the Nature and Causes of the Wealth of Nations* (London: Strahan and Cadell; Modern Library edn, Edwin Cannan, ed, New York: Random House).
Taylor, W.L. (1965) *Francis Hutcheson and David Hume as Predecessors of Adam Smith* (Durham, North Carolina: Duke University Press).
Thomson, H.F. (1965) 'Adam Smith's philosophy of science.' *Quarterly Journal of Economics* 79, 212–33.
Viner, J. (1958) *The Long View and the Short* (Glencoe, Illinois: Free Press).
Viner, J. (1968) 'Smith, Adam.' In David L. Sills, ed., *International Encyclopedia of the Social Sciences* 14, 322–8.
Walras, Auguste (1831/1938) *De la nature de la richesse et de l'origine de la valeur* (Paris: Johanneau; 2d edn, ed. Gaston Leduc, Paris: Alcan).
Walras, L. (1860) *L'économie politique et la justice* (Paris: Guillaumin).
Walras, L. (1874–77/ . . .) *Eléments d'économie Politique pure ou Théorie de la richesse sociale* (1st ed. [in two instalments], Lausanne: Corbaz, 1874–77; 2d ed., Lausanne: Rouge, 1889; 3rd ed., Lausanne: Rouge, 1896; 4th ed., Lausanne: Rouge, 1900; definitive ed. (published posthumously), 1926. Reprinted Paris: Pichon and Durand-Auzias, 1952. English translation by William Jaffé, *Elements of Pure Economics,* London: Allen and Unwin, 1954 [Reprints of Economic Classics, New York: Augustus Kelley, 1969]).
Walras, L. (1880) 'Théorie mathématique du billet de banque.' *Bulletin de la société vaudoise des sciences naturelles* 2d Series, 16 (80), 553–92. Republished in Walras (1898/1936, 339–75).
Walras, L. (1898/1936) *Etudes d'économie politique appliquée (Théorie de la production de la richesse sociale)* (Lausanne: Rouge. 2nd edn, ed. G. Leduc, Paris: Pichon and Durand-Auzias).
Walras, L. (1908) 'Un initiateur en économie politique: A.A. Walras.' *Revue du Mois* 6 (2), 170–83.
Walras, L. (1909) 'Economique et mécanique.' *Bulletin de la société vaudoise des sciences naturelles* 5th Series, 45 (166), 313–27.

6

LEON WALRAS AND HIS RELATIONS
WITH AMERICAN ECONOMISTS

What can be said that is new about the School of Lausanne to professors and students of the University of Lausanne? You must have heard before almost anything I can present. Nevertheless, I dare hope that my research will at least enable me to throw a special light upon certain familiar matters.

There are some facts about Walras's life that are not recorded in the archives of Lausanne, archives that in other respects are so rich. For example, I could mention his private life, which was so carefully hidden by him and his daughter, Aline, from their Swiss contemporaries. Fearing that their friends in the canton of Vaud, who were models of decorum and propriety, would mistakenly think ill about her father, Aline Walras sent most of his private correspondence to Lyons, where I found it preserved in the law school. That correspondence put me on the track of other materials, which I uncovered in the archives of Montpellier, in the records of the cemetery in Paris, and in the register general's archives devoted to the Walras family. I hasten to add that if the facts uncovered by this search would have caused some frowns in certain quarters in the time of Walras, they were not scandalous facts, although they ran counter to social conventions. Some years ago, at Chartres, when I revealed to the late Canon Yves Delaporte, a second cousin of Léon Walras, that the latter's first marriage was to an unmarried mother who was herself a natural child, and when I revealed how Walras had recognized, at the time of the marriage, the natural child who was not his, the venerable Canon exclaimed: "How generous he was!" In actuality, the Canon was grateful to me for these revelations, since for the first time in his long life he understood the veiled allusions that his parents had whispered about when he was a little child. I myself was moved when the Canon said to me: "Walras no longer belongs to us. He belongs to history. You have not only the right, but the duty to publish everything."

This paper was delivered at a conference given on June 12, 1959, under the aegis of the School of Social and Political Sciences of the University of Lausanne and the Swiss-American Society for Cultural Relations. The article was translated from the French by Donald A. Walker.

Even with that solemn authorization, I have not chosen as the subject of this study the private life of the man who lived at Lausanne for some forty years, from 1870 to 1910, nor to speak of his Dutch ancestry, nor to tell you how I discovered that the name Walras is a corruption of the name Walraevens, well known in Holland and in Flemish regions. Why have I refrained from treating these subjects? Because Walras was an economist. It is in that way that his children described him on his tomb at Clarens, without doubt following the desire of their father. But what is an economist? He is a professor or a practitioner of a science that in England has acquired the reputation of a "dismal science," that is to say a sad and boring science. One therefore expects that those professors and practitioners, in order to be worthy of their science, must be boring also, that their lives must be completely irreproachable and follow doleful and severe conformist principles. Since it cannot be believed that the works of an economist could be serious and important unless his life is totally devoid of interest from any other point of view, I have decided that it would be wiser not to insist upon the intimate and private episodes in Walras's life. If he had distinguished himself as a poet, dramatist, novelist, or painter, it would be generally recognized that his work could not be understood without probing all the events of his life and all aspects of his personality; but in economics the fashion is rather to create the illusion that absolute truths exist completely independent of the human character of those who have formulated its principles and doctrine.

We are therefore going to consider Walras exclusively as an economist and in his relationships with other economists of his time. Joseph Schumpeter said that of all the theoretical economists, Walras was the greatest in the history of our science. His theory of general equilibrium couched in systems of simultaneous equations still furnishes the base of almost all theoretical studies that are pursued today the entire world over, from America to Japan. It is not without reason that, shortly before Walras's death, at the entrance of this building in which we find ourselves, a plaque was placed that reads:

To Léon Walras, born in Evreux in 1834, professor at the academy and University of Lausanne, who first established the general conditions of economic equilibrium, thus founding the School of Lausanne. In honor of fifty years of disinterested work.

We now acknowledge that consciously or unconsciously, directly or indirectly (and when I say indirectly, I mean above all via Pareto's work) almost all economists and econometricians follow the route that Walras traced. Even those who would prefer another theoretical course are obliged to recognize Walras's strong current influence. For example, an

American professor, Milton Friedman of the University of Chicago, who believes that the theories of Alfred Marshall are superior to those of Walras, exclaimed several years ago in vexation: "We curtsy to Marshall, but we walk with Walras." Other English-speaking economists, such as Hicks in England and Samuelson in America, are proud to acknowledge their debt to Walras and refer to the School of Lausanne as their authority.

Walras was an economist to the very marrow. The fact that he was raised by a father who was an economist and by a mother who was economical as only someone from Normandy can be explains in part his character. Of his mother, Walras said that she belonged to the race of economist ants. These facts also perhaps explain how in his youth, before consecrating himself to the study of economics, when he still hoped for a purely literary career, he published a short story entitled "The Letter" in the *Revue francaise* in 1859, in which he wrote:

Henri Chevreux (the hero of the story) lived in Paris on four hundred francs per month, two hundred and fifty francs provided by his father, and a hundred and fifty francs earned as his salary. To tell the truth, he did not understand that it was possible to live on much less, but, on the other hand, he did not wish to spend more. He was 28 years old, and as a lawyer and notary's clerk he worked very hard. . . . This makes one suspect that a passionate love of order was the basis of his character, and that in fact was the case. An account of his attitude reveals the intimate recesses of his nature. After an unavowed first love when he was eighteen, Chevreux went to Paris and took a mistress. He broke off with her in a decent manner, more alarmed for the future than dissatisfied with the present, when, one fine day, calculating the balance of happiness that she gave him on the one hand against the loss of time and financial expenses that she caused him on the other, he coldly recognized a deficit.

Is this not marginalism in embryo? The passage, imbued with an almost mathematical reasoning, preceded by at least twelve years the beginning of the marginalist school in England and Austria, as well as Walras's serious study of economic theory.

That is not all. During the same period, he wrote a letter dated August 26, 1860, to his dear (future wife) Aline, to offer his apologies for having neglected her so much because of his work. He said to her:

Remember, my dear, that love is an inexhaustible treasure when it is spent wisely, but quickly exhausted if it is squandered. If you knew economics, I would say to you that love is a capital of which only the income should be consumed; but perhaps you would not understand me, and perhaps also my comparison would strike you as ridiculous. Forgive my pedantry.

Thus Walras was not only an economist; he was a living example of the *homo economicus* whose existence was denied and described as an absurdity by critics of economic theory.

Early in his career as an economist, when he tried to earn his living as a journalist after renouncing his literary ambitions, Walras turned his eyes toward America. One is struck by his profound and sympathetic comprehension of the economic situation in America on the eve of the outbreak of the Civil War, although that situation had unpleasant repercussions in France. It was a time when the price of cotton had collapsed, which led English and French speculators to discount their commercial paper for gold at the Bank of France to such an extent that the bank was obliged to raise the rate of discount several times. Walras, like many of his contemporaries, attributed the cause of this crisis to the anarchy that reigned at that time in banking practices in the United States. But, while Alfred Darimon, his colleague and rival at the journal *La Presse,* made an appeal to create an international organization that would have control over American banks and introduce order into their lending policies, Walras wrote on February 15, 1861:

The monetary crises of the United States have an impact upon us, namely, they cause an increase in the rate of discount at the Bank of France. So far as I am concerned, I accept this repercussion. Mr. Darimon, for his part, seeks "measures designed to put an end to the crises." I try to determine the strictly necessary extent to which we ought to allow the rate of discount to rise as a result of the American crises. Mr. Darimon calls for an international congress, and wants "an international agreement to adopt a common medium of exchange and credit."

To put an end to crises! Very well! So be it. But it should be borne in mind that to do so would at the same time be to kill work, industry, commerce, speculation, and economic development in the United States. And, in effect, these two conditions: the crises on one hand, and the growth of wealth on the other, arise simultaneously from the same circumstance: the organization of credit and of banking in America on the basis of a degree of liberty which borders upon license and an audacity which verges upon folly. The Americans are not unaware of it: far from it, they know it perfectly well. They forecast, they undergo, and they periodically forget their commercial and monetary crises, proud that they are able to show the world that their wealth, begotten only yesterday, is comparable to ours which is ten times older.

. . . Let each nation organize government, the family, property, and credit in its own way, and pursue social progress as it thinks best. . . . In France, up till now authority alone determined the direction of our economic education. When that education is finished and we are able to choose freely what is best for us, we shall probably adopt a system of credit less formal, more supple, more fertile; and, in America, when its wealth becomes large and well established, the banks will assuredly make loans with less haste and more precaution. Then there will be no more repercussions, no more raising of the discount rate on one side and then on the other side of the ocean.

I have cited this passsge from *La Presse* not as a definitive expression of the monetary policies advocated by Walras, but simply in order to show that whatever may have been his doctrine *in abstracto,* when it was a question of a concrete case, he had a sense of the relativity of historical events.

Much later, in 1898, at the time of the Free Silver movement in the United States, that is, at the moment at which William Jennings Bryan placed himself at the head of a political party that was in favor of the free coinage of silver, Walras published an article in the *Revue socialiste* for July 15, 1898, entitled "The Bimetalist Peril," in which he denounced the silver interests in the United States and warned the world of the inflationary danger of such a policy. As far as I know, the article in *La Presse* of 1861 and that in the *Revue socialiste* of 1898 on "The Bimetalist Peril" passed totally unnoticed in America, where neither economists nor the public had the habit of reading French journals and periodicals. If the policy of the free coinage of silver failed to be adopted, it was for reasons that had nothing to do with Walras's warnings. That failure resulted, it is true, in the establishment of a gold standard with silver coinage, but not the regulatory coinage of silver that Walras recommended.

In 1898 Walras's name was not, however, completely unknown in the United States. In 1892, he had received a letter from the secretary of the American Economic Association, dated September 14, which read:

I have the honor to inform you that at the meeting of the American Economic Association from the twenty-third to the twenty-sixth of August, its Council, in recognition of the eminent services that you have given to the cause of economics, has elected you an honorary member of the Association.

That same year, the annals of the American Academy of Political and Social Science published Walras's *Théorie géométrique de la détermination des prix* in English. It was as a pure theoretician and not as a proponent of some economic policy, monetary or otherwise, that he was honored in America during his life, and for which he is honored today.

Nevertheless, even his policy proposals gave rise to an exchange of letters with American economists. For example, as early as September 1877, he was visited at Ouchy by the American S. Dana Horton, a visit that was followed by a fairly lengthy correspondence devoted mainly to monetary questions. At that time Horton was leading an intense campaign in favor of international bimetalism and sought Walras's support. Referring to his visit, Horton wrote in French: "I ask that you not permit your preoccupation with science to prevent you from making your influence felt on present policy in economic matters." The correspondence with Horton was not very important, because Horton, very pompous, very eloquent, and very prolix, was more advocate than scholar. It can be seen that Walras, on his side of the relationship, used Horton to obtain information on the economic situation in America; but he mistrusted Horton because he believed him to be a supporter of the "silver interests," that is to say, of the owners of silver mines. Besides, Horton would have never been able to understand Walras's mathematical *Theory of Bimetalism,* a little masterpiece of economic analysis that was published for the first time in 1881 in the *Journal des Economistes.*

Walras's correspondence with the American economists General F. A. Walker and J. Laurence Laughlin is much more interesting and revealing. There it becomes more and more plain that questions of economic policy were not Walras's fundamental concern. He sought out every possible opportunity to raise himself above the ephemeral questions of policy in order to reach the rarefied but more general and lasting atmosphere of pure theory. One day he made a confession that, in my opinion, showed his true colors, not to an American correspondent, but to a German, Ludwig von Winterfeld, who was then translating Walras's early essays into German, subsequently published under the title *Mathematische Theorie der Preisbestimmung der wirtschaftlichen Güter.* Von Winterfeld had raised objections to certain social ideas that were implicit in Walras's favorite policy proposal, that privately owned land be purchased by the state. In a letter dated October 14, 1881, Walras answered:

I must admit that I am myself a little frightened by my conclusions, and that, if I were free to do as I please, I would voluntarily confine myself to studies in pure economic theory. But I cannot do that, I must give a complete course. [Walras, it should be remembered, was then professor of economics at Lausanne.] Furthermore [he went on], people who are capable of appreciating pure theory are very rare, especially these days. Pure theory is appreciated only because of the practical conclusions that can be drawn from it. You are one of the few minds capable of disinterested and scientific thought, and you have been able to appreciate the intrinsic interest of a rigorous and mathematical theory of the determination of prices under a hypothetical regime of absolute free competition; but you will see that that theory will be neither read nor discussed seriously until the day when it is recognized that it results, among other things, in theories about the rise of rent in a progressive society, which is the point of departure for the proposal to have land bought up by the state. Thus one supports or one disputes the truth according to whether one is a partisan or an adversary of the purchase policy.

Even more remarkable is that as early as 1865, when Walras was manager of a popular bank for producers' cooperatives in Paris and not yet an economic theorist, he wrote a review, published in the *Journal des Economistes,* of Victor Bonnet's book, *Credit and Finance.* In the review the following phrase appeared: "For me, I must confess, it is not by its timely and practical qualities but by its scientific quality that Mr. Bonnet's book has captivated me."

We admit that many public declarations of Walras can be found which contradict the avowal. We even admit that at the beginning of his career, and throughout the course of it, even while insisting upon the primary importance of pure theory, he took a deep interest in current economic policies, such as the development of cooperative societies, the nationalization of land, the elimination of the abuse of the issuance of paper money, a gold standard with silver coinage used as a regulating device, and the growth of the role of the state in sectors of the economy in which free competition cannot operate. We admit all that, but, as soon as he found himself with some freedom of choice, even if limited, he concentrated the greater part of his attention on contributions to pure science. Thus, during his life, he produced five editions of his only formal treatise, the *Elements of Pure Economics,* each successive edition of which embodied considerable revisions, while his *Social Economics* (1896) and his *Applied Economics* (1898), which he published at the end of his scientific career, were no more than collections of articles and memoirs, most of which had already appeared in various journals during the course of the preceding thrity-three years. He said himself in the foreword of his *Social Economics* (1896) that his failing strength prevented him from completing the transformation of the volume, and his *Applied Economics* also, into formal treatises.

How can we explain such an unequal division of his energy between pure economic theory and economic policy? Perhaps it was because of two warnings that he had received, one from his father in 1859 and the other from the University of Lausanne in 1870. At the time when he was writing his first book on economics, *Economics and Justice* (1860), a critical examination and refutation of the doctrines of P.-J. Proudhon, Walras's father told him in a letter dated October 29, 1859, to be careful not to touch upon topics that were politically sensitive. Similarly, when he was hired at Lausanne in 1870, initially with a provisional one-year appointment, he recognized that if he wished to retain his post, it would be better not to publicize his advanced ideas, because they would alarm certain members of the commission that was charged with filling the chair at Lausanne. Whatever may have been the psychological origins of his infatuation with pure economic theory in mathematical form, it is nevertheless the case that the major part of his efforts was directed toward the development of it; and even today Walras's high reputation among economists the world over, with few exceptions, is founded upon his original and fruitful discoveries in that domain.

In this regard, it is interesting to turn to the correspondence that Walras conducted with Francis Amasa Walker and J. Laurence Laughlin. Although Walker was known primarily for his writings on monetary policy, Walras insisted in his letters on trying to persuade Walker of the value of his purely theoretical conception of the definition of the entrepreneur, a conception that plays a significant role in Walras's theory. In his correspondence with Laughlin, who had also achieved distinction by his profound contributions to monetary policy, and who was then teaching economics at Harvard University, Walras hardly mentioned questions of applied economics, but totally different matters. Because his efforts to try to explain and disseminate his system of general equilibrium in England had failed, partly because of British insularity and partly because of the dominant and exclusive influence of Alfred Marshall, whom he once called "the great white elephant of economics," Walras made an appeal to Laughlin in a letter dated June 12, 1887, couched in the following manner:

Mr. Marshall says that he wrote his *Economics of Industry* in order to show "that there is a unity underlying all the different parts of the theory of prices, wages and profits. . . ." I do not believe any more than you that he attained his goal; but since you appear to attach to the great problem of the relation of the prices of *products* to the prices of productive *services* all the importance that it merits, I should like you to demonstrate to yourself exactly how I tried to resolve it through my theory of production and of the two markets for products and for services (. . .), and to that end, I am taking the liberty of sending you a copy of my *Elements of Pure Economics. . . .*

Mr. Marshall promises us "a larger book" in which he will give himself "more room" and make his thought "clearer." Previously, in 1879, in the preface of the second edition of his *Theory of Political Economy* (p. XLVIII), Jevons, when he posed (in what I believe is an admirable manner) the important problem in question, said: "The working out of a complete system based on these lines must be a matter of time and I know not when, if ever, I shall be able to attempt it." And, nevertheless, prior to that time, I had furnished a general theory of the simultaneous determination of the price of products and of productive services in my *Elements* which appeared in 1874 and 1877; and it seemed to me that this theory was at least worth the trouble of being cited and discussed. Since the occasion is now offered to me to call this point to the attention of a person whom I believe is as impartial as he is competent, I decided, after fully considering the matter, not to let the opportunity escape, and to declare to you that if, having examined the problem, you are able to relieve me of what would be, for me, the rather delicate task of publicly informing Mr. Marshall that he is preparing himself to break down a door that is already open, you would earn an unshakeable claim upon my gratitude and my friendship.

In sending a copy of his *Elements* to Laughlin, Walras was following a systematic practice that he had long adopted to make himself known to economists in all countries. We know from his personal financial accounts that he spent almost three quarters of his inheritance in publishing and disseminating his books. That practice enabled him to have at least nineteen correspondents in the United States. I now turn to two more: Irving Fisher and Henry Ludwell Moore.

The correspondence of Walras with Irving Fisher began in 1892, when Walras was fifty-eight years old and Fisher twenty-five. In fact, it was Fisher who took upon himself the responsibility of translating the *Geometrical Theory of the Determination of Prices* into English, a translation that appeared in America in 1892. He added some critical notes in that translation. In one of them, he reproached Walras for having abstracted too much from time in his theory of prices, and, in another, he took exception to Walras's narrow conception of the theory of marginal utility or of *rareté*, a doctrine in which no account was taken of complementary or substitute commodities. Walras then answered his young critic, in generous and frank terms, by a letter dated July 28, 1892, of which an abstract follows:

> Please believe that I am very far from wanting to argue against the value of your observations. I have considered the element of *time* in my work. I have studied and made notes on the utility of complementary goods (and also of substitute goods), as well as on ways of incorporating the permanent profits of productive enterprise in the equations that state the cost of production. But I have let all that to one side in the interests of simplification. It seemed to me that in taking up for the first time the general problem of economic equilibrium, I ought to limit myself to trying to solve it in broad and general terms, and to leave to another generation of economist-mathematicians the task of correcting the details and filling in the gaps. I see by your work that you are fully qualified to accomplish that task, and I look forward to reading attentively your *Mathematical Theory of Value and Prices* when it appears.

We know also that Fisher had met Walras at Pareto's house on January 30, 1894, because the meeting is mentioned in a letter of Madame Pareto's. We do not know what happened at Pareto's, but there is every reason to believe, in the light of a correspondence that was friendly and scientific, and that was maintained until 1909, the eve of the death of Walras, that he and Fisher must have enjoyed each others' company. In acknowledging the receipt of the third edition of the *Elements of Pure Economics,* Fisher observed in a letter of April 15, 1896, that "the only thing that was new to him in that edition was the third appendix on Wicksteed."

Fisher was one of the rare defenders of the third appendix, which created and still creates a scandal because it contains a barely veiled accusation of plagiarism against Wicksteed, an English economist who was also a Unitarian minister. In a review published in the *Yale Review* for August 1896 in which he considered both the third edition of the

Elements of Walras and the *Essay on the Coordination of the Laws of Distribution* of Wicksteed, Fisher echoed Walras's accusation against Wicksteed. In harsh terms he wrote:

> ...We regret that the author [Wicksteed] did not take the trouble of mentioning the historical development of the theory and has not rendered homage to previous writers, notably Walras. The author mentions few of his predecessors, with the exception of Marshall...

It should be noted in passing, however, that Walras, in his third appendix, had not claimed priority in developing the law of marginal productivity for himself, but rather for Stuart Wood, J. A. Hobson, John Bates Clark, Enrico Barone, and Vilfredo Pareto. Fisher's review delighted Walras, who thanked Fisher in November 1896 for his "excellent and charming article."

Although Irving Fisher, as an economist-mathematician, greatly esteemed Walras's works, he was not inspired as much by Walras as by Cournot, Auspitz, and Lieben. It was another American, Henry Ludwell Moore, professor at Columbia University, who declared himself quite simply to be a follower of the School of Lausanne. We read, for example, in his book *Synthetic Economics* (1929), that he took the position of the School of Lausanne as his point of departure:

> It is desirable, in the interest both of science and of personal loyalty, to adhere as far as possible not only to Walras' terms but also to his symbols. His terms are in some cases uncommon, but the use of them has been continued by his most distinguished disciples; his symbols, for the most part, have been retained, and where substitutes have been offered the innovations have seldom proved to be betterments.

This declaration of personal loyalty to Walras has interesting origins in an exchange of letters that began in June 1903, when Moore wrote to Walras to ask him if he could visit him to discuss the manuscript of Cournot's *Souvenirs* that he had discovered.

Had I more time I would cite the letters in which Walras tried to persuade Moore to translate or to have translated into English his *Elements of Pure Economics,* or at least his abridgment of the *Elements,* which at that time had not yet been published. Declining the task, Moore answered on January 26, 1906, that Walras underestimated the difficulty of his work. I can recall how many times that opinion came to my mind when, much later, I myself struggled with its difficulty when translating it, and how many times I said to myself that "fools rush in where angels fear to tread."

It would be necessary to cite a number of Moore's letters in which he insists on the importance that he attached to the publication of a biography of Walras, which, according to Moore, would be a source of inspiration for the community of scholars.

It is time now to conclude, and in so doing to recall that it was in Switzerland, a country faithful to the ideal of intellectual liberty, that Léon Walras, a Frenchman who was misunderstood and unrecognized in his own country, found a refuge that encouraged his research. It was a great Swiss statesman, Louis Ruchonnet, who had that singular person Walras named to the chair of economics newly created at Lausanne. From the moment of his arrival at that university, which was then only a simple academy, Walras found among his Swiss colleagues a Paul Piccard, a Herman Amstein, a Charles Secrétan, who generously gave him friendly aid by providing him from time to time with technical advice without which he would never have been able to develop his theory of general equilibrium. When one thinks also of the encouragement that he received from the Vaud Society for Natural Science during the forty years that he lived in this country, one recognizes that the great Walrasian contribution to present economic science is truly a contribution of the School of Lausanne as a whole.

PART III

THE SCOPE OF WALRAS'S WORK

7

LEON WALRAS AND HIS CONCEPTION OF ECONOMICS

Monsieur le President
Mesdames, Mesdemoiselles, Messieurs,

I should like to begin by thanking Monsieur Jacques Peyréga, Dean of the *Faculté de Droit* of Algiers, and his colleagues for the honor that they have done me by inviting me to occupy the *Chaire des Actualités Scientifiques* at the University of Algiers. I should also like to tell them how appreciative I am of the warm welcome that I have received from the moment that I came under Algierian skies. I must admit that what moves me most is the privilege of giving a course on the history of Walrasian theories. Indeed, that is the subject that I most prefer, one to which I have dedicated a large part of my professional life. My feelings in this respect are not entirely personal. Having done so much research on Walras's life by studying his unpublished manuscripts and especially his personal letters and his scientific correspondence, I feel that I have achieved an intimate understanding that gives me the right to speak to some extent in his name. I can state that my course will be the realization of a long-cherished ambition of the great master, Léon Walras.

Walras was never asked to teach in France, his native country. At one time in 1879 after the death of Michel Chevalier, he hoped to return from Lausanne and occupy a chair at the *Collège de France*. With this in mind, he wrote the following letter to an important official in the Ministry of Public Instruction:

Permit me to submit to you a statement of my professional faith. If I had the honor of becoming a professor of economics at the *Collège de France,* I would devote myself entirely to my teaching. I would not be the member of any deliberative assembly, nor an editor of any review or journal, nor the administrator of any financial company. I would not add any other teaching appointment to the one that I held. I would give a regular and complete course in economics over a period of years, always intellectually accessible to the students. I would use my vacations to enhance successively the various parts of the course in such a manner as to perfect it and enrich it from year to year. I would strive to

A lecture delivered to the *Faculté de Droit* of the University of Algiers, March 9, 1956, and translated from the French by Donald A. Walker.

leave after me some theories and some students who adhere to my views and who would do justice to my work, which is, in my opinion, the only serious and worthy testimonial that a professor ought to desire.[1]

In spite of this moving profession of faith, in spite of many attempts made directly by Léon Walras and indirectly by his friend Jules Ferry, he did not succeed in finding a suitable position in a French university. Finally, he wrote in 1880 to his friend Louis Lacour de la Pijadière of Montpellier: "I have definitely renounced the idea of returning to France."[2] Until the end of his life, however, he nursed the conviction that after his death his country would recognize the value of his work. In 1903, he wrote to his friend, Madame Georges Renard:

> The 16th and 23rd of August marks 30 years since I read my memoir, *Principles of a Mathematical Theory of Exchange,* at the Institute. On the basis of that work I subsequently constructed the whole mathematical theory of economic equilibrium. The only result, insofar as France is concerned, is that I have used up three-quarters of my inheritance, and fallen victim to cerebral neurosis. I am not complaining. Posthumous successes are best, because, resulting from a reaction to the previous neglect, they do not come to an end. Besides that, I am a man of science: I have sought the truth; I believe that I have found it; I am recompensed.[3]

Let it be said in passing that his "cerebral neurosis" was a subject of pride of Walras, like everything that he could attribute to a cerebral origin. Five years earlier, he had written to his Russian disciple, Ladislaus Bortkiewicz:

> I hope to live long enough to see the dawn of scientific political economics and social economics. And what is more, I am certain that I already see it coming. Of the four founders of economics, I am the only one still surviving. Cournot and Gossen died unknown; Jevons died unrecognized; and when the same thing happens to me, it will only have the effect of preparing the way later on for a magnificent reaction in favor of my ideas.[4]

[1] This extract, like most of the extracts given below, is taken from the unpublished letters preserved in the *Bibliothèque Cantonnale et Universitaire de Lausanne.* The *Fonds Walras* is composed of several parts. F.W. I contains the rough drafts of Walras's letters to his correspondents, and F.W. II is constituted of the letters addressed to Walras. It was thanks to the aid received from the Social Science Research Council, the American Philosophical Society, and Northwestern University that I was able to examine these documents at Lausanne and to make photocopies of them for the purpose of preparing a book that I am writing on the life and works of Léon Walras. In addition, a Fulbright Grant enabled me to examine in the same fashion a collection of personal letters and other documents that are deposited at the *Faculté de Droit* of Lyons. The quoted material is from the *Fonds Walras* at Lausanne. The extract given above is from a letter to Albert Dumont, dated December 4, 1879 (F.W. I, 163).
[2] Unpublished letter, May 18, 1880 (F.W. I, 300).
[3] Unpublished letter, Nov. 29, 1903 (F.W. I, 475).
[4] Unpublished letter, March 25, 1898 (F.W. I, 66).

Of course, the reaction in favor of Walras's ideas did not have to wait for me to start it here, for the University of Algiers can take pride in having already worked in that direction through the contributions of Professor Bousquet[5] on the subject of Vilfredo Pareto's theories. I believe that it was by his own percipience that Professor Bousquet recognized Vilfredo Pareto to be the great successor of Léon Walras. Furthermore, France has rendered justice to Léon Walras, although tardily, especially in the teaching of celebrated writers and professors such as Etienne Antonelli, Aupetit, Bompaire, and Gaëtan Pirou.[6] In 1952, I myself had the honor of participating in a series of conferences organized in Paris by Professor François Perroux, Director of the Institute of Applied Economic Science.[7] It must be admitted, however, that Walras's success has always been greater in foreign countries – first in Italy, then in the United States – than in his own land. Among the American economists who have been inspired by Walras and Pareto, I should mention Irving Fisher, Henry Ludwell Moore, Henry Schultz, Wassily Leontief, Paul Samuelson, and Don Patinkin. And now, since my annotated English translation of Léon Walras's *Elements of Pure Economics,* which appeared in 1954,[8] the number of journal articles dealing with our master has grown considerably. It may be asked if the Austrian economist Joseph Schumpeter was not right to declare solemnly that in pure economics Léon Walras was the greatest of all the economists who had ever lived.[9]

Now it will be understood why I venture to rejoice in the name of Léon Walras to see a semester devoted to a study of the history of the Walrasian theories here at the *Faculté de Droit* of Algiers.

I will pass very quickly over his life,[10] because if I give way to the

[5] Cf., for example, his *Vilfredo Pareto, sa vie et son oeuvre* (Paris, 1929), and his *Introduction à l'Etude du Manuel de Vilfredo Pareto* (Paris, 1927). Professor Bousquet has developed and broadened general equilibrium theory in his *Cours d'économie pure* (1927), his *Essai sur l'évolution de la pensée économique,* and his *Institutes de sciences économiques* (1930–6).

[6] Etienne Antonelli, *Principes d'economie pure,* Paris, 1914, and *L'Economie pure du capitalisme,* Paris, 1939; Albert Aupetit, *Essai sur la théorie générale de la monnaie,* Paris, 1901; F. Bompaire, *Du principe de liberté économique dans l'oeuvre de Cournot et dans celle de l'Ecole de Lausanne (Walras, Pareto),* Paris, 1931; Gäetan Pirou, *Les théories de l'équilibre économique,* *Walras et Pareto,* 3rd edition, Paris, 1946.

[7] Cf. my article, "La théorie de la capitalisation chez Walras dans le cadre de sa théorie d'équilibre général," *Economie Appliquée,* vol. VI, nos. 2–3, April–Sept. 1953, pp. 290–317.

[8] Published under the auspices of the American Economic Association and the Royal Economic Society by Irwin, Homewood, Ill. and Allen and Unwin, London.

[9] "So far as pure theory is concerned, Walras is in my opinion the greatest of all economists." Joseph A. Schumpeter, *History of Economic Analysis,* New York, Oxford University Press, 1954, p. 827.

[10] Cf. Marcel Boson, *Léon Walras, Fondateur de la politique économique,* Paris and Lausanne, 1915, pp. 17–24, and my article "The Unpublished Papers and Letters of Léon Walras," *Journal of Political Economy,* vol. XLIII, no. 2, April 1935, pp. 187–207.

temptation to expose the details of Walras's private life as revealed, not in his well-known autobiography published in the *Giornale degli Economisti* in 1908, but in his private letters, which are to be found at the University of Lyons, I would never be able to start the task of tracing for you the outline of his theory of general equilibrium, which is his masterpiece.

Léon Walras was born on December 16, 1834, at Evreux. He was the eldest son of Auguste Walras, who was also a great economist and who was then principal of the *Collège d'Evreux*. His mother, Louise Aline de Sainte-Beuve, was not related to the great French literary critic, although several authors have said that was the case. It was Canon Yves Delaporte of Chartes Cathedral, a distant cousin of Léon Walras, who told me that the Sainte-Beuve family from which Léon Walras descended was not the family of Charles Augustin Sainte-Beuve. As for the Walras family, its origins are quite obscure. At the beginning of the nineteenth century, the family had established itself in Montpellier, where Léon Walras's grandfather was a minor municipal official. Léon Walras wrote that he had heard it said during his childhood that his great-grandfather or great-great-grandfather had emigrated from East Prussia. What interests us most regarding his ancestry is the fact that his father, Auguste Walras, was the author of two books on economics that are very important from the viewpoint of the history of doctrine. The first, *Of the Nature of Wealth and the Origin of Value,* appeared in 1831, and the second, *The Theory of Social Wealth,* appeared in 1848. Furthermore, Auguste Walras had in his library a book by one of his schoolmates at the *Ecole normale supérieure,* a book that we recognize today as being of primary importance, but which, at that time, had not attracted any attention. It was the *Investigations into the Mathematical Principles of the Theory of Wealth* by Antoine Augustin Cournot. It was in that work that Léon Walras first came in contact with the application of mathematics to economic analysis.

Although the environment in which he was raised was very conducive to his becoming an economist, Léon Walras initially had other ambitions. Moreover, his mother, seeing that her husband had not been able to profit, so far as his career was concerned, from his preoccupation with economics, wanted her oldest son to follow a less risky career. In fact, Léon Walras was for some time a student at the School of Mines; but the profession of an engineer did not interest him at all. Impelled by his literary ambitions, in 1858 he published a novel titled *Francis Sauveur,* which cannot be said to have been a success. But from our point of view, the novel is interesting because it enables us to learn about the intellectual development of the young author and the influence that the social ideas of the revolution of 1848 had upon him. In the copy of *Francis Sauveur* that is in the archives of the *Faculté de Droit,* I discovered some penciled notations in Léon Walras's handwriting. I believe that these annotations date from 1882 or thereabouts, nearly a quarter of a century after the publication of the novel. The first of the notes is worth being cited without comment:

> My opinion on universal suffrage has been modified as a result of the distinction that I have come to draw between social theory or science on the one hand, and actual practice or policy on the other. I have always believed that universal suffrage is a scientific truth in the sense that it has its place in an ideal society as a condition of its rational organization, but I also believe that its premature adoption and its operation in a disorderly and brutal fashion has been a political misfortune from which French democracy may never recover.

After Walras had tried literature, and after he took note that the critics did not acclaim him as a budding genius, it is not surprising that his father was able to persuade him to abandon literature in order to devote himself to economics. I pass over the ten years between 1860 and 1870, during which he pleaded in vain for an economics professorship in France. He earned his living successively as a journalist, as an employee of the Ministry of Northern Railways, as an administrator and director of a popular bank for producers' cooperatives, and finally as an employee in a private bank in Paris, until he resigned in order to accept the chair of economics at the University of Lausanne.

I would like to draw your attention to a single incident at that time, because I believe that we will find in it the psychological reason for his great attraction to pure economic theory, even though he was passionately interested in political and practical questions, such as the nationalization of land, the cooperative movement, and the single tax. Toward the end of 1859, when he was writing a book entitled *Economics and Justice, A Critical Examination and Refutation of the Economic Doctrines of M. P.-J. Proudhon* (Paris, 1860), his father wrote to him:

> If you decide to publish your work, re-read it with care; don't allow anything to remain in it that could give even the slightest offense from a political point of view. Place yourself and keep yourself always on scientific ground. Arrange matters, in a word, so that if by chance anyone decides to lodge charges against you, the Imperial Prosecutor would be obliged, in order to have you condemned, to maintain that the world does not turn, that the sun is no bigger than a pumpkin, that thunder is a bar of iron forged by the Cyclops and hurled by Jupiter.[11]

[11] Letter postmarked Pau, October 29, 1859, published in *La Révolution de 1848, Bulletin de la Société d'Histoire de la Révolution de 1848,* vol. 9, no. LII, Sept.–Oct. 1912, pp. 299–300.

Léon Walras tried to follow the wise counsel of his father even in his first economic writings. In particular, he always sought to base the reforms that he recommended between 1860 and 1870 upon a systematic and closely reasoned analytical structure. This was true, for example, of the nationalization of land, and measures for the improvement of the condition of the working class by the cooperative movement, but his reasoning remained unrigorous and was diluted with moral exhortations. His heterodox economic policies did not cause his candidacy for the chair of economics at Lausanne to fail,[12] and after a year of teaching, it could be seen that Léon Walras was above all a scholar and not a dangerous agitator.

He fulfilled the duties of a professor for twenty-two years. Worn out by his work, he took an early retirement in 1892, but continued his research until 1902. His career was triumphantly crowned by the ceremonies observing his jubilee on June 10, 1909. Some months later, on January 6, 1910, he died at his retreat in Clarens, near Lausanne.

However interesting the life and works of Léon Walras may be, it is reasonable to ask how a course in the history of Walrasian theory can be justified in terms of present-day scientific interests. It is now [1956] 122 years since Walras was born, and 46 years since he died. His principal works appeared between 1873 and 1902. These facts do not give the impression that Walras's work has relevance for the modern era.

I believe there is nevertheless a profound and very real justification for viewing the Walrasian theories as present-day theories. The evidence is found in current literature, in the economics journals of all countries in which a critical discussion of the Walrasian theories is becoming more vigorous each day. My course will deal above all with the history of Walrasian theories since the time of Walras, including the present. Walras knew well that he was in advance of his time, and we can now see that it is only in recent times that we have begun to understand Walras and to discern the weak points as well as the strong points in his work. We now recognize that consciously or unconsciously, directly or indirectly (and when I say indirectly, I mean especially in considering the path that theory has taken through Pareto), almost all the economists and econometricians of our time follow the route that Léon Walras traced. Even those who would prefer another brand of theory are obliged to recognize Walras's strong influence on the present.[13] Thus we find ourselves in the midst of a debate between the supporters of Marshall and those of Walras. In my course, I shall try to give a

[12] See Fermin Oulès, *L'Ecole de Lausanne, Textes choisis de L. Walras et V. Pareto*, Paris, 1950, pp. 118–21.
[13] Milton Friedman, "The Marshallian Demand Curve," *Journal of Political Economy*, vol. LVII, no. 6, Dec. 1949, p. 489.

technical analysis of that debate, and I believe that I can demonstrate that it is, in the last analysis, a false issue.

I wish now to sketch in a few words Walras's overall conception of economics. He had the idea, from the very beginning of his career as an economist, of dividing economics into three parts, corresponding to the triple point of view of the True, the Useful, and the Just.[14] Permit me to examine these three points one after another, in an effort to interpret the profound thought of Léon Walras according to my own notions.

In the first part, which constitutes pure economic theory, the problem is to investigate the ineluctable conditions that are imposed by the nature of things. This part consists of an application of logic to economic propositions. In postulating any hypothesis, it must be asked, in pure science, what must *necessarily* follow from it. Given the fact that economic propositions have in general a quantitative implication, in the sense that they are almost always concerned with the relationships between quantities, it is natural to use mathematics in seeking the implications of the propositions. As early as 1831, in his work entitled *Of the Nature of Wealth and the Origin of Value,* Auguste Walras, the father of Léon Walras, had glimpsed the possibility of creating a mathematical economic science.[15] That is a fundamental reason why so many economists, especially since the time of Cournot, have used the mathematical method. Walras himself, who was not a good mathematician and whose knowledge of mathematics was hardly more than what is taught in a high school, adopted that method with the fervor of a novice. But he knew how to avoid certain pitfalls that have not been recognized by many present-day mathematical economists. In 1894, on a letter that he had received from the great Italian economist Enrico Barone in which he had set forth his theory of marginal productivity, Walras penciled the following words: "Here is the (mathematical) formulation of marginal productivity, but the economic foundation is bad."[16] In this remark, we see clearly the

[14] Letter to Du Mesnil Marigny, dated Dec. 23, 1862 (F.W. I, 162).

[15] "Furthermore, everyone knows that wealth can be counted and measured, and that economics involves the use of arithmetic. It is for those reasons that economics fulfills the hopes of alert intellects, who correctly believe that one day they will see it placed among the mathematical sciences, and achieve the degree of certainty which characterizes, so advantageously, that important branch of our knowledge." See p. 270, cited by Boson, op. cit., p. 99. Auguste Walras, however, did not realize that, as Antoine Augustin Cournot said: "Those versed in mathematical analysis know that it is not only used for the purpose of calculating numerical magnitudes; that it is also used for finding relationships between variables that cannot be measured numerically, between functions whose characteristics cannot be expressed in algebraic symbols" (*Recherches sur les principes mathématiques de la théorie des richesses,* new edition published with an introduction and notes by George Lutfulla, Paris, 1938, p. VIII). Léon Walras, in contrast, was well aware of this.

[16] Unpublished letter from Enrico Barone to Léon Walras, dated Sept. 20, 1894 (F.W. II, 1848).

criterion that I shall use in my course to aid us to distinguish between good and bad uses of mathematics in economics. The debate between those who support and those who oppose the application of mathematics to economics is now out of date; but we should recognize that to be good at mathematics does not necessarily make one an economist. Whether one expresses oneself in mathematics or in ordinary language, it is always necessary to examine very closely whether the economic foundation is secure. It is one of Walras's great achievements to have been able to create, despite the use of relatively primitive mathematical tools, an entire system of equations that can be seen to have a remarkably solid economic foundation. Thus, it was with the aid of mathematics that he created his pure economic theory, which consists, as I remarked earlier, of an application of logic that is not only rigorous, but also systematic, to propositions of an economic nature.

The second part of economics is called applied economics. This examines the subject matter from the point of view of what is useful. In this part, a given practical goal is posited, and an effort is made to determine the best manner of achieving that goal. It is here that a judgment can be made as to whether the reasoning developed in the first part, that is to say in pure economic theory, is relevant to the real world. We may quote Walras:

> If the pure theory of economics or the theory of exchange and value in exchange, that is, the theory of social wealth considered by itself, is a physico-mathematical science like mechanics or hydrodynamics, then economists should not be afraid to use the methods and language of mathematics. . . . We shall see, however, that the truths of pure economics yield solutions of very important problems of applied economics and social economics, which are highly controversial and very little understood.[17]

Nevertheless, there is no way to obtain a solution to practical questions even if the cause of the problem is fully known, without having first constructed an economic theory.[18] It was for this reason that Léon Walras turned away in his youth from Saint-Simon's socialism, which seemed to him too vague and lacking a logical basis.

Finally, we turn to the third part, which Walras called social economics. Here he dealt with economic phenomena from the standpoint of

[17] Léon Walras, *Eléments d'économie politique pure,* definitive edition, new printing, 1952, pp. 29–30. [The translation given in the text is from Léon Walras, *Elements of Pure Economics,* translated and annotated by William Jaffé, Irwin, Homewood, Ill., 1954, pp. 71–72.]

[18] Cf. Cournot, op. cit., p. IX: " . . . I believe that if this essay proves to be of some practical use, it will be principally in making us realize that we are seriously deficient in the knowledge that is needed to obtain solutions to the many questions which are boldly settled every day."

justice. We recall that in applied economics the investigation begins with a given goal, without asking if the goal is good or bad. Indeed, economics is incapable of answering questions about justice or injustice. These questions are considered, as has recently become well known, in the new contributions of welfare economics. In his *Social Economics*, Léon Walras perceived clearly the manner of handling the problem. He postulated various principles of justice, and, in the light of them, judged the different social goals that were proposed during his time. It must be recognized that such an investigation leaves economics proper and enters the domain of moral inquiry. I believe that a doctoral candidate, if he has a liking for philosophy, would find an interesting subject for a dissertation in an analytical inquiry into the normative bases of Léon Walras's social economics.

There are certain problems of applied and social economics that I shall touch upon only in passing in my course at the *Faculté de Droit* of Algiers. I shall devote myself almost entirely to pure economic theory, for that is the part of Walras's work that has had the greatest impact and is most relevant in the present. It is also the most aesthetically pleasing part. Any great scholar, whether it be a Newton, or a Henri Poincaré, or an Einstein, is a poet who creates beauty. For me, the principal attraction of Walras's theory of general equilibrium is its aesthetic aspect. When one thinks of the structure of the Walrasian system, which includes a theory of exchange, a theory of production, a theory of capital goods, and a theory of money, and sees that all the parts are intimately linked by a single principle, the principle of the maximization of utility, one cannot help thinking of a mystical English poet, Francis Thompson, who expressed the same idea in the following way:

> *All things by immortal pow'r*
> *Hiddenly to each other linked are,*
> *That thou cans't not stir a flow'r*
> *Without troubling of a star.*

It can be seen in studying closely the imposing system that Léon Walras created why he scribbled one day on a piece of paper that I found in the Walras Collection at Lausanne: "I am not an economist, I am an architect; but I know economics better than the economists do."

By its very nature, no science is ever complete; and all scientific effort consists precisely in a ceaseless effort to create and improve our conceptual models in order to improve our understanding of the universe. In his role as an architect, Léon Walras designed a plan, magnificent in its conception. It was also inevitable that Walras, like the great architects of the cathedrals of the Middle Ages, left his edifice uncompleted. We, the heirs of Léon Walras's great work, have the task of trying to add a stone or two to the edifice and of trying to add to its beauty.

You see now, ladies and gentlemen, why I am so happy to be installed in the *Chaire des Actualités scientifiques* of the University of Algiers for the purpose of giving a course on the history of the Walrasian theories. I thank you, one and all.

8

LEON WALRAS

For many years Walras thought that his chief title to fame lay in his marginal utility theory, which was certainly more rigorous and elegant than that of either Jevons or Menger. He did not realize the full significance of the unique character of his general equilibrium system until Barone hailed it in the *Giornale degli economisti* (1894, p. 407) as "the most general, most comprehensive and most harmonious" that had yet appeared. Already in the 1870s, in the first edition of the *Éléments*, Walras had laid the groundwork for a unified model, comprising the theories of exchange, production, capital formation, and money. In the subsequent revisions of the *Éléments*, he strengthened the model by applying the principle of utility maximization throughout. Moreover, to link his model to the real world, he followed up each of his successive cumulative submodels describing the static *determination* of equilibrium with a related quasi-dynamic theory of the emergence (or *establishment*) of equilibrium via the operation of the competitive market mechanism. He called the process of automatic adjustments of the network of real markets to equilibrium one of *tâtonnement*, that is, of groping without conscious direction. His argument that the process would culminate, under his assumptions, in a stable equilibrium was, nevertheless, intuitive, without any semblance of a rigorous demonstration. Despite this and other defects, lacunae, and inconsistencies in detail, which were inevitable in so immense a pioneer work produced with primitive mathematical tools, Walras' general equilibrium model earned for him the supreme encomium of Joseph Schumpeter, who said that "as far as pure theory is concerned, Walras is in my opinion the greatest of all economists" (1954, p. 827).

The idea of general equilibrium was not new with Walras. It had already been enunciated in 1690 by Nicholas Barbon; there were descernible adumbrations of the theory in Petty, Boisguilbert, Cantillon, and especially in Turgot and Quesnay; and an implicit pattern of mutually interdependent relationships underlies the writings of the great classical founders of economics, Adam Smith, Ricardo, and Jean Baptiste Say. It is altogether unlikely, however, that Walras derived direct inspiration for his multiequational model of interdependence from these precursors. He himself liked to give the impression that his father and Cournot had furnished the principal elements of his economic theory, but Cournot had mentioned the interconnection of all the parts of the economic system only to recoil from it as surpassing "the powers of mathematical analysis," and Auguste Walras had furnished nothing but vague hints of general equilibrium.

The true *fons et origo* of Walras' multiequational formulation of general equilibrium was Louis Poinsot's once famous textbook in pure mechanics, *Éléments de statique* (1803), which, as Walras confided to a friend in 1901, he first read at the age of 19 and then kept by him as a companion book throughout his life. In Poinsot we find virtually the whole formal apparatus that Walras later employed in his *Éléments d'économie politique pure*. Poinsot's *Éléments de statique* bristles with systems of simultaneous equations, some of them equilibrium equations proper and others equations of condition (constraints or definitional identities), and contains the postulate that these systems have determinate solutions if they consist in as many independent equations as unknowns. Isnard's *Traité des richesses* (1781)—which Walras rescued from oblivion by inserting it in the list of writings on mathematical economics compiled by Jevons (1871)—also appears to have played a part in shaping Walras' formulation of his system. Walras praised Isnard for having correctly stated algebraically the inverse proportionality of values to quantities exchanged. Both in his unpublished juvenile essays of the 1860s and in the opening algebraic treatment of exchange in the *Éléments*, Walras' simultaneous equations bear a remarkable resemblance to Isnard's. Notable, too, was Isnard's anticipation of the Walrasian proposition that the use of a standard unit of account obviates the need for recourse to arbitrage in a competitive, multicommodity model.

Although Walras was not really indebted to his father or to Cournot for his composite model, his pure theory does bear the sharp imprint of their influence. Walras took over, for better or worse, a good part of his father's terminology, his taxonomy, and his conception of the object of economics. From Cournot he first learned the meaning of functional relations between variables; it was precisely his growing dissatisfaction with Cournot's particular demand function that first led him to seek a wider framework within which to express the quantity demanded of a commodity as a function not of the price of that commodity alone, but of the entire constellation of prices. This was the point of departure for his general equilibrium model.

LATER LIFE AND WORK

Soon after the publication of the first edition of the *Éléments,* Walras' wife was stricken by a fatal illness and his financial situation deteriorated. His academic salary, which had been raised to 1872 from the initial 3,600 francs per annum to 4,000 francs, still proved inadequate. To eke out the income he required for his family needs and his research and publication expenses, he had to give supplementary courses at Geneva and Neuchâtel, to serve as a regular consulting actuary for a Swiss insurance company, to write fortnightly feature articles (under the psudonym "Paul") for the *Gazette de Lausanne,* to contribute weighty articles to the *Bibliothèque universelle,* and to borrow. When in 1879 his old friend Jules Ferry became minister of public instruction in France, Walras thought he had a chance to obtain a university post in his native country and to improve his financial situation. His efforts in this direction proved vain, notwithstanding his offer to help Ferry modernize the whole French university system and, by the same token, pull the teaching of economics out of the law-school rut and give it the status of a science. In 1881 the Academy of Lausanne increased his salary to 5,000 francs. But it was only after his second marriage in 1884 (his first wife having died in 1879), that his financial condition took a substantial turn for the better. His second wife, Léonide Désirée Mailly, a French spinster who had lived for many years in England, brought with her an annuity which more than doubled the income of the Walras household.

Relieved now of private financial worries, Walras returned to his work with a burst of renewed energy. He ventured upon a fundamental revision of his theories of money and capital and took up the cause of monetary reform. In his monetary theory, he substituted the conception of a demand for cash balances *(encaisse désirée)* for his earlier conception of the demand for money as depending on the volume of transactions to be cleared *(circulation à desservir).* As Arthur Marget pointed out, this entailed the substitution of his earlier Fisherian equation of exchange by an equation essentially Keynesian in form (1931). The change was made in the interests of symmetry and over-all coherence in the general model, for now the same *primum mobile*—the maximization of utility— could operate in the theory of money as in the rest of his system. Walras' new monetary theory, first announced in his paper "Équations de la circulation" (1899), was very soon incorporated into the fourth edition of the *Éléments.* Into this edition, he also introduced his revised conception of the role of interest as an equilibrating factor between the aggregate demand for cash balances and the existing quantity of money.

Walras' revision and extension of his theory of capital formation were similarly motivated. In the fourth edition of the *Éléments,* in order to avoid the dilemma of either continuing to use his earlier empirical savings function unrelated to the utility maximization principle or of complicating his postulates with time preference functions, Walras chose to consider savings and investment, as he did consumption and production, exclusively at the moment of decision making. He envisaged the decisions theoretically as bearing on a fictive commodity, "perpetual net income" (net of depreciation and insurance charges), each unit of which represents a perpetual yield of one unit of *numéraire* per annum from whatever assets, human as well as marketable, an individual possesses. This commodity, having a utility function of its own, enters into the general equilibrium model on the same footing as any other commodity and renders the entire system homogeneous.

In his writings on monetary reform, Walras focused his attention upon the questions, then current, of bimetallism and bank note issue. His work *Théorie mathématique du bimétallisme* (1881) presented, in the form of an *ad hoc* model, a complete theory of the bimetallist standard with a fixed ratio. Basing his proposal on this model, as well as on his utility theory and his conception of "justice," he advocated a symmetallist system in the form of a gold standard with a regulatory silver token currency. The state would regulate the quantity of a special silver token currency in such a way as to counteract the long wave fluctuations in the value of money. In the matter of bank note issue, Walras maintained that any system that fell short of 100 per cent metallic coverage was dangerous.

These arduous labors exhausted Walras. By 1892 he felt he could no longer go on with his teaching. The inheritance he received from his mother in that year enabled him to purchase an annuity and repay his old debts, incurred mainly in the publication and free distribution of his books and economic papers. Thereupon, he retired from the university on a pension of 800 francs a year and was succeeded in his chair by his protégé Vilfredo Pareto. He did not, however, lay down his pen. In the decade 1892–1902, as has been seen, he made some of his most important innovations in the theory of capital and money. He could not, however, find strength to write the systematic treatises he had planned on applied economics and social economics. Instead, he published two volumes of collected papers, *Études d'économie sociale* in 1896 and *Études d'économie politique appliquée* in 1898. From 1902 on, after completing his notes for what ultimately became the definitive edition of 1926, he devoted himself to puttering and to propaganda in favor of his theory. Upon the death of his second wife in 1900, her annuity ceased, and Walras and his unmarried daughter, Aline, moved, without regrets, to a modest apartment at Clarens, near Montreux, where he died on January 5, 1910. Six months before his death, the University of Lausanne celebrated his jubilee as an economist, on which occasion he was acclaimed in messages from all over the world as the founder of the general equilibrium school.

Though Walras had received occasional marks of recognition before his death, it was only posthumously that his reputation and influence grew to their present proportions. After 1910, Étienne Antonelli championed the Walrasian model in his lectures and writings in France. Elsewhere, Walras' model has been the subject of continued emendations, controversy, and fluctuating evaluations. His crabbed notations have been streamlined; his crude mathematics polished, perfected, and modernized; his utility theory superseded by a theory of ordinal preference unencumbered by assumptions of cardinal measurement and independence; his production theory freed from implications that had left the distinction between free and scarce goods empirically hazy; his production functions generalized to admit more easily of variable coefficients of production; his investment theory disassociated from postulates of certainty of outcome; and his unwarranted premise that equality between the number of unknowns and the number of independent equations is sufficient for a determinate solution supplanted by rigorous existence theorems. For all that, the main lines of the Walrasian model remain intact, and its authority is such that in 1949 Milton Friedman was forced to admit, "We curtsy to Marshall, but we walk with Walras" (p. 489). Some critics, while conceding the aesthetic qualities of the general equilibrium model, hold it to be sterile, little realizing that pure economics is no more intended for direct application to practical problems than pure mechanics is intended for guidance to machinists. Besides, it is putting a strange construction upon the word "sterility" to apply it to an over-all theory that is the acknowledged forebear of input-output analysis and that directly begot the modern conceptions of exchange, production, saving, investment, interest, and money and fitted them neatly into a single, coherent framework. This was the achievement of Walras, a lonely, cantankerous savant, often in straitened circumstances, plagued with hypochondria and a paranoid temperament, plodding doggedly through hostile, uncharted territory to discover a fresh vantage point from which subsequent generations of economists could set out to make their own discoveries.

PART IV

SPECIAL TOPICS IN WALRAS'S ECONOMICS

9

LEON WALRAS' THEORY OF CAPITAL ACCUMULATION

The object of this paper is to expound a much-neglected chapter in the history of economic theory. Special interest attaches itself at present to Léon Walras' discussions of capital,[1] interest, and money because of the affinities which Marget[2] and Lange[3] have shown to exist between these older Walrasian theories and their independently discovered Keynesian counterparts.

What Walras actually had to say about capital accumulation is very difficult to grasp. Part of the difficulty arises from the way in which this particular discussion was incorporated into the whole structure of general static equilibrium. But even more troublesome are the obscurities and lacunae of the discussion itself.

Walras arrives at his theory of capital accumulation as follows. First he develops a pure theory of exchange, which bears a remarkable resemblance in essence to Marshall's "Temporary Equilibrium of Demand and Supply." In this part of Walras' treatise the stocks of exchangeable commodities are held constant. Then follows the pure theory of production, which corresponds approximately to Marshall's "Equilibrium of Normal Demand and Supply" in the short period. Here the commodities of the former part are viewed as products, and their quantities are subject to variations; but the quantities of productive services and, consequently, of the capital goods yielding productive services are assumed constant. It is not until we arrive at the part entitled "Théorie de la capitalisation et du credit" that the assumption of fixed quantities of capital goods and services is dropped. The whole development up to and including this point presupposes a barter or moneyless economy, for Walras' standard commodity (*numéraire*) is on a par with all other commodities or products, except that its value is taken

---

[1] Léon Walras, *Eléments d'économic politique pure* (4th ed. [definitive ed.]; Lausanne and Paris, 1900 [1926]), Part V.
[2] A.W. Marget, "Léon Walras and the 'Cash Balance Approach,' " *Journal of Political Economy*, XXXIX (1931), 569–600, and "The Monetary Aspects of the Walrasian System," *ibid.*, XLIII (1935), 145–86.
[3] O. Lange, "The Rate of Interest and the Optimum Propensity to Consume," *Economica* (N.S.), No. 17, pp. 20–23.

as a standard of measurement of values. Money and, therefore, interest, properly speaking, do not enter into Walras' general system until after he had evolved his theories of exchange, production, and capital accumulation without money. Monetary phenomena are then seen to affect the total equilibrium through the influence of cash balances, the demand for and offer of which must be equal if the rest of the system is to remain in a balanced state. Finally Walras discusses the conditions and consequences of economic progress. It is here that we first encounter the marginal productivity theory. In the theory of production Walras had provisionally assumed the technical coefficients fixed. Without technical progress, with fixed quantities of service-yielding factors, with a fixed population and fixed tastes, the technical coefficients might well be assumed constant in his theory of production. It would have been logically incongruous to assume anything else at that stage of the argument, for, until the theory of capital accumulation is reached, the technical coefficients in the theory of production cannot be considered as variable since this variation involves variations in the quantities of the capital goods which give rise to them. Nor could Walras have included the marginal productivity theory in his chapters on capital accumulation, for there he described only the mechanism of capital accumulation, not the reasons for it. These reasons are found in the section on economic progress. If the state of the industrial arts is unchanged, there can be no inducement to modify the technical proportions in which the productive services are combined unless population increases while the quantity of land remains fixed. When land becomes increasingly scarce, then there are inducements to change the technical proportions with a view to minimum costs, and the reasons for capital accumulation become evident.

So much for the setting of the particular discussion of capital accumulation within the total Walrasian system. For the purpose of this paper only one phase of Walras' exposition need be presented—namely, that in which Walras defines equilibrium and shows how it is mathematically *determined*. Another phase, which I am passing over in silence, is that of the *emergence* of equilibrium *ab ovo*, the egg being a random or inherited state most probably not in equilibrium.

The condition of equilibrium in production is the starting-point for Walras' consideration of capital accumulation. This equilibrium is made up of the following elements:

Given: (1) A number of individuals in a community each characterized by a group of utility functions, which are conceived in such a way that the marginal degree of utility (rareté) of each commodity is a function of the quantity of that commodity only. These marginal degree of utility functions are the ϕ's in system (1) of the equations below.[4]

(2) Each individual of our community is further characterized by the resources he possesses at the moment under consideration. If there are n different types of resources (T), (P), (K), $[n = 3]$, each individual has, to start with, q_t of (T), q_p of (P), and q_k of (K). These resources may be envisaged as disposal over so much flow of the corresponding services or they may equally well be envisaged as possession of so much capital goods whence these services flow. This assumption implies that the total stock of capital goods is given and constant.

(3) m different kinds of consumers' goods (A), (B), (C), $[m = 3]$, (A) being the standard commodity.

(4) n different kinds of producers' goods (T) land, (P) persons; (K), capital goods in the narrow sense. $[n = 3]$.

(5) nm technical coefficients a_t a_p a_k, b_t b_p b_k, c_t c_p c_k.

Unknown: (1) $m-1$ prices of consumers' goods: p_b, p_c, $(p_a = 1)$.

(2) n prices of productive services: p_t, p_p, p_k.

(3) m quantities of consumers' goods demanded, D_a, D_b, and D_c being sums of the individuals d_a's, d_b's, and d_c's.

(4) n quantities of productive services supplied, O_t, O_p, O_k being sums of the individual o_t's, o_p's, o_k's.

Such are the symbols which Walras uses. While he refrains from defining numerically the large, but finite, quantity of categories of commodities and productive services, it has been found convenient here to reduce the number in each case to manageable proportions. Now it is possible to present in brief and simple form, without sacrifice of principle, the following sets of Walrasian equations portraying equilibrium in production both for the individual and for society as a whole.

INDIVIDUAL CASE

$$\frac{\phi_t (q_t - o_t)}{p_t} = \frac{\phi_p (q_p - o_p)}{p_p} = \frac{\phi_k (q_k - o_k)}{p_k} = \frac{\phi_a (d_a)}{1} = \frac{\phi_b (d_b)}{p_b}$$

$$= \frac{\phi_c (d_c)}{p_c} = \frac{\Phi_e (q_e + d_e)}{p_e} . \tag{1}$$

[4] The boldface symbols should be ignored until they are specifically referred to.

$$o_t p_t + o_p p_p + o_k p_k = d_a + d_b p_b + d_c p_c + \mathbf{d_e p_e} \tag{2}$$

$$o_t = f_t(p_t,\, p_p,\, p_k,\, p_b,\, p_c,\, p_d,\, \mathbf{p_e}); \quad o_p = f_p(\ ); \quad o_k = f_k(\ ) \tag{3}$$

$$d_b = f_b(\ ); \qquad d_c = f_c(\ ); \qquad \mathbf{d_e} = \mathbf{f_e}(\ ) \tag{4}$$

$$d_a = o_t p_t + o_p p_p + o_k p_k - (d_b p_b + d_c p_c + \mathbf{d_e p_e}) \tag{5}$$

SOCIAL CASE

$$\left.\begin{array}{l} O_t = F_t(\ ); \quad O_p = F_p(\ ); \quad O_k = F_k(\ ); \\[2mm] \mathbf{D_e p_e} = \mathbf{F_e}(\ )\mathbf{p_e} = \mathbf{F_e}(\mathbf{p_t},\, \mathbf{p_p},\, \mathbf{p_k},\, \mathbf{p_b},\, \mathbf{p_c},\, i) \end{array}\right\} \begin{array}{c} n \text{ equations} \\ + \\ 1 \text{ equation} \end{array} \tag{I}$$

$$\left.\begin{array}{l} D_b = F_b(\ ); \quad D_c = F_c(\ ); \\[2mm] D_a = O_t p_t + O_p p_p + O_k p_k - (D_b p_b + D_c p_c + \mathbf{D_e p_e}) \end{array}\right\} \begin{array}{c} m - 1 \text{ equations} \\ + \\ 1 \text{ equation} \end{array} \tag{II}$$

$$\left.\begin{array}{l} a_t D_a + b_t D_b + c_t D_c + \mathbf{k_t D_k} = O_t \\ a_p D_a + b_p D_b + c_p D_c + \mathbf{k_p D_k} = O_p \\ a_k D_a + b_k D_b + c_k D_c + \mathbf{k_k D_k} = O_k \\ \mathbf{D_k P_t} = \mathbf{D_e p_e} = \mathbf{E} \end{array}\right\} \begin{array}{c} n \text{ equations} \\ + \\ 1 \text{ equation} \end{array} \tag{III}$$

$$\left.\begin{array}{l} a_t p_t + a_p p_p + a_k p_k = 1 \\ b_t p_t + b_p p_p + b_k p_k = p_b \\ c_t p_t + c_p p_p + c_k p_k = p_c \\ \mathbf{k_t p_t} + \mathbf{k_p p_p} + \mathbf{k_k p_k} = \mathbf{P_k} \end{array}\right\} \begin{array}{c} m \text{ equations} \\ + \\ 1 \text{ equation} \end{array} \tag{IV}$$

$$\mathbf{P_k} = \frac{\mathbf{p_k}}{i + \mu + \nu} \qquad \left.\right\} 1 \text{ equation} \tag{V}$$

Of the $2m + 2n$ equations of systems (I) to (IV) (exclusive of the boldface symbols), one can be shown to be redundant; so that we have at least one of the conditions necessary for a solution, namely, that the number of independent equations is equal to the number of unknowns.

Walras' whole theory of capitalization and capital accumulation consists in an extension, pure and simple, of this composite system in order to include the prices and quantities exchanged of capital goods. It is my contention that, while it is perfectly possible to extend this static system to include the pricing of old capital goods, it is not possible to bring within the static structure a theory of capital accumulation without damaging both the structure and theory.

Walras quite correctly feels that, before discussing the logic of price determination in the case of capital goods, it is necessary to establish a *raison d'être* for a capital goods market. He finds a *raison d'être* consistent with the static scheme by simply assuming that at all times some persons are eating into their capital by spending more than their incomes, while others are spending less than their incomes and buying up the spendthrifts' capital goods. Assuming this state of affairs, we may ask: What would anyone be willing to pay for a capital good (now to be distinguished from its service),[5] in view of the fact that the capital goods under consideration have no direct utility of their own, which precludes the possibility of their prices being determined on the basis of systems (I) and (II) of the production equilibrium equations (exclusive of boldface symbols)? Capital goods, if demanded at all, are wanted not for their utility, which does not exist, but for the incomes they yield; and then again not for their whole income but for their net income, these incomes begin in the form of productive services. If we designate the gross income of a unit of capital good, priced in terms of the standard commodity, by p_k; the price of the capital good by P_k; the rate of depreciation as a technologically given percentage ν_k of P_k; and the rate of insurance as an actuarially given percentage μ_k of P_k, then the net income is

$$\pi_k = p_k - (\mu_k + \nu_k)P_k ,$$

from which we can obtain a rate of net income

$$i = \frac{\pi_k}{P_k} = \frac{p_k - (\mu_k + \nu_k)P_k}{P_k} .$$

By transposing, we may express the price of the capital good as

$$P_k = \frac{p_k}{i + \mu_k + \nu_k} = \frac{\pi_k}{i} ,$$

for any given i. In the case of land μ and ν are zero.

This is capitalization in the familiar sense of the term. While it furnishes a concept necessary for the discussion, it explains nothing, for

---

[5] It should be carefully noted that the theory of production gives the prices of the *services* of capital goods but not of the capital goods themselves. The equations of production (exclusive of the boldface symbols) on p. 40 show how the prices of even those productive services which have no direct utility are determined. Walras' "Théorie de la capitalisation" was designed particularly to enlarge the machinery of price determination in order to include the prices of capital goods as well as the prices of their services.

it still does not tell us why there should be a demand for, and supply of, capital goods. If all persons in our community just lived within their gross incomes, so that there were no spendthrifts and no savers in any sense, the result would be twofold: (1) there would be no buying or selling of existing capital goods and (2) there would be no replacement of worn-out and accidentally destroyed capital goods. The net conse-quence would be a gradual diminution in the stock of capital goods and hence a gradual shrinkage of incomes. We should, then, have not a static state but a retrogressive state. The demand for capital goods is, therefore, a necessary condition for the existence of a static society, for dissavers are not only those who sell their capital assets in exchange for the unconsumed consumers' goods of savers but also those who fail to provide for replacements. If individuals provide for replacements, it is not because they are interested in utilityless capital goods but because they are concerned about their incomes. To keep income intact in the future the individual would have to distribute his present income, that is, $q_i p_i + q_p p_p + q_k p_k$, among: ($\alpha$) the productive services retained for his own use; (β) consumers' goods purchased; and (γ) capital replacements, as follows:

$$q_i p_i + q_p p_p + q_k p_k = \overbrace{(q_i - o_i)p_i + (q_p - o_p)p_p + (q_k - o_k)p_k}^{\alpha}$$

$$\overbrace{+ d_a + d_b p_b + d_c p_c}^{\beta} + \overbrace{q_k(\mu_k + \nu_k)P_k}^{\gamma},$$

which, when simplified, becomes

$$\underbrace{o_i p_i + o_p p_p + o_k p_k - (d_a + d_b p_b + d_c p_c)}_{e} = q_k(\mu_k + \nu_k)P_k .$$

It is curious to note that Walras appears to take it arbitrarily for granted under the blanket assumption of a progressive state that, for the community as a whole, the left member of the above equation, which he designates as e (= *excédent*), will not merely equal the right member, but will be more than equal, so that, if there are Θ individuals in our community, we have

$$\sum_{j=1}^{j=\Theta} e_j > \sum_{j=1}^{j=\Theta} q_{k,j}(\nu_k + \mu_k)P_k .$$

Neither the provision for maintenance capital nor the provision for additional capital is as arbitrary as it seems, for it is easy enough to subsume both under the next argument which deals with the demand for more net income. In other words, if we can find a way to set up a demand function for additional net income, similar to the demand functions for anything else, the point at which the aggregate quantity demanded of new net income is zero defines the stationary state; the points at which this quantity is negative define the retrogressive state; and the points at which it is positive define the progressive state.

In the first three editions of the *Eléments* the argument did not take this course. There was no reference at all to the demand for net income. Walras simply set down an arbitrary, or what he called an empirical, gross savings function, in which the independent variables were the prices of all the products and services and also the rate of net income. He added that, if we wished to derive such a savings function from his general system, we should have to look upon utility in a new light and distinguish between present and future utilities. But actually he himself did nothing beyond asserting the possibility of such a derivation.

In his fourth edition, however, he boldly included his savings function in his total system which rests on a foundation of utility functions; but he deals here not with gross savings but with net savings which he puts in the form of what is spent on acquiring additional net income. Although he drops all reference to the difference between present and future utility, we must be careful not to interpret this as meaning that Walras repudiated or denied the element of time in his theory of savings. Given the whole structure of his general equilibrium theory, which is, as Wicksell so aptly points out, a cross-section in time of the processes involving exchange, production, capital accumulation, and circulating media, it would have been irrelevant for Walras to include any function of a lapse of time explicitly. Moreover, in a letter to Böhm-Bawerk, dated May 5, 1889, and in the Preface to the second edition of the *Eléments*, dated the same year, he indicated that he could not take the difference in value between present and future goods as a datum, for that very difference in Walras' system is a variable, functionally related to all other variables, including income. That did not preclude him, of course, from taking the preference function itself as a datum.

The precise manner in which Walras introduces his savings function into his system is this. He invents an imaginary commodity, E, which consists of perpetual annuity shares, each entitling the holder to the equivalent of one unit of standard commodity per annum. Referring back to the capitalization equation

$$i = \frac{p_k - (\mu_k + \nu_k)P_k}{p_k} \, ,$$

and replacing the numerator by unity and the denominator by p_e, representing the price of the income-yielding perpetual annuity, we obtain

$$i = \frac{1}{p_e}, \qquad \text{or} \qquad p_e = \frac{1}{i} \cdot$$

This is the same thing as the formula for the discounted present value of an infinite series of net incomes. Furthermore, at the moment at which we are trying to obtain a cross-section portrayal of relationships, any individual may be regarded as possessing a certain stock of these shares, which will be numerically equivalent to his net income also expressed in terms of the standard commodity, according to the following equation:[6]

$$q_e = q_i p_i + q_p p_p + q_k \pi_k \cdot$$

Each individual has not only a given net income at any moment of time but also a desire for net income. Although the net income is to be received in the future, the desire is felt now; and this desire will express itself now, according to the Walrasian scheme of things, as a function of the quantity of net income possessed, or $\phi_e(q_e)$. We may look at this as the marginal degree of utility function for perpetual annuity shares. And our individual, having regard to his income and the general price constellation, will decide to demand more or less of these shares—he may even decide to offer some—until equation (1) of maximum satisfaction is extended to include $[\phi_e(q_e + d_e)]/p_e$.[7] Assuming that he demands some of these shares, the quantity demanded times price must enter into our budgetary equation (2) as $d_e p_e$ on the right side. In this way Walras attempts to handle an essentially dynamic concept with the aid of the tools of static theory. What the individual is purchasing when he buys a hypothetical perpetual annuity share is betterment. And in Walras' static system betterment is a commodity which can be bought and sold like any other commodity and for which an individual is presumed to have a desire or utility function like any other desire or utility function. The price of a unit of betterment (the reciprocal of the rate of capitalization) is thus determined in the same way as all other prices. Equations (1) and (2) as now amended are extremely interesting, for they make quite plain that there is no antithesis between Adam Smith's desire to better one's condition and Walras' desire to maximize satisfaction, for at any moment of time an individual can only undertake to better his

---

[6] I have modified Walras' statement slightly by changing his π_p to p_p in order to avoid subsidiary issues not immediately relevant to the present argument.
[7] See first system of equations, (1), on p. 144, boldface addendum.

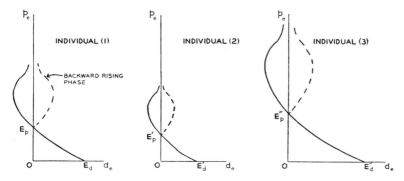

Figure 1. Individual demand and supply of perpetual annuity shares

condition within the limits of the resources he has at his disposal. From our modified (1) and (2) we obtain an additional demand function for equation (4), viz., $d_e = f_e (\ \ )$, after suitably amending the other demand and supply functions to include the price of the standard commodity among all the other prices. This demand function will behave like all other Walrasian demand functions and will become a supply function as the price continues to rise.

Walras describes a geometrical representation of this theory demand,[8] which I am giving on Marshallian axes (Fig. 1) to make it look a little more familiar to readers brought up in the Cambridge tradition. It will be recognized at once that offer segments of these continuous curves are really dissaving functions. Hence the intersection of the aggregate social demand and social supply curves for these shares (Fig. 2) will only give us the price of the share $D'_e\beta = p'_e$ at which dissaving is exactly equal to saving. The p'_e is, therefore, the price of the share in the stationary state. To obtain a demand curve for new shares, we must subtract horizontally the $\alpha\beta$ segment of the supply curve from the demand curve $E''_p \Sigma E_d$ which gives us the curve $p'_eG \Sigma E_d$. This is the curve of net demand for

    [8] *Eléments*, pp. 251–52. In Fig. 1, OE'_d, OE'_d, and OE''_d represent the amounts of perpetual annuity shares taken by individuals (1), (2), and (3), respectively, when the price per share p_e is zero. These amounts decrease as p_e rises, and become zero for our individuals at E_p, E'_p, and E''_p, respectively. At still higher prices our individuals no longer demand, but offer, the shares. For example, as p_e rises above E_p, individual (1) first offers increasing amounts and then decreasing amounts. This is shown by the continuation of the E_dE_p curve to the left of the vertical axis. The offer segment when pivoted around the vertical axis is brought (in the form of the broken-line curve) into the same quadrant as the demand curve. This is done for each individual. Figure 2 is, then, constructed by the horizontal summation of the individual demand curves, giving the social demand curve $E''_p \Sigma E_d$, and by the horizontal summation of the individual offer curves, giving the broken-line social supply curve $\alpha\beta\gamma$.

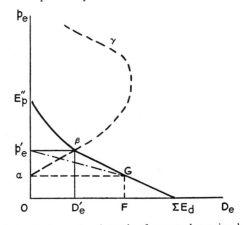

Figure 2. Social demand and supply of perpetual annuity shares

more perpetual annuity shares in our community, and the equation of that curve is

$$D_e = F_e(p_t, p_p, p_k, p_b, p_c, p_e) .$$

If we multiply both sides of this equation by p_e , we obtain the supply function of savings

$$D_e p_e = F_e(p_t, p_p, p_k, p_b, p_c, p_e)p_e ,$$

which may also be expressed — in view of the fact that $p_e = 1/i$—as

$$D_e p_e = \mathbf{F}_e(p_t, p_p, p_k, p_b, p_c, i) .$$

This we may add to our system of equations (I), at the same time that we add p_e to the independent variables of the supply and demand equations of systems (I) and (II).

Furthermore, we can translate geometrically our demand curve for perpetual annuity shares $p'_e G \Sigma E_d$ into a supply curve of savings as a function of the rate of net income $i = 1/p_e$. A decision to purchase, say, αG units of perpetual annuity shares is tantamount to a decision to save or set aside the equivalent of $O\alpha GF$ units of standard commodity when the rate of new income is $1/O\alpha$. Following this through for the reciprocals of all values of p_e from O to p'_e, and setting up abscissas proportional to the inscribed rectangles, we obtain the $i'\epsilon T$ curve shown in Figure 3. It is obvious that in order to find an equilibrium rate of net income that would correspond to an equilibrium rate of capital accumulation, we must have a demand for these net savings. Walras gives one, namely,

$$\frac{D_k \pi_k}{i} = D_k \frac{p_k}{i + \mu_k + \nu_k} = D_k P_k ,$$

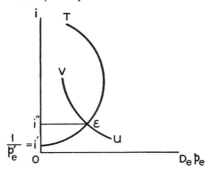

Figure 3. Supply and demand curves of net savings as a function of i, other
things remaining equal

which is obviously a decreasing function of i and which is represented
by the curve $V\epsilon U$. Where the two curves intersect, $D_e p_e = D_k p_k$. Here D_k
is defined by Walras as the quantity of capital goods *to be* manufactured;
and this quantity is determined at the point where the capitalized value
of a unit of capital good is equal to its cost of production:

$$P_k = \frac{p_k}{i + \mu_k + \nu_k} = k_t p_t + k_p p_p + k_k p_k .$$

All this has the *appearance* of giving a satisfactory solution to the whole
problem of capital accumulation. It gives us the negatively inclined
demand curve $V\epsilon U$ of our Figure 3. Also it enables us to add enough
new equations to the system with which we started to make it mathematically determinate.

New Unknowns	New Equations
D_e	$D_e p_e = \mathbf{F}_e(\ )$
D_k	$D_k P_k = D_e p_e$
P_k	$P_k = k_t p_t + k_p p_p + k_k p_k$
$P_e = \dfrac{1}{i}$	$P_k = \dfrac{p_k}{i + \mu_k + \nu_k}$

In spite of this apparent determinacy, it is not at all clear, to me at
least, where the D_k came from. It seems to me to be an adventitious
element which is neither directly nor indirectly related to the utility
functions which constitute, as it were, the primary motive for the whole
system. Walras went to a great deal of trouble to make decisions to save
an integral part of his equilibrium structure, but he gives no clue at all
to the reasons for decisions to manufacture, or decisions to invest in,
new capital goods. Whatever rationally determined demand for savings

there was has already been taken care of in the dissaving function. The demand for still more savings on the part of the manufacturers of capital goods is not given a rational basis in Walras' system. If this view is correct, Walras' theory of capital accumulation remains indeterminate. And if I am right, the indeterminacy is due either to an inherent defect in Walras' static system or to an unfortunate attempt to squeeze an essentially dynamic phenomenon[9] into a static framework. I think the latter reason is more probable.

[9] Walras' theory of capital formation has every appearance of a static theory in that the mere decision of an individual to spend part of his income on some means of increasing his income has no effect at the moment of decision upon his *resources* and in that the mere decision to add to the existing stock of utilityless capital goods can neither arise from any change in *tastes* nor give rise immediately to any change in *technique*. If, however, these decisions are affected by *uncertain expectations* as to the future income to be derived from investments of savings in view, i.e., additional capital goods, then the phenomenon belongs properly to the realm of dynamics (see J. R. Hicks, *Value and Capital,* [London: Oxford University Press, 1939] chap. IX). Though Walras failed to incorporate the concept of expectations in his theoretical structure, he recognized its importance as an afterthought. At the very close of his discussion of capital accumulation we find the following passage, which I have translated, from pp. 292 and 293 of the *Eléments:* "We must remember that the income of new capital goods is not known with the same degree of certainty as that of existing capital goods. It may prove to be larger or smaller than anticipated; in short, it is more problematical. . . . Then, too, we must remember that the price of capital goods varies by reason, not only of past changes, but also of expected changes in gross income or in rates of depreciation and insurance; and that, so far as future changes are concerned, the expectations differ from individual to individual."

10

WALRAS'S THEORY OF CAPITAL FORMATION IN THE FRAMEWORK OF HIS THEORY OF GENERAL EQUILIBRIUM

Probably the most difficult component of the *Elements of Pure Economics* is Part V of the definitive edition, entitled "Theory of Capital Formation and Credit." The proof of its difficulty, even for its most erudite readers, is revealed by the paucity of commentaries published on that part and by the abundance of unpublished correspondence that deals with that aspect of the Walrasian system. That it constituted for Walras himself a veritable stumbling block is equally well demonstrated by the numerous revisions that he made to his theory of capital formation in the course of the successive editions of the *Elements* that appeared during his lifetime. These revisions not only dealt with the substance but also affected the location of the theory in his system of general equilibrium. In fact, if one wishes to achieve a better comprehension of the theory, it is necessary to follow it through the changes to which it has been submitted in its successive versions, and to consider it from the point of view of the place it occupies in the totality of Walras's system. This is what I propose to do in this study.

If we refer to the first edition (1874–7), we see that Walras posed the problem but did not get very far in his efforts to solve it. He posed the problem at the very beginning of Part V of the first edition, entitled "Conditions and Consequences of Economic Progress." This should not be confused with Part V of the fourth edition (1900) or of the definitive edition (1926), which is entitled "Theory of Capital Formation and Credit," and which is placed considerably before a new Part VII that carries the title "Conditions and Consequences of Economic Progress."

Walras began the 45th Lesson of the first edition with a significant paragraph that reads: "The existence of different kinds of income (T),

This paper was read at the Institute of Applied Economic Science in Paris on October 29, 1952, during the course of the first of three "Walrasian days," devoted to the life and works of the great economist. My research was made possible by a Fulbright grant, a grant from the Social Research Council, and my stay at the Institute of Applied Economic Science. The article was translated from the French by Donald A. Walker.

(T′), (T″) . . . (P), (P′), (P″) . . . (K), (K′), (K″) . . . from land, persons
and capital proper presupposes the existence of landed capital, personal
capital and capital goods of corresponding categories. In the preceding
pages we have determined the prices of various types of income, but we
have not yet determined the prices of the capital goods yielding these
incomes in the form of uses and services. The determination of the
prices of capital goods is the third major problem of the mathematical
theory of social wealth. It is with this problem that Part V is now
concerned."[1] This clear statement of the problem remains unchanged
throughout the five editions of the work – except for the number given to
the section.[2]

The changes in the place that Walras assigned in his *Elements* to this
problem are of more than philological interest, for they reflect the long
and painful hesitations that he experienced during the whole of a
quarter of a century in his efforts to insert the theory of capital formation
into his larger conception of general equilibrium. Where, then, is the
theory of capital to be situated? This question does not arise with respect
to the theory of pure exchange, that is to say, with respect to the theory
of determination of the price of commodities, nor with regard to the
theory of production, that is to say, the theory of the determination of the
prices of productive services. Subject to certain reasonable assumptions,
these theories easily find their place in a static framework. The same
cannot be said of the theory of capital formation, which is concerned not
only with the determination of the prices of capital goods, but also with
the formation of capital. We know that *Value and Capital,* the title of the
book by Professor John R. Hicks, tries to evoke the idea of statics and of
dynamics, the word capital symbolizing, as a synecdoche, the whole of
the dynamic part of Hicks's theory. In fact, the author tells us that
economic statics is "quite incompetent to deal properly with capital, or
interest, or trade fluctuations, or even money."[3] It can be said that it is
generally recognized that the study of the phenomenon of capital is part
of economic dynamics and not of statics, however these terms may be
defined. That seems to have been the position of Walras in the first
edition, because he placed the theory of capital formation under the
heading of economic progress. This procedure confronted him, however, with a serious dilemma and explains why he agonized over the
subject without ever reaching complete peace of mind. Either he was
obliged to consider capital goods as a purely dynamic concept, in which

[1] First edition, p. 273. [The wording of this quotation is taken from Léon Walras,
Elements of Pure Economics, translated and annotated by William Jaffé, Irwin, Homewood,
Ill., 1954, p. 267.]
[2] Definitive edition, section 231, p. 241.
[3] *Value and Capital,* Oxford University Press, Oxford, 1939, p. 116.

case he could not integrate it into his model of static equilibrium, or he was forced to treat capital goods as a static phenomenon, in which case it would no longer be relevant for the topic of economic progress. In his first edition he forced himself to hold both these positions simultaneously; but the changes that he introduced into the second show how much that attempt left him ill at ease.

What exactly does the first edition say?[4] To begin with, we note that because Walras speaks of the determination of the prices of capital goods, he ought to establish a raison d'être for their purchase and sale and, consequently, for their prices. Capital goods are not, in general, demanded for themselves. Only consumer goods and services satisfy needs. Nevertheless, because consumption goods and services are, for the most part, commodities that result from productive services that are produced by the factors of production, it is necessary to have land, labor and capital proper, for these are the source of the services provided by consumption goods and the services provided by the producers' goods. Up to this point all is well. We have limited ourselves to the declaration of a physical condition, but this leaves unanswered the entire question of why capital goods have prices. One category of capital, namely human beings, which Walras called personal capital, does not have an effective price, except in a system of slavery – but it must have a virtual price. What of the other sorts of capital, such as land and capital proper? Why should they be objects of exchange and have rates of exchange? If we suppose that the quantities of land, of labor, and of capital proper are fixed and that they are distributed in a given manner, there is no imperative reason why there must exist a market for each of them. Whoever is not an owner of them need only demand the services of a factor of production and not the factor itself.

Under these conditions, those who do not own the factors of production need only buy capital services or hire the factors – as is done in the case of personal capital. This gives rise to prices for factor-services and to fees for hiring different sorts of factors, but not to prices for capital goods themselves determined in markets for them. It was at this point that Walras found it necessary to abandon the stationary state and to take up the notion of a progressive state in which personal capital and capital proper are not fixed quantities, but are capable of growth. In a progressive state there must be entrepreneurs who are engaged in the production of new capital goods and services. The difference between income and consumption is then utilized to purchase capital goods. We should not lose sight of the fact that throughout his exposition at this stage of his argument Walras was abstracting from the existence of

[4] Lessons 45 to 49.

money as a store of value, using a *numéraire* that has no other function than that of a measure of exchange values. It follows that savings necessarily equal investment in new capital goods. Indeed, if we examine the question from a social point of view, on a simplifying assumption of that nature, the act of saving appears identical to the act of creating new capital goods. But if we turn to the point of view of individuals, it appears that those who "save" out of their incomes can be perfectly separate and distinct from those who construct new capital goods. Furthermore, competition will adjust the market price of capital proper to its cost of production. It is also the case that arbitrage will equalize the net rates of return of all capital goods, however varied they may be. These equalities previously established by Walras in the theory of exchange and in the theory of production constitute, according to Walras, the essential and necessary elements of the determination of the prices of capital goods. But they are not sufficient conditions, for it is clear that nothing in what has been said up to this point explains the fact of saving or the demand for capital goods.

All the first edition does is to indicate the existence of an individual savings function and an aggregate savings function. The individual savings function in the first edition has the following form:[5]

$$e = f_e(P_t \ldots P_p \ldots p_k, P_{k'}, P_{k''}, \ldots P_b, P_c, P_d, \ldots i) \qquad (\alpha)$$

in which e is the excess of income over consumption, $p_t \ldots p_p \ldots p_k$, $p_{k'}, p_{k''} \ldots$ are the prices of the productive services of land, labor, and capital proper, and i is the common rate of net return of all capital goods, with all prices expressed in terms of the *numéraire* commodity (A). Walras's own comments on this individual savings function read as follows: "We present that savings equation empirically. . . . We might, of course, have investigated the arguments of the savings function, as we did the arguments of the effective demand function. Evidently, in order to do so it would be necessary to consider utility from a new point of view, distinguishing *present* and *future* utility. Without denying for a moment the possibility of tracing the function back to its causal elements, we shall, nevertheless, not do so, but remain with its empirical representation, for that is all we need for the present. It suffices to postulate that the function is increasing or decreasing according as the value of i increases or decreases, inasmuch as it would be absurd to suppose that a man who decides upon a certain amount of savings under given conditions of net income would be unwilling to save at least as much under better conditions."[6]

With the use of similar individual savings functions, Walras has no

[5] First edition, p. 283.   [6] Ibid., pp. 283–4.

difficulty in obtaining $E = F_\epsilon (\dots)$ as an aggregate savings function by simple addition. Then, $D_k, D_{k'}, D_{k''}, \dots$, being the respective quantities of new capital goods (K), (K'), (K''), ..., he writes the equation[7]

$$D_k P_k + D_{k'} P_{k'} + D_{k''} P_{k''} + \dots = E \qquad (\beta)$$

in which $P_k, P_{k'}, P_{k''}, \dots$, are the prices of capital goods. In equilibrium, each such price is equal to the cost of production of the capital good and to the capitalized value of the stream of net income generated by the capital good.

It is, *grosso modo*, at this point that Walras leaves the important subject of the determination of the equilibrium prices of capital goods in the first edition of his work. He establishes a system of eight equations containing as many unknowns as there are equations, so that it appears, at first glance, to solve the problem satisfactorily. On closer examination, however, it is seen to be inadequate for a number of reasons, but above all because $D_k, D_{k'}, D_{k''} \dots$, represent specific quantities demanded which, although mathematically determinate in the system of eight equations, lack any economic rationale. The quantities demanded of consumption goods are, in the last analysis, derived in a rigorous fashion from their utility functions. But, in the first edition of the *Elements,* the demand for capital goods is only vaguely linked to the idea of economic progress.

Before turning to the subsequent editions of the *Elements,* I wish to call special attention to a particular point, namely, the definition that Walras gave to savings, because it is important to be mindful of that definition when one discusses the later versions of Walras's theory of capital formation. He defined savings as "the positive difference between the excess of income over consumption, on the one hand, and the amount necessary to cover the depreciation and insurance of capital goods proper, on the other hand.[8] Thus by the word "savings" he meant *net* savings corresponding to *net* growth of capital. It is only when net savings and net growth of capital exist that we have a progressive economy. The *e* of equation (α) and the E of equation (β) of the first edition do not represent savings, but only the excess of income over consumption. It follows that equation (β) is compatible with a stationary economy or even a regressive one, if E is equal to or less than the depreciation and insurance charges. This fact, which is characteristic of the whole mathematical apparatus employed by Walras in that section of the first edition, is symptomatic of the problem. It underscores a fundamental inconsistency in the 1877 exposition of his theory of capital

[7] Ibid., p. 284.   [8] Ibid., p. 282.

formation. Although he postulated in principle a dynamic economy, his analysis nevertheless remains static.

I leave to one side the problem of the *tâtonnements,* that is to say of the adjustments toward equilibrium that Walras called the process of the establishment of equilibrium in order to distinguish it from the determination of equilibrium,[9] and I confine myself to the determination or to the definition of equilibrium. The fact that the equations of capital goods are established in these terms confirms the statical character of that analysis.

The second edition of the *Elements* appeared in 1889. In that edition we find not only significant changes in certain details of the theory presented in the first edition, but also a very important innovation dealt with in a new lesson, the 26th in the second edition, which improved upon the integration of the theory of capital formation within the first Parts of the *Elements.*

In the second edition, the lessons that dealt with capital formation formed a distinct section and no longer appeared under the title "Conditions and Consequences of Economic Progress." The new Part IV is titled "Theory of Capital Formation and Credit." In fact, the second edition does not contain any section dealing with economic progress, but only a lesson numbered 28, which follows the lessons on capital formation in Part IV and which has as its title: "Of the Increase in the Quantity of Products. The Laws of the General Variation of Prices in a Progressive Society." Nevertheless, the economy treated in the lessons on capital goods is still a progressive economy, because new capital goods appear in that section, representing the net growth of total capital; and the growth in the quantity of output is a necessary consequence of this fact. The analysis of the second edition is, however, even more static than in the preceding one.

Two matters of detail are worth remembering in considering Walras's reformulation of the material of the first edition. The first concerns the form of the function that connects the excess of income over consumption to the rate of net revenue i. In the first edition, it is defined as a "function that increases or decreases with the increasing or decreasing value of i."[10] In the second, its definition conforms more to the Walrasian theory of supply functions. It is generally presented as a "successively increasing and decreasing function of i, from zero to zero."[11] The second change in the details of the exposition is more interesting, because it gives an idea of the way in which Walras anticipated Keynes.

---

[9] Lessons 48 and 49 of the first edition (Lesson 25 in the following editions).
[10] Part V, p. 293, n. 1, *supra.*   [11] Second edition, p. 285.

In the first edition, when Walras set down the equation that we have numbered (α), e was defined for any given individual:

$$e = (o_t P_t + \ldots + o_p P_p + \ldots + o_k P_k + o_{k\prime} P_{k\prime} + o_{k\prime\prime} P_{k\prime\prime} + \ldots) -$$

(Individual income)

$$- (d_a + d_b p_b + d_c + P_c + \ldots)$$

(Individual consumption)

This is an equation in which $o_t \ldots, o_p \ldots, o_k, o_{k\prime}, o_{k\prime\prime} \ldots$, are the quantities of the various services that are sold; $p_t \ldots, p_p \ldots, p_k, p_{k\prime}, p_{k\prime\prime} \ldots$, are the prices per unit for these services; $d_a, d_b, d_c \ldots$, are the quantities of the consumption goods purchased, and $p_b, p_c \ldots$, are the prices per unit of these commodities, all prices being expressed in terms of (A), so that $p_\alpha = 1$. We have, in consequence, for the economy as a whole:

$$E = (O_t p_t + \ldots + O_p p_p + \ldots + O_k p_k + O_{k\prime} p_{k\prime} + O_{k\prime\prime} p_{k\prime\prime}) -$$

(Total income)

$$- (D_a + D_b p_b + D_c p_c + \ldots)$$

(Total consumption)

It follows that:[12]

$$D_a = (O_t p_t + \ldots + O_p p_p + \ldots + O_k p_k + O_{k\prime} p_{k\prime} + O_{k\prime\prime} p_{k\prime\prime}) -$$

$$- (E + D_b p_b + D_c p_c + \ldots) \qquad (\gamma)$$

This last equation is significant because (A) is the commodity that serves as *numéraire*. Thus, given the fact that "capital goods proper are rented in the form of money" and that "the capitalist accumulates his capital by saving in money,"[13] we are obliged to recognize the existence of an intermediate market in which savings are exchanged for capital goods, and to take cognizance of the money market where credit transactions take place. Although Walras abstracted from money in Part IV of the second edition, because he did not discuss monetary theory before Part V—a procedure that does not involve a question of principle

[12] First edition, pp. 287 and 292.   [13] Ibid., p. 277.

but only a method of exposition — the *numéraire* in the theory of capital formation is truly a commodity money, and fulfills all the functions of money. Thus the market in which *numéraire*-capital is lent appears as an extension of the market for capital goods, similar to the money market. Walras described the left member of equation (β) as being "the demand for *numéraire*-capital by the entrepreneurs who produce products and who would just as soon borrow *numéraire*-capital as rent existing capital goods," and the right member as being "the offer of *numéraire*-capital by those who create the excess of income over consumption,"[14] but equation (γ) in fact expresses nothing other than the demand for (A) as a consumption good, just like the demand function of all the other consumption goods (B), (C), etc. There is, therefore, no way to express the demand for (A) as *numéraire*-capital. Everything is presented as if the *numéraire*-capital (A) is *immediately* converted into capital goods, without any interval of time being provided for its accumulation.

It is clear that when Walras prepared the second edition of his work, he understood that the assumption implicitly contained in equation (γ), that is to say, the assumption that *numéraire*-capital is immediately converted into capital goods, is equivalent to assuming away the existence of the intermediate credit market. This explains why he made a very clear distinction in sections 250 and 251 of the second edition between the market for *numéraire*-capital and the market for capital goods, showing at the same time the relations that exist between the two markets. The reason for a "preference for liquidity" in terms of (A) was not given before the fourth edition, in which he developed the concept of the utility of availability in Part VI, which deals with the theory of circulation and money. But, given the existence of any demand whatsoever for (A) that is not destined for immediate consumption, D_a cannot represent the total demand for (A) and the total demand cannot be determined by the system of equations for the demand for consumption goods alone. Furthermore, we no longer find equation (γ) in the second edition among the equations of the demand for consumption goods. The equation containing D_a is relegated to the very end of the system of equations that determines the prices of consumption goods, productive services, and capital goods. It is formulated in the following manner:[15]

$$\Omega_a p_a + D_k P_k + D_{k'} P_{k'} + D_{k''} + P_{k''} + \ldots = D_a + E \qquad (\delta)$$

where Ω_a is the quantity produced of (A), and p_a is the cost of the

[14] Ibid., p. 299.
[15] Cf. p. 292 of the first edition with pp. 282–3 of the second edition.

production of (A), which in equilibrium is equal to unity and can therefore be neglected in the present inquiry. It follows that

$$\Omega_a - D_a = E - (D_k P_k + D_{k'} P_{k'} + D_{k''} + P_{k''} + \ldots) \qquad (\epsilon)$$

which represents the aggregate of the noninvested excess of income over consumption held at any moment of time and not destined for consumption, expressed in terms of (A).

We shall say no more about the corrections that are to be found in the second edition; instead we now consider its innovations. First of all, we recall that in the first edition D_k, $D_{k'}$, $D_{k''}$ . . . , although mathematically determinate, do not appear to have an economic rationale. It was in this respect that the Walrasian system had a serious deficiency, one to which I called attention for the first time in my article "Léon Walras' Theory of Capital Accumulation," which appeared in the Henry Schultz memorial volume published in 1942 with the title *Studies in Mathematical Economics and Econometrics,* edited by Oskar Lange and others.[16] Although that article was based upon the definitive edition of the *Elements* (1926), I did not notice that the deficiency had occurred as early as the second edition. The significance of the 26th and 27th lessons of the definitive edition, which were only an extension of the subject of the 26th Lesson of the second edition, was not perfectly clear to me. I want to take the present opportunity to correct my error, and, at the same time, to explain it, because that explanation may help others to achieve a better understanding of Walras's theory of capital formation.

One of the titles of the 26th Lesson of the second edition is: "The Theorem of the Maximum Utility of New Capital Goods." Walras directed his attention specifically, in the first part of this lesson, to furnishing for the demand for capital goods a basis identical to that which he had furnished for the demand for consumption goods. That basis is *rareté,* which Walras had always considered as "the cause of exchange value."[17] Because capital goods have exchange value, the cause of that value must be, in the last analysis, the same as the cause of the exchange value of consumption goods. If there is a difference, it arises from the circumstance that the utility of capital goods that yield productive services is derived rather than direct. Only consumption goods and services have a direct utility, but they are generally produced by capital goods, which therefore have an indirect utility. In all the versions of this new aspect of Walras's theory of capital formation, from the second edition to the definitive edition, the mathematical formula-

[16] Chicago, University of Chicago Press, pp. 37–48 [chapter 9 of this volume].
[17] Lesson 18 in the first edition (Lesson 10 in the others).

tion is so fuzzy and muddled that it is almost impossible to understand its complete significance. What Walras succeeded in doing – although in an extremely clumsy fashion – was to advance by one more step to the integration of the theory of capital formation with the rest of his theory of general equilibrium. To the extent that he succeeded in doing this, his analysis of an essentially dynamic phenomenon became more and more static. On the other hand, he approached closer to achieving an extraordinary architectonic unity throughout the whole of his system. That objective was not realized before the fourth edition, in which he took a new step in this direction which, as we will see, was extremely bold. It implied, in effect, Walras's transformation of his primitive and deliberately empirical savings function into a savings function that could be founded, in the last analysis, upon utility functions. I will show the significance of these two new steps when I examine the fourth edition and the definitive edition, which give us the total Walrasian vision in its final form.

It is not necessary to analyze the third edition of 1896, because it is practically identical to the second edition with regard to its treatment of the theory of capital formation.

It is in the fourth edition of 1900 that Walras's theory of capital formation was definitively integrated into the system of general equilibrium. In the last two editions, the lessons on capital formation and credit constitute a distinct part, Part V, from which the lessons on the "Conditions and Consequences of Economic Progress" are totally excluded. The latter issues are relegated to a new Part VII in which the central concept is no longer the formation of capital but marginal productivity. The place finally assigned to the theory of capital formation unequivocally places it within the static framework of analysis. It is easy to charge Walras with inconsistency in this matter, because he continued to consider a progressive economy, new capital goods, and net savings precisely as he had in the first edition. He succeeded nevertheless in taking an instantaneous view of a progressive economy at a given moment and showed the character of general equilibrium at that given moment. What he said about his theory of circulation and money is perfectly applicable to his theory of capital formation. He indicates to us in effect that he poses the problem without leaving the *static* point of view, while at the same time approaching as closely as possible to the *dynamic* point of view.[18]

How did he do that? This is what we are going to try to show in giving an exposition first of his new theory of the savings function, and second of his theory of the maximum utility of capital goods.

[18] Definitive edition (identical in this regard to the fourth), p. 298.

When Walras came to his fourth edition, he was no longer satisfied with his initial summary explanation of the existence of a capital market. That first explanation was based, as we have seen, on the arbitrary hypothesis that some individuals save and that some entrepreneurs produce new capital goods. But we are not told this. In the fourth edition of 1900, Walras not only threw light on this question, but gave explanations that were valid as much for a stationary state as for a progressive state.[19] All he needed to do was to suppose that some people break into their capital by spending more than their current income on consumption goods, whereas others do not spend all their income on consumption goods and instead use their savings to purchase capital goods from those who are dissaving. This is sufficient to cause the formation of a market for capital goods even under the most static conditions that it is possible to conceive, and even if all capital goods by their very nature have a perpetual existence.

Supposing these conditions to be realized, we can pose the following question: what would a person be willing to pay for a capital good, taking account of the fact that capital goods do not themselves have direct utility? Capital goods, insofar as they are demanded, are not desired because of their utility, which does not exist, but because of the income they yield. This refers not to their gross income, but to their net income in the form of productive services. It we designate the gross income from a unit of capital goods, measured in *numéraire,* by p_k; the price of the capital good by P_k; and if we consider the rate of depreciation as a technologically determined percentage μ_k of P_k, and the insurance rate as an actuarially determined percentage ν_k of P_k, the net income will be

$$\pi_k = p_k - (\mu_k + \nu_k)\, P_k$$

from which we obtain a rate of net income

$$i = \frac{\pi_k}{P_k} = \frac{p_k - (\mu_k + \nu_k)\, P_k}{P_k}.$$

By transposing, we can express the price of the capital good as

$$P_k = \frac{p_k}{i + \mu_k + \nu_k} = \frac{\pi_k}{i}$$

for any given value of i. In the case of land, μ and ν are equal to zero.

The foregoing describes capitalization in the familiar sense of the term. That furnishes us a useful concept for our inquiry, but it explains nothing, because it still does not tell us how the demand for and supply

[19] Ibid., p. 244.

of capital goods arise. If all the members of our economic community lived within the limits of their gross incomes, so that there were neither dissavers nor savers, there would be two results: First, there would be neither sale nor purchase of existing capital goods, and, second, there would never be replacement of obsolete or accidentally destroyed capital goods. The consequence would be a gradual diminution of the stock of capital goods, and consequently a gradual shrinking of incomes. When this happens, we should no longer be in a static state but in a regressive state. It follows that the demand for capital goods is a condition that is necessary for the existence of a static society, for the dissavers are not only those who sell their capital goods in exchange for consumption goods which are not consumed by the savers; there are also those who do not provide the necessary replacements. If certain individuals do provide for these replacements, it is not that they are interested in capital goods as such without utility, but because they are concerned with their income. In order to preserve his income intact in the future, an individual must distribute his present gross income, that is to say the value of the services of land, of labor, and of capital at his disposal, $q_t p_t + q_p p_p + q_k p_k{}'$, between: (a) the productive services that he retains for his personal use; (b) the consumption goods that he purchases; and (c) the replacement of capital. This he will do in the way indicated by the following equation:[20]

$$\overbrace{\hspace{8cm}}^{(a)}$$

$$q_t p_t + q_p p_p + q_k p_k = (q_t - o_t)\,p_t + (q_p - o_p)\,p_p + (q_k - o_k)\,p_k +$$

$$\overbrace{\hspace{4cm}}^{(b)} \qquad \overbrace{\hspace{4cm}}^{(c)}$$

$$+\, d_a + d_b p_b + d_c p_c + q_k\,(\mu_k + \nu_k)\,P_k$$

which, after simplification, becomes

$$o_t p_t + o_p p_p + o_k p_k - (d_a + d_b p_b + d_c p_c) = q_k\,(\mu_k + \nu_k)\,P_k$$

As we have already noted, Walras arbitrarily considered it to be evident from the given assumption of a progressive state that, for the community as a whole, the left part of the foregoing equation, which he designates by e (= excess), would not merely be equal to the right member, but greater, in such a manner that if there are θ individuals in the community, we will have

$$\sum_{j=1}^{j=\theta} e_j > \sum_{j=1}^{j=\theta} q_{kij}(\mu_k + \nu_k)P_k \qquad (\text{\textfractionsolidus})$$

Neither the provisions for the maintenance of capital nor the provisions for additional capital are as arbitrary as they might seem, for it is easy enough to bring them together in the analysis of the demand for an increment of net income. In other words, if we can succeed in establishing a demand function for additional net income, similar to the demand functions for other things, the point at which the total quantity of additional net income demanded is equal to zero defines the stationary state; the point at which that quantity is negative defines the regressive state; and the point at which it is positive defines the progressive state.

In his fourth edition, Walras succeeded in establishing a demand function for additional net income similar to his other demand functions, boldly basing his new function on *rareté* functions. Although he abandoned all reference to the difference between present and future utility, we ought to guard carefully against interpreting this fact as implying that Walras repudiated or denied the element of time in his theory of savings. Given the structure of his theory of general equilibrium, which is, as we have seen, a cross-section of the continuum of exchange, production, capital formation, and demand for monetary assets, viewed at a moment in time, it would have been illogical of Walras to have inserted a function of time explicitly into that picture. Furthermore, in an unpublished letter to Böhm-Bawerk, dated May 5, 1889, and in the preface to the second edition of the *Elements,* dated the same year, he indicated that he could not take the difference in value between present and future goods as a datum, because that difference is a variable in his system, functionally related to all the other variables, including the rate of net income. Obviously, this did not prevent him from considering the preference function for additional net revenue as given.

We shall now examine exactly how Walras introduced his demand function into his system. He invented an imaginary commodity (E), which should not be confused with the E of equation (β). Commodity (E) consists of perpetual annuity shares, each unit of which yields a unit of *numéraire* per annum in perpetuity.[21] (The term "shares" includes capital proper, personal capital, and landed capital.) Returning again to the capitalization equation

$$i = \frac{p_k - (\mu_k + \nu_k)\, \mathrm{P}_k}{\mathrm{P}_k}$$

and replacing the numerator by unity, and the denominator by p_e, which represents the price of a perpetual annuity share income, we have

$$i = \frac{1}{p_e}, \quad \text{or} \quad p_e = \frac{1}{i}$$

This formula is the same as that of the present discounted value of an infinite series of net incomes. Furthermore, at the moment at which we are examining a cross-section of the economic system, and trying to obtain a representative view of the existing set of relationships, each individual can be considered as possessing a certain number of these securities, which are numerically equivalent to his net income. The latter is also expressed in *numéraire*, according to the following equation:[22]

$$q_e = q_i p_i + q_p \pi_p + q_k \pi_k$$

Each individual therefore has, at each moment of time, not only a given net income, but also a desire for net income. Although he does not receive the income until later, the desire that he has for it exists in the present; and it is expressed at the present time, according to the Walrasian scheme, as a function of the quantity of income that he possesses, or $\phi_e (q_e)$. We can consider this as being the *rareté* function for the perpetual securities. And our individual, taking into account his present income and the general set of prices, will decide to demand more or less of these shares – perhaps even to sell some of them – until the equation of maximum satisfaction includes $[\phi_e (q_e + d_e)]/p_e$:

$$\frac{\phi_i(q_i - o_i)}{p_i} = \frac{\phi_p(q_p - o_p)}{p_p} = \frac{\phi_k(q_k - o_k)}{p_k} = \ldots = \frac{\phi_a(d_a)}{1} =$$

$$= \frac{\phi_b(d_b)}{p_b} = \frac{\phi_c(d_c)}{p_c} = \ldots = \left[\frac{\phi_e(q_e + d_e)}{p_e} \right] \quad (\eta)$$

If the individual demands some shares, the quantity demanded multiplied by the price appears in the budget equation as the term $[d_e p_e]$ in the right-hand member:

$$o_i p_i + o_p p_p + o_k p_k + \ldots = d_a + d_b p_b + d_c p_c + \ldots + [d_e p_e] \quad (\theta)$$

It was in this way that Walras strove to handle an essentially dynamic concept with the aid of the tools of static analysis. When an individual buys a hypothetical perpetual annuity share, he is purchasing a net amount or surplus. Now, in Walras's static system, a surplus is a commodity that one can buy and sell like any other commodity, and with respect to which it can be presumed that an individual experiences a desire and has a utility function like any other utility function. The price

[22] Ibid., p. 251.

of a unit of the surplus (which is the reciprocal of the rate of capitalization) is thus determined in the same manner as all other prices. The equations (η) and (θ) amended in this way are extremely interesting because they show clearly that there is no contradiction between the desire of an individual to improve his situation in the way described by Adam Smith, and the desire to maximize utility in the way described by Walras. In actuality, at any moment of time, an individual can try to improve his situation only within the limits of the resources that he possesses.

From our equations (η) and (θ) we obtain a demand function for the perpetual security (E), that is to say,

$$d_e = f_e(p_t \ldots p_p \ldots p_k,\, p_{k'},\, p_{k''},\, \ldots p_b,\, p_e \ldots p_e)$$

similar to the other demand functions in the Walrasian system, but which now includes the price of the perpetual securities among the other prices that appear in the function. That demand function will become a supply function in the familiar manner when the price of the perpetual security becomes sufficiently high. By rearranging in a suitable fashion the market demand curve and the market supply curve for the perpetual security, we can obtain the momentary equilibrium value of p_e or of i, since $p_e = 1/i$, as I did in my 1942 article, "Léon Walras' Theory of Capital Accumulation," to which I referred above.[23]

As I have already said, it seemed to me at the time I wrote that article that the D_k, $D_{k'}$, $D_{k''}$, ... of equation (β) were adventitious variables having no relation to the rareté functions. My error resulted, in part, from the fact that I did not understand the 27th Lesson of the definitive edition of the *Elements*. When I tried more recently to find my way step by step through the labyrinth of equations in that lesson, it still appeared impossible for me to understand the mathematical procedure followed by Walras, even with the aid of a mathematician and economist as remarkable as Mr. G. Th. Guilbaud, who is attached to the Institute of Applied Economic Science. Mr. Guilbaud has given me to understand that Walras's mathematics is muddled mainly because of his lack of mastery of the techniques necessary for the accomplishment of his objectives. Nevertheless, thanks to the helpful suggestions of Mr. Guilbaud, and to a pertinent comment by Professsor Samuelson, I have been able to reconstruct the theory in a form which is, I hope, comprehensible. As far as possible, I have retained Walras's notation and employed only the simplest mathematical tools. It is with this mathematical reconstruction that I bring this article to a close.

The object of the 27th Lesson is to relate the demand for capital goods to the rareté functions of the consumption goods that they help to

[23] Op. cit., p. 47 [p. 149 of this volume].

produce. Suppose, for simplicity, that there are only three consumption goods (A), (B), and (C), of which the quantities $\delta_a, 1$, $\delta_b, 1$, $\delta_c, 1$ are consumed by individual $(_1)$. Let $\Phi_{a,1}$ $(\delta_{a,1})$, $\Phi_{b,1}$ $(\delta_{b,1})$, $\Phi_{c,1}$ $(\delta_{c,1})$, be the total utilities, which Walras called the effective utilities, of the various commodities for the individual in question. The sum of these effective utilities is then

$$\Phi_{a,1} (\delta_{a,1}) + \Phi_{b,1} (\delta_{b,1}) + \Phi_{c,1} (\delta_{c,1})$$

For that sum to be a maximum, it is necessary that

$$\Phi'_{a,1} (\delta_{a,1}) \, d\delta_{a,1} + \Phi'_{b,1} (\delta_{b,1}) \, d\delta_{b,1} + \Phi'_{c,1} (\delta_{c,1}) \, d\delta_{c,1} = 0 \qquad (1)$$

for all the admissible values of $d\delta_{a,1}$, $d\delta_{b,1}$, $d\delta_{c,1}$ subject to the budgetary constraints on the individual in question. As a consequence, any change, such as $\pm \ d\delta_{a,1}$ in the consumption of (A), for example, by individual $(_1)$, will necessarily entail a change of the opposite sign, such as $\mp \ d\delta_{b,1}$, in his consumption of at least one other good, for example (B).

Thus, in the simplest case in which the compensating variations of consumption occur only between pairs of commodities, the criterion for the admissible values of the differentials in equation (1) above is given by:

$$\Phi'_{a,1} (\delta_{a,1}) \, d\delta_{a,1} = - \ \Phi'_{b,1} (\delta_{b,1}) \, d\delta_{b,1}$$
$$\Phi'_{a,1} (\delta_{a,1}) \, d\delta_{a,1} = - \ \Phi'_{c,1} (\delta_{c,1}) \, d\delta_{c,1} \qquad (2)$$

It is important to note that any increase in the consumption of (A) by individual $(_1)$ entails a corresponding increase in the services of capital, and therefore in the capital goods employed for the production of the surplus of (A) consumed by individual $(_1)$.

In order to complete this account, we now take into consideration not only capital goods proper, which we assume for simplicity to be three in number, (K), (K'), (K''), but also personal capital, of which we assume, also for simplicity, that there is a single sort, (P). We do not take account of landed capital, (T), because the total quantity is constant by definition. Because, except in a slave economy, there cannot be a market for personal capital, there is nothing to prevent an individual, in the conduct of his personal economic affairs, from investing part of his savings in improving his own or his family's capacity to produce. He can do so either by assigning an increased amount of his total savings to that purpose, or by allocating to (P) a greater part of a given amount of savings, at the expense of (K), (K'), (K''). Because the aggregate quantity of (P) can, unlike (T), be increased or decreased within the economy as a whole, personal capital becomes an important variable in our problem. We can then write the relations:

$$d\delta_{p,1,a} = a_p \, d\delta_{a,1}$$
$$d\delta_{k,1,a} = a_k \, d\delta_{a,1} \tag{3}$$
$$d\delta_{k',1,a} = a_{k'} \, d\delta_{a,1}$$
$$d\delta_{k'',1,a} = a_{k''} \, d\delta_{a,1}$$

in which the first member expresses the differential increments in the quantities of (P), (K), (K′), (K″), necessary for a given increase in the consumption of (A) by individual ($_1$), and the coefficients a_p, a_k, $a_{k'}$, $a_{k''}$ of the second member are the coefficients of production, assumed here to be constants. Analogous equations can be written to relate the differential increments of consumption by ($_1$) of (B) and (C) to the capital goods employed in their production. In consequence, all changes in the direct consumption of (A) by ($_1$) and the compensating changes in the consumption of (B), for example, lead to changes in the indirect consumption of (P), (K), (K′), (K″) *via* (A) designated by:

$$d\delta_{p,1,a}, \quad d\delta_{k,1,a}, \quad d\delta_{k',1,a}, \quad d\delta_{k'',1,a},$$

and at the same time to the compensating changes, with opposite signs, in the direct consumption of (P), (K), (K′), (K″) *via* (B), designated by:

$$d\delta_{p,1,b}, \quad d\delta_{k,1,b}, \quad d\delta_{k',1,b}, \quad d\delta_{k'',1,b}$$

The problem is therefore, as Walras clearly established, to extract from the differential equations (1) and (2) the interrelated differentials of (P), (K), (K′), (K″) implicit in the differentials of (A), (B), and (C), so as to show how the distribution of a given aggregate excess of income over consumption among the different types of investments (P), (K), (K′), (K″) is governed, in the last analysis, by the acts of individuals in their search for maximum utility given the limits of their incomes. In this exposition, to achieve brevity we give the name "savings" to the aggregate excess of income over consumption, even though the present discussion deals only with the stationary state in which there is no net difference between income and consumption over and above what is necessary to maintain the capital goods of the economy intact. It should be recalled that Walras limits his use of the word *savings* to the net excess.

Since $\Phi' = r$, we rewrite equation (1) in the form

$$r_a \, d\delta_{a,1} + r_b \, d\delta_{b,1} + r_c \, d\delta_{c,1} = 0 \tag{4}$$

We now substitute in (4) the prices of (A), (B), and (C) in place of the *raretés* to which they are proportional in equilibrium:

$$\frac{r_{a,1}}{p_a} = \frac{r_{b,1}}{p_b} = \frac{r_{c,1}}{p_c}$$

Next, substituting in (4) the unit costs of production for the prices to which they are proportional in equilibrium (neglecting, for simplicity, the costs of the services of land), we obtain:

$$
\begin{aligned}
& (a_p p_p + a_k p_k + a_{k'} p_{k'} + a_{k''} p_{k''})\, d\delta_{a,1} \\
+\ & (b_p p_p + b_k p_k + b_{k'} p_{k'} + b_{k''} p_{k''})\, d\delta_{b,1} \\
+\ & (c_p p_p + c_k p_k + c_{k'} p_{k'} + c_{k''} p_{k''})\, d\delta_{c,1} = 0
\end{aligned}
\tag{5}
$$

which is an alternative formulation of equation (1). Removing the parentheses, we obtain:

$$
\begin{aligned}
& a_p p_p d\delta_{a,1} + a_k p_k d\delta_{a,1} + a_{k'} p_{k'} d\delta_{a,1} + a_{k''} p_{k''} d\delta_{a,1} \\
+\ & b_p p_p d\delta_{b,1} + b_k p_k d\delta_{b,1} + b_{k'} p_{k'} d\delta_{b,1} + b_{k''} p_{k''} d\delta_{b,1} \\
+\ & c_p p_p d\delta_{c,1} + c_k p_k d\delta_{c,1} + c_{k'} p_{k'} d\delta_{c,1} + c_{k''} p_{k''} d\delta_{c,1} = 0
\end{aligned}
\tag{6}
$$

Then, factoring out the prices of the inputs, we obtain

$$
\begin{aligned}
p_p\,(a_p\, d\delta_{a,1} + b_p\, d\delta_{b,1} + c_p\, d\delta_{c,1}) + p_k\,(a_k\, d\delta_{a,1} + b_k\, d\delta_{b,1} + c_k\, d\delta_{c,1}) \\
+\ p_{k'}\,(a_{k'}\, d\delta_{a,1} + b_{k'}\, d\delta_{b,1} + c_{k'}\, d\delta_{c,1} \\
+\ p_{k''}\,(a_{k''}\, d\delta_{a,1} + b_{k''}\, d\delta_{b,1} + c_{k''}\, d\delta_{c,1} = 0
\end{aligned}
\tag{7}
$$

But, if we write

$$
\begin{aligned}
a_p\, d\delta_{a,1} + b_p\, d\delta_{b,1} + c_p\, d\delta_{c,1} &= d\delta_{p,1} \\
a_k\, d\delta_{a,1} + b_k\, d\delta_{b,1} + c_k\, d\delta_{c,1} &= d\delta_{k,1}
\end{aligned}
$$

etc.; and if we substitute into (7), we obtain:

$$
p_p\, d\delta_{p,1} + p_k\, d\delta_{k,1} + p_{k'}\, d\delta_{k',1} + p_{k''}\, d\delta_{k'',1} = 0
\tag{8}
$$

which is now the necessary condition for maximization of effective utility by individual $(_1)$. Analogous equations are obtained for individuals $(_2)$, $(_3)$.

Setting

$$
\begin{aligned}
d\delta_{p,1} + d\delta_{p,2} + d\delta_{p,3} &= dD_p \\
d\delta_{k,1} + d\delta_{k,2} + d\delta_{k,3} &= dD_k \\
d\delta_{k',1} + d\delta_{k',2} + d\delta_{k',3} &= dD_{k'} \\
d\delta_{k'',1} + d\delta_{k'',2} + d\delta_{k'',3} &= dD_{k''}
\end{aligned}
$$

We can now write:

$$p_p \, d\mathrm{D}_p + p_k \, d\mathrm{D}_k + p_{k'} \, d\mathrm{D}_{k'} + p_{k''} \, d\mathrm{D}_{k''} = 0 \qquad (9)$$

for the entire economy.

From the macroeconomic point of view, our assumed stationary state required that there be an annual "savings" exactly equal to the cost of maintaining the capital equipment of the economy intact. If we designate that constant amount of savings by E^*, we can write

$$\mathrm{P}^*_p \, \mathrm{D}_p + \mathrm{P}^*_k \, \mathrm{D}_k + \mathrm{P}^*_{k'} \, \mathrm{D}_{k'} + \mathrm{P}^*_{k''} \, \mathrm{D}_{k''} = E^* \qquad (10)$$

where P^*_p, P^*_k, $\mathrm{P}^*_{k'}$, $\mathrm{P}^*_{k''}$ represent the *cost to the consumer* of the corresponding capital goods (which are not necessarily equal, as we shall see later on, to Walras's P_p, P_k, $\mathrm{P}_{k'}$, $\mathrm{P}_{k''}$) and D_p, D_k, $\mathrm{D}_{k'}$, $\mathrm{D}_{k''}$ represent the aggregate quantities of the different varieties of new capital goods that are annually demanded. Assuming that P^*_p, P^*_k, $\mathrm{P}^*_{k'}$, $\mathrm{P}^*_{k''}$ and E^* are already determined and constant, so that the quantities demanded are the only variables in our present problem, we have

$$\mathrm{P}^*_p \, d\mathrm{D}_p + \mathrm{P}^*_k \, d\mathrm{D}_k + \mathrm{P}^*_{k'} \, d\mathrm{D}_{k'} + \mathrm{P}^*_{k''} \, d\mathrm{D}_{k''} = 0 \qquad (11)$$

The differentials of equation (11) must be such that, *at least for any pair of them,* including any given capital good and each of the other capital goods successively, the following equations are satisfied:

$$\begin{aligned}
\mathrm{P}^*_k \, d_k + \mathrm{P}^*_p \, d_p &= 0 \\
\mathrm{P}^*_k \, d_k + \mathrm{P}^*_{k'} \, d_{k'} &= 0 \\
\mathrm{P}^*_k \, d_k + \mathrm{P}^*_{k''} \, d_{k''} &= 0
\end{aligned} \qquad (12)$$

Inasmuch as we suppose that the quantities of capital goods are numerically equal to the quantities of corresponding services furnished by the capital goods, and that the prices of the services are, at this stage of the inquiry, already determined, we may also write:

$$\begin{aligned}
p_k \, d\mathrm{D}_k + p_p \, d\mathrm{D}_p &= 0 \\
p_k \, d\mathrm{D}_k + p_{k'} \, d\mathrm{D}_{k'} &= 0 \\
p_k \, d\mathrm{D}_k + p_{k''} \, d\mathrm{D}_{k''} &= 0
\end{aligned} \qquad (13)$$

as a supplementary restriction on (9). This expresses the condition that, from the aggregate or macroeconomic point of view, individuals can maximize their total effective utility only within the limits imposed by the total quantity of "savings" available for investment in the various kinds of capital goods that are necessary for the production of consumption goods. Thus the maximization of utility expressed by equations (1) and (9) is subject to two constraints: the microeconomic constraint given by the individual budget equation, and the macroeconomic constraint given by an aggregate "investment = savings" equation. The macroeconomic constraint on (11) can also be expressed by other systems. In these we eliminate the algebraic sums that include any given capital good associated with all the combinations of two, three, or more of the others. System (12) therefore constitutes a sufficient but not a necessary condition for the maximum in question.

From (12) and (13) we derive

$$\frac{p_p}{P^*_p} = \frac{p_k}{P^*_k} = \frac{p_{k'}}{P^*_{k'}} = \frac{p_{k''}}{P^*_{k''}} \tag{14}$$

for each individual. In other words, for each individual who consumes the services of capital goods, directly or indirectly, to raise his effective total utility to a maximum, it is necessary that the relation of income to cost be the same for all new capital goods.

Thus the demand for the productive services of capital goods, and consequently the demand for capital goods that in themselves have no utility, are not superadded onto Walras's system, as I formerly asserted, but are rigorously tied to the utility functions, which constitute, so to speak, the fundamental motor of the entire system.

We cannot stop at this point, however, because we have no reconcile our equations (14) with the fact, mentioned above, that arbitrage in the market for capital goods results in the equality of the rate of net income on all new capital goods.

Walras expresses this fact in the following manner:[24]

$$\frac{\pi_k}{P_k} = \frac{\pi_{k'}}{P_{k'}} = \frac{\pi_{k''}}{P_{k''}} \tag{15}$$

and then juxtaposes these equations with the following ones:

$$\frac{p_k}{P_k} = \frac{p_{k'}}{P_{k'}} = \frac{p_{k''}}{P_{k''}} \tag{16}$$

which are not identical to equations (14), because the P_k variables written by Walras do not have our asterisks. Equations (16) show that Walras did not employ any symbol to distinguish what I call "the cost of a capital good to the consumer" from the market price of that capital good, which, in equilibrium, is equal to its cost of production. Walras's juxtaposition of equations (15) and (16) posed great difficulties for his first critics, as is shown by a series of unpublished letters between Walras and von Bortkiewicz and Edgeworth during the period January 9 to September 14, 1889, on which date Walras wrote to von Bortkiewicz: "At the present moment, my mind is tired."

---

[24] Definitive edition, p. 286.

I am going to show that neither the difficulties of his readers nor
Walras's mental fatigue were necessary to achieve mutual understanding, because the difficulty did not arise from an internal contradiction in
his argument, but in a genuine *lapsus calami,* and in the ineptness of his
exposition. Walras defined – and this is the *lapsus calami* – the terms P_k,
$P_{k'}$, $P_{k''}$ as the supply prices of the corresponding capital goods.[25] Taken
together, the two equations (15) and (16) then become irreconcilable if
the πs and ps are not proportional. If each π_k were equal to the
corresponding p_k, which would be the case for infinitely durable and
indestructible capital goods, the problem would be automatically resolved; but the theorem would be without interest because under those
conditions the only capital goods would be landed capital, and there
would not be, following Walras's terminology, any "capital proper."[26]
The only means of retaining goods that are "capital proper," while also
preserving the proportionality of π_k and p_k, would be to suppose that the
combined rates of depreciation and insurance, that is to say

$$(\mu_k + \nu_k), \quad (\mu_{k'} + \nu_{k'}), \quad (\mu_{k''} + \nu_{k''})$$

are the same for all the varieties of capital goods. This would be a wholly
meretricious hypothesis that could not be applied to the real world, in
which these rates differ greatly from one capital good to another. It
would be even more unfortunate because it would hide the relationships
that form the heart of our problem. A formal contradiction therefore
exists when the values of $(\mu_k + \nu_k)$ are neither zero nor equal for all
capital goods. Because

$$\pi_k = p_k - (\mu_k + \nu_k) \; P_k$$
$$\pi_{k'} = p_{k'} - (\mu_{k'} + \nu_{k'}) \; P_{k'}$$
$$\pi_{k''} = p_{k''} - (\mu_{k''} + \nu_{k''}) \; P_{k''}$$

equations (15) can be written

$$\frac{p_k - (\mu_k + \nu_k) \; P_k}{P_k} = \frac{p_{k'} - (\mu_{k'} + \nu_{k'}) \; P_{k'}}{P_{k'}} = \frac{p_{k''} - (\mu_{k''} + \nu_{k''}) \; P_{k''}}{P_{k''}} \quad (17)$$

which are clearly incompatible with equations (16), if any two of the
expressions in parentheses in (17) are not equal.

But, in Walras's formulation, that incompatibility is purely formal
and does not destroy the fundamental structure, because, at the precise
point at which the danger of the contradiction appears, Walras made the
necessary additions to the denominators of system (16).[27] And it is there
that the ineptness of his exposition can be clearly seen. It was sufficient
for me, in order to avoid difficulties in my reformulation of Walras, to

[25] Ibid., p. 285.   [26] Ibid., p. 258.   [27] Ibid., pp. 246–7.

choose a group of different symbols: P^*_k, $P^*_{k'}$, $P^*_{k''}$, in order to represent the P_k, $P_{k'}$, $P_{k''}$ that Walras employed *plus* the provision of supplementary capital that consumers must make for each unit of each new capital good in order to ensure a regular flow of income to cover the depreciation and insurance charges of that capital good. This is why I defined the P^*_k as the *costs to the consumer*. Because in a stationary state the cost to the consumer of a new capital good that ultimately wears out is not equal to the market price received by the producer of such a good, it is the P^*_k values and not the P_k that appear in the calculations made by the consumer to achieve a maximum of his effective utility. Furthermore, what is of concern to the producer of a new capital good in his search for maximum profits are the P_k values. It is therefore the P_k values, and not the P^*_k, which ought to appear in equations (15) or (17), which give a necessary equilibrium condition in the market for capital goods. Walras's inept procedure was to assume, first, that all the capital goods were infinitely durable or that the provision for depreciation and insurance was assumed by a *deus ex machina,* which enabled him to write (15) and (16) with the same denominator, for in this case the p_k and the π_k are equal. Then, abandoning that assumption, he added to each denominator of (16) the respective values of $[(\mu_k + \nu_k) P_k]/i$. It is precisely this addition that constitutes, in my reformulation, the difference between the P^*_k and the P_k.

As soon as equations (16) are replaced by:

$$\frac{p_k}{P_k + \dfrac{(\mu_k + \nu_k)P_k}{i}} = \frac{p_{k'}}{P_{k'} + \dfrac{(\mu_{k'} + \nu_{k'})P_{k'}}{i}} = \frac{p_{k''}}{P_{k''} + \dfrac{(\mu_{k''} + \nu_{k''})P_{k''}}{i}} \quad (18)$$

the reconciliation for which we have searched is attained, because equations (18) lead to equations (15). As a matter of fact, i is the general rate of net income in equilibrium, equal for all capital goods, and in consequence, it is the factor of proportionality that obtains between the π_k and the P_k:

$$i = \frac{\pi_k}{P_k} = \frac{\pi_{k'}}{P_{k'}} = \frac{\pi_{k''}}{P_{k''}}$$

Then:

$$\frac{p_k}{P_k + \dfrac{(\mu_k + \nu_k)\, P_k}{i}}$$

for example, can be written:

$$\frac{p_k}{\dfrac{\pi_k}{i} + \dfrac{(\mu_k + \nu_k)\,P_k}{i}}$$

or,

$$\frac{p_k}{\dfrac{p_k}{i}} = i = \frac{\pi_k}{P_k}$$

because

$$\pi_k + (\mu_k + \nu_k)\,P_k = p_k$$

We can explain the new denominators that appear in equation (18) by imagining that at the beginning of a year a unit of particular capital good (K) has to be replaced in order to maintain a constant flow of consumption goods. The consumers must therefore not only utilize whatever is necessary of their savings in order to pay for that unit of (K), but also provide an annual amount of saving in each future year sufficient to replace that unit when it is used up or destroyed. That annual provision, which must be made for all future time if the stationary state is to be preserved, is equivalent to the permanent investment of a sufficient amount of capital to produce that annual provision each year. In adding this capital to the market price of the new unit of capital goods (K), we obtain

$$P_k + \frac{(\mu_k + \nu_k)\,P_k}{i} = P^*_k$$

which represents the total cost that has to be borne directly or indirectly by the consumer if he is to receive an annual flow of services that are always worth p_k. This is why the relationship

$$\frac{p_k}{P^*_k} = \frac{p_k}{P_k + \left(\dfrac{\mu_k + \nu_k}{i}\right)P_k}$$

was referred to above as the relationship of income to cost to the consumer. Furthermore, it folows that

$$P^*_k - P_k = \frac{(\mu_k + \nu_k)\,P_k}{i} \tag{19}$$

for (K) and, similarly, for the other capital goods (K') and (K").

There still remains a gap that needs to be filled in the reasoning. In passing from the microeconomic equilibrium to the macroeconomic condition of the stationary state, it is not clearly seen in Walras's Lessons 26 and 27 how he took account, in the equation "savings = investment," of the additional capital that is necessary for the continued maintenance of new capital goods. Walras expressed this restriction by his equation (2) in sections 262 and 263:

$$D_k\, P_k + D_{k'}\, P_{k'} + D_{k''}\, P_{k''} = E \qquad (20)$$

which we earlier called equation (β), and which could have been written in the following manner:

$$D_p\, P_p + D_k\, P_k + D_{k'}\, P_{k'} + D_{k''}\, P_{k''} = E \qquad (21)$$

if Walras had considered it appropriate to take into consideration personal capital, which is not marketable. In each of the two cases, that equation could not serve Walras's purposes unless he assumed that depreciation and insurance charges were not paid by the consumer. On the other hand, when that assumption is abandoned, equation (20) or (21) is no longer appropriate. Another equation, such as (10), must then be used. The difference between (10) and equation (21)

$$E^* - E = D_p\,(P^*_p - P_p) + D_k\,(P^*_k - P_k) + D_{k'}\,(P^*_{k'} - P_{k'}) +$$
$$+ D_{k''}\,(P^*_{k''} - P_{k''}) \qquad (22)$$

is equal to

$$D_p \left[\frac{(\mu_p + \nu_p)\, P_p}{i}\right] + D_k \left[\frac{(\mu_k + \nu_k)\, P_k}{i}\right] + D_{k'} \left[\frac{(\mu_{k'} + \nu_{k'})\, P_{k'}}{i}\right] +$$

$$+ D_{k''} \left[\frac{(\mu_{k''} + \nu_{k''})\, P_{k''}}{i}\right] \qquad (23)$$

as equation (19) demonstrates.

I have, it is clear, deliberately restricted my reconstruction of the theory presented by Walras in Lesson 27 to the case of a stationary state. I have done so simply in order to render the exposition more simple. Nevertheless, the analysis is general, and applies just as well, after appropriate modifications, to a progressive state. If the left member of equation (22) is greater than the right member, and if the difference between them is made equal to the positive aggregate demand for perpetual net income shares and to the value of the net production of new capital goods, all the supplementary necessary conditions for equilibrium in a progressive state are given.

It is interesting to note, in conclusion, that although Walras's structure of empirical reasoning may be static, it lends itself very well to the solution of the type of dynamic problems that Richard M. Goodwin described in his article "Iteration, Automatic Computers and Economic Dynamics," (*Metroeconomia,* April 1951, pp. 1–7). In Lesson 25 of the definitive edition, where Walras deals with the law of the establishment of the rate of net income, he shows how his equations of capital goods and credit are automatically solved in the real market by the *tâtonnement* process. In Lesson 28, on the other hand, Walras admits that such a solution can be attained "in an economy in normal operation which has only to maintain itself in an equilibrium state," and not otherwise.[28] He recognized that "in a society that has just been economically disrupted by a war, a revolution, or a crisis,"[29] it cannot be expected that the normal functioning of the market will lead to the sort of consistent solution that he described for the equilibrium equations. A complete discussion of these matters would go beyond the limits of this study.

[28] Ibid., p. 280.   [29] Ibid., p. 290.

11

NEW LIGHT ON AN OLD QUARREL: BARONE'S UNPUBLISHED REVIEW OF WICKSTEED'S "ESSAY ON THE COORDINATION OF THE LAWS OF DISTRIBUTION" AND RELATED DOCUMENTS[1]

The old quarrel with which this paper deals is of significance for the light it sheds on the authorship of the marginal productivity theory in its modern mathematical form. The *locus classicus* of the quarrel is Léon Walras's "Note sur la réfutation de la théorie anglaise du fermage de M. Wicksteed"[2] (hereinafter referred to as his "Note"), published in the 3rd edition (1896) of his *Eléments d'économie politique pure* as Appendix III. What did Walras mean by the charge, at the close of his "Note," that Mr. Wicksteed "might have been better advised had he not persisted in

In Dr. Jaffé's original article, almost all the quotations from European writers were in French. These have been translated by Donald A. Walker, except for a few phrases of obvious meaning that have been left in French.

[1] The research on which this paper is based was made possible by a John Simon Guggenheim Memorial Foundation Fellowship, a Ford Foundation Grant to the Economics Department of Northwestern University and a Rockefeller Foundation Grant. This aid is gratefully acknowledged, as is my debt to M. Charles Roth, Keeper of Manuscripts at the Bibliothèque Cantonale et Universitaire de Lausanne, and his colleagues for their unfailing courtesy in facilitating my access to the archives and other sources of information in Lausanne. Thanks to the intervention of the late Bernard Chait of Antwerp and of Professor Léon H. Dupriez of the University of Louvain, and to subsidies granted by the Belgian Fonds National de la Recherche Scientifique and by the French Centre National de la Recherche Scientifique, I have received invaluable aid from Mme Livia Thür-Rechnitzer formerly of Louvain, now professor at the Université de Montréal, M. Pierre Lebrun at Liège and Melle Angèle Frenkel at Strasbourg in deciphering the letters here cited as well as other letters to be published under the auspices of the Royal Netherlands Academy of Science in three volumes (in press) of the *Correspondence of Léon Walras and Related Papers* which I have selected, edited and annotated.

[2] The "Note" first appeared in the *Recueil publié par la Faculté de Droit de l'Université de Lausanne à l'occasion de l'Exposition nationale suisse*, Geneva, Viret-Genton, 1896, pp. 1–11, and was soon reprinted with only one minor change as "Apendice III" in the third edition of Léon Walras's *Eléments d'Economie Politique Pure*, Lausanne, Rouge, 1896, pp. 485–492. This Appendix, however, was dropped from the subsequent editions of the *Eléments*. An English version of Appendix III was added to my translation of the definitive edition (1926) of the *Eléments* (Léon Walras, *Elements of Pure Economics*, London and Homewood, Illinois: Allen & Unwin and Irwin, 1954), pp. 489–495. My bracketed insertion in Footnote 1 on p. 489 of the translation is an error; the Post-Script to the Appendix is, in fact, found in the above-mentioned *Recueil*.

appearing ignorant of the work of his forerunners"? Did Walras mean to include himself among the forerunners he thought were deliberately ignored in Philip H. Wicksteed's *Essay on the Coordination of the Laws of Distribution*?[3] If so, what did Walras conceive his contribution to be? The answers to these questions thus far given have been contradictory and at times heated.[4] Fortunately, several hitherto unpublished documents and letters preserved in the *Fonds Walras* of the Bibliothèque Cantonale et Universitaire de Lausanne illuminate the issues involved.

The most important of these documents is, undoubtedly, Enrico Barone's review article, "Sopra un recente libro del Wicksteed," originally written for the *Economic Journal,* but rejected by Edgeworth in 1895

---

[3] London, Macmillan, 1894; reprinted as No. 12 of the Series of Reprints of the London School of Economics and Political Science (London, 1932). Wicksteed later withdrew the central argument of his *Essay.* In his review of Vilfredo Pareto's *Manuale di economia politica,* he wrote:

> Professor Pareto exposed (in his *Cours* and in his *Anwendungen der Mathematik auf Nationalökonomie*) the fallaciousness of some of the reasoning in my own Co-ordination of the Laws of Distribution. And it was by an implicit application of the same principle that Prof. Edgeworth performed the same task elsewhere. I should like to take this opportunity of acknowledging the justice of both their criticisms. (*Economic Journal,* December 1906, vol. 16, No. 64, p. 554 *n.*)

The story of Wicksteed's recantation lies outside the scope of this paper. *Cf.* George J. Stigler, *Production and Distribution Theories,* New York, Macmillan, 1941, pp. 332–335.

[4] For example, *cf.* Lionel Robbins:

> How far this result [Wicksteed's statement of the marginal productivity theory in the *Essay*] had been reached independently of the work of others it is difficult to say. ... [T]he productivity theory of distribution was 'in the air' and different variants had been put forward by Marshall, Clark and others. It is certain that Wicksteed was acquainted with Marshall's work in this field, for there are footnote references to it in the *Essay.* But it is probable that his solution was reached as a result of his studies of Jevons, which were carried out before Marshall's *Principles* were published. This is what seems to follow from Wicksteed's own account of his discovery [*Essay*, p. 43], and we may be sure that a man so scrupulously honest and so modest about his own achievements would have acknowledged the debt had it existed. (Lionel Robbin's Chapter, "The Economic Works" in C.H. Herford, *Philip Henry Wicksteed, His Life and Work,* London, Dent, 1931, pp. 232–33);

and George J. Stigler:

> Walras did not have a marginal productivity theory before Wicksteed's brochure appeared. Walras, therefore, could not and did not prove that rent as a residual is equal to rent as a marginal product. We may charitably attribute to self-confusion his belief that he possessed a marginal productivity theory, but his charge of plagiarism (which would of course be improbable in any case in the light of Wicksteed's character) can be characterized only as gross impertinence. (*Op. cit.,* p. 370);

and Joseph A. Schumpeter:

> The irritation that Walras displayed in his 'Note sur la réfutation de la théorie anglaise du fermage (rent of land) de M. Wicksteed' ... is ... less unjustified than Professor Stigler declares it is. Moreover it is a misunderstanding to think that Walras claimed personal priority for the theory of marginal productivity as defined by himself. As far as this goes, the note on p. 376 of the *Eléments* [definitive edition, 1926] is conclusive. (*History of Economic Analysis,* New York, Oxford University Press, 1954, p. 1033, Footnote 18.)

See Note 66, *infra.*

and then lost from sight.[5] Were it not for the fact that Barone's manuscript had been lent to Walras, who made a French translation of it which is preserved in the Fonds Walras of the Bibliothèque Cantonale et Universitaire de Lausanne,[6] all trace of this review would have been obliterated. Nor would it have been possible to determine the precise part Barone played in shaping Walras's "Note" on Wicksteed.

In the first part of this paper we shall present Walras's translation of Barone's review, citing at the same time the revelant passages in the Walras-Pareto and Walras-Barone correspondence which recount the circumstances that led Walras to write and to publish his harsh "Note." The Barone correspondence, in particular, is of interest not only because of the analytical argument it contains, but also as a record of Barone's dramatic effort to curb Walras's public attack on Wicksteed. Then, drawing again upon unpublished material, we shall see how closely Walras came to formulating a marginal productivity theory himself and how Pareto and Barone developed Walras's early suggestions before Wicksteed's *Essay* appeared. Finally we shall look into the private reactions of economists who wrote to Walras regarding the "Note" as it appeared in Appendix III to the 3rd edition of the *Eléments*.

Wicksteed's *Essay* was first mentioned in the Walras correspondence in a brief message Léon Walras sent to Vilfredo Pareto, his successor at the University of Lausanne, on October 5, 1894: "Have you read the little volume of M. Wicksteed's that has just appeared? I've read it attentively, and I've drafted a short note on which I would like to get your advice."[7] Walras had just been engaged in an epistolary discussion with Pareto on the question of the determination of variable coefficients of

[5] Efforts made in Italy and elsewhere to find the original Italian version of Barone's review, to which Walras alluded in the Post-Script to his "Note," have proved unavailing. Professor Francesco Spinedi, editor of Barone's *Opere economiche*, Bologna, Zanichelli, 1936, informed me that Barone's papers have not been preserved.

[6] Catalogued in the Fonds Walras of the Bibliothèque Cantonale et Universitaire de Lausanne under the classification mark, F.W. V, 1. The F.W. V series of the *Fonds Walras* contains a miscellany of Walras's manuscripts as well as some of his correspondence not individually catalogued or ordered in any consecutive way. The Arabic numbers after F.W. V refer to the particular boxes in which the documents are found. The manuscript translation of Barone's review is a clear copy in Walras's best hand, written on both sides of two double sheets of ruled copy-book paper folded lengthwise, thus forming eight pages.

[7] Catalogued in the Fonds Walras under the classification mark F.W. I, 428. The F.W. I series contains Walras's rough drafts of the letters to his correspondents and are arranged in the alphabetical order of their names. The arabic numbers after F.W. I refer not to the separate letters but to the separate folders in which the drafts of letters addressed to each correspondent are preserved. In this paper the letters from Walras will only be identified by their dates, after the classification mark for a correspondent has once been given.

In those rare instances (which do not include any of the letters quoted in this paper), where it has proved possible to compare the drafts with the autograph letters Walras

production in relation to maximum social utility, a subject which Pareto treated in his article, "Il massimo di utilità dato dalla libera concorrenza."[8] There Pareto referred to Walras's earlier allusions in the *Eléments* to the determination of variable coefficients by the condition of minimum cost of production to the entrepreneur.[9] Moreover, about a fortnight before he sent his anxious message to Pareto, Walras had written critical private comments in pencil across a letter from Enrico Barone, dated September 20, 1894, which also dealt with the marginal productivity theory. True, Barone had mentioned Wicksteed's name (curiously misspelled), but as is seen from the following paragraph of this letter, Wicksteed was simply listed as one of five forerunners in the development of the theory.

At present I am occupied with questions about the distribution of output among the productive services. In taking up and developing observations that Thünen, Jevons, Marshall, Clark, Weeckstead [*sic*] have already made, it seems to me that I have succeeded in formulating a fairly simple theory of distribution in general and of the profit of the entrepreneur in particular, on the basis of a new theorem of the entrepreneur's maximum net product.[10]

---

actually sent, the concordance appears perfect. This creates a presumption in favor of the reliability of the whole F.W. I series as representing the final version; but since the rough drafts are often barely decipherable, it has been found necessary to enclose doubtful readings of Walras's scribble in square brackets.

The letters received by Walras are contained in the F.W. II series. These are arranged in chronological order in the *Fonds Walras;* and each letter is identified separately by an arabic number following F.W. II.

The entire collection of 61 letters *from* Pareto *to* Walras preserved in the *Fonds Walras* was first published by Tommaso Giacalone-Monaco as "Le lettere di Vilfredo Pareto a Léon Walras (1891–1901)" in the *Rivista internazionale di scienze economiche e commerciali,* July–August 1958, vol. 5, No. 7-8, pp. 687–721, with an introduction by Tullio Bagiotti (pp. 685–86). The letters were then republished in Giacalone-Monaco's book, *Pareto-Walras. Da un carteggio inedito (1891–1901),* Padua, Cedam, 1960, prefaced by a detailed commentary on the relations between Pareto and Walras.

[8] *Giornale degli economisti,* July, 1894, pp. 48–66, reprinted in V. Pareto, *Scritti teorici,* edited by Giovanni Demaria, Milan, Rodolfo Malfasi, 1952, pp. 276–294. The letters from Walras to Pareto discussing Pareto's article are dated July 19 and July 22, 1894; while Pareto's replies on the subject are dated July 20 and July 23 (F.W. II, 1843 and 1844 respectively). This exchange of letters probably took place before Walras had seen Wicksteed's *Essay,* for the date of his note of "remerciements empressés" to Wicksteed is September 14, 1894 (F.W. I, 612).

[9] *Eléments,* 2nd edition (1889), §247. *Cf.* the collation of Walras's five editions of the *Eléments* in the *Elements of Pure Economics, op. cit.,* pp. 559–610.

[10] F.W. II, 1848. What Walras objected to in Barone's letter was the derivation of proportionality between the marginal productivities of the services and their prices from the condition of maximum entrepreneurial profits. "Voilà bien la formule des productivités marginales," he scrawled on the letter, "mais ıe fondement économique est mauvais." He presumably meant by this that though the proportionality characteristic of the marginal productivity theory can be mathematically derived from the condition of maximum profit, nevertheless in an economic model of general equilibrium adapted to a real world which works by *tâtonnements* in separate markets (for finished products, for productive services, etc.), it should be derived from the condition of minimum cost of production. *Cf.* Walras's letter of October 30, 1895 *(infra)* to Barone and Translator's Note

When, therefore, Wicksteed's *Essay* reached Walras in the midst of his discussion with Pareto and Barone on their contributions to the marginal productivity theory, it is not surprising that he wanted immediately to consult with Pareto, who was close by, on his first impressions of the new book which claimed to outline "a new theory of Distribution in its entirety." Pareto replied at once, on October 7th, to Walras's call by saying that he had not yet had time to read Wicksteed's "petit volume," which he had just received from Paris, but that he had already heard about it from Pantaleoni, who had written to him that it contained nothing new ("qu'il n'y a dedans que des choses déjà connues").[11] Pareto suggested that Walras submit his note to Pantaleoni's *Giornale degli economisti*. This Walras declined to do because, as he explained in the following letter to Pareto dated October 9, 1894, he did not feel sure enough of himself:

Here is my note. I didn't write it for publication, but in order to get your advice on the following points:

If we assume that (T) and (K) are the two productive services that make a product (B), as Wicksteed does, we have in our system of notation:[12]

---

[1] to Lesson 36 in *Pure Economics*, p. 533. *Cf.* also Paul Samuelson, *Foundations of Economic Analysis*, Chapter IV.

Barone persisted, however, in thinking of the two conditions as perfect alternatives, as is seen in the *Note matematiche* to his "Studi sulla Distribuzione," *Giornale degli economisti*, vol. XII, 2nd Series, February, 1896, p. 154 (E. Barone, *Opere economiche, op. cit.*, vol. I, p. 221), where he says they amount to the same thing ("ciò che torna lo stesso"). Nevertheless, nothing but the condition of minimum cost is mentioned in his article, "Il Ministro della produzione nello stato collettivista," *Giornale degli economisti*, vol. XXXVII, 2nd Series, September and October, 1908, pp. 267–293 and 391–414 (*Opere,* vol. I, pp. 229–297), which has been published in English in *Collectivist Economic Planning*, edited by von Hayek, London, Routledge, 1935, where see especially p. 251.

In his letter of September 20, 1894, which makes no mention of Wicksteed's *Essay,* Barone insisted that the production function is not ordinarily a linear homogeneous function and that only at what he vaguely called the margin of production is the entire product absorbed in the distributive shares paid out to the factors of production. Before this marginal point is reached, there is a profit for the entrepreneur.

To this same letter Barone added a post-script apologizing for his imperfect French. [In the letters quoted by Jaffé in his original article no attempt was made to correct Barone's French or that of any other of Walras's foreign correspondents.]

[11] F.W. II, 1849.

[12] To take Walras's symbols first, b_t, b_p and b_k are technical coefficients of production, i.e. quantities of the inputs (T), (P) and (K) respectively per unit of output of a given product (B); p_t, p_p, p_k, p_b the prices per unit of (T), (P), (K) and (B) respectively; $\varphi(b_t, b_p, b_k) = 0$ Walras's original implicit "production equation" with the rate of output unspecified; $b_t = \Theta(b_k)$ the explicit relation between two of the coefficients considered. In Wicksteed, c stands for the units of a composite factor, "Capital + Labor," employed per unit of land; p_t the total product of Labor + Capital employed on a unit of land and hence equal to $F(c)$; and $F'(c)$ the rate at which the total product increases with an increase of the compositive "Capital + Labor" employed on a unit of land. It is interesting to note that Walras's $F'(x)$ in §355 of the definitive edition (1926) of the *Eléments,* which had made its first appearance in the 2nd edition (1889), §303, was, bar the name, nothing more or less than the marginal productivity of capital, precisely analogous to Wicksteed's $F'(c)$.

$$p_b = b_t p_t + b_k p_k$$

with the relation

$$b_t = \Theta(b_k)$$

from which it follows

$$p_t = \frac{p_b}{\Theta(b_k)} - \frac{b_k}{\Theta(b_k)} \cdot p_k \cdot$$

If you grant me, after studying the matter, that Wicksteed's symbols and relations c, $p_t = F(c)$, $F'(c)$ are the same as my $b_k/\Theta(b_k)$, $p_b/\Theta(b_k)$, and p_k, I can state that the criticism of the English theory of rent "in its second form" is substantially that of my *Eléments* with a simple change of notation and some minor differences of details.

I would also like you to tell me if there is anything other than ambiguity between the *physical* product and the *value* product in the relation

$$P = \frac{dP}{dA} A + \frac{dP}{dB} B + \frac{dP}{dC} C + \ldots$$

in contrast to stating

$$p_b = b_t p_t + b_p p_p + b_k p_k + \ldots$$

with the relation

$$\varphi(b_t, b_p, b_k \ldots) = 0.$$

I don't think so. And I find, on the contrary, that the latter form is advantageous because it separates the two relationships of value and of physical product.

Take all the time that you need to examine these points. We can talk about them after my return to Lausanne, which will be in eight days.

I almost reproach myself for imposing on you this additional amount of work, however small it be, when I see how much you have before you. I ought rather to do for you something like what my mother used to do for me in my youth, when she surprised me studying after midnight. She would take away my lamp and leave me to go to bed in the dark.

Beyond this we have nothing in the surviving correspondence between Walras and Pareto on the subject of Wicksteed's *Essay*. It seems highly probable that they had ample opportunity to discuss the matter *viva voce*. This surmise is confirmed by the following passage from a letter Walras sent to Barone more than a year later, on October 23, 1895.

Since the dean of our School of Law asked if he could include some pages of mine in a *Recueil Universitaire* intended for the Geneva Exposition, I sent him on

September 30 a *Note on the Refutation of M. Wicksteed's English Theory of Rent* that I prepared while I was staying in the country last summer and that I have recopied this summer for the occasion.

On returning to town, I went on Sunday to see M. Pareto, who gave me your own note *Sopra un recente libro del Wicksteed,* intended for the *Economic Journal,* which I read with pen in hand, making a French translation of it.

These two notes are not useless repetition. I have put my equation in opposition to M. Wicksteed's, but only to show that he was wrong to say as he did in his introductory lines: "I am not aware that any satisfactory attempt has been made to state what may be called the new theory of Distribution in its entirety; and still less have its relations to the old theory been defined"; and in expressly setting aside the question of "the identicality of the rate of remuneration of each of the factors of production with the partial differential coefficient of output with respect to [the quantity of] each factor," which is precisely the question that you treat and that you solve perfectly under the title of "The Theory of Marginal Productivity." Thus our two notes complement each other. If you want to convince yourself of this *de visu,* I will send you a copy of mine that I have kept. I ask only that you take good care of it.[13]

Walras's translation of Barone's lost review of Wicksteed's *Essay* ran as follows:

ON A RECENT BOOK BY WICKSTEED

1. M. Wicksteed, in his valuable little book, "An Essay on the Coordination of the Laws of Distribution" (London, Macmillan, 1894), proposes to develop and to state precisely, in deducing some of its important consequences, that *Law of marginal productivity* of which traces can be found in the work of a few writers, especially in Thünen, Jevons, and Marshall. The generality of this Law has recently been glimpsed more or less clearly by a group of American economists such as Hobson [*sic*], Wood, Carver, and especially Clark (*Quarterly Journal of Economics,* Vol. III, V, VIII).

But two things are detrimental to the cogency of Wicksteed's thesis: the somewhat convoluted and artificial manner in which the research is conducted; and, above all, the fact that the author has taken an arbitrary premise as a basis for his reasoning. The result is that his study uses a point of departure that may be very controversial in order to arrive at a conclusion that is nevertheless exactly true.

Persuaded as I am that the theory of marginal productivity can be very seminal in the science – and hoping to present an essay of my own on the subject before long – I am going to undertake in this short note to correct Wicksteed's reasoning in order to eliminate the possibility that his inexactitude and uncertainty may cast doubt upon the validity of the theory.

Furthermore, I will show in a few words that the law of marginal productivity is included within Walras's theory, and that a simple transformation is sufficient to derive it explicitly.

2. Let (A), (B), (C) . . . be *all* the factors that cooperate in the production of a certain product (P). And let

[13] F.W. I, 27

$$P = \varphi(A, B, C \ldots)$$

be a relation between the quantities of the factors and the quantity of the product. In this relation both the quantity of the product and the quantities of the factors are expressed in the appropriate units, and are not aggregated in groups of heterogeneous elements in the manner of the usual classification of land, labor, and capital.

The law of marginal productivity says this: *Under conditions of perfect free competition, each factor receives in remuneration a part of the output determined by the marginal productivity of the factor; and remuneration according to marginal productivity does not leave any undistributed residuum.*

That is to say:

a) The payments to (A), (B), (C)... are respectively

$$\frac{\partial \varphi}{\partial A} A, \quad \frac{\partial \varphi}{\partial B} B, \quad \frac{\partial \varphi}{\partial C} C \ldots$$

b) and

$$P = \frac{\partial \varphi}{\partial A} A + \frac{\partial \varphi}{\partial B} B + \frac{\partial \varphi}{\partial C} C + \ldots$$

It is easy to see that, because in a real market it is not the *product* that is distributed but its value in *numéraire*, the law amounts to saying in effect that if π is the price of the product [and] p_a, p_b, p_c... are the prices of the various factors, it will be true in a system of free competition that

$$\frac{\partial \varphi}{\partial A} = \frac{p_a}{\pi} ; \quad \frac{\partial \varphi}{\partial B} = \frac{p_b}{\pi} ; \quad \frac{\partial \varphi}{\partial C} = \frac{p_c}{\pi} \ldots$$

and

$$\pi P = p_a A + p_b B + p_c C + \ldots$$

and it is precisely the truth of that equality that must be demonstrated.

3. Let us see how Wicksteed proceeds.

He begins by affirming that if *all* the factors appear in the function $\varphi(A, B, C\ldots)$, and if they are distinct from each other, then if all the factors are increased in the same proportion (for example, if they are all doubled), the output will increase in the same proportion (for example, will double). "Now it must of course be admitted that if the physical conditions under which a certain amount of wheat, or anything else, is produced were exactly repeated, the result would be exactly repeated also, and a proportional increase of the one would yield a proportional increase of the other." (Page 32).

It is true that

$$\varphi(A, B, C \ldots) + \varphi(A, B, C \ldots) = 2\varphi(A, B, C \ldots),$$

but it does not follow from this truism, as Wicksteed believes, that

$$\varphi(A, B, C \ldots) + \varphi(A, B, C \ldots) = \varphi(2A, 2B, 2C \ldots)!$$

That transition is arbitrary. It is not legitimate except under the condition that a particular assumption is made about the nature of the function φ, namely, to assume that function is a homogeneous function. And that it is such a function is not demonstrated.*

Nor is there to be found all the necessary scientific rigor in the second part of his argument in which (pages 34–38), moving from the proposition that the proportional increase of all the factors results in a proportional increase in the *quantity* of the product, the author passes to the proposition, in order to complete his demonstration, that the proportional increase in the quantity of the product also implies, under a regime of free competition, a proportional increase in the *value* of output expressed in *numéraire*.

This reasoning is not rigorous because it is based upon the presupposition that the price of the product depends *exclusively* on the quantity of it that is available; whereas we know that the relations between the price and the available quantity are much more complex and that the demand function reduces to a simple relation between the price and the quantity only when that is admissible in certain cases and in certain questions, and not in others.

That part of Wicksteed's argument boils down to the following propositions: a proportional increase in the factors of production results in a proportional increase in the quantity of output; that increase in the quantity of output has the effect of lowering the price of the product in *numéraire*; but if the product is not monopolized, that is to say if the entire demand in the market is satisfied not by one but by several producers, an increase of production by one of them will not appreciably change the price; thus a proportional increase of all the factors corresponds rigorously to a proportional increase in the quantity of output and *approximately* a proportional increase in its value in *numéraire*. Thus "under ordinary conditions of competitive industry, it is sensibly or approximately true that if every factor of production draws a remuneration determined by its marginal efficiency or significance, the whole product will be exactly distributed." (p. 38).

It is sufficient to reflect a little on the course of the second part of Wicksteed's demonstration to become convinced that it is also defective because it does not

---

*We note the following. If, like Wicksteed, we assume that φ is a homogeneous function, that is to say that

$$\varphi(nA, \ nB, \ nC \ . \ . \ .) = n\varphi(A, \ B, \ C \ . \ . \ .) \tag{α}$$

the condition

$$\varphi(A, \ B, \ C \ . \ . \ .) = \frac{\partial \varphi}{\partial A} A \ + \ \frac{\partial \varphi}{\partial B} B \ + \ \frac{\partial \varphi}{\partial C} C \ + \ . \ . \ . \tag{β}$$

follows immediately without need of introducing the equations on pages 24 to 31. In effect, in taking the derivatives of the two sides of the equation (α) with respect to n, a variable that is independent of A, B, C . . ., we have

$$A\varphi'_A(nA, \ nB, \ nC \ . \ . \ .) \ + \ B\varphi'_B(nA, \ nB, \ nC \ . \ . \ .)$$
$$+ \ C\varphi'_C(nA, \ nB, \ nC \ . \ . \ .) \ + \ . \ . \ . = \ \varphi(A, \ B, \ C \ . \ . \ .)$$

for all values of n. And also for n $=$ 1. Equation β follows from this.

take account of the mutual and complex interdependence of diverse economic variables, such as exist in a market in equilibrium subject to the operation of free competition, and in addition completely neglects certain conditions that are characteristic of free competition. Furthermore, under the conditions postulated, the proposition is not only "approximately true": it is *rigorously* true.

For all these reasons the proof of the thesis as given by Wicksteed is uncertain, not very correct, not very persuasive.

4. The way to arrive at a correct proof of the thesis appears to me to be as follows.

Let π, p_a, p_b, p_c. . . . be the *equilibrium* prices in *numéraire* of the product and of the various factors of production.

If, in enumerating the various factors of production, account is taken of *all* of them, it will necessarily be true under conditions of free competition that:

$$\pi P = p_a A + p_b B + p_c C + \ldots \tag{1}$$

That is to say that *all* the output in *numéraire* will be distributed among the factors of production. It is not possible to conceive of free competition without that result. If, after *all* the factors of production have been paid at their market equilibrium prices, there remains an undistributed part of the *numéraire* value of the output, all the participants will begin to undertake this agreeable occupation: to seize upon remuneration without being *in any respect* involved in the productive process or in putting the product at the disposal of the consumer. That would be possible in a monopoly; it is inconceivable in a regime of free competition.

Equation (1) is our point of departure.

Another important effect of free competition is this: At the margin of production, an increment of any factor of production ought to give an increment of output of which the *numéraire* value is equal to the remuneration in *numéraire* of the increment of the factor, because if that were not the case, equilibrium could not exist in the distribution of all the factors among different economic activities. Thus, if it is true that

$$\Delta A \cdot p_a = \frac{\partial \varphi}{\partial A} \Delta A \cdot \pi$$

and similarly for all the other factors, then

$$\frac{\partial \varphi}{\partial A} = \frac{p_a}{\pi} \; ; \; \frac{\partial \varphi}{\partial B} = \frac{p_b}{\pi} \; ; \; \frac{\partial \varphi}{\partial C} = \frac{p_c}{\pi} \ldots \tag{2}$$

Equations (1) and (2) immediately give

$$P = \frac{\partial \varphi}{\partial A} A + \frac{\partial \varphi}{\partial B} B + \frac{\partial \varphi}{\partial C} C + \ldots .$$

from which it is seen that the thesis is proved.

5. I am now going to show, as I have already stated (paragraph 1), that the law of marginal productivity is a part of Walras's theory and that it can be found in substance in the equations that appear in another form in Walras's system.

Walras's ideal entrepreneur who makes neither profit nor loss after having paid for all the services that he hires (and also the real entrepreneur to whom he gives the profits) corresponds precisely to the concepts symbolically represented by the equation

$$\pi P = p_a A + p_b B + p_c C + \ldots$$

except that Walras wrote that equation in the form

$$\pi = a\, p_a + b\, p_b + c\, p_c + \ldots$$

in which a, b, c . . . are the coefficients of production equal to our $\dfrac{A}{P}, \dfrac{B}{P}, \dfrac{C}{P} \ldots$

He then said – I am taking account of the refinements that Prof. Pareto has made to Walras's theory – that between the coefficients of production there is a relation into which the quantity of production also enters, because the optimum coefficients of production depend also on the quantity of output that they enable to be produced:

$$\Theta(a, b, c \ldots P) = 0 \tag{3}$$

This relation determines a, b, c . . . with the condition that, given the prices of the factors of production and the quantity produced, the average cost of production must be a minimum, the value to which the price of output is made equal by the effect of free competition.

It is easy to see that the conditions for a minimum are

$$\frac{\partial\Theta}{\partial a} : p_a = \frac{\partial\Theta}{\partial b} : p_b = \frac{\partial\Theta}{\partial c} : p_c = \ldots \tag{4}$$

These relations and equation (3) determine the coefficients of production.

Now, if it is recalled that $\quad a = \dfrac{A}{P}, \; b = \dfrac{B}{P}, \; c = \dfrac{C}{P} \ldots$, the identity of the implications of Walras's system with the implications of the law of marginal productivity is evidenct.

$$\Theta(a, b, c \ldots P) = 0 \qquad\qquad \varphi(A, B, C \ldots) - P = 0$$

$$\frac{\partial\Theta}{\partial a} : p_a = \frac{\partial\Theta}{\partial b} : p_b = \frac{\partial\Theta}{\partial c} : p_c = \ldots \qquad \frac{\partial\varphi}{\partial A} : p_a = \frac{\partial\varphi}{\partial B} : p_b = \frac{\partial\varphi}{\partial C} : p_c = \ldots$$

$$\pi = a p_a + b p_b + c p_c + \ldots \qquad\qquad \pi P = p_a A + p_b B + p_c C + \ldots$$

Enrico Barone[14]

At the end of the manuscript containing the translation, Walras added in colored pencil a note reading, "Envoyé à Edgeworth pour l'*Economic Journal*," which clearly indicates that at the time he made the translation he had not yet heard of Edgeworth's rejection of Barone's review. The story of this rebuff was conveyed to Walras by the following letter from Barone of October 26, 1895, in reply to Walras's letter of October 23rd:

[14] See Notes 5 and 6, *supra*.

I thank you for your very kind letter. My friend M. Pareto will have perhaps already told you why my note will not be published in the *Economic Journal*. M. Edgeworth, after having asked me to examine M. Wicksteed's work, and to enlarge upon, in an article, the observations that I had made in one of my letters to M. Edgeworth himself; after having written to me to tell me that my note was, in his opinion, a new ray of light on a very important question, one fine day he informed me that it was impossible for him to publish it. My note has, evidently, shocked those gentlemen who have understood neither your theory nor the role of the entrepreneur in it. It is evident: my note has not had the good fortune of being acceptable to the pontiff of English economists, M. Marshall; and poor M. Edgeworth finds himself embarrassed! It's of no significance. I will continue on my course; I study science only to discover truth and not to succeed in being agreeable to this or that person. For me it is sufficient satisfaction that my ideas have full approval from you and from M. Pareto, the only persons with whom I can discuss things without fear of not being understood.

I don't know if you have translated my note with the intention of publishing it as an *appendix* to yours in the *Recueil Universitaire*. If so, I'll be very flattered; and, in that case, I would like to ask you to let me have the rough draft when it is ready, because I would like to add a few words in order to explain more clearly the role of the entrepreneur, which the English authors have so much difficulty in understanding. After that I will present the Italian translation of my note in the *Giornale degli Economisti*. . . .

I will read your note with great eagerness; I'll guard it with all possible care.[15]

Walras's first reaction to this news was quite restrained in comparison with what was to follow. On October 30, 1895, Walras wrote Barone a letter that consisted mainly of a critical discussion of Barone's review:

I am sending you my little note included with this letter. . . . I am not at all astonished by what happened to you at the *Economic Journal;* on the contrary, I would have been very astonished if it had been published there.

I have sent to M. Pareto the manuscript copy of your note that he had lent to me. As for my translation, I don't believe that it would be appropriate to offer something like that to an Anthology of choice pieces emanating from our University to represent it in a national Exposition, and appearing no one knows when. But I plan to make a short résumé of it which I will attach as an appendix at the end of my piece.[16] I will wait to write this résumé until you have developed and completed your theory in the way that you find satisfactory for submission to the *Giornali degli Economisti*.

[15] F.W. II, 1877. *Cf.* Note 10, *supra,* last paragraph.

[16] In carrying out this intention, Walras added to his "Note" a Post-Script found on pp. 489–492 of the third edition of the *Eléments* (*cf.* Note (2), *supra*, and *Eléments of Pure Economics*, pp. 493–95. The Post-Script was not presented as a summary of Barone's review, but rather as a statement of Walras's understanding of it. This Post-Script, as published, was dated, "Octobre 1895," which would mean either that Walras composed it the very next day after writing to Barone or that he had already prepared it – in any case, without waiting, as he said he would, for any further developments of Barone's theory.

Until then, I'm going to study the issue again; for I ought to admit that there is one point on which I am not sure that I am totally in agreement with you. It does not seem to me that the equations

$$\Delta A \cdot p_a = \frac{\partial \varphi}{\partial A}\Delta A \cdot \pi$$

express, as you maintained, "the state of equilibrium in the distribution of all the factors among the various economic activities." I believe that these equations instead express the "minimum average cost of production" obtained through *tâtonnement* by the entrepreneur who does not know the function φ or Θ, doesn't amuse himself by making a distinction between them, but who increases the quantity of service A as long as

$$\Delta A \cdot p_a < \frac{\partial \varphi}{\partial A}\Delta A \cdot \pi$$

and who decreases it as long as

$$\Delta A \cdot p_a > \frac{\partial \varphi}{\partial A}\Delta A \cdot \pi.$$

Thus it is quite clear that the theory of *marginal productivity* is not only "included" within my theory; it *is* my theory, [indicated] by the differentiation of my equations

$$p_b = b_t p_t + b_p p_p + b_k p_k + \ldots$$
$$\varphi(b_t, b_p, b_k \ldots) = 0$$

in consideration of the minimum value of p_b. I remarked upon that differentiation (*Eléments,* par. 200, 274),[17] leaving to others the task of making it. This all deals with a point on which I ought to reflect very calmly because my head is very tired and refuses to undertake any work that is somewhat intense and closely reasoned.

It should be observed, however, that in the rough draft of the above letter there is a second paragraph that Walras crossed out and that began:

[17] Ed. 2, 1889 (*cf.* §§204 and 325 of the fourth definitive edition; and *Elements of Pure Economics,* p. 582, Collation Note [f] to Lesson 20, and p. 604, Collation Note [o] to Lesson 36). The passages in the *Eléments* referred to contain a virtual repetition of the same idea he had already expressed in 1876 in his memoir entitled, "Equations de la Production," read before the Société vaudoise des sciences naturelles on the 19th of January and the 16th of February, 1876, published in the *Bulletin* of that Société, vol. XIV, No. 76, October, 1876, pp. 395–430, and republished in the *Théorie mathématique de la richesse sociale,* Lausanne, Corbaz, 1883, where on p. 66 we find:

The respective quantities of each of the productive services that therefore are combined into a unit of output of each of the commodities are determined only after the determination of the prices of productive services by the condition that the average cost of production of the products be minimized.

You must treat these people as I do. When I saw that they had decided not to make my theory known in England, I turned toward the Americans.

The initial caution which dictated this deletion arose, one would guess, from an easily understandable diffidence in communicating one's more violent sentiments to a stranger, for Walras never met Barone.

Then Walras received a series of letters from Barone which must have warmed the cockles of his heart and which finally, as we shall see, broke down all reserve. In the first of these letters from Barone, dated November 8, 1895, we read:

I have just read your note on Wicksteed's book. I fully share the opinion that you have expressed on the work of that author.

With respect to the equation

$$\Delta A.p_a = \frac{\partial \varphi}{\partial A} \Delta A.\pi$$

you are right. It expresses "the minimum average cost of production" and not "the state of equilibrium in the distribution of all the factors among the various economic activities." I don't know how that last statement escaped me. It is evidently my fault.

Also, I entirely agree with you that the theory of marginal productivity is none other than the development of what you had already indicated in §§200 and 274 of your *Eléments*. That was precisely my thought when I wrote my note. If that thought isn't expressed with sufficient clarity, I will try to make it better understood in the *Giornale*.[18]

To this Walras responded, still soberly, on November 11, 1895:

Yesterday I received your kind letter of the 8th, with the copy of my note.

Because we are absolutely in agreement, as far as I can see, on the principal points of this question of marginal productivity, it seemed to me that I could draft my Post-Script to my note here and now.[19] I send you that draft, asking you to be so kind as to look it over, and to give me all your comments on it. I will receive them with the same good faith that you have shown in welcoming mine.

Barone then reiterated and improved upon his laudatory attribution of priority to Walras, and made more emphatic than ever his denial of Wicksteed's claim to being the first to coordinate the laws of distribution. This was not intended merely to humor Walras; for, as can be seen in the following passges from Barone's letter of November 13, 1895, he did not hesitate either to take sharp issue with his "maestro"[20] on a

---

[18] F.W. II, 1879.   [19] *Cf.* Note 16, *supra*.

[20] It was in a letter from Barone to Knut Wicksell, dated November 23, 1895, that Barone referred to Walras as his "maestro":

Io pienamente e profondamente deploro le controversie fra il mio maestro ed il Prof. Marshall ed il Prof. Edgeworth tanto che, come Ella avrà visto, l'opera scientifica mia à stata in parte rivolta fino ad ora a mettere pace fra di essi.

I am indebted to Professor Torsten Gårdlund of Stockholm for a photocopy of this letter.

matter of analytical importance or to define the limits of what he conceived to be Walras's original contribution.

I have read your note with great care. I don't have anything to say about it, except for something about what you say on page [c1]. I don't understand, for example, why in the study of distribution you attribute less importance, so to speak, to the equations that determine the coefficients of production than to other equations, and why you say that the determination of those coefficients "assumes that the prices of these services are determined because they are based on the differentiation of the equations of the average cost of production." I believe that all that is not exact; to my mind it is not at all necessary to suppose that the prices of services are *determined in order to determine in their turn the values of those coefficients*. All these variables *are mutually determined at the same time;* and it is precisely one of your greatest merits to have demonstrated that "rent, wages, interest, prices of products and the *coefficients of production,* all being unknowns in the same problem, must be determined all together. . ." (*Eléments,* p. 358 [ed. 2]).[21]

The truth is that you saw perfectly how to determine those coefficients; and that you did not enlarge upon the details of this matter, because you are looking at the problem of the true coordination (that M. Wicksteed claims to have just furnished us with!) in its entirety, a problem of the entire system that you have solved perfectly. In examining your theory and your question regarding the coefficients of production, in making the differentiations that you accurately indicated were appropriate, some very elegant propositions are found. They alone, however, are not at all sufficient to make the problem determinate. That is the whole truth. The theory of marginal productivity is only a new manner of expressing two of the relations that make the problem determinate; that is to say, the condition of the price of output being equal to the average cost of production, and the condition that the average cost to the entrepreneur be at a minimum.[22]

With only the published text of Walras's "Note" in Appendix III before one, it is difficult to see what Barone's critical remarks in the first of the above paragraphs could have referred to. Luckily, there is found preserved among the manuscripts at Lausanne the following paragraph which contains the passage Barone quoted in his letter and which is described in Walras's hand as "eliminated from the last part of the appendix on Wicksteed":

Thus, assuming that the coordination of the laws of distribution depends upon the theory of marginal productivity, that coordination would have been, if not completed, at least a long way toward being completed before Wicksteed's work – work that has not resulted in perfecting the subject. It would have been better if he had been motivated to render more justice to those who had

---

[21] *Cf.* §362 of the fourth definitive edition of the *Eléments;* and p. 607 of the *Elements of Pure Economics,* Collation Note [o] to Lesson 39.

[22] F.W. II, 1880.

preceded him. But does the coordination of the laws of distribution depend upon the theory of marginal productivity? I leave the discussion of that question to others. It seems to me that it is rather the contrary that is true. Once the theory of marginal productivity is elucidated, as it is in all essentials in the Note of M. Barone, one sees immediately that it introduces into the theory of production a certain number of unknowns that are the coefficients of production $b_1 \ldots b_p \ldots b_k \ldots$, which are assumed to be variable, and which depend not only on each other, but also on the quantity of output. The theory also provides an equal number of equations. The equations of marginal productivity are none other than the equations of minimum average cost of production that were indicated but not furnished by me (*Eléments*, §§200, 274).[23] As for the unknowns that are the prices of services $p_1 \ldots p_p \ldots p_k \ldots$, and as for the equations that serve to determine them, they are the subject of another part of the theory of production. Now that other part can be developed without taking account of the determination of the coefficients of production; whereas the determination of the latter, on the contrary, *assumed that the prices of services are determined, because they depend upon the differentiation of the equation of the average cost of production.* The more I think about it, the more I believe that M. Wicksteed, in giving us the theory of marginal productivity with the objective of coordinating the laws of distribution, tries (without at all succeeding) to furnish us with the equations of the minimum average cost of production with a view to determining the prices of services, thanks to which confusion he still has one foot lodged in the theory of Ricardo, from which he believes himself completely liberated. But there it is! He applies himself particularly to solving the problem that I had already solved; and this is why he has only half-solved the problem that remains in need of solution. MM. Pareto and Barone proceed in another manner: they don't claim to refute me by proving that I haven't created pure mathematical economics all alone, and they don't give themselves the task of doing again what I have already done. They take the science at the point to which I have brought it and left it, and they proposed to continue on beyond me; and consequently they achieved important and new results that are complete and definitive.[24]

How Walras came to delete this paragraph is seen in his next letter to Barone, dated November 16, 1895, where he wrote:

This morning I received . . . your letter of the 13th of this month, in consequence of which I'm going to eliminate from the P.S. to my *Note* on Wicksteed everything that deals with the relation of the theory of marginal productivity to the coordination of the laws of distribution, a relation that I will leave to you to set forth, if you so desire, in the *Giornale degli Economisti*. I am all the more willing to do this because you indicate those relations in your letter in a way that fully satisfies me.

Nevertheless, Walras could not really bring himself to abandon all idea of publishing the stinging rebuke of Wicksteed contained in the deleted paragraph; for it eventually reappeared, as we have seen, in the closing lines of the published Post-Script to his "Note."

[23] *Cf.* Note 17, *supra.*   [24] F.W. V, 1.

To Walras's letter of November 16th, which also carried an offer to lend Barone copies of his rare early publications, Barone replied on November 20th, "Je vous remercie bien de la confiance que vous avez en moi . . . ."[25]

By this time Walras probably felt that here was a kindred spirit, and, abandoning all reserve, he gave full vent to the deep-rooted resentment he bore against the English in general, a resentment he had inherited from his father, whose childhood coincided with the Napoleonic Wars. This we see in the second part of his letter of November 24, 1895. In the first part, he referred Barone to Ladislaas Bortkiewicz's answer[26] to Edgeworth's criticism of Walras's method of assuming certain variables *provisionally* as constants and then gradually dropping these assumptions as he passed from one stage to the next in the unfolding of his general equilibrium model. Then in the second part of the letter, Walras went on to say:

All that I wished to say in the conclusion that I have eliminated from my Note on Wicksteed follows from the fact that M. Bortkévitch's observation is equally applicable to *coefficients of production* as to *quantities of output produced,* as to *quantities of artificial capital,* etc.

I am enclosing two additions to the Note on Wicksteed that I am tempted to make before giving it to the printer. The first is a little note in which I demonstrate your theorem by a method that I have already employed in the *Eléments*. . . . The second would be a short Preface that I wrote upon the receipt of your letter of October 26 without the intention of publishing it. Above all, I wrote it, as I often do, in order to relieve my mind of an idea that obsesses me, by throwing it out onto the paper. Having thought the matter over completely, however, I would like, so far as I am concerned, to make it precede my note, if that's agreeable with you. What makes up my mind on this matter is the consideration that one doesn't get anything from the English except by refusing to allow oneself to be troubled by them and by putting them in their place. It would not be impossible that some people may be shocked by the behavior of Marshall and Edgeworth and tempted not to associate with them. I know by experience that when one has the English against one, one does well to welcome the Americans, who are generally very well-disposed in our favor. . . .

Of the first of the proposed additions he sent to Barone, I have not been able to find any trace among either Walras's letters or his papers.[27]

---

[25] F.W. II, 1881.

[26] Bortkiewicz's review of the second edition of Walras's *Eléments* (1889), *Revue d'Economie Politique,* January–February, 1890, pp. 80–86. Bortkiewicz is usually transliterated "Bortkévitch," in French.

[27] Though the following undated note found on a small separate sheet among Walras's letters to Barone contains an analysis linking Barone's theorem of marginal productivity to Walras's earlier work on Ricardo's theory of rent, it could not have been the addition in question because it refers to equations in §326 that did not appear until the 4th edition of

But we do have the second, at least so I judge from the date, content, and explosive tenor of the following manuscript:

I wrote the *Note* that follows in September 1894, immediately after having read M. Wicksteed's volume, and solely in order to clarify my opinion on a subject that was of interest to me. I sent it only to M. Pareto.

During this month [October 1895], M. Pareto sent me in turn a note of M. Barone's intended for the *Economic Journal,* which seemed to me to complete the study of the question, and which I summarized and placed at the end of mine.

Now I learn that M. Edgeworth, the editor of the *Economic Journal,* who, in his discussions with us has always very carefully abstained from answering us in his own journal, and who has found in the journals of our friends an unlimited hospitality extended to explanations of his own that are more prolix than penetrating, refuses to insert M. Barone's *Note* of four or five pages in which the author illuminates completely, by means of an original demonstration, a theory that is of evident importance. I strenuously protest this action and at the same time I am publishing my own *Note* and its *Post-Script.*

In the meeting in which the *British Economic Association* and its organ the *Economic Journal* were founded, on November 21, 1890, apropos of the hope expressed by some persons "that these institutions would exercise a salutary influence," Marshall, signatory of the report of the meeting, expressed himself as follows in the name of the founders: "That was the one thing which he hoped they would not set themselves to do. Their desire was not *to exert a wholesome influence* in the sense of setting up a standard of orthodoxy, to which all contributors had to conform; economics was a science and *an orthodox science* was a contradiction in terms. Science could be true or false, but could not be orthodox; and the best way to find out what was true was to welcome the criticisms of all people who know what they were talking about. . . etc., etc." Marvelous! Only, it can now be seen that these emphatic declarations carry an unspoken restriction, namely that in regard to mathematical economics, the

---

the *Eléments* (1900).

For a commodity (B) produced by two services (T) and (K), [3] and [4] of the marginal productivity theorem (326) imply

$$\frac{P_t}{P_b} T = Q - \left(\frac{d\varphi}{dK}\right) K \qquad \ldots [1]$$

If it is assumed that Q = H, so that T = Hb = 1, and K = x; the function Q = w(T, K) becomes H = F(x), and the partial derivative $d\varphi/dK$ becomes F'(x). Then equation [1] becomes

$$\frac{P_t}{P_b} = F(x) - xF'(x) \qquad \ldots [2]$$

which is identical to Ricardo's mathematical theory of rent. (361) [i.e. §361 of the fourth edition of the *Eléments*].

Whereas his theory uses equation [2] for the determination of P_t/P_b, the theory of marginal productivity uses equation [1] together with the equation Q = F(T, K) for the determination of b_t and b_k.

Cf. footnote added to fourth definitive edition of the *Eléments* 1926, p. 414; and the *Elements of Pure Economics*, p. 418, note 1.

readers of the *Economic Journal* will hear only one side of the question, the side of the influential members of the editorial committee.

October 31, 1895.   L. W.[28]

A teasing psychological problem is raised by the discrepancy between the date on which Walras first submitted his "Note sur la réfutation..." (to start with, without the Post-Script) for publication in the *Recueil*[29] and his frequent protestations that he resolved to publish his "Note" only as a protest after he had learned of Edgeworth's rejection of Barone's review. That these protestations referred to his entire "Note" and not merely to the proposed "petite Préface" or the Post-Script is clear from the retracted addition dated October 31, 1895, which is quoted above, and from the following footnote, which he first added in pencil and then crossed out on the page proofs of the "Note" (containing the Post-Script) intended for the *Recueil:*

I wrote these few pages for myself alone. I seized the occasion of publishing them on learning that the editors of the *Economic Journal* had refused to publish M. Barone's Note.[30]

Later, on March 29, 1897, he wrote to Professor Ernest Mahaim of Liège, commenting on the separately bound offprint of the three appendixes to the 3rd edition of the *Eléments:* "Apropos of my brochure, I ought to tell you that Edgeworth, evidently under the influence of Marshall and of Wicksteed, has rejected Barone's theorem, after having first accepted it eagerly for his Review. That is why I decided to publish Appendix III in the form that you will find it."[31] The facts, however, are: (1) that on September 27, 1895, Walras informed Dean Jacques Berney of the Faculté de Droit at Lausanne that he was ready to send him the "Note sur la réfutation..." for publication in the forthcoming *Recueil;*[32] (2) that according to Walras's letter to Barone of October 23, 1895 (quoted above), the manuscript of the "Note" was sent on September 30; (3) that both in the *Recueil* and in Appendix III of the *Eléments,* the "Note" preceding the Post-Script is dated "Septembre 1894" (the Post-Script itself being dated, as we have seen, "Octobre 1895"); (4) that the "Note" (*sans* Post-Script) must have been submitted for publication *before* Walras had heard from either Pareto or Barone of Edgeworth's rejection of Barone's review. As for the Post-Script, it was not submitted to Dean Berney to be added to the "Note" until December 2, 1895, as

---

[28] F.W. V, 1.   [29] *Cf.* Note 2, *supra.*

[30] These page proofs which are in my possession, having been presented to me by Walras's daughter, the late Aline Walras, were rubber-stamped by the publisher of the *Recueil,* "January 25, 1895," but this is obviously a mistake in the stamp, for the year must have been 1896. *Cf. Elements of Pure Economics,* p. 610.

[31] F.W. I, 357.   [32] F.W. I, 41.

we learn from Walras's covering letter of that date to Dean Berney, which began: "*Voici le Post-Scriptum* à ma *Note.* Il n'y aura pas de Préface ..." Walras's letter to Barone of October 23rd, the notation he made in colored pencil at the end of his translation of Barone's review, and the month of October set down but then deleted (hence the square brackets) in the second paragraph of the proposed "petite Préface," all show unmistakably that he had not heard of the rejection before October, certainly not before October 23rd and very probably not until October 28th, when, according to his notation, he received Barone's letter of October 26th. Why then did Walras pretend to himself or to others that he had had no intention of ever publishing his "Note" until he was moved to do so as an expression of righteous indignation against Edgeworth's mistreatment of Barone? Perhaps his protestations betoken an uneasy conscience trying to justify to itself a publication in questionable taste.

Whether or not Barone perceived this discrepancy, Walras's wrath[33] was too much for Barone. Though he felt himself deeply aggrieved by Edgeworth's refusal of his review, though he conceded that Walras was right in his private complaint about Wicksteed's failure to mention Walras's earlier contribution to the theory of the coordination of the laws of distribution, Barone envisaged his rôle as that of a peacemaker among rival mathematical economists.[34] Thus he replied immediately to Walras on November 26th:

As for the two notes, I would be obliged if you would *not* publish the second. I don't care about myself; I care above all about science; and from these polemics, which are totally personal, I believe that science has nothing to gain.

[33] Repeated private jottings in the same vein show how hard Walras must have found it really to clear his mind of a sullen obsession. One of these jottings found on a small piece of paper among the letters to Barone reads:

The theory of marginal productivity is especially important to me because it provides in the most striking fashion the complete and thorough conclusion of the critique of Ricardo's theory of rent that has cost me a great deal of trouble. I wrote that critique in 1877 (24 years ago) in the first edition of *Eléments d'économie politique pure,* and M. Wicksteed drew upon much of it (17 years later) in 1894 without giving me credit. (Having said that, it will be understood why I do not give up my interest in science, which is always a source of delight, and why I am going to try to disengage myself as much as possible from relationships with scientists – relationships that are more often than not a source of unpleasantness.)

Another jotting, scrawled on a still smaller piece of paper and preserved among the manuscripts in F.W. V, 1, refers to Marshall's alleged part in the rejection of Barone's *Note,* and reads:

In order to understand Marshall's villainy with respect to Barone, it is necessary to read the two articles in the *Giornale degli economisti,* "Sulla Consumers' Rent" (September 1894) [and] "Sul trattamento di quistioni dinamiche" (November 1894) [in which Barone came out in defense of Marshall's theories].

[34] *Cf.* Note 20, *supra.* What makes this role as peacemaker all the more interesting is the fact that Barone was at this time a career army officer attached to general headquarters.

Victory must be obtained for the mathematical method, and for mathematical economists to tear each other to pieces is not the best way of obtaining it. Let us leave M. Edgeworth alone, especially because when hs sent me back my work, he did so along with a letter in which he didn't hide his embarrassment. We can support our thesis totally objectively, and that would be best for the prestige of the mathematical school.[35]

Walras was apparently abashed by this and at once softened his tone, as if nothing had ever been further from his thought than to air his personal grievances in public. Thus on December 1st, 1895, he wrote Barone:

I am all the more able to understand your wishes regarding the attitude that should be taken vis-à-vis MM. Marshall and Edgeworth because those wishes have been mine for a long time.[36] My little Preface will remain unpublished.

From here on, in any case, the flow of correspondence between Walras and Barone, which had begun in September, 1894, and swelled to flood proportions during November, 1895, dwindled into dull driblets that became fewer and farther between. The next letter we have is again one from Walras dated March 15, 1896, saying merely that he had sent his "Note" to Professor John Bates Clark along with a letter strongly recommending Barone, who was then angling for an academic post in the United States,[37] as a mathematical economist of great promise. He also asked Barone to send him a copy of his forthcoming article in the *Giornale degli economisti* on marginal productivity.[38] Barone then wrote to

[35] F.W. II, 1882.

[36] True! Some five years back, Walras had expressed much the same sentiments in a letter to Maffeo Pantaleoni written on August 17, 1889 (F.W. I, 427):

It is clear to me that Jevons himself acted quite peculiarly in giving himself the air, in the 10 last pages of the Preface to his 2nd edition of his *Theory of Political Economy*, of having discovered independently the principle of the determination of the prices of productive services in accordance with the prices of products, when he had quite simply found it in the 1st edition of my "*Eléments d'économie politique pure.*" I find that M. Marshall has acted quite peculiarly in having his theories printed "for private circulation," thus establishing his rights of priority without publishing anything, so as to be able to continue his research at his leisure, without anyone being able to take precedence of him. All that is clear to me and other things also. But I also recognize that it is a good policy, because we are so few in numbers and so lacking in influence, to close ranks together somewhat, rather than to bicker with each other. The time will come later to write the history of the science, and then our merits and our individual behavior will become known.

This is my private opinion. I am communicating it to you because you ask it of me, on the condition that it is confidential.

[37] In his letter of November 26, 1895, already cited in another connection, Barone had written to Walras: "I am hunting for a chair, and to have one I would even go to America. My love for science makes me ready to sacrifice my brilliant military career [*cf.* Note 34, *supra*]; but I'm not rich, and if I want to devote myself totally to science, a chair is necessary."

[38] "Studi sulla distribuzione," *op. cit.*

Walras on April 27th, 1896, to apologize for his delay in acknowledging receipt of the 3rd edition of the *Eléments*, explaining that he had been snowed under with work since his recent appointment as Professor of Strategy and Military History at the military staff college in Turin.[39] Walras apparently did not reply to this until November 11, 1896 when he promised to send Barone one of the first copies of the forthcoming *Etudes d'Economie Sociale* (1896) and added:

I have recently received, regarding the theory of marginal productivity, communications from some of my best correspondents who are in agreement in finding it remarkable in itself and definitive from the point of view of the mathematical theory of production. The fact is that you have, in my opinion, comprehended better than anyone what it is, the essence and the character of that theory; and I regret bitterly that you are writing military history instead of writing the history and the criticism of economic theory. But there is an inevitable end for economic theory. It is inevitable that it will triumph only after our society has ceased to exist.

Barone sent a banal missive in response on November 23rd, 1896, thanking Walras in advance for the promised copy of the *Etudes d'Economie Sociale* and ending with the following inauspicious paragraph:

I also, my dear Professor, regret being obliged at present to put economic theories somewhat to one side; but I hope that a little after the end of this year – when I have prepared all my 120 (!) lessons in Military History and Strategy, I will be able to return to it.[40]

This is, indeed, the last letter we have from Barone to Walras, though Walras later referred to a card received in 1900 of which there is no trace in the archives. Barone's preoccupation at the military staff college could hardly have been the whole reason for the final cessation of all communication with Walras. We know that Barone never relaxed his interest in economics, though he had to wait until 1907 to become a professor of economics.[41]

More than five years elapsed before Walras wrote to Barone again. At the end of 1901, when Walras was preparing his final revision of the *Eléments* for the definitive edition, he made one last, desperate attempt to reestablish contact with Barone. This final letter has already been

---

[39] F.W. II, 1898.   [40] F.W. II, 1930.

[41] In 1907, Barone became professor of economics at the Instituto de scienza economiche in Rome. His *Principi di economia politica* (1908), and his well-known article, "Il Ministro della produzione nello stato collettivista" (*op. cit.*) published in the same year, give unmistakable evidence that Barone must have kept his hand in the subject in the interval between 1896 and 1907, and that he continued to draw inspiration from the Walras-Pareto general equilibrium model.

published,[42] but the version given below is closer to the text of Walras's draft.

> Lieut.-Colonel Barone
> Professor at the School of War,
> Turin, Italy
> Les Brayères sur Clarens,
> Vaud
> December 10, 1901

Monsieur le Colonel,

In a letter dated September 20, 1894, which I have before me, you sent me the equations of marginal productivity, represented as "equations of maximum net product." I find the equations sound but incorrectly rationalized.

In a *note* sent by you to M. Edgeworth, refused by him, communicated to me by M. Pareto in October 1895, and which I also have, in translation, before me, you provide the same equations as "equations of equilibrium in the distribution of all the factors among various economic activities." I wrote to you on October 30 that, in my opinion, they were "equations of the minimum average cost of production." And you answered me on November 8 that you were giving up your own opinion and adopting mine.

I tried sincerely to take an exact account of all these circumstances when I introduced the *Theorem of Marginal Productivity* in the 4th edition of my *Eléments d'économie politique pure*.

Now, in a note (p. 10) of a short work entitled *Economic Theory*[43] that he published recently, M. Pareto said this:

"We have given, in the *Cours* §719 note, the equations that determine the coefficients of production.

"The theory that claims to determine them by consideration of marginal productivity is erroneous. Quantities that are not independent variables are treated as though they are, and the equations that are written to determine the minimum are not admissible. This is the case with equations (3) of the *Eléments d'économie politique pure* of M. Walras, 4th edition, p. 375."

In response to these assertions, I want to state that, during the entire course of production *tâtonnements*, the quantity produced of commodity (B), $Q = \varphi(T, P, K)$, initially fixed at random at the level Ω_b (*Eléments* §208 [4th edition], then successively equal to Ω'_b (§211) ... D'_b (§212), D''_b (§218), D'''_b (§219) ..., is

---

[42]The letter was published in Henri Schultz's article "Marginal Productivity and the General Pricing Process," *Journal of Political Economy*, Vol. XXXVII, No. 5, October, 1929, pp. 547–551. This previously published version differs substantially from mine. Professor Schultz did not have the rough draft at his disposal, but only a garbled transcription made by Walras's daughter, Aline, who had no understanding of the technical passages which are, at best, extremely difficult to decipher from Walras's crabbed draft. It is not surprising that Schultz's commentary on the letter was quite unsatisfactory. *Cf.* M. Georgescu-Roegen, "Fixed Coefficients of Production and Marginal Productivity Theory," *Review of Economic Studies*, Vol. 3, No. 1, October, 1935, pp. 40–49; and H. Neisser, "A Note on Pareto's Theory of Production," *Econometrica*, Vol. 8, No. 3, July 1940, pp. 253–262.

[43] Reprinted in *Metroeconomica*, Vol. VII, April, 1955, pp. 1–15. The passage quoted is found on p. 9 of this reprint.

always determined in a special manner and is, like the prices of the services, a *given datum* and not *an unknown* in the problem of the determination of the coefficients of production. From this it follows, it seems to me, that $T = Qb_t$, $P = Qb_p$, $K = Qb_k$ ... are, in that latter problem, variables that are as independent as b_t, b_p, b_k. ... Contrary to the opinion of M. Pareto, I continue therefore, by reason of the conception that I have created of the establishment of economic equilibrium, to believe that equations [3] on p. 375 of my *Eléments* are perfectly admissible and that the theory of marginal productivity with which they are in harmony is a theory of "capital importance in economics," one that you have so commendably introduced in a rational manner into the science by providing it with the most appropriate mathematical expression.

I asked you to tell me if the argument that I have just presented seems sound to you, and if, in consequence, you would like to take the responsibility, and, what is in my opinion the honor, of having formulated the equations [1], [2], [3], and [4] of the "determination of the coefficients of production under the condition of a minimum average cost of production," equations that we set forth and agreed upon in 1895. If so, the part of my text numbered 326 will remain as it is so far as it concerns you. In the contrary case, I will claim those equations as my own.

Please accept the assurance of my best wishes.

Léon Walras.

There was no response. Walras recorded his dismay in two pencilled notes characteristically scrawled on the blank inner surface of a used envelope cut open at three edges and unfolded to serve as economical jotting paper:

I have vainly awaited a response from M. Barone up to the present day, March 6, 1902. Thus far I have held back from the printers the corrections to pages 375–76 of my *Eléments*.

March 6, 1902
Léon Walras.

and

It is now October 4, and still nothing. I am sending the corrections to the printer. See his card (1900).

L. W.

The first of these notes refers to proofs of the revised pages 375 and 376 of which Walras had the type set up in advance in 1902 for the eventual "édition définitive" of the *Eléments,* which actually did not appear until after his death, in 1926. At the foot of page 376 of the "édition définitive," there is a new note (referred to at the end of §326) reproducing, almost word for word, the whole analytical argument contained in Walras's letter of December 10, 1901, quoted above. Of this I shall have more to say in what follows.

The contrapuntal interweaving of private sentiments, caustic accusa-
tions and theoretical analysis in the above correspondence makes it
necessary to separate out the purely analytical considerations in order to
clarify the particular phase of the history of the marginal productivity
theory with which we are concerned.

One thing is clear: Léon Walras neither invented nor ever said he
invented the marginal productivity theory. Neither in the first three
editions of the *Eléments* (apart from the Post-Script to Appendix III of the
3rd edition) nor in any other of his published writings (apart from his
contribution to the *Recueil*,[44] which appeared in the same year as the
third edition of the *Eléments*), do we find any mention of a marginal
productivity theory. Moreover, in his "Note sur la réfutation...,"
whatever Walras has to say about the marginal productivity theory is
presented merely as his reformulation and interpretation of Barone's
unpublished review. This is precisely what has confounded and misled
his readers, for, without any clue to the contents of Barone's review, it
has proved impossible, as George J. Stigler discovered,[45] to tell what
part of the argument in the Post-Script was Barone's and what part
Walras's. This confusion, which, it must be admitted, Walras himself
created, was not deliberate. If it were, he would not have written for the
leaflet put out by the Librairie Pichon, the Paris distributor of the third
edition of the *Eléments,* that Pareto and Barone "are busy completing
this system [i.e., Walras's system] by studying the variations of the
coefficients of production...," coefficients which Walras in his own
model had assumed to be constant quite explicitly as a first approximation. Nor would he have written to Luigi Einaudi on February 4, 1900:

M. Barone is the man who has profited most by my works in order to open
new perspectives even to me. His theorem of "marginal productivity" by which
he provides the system of equations that determine the coefficients of production, and which I introduce in the new text of my work, extends considerably
the theory of economic equilibrium that I have created.[46]

[44] *Cf.* Note 2, *supra.*
[45] George J. Stigler, *op. cit.,* p. 362. John R. Hicks, on the other hand, seems to have
attributed what exposition of the marginal productivity theory there is in Walras's
Appendix III all to Walras, without mentioning Barone. In his *Theory of Wages* (London,
Macmillan, 1932, pp. 233–34), Hicks wrote, apropos of Wicksteed's *Essay:*
    The solution which Wicksteed himself offered to his own problem is unsatisfac-
    tory, as, indeed, he admitted on subsequent occasions. But it is not true, as most
    English and American economists seem still to imagine, that the problem remained
    unsolved. Within a few months of the publication of Wicksteed's Essay, Léon Walras
    put forward a solution which is altogether free from the objections to which
    Wicksteed's own solution is liable. But unfortunately, Walras expressed himself in so
    crabbed and obscure a manner that it is doubtful if he conveyed his point to anyone
    who did not possess some further assistance. Anyone who knows the answer can see
    that Walras has got it; but anyone who does not must find it almost impossible to get
    it from Walras.
[46] F.W. I, 171.

When Walras, upon dropping his Appendix III, incorporated the marginal productivity theory into the text of the fourth edition of the *Eléments* (1900), he explicitly attributed the mathematical equations he used to Barone, and credited Pareto as well as Barone with having rescued the theory from its pristine empirical immaturity. The final paragraph of §326 of the fourth edition of the *Eléments* ran:

That theory of marginal productivity, the germ of which is found in chapters VI and VII of Jevons's *Theory of Political Economy,* has been touched upon by various American and Italian economists, notably by MM. Wood, Hobson, Clark, and Montemartini. But it remained empirical in nature until MM. Pareto and Barone connected it with the equation of production (325) by first modifying that equation in such a way as to introduce the quantity of output into it, in order to be able to assume that the coefficients of production vary with that quantity. They then differentiated the equation of the average cost of production and the modified equation for output, in order to maintain the minimum average cost of production. M. Barone sent me equations [1], [2], [3], and [4] in 1894 and 1895; I have discussed them with him; and we reached agreement that the third should be derived from the first two in the manner shown above. I displayed them in that way in my *Note on the Refutation of Wicksteed's English Theory of Rent,* inserted in the *Recueil publié par la Faculté de Droit de l'Université de Lausanne* (1896).

To this he added the following footnote:

I am adding number 326 to the 4th edition of the *Eléments,* from which I am eliminating Appendix III of the 3rd edition, which contains the *Note on the Refutation of Wicksteed's English Theory of Rent.*

Finally, when in 1901 and 1902 he came to prepare the definitive edition of the *Eléments* for eventual publication, he made every effort to persuade Barone to take "responsibility" for equations [1], [2], [3], and [4] of §326 of the *Eléments*.[47] Only after failing to get any response at all from Barone, which Walras took as a sign that Barone must have fallen under the baneful influence of Pareto, did Walras reluctantly assume the "responsibility" himself. Thus Walras never claimed to have been the progenitor of the marginal productivity theory,[48] but merely to have adopted it as a misunderstood waif forsaken by its natural parents.

How then could anyone have gained the impression that Walras had

[47] Walras's equation [4] of §326 in the fourth edition of the *Eléments,* where the parentheses denote partial derivatives, was suppressed in the "édition définitive." *Cf. Elements of Pure Economics,* p. 605, Collation Note [f] to Lesson 36.
[48] Referring to Giovanni Montemartini's brochure, *La teorica delle produttività marginali* (Pavia, 1899) in a letter to Léon Winiarski dated September 28, 1899 (F.W. I, 619), Léon Walras wrote: "It could give rise to a solid work on marginal productivity, the germ of which is found in Ricardo's theory of rent . . . , and the mathematical formulation of which has been given for the first time by Jevons in his 'Theory of Political Economy,' and which was stated definitively by Barone."

laid "claim to priority in the formulation of the general marginal productivity theory," as Professor Stigler alleged?[49] Conceivably a reader, blinded by indignation at Walras's personal attack on Wicksteed, might mistake Walras's assertion that Wicksteed's $\partial P/\partial A$, $\partial P/\partial B$, $\partial P/\partial C$ ... *correspond respectively to* ("correspondent respectivement à") his $p_t \ldots p_p \ldots p_k \ldots$,[50] for an assertion that

$$" \frac{\partial P}{\partial A} = p_t, \frac{\partial P}{\partial B} = p_p, \ldots "^{51}$$

But a closer reading would reveal that what Walras meant by his equivocally drawn parallel was that if within the framework of his general equilibrium theory of exchange and production one replaces Walras's $p_t \ldots p_p \ldots p_k \ldots$ by Wicksteed's $\partial P/\partial A$, $\partial P/\partial B$, $\partial P/\partial C$ ..., or its equivalent in Walras's notation, then Wicksteed's theorem is revealed as no more than a generalized formulation of Walras's system of coordinated relationships. Since this system had been published by Walras as far back as 1876 and repeated with minor revisions in the 1877[52] and 1889 editions of the *Eléments;* and since Wicksteed had read the latter edition in proof and commented upon part of it in his correspondence with Walras in 1889,[53] Walras, always tiresomely touchy in such matters,[54] felt he had grounds for complaint when Wicksteed announced in the Prefatory Note of his *Essay* that, "no satisfactory

[49] George J. Stigler, *op. cit.*, p. 369.
[50] §2 of Walras's "Note."
[51] George J. Stigler, *loc. cit. Cf.* Note 12, *supra.* If Walras was anywhere unfair to Wicksteed, it was certainly in his statement in §2 of Appendix III that Wicksteed reserved the right to interpret P (the product) *"ad libitum"* as a physical quantity or as a "commercial value." (*Cf.* Walras's letter to Pareto of October 9, 1894, pp. 66–67, *supra*). Actually, on pp. 35–38 of Wicksteed's *Essay,* we find a developed argument, quite remarkable for its time, restricting the conditions under which it is admissible to assume that the "commercial product," like the physical product, will increase *pari passu,* at least approximately, with an equi-proportional increase in all the factors of production. These conditions, which Wicksteed expressed in his clumsy mathematics as if they were mutually-exclusive alternatives, amount to either a very high elasticity of demand for the product or so large a number of (small) competitive firms that the increase in output of any one firm is bound to be too small to affect the price of the product perceptibly. This argument is a far cry from taking the product *"ad libitum"* as either a quantity or a value. Barone, as his review shows, appreciated Wicksteed's point which apparently escaped Walras completely.
[52] *Cf.* Note 17, supra. The 1st edition of the *Eléments* was published in two instalments: the first in 1874, and the second in 1877. The latter contains virtually the same theory of production that appeared in 1876.
[53] On April 2, 1889, Wicksteed wrote to Walras enclosing nine pages of detailed comments on the proofs of the second edition of the *Eléments* which Walras had sent him for criticism, but these comments dealt only with the theory of exchange, the last of them referring to page 179 of the page proofs. The letter is preserved at Lausanne under the classification mark F.W. II, 1397, and the nine pages of notes under F.W. V.
[54] The late 19th Century was marked by a *Prioritätstreit* almost as much as by a *Methodenstreit.* Only Walras was a little more strident than his contemporaries. Others,

attempt had previously been made to recast the Theory of Distribution in systematic form." The quarrel was then not over the marginal productivity theory, but over a generalized theory of "Distribution" in which the theory of marginal productivity could find an appropriate place.

Walras did not, however, regard himself as a total stranger to the genesis of the marginal productivity theory. In Appendix III, he pointed out that Pareto and Barone took his equation of cost of production and his production function (modified by Pareto to include an explicit variable representing quantity of output) as their starting point. Moreover, in the penultimate sentence of the Post-Script to Appendix III Walras inserted a clause not found in the *Recueil,* referring to Lesson 31 of the *Eléments,* p. 358, line 20 (3rd edition),[55] which, he intimated, foreshadowed the importance of marginal productivity for the determination, not of the prices of productive services, but of the coefficients of production. Actually the sentence beginning on line 20 of page 358 follows another sentence in which Walras described in general terms the equations required for the determination of the prices both of products and of productive services. Then he added as a separate proposition: "The equations for output will serve to determine the coefficients of production." He could have made a better case for himself had he referred to a passage earlier in the 3rd edition, in lesson 20, p. 232, where after defining his coefficients of production, he declared that these coefficients, provisionally assumed constant, were really variables and could be determined by the condition of minimum cost of production. He had said this not only in the 3rd edition, but in the previous editions as well, and indeed as far back as 1876 in his memoir, "Equations de Production."[56] Though marginal productivity as such

like Alfred Marshall and John Bates Clark, were content to make their immodest claims with disarming modesty. John Bates Clark, for example, wrote to Walras on February 28, 1896 (F.W. II, 504):

> I suppose — though of course I cannot be quite certain — that the paper printed in the [i.e., his own] *Wages* Monograph contains the earliest expression of the Final Productivity theory of wages and interest. . . . The paper was read before the American Economic Association in December 1888, and published in March 1889. The admirable work of Professor Wieser, which has points of kinship with the theory, though it is not identical with it, appeared almost at the same time. . . . Excuse this too extended reference to my own work.

Walras, on the other hand, always felt frustrated or cheated in the race for recognition. Toward the end of his life, he wrote of himself:

> I have lived through two periods, one during which I was a madman, and one during which everyone made my discoveries before me. (From jottings copied by his daughter, Aline Walras, and preserved at the Faculté de Droit de Lyon.)

[55] The end of the long penultimate sentence in Appendix III reads: " . . . the consideration of marginal productivity is relevant for the determination of the coefficients of production, and not for the determination of the prices of services, *exactly as I said in my 31st Lesson* (p. 358, 1. 20)." (My italics to indicate the clause added in Appendix III.)
[56] *Cf. Elements of Pure Economics,* p. 582, Collation Note [f] to Lesson 20.

had not been mentioned, its place and its rôle in the general equilibrium model were clearly marked out.[57]

As we have already observed, Pareto and Barone both acknowledged the part Walras played in inspiring them by pointing the way to the marginal productivity theory. Barone continued to express his indebtedness to Walras in this respect even when his correspondence with Walras began tapering off. For example, in 1896, in his "Studi sulla Distribuzione," after referring to Wood, Carver, Clark and Wicksteed as his forerunners, Barone declared:

> But the work that has left the deepest impression on this article is that of Walras, for the theories that I am presenting here are intended as a continuation, in simpler form, and an amplification of Walras's contribution. . . . The theory. . . , as expounded by Walras, contains, as we shall see, more than mere germs of the new theory of marginal productivity.[58]

Even had Walras deluded himself into believing that he was the first to have uncovered the marginal productivity theory in a modern mathematical form, he might have found some justification for this in certain items of his past correspondence, which he seems to have overlooked at the time of his quarrel with Wicksteed. The following two items, preserved among the treasures in the Lausanne archives, constitute two extraordinary documents, the first of which, though undated, was obviously written as a memorandum shortly before the second, since it records Walras's question, probably posed orally, to which the second, a letter, furnishes the answer.

> The point on which I would like to have M. Prof. Amstein's advice relates to the *coefficients of production*
>
> $$a_t a_p a_k \qquad b_t b_p b_k \qquad c_t c_p c_k \qquad d_t d_k d_p$$
>
> introduced in §III of the Mémoire no. 3 (Equations of Production) (page 408 of the Bull . . .).[59] I assume that they are constant and known in my mémoire for added simplicity. In reality they are variable and unknown, but they can be assumed to be interrelated in regard to the production of a commodity (B), for example, in the way given by an equation of the form,
>
> (1) $$F(b_t, \ b_p, \ b_k \ . \ . \ .) = 0$$
>
> Their interrelationship may have the explicit form
>
> $$b_t = \Psi(b_p, \ b_k \ . \ . \ .)$$
> $$b_p = \chi(b_t, \ b_k \ . \ . \ .)$$
> $$b_k = \Theta(b_t, \ b_p \ . \ . \ .)$$
> . . . .

---

[57] *Cf. ibid.*, pp. 549–53, Translator's Note [1] to Lesson 36 for a detailed analytical discussion of the manner in which Walras had prepared the niche for the marginal productivity theory.

[58] *Op. cit.*, p. 110, footnote 1.   [59] *Cf.* Note 17, *supra*.

from which it follows that the average cost of production

$$b_t p_t + b_p p_p + b_k p_k + \ldots = p_b$$

would take the form

$$\Psi(b_p, b_k)p_t + \chi(b_t, b_k)p_p + \Theta(b_t, b_p)b_k + \ldots = p_b$$

It seems to me that the condition that the average cost must be minimized ought to furnish the number of equations that are necessary to determine b_t, b_p, $b_k \ldots$ [60]

Professor Hermann Amstein,[61] one of Walras's mathematical colleagues at Lausanne, replied on January 6, 1877:

If I have properly understood the question on which you ask my advice, it has to do with determining the quantities b_t, b_p, $b_k \ldots$ in such a way that the average cost of production p_b of commodity (B) is minimized, recognizing that

$$p_b = b_t p_t + b_p p_p + b_k p_k + \ldots$$

and at the same time

$$F(b_t, b_p, b_k \ldots) = 0.$$

If we write, in order to simplify calculations,

$$b_t = x_1, \quad b_p = x_2, \quad b_k = x_3 \ldots$$
$$p_t = p_1, \quad p_p = p_2, \quad p_k = p_3 \ldots$$

then p_1, $p_2 \ldots p_n$ can be regarded (if I have understood matters properly) as known, and it is necessary to find values of x_1, $x_2 \ldots x_n$ such that

$$p_b = x_1 p_1 + x_2 p_2 + x_3 p_3 + \ldots + x_n p_n$$

is minimized, and at the same time $F(x_1, x_2, \ldots x_n) = 0$.

Thus we are here concerned with a relative maximum or a relative minimum, because one of the conditions is an equation $F(x_1, x_2 \ldots x_n) = 0$. The n variables $x_1 \ldots x_n$ are therefore not all independent. One can transform the problem into that of finding an absolute maximum or an absolute minimum by eliminating from p_b, through the use of the equation $F(x_1 \ldots x_n) = 0$, one of the variables, for example x_r. Then p_b is a function of (n - 1) variables, all independent. The maximum or the minimum value of p_b is obtained by setting the (n - 1) partial derivatives equal to zero with respect to the (n - 1) independent variables. That furnishes (n - 1) equations to determine the (n - 1) variables,

$$x_1, x_2, x_3 \ldots x_{r-1}, x_{r+1} \ldots x_n.$$

[60] F.W. V, 5.
[61] Hermann Amstein (1840–1922), born in Zurich, became professor of mathematics at the Ecole d'ingénieurs of Lausanne in 1875 and later at the Faculty of Science of the University of Lausanne. He took an active part in initiating the publication of the definitive edition of the works of Leonhard Euler, and published some twenty mathematical articles of his own which appeared in the *Bulletin de la Société vaudoise des sciences naturelles,* the *Bulletin de la Société helvétique des sciences naturelles,* and in various other publications of the University of Lausanne and the Ecole d'ingénieurs. Amstein's letter to Walras is preserved in F.W. V, 5.

When these have been determined, x_r is found with the equation $F(x_1, x_2 \ldots x_n)$ = 0. By inserting the values found in p_b, the desired maximum or minimum is obtained.

A more symmetrical and more elegant method is given by the following.

Instead of maximizing or minimizing p_b, define $p_b - \lambda F$ (where λ is a constant that is to be determined), which evidently amounts to the same thing, since F is necessarily $= 0$ for all values of x_1, $x_2 \ldots x_n$, that are compatible with the problem. The introduction of the constant λ is equivalent to the elimination of one of the variables $x_1 \ldots x_n$ of p_b. All the n variables and $p - \lambda F$ can now be considered as independent, that is to say we are now concerned with an absolute maximum or an absolute minimum. Thus we have for the determination of the $(n + 1)$ unknowns $x_1 \ldots x_n$ and λ, the $(n + 1)$ equations

$$\frac{\partial p_b}{\partial x_1} - \lambda \frac{\partial F}{\partial x_1} = 0$$

$$\frac{\partial p_b}{\partial x_2} - \lambda \frac{\partial F}{\partial x_2} = 0$$

$$\vdots$$

$$\frac{\partial p_b}{\partial x_n} - \lambda \frac{\partial F}{\partial x_n} = 0$$

$$F(x_1, x_2, x_3 \ldots x_n) = 0.$$

(In order to indicate partial derivatives the ∂ symbol is preferred.)

For all its shortcomings, this piece of analysis, giving what is probably the first instance of the use of the Lagrange multiplier method in economics, is remarkable especially when one considers its date: 1877. This was fully seventeen years before Wicksteed's *Essay* appeared, and indeed more than a decade before *any* of the first attempts at a modern formulation of the marginal productivity theory was made. Surely, on the principle of *prudens interrogatio dimidium scientiae,* much credit is due to Walras. The very aptness with which he posed the problem evoked an answer from Amstein which lacked only the specification of quantity of output to be as complete and general a mathematical expression of the marginal productivity theory as we know it today.

The question, however, arises: Why did Walras fail to develop a marginal productivity theory himself when he was so close to it in 1877? Why did he not exploit Amstein's suggestion, as he had already exploited the suggestion of another mathematical colleague, Paul Piccard,[62] in the early 1870s, when he formulated his marginal utility theory? The trouble is that Walras did not know enough mathematics at

---

[62] Antoine Paul Piccard (1844–1902?), an uncle of the twin brothers Auguste Piccard and Jean Félix Piccard, both physicists well known for their astronautic and bathyspheric exploits, was himself an engineer and professor of mechanics at the Academy of Lausanne from 1869 until 1881. Piccard played more than a casual role in bringing mathematical

the time to understand Amstein's letter. Piccard, unlike Amstein, had made an effort to expound the principle of maximization of utility in non-rigorous terms, illustrating the little calculus he used by simple, heuristic geometric devices.[63] That brought the demonstration down to Walras's level, for he had at that time hardly progressed in mathematics beyond the stage of elementary analytical geometry and had only just begun teaching himself the rudiments of calculus. Amstein's rigorous demonstration, with its partial derivatives and its use of a Lagrange multiplier, was then far beyond Walras's ken.

Only later, as Walras's pencilled notes added at the end of Amstein's letter show, was he able to gain some glimmering of Amstein's solution. We know that he must have made these notes long after receiving Amstein's letter, not only because they mentioned Barone and alluded to the 4th edition (1900) of his *Eléments,* but also because the rewritten Amstein equations contained a new parameter, Q, to designate the quantity of output. It is doubtful whether Walras ever realized that his original model for the theory of production and Amstein's demonstration designed to fit this model implied the very homogeneous production function of first degree in all the inputs which Barone rejected, with Walras's blessing.[64]

It remains now to see what exactly were the initial reactions of economists to the publication of Walras's Appendix III in the third edition of the *Eléments.* It will be recalled that in his letter to Barone of November 11, 1896, Walras had boasted that his "best correspondents" found the marginal productivity "remarkable" in itself and "decisive" for the mathematical theory of production. In fact, all we find in the Lausanne archives relating to the reception of Appendix III, which is the only place in the 3rd edition where the marginal productivity theory is mentioned at all, are three communications. The first, dated February 28, 1896, was from John Bates Clark:

I thank you for the copy of the criticism of Mr. Wicksteed's theory. . .

light to Walras, who publicly acknowledged his assistance on several occasions, e.g. Léon Walras, *Etudes d'économie sociale,* Lausanne, Rouge, 1896 (édition définitive, edited by Gaston Leduc, 1936), p. VII.

[63] In the Lausanne archives, under the classification marks F.W. V, 5, there is found a private note, two foolscap pages in length and signed by Paul Piccard, explaining to Walras, both in diagrammatic and analytical terms, the elementary principle of maximization applied to the problem of utility. Though the note is undated, I place it *circa* 1871. A significant feature of Walras's writings is the almost complete absence of any calculus notation until the appearance of the 2nd edition of the *Eléments* (1889).

[64] For proof, *cf.* Vilfredo Pareto, *Cours d'économie politique,* Lausanne, Rouge, 1896–97, volume II, pp. 83–84, note (714); Henry Schultz, *op. cit.,* pp. 543–545; and H. Neisser, *op. cit.,* p. 254, note 4.

That was all J. B. Clark had to say on this subject, apart from making a claim of his own to priority in discovering the marginal productivity theory.[65] The second communication, dated April 13, 1896, was from Irving Fisher:

> I am greatly obliged for a copy of your Third Edition of '*Eléments d'économie politique pure.*' The only thing in this edition which will be new to me is the Third Appendix on Wicksteed . . . [66]

And the third, dated November 7, 1896, was from Bortkiewicz, who was then teaching mathematical statistics at Strasbourg:

> I have greatly enjoyed your appendixes to the *"Eléments"*. . . . What interests me most is Appendix III, for I know it well as a result of having often reread the 31st Lesson[67] of the *Eléments;* if I haven't had the occasion to mention it during the course of our correspondence, it is because I haven't found anything to add to it. The characteristics of the Wicksteed incident will bring out the solidity of your system in as much as it is concerned with "essential elements," as you say on p. 17 of the "appendixes." With respect to the complications, I am not entirely sure that the mathematical method is of great utility. That is one of the reasons why I have not tried to cultivate the field that you have reserved to the young. . . . [68]

All three communications, added together, can hardly be said to constitute an enthusiastic reception. What did call forth an expression of unmistakable enthusiasm was the dropping of Appendix III from the 4th edition (1900) of the *Eléments*. Knut Wicksell, who might surely be numbered among Walras's "best correspondents," wrote, on October 28, 1900, to congratulate Walras on the appearance of the new edition and added:

> I am pleased to have seen that you have eliminated the note concerning M. Wicksteed. M. Barone's critique, which you gave in that note, hasn't seemed to me totally just. The restriction of the theorem of marginal productivity to the case in which total output is a homogeneous function of the first degree of the factors of production (land, work, etc.), introduced by M. Wicksteed, and which seemed so superfluous to M. Barone, is in reality nothing other than your own assumption of unlimited competition among the entrepreneurs, because

[65] *Cf.* Note 54, *supra.*
[66] F.W. II, 1896. Later Irving Fisher pointed out, in a joint review of Wicksteed's *Essay* and of the third edition (1896) of Walras's *Eléments,* that many other economists had previously and independently been led to conclusions similar to those of Wicksteed and he expressed the regret that Wicksteed had not taken "pains to trace the development of the theory or to give credit to previous writers, particularly to Walras" (*Yale Review,* August 1897, vol. V, no. 2, pp. 222–23).
[67] Leçon 31 of the second edition of the *Eléments* was entitled, "Exposition et réfutation de la théorie anglaise du fermage." *Cf.* Leçon 39 of the definitive edition.
[68] F.W. II, 1929. Ladislaus von Bortkiewicz (1868–1931), a trained mathematician, toyed in his youth with the idea of becoming an economic theorist before turning, much to Walras's disappointment, to statistics, in which he attained high repute.

that kind of competition evidently cannot occur unless production on a small scale is proportionately as lucrative as on a large scale, and that is precisely the meaning of Wicksteed's restriction.[69]

As George J. Stigler pointed out,[70] a similar defense of Wicksteed is found in Wicksell's article, "Om gränsproduktiviteten sasom grundval för den nationalekonomiska fördelningen" ("Marginal Productivity as the Basis of Distribution in Economics") which appeared the same year as this letter in the *Ekonomisk Tidskrift,* (1900), vol. II, pp. 305–337. The revelant passage of the article, which was overgenerous to Walras in that it made no mention of Barone's contribution, reads, in Reginald S. Stedman's English translation, as follows:

> Walras contends, and rightly I think, that the fundamental features of Wicksteed's theory are to be found in Walras's own theory of economic production. But he also maintains that his theory is more generally valid than Wicksteed's: Wicksteed is said to have established the law of marginal productivity only for the case where the total product is a linear and homogeneous function of the productive factors (as I have just pointed out, this is the mathematical expression of the fact that production yields the same return on a small scale as on a large), whereas Walras considers that he himself has proved the proposition 'dans sa plus grande généralite,' without any restrictions. In this he is mistaken, however. Actually, he makes what he regards as a self-evident assumption, that competition between entrepreneurs makes the entrepreneurial profit tend steadily to zero, unless there is monopoly. But it is not difficult to see that this assumption involves the very condition that we postulated, namely, that the product is independent of the scale of production. If such is not the case, but if instead an enterprise on a larger scale is, say, more profitable than one on a smaller scale, the entrepreneurial profit cannot disappear or even tend to zero; for either the smaller enterprise will simply run at a loss or the larger shows a positive surplus over and above production costs, wages and rent (together with interest). So Wicksteed's treatment of the problem is particularly commendable, and not at all deserving of the scornful dismissal accorded it by Walras.[71]

Two years later, Wicksell withdrew this argument, at the same time giving credit to Barone where credit was due, in another article, "Till

[69] F.W. II, 2246. Walras's reply to Wicksell, dated November 2, 1900 (F.W. I, 611), contains the following passage, remarkable for its succinctness in summarizing what he conceived to be the essence of his contribution to theory:

> Your observation regarding marginal productivity deserves a serious examination. I am not entering any longer into that controversy for the same reason that led me to eliminate the appendix on Wicksteed: Namely, that not having made an exhaustive study of the question, I prefer to do no more than to refer to it, while keeping it outside of my theory. As for my own theory, I can state that it is the theory of *Genznutzen traced through all the details of economic equilibrium.* I have spent 40 years developing it, and I deliver it confidently to the examination of the generation of economists upon whom the task of undertaking the science will devolve.

[70] George J. Stigler, *op. cit.,* p. 375.

[71] Knut Wicksell, *Selected Papers on Economic Theory,* edited by Erik Lindhal, London, Allen & Unwin, 1958, p. 100.

fördelningsproblemet" ("On the Problem of Distribution"), *Ekonomisk Tidskrift*, 1902, vol. IV, pp. 424–433. Referring to his 1900 article, Wicksell acknowledged that he had been in error:

> I have found on further reflection, however, that on this point [i.e. the point that the total product is exhausted in distributional shares only under Wick-steed's assumption of constant returns to scale] I did Walras – or rather his collaborator, Barone – an *injustice,* and that the law of marginal productivity actually has a far greater field of application theoretically than either Wicksteed or I had hitherto imagined.[72]

The position Wicksell took in his 1902 article was confirmed and elaborated upon in his *Lectures on Political Economy,* where, speaking of the necessary condition for the exhaustion of the total product in distributive shares without any pure profit residue, Wicksell wrote, "This condition may be *either* that large-scale and small-scale operations are equally productive, so that, when all the factors are increased in the same proportion, the total product increases exactly proportionately; *or* at least that all productive enterprises have already reached the limit beyond which a further increase in the scale of production will no longer yield any advantage.[73]" At the close of his discussion of the second alternative, Wicksell added in a footnote, "The basis of this argument is due to Enrico Barone; cf. Walras, *Eléments d'Economie Politique Pure,* 3rd edition, p. 489 *et seq.* . . ."[74]

As Knut Wicksell slowly discovered, the contributions of Léon Walras were extensive enough without attributing to him what Walras himself insisted was due to others. With the present publication of Barone's lost review of Wicksteed's *Essay,* the genesis of the modern formulation of the marginal productivity theory and the limited part that Walras played in it should now be clear.

Underlying Walras's quarrel with Wicksteed over the latter's *Essay on the Coordination of the Laws of Distribution* is a curious paradox. Neither Walras nor Wicksteed were really concerned in their analytical argument with the problem of Distribution as Ricardo understood it: "To determine the laws which regulate" the division of "the produce of the earth – all that is derived from its surface by the united application of labor, machinery, and capital . . . among three classes of the community; namely, the proprietor of the land, the owner of the stock or capital necessary for its cultivation, and the laborers by whose industry it is

---

[72] *Ibid.,* p. 122.
[73] Knut Wicksell, *Lectures on Political Economy,* edited by Lionel Robbins, 2 vols., London, Routledge, 1934–35 (translated by E. Classen from the third Swedish edition of Knut Wicksell's *Föreläsningar i nationalekonomi,* ed. 1, 1901–6), vol. 1, p. 126.
[74] *Ibid.,* vol. 1, p. 131.

cultivated."[75] True, Wicksteed briefly mentioned this problem to start with, but quickly turned from it to another problem which was the main concern of his *Essay*: that of the exhaustion of the product without any residue under the operation of the marginal productivity theory.[76] And he as much as confessed, toward the close of the *Essay*, that in its strict form the marginal productivity theory "is not a law of distribution, but an analytical and synthetical law of composition and resolution of industrial factors and products, which would hold equally in Robinson Crusoe's island, in an American religious commune, in an Indian village ruled by custom, and in the competitive centers of the typical modern industries."[77] His vague attempts to link the two problems remain unconvincing. As for Walras, he kept himself completely aloof, in his *Eléments*, from the problem of Distribution proper.[78] Not a single title of the eight major parts of the definitive edition of the *Eléments* or of its forty-two "Leçons" (as he called the chapters), contains the word "Distribution" or its equivalent in the relevant sense. His Leçons 39 and 40 in that edition, dealing with Rent, Wages and Interest are little more than critical reexaminations of the classical literature on these subjects and make no pretense of being anything else. The omission of Distribution from the *Eléments* not only represented a notable departure from the practice of earlier treatises on economic theory, but also established a precedent which was followed, for example, by John R. Hicks in his *Value and Capital*,[79] and by Paul A. Samuelson in his *Foundations of Economic Analysis*,[80] where there is no section or chapter on Distribution either.

It must not be assumed, however, that Walras was unaware of, or insensitive to, the problem of Distribution proper. Rather, in the spirit of John Stuart Mill, who regarded the "Distribution of wealth" as "a matter of human institution solely" in contradistinction to Production, the laws of which, he said, "partake of the character of physical truths,"[81] Walras thought of Distribution as a socio-ethical problem and not one for which a solution could be ground out simply by turning the crank of an analytical engine. This is evident in Walras's *Etudes d'économie sociale*, a collection of his papers on social philosophy which he

[75] David Ricardo, On the Principles of Political Economy and Taxation, Preface.
[76] *Cf.* §§1–3 of Wicksteed's *Essay*.   [77] *Ibid.,* p. 42.
[78] *Cf.* Edwin Cannan, *A History of the Theories of Production and Distribution in English Political Economy from 1776 to 1848*, ed. 3, 1917 (Reprinted by the Staples Press, 1953), chapters VII and VIII. Cannan placed the problem of the determination of "wages per head, profits per-cent, and rent per acre" under the heading of "Pseudo-Distribution" (Chapter VIII).
[79] Ed. 2, Oxford, Clarendon Press, 1946.
[80] Cambridge, Harvard University Press, 1947.
[81] John Stuart Mill, *Principles of Political Economy*, Book II, Chapter I, §1.

published in 1896 with the significant sub-title, "Théorie de la répartition de la richesse sociale." For Walras, the theory of marginal productivity was, in essence, nothing more than an emendation of his theory of
Production, i.e. a theory of the determination of the prices of productive
services, which he had originally formulated under the assumption of
constant coefficients of production, but which now could be generalized
to include variable coefficients.

The quarrel was, therefore, not over the theory of Distribution, but
over the theory of Production.

12

THE WALRAS-POINCARE
CORRESPONDENCE ON
THE CARDINAL MEASURABILITY OF
UTILITY

It is surprising that in the very period when modern 'mathematical economics' was burgeoning forth so auspiciously as a novel science, there was, it appears, only one occasion on which Henri Poincaré (1858–1912), universally acclaimed for his versatility in applied as well as pure mathematics, brought his genius directly to bear on the application of mathematics to economics.[1] His single passing glance in this direction is, nonetheless, of considerable interest, revealing, as it does, a profound insight on Poincaré's part into the *economic* implications of the question he was called upon to examine. This occurred when Léon Walras invited Poincaré to pronounce upon his controverted assumption of cardinal measurement of utility when it ran into more serious opposition than usual.[2]

Walras had first made this assumption in 1873, in his maiden analytical paper, 'Principe d'une théorie mathématique de l'échange,'[3]

The research was supported by a Killam Senior Research Scholarship (1975–6) of the Canada Council. Thanks are also due to my colleagues John Buttrick and Michael D.G. Copeland for editorial advice and Rasesh B. Thakkar who guided my faltering mathematical hand and gave me invaluable assistance in crucial matters of interpretation, thus reducing the shortcomings of this paper for which I alone must bear responsibility. I am no less grateful to the two anonymous referees of the *Canadian Journal of Economics* whose painstaking and constructive comments have helped improve the presentation of the paper. I had previously benefited by a discussion of the same topic as I presented it at a Symposium on Walras Studies in Hakone, Japan, on 29 October 1974.

[1] Jules Henri Poincaré, better known simply as Henri Poincaré, is rarely encountered in economic literature. Where his name does crop up in this literature, as in Hutchison (1938, *passim*), in Schumpeter (1954, 17, 776, 828, 1055), and in Samuelson (1972, 127, 135, 324), it is almost always to credit him with having performed, quite unawares, an ancillary mathematical or methodological service for economists. In the one place (Schumpeter, 1954, 1055, n. 1 to §2 of Appendix to chap. 7) where Poincaré is spoken of as concerning himself directly with economic theory, his name is coupled with that of Léon Walras, who propounded the question of cardinal utility to Poincaré. Schumpeter, who probably came upon Poincaré's response in Walras (1909, 326–7), unfortunately drew a wrong inference from it. It will be seen in the above paper, that Walras did not wait either to convince himself 'eventually' or to be convinced by Poincaré, as Schumpeter alleged, that 'utility, though a quantity, was unmeasurable.' He knew it all along.

[2] Jaffé, ed. 1965 (cited hereafter as *Correspondence*), 3, 161–2, Letter 1495.

[3] Walras 1874/1883.

which he read in August of that year before the Académie des sciences morales et politiques in Paris. The relevant passage reads:

At this juncture, I seem indubitably to be straying from the straight and narrow path of science into regions of the unmeasurable. I hope to demonstrate that this is not the case. Of the two elements I have just mentioned [as data in the derivation of the demand curves], one is perfectly measurable, namely the quantity of each commodity initially owned by each trader. The other element, however, namely the utility of each commodity to each trader, certainly stands in no direct or measurable relation to either space or time. It would appear, therefore, that we cannot proceed any further. But we can. The circumstance which obviously precludes numerical measurement does not by any means rule out pure and simple mathematical expressions. In physics as in mechanics, one operates mathematically with entities, such as mass, which are not directly measurable either. Let us follow the same procedure. We need only suppose that utility is measurable and we are at once able to give an exact, mathematical account of the influence utility exerts, along with the quantity [initially] owned, on demand curves and hence on prices.[4]

Walras was immediately attacked by the bigwigs of the Académie.[5] One of its leading figures, Emile Levasseur, charged that it was 'false and dangerous' to treat imponderables mathematically. Though irritated, Walras did his best to shrug off such criticisms as long as they came from the mathematically ignorant. When, however, in 1900, a distinguished French mathematician, Hermann Laurent, denounced Walras's attempt to derive a theory of price determination from the principle of maximization of measurable utility,[6] Walras was cruelly shaken. Finally, on 10 September 1901, he appealed to Poincaré, as to a supreme arbiter, sending him a copy of the fourth edition of the *Eléments d'économie politique pure* with a letter in which he candidly acknowledged that while he thought his accomplishments in economics were fairly substantial, his attainments in mathematics were extremely modest.[7]

This avowed weakness in mathematics is confirmed, if by nothing else (and there is much else), by Walras's long drawn out struggle to formalize the assumption of cardinal measurement of utility he first broached in 1873. It was not until the second edition of the *Eléments* (1899) that he made a first attempt to express the idea analytically.[8] In 1902, he was still tinkering with the formulation in a final effort to present his theorem more rigorously for an eventual definitive edition he

---

[4] Ibid., p. 19 of the 1883 republication; my translation.
[5] Cf. *Correspondence* 3, 334–6, Letter 232, n. 7.
[6] Ibid., 3, 113, Letter 1448, n. 2.   [7] Ibid., 3, 158–9, Letter 1492.
[8] Walras 1874/ . . . , 2nd ed, §81. Both in his 'Principes d'une théorie mathématique de l'échange' of 1973 (see above n. 3) and in the first edition of the *Eléments,* the demonstration was entirely geometrical, the conclusions alone being stated in analytical symbols. The curves were *rareté* (marginal utility), not total utility, curves. Though Walras described the appropriately bounded areas under the curves as representing

was then preparing.[9] In §82 of the fourth edition (1900), the one he presented to Poincaré, he wrote the 'effective' utility for a given individual (designated by the second subscript) as the sum of the separate independent utilities of commodities A and B, in the simple two-commodity case, as follows:

$$\Phi_{a1}(d_a) + \Phi_{b1}(\overline{q}_b - o_b), \tag{1}$$

where the *capital* Φ's are total (not marginal) utility functions. In this expression, the individual, Mr 1, who possesses initially $\overline{q}_b$ of B and none of A, is assumed to exchange o_b of B for d_a of A at a given current price $\overline{p}_a$ of A in terms of the numéraire B, whence $\overline{p}_b \equiv 1$.[10] At the same time Walras introduced the individual's budget constraint,

$$d_a\overline{p}_a + (\overline{q}_b - o_b) = \overline{q}_b, \tag{2}$$

subject to which (1) is to be maximized via the process of market exchange. To describe this maximum in analytical terms, Walras used the standard method of differential calculus and equated to zero the sum of the differential increments of utility, thus obtaining

$$\Phi'_{a1}(d_a)dd_a + \Phi'_{b1}(\overline{q}_b - o_b)d(\overline{q}_a - o_b) = 0, \tag{3}$$

which he held subject to the differential form of the budget equation,

$$\overline{p}_add_a + d(\overline{q}_b - o_b) = 0, \tag{4}$$

where, in Walras's characteristically awkward notation, the d without a subscript is the symbol for the operation of differentiation, while d_a and o_b are respectively the quantity demanded of A and the quantity offered of B. Though as early as 1888, when the second edition was still in proof, Bortkiewicz had alerted Walras to the need for the explicit mathematical incorporation of second-order conditions of a maximum into his proof, it was not until the fourth edition that Walras filled the gap.[11] Technical proficiency in mathematics was never Walras's forte.

'effective' (i.e. total) utilities, he did not express these areas in analytical notation in his two initial expositions of the theory. In his 'Principes d'une théorie mathématique de l'échange,' he admitted: 'Je n'en ferai pas la démonstration rigoureuse qui est une démonstration de calcul infinitésimal; je ferai seulement une démonstration succincte qui, dans l'espèce, sera suffisante' (§V). In the second edition of the *Eléments* (1889), of which he sent proofsheets in advance to Bortkiewicz for comment, and again in the third edition (1896), he used the definite integral $\int_o^q \phi(q)dq$ to represent total utility functions.

[9] A marked copy of the fourth edition of the *Eléments* with projected corrections and emendations noted in the margins and dated 1902 in Walras's hand is found in the *Fonds Walras* at Lausanne (see *Correspondence* 1, xii). The 'édition définitive, revue et augmentée par l'auteur,' appeared posthumously in 1926.

[10] Since the individual as such is assumed to be nothing but a quantity adjuster, I have placed a bar over the letters (for market price and initial endowment) to denote parametric constants in the individual's adjustment process.

[11] *Correspondence* 2, 248–9, Letter 831. Cf. Walras 1874/ ..., English translation, 567–71, Collation Notes to Lesson 8, especially [m].

It may help explain the particular turn the Walras-Poincaré correspondence took to note that after Lesson 8 of the *Eléments*, where §82 is located, and apart from Lessons 26 and 27 on the 'Theorem of Maximum Utility of New Capital Goods,' Walras never again used his capital Φ 'effective' utility functions, and that nowhere, after having more or less casually mentioned it in §82, did he take into account the second-order conditions of 'maximum satisfaction.' Whenever he invoked the marginal utility principle in the mathematical portrayal of his theories of multicommodity exchange, production, and money, he took as his point of departure the derivatives of total utility of the commodities considered, which he called their 'raretés' and which he wrote no longer as capital Φ'_{a1}, $\Phi'_{b1} \ldots$, but as *lower case* ϕ'_{a1}, $\phi'_{b1} \ldots$, each defined as 'the intensity of the last want satisfied by any given *quantity consumed* [Walras's italics] of a commodity.' Moreover, Poincaré may have been misled by the fact that Walras chose to express cardinal utility, not in units of utility, but in units of its derivative, or, in his words, units 'of the intensity of wants (or intensive utility).'[12] Besides that, the sole reference in the whole of the *Eléments* to second-order conditions of an extremum is that which he tacked on at the end of §82, after mulling over Bortkiewicz's suggestion for more than a decade. It reads:

It will be seen that the root of this derived equation $[\phi_{a1}(d_a) - \bar{p}_a\phi_{b1}(\bar{q}_b - d_a\bar{p}_a)$ $= 0$, derived from equations (3) and (4) above], always corresponds to a maximum and not a minimum, because the functions $\Phi'_{a1}(q)$ or $\phi_{a1}(q)$ and $\Phi'_{b1}(q)$ or $\phi_{b1}(q)$ are by their nature decreasing and the second derivative

$$\phi'_{a1}(d_a) + \bar{p}_a^2\phi'(\bar{q}_b - d_a\bar{p}_a) \tag{5}$$

is necessarily negative.

Walras's laboured and inelegant notation makes it all too easy for a hasty reader to overlook the fact that when Walras expressed his postulate of diminishing marginal utility as negative first derivatives of his lower case ϕ functions, he was really speaking of the postulated sign of second derivatives of his upper case Φ functions. Poincaré may well have been

---

[12] Ibid., §74. The crucial sentence defining this standard reads in the original; 'Je suppose qu'il existe un étalon de mesure de l'intensité des besoins ou de l'utilité intensive, commun non seulement aux unités similaires d'une même espèce de richesse mais aux unités différentes des espèces diverses de la richesse.' In other words, the standard is conceived to be usable for making intercommodity comparisons of utility, but only, Walras was careful to add, in relation to a given individual (see below n. 19). Since Walras's further assumption that the *rareté* of each commodity is independent of the *raretés* of other commodities, the analytical objection to cardinal measurability in the case of interdependent marginal utilities cannot be raised against Walras's theory, however inadequate on other grounds one may find a model, such as his, restricted to gross substitutes. This was conceded in Walras's day by Irving Fisher (1892/1926, Part I; cf. Fisher's Translator's Note in Walras, 1892, 45–7) and by Vilfredo Pareto (1906, §8 of the Appendix; Pareto, 1909, chap. 3, §35, and §10 of the Appendix).

just a hasty reader or may have regarded the matter too trivial to notice.

When Poincaré responded to Walras's overture of 10 September 1901 with the statement that a priori he had no objection to the application of mathematics to economics 'provided that certain limits were not exceeded,'[13] Walras asked Poincaré point blank, in a letter dated 26 September 1901,[14] whether he had exceeded these limits in assuming the cardinal measurability of utility. Walras's letter ran, in part:

I have supposed *rareté* (or intensity of the last want satisfied) to be 'a decreasing function of the *quantity consumed* of a commodity,' and I added that while this *rareté* is not a measurable magnitude, it suffices to think of it as such in order to derive the principal laws of political economy from the fact that *rareté* decreases. Whereupon Laurent exclaimed, 'How can one believe that satisfaction is capable of being measured? Never will a mathematician agree to that!'

Certainly, for the present, I exclude any thought of *numerical evaluation* for practical purposes and confine myself to the idea of a *mathematical expression* for theoretical investigation only.

To this Poincaré replied[15]

Your definition of *rareté* impresses me as legitimate. And this is how I should justify it. Can satisfaction be measured? I can say that one satisfaction is greater than another, since I prefer one to the other,[16] but I cannot say that the first satisfaction is two or three times greater than the other. That makes no sense by itself and only some arbitrary convention can give it meaning. Satisfaction is therefore a magnitude but not a measurable magnitude. Now, is a non-measurable magnitude *ipso facto* excluded from all mathematical speculation? By no means. Temperature, for example, was a non-measurable magnitude – at least until the advent of thermodynamics which gave meaning to the term absolute temperature. The measurement of temperature by the expansion of mercury rather than the expansion of any other substance was nothing but an arbitrary convention. One could just as well have defined temperature by *any* function of temperature . . . *provided that the function was monotonically increasing.* Similarly you [on your side] can define satisfaction by any arbitrary function providing the function always increases with an increase in the satisfaction it represents.

Among your premises, there are a certain number of arbitrary functions; but once given these premises you have the right to draw consequences from them mathematically. If the arbitrary functions still appear in the conclusions, the

[13] *Correspondence* 3, 160–1, Letter 1494.

[14] Ibid., 3, 161–2, Letter 1495. My translation of the extract which follows in the above text. The italics represent Walras's own underlining for emphasis.

[15] Ibid., 3, 162–3, Letter 1496 (cf. ibid., 164–5, Letter 1496 *bis*); my translation. Poincaré's letter is undated, but marked in Walras's hand, 'Paris 30-7bre [Septembre], reçue 1er 8bre [Octobre]. L.W.,' the first date being probably that of the postmark. Apart from the italicized foreign expressions, the italics represent Poincaré's emphatic underlining.

[16] Walras was impressed by Poincaré's use of the word 'prefer' in this passage (Walras, 1909, 315, n 2). We seem to be brought here (in 1901) to the threshold of the modern ordered preference analysis of consumer's behaviour.

conclusions are not false, but they are totally without interest ['dénuées de tout intérêt'] because they depend upon the arbitrary conventions made at the start. You ought, therefore, to do your utmost to *eliminate* these arbitrary functions, and that is what you are doing.

In point of fact, Walras did not succeed in eliminating his arbitrary functions from his conclusions. In his own proof of the fundamental theorem of proportionality of marginal utilities to parametric prices as a condition of equilibrium (i.e. of 'maximum satisfaction' for each and every trader), the arbitrary assumption of diminishing utility remains embedded in the conclusion and entails the retention throughout of the further arbitrary assumption of cardinally measurable utility. It is readily seen in the above restatement of Walras's theory of the two-commodity exchange that unless at least one of the lower case ϕ' functions in the polynomial (5) is negative (and of proper magnitude) there can be no assurance that the extremum is a maximum. The same principle can be extended to include any number of commodities. But these lower case ϕ' functions are really upper case Φ'' functions; and, as is well known, once the requisite solution hinges on the sign of the second derivative of utility functions, the cardinal measurability of utility, whether stated or not, is necessarily implied and cannot be eliminated from the conclusion.[17]

Though Poincaré apparently overlooked all this, perhaps indeed because he did so, he perceived at once – in all probability without the benefit of acquaintance with previous literature on the subject[18] – that arbitrariness is removed from the quantitative consideration of utility when it is taken to be an ordinal magnitude, i.e. when the magnitude is assumed measurable up to a monotonic transformation and no further. In that case only the sign of the first derivative of the utility function has an operational significance.

Poincaré's remarkable premonition of subsequent trends in microeconomic theory was not confined to the replacement of cardinal by ordinal utility functions. In the same letter to Walras, Poincaré went on to say:

I can tell whether the satisfaction experienced by the same individual is greater under one set of circumstances than under another set of circumstances; but I have no way of comparing the satisfactions experienced by two different individuals. This increases the number of arbitrary functions to be eliminated.

When I spoke of 'proper limits,' that is not all I wanted to say. What I had in mind was that every mathematical speculation begins with hypotheses, and that if such speculation is to be fruitful, it is necessary (as in applications to physics) that one be aware of these hypotheses. If one forgets this condition, one oversteps the proper limits. For example, in mechanics one often neglects

---

[17] See, for example, Allen (1959, 670-2); cf. Majumdar (1958, 37-54 and also 144-9 for a select bibliography).

[18] For example, Antonelli (1886/1952) and Fisher (1892/1926).

friction and assumes the bodies to be infinitely smooth. You, on your side, regard men as infinitely self-seeking ['égoïstes'] and infinitely clairvoyant. The first hypothesis can be admitted as a first approximation, but the second hypothesis calls, perhaps, for some reservations.

Thus Poincaré perceived in Walras's submission not only the usual assumption of undiluted individual self-interest but also the exclusion of interpersonal comparisons of utility[19] and, more importantly still, the abstraction from uncertainty.

Presumably no one will disagree with Poincaré that scientists should make every effort to be aware of the assumptions, explicit or implicit, underlying their models. This applies as much to economists as to other scientists. Nor would anyone quarrel, I imagine, with Poincaré's warning that gratuitous presuppositions, indispensable though they be in the course of construction of a theoretical model, may very well render the model trivial unless they are eliminated in the final analysis. If Poincaré's phrase 'without interest' ('dénué d'intérêt') means 'without empirical relevance,' then the problem becomes, in principle, an econometric problem.

So at least Hicks sees it in his *Revision of Demand Theory* (1956), where he says, almost as an echo of Poincaré's letter to Walras: 'A theory which is to provide the econometrist with tools which he can use, which is to ask questions which he is to have some hope of being able to answer, must if it is to be based on cardinal utility, extrude these cardinal properties before it reaches its conclusions . . . It is possible that it might be more convenient to use the cardinal properties as a sort of scaffolding useful in erecting the building, but to be taken down when the building has been completed.'

REFERENCES

Allen, R.G.D. (1959) *Mathematical Economics,* 2d ed. (London: Macmillan).
Antonelli, G.B. (1886/1952) *Sulla teoria matematica della economia politica* (Pisa, Folchetto; republished with an introduction by G. Demaria and Comments by G. Ricci, Milan: Falfari, 1952).

[19] Walras insisted in all editions of the *Eléments* that *'rareté'* must be considered 'personal [*'individuelle'* in the first edition] or *subjective,'* and that 'it is only with respect to a given individual that we can define *rareté* in terms of *effective utility* and *quantity possessed'* (§101). Though Walras did speak in the *Eléments* of the *average rareté* of a given commodity over a whole population (§§101, 135, 226, 265), which would imply that the *raretés* of different persons are addible, he consistently used these hypothetical average *raretés* only in ratios. The ratios of the average *raretés* played no other role than that of a factor of proportionality in defining general market equilibrium, the numerical values of the terms in the ratios of average *raretés* being entirely arbitrary. See Walras (1874/ . . . ; 511 of the English translation, Translator's Note [1] to Lesson 10). On the other hand Walras (1896, 207–11) gave numerical examples involving genuine interpersonal comparisons of utility, but it should be noted that he was in this instance expounding Gossen's theory of maximum social satisfaction, not his own.

Fisher, Irving (1892/1926) *Mathematical Investigations in the Theory of Value and Prices. Transactions of the Connecticut Academy* 9 (reprinted New Haven: Yale University Press, 1926).

Hicks, John R. (1956) *A Revision of Demand Theory* (Oxford: Clarendon Press).

Hutchison, T.W. (1938) *The Significance and Basic Postulates of Economic Theory* (London: Macmillan).

Jaffé, William, ed. (1965) *Correspondence of Léon Walras and Related Papers* 3 vols (Amsterdam: North Holland, for Royal Netherlands Academy of Sciences and Letters).

Majumdar, Tapas (1958) *The Measurement of Utility* (London: Macmillan).

Pareto, Vilfredo (1906) *Manuale di economia politica con una introduzione alla scienza sociale* (Milan: Società editrice libraria; No. 13 in the Piccola biblioteca scientifica).

Pareto, Vilfredo [1909] *Manuel d'économie politique* translated from the Italian edition by Alfred Bonnet and revised by the author. (Paris: Giard et Brière, n.d.).

Samuelson, P. (1972) *Collected Scientific Papers* 3, edited by R.C. Merton (Cambridge, Mass.: MIT Press).

Schumpeter, Joseph A. (1954) *History of Economic Analysis* (New York: Oxford University Press).

Walras, Léon (1874/1883) 'Principe d'une théorie mathématique de l'échange.' *Séances et travaux de l'Académie des Sciences morales et politiques* Jan. 1874, vol. 101 of the *Collection,* 33rd Year of the New Series, Part I, 77–116. Followed by 'Observations relatives au Mémoire de M. Walras.' 117–120. Republished without the 'Observations' in Walras (1883, 7–25).

Walras, Léon (1874/ . . .) *Eléments d'économie politique pure ou Théorie de la richesse sociale* (1st ed [in two instalments] Lausanne: Corbaz, 1874–77; 2d ed Lausanne: Rouge, 1889; 3d edn Lausanne: Rouge, 1896; 4th edn Lausanne: Rouge, 1900; definitive edn (published posthumously) Paris: Pichon and Durand-Auzias, 1926, and Lausanne: Rouge, 1926. Reprinted Paris: Pichon and Durand-Auzias, 1952. English translation by William Jaffé, *Elements of Pure Economics* London: Allen and Unwin, 1954; Reprints of Economic Classics, New York: Augustus Kelley, 1969).

Walras, Léon (1883) *Théorie mathématique de la richesse sociale* (Lausanne: Corbaz).

Walras, Léon (1892) 'The geometrical theory of the determination of prices.' *Annals of the American Academy of Political and Social Science* 3 (63), 45–64.

Walras, Léon (1896) 'Théorie de la propriété.' *Revue Socialiste* 23 (138), 668–81, and 24 (139), 23–5 (republished with minor changes in Walras 1896/1936, 205–39).

Walras, Léon (1896/1936) *Etudes d'économie sociale (Théorie de la répartition de la richesse sociale)* (1st edn Lausanne: Rouge; 2d edn, edited by G. Leduc, Paris: Pichon and Durand-Auzias, 1936).

Walras, Léon (1909) 'Economique et mécanique.' *Bulletin de la Société vaudoise des Sciences naturelles,* 5th Series, 45 (66), 313–27.

13

WALRAS' THEORY OF *TÂTONNEMENT:* A CRITIQUE OF RECENT INTERPRETATIONS

In 1956 Don Patinkin described Léon Walras' theory of *tâtonnement* as "one of his most imaginative and valuable contributions to economic analysis," and rightly lamented its neglect and disparagement up to that date (Patinkin, 1956, p. 377). Since the appearance of Patinkin's authoritative exposition of the theory in the first edition of his *Money, Interest and Prices,* there has been a profusion of ingenious articles on *tâtonnement,*[1] so that the repetition of this lament in 1965, in the second edition of his treatise (Patinkin, 1965, p. 531), now appears an anachronism. On the other hand, when Patinkin repeats his complaint that Walras' theory of *tâtonnement* has been misunderstood, he is surely justified. The current reformulations of the theory, though they proudly bear the Walras patronymic, display only a distant family resemblance to their ancestral prototype, for the infusion of new technical refinements has all but obliterated any recognizable similarity between the descendant theories and their progenitor. Moreover, the latter-day emendations and the niceties of modern analysis have so colored the recent exegetical comments on Léon Walras' own theory that the criticism has often been misdirected, finding fault with Walras' handling of subtle issues which, for want of hindsight and the techniques of a late twentieth-century economist, he had not even raised. This is my excuse for retracing and reappraising once more Léon Walras' theory of *tâtonnement* as it was first developed in the *Éléments d'Économie Politique Pure.*[2] To keep the argument within reasonable bounds, I shall restrict

This work was supported partly by a Social Science Research Council Grant-in-Aid of Research and partly by a National Science Foundation award for which I wish to express my gratitude. I am also greatly indebted to Professor Lester B. Lave of the Carnegie Institute of Technology, visiting Northwestern University 1965–66, and to Professor George J. Stigler of the University of Chicago for their helpful suggestions and for their valuable comments on earlier drafts of this paper.
  [1] See Takashi Negishi's list of bibliographical references on the last four pages of his article (1962).
  [2] Léon Walras, *Éléments d'Économie Politique Pure* (1874–1952). The definitive edition (1926) was translated and annotated with a collation of editions by William Jaffé (1954, reprinted 1965). Walras' original French work will be referred to henceforth as *Éléments* and the English translation by the initials *E.P.E.* The references to the section numbers

my discussion to the theory of *tâtonnement* in exchange and production, leaving to one side its applications to capital formation and money.[3]

At the point where Walras first introduced his theory of *tâtonnement* explicitly, he stated the purpose of this theory in the following terms: "What must we do in order to prove that the theoretical [that is, mathematical] solution [of the problem of the determination of equilibrium prices in a multicommodity universe] is *identically* the solution worked out by the market [*'que la solution théorique et la solution du marché sont identiques'*]? Our task is very simple: we need only show [in the case of pure exchange] that the upward and downward movements of prices solve the system of equations of offer and demand by a process of groping [*'par tâtonnement'*]."[4] Walras' underlying motive in framing this theory was to lend an air of empirical relevance to his abstract mathematical model of general equilibrium at each stage of its development.

The question is now whether Walras succeeded in proving what he set out to prove, namely, that the relative prices which emerge from the process of free competition in an assumed perfectly competitive market are identically the same as the roots of his system of equations, in which the unknowns are the equilibrium prices and quantities exchanged. The market is represented as achieving this result *"par tâtonnement,"* that is to say, by groping, by blindly feeling its way, since no one in the actual world is presumed to know in advance the parameters or the solution of the equations. Once the complete solution is reached, the parameters and the market structure remaining constant, all chance of pure profits is gone and with it all risk of loss. It is the impersonal mechanism of pure competition in a perfect market, "ever unconscious, an automatic sense, unweeting why or whence," which imposes, as Walras saw it, the selfsame solution which only a computer-like *intellectus angelicus* knowing all the parameters could arrive at algebraically. This is what Walras attempted to prove.

Actually Walras failed in this attempt. The failure was due to a conceptual oversight on his part and not merely to his inept mathematical handling of the problem. Though he allowed for trading at "false

preceded by the sign § are designed to facilitate a comparison of passages cited in the translation with the original version in the French editions.

[3] For these applications, see *E.P.E.,* pp. 282–95 (§§251–60); pp. 316–19 (§§273–74); pp. 326–27 (§278); p. 332 (§281); pp. 380–81 (§322).

[4] *E.P.E.,* p. 170 (§125), italics added. Discriminating critics of the English translation have indicated that, as a matter of taste, they would have preferred the retention of the French word *tâtonnement* instead of its English equivalent "groping." At the time the translation appeared (1954), the term *tâtonnement* had not yet become common coin in the literature and might have been puzzling to readers unacquainted with French. Besides, "groping" renders precisely the intended meaning, as will be seen below in the text.

prices" in his preliminary description of the operation of the mechanism of competition in the real market,[5] he overlooked it completely in his analytical discussion of *tâtonnement*. Had Walras taken trading at "false prices" into account in his analytical argument, he might have noticed that such trading generally entails a change in the value of the assets when reckoned in *numéraire* either at the initial set of prices or at equilibrium prices or, for that matter, at any arbitrary set of prices. These changes in the value of the assets, which are of the nature of "income effects," are most appropriately designated in the theory of exchange as "endowment effects," a term introduced by Peter Newman (1965, p. 94) because, as he rightly observes, there is no income in the strict sense of a flow in a pure exchange model. That invariance in the value of each individual's asset endowment is at least a sufficient condition of a unique market solution of the price system was recognized by Walras himself in his "theorem of equivalent redistributions of commodity holdings."[6] The theorem reads, "Given several commodities in a market in a state of general equilibrium, the current prices of these commodities will remain unchanged no matter in what way the owner-ship of the respective quantities of these commodities are redistributed among the parties to the exchange, *provided, however, that the value of the sum of the quantities possessed by each of these parties remains the same.*"[7] It follows from this theorem that if, for any reason, the values of the collections of assets of the several market participants are affected in the course of the *tâtonnement* process and do not remain unchanged, the prices in which the process culminates must also be affected, so that a variety of market solutions is possible, rather than a unique solution identical with the mathematical solution. The inevitable consequence of trading at "false prices" is that the resulting redistribution of ownership of assets cannot remain "equivalent" unless some device like recontract-ing (which will be considered below) is employed to eliminate the "endowment effects" or unless "endowment effects" by chance elimi-nate themselves as would happen if the "endowment effects" of "false

---

[5] *E.P.E.*, pp. 84–86 (§42).

[6] *E.P.E.*, pp. 182–85 (§§139–44). In line with Marshallian reasoning, if all consumers had identical tastes and similar income elasticities, again the same unique solution of the price system would emerge.

[7] *Ibid.*, p. 185 (§143). This same idea of the need for invariance in the value of individual endowments for a unique equilibrium solution is brought out again by Walras himself in those passages in the *É.P.E.* (pp. 178–81 [§§137–38] and pp. 256–60 [§§223–27]) where he points out that variations in the individual endowments parameter will lead to variations in the equilibrium prices unless there are compensating variations in other parameters. There is, however, not the slightest hint in all this of the possibility of "endowment effects" or of individual endowments ending up as endogenous variables in the system.

trading" at one stage of the market adjustment process were precisely compensated by reverse "endowment effects" at a subsequent stage of "false trading" with a different set of non-equilibrium prices. It is not surprising that Walras missed perceiving the relevance of his "theorem of equivalent redistributions of commodity holdings" to his theory of *tâtonnement,* since the proof he formulated for the theorem begs the question. He calculated the value of the equivalent commodity holdings in terms of the mathematically determined prices, which *ipso facto* guaranteed a solution at the same equilibrium prices! Had he calculated the value of the commodity holdings at another set of prices, the solution would not have been the same.[8]

It follows, therefore, that so long as trading at "false prices" is regarded as essential to real *tâtonnement* in actual markets, whatever equilibrium is arrived at in the competitive market via *tâtonnement* cannot, except by accident, be the same as the equilibrium determined mathematically from a system of equations. In the mathematical solution, the parameters to be held constant are not only *tastes* (utility functions or preference scales), not only the total *resources* (total quantities of each of the different commodities in the theory of pure exchange, or total quantities of available productive services in the theory of production), not only the *technology* (relevant only for the theory of production), but also the *distribution of wealth among the traders* (that is, "the values of the sum of the [initial] quantities possessed" by each of the traders, actual or potential). When this last parameter is allowed to shift, as it must when trading at "false prices" takes place, the equilibrium (if it exists) is unlikely to remain unchanged.[9]

The allegation made above that Walras completely overlooked "false trading" in his analytical discussion of *tâtonnement* runs counter to Peter Newman's (1965, p. 102) assertion that Walras did take trading at "false prices" into account. Newman adduces pages 84–86 (§42) of Walras' *E.P.E.* to prove that Walras "explicitly states that trading does take place at false prices." Newman is quite correct in what he has to say of pages 84–86 of the *E.P.E.* But he is quite incorrect in supposing that Walras meant to carry over the "false trading" he portrayed on pages 84–86 into his analytical discussion of the process of *tâtonnement* in multicommodity pure exchange on pages 169–72 (§§125–30). At the

[8] See below (n. 35), where it is seen from H. Uzawa's (1960) mathematical proof that the aggregate excess demand for each of the several commodities is a function of the vector of individual endowment values as well as of the vector of prices, and hence the equilibrium set of prices is partially, but directly, dependent on the distribution of individual endowment values.

[9] The question of the existence of an equilibrium solution falls outside the purview of this article. Cf. Arrow and Debreu (1954) and McKenzie (1959).

very start of his exposition of the theoretical determination of equilibrium price, beginning with the two-commodity case,[10] Walras explicitly disassociated what he had to say on pages 84–86 of the *Éléments* from his analytical argument. He rejected the example of the market for *rentes* (the French equivalent of British consols) he had invoked for his quasi-anecdotal narrative of the working of a well-organized market as unsuitable for the type of analysis he had in mind because, as he saw it, special dynamic factors operating in the *rentes* market entailed a monotonically increasing offer curve[11] which would preclude multiple equilibria and, consequently, all consideration of stability and instability in the static sense. Though Walras denied the possibility of multiple equilibria in the case of exchange involving more than two commodities,[12] which was the very case where he first took up the analysis of *tâtonnement,* still he gave no indication of reverting to the concrete instance of trading at "false prices" which he had described in the *rentes* market. From all the evidence available, it appears that Walras was completely unaware of the special theoretical significance to be attached to this phenomenon.[13] This same unawareness characterizes his analysis of the market adjustment process, not only in his theory of multicommodity exchange, but also in his theories of production, capital formation, and money. In the theory of production, he explicitly confronted the problem of producing what may be called "false quantities" when the market is in disequilibrium, but that is a different story which will be taken up later in this article.

Another ground for rejecting any attribution to Walras of a consider-

[10] *E.P.E.,* pp. 90–91 (§47).
[11] *E.P.E.,* p. 48 (final par. of §47), Lesson 6 (*Leçons* 11 and 12 of the 1st ed.); and pp. 311–12 (§§270–71, §§264–65 of the 2nd and 3d eds.; §§296–97 of the 1st ed.). From the fourth edition of the *Elements* on, all other offer curves are re-entrant, even the offer curve of the hypothetical perpetual annuity shares representing units of capital yielding one franc of net income forever (§242). All these offer curves, however, are derived from purely static assumptions. In the stock market, on the other hand, where purchases and sales of *rentes* are determined by considerations of expected future changes in the rate of yield, the dynamic phenomena of risk and uncertainty influence the fluctuations in their price. Walras argued in §§270–71 of the fourth edition (*E.P.E.,* pp. 311–12), and similarly in the earlier editions, that if, in the course of speculative bidding, the price of *rentes* in the stock market should rise to such an extent that the rate of yield falls appreciably below the current rate of net return on capital investments, holders of *rentes* would sell them and reinvest in capital goods with a higher yield; and the greater the positive discrepancy between the price of the *rentes* and the capitalized value of their coupon interest, the larger the quantity of *rentes* which would be offered for sale.
[12] *E.P.E.,* p. 200 (§156).
[13] Newman (1965) further infers from a passage in Walras alluding to the rapidity with which markets, whether highly organized or not, settle upon prices which then remain current until the markets are cleared (*E.P.E.,* p. 106 [§61]), that Walras must have had effects of "false trading" in mind but deliberately neglected them because he thought, according to Newman's surmise, that the speed with which the market arrives at equilibrium prices prevents these effects from becoming "serious." This, I submit, is straining conjecture to the breaking point.

ation of "false trading" in his analysis of *tâtonnement* lies in the complete absence of recontracting from his theory of exchange. Don Patinkin pointed this out in Supplementary Note B, "Walras' Theory of *"Tâtonnement"* (1956, pp. 379–80; 1965, pp. 533–35). If Walras had considered trading at "false prices" at all, he would have been compelled to resort to the device of recontracting or to some other artifice designed to eliminate or neutralize the effects of "false trading"; otherwise the prices established in the market by a process of *tâtonnement,* including effective intermediary "false trading," could hardly be the same as the prices mathematically determined by solving the multiequational system.

Quite apart from the question of whether Walras took "false trading" into account, his treatment of the process of *tâtonnement* was wholly inadequate, as has been frequently noted.[14] In this instance, Walras fell far short of his declared ideal of rigorous demonstration.[15] What he did on pages 170–72 (§127) of the *E. P. E.* amounted to nothing more than a gratuitous assertion that "it will appear probable [*'cela paraîtra probable'*]" that when a multicommodity exchange system is not in equilibrium— say, because there is a positive or negative excess demand in the case of one of the n commodities in the system—all the prices in the interdependent system will so adjust themselves through the market mechanism that positive or negative excess demand will be reduced to zero everywhere so that the system will converge to equilibrium.[16] What equilibrium he does not say. We must assume, however, that he meant it to be the same as the equilibrium of his mathematical solution, for nothing else would be consistent with the purpose of the theory of *tâtonnement* he announced at the outset. It is evident also from his model of the adjustment process in the theory of production that he had this same purpose constantly in mind.

[14] For example, Robert Solow wrote in his review (1956) of the *E.P.E.,* "The famous *tâtonnements,* by the way, are a swindle, rigorously speaking, and I suspect Walras knew it. ... But Walras' failure on this point was itself creditable. His instinct was right; he saw what the problem was, and the rough outline of its solution" (p. 88). In particulr, the algebra of Lesson 21 of the *E.P.E.* (§§208–20), where Walras tried to work out the adjustment process for production mathematically, is incoherent and defies precise restatement. A collation of the editions of the *Éléments* (§§250–62 of the 1st ed.; §§204–16 of the 2d and 3d eds.) shows that much of the confusion of the definitive version is the consequence of ill-managed tinkering with the earlier versions, imperfect though they were, when Walras introduced the use of "tickets" (of which more below) into the fourth edition in analyzing the process. The second and third paragraphs of §212 of the *E.P.E.,* for example, were carried over verbatim from §208 of the second and third editions, though they were no longer relevant in a situation without effective transactions and without the effective production of "false quantities."

[15] *E.P.E.,* p. 471 (§4 of Appendix I).

[16] Walras' argument ran as follows: If there is a positive or negative excess demand for one of the n commodities in the system, while the markets for all other commodities are in equilibrium (as one would gather in one place where Walras says "ces prix étant supposés déterminés, et (p_b) restant seul à déterminer," though a little further on, in setting $F(p'_b, p'_c, p'_d \ldots) \lessgtr 0$, it appears that all the prices, $p'_b, p'_c, p'_d \ldots$, are initially unadjusted

Walras' enlargement of his general equilibrium model to include production as well as exchange consisted essentially in the introduction of two new sets of unknowns: (1) prices of productive services and (2) quantities produced (rates of output) of consumers' goods; and hence the addition of corresponding sets of equations to render the system determinate.[17] This entailed the abandonment or modification of assumptions peculiar to the theory of exchange, where the "resources" parameter was made up of exogenously given and fixed total quantities of consumers' goods, where the total quantity of each consumers' good was distributed initially in some definite but arbitrary way among the individual market participants, and where the collection of the various items falling to each individual in the inaugural distribution constituted his original endowment. In the theory of production, on the other hand, the characteristic exogenously given "resources" parameter consists no longer of total stocks of consumers' goods, but rather of total "stocks" of productive services of various types, again distributed among the individual market participants in some definite but arbitrary way and constituting their respective endowments. Consumers' goods are now considered, not as originating in primordial stocks, but as products flowing from fields, factories, and workshops at rates which can be varied subject only to the constraints imposed by a given technology (production function) and by the new "resources" parameter. Since services are themselves by their very nature flows and not stocks, the

prices), then, given general interdependence, the competitive mechanism, while bringing about a price adjustment in the one market which is out of equilibrium, will impair the previously established equilibria in the remaining $n-1$ markets. The ensuing adjustments in the prices of the remaining $n-1$ commodities until their induced positive or negative excess demands vanish will, in turn, upset the newly obtained equilibrium in the first market. This will call for secondary readjustments in that market; and again the remaining $n-1$ markets will be thrown into disequilibrium; and so on. All this is well and good up to the point where Walras assigns to this process analysis the property of convergence and, not only that, but convergence to the very equilibrium defined by the mathematical solution of his multi-equational system. Walras' sequential analysis is so slipshod and vague that it cannot be called a proof, not even an erroneous proof. The whole line of argument was probably suggested to Walras (as Kuenne [1963, p. 118, n. 58] aptly indicates) by a passage in Cournot, which, though it was not confined to pure exchange and referred to production, contained the postulate that the interacting adjustments in a multi-product universe take place "with decreasing amplitude" (Cournot, 1897, pp. 130–31), thus rendering the process convergent. Cournot, however, did not invoke this analysis, as Walras did, to argue that the process culminates in some unique equilibrium set of prices, but only to illustrate the extreme complexity of general, as compared with partial, equilibrium analysis, a complexity which he thought was so great as to "surpass the powers of mathematical analysis and of our practical methods of calculation, even if the values of all the constants could be assigned to them numerically" (Cournot, 1897, p. 127). If Walras was inspired, as it appears, by Cournot's example, he nevertheless seems to have missed an essential ingredient of Cournot's analysis at this point, namely, Cournot's stress on the income effects of the adjustments on both consumers and producers.

[17] *E.P.E.,* Lesson 20.

"resources" parameter for the theory of production might be more
accurately described as consisting of a given and fixed set of quantities
of various types of service-yielding capital goods (landed capital and
human capital as well as capital in the narrow and conventional sense),
but if it is assumed, for simplicity, that each type of capital good
invariably yields a rate of flow of a corresponding type of service in
exact proportion to the quantity of the capital good from which it
emanates, then there is no harm done in speaking elliptically of
quantities or "stocks" of services in the present context. The services
are bought and sold in a market for services, where they are demanded
partly for the direct utility they may have for consumers, but more
importantly for what they can contribute as inputs in the production of
consumers' goods. These latter services are sold in the market in
exchange for products to the extent that such exchanges serve to
maximize the satisfactions of the original possessors of the services. The
buyers of services to be used as inputs are the entrepreneurs, to whom
Walras assigns a role resembling that of catalytic agents who perform an
indispensble function in the scheme of production but remain unchanged in their original endowments under static equilibrium conditions. Qua entrepreneurs, their function is to buy productive services in
the services market for a profit which, under perfect competition, turns
out to be a will-o'-the-wisp, vanishing to zero as soon as static equilibrium is approached. Dynamic phenomena being excluded by hypothesis
from Walras' production model, entrepreneurs must operate within the
constraints of a given immutable technology, which, for simplicity, is
assumed to admit of fixed technical coefficients of production only,[18]
that is, of fixed quantities of the inputs per unit of output, irrespective
of the scale of output.

In the pure exchange model, general equilibrium was determined by
two systems of equations: (1) a system of separate systems for each and
every trader equating, in accordance with his private utility functions,
the ratio of the *raretés* (that is, of the marginal degrees of utility) of the
various goods he consumes to the ratio of their respective prices, thus
marking for all traders simultaneously the point of maximum satisfaction they can attain within the limits of the *numéraire* value of their
original endowments by exchanging commodities for one another in the
market; and (2) a system equating the total quantities demanded of the
several consumers' goods with the total quantities offered in their
respective commodity markets where the competitive mechanism raises
or lowers the price of each commodity according to whether its excess
demand is positive or negative. In the production model in which, as we

[18] *Ibid.,* p. 240 (§204); and p. 527, n. 3 to Lesson 20.

have seen, consumers' goods are products and productive services (utilizable also in direct consumption) replace consumers' goods as the ingredients of the initial endowments, general equilibrium is now determined by four systems of equations. Two of these systems are carried over, with appropriate modifications, from the pure exchange model, the offers of consumers' goods, however, now becoming supplies (rates of output). In addition, the two specifically production systems are: (1) a system of separate equations for each and every product equating its selling price to its cost of production in the products market upon which the competitive mechanism imposes this equality by inducing or compelling actual or potential entrepreneurs to expand or contract the output of a product according to whether the difference between its selling price and its cost of production is positive or negative; and (2) a system of separate equations for each and every service equating the total quantity demanded with the total quantity offered in the services market where the competitive mechanism raises or lowers the price of each service according to whether its excess demand is positive or negative.

Thus the mathematical production model defines general equilibrium. Then, under the heading of "The Law of the Establishment [= emergence] of the Prices of Products and Services,"[19] Walras undertook to show that "for equilibrium in production as for equilibrium in exchange, this problem [of the determination of the relevant equilibrium quantities and relative prices in terms of *numéraire*] to which we have given a theoretical solution is the self-same problem which is solved in practice in the market by the mechanism of free competition."[20] Though he did not state it explicitly, his aim was, we may be certain, no different in the theory of production from what he had proclaimed it to be in the theory of exchange, namely, to show that the market solution of the problem of production is identically the same as the mathematical solution. How else can one explain Walras' sudden awareness in the fourth edition (1900) of the *Éléments*[21] that a "complication" specific to production, which he had first recognized in the second edition (1889) of the *Éléments*[22] constituted such a snag that he felt obliged to redesign his model of the *tâtonnement* process in order to circumvent it? As will be seen, the snag would not necessarily have prevented the system with production from converging to *an* equilibrium; but it would certainly have interfered with convergence to *the* equilibrium given by the mathematical solution.

[19] *Ibid.*, pp. 242–54 (§207–20).
[20] *Ibid.*, pp. 241–42 (§206).   [21] Pp. 214–15; cf. *E.P.E.*, §207.
[22] Pp. 234–35 (§203); cf. *E.P.E.*, p. 582, Collation Note g to Lesson 20.

In the first edition (1874–77) of the *Éléments,*[23] Walras described the process of *tâtonnement* in production along very much the same lines that he had laid down for *tâtonnement* in exchange. He simply made it more comprehensive to include (1) adjustments in the rate of output of products forced upon entrepreneurs by competitive pressures until the selling prices of products everywhere equaled their costs of production and (2) market adjustments in the prices of productive services until the total quantities demanded of the several services (including the quantities demanded for direct consumption) everywhere equaled the total quantities offered. Thus the simple operation of the competitive mechanism was regarded in the first edition as sufficient for the system to culminate in a unique equilibrium. Within this mechanism, each seller of services and each buyer of products (and consumers' services) was regarded in all editions of the *Éléments* as maximizing his satisfaction subject to his budget constraint which, in the theory of production, is identically equal to the value in *numéraire* of his receipts. His expenditures on products cannot fall short of these receipts, since negative or positive savings have no place in Walras' general equilibrium model until it is enlarged to include capital formation. Moreover, at equilibrium the values of the services bought by entrepreneurs must equal the value of the services sold by them in the form of products, since, in final analysis, services are exchanged for services embodied in products.

The snag that Walras perceived when he came to his discussion of *tâtonnement* in production in the fourth edition (1900) of the *Éléments* was that, unless all prices of services and products were *the* equilibrium prices *ab initio,* entrepreneurs would produce non-equilibrium quantities of products at successive stages of the groping process and that these "false quantities" once produced would have the effect of changing the parameters which he insisted (presumably in order to guarantee that the system converge to *the* equilibrium) must be held constant. In the fourth edition, Walras did not specify what parameters would be affected by the production of "false quantities." It could not have been the "resources" parameter, or the technology parameter, or indeed the "tastes" parameter (that is, the utility functions). What would, in fact, change would be the "distribution" parameter, that is, the distribution of the asset values of the original endowments held by the individual participants in the system, though the quantities of the physical items making up each separate endowment might or might not remain unchanged. The *numéraire* values of the various items in each original endowment would have to change with the changing *numéraire* prices of the productive services in the course of effective *tâtonnement.* As the

[23] Pp. 251–65 (§§249–62); cf. *E.P.E.,* pp. 583–85, Collation Notes to Lesson 21.

numéraire prices of the services emanating from various types of capital goods undergo adjustments on the way to equilibrium—if there are effective transactions at prices other than the equilibrium prices—then in terms of any arbitrary set of prices the incomes received in the form of products in return for the services sold will increase for some participants and decrease for others, depending upon whether the effective prices of the services they sell are above or below the equilibrium level and depending upon whether they are buyers or sellers at these prices. Since each participant's demand for products and offer of services are functions of his income as well as of market prices, whatever equilibrium the market converges to—if it converges at all—must be different from the equilibrium that would result if there were no change in the values of the incomes or assets of the traders.

In the fourth edition (1900) of the *Éléments* there is no direct evidence of any awareness of the distributional effects of the process of *tâtonnement* in production. All Walras said in that edition is "the process of groping [*tâtonnement*] in production entails a complication which was not present in the case of exchange. . . . In production, productive services are transformed into products. After certain prices for services have been cried and certain quantities of products *have been* manufactured ['certains prix de services étant criés, et certaines quantités de produits étant fabriquées'], if these prices and quantities are not equilibrium prices and quantities, it will be necessary not only to cry new prices but also to manufacture revised quantities of products."[24] Why this should constitute a "complication" he did not explain in the fourth edition; nor did he attempt to trace the effects of the "complication" on the unfolding of the *tâtonnement* process. He simply went on to tell us:

In order to work out as rigorous a description of the process of groping [toward equilibrium] as we did in exchange and yet take this additional circumstance into account, we have only to imagine, on the one hand, that entrepreneurs use *tickets* [*"bons"*] to represent the successive quantities of *products* which are first determined at random and then increased or decreased, according as there is an excess of selling price over cost of production or vice versa, until selling price and cost are equal; and, on the other hand, that landowners, workers and capitalists also use *tickets* to represent the successive quantities of *services* [which they offer] at prices first cried at random and then raised or lowered, according as there is an excess of demand over offer or vice versa, until the two become equal. . . . Thus equilibrium in production will first be established *in principle*. Then it will be established *effectively* through reciprocal exchange between

[24] *E.P.E.*, p. 242 (§207). In the translation of "étant fabriquées" as "*have been* manufactured," italics are here inserted to stress the difference between this expression and Walras' phrase, "*quantités à fabriquer*" (*Éléments*, 4th ed., p. 216 [§208]), which he used to designate quantities *not* effectively manufactured, but provisionally in prospect and represented by "tickets."

services employed and products manufactured *within a given period of time* during which *no change in data is allowed.*[25]

So we are left vaguely to infer that a modification in the design of the *tâtonnement* process is necessary, once the complication is taken into account, in order that the description of the process may be worked out rigorously without any change in the "data of the problem."

Strange as it may seem, what is left only to inference in the fourth edition (1900) had been spelled out in the corresponding passage in the second edition (1889) of the *Éléments,* where we read:

We propose to arrive at equilibrium in production in the same way that we arrived at equilibrium in exchange, that is by assuming the data of the problem invariable over the whole period during which our *tâtonnements* take place. . . . But *tâtonnement* in production runs into a complication which was not present in the case of exchange. In exchange, commodities do not undergo any change ["il n'y a pas de modification des merchandises"]. When a price is cried and the effective demand and offer corresponding to this price are not equal, another price is cried giving rise to a new effective demand and a new effective offer. In production [on the other hand], productive services are transformed into products. After certain prices for services have been cried and certain quantities of products have been manufactured, if these prices and quantities are not the equilibrium prices and quantities, it will be necessary not only to cry new prices but also to manufacture other quantities of products. Taking this necessity into account, we must suppose that at each renewal [*"reprise"*] of *tâtonnement* our entrepreneurs will find in the home country landowners, workers and capitalists possessing unchanged [*"les mêmes"*] quantities of services and having unchanged [*"les mêmes"*] needs for services and products. A cycle of *tâtonnement* runs its course as follows. At certain prices first cried at random and then rising or falling according to circumstances, our entrepreneurs will borrow from landowners, workers and capitalists the quantities of productive services required for manufacturing certain quantities of products which are first determined at random and then increased or decreased according to circumstances. Then they will sell these products in the products market, through the mechanism of free competition, to the same landowners, workers and capitalists who possess the same quantities of services as before and have the same needs for products as before. The *tâtonnement* process will be completed when, in exchange for the products they have manufactured, the entrepreneurs obtained from the landowners, workers and capitalists precisely those quantities of land-services, labor-services and capital-services which they owe to the landowners, workers and capitalists and which they have used in the manufacture of the products, so that [in the end] either they will repay their debts and shut up shop, or, more likely, they will continue their production indefinitely at the rate to which it has now become adjusted, so long as there is no change in the data, that is to say, in quantities possessed of the services and in the utilities of the products.[26]

[25] *Ibid.*
[26] See n. 22 above. It will be noted that in this fiction (in the second and third editions of the *Éléments*) involving the borrowing of productive services for the period of

For all its ingenuity, this model of the working out of the *tâtonnement* process is slipshod. In the first place, Walras failed to specify whether by "the quantities possessed of services" which need to be held constant he meant *(a)* the total quantities of the several services in the hands of all participants taken together or *(b)* the quantities of these services in the hands of each individual considered separately. Holding the former constant is a necessary but not a sufficient condition for the culmination of the process in *the* equilibrium, while holding the latter constant is neither necessary nor sufficient for a unique solution. In the second place, after calling attention to the "complication" occasioned by the production of "false quantities," Walras immediately proceeded to ignore it in his model as if it sufficed to assume "the data" constant to get rid of the untoward effects of the "complication" on the endowments parameter. At all events, in the second (1889) and third (1896) editions of the *Éléments*, Walras' analysis of the *tâtonnement* process was very much the same as that of the first edition (1874–77),[27] no further account being taken of the new "complication."

Apparently, Walras realized when he came to revise his *Éléments* for the fourth edition (1900) that it would not do simply to assume away the effects of the manufacture of "false quantities" on the parameters while retaining his original design of the *tâtonnement* process. The initial purpose of this design, it should be remembered, was to demonstrate how a market system automatically achieves by groping the very equilibrium solution that is derived mathematically from an appropriate

production and the subsequent repayment of the borrowed services in kind after receiving like services again in exchange for products there is no allusion to interest. What this amounts to is an implicit abstraction from time (made explicit in the fourth edition of the *Éléments*), probably because Walras wished to reserve the inclusion of interest for the more comprehensive *tâtonnement* model (*E.P.E.*, Lesson 25) in Part V, "The Theory of Capital Formation and Credit."

[27] The analysis worked out in *Leçon* 21 of the second edition of the *Éléments* and repeated in the same *Leçon* of the third edition did not differ in its essential argument from what is found in *Leçons* 42 and 43 of the first edition, though in place of the fiction of borrowing productive services from landowners, capitalists, and workers within a self-contained economy, Walras had resorted to a different fiction in the first edition. In all five editions, for expository convenience, Walras divided his analysis into two steps: In the first step he wanted to show how the *tâtonnement* process eventuates in equality *in the aggregate* between the total value of all inputs and the total value of all outputs via the extrusion of profits and losses through the competitive mechanism; in the second step his object was to show how the *tâtonnement* process results at the same time in equality between the quantity of each and every productive service used by entrepreneurs and the quantity offered, item by item. In the first edition, in order to proceed with his first step without disturbing the parameters which had to be held constant for the second step, he supposed the entrepreneurs to purchase the productive services they needed from abroad where their elasticities of supply were assumed to be infinite at an arbitrarily given set of prices, and then he supposed the entrepreneurs to restitute these services not in the same quantities but in quantities having the same value in total. It was in order to simplify this artifice that Walras introduced the fiction of borrowing and lending at home into the second edition (see n. 26 above) and finally the fiction of "tickets" into the fourth edition.

simultaneous equation system. True, the real market system Walras had in mind was not a replica of the infinitely complex network of the heterogeneously organized markets of the real world, but a simplification of that network idealized in the sense that it was assumed to operate as a perfectly competitive mechanism. This in itself by no means detracts from the pragmatic significance of Walras' theory of *tâtonnement*, for it is of no little importance from the standpoint of policy to know how a perfectly competitive mechanism would work, whether or not the results are to one's liking (Hicks, 1965, pp. 9–10). Another simplification, one that Walras had not introduced explicitly into his theory of *tâtonnement* in production until the fourth edition (1900), was the provisional exclusion of the element of time required for production.[28] This he could do without loss of generality, since by discounting the relevant variables spread over the production period to a given moment of time, it is possible to treat production as if it were instantaneous. What no feat of theoretical ingenuity would permit him to do, however, as Walras seems to have learned on mature reflection, was to abstract from the perverse consequences essentially inherent in his original design of a quasi-realistic *tâtonnement* process. Without giving his reasons—and it is doubtful that he had ever learned to work out these reasons—he announced in the Preface to his fourth edition: "In the theory of production, I no longer represented the preliminary groping toward equilibrium as it takes place effectively, but I assumed, instead, that it was done *by means of tickets* [*'sur bons'*] and I then carried this fiction through the remainder of the book."[29]

This change in the design of the model, which was first made in the fourth edition (1900) of the *Éléments*, cannot be considered as a further idealization of the real market system. It is, in fact, an abandonment of realism, and with this abandonment the initial purpose of the theory of *tâtonnement* is lost from sight. In any case, Walras was no longer under the illusion that the endogenous operating forces within his earlier quasi-realistic model of *tâtonnement* would allow the parameters he wanted fixed to stay fixed. Hence the new design of his model with its *"bons"* or tickets, which Walras meant to be *imaginary* ("il n'y a qu'à supposer," he wrote). These tickets are, in essence, provisional contracts

[28] The relevant *E.P.E.* passage (p. 242 [§207]) of the fourth edition of the *Éléments* runs as follows: "There is still another complication.... Production [as contrasted with exchange]...requires a certain lapse of time. We shall resolve this...difficulty purely and simply by ignoring the time element at this point. And later on, in Part VI, ["Theory of Circulation and Money"], we shall bring in *circulating capital* and *money* and thereby make it possible for productive services to be transformed into products instantaneously, provided that the consumers pay the interest charges on the capital required for this sort of transformation."

[29] *E.P.E.*, p. 37.

to buy or to sell given quantities of services or products at a given set of prices first "cried" at random. The provisional character of these contracts lies in the implied stipulation that they are binding if and only if a battery of totalizators, as it were, shows that the aggregate excess demands are everywhere zero simultaneously. Otherwise the contracts are declared null and void; and a new set of prices must be "cried," some higher, others lower, depending in each case upon whether the excess demands at the previously "cried" price were positive or negative. Walras' *"bons"* or tickets are, in a sense, like the provisional contracts in an auction "by inch of candle," where a bid recognized by the auctioneer constitutes a provisional contract between a bidder and the seller that becomes null and void if a higher bid is made before the candle burns out, in which case the auctioneer recontracts with the new bidder, and so on—the final bid alone constituting a binding contract. It should be noted that, under the rules of the provisional contracts in the form of Walras' tickets, no productive services are hired and consequently *no production takes place* until or unless the entire system is in equilibrium. Similarly, until equilibrium is reached, there is no effective purchasing or selling of products either. Thanks to this arrangement, which is a variant of Edgeworth's fanciful scheme of recontracting (Newman, 1965, p. 68), Walras circumvented the snag of "false quantities" with all their disturbing effects on the parameters.

What literature there is bearing directly on the theory of *tâtonnement* as Walras expounded it is bedeviled by the failure to mark out clearly and unmistakably the distinction between his two designs of the *tâtonnement* process: the one without tickets, as Walras had it in the theory of exchange throughout all editions of the *Éléments,* and the other with tickets, as it first appeared in the fourth edition (1900) in connection with the theory of production. Takashi Negishi (1962, pp. 646–47) did notice the difference, but the way he labeled the two designs of *tâtonnement* fails to reflect accurately the development of the theory in Walras' hands and thus constitutes a gratuitous break with the past from which Negishi derived the very problem he surveyed. Negishi, for some impenetrable reason, chose to designate as "a non-tâtonnement process" the down-to-earth *tâtonnement* in which "some trade out of equilibrium is permitted according to certain transaction rules," while reserving the term "tâtonnement process" proper for the hypothetical market adjustments in which "recontract is always possible and no actual trade of commodities is permitted (Walras suggests the use of tickets) until the equilibrium is reached" (Negishi, 1962, p. 647). Taking his cue from Hicks (1946, pp. 127–29), Negishi correctly observed that "on account of the redistribution of incomes among individual participants due to changes of prices in the midst of trading, the competitive equilibrium reached by a non-tâtonnement process [in Negishi's sense: without recontracting or tickets] is generally different from the one reached by a *tâtonnement* process [in Negishi's sense: with recontracting or tickets]" (Negishi, 1962, p. 648). But is this any reason for reversing the labels that a study of Walras' theory in the successive editions of the *Éléments* clearly suggest should have been placed the other way round? From this standpoint, would it not have been more appropriate to attach the term *tâtonnement* proper to the trial and error adjustments involving effective transactions in the competitive market, whether or not these adjustments could be shown to converge to a unique equilibrium? And, again from the same standpoint, would it not have been more suitable to apply the term "non-tâtonnement process" to Walras' makeshift involving the fictive use of tickets to which he had recourse in order to bypass the snags he vaguely perceived, since in so doing he lost all contact with anything like a real market and thus departed from his original purpose of identifying the real market solution with his mathematical solution?

The only model of a market system to which Walras' *tâtonnement* with tickets might be conceivably relevant is the one that Robert E. Kuenne (1963, p. 199, n. 3) suggested, a model consisting exclusively of "future markets, with contracts made on the market day having relevance to consumption and production for the forthcoming week," when "planned production and consumption always equal realized production and consumption." This ingenious suggestion of Kuenne's is in line with a fashion among econometricians of contriving market models to elucidate mathematical systems instead of developing mathematical models to elucidate market systems. Walras' *tâtonnement* with tickets, even when viewed in the light of Kuenne's model, boils down essentially to a mathematical solution by an iterative process of successive approximations, rather than a realistic trial and error market solution (see Goodwin, 1951).

Peter Newman's (1965) attempt to clarify some of the issues inherent in Walras' discussion of adjustment mechanisms can hardly be credited with having succeeded in dissipating the confusion which still reigns on the subject.[30] The reasons Newman alleges for Walras' employment of the device of *tâtonnement* in multicommodity exchange are seriously open

---

[30] Newman, 1965, pp. 101–3. In a private letter, Newman withdrew the suggestion he made in his *Theory of Exchange* that I held the "standard view" that Walras employed the device of *tâtonnement* in order to deal with "false trading" in exchange. My Translator's Note 6 to lesson 20 (*E.P.E.*, pp. 528–29) relates to the theory of production and not to the theory of exchange, and the device I referred to in that note as an artifice for evading the "problem of the path" was not the *tâtonnement* of Walras' theory of exchange, but rather the tickets (or *"bons"*) Walras used in place of *tâtonnement* involving effective production.

to question. He insists that the problem Walras' *tâtonnement* without tickets "was meant to cope with . . . was the problem of convergence of the 'excess demand' mechanism in *multiple market* situations, where interrelations of substitutability and complementarity make the analysis of convergence in simple two commodity markets just too simple to apply without considerable change." Surely this cannot be so.[31] In no part of the *Éléments,* whatever edition one may consult, does Walras allude to or consider interrelated demands. The manner in which he sets up his utility functions entirely precludes this. The utility function for any individual is considered by Walras as the sum of independent utility functions pertaining to each good separately.[32] He never deviated from this postulate. Walras' mind was set in the mold of what Metzler (1945, pp. 285–86) has called "gross substitutes," all commodities being such that, in Metzler's words, "a rise in price of the ith commodity, all other prices remaining unchanged, reduces the excess demand for that commodity and increases the excess demands for all other commodities." When Walras' attention was called by Leroy-Beaulieu, F. Y. Edgeworth, Irving Fisher,[33] and Pareto to his neglect of complementary and competitive goods, he took refuge in the claim that he concerned himself exclusively with "the general case" and not with special cases, which, he added, were of secondary importance and could readily be analyzed by means of a more complicated mathematical method than he had employed.[34] Whatever drawbacks Walras' assumption of independence of

[31] Nor, as Newman assures me in the private letter mentioned above (n. 30), did he intend his reference to "interrelations of substitutability and complementarity" to be understood in this context as "necessarily arising from the structure of individual prefereces." What Newman meant to attribute to Walras was simply an undefined sense of the complexity of market interrelations once one passes from the two-commodity case to the multicommodity case.

[32] *E.P.E.,* Lesson 8, and pp. 461–71 (§§71–84, and Appendix I, §§1–4). Cf. Hicks, 1946, pp. 43–50. Though there are passages in the *E.P.E.* (p. 171 [§128]; cf. §126 of 2d and 3d eds.), which may be interpreted as deliberately excluding from consideration the concepts of substitutability and complementarity in the Paretian and Hicksian sense, it is doubtful whether Walras fully understood the implications of these passages.

[33] Among Irving Fisher's comments in his "Translator's Note" which preceded Walras' "Geometrical Theory of the Determination of Prices" (1892), the comment on Walras' independence hypothesis reads as follows: "Although Professor Walras clearly recognizes that the demand and supply of each commodity is a function of the prices of all commodities, he omits to state that the *rareté* to a given individual of a given amount of one commodity is a function of the quantities not only of that commodity, but of all others. Hence the curves he employs are not independent, but the shape of the A curve in Fig. 1 [that is, the marginal utility of '*rareté*' curve of commodity A as a function of its quantity alone] will change according to what point is selected on the B curve [that is, the marginal utility or '*rareté*' curve of commodity B]. The A curve could not be said to be given until the demand for B, C, D, etc., was each given. The utility of bread, it is true, decreases with the amount of bread, but the *law* of that decrease depends on the amount of butter; in general the utility of the same quantity of bread increases as the amount of butter increases" (p. 46).

[34] Cf. Jaffé, 1965, Vol. II, Letter 999; Vol. III, Letter 1685, n. 5.

utility functions and gross substitutability may have from an econometric standpoint, it has the considerable advantage, as has been shown by
Metzler (1945, pp. 285–90) and Negishi (1962, pp. 649–56, 659–60), of
rendering the *tâtonnement* process without recontract "quasi-stable" (that
is, stable at *any* equilibrium set of prices to which the system may
converge without recontract), and the *tâtonnement* process with recontract
"globally stable" (that is, stable at *the* equilibrium set of prices to which
the system converges with recontract). The stability conditions of
tâtonnement lie, however, outside the interest of this paper.

From the standpoint of the present argument, which is concerned
with the interpretation of Walras' original model rather than with
attempts to substitute new, up-to-date theories of *tâtonnement* for the old,
it is important not only to avoid misconstruing the whole tenor of
Walras' theory but also to take care not to slip into an equivocal
terminology that opens the door to unnecessary ambiguities. For example, in the above-quoted passage from Negishi (1962, p. 648), which is a
passage taken from his discussion of *tâtonnement* in "the case of pure
trade," the term "incomes" appears in his allusion to the distribution
effect of changes in prices; and, again in H. Uzawa's (1960) admirably
lucid mathematical interpretation of Walras' theory of *tâtonnement* in
exchange, the term "income" is employed to designate the value of the
initial holdings of the individual market participants.[35] The use of the

---

[35] Uzawa's analysis of the dependence of excess demand on changes in the values of
the individual endowments runs as follows. Using vector notation, Uzawa describes the
initial quantities of consumers' goods or commodities held by individual r ($r = 1, \ldots,$
R) as $y^r = (y^r_0, y^r_1, \ldots, y^r_n)$, there being $n + 1$ commodities, commodity $i = 0, 1, \ldots n$.
It is immediately obvious that one cannot speak meaningfully of an increase (or decrease)
in y^r unless at least one component increases while none decreases (or at least one
component decreases while none increases). Uzawa then writes individual r's demand
function for commodity i as $x^r_i(p, M^r)$, where $p = (p_0, p_1, \ldots, p_n)$ is "a market
(accounting) price vector," and M^r is what Uzawa calls "income," that is, the value of the
initial endowment collection held by individual r. Once a market price vector $p = (p_0, p_1, \ldots, p_n)$ has been announced, then the value of r's endowment becomes

$$M^r(p) = \sum_{i=1}^{n} p_i y^r_i;$$

and his demand function for commodity i becomes $x^r_i[p, M^r(p)]$. Writing the aggregate
demand function as

$$x_i(p) = \sum_{r=1}^{R} x^r_i[p, M^r(p)].$$

Uzawa defines the aggregate excess demand function, $z(p) = [z_0(p), \ldots, z_n(p)]$, as $z_i(p)$
$= x_i(p) - y_i$, where

$$y_i = \sum_{r=1}^{R} y^r_i.$$

Since $x_i(p)$ is a function of $M^r(p)$ as well as of p, the dependence of the excess demand $z_i(p)$

term "income" in this context is disconcerting, for by blurring the distinction between stocks and flows, it also blurs the distinction between the pure exchange model and the production model. In Walras' model of pure exchange, there are no incomes or flows; there are only stocks consisting of holdings of consumers' goods.[36] It is, of course, possible to suppose each individual endowment collection to be renewed periodically by some exogenous agent and thus denominate the endowment parameters as "income"; but to do so without distorting Walras' original model of *tâtonnement* in the case of pure exchange, it would be necessary to stipulate that the *tâtonnement* process must be independently completed prior to each renewal of the endowments and that there is no subsequent trading without renewal of endowments. If there were any point in emending the pure exchange model in this way, it would be necessary also to stress the exogenous source of the "income," lest the term appear as an illicit importation from the theory of production. Income proper only appears in the production model, where each individual's endowment consists of a flow of services, or better, of a stock of capital goods yielding a flow of services, the value of which per unit of time constitutes his rate of income.

If some of Patinkin's interpretations of Walras' theory of *tâtonnement* are open to question, it is more a reflection on the obscurities and ambiguities inherent in Walras' pioneer work than on Patinkin whose meticulous scrutiny of the original text conforms to the highest standards of scholarship. Nevertheless, in the following passage, Patinkin leaves an important analytical distinction in limbo:

In general, what is an equilibrium set of prices for one array of initial endowments will not be an equilibrium set for another. For assume that we begin with a market in equilibrium at a certain set of prices. Assume now that there occurs an arbitrary change in initial endowments, either in their distribution among individuals in the economy and/or in the sum total of initial

and consequently of the adjustment in prices in the course of *tâtonnement* on changes in the value of the endowment parameter M is demonstrated.

[36] Walras illustrates the nature of the endowment scheme he has in mind for exchange by the following example: "Let us imagine that Robinson Crusoe, instead of being the sole survivor, came ashore with a hundred or so sailors and passengers, some of whom had salvaged rice, others rum, etc. If all these survivors held a market on the beach in order to exchange their commodities with each other, the commodities would have current prices perfectly determined and entirely independent of the costs of production. This is the problem of exchange and shows how prices depend only on the *rareté,* i.e., the utility, and the quantity possessed of the commodities. But if afterwards, upon discovering the requisite productive services on the island, they proceeded to manufacture the same kinds of commodities and carried them to the market, those products whose selling prices exceeded their costs of production would be produced in larger quantities and those products whose cost of production exceeded the selling price would become scarcer until equality was established between selling prices and costs of production. This is the problem of production, and shows how cost of production determines the quantity and not the price of the products" (*E.P.E.,* p. 476, n. 1).

endowments of one or more goods. From our discussion of the market excess-demand functions, we know that under these circumstances there will be changes in the amounts of excess demands. Hence, at the original set of prices, there will not exist positive or negative amounts of excess demands in at least some of the markets. Hence this original set is no longer an equilibrium one. Thus the term "equilibrium prices" must always be expressly or tacitly qualified by the phrase "at a given array of initial endowments." The same qualification must be made, *mutatis mutandis,* for the other independent variables of the analysis [Patinkin 1956, p. 33; 1965, p. 35].

From this it is by no means clear that only if the redistribution of individual endowments of which Patinkin speaks affects their values will a change in the set of equilibrium prices ensue. Otherwise the equilibrium set is invariant with respect to redistributions of the physical items making up to separate endowments, provided always that the total quantity of each commodity remains constant over the entire "array of endowments." This, as has been seen, follows from Walras' "theorem of equivalent redistributions." It is again for want of attention to this theorem that Patinkin couched his criticism of Walras' asymmetrical treatment of *tâtonnement* in exchange and *tâtonnement* in production in the following terms: "Walras seems to forget that the given data of a production economy are not the quantities of commodities, but the quantities of productive services; hence just as the *tâtonnement* does not affect the given data of the exchange economy, so does it not affect those of the production economy. Hence there can be no difference between these two economies with respect to the logical necessity of tickets in analyzing their workings" (Patinkin, 1956, p. 380; 1965, pp. 534–35). It is quite true, as we have seen, that "logical necessity" would call for the use of tickets in the case of pure exchange as in the case of production if *tâtonnement* is to culminate in a unique equilibrium; but this is only because in exchange no less than in production the effect of trading at "false prices" is generally to change the *values* of the endowment collections of at least two individuals and not because of any change in *quantities* of the physical components of these collections. Patinkin perceives perfectly that it makes no difference whether the individual endowments are made up of a distribution of fixed total quantities of various consumers' goods or of a distribution of fixed total quantities of productive services; if recontracting is required in the one case, it is also required in the other. Patinkin, however, leaves one with the impression that what is needed is constancy in the quantities of the physical components of the individual endowment collections, when in fact what is required for a unique equilibrium is constancy in the values of these separate endowments plus constancy in the sum total over all individuals of the physical quantities of the several commodities or services making up their initial endowments.

In his discussion of Walras' recourse to tickets in the model of *tâtonnement* in production, Patinkin observes at one point, where he refers to the passage quoted above (see n. 25 above), "It is noteworthy that this passage does *not* make provision for consumers also to make use of tickets" (Patinkin, 1956, p. 379; 1965, p. 534). Patinkin does not explain why this is particularly "noteworthy," but he leaves the reader with the ominous feeling that the omission is a defect, that the model is not consistent. Certainly if Patinkin had in mind Walras' failure to make provision for the use of tickets by consumers in the direct trading of their services among themselves for immediate consumption, he would be quite right in pointing to a gap, but it is hardly a significant or "noteworthy" gap. If, on the other hand, Patinkin had in mind to reproach Walras for not stipulating the use of tickets to represent quantities demanded of consumable products (as distinguished from consumable services) at quoted prices, then the reproach would be misplaced. A close examination of Walras' *tâtonnement* model in production reveals that he actually did make provision, albeit indirectly, for consumers to make use of tickets in bidding for products. In terms of Walras' model of *tâtonnement* in production, there is no trading of products among consumers, so that the only way consumers can obtain products is to purchase them from entrepreneurs in exchange for productive services. Since consumers are none other than Walras' "landowners, workers and capitalists," the tickets they use to represent their offer of services in exchange for products implicitly represent their demand for consumable products. It would, therefore, have been redundant "for consumers [qua consumers] also to make use of tickets" in the case of production.

In view of the current predisposition on the part of authors "of some of the best work of the present generation" (as Marshall phrased it) to ignore or deal cavalierly with the older sources of their inspiration, it may not be superfluous to point out what is obvious to the historian of economic analysis, that the general idea of *tâtonnement* is quite an ancient one. Léon Walras did not originate it, though he was doubtless the first to elaborate upon it in a manner that set in motion its modern refined analysis. Adam Smith, for example, a century before Walras, formulated the concept in this way: "The natural price, therefore, is, as it were, the central price, to which the prices of all commodities are continually gravitating. Different accidents may sometimes keep them suspended a good deal above it, and sometimes force them down even somewhat below it. But whatever may be the obstacles which hinder them from settling in this center of repose and continuance, they are constantly tending towards it" (Smith, 1920, I, 60). The germ of the idea is unquestionably to be found still further back, in Richard Cantillon's (1755) *Essai sur la nature du commerce en général,* and so on ad infinitum. It is, of course, otiose to try to trace the genealogy of the broad concept of *tâtonnement* to Adam and Eve, but in the case of the direct and acknowledged filiation of analytical arguments here considered, a painstaking and exact investigation of the line of filiation would seem imperative.

The example set by Alfred Marshall teaches us that even economic tales should have a moral. The moral of this tale was best expressed by Jonathan Swift, who I imagine would not deny its applicability to the present instance: "Because memory, being an employment of the mind upon things past, is a faculty for which the learned in our illustrious age have no manner of occasion, who deal entirely with invention, and strike all things out of themselves, or at least by collision from each other: upon which account we think it highly reasonable to produce our great forgetfulness as an argument unanswerable for our great wit" (Swift, 1704, sec. VI).

REFERENCES

Arrow, K. J., and Debreu, G. "Existence of an Equilibrium for a Competitive Economy," *Econometrica,* XXII, No. 3 (July, 1954), 265–90.
Cournot, A.A. *Researches into the Mathematical Principles of the Theory of Wealth.* Translated from the original French ed. of 1838 by D. T. Bacon. New York: Macmillan, 1897.
Goodwin, Richard M. "Iteration, Automatic Computers and Economic Dynamics," *Metroeconomica,* III, No. 1 (April, 1951), 1–7.
Hicks, John R. *Value and Capital.* 2d ed. Oxford: Clarendon, 1946.
Hicks, John R. *Capital and Growth.* Oxford: Clarendon, 1965.
Jaffé, William (ed.). *Correspondence of Léon Walras and Related Papers.* 3 vols. Amsterdam: North-Holland Publishing, 1965.
Kuenne, Robert E. *The Theory of General Equilibrium.* Princeton, N.J.: Princeton Univ. Press, 1963.
McKenzie, Lionel W. "On the Existence of General Equilibrium for a Competitive Market," *Econometrica,* XXVII, No. 1 (January, 1959), 54–71.
Metzler, Lloyd A. "Stability of Multiple Markets: The Hicks Conditions," *Econometrica,* Vol. XIII, No. 4 (October, 1945).
Negishi, Takashi. "The Stability of a Competitive Economy: A Survey Article," *Econometrica,* XXX, No. 4 (October, 1962), 635–69.
Newman, Peter. *The Theory of Exchange.* Englewood Cliffs, N.J.: Prentice-Hall, 1965.

Patinkin, Don. *Money, Interest and Prices*. 1st ed. Evanston, Ill.: Row, Peterson, 1956.

Patinkin, Don. *Money, Interest and Prices*. 2d ed. New York: Harper & Row, 1965.

Smith, Adam. *Wealth of Nations*. Cannan ed. 2d ed. London: Methuen, 1920.

Solow, Robert. Review of *Elements of Pure Economics,* in *Econometrica*, Vol. XXIV, No. 1 (January, 1956).

Swift, Jonathan. *A Tale of a Tub*. London: John Nutt, 1704.

Uzawa, H. "Walras' Tâtonnement in the Theory of Exchange," *Rev. Econ. Studies*, XXVII (3), No. 74 (June, 1960), 182–94.

Walras, Léon. *Éléments d'Économie Politique Pure*. Lausanne: 1st ed. (in 2 instalments), 1874–77; 2d ed., 1889; 3d ed., 1896; 4th ed., 1900; definitive ed. (published posthumously), 1926. Reprinted; Paris, 1952.

Walras, Léon. "Geometrical Theory of the Determination of Price," *Ann. American Acad. Polit. and Soc. Sci.*, III (July, 1892), 45–64.

Walras, Léon. *Elements of Pure Economics*. Translated by William Jaffé. London: Allen & Unwin; Homewood, Ill.: Irwin, 1954 (reprinted 1965).

14

ANOTHER LOOK AT LEON WALRAS'S THEORY OF *TÂTONNEMENT*

Two considerations have prompted me to have another look at Léon Walras's (L. W.'s) theory of *tâtonnement*. One is my growing dissatisfaction with my own prior look that goes back to 1967 when my article, "Walras's Theory of *Tâtonnement:* A Critique of Recent Interpretations,"[1] was published; the other is my present disagreement with Professor Michio Morishima's recent interpretation of the same theory in Chapter 2, "The *Tâtonnement,*" of his *Walras' Economics: A Pure Theory of Capital and Money,* published in 1977.

My purpose is not to pick a quarrel with Morishima's or anyone else's Walras-like theories of *tâtonnement,* which, indeed, are often better than the original, especially from the standpoint of econometrically motivated analysis. My sole aim is to show that the 'present-mindedness' of our contemporaries tends to blind them to the original purport of past texts. The principle of historical integrity is too dear to the heart of a practiced historian to allow textual misinterpretations (his own included) to pass unnoticed.

L. W. could not have found a better label than *tâtonnement* to attach to his theory of the emergence of multi-market equilibrium. It describes perfectly how he reached for the theory, though it is a misnomer for the theory itself, especially in its definitive version. From edition to edition of the *Eléments,*[2] beginning with the first part of the first edition of 1874–1877, he groped and groped for an answer to his problem, and, in the end, he shifted his ground and actually, perhaps without quite realizing it, gave up the quest. He left us finally with a theory of market groping without any groping in it.

In §124 of the posthumously published definitive edition (1926), L. W. reiterated the announcement made in his previous editions, that, having now defined mathematically the conditions of general equilibrium in multi-commodity exchange, he was moving on to show how the equilibrium solution emerges[3] in practice ["pratiquement" or "empiri-

---

[1] Jaffé (1967).   [2] Walras (1874, etc.).
[3] Cf. Translator's Note [11] to Lesson, 6, p. 501, of the *Elements of Pure Economics* (Walras 1874, etc.), referred to below as the *E.P.E.*

quement"] by virtue of the forces at work within the competitive market mechanism. The whole tenor of §124 suggests a transition from the abstract to the real, from theory to the world of experience. This impression is reinforced by (1) a previous intimation in the last paragraph of §116, reading,

In this way [i.e. by the immediately preceding system of equations of general equilibrium in multi-commodity exchange] ... prices are determined mathematically. Now there remains only to show—and this is the essential point—that the problem of exchange for which we have just given a theoretical solution is the selfsame problem that is solved in practice on the market by the mechanism of free competition.[4]

(2) the opening words of §125,

First of all, what takes place in the market is that the m (m -1) prices of m commodities in terms of one another are reduced precisely ... to m $-$ 1 prices of m $-$ 1 of the m commodities in terms of the m-th.[5]

(3) L. W.'s fourth sentence in the same §125,

These decisions [to transact] are arrived at upon reflection, but without finespun calculation, and yet turn out as if they had been reached by the mathematical solution of the system of equations ...."[6]

(4) the penultimate sentence of §125,

What must we do in order to prove that the theoretical solution is identically the solution worked out by the market?[7]

and again, (5) the last sentence of §206, leading up to the theory of *tâtonnement* in production,

---

[4] Reading in the original, "Voilà comment ... les prix en résultent mathématiquement. Reste seulement à montrer, et c'est là le point essentiel, que ce même problème de l'échange dont nous venons de fournir la solution théorique est aussi celui qui se résout pratiquement sur le marché par le mécanisme de la libre concurrence." This passage first appeared in §115 of the 2d edition of Walras (1874, etc.).
    So much of the present argument hinges on the very wording of the original text that I have felt it is necessary to give the French in footnotes to my translations. At best a translation can only be an approximation of the original and rarely will any two translators agree on the closeness of one approximation as compared with another. The same translator viewing a passage in a different light at different times, may render the same passage differently at different times, as I have done here in offering translations which sometimes differ from the *E.P.E.*
    [5] Reading in the original, "Et d'abord, sur le marché, on réduit précisément ... les $m(m$ $-$ 1) prix des m marchandises entre elles aux m $-$ 1 prix de m $-$ 1 d'entre elles en la m-ième."
    [6] Reading in the original, "Cela (i.e. the arrival at decisions to transact) se fait après réflexion, sans calcul, mais exactement comme cela se ferait par le calcul en vertu du systeme des équations ...."
    [7] Reading in the original, "Que faut-il donc prouver pour établir que la solution théorique et la solution du marché sont identiques?"

246   Special topics in Walras's economics

It . . . remains to be shown for equilibrium in production as was shown for equilibrium in exchange that [the] problem to which we have just given a theoretical solution is the same problem which is solved in practice on the market by the mechanism of free competition.[8]

All but the first of the above passages in the definitive edition are survivals from the first edition of the *Eléments,* though L. W.'s account of the *tâtonnement* process had, in the meantime, undergone substantial changes which made it less and less susceptible of interpretation in terms of real phenomena. Even in the first edition of 1874–1877, there are signs of ambivalence. After declaring in §126 of the first edition, which corresponds to §125 of the definitive edition, that markets solve his equilibrium equations "exactly," he ended up with the sentence, "Voici comment cela peut se faire," i.e., "Here is how this can be done." Thus he did not claim to describe what actually takes place even in the first edition.

On rereading page 2 of my previous article on *tâtonnement,* I find I am not at all as sure as I was in 1967 that "Walras's underlying motive in framing this theory was to lend an air of empirical relevance to his abstract mathematical model of general equilibrium . . . ." In the light of L. W.'s 'normative bias' implicit in his model[9] I am now more inclined to consider that the underlying purpose of L. W.'s *tâtonnement* theory was to portray an empirical possibility or feasible desideratum rather than an empirical fact. L. W. must bear part of the blame for my vacillation inasmuch as he delivered his theory of *tâtonnement* in snatches[10] scattered throughout the *Eléments* and nowhere as a straightforward, self-contained and unified piece of analysis. Add to that his inconsistencies from edition to edition, and the problem of figuring out what he really said, let alone what he really *meant,* becomes a daunting one.

My earlier view could perhaps be defended if I had confined my attention to the first edition of the *Eléments,* for in §42 of that edition (corresponding to §42 of the subsequent editions), where he described concretely how positive or negative excess demands for a security in stock exchange trading give rise to price adjustments in the direction of equilibrium, he said nothing which would preclude effective transactions at 'false prices.' In the second edition (1889) and subsequent editions, however, he inserted not only the sentence, "Theoretically, trading should come to a halt" ["Théoriquement, l'échange doit être

---

[8] Reading in the original, "Reste . . . à montrer, en ce qui concerne l'équilibre de la production comme en ce qui concernait celui de l'échange, que ce même problème dont nous avons donné la solution théorique est aussi celui qui se résout pratiquement sur le marché par le mécanisme de la libre concurrence."
[9] See Jaffé (1977).
[10] See Index of Subjects under "Groping," p. 614, of the *E.P.E.*.

suspendu"] when at a quoted price the quantity demand of the security exceeds the quantity offered, but also the sentence, "Trading suspended" ["Suspension de l'échange"] when the quoted price is such that the quantity offered exceeds the quantity demanded. These insertions appear unheralded and without explanation, like a passing remark uttered *sotto voce,* so unobtrusively that they apparently escaped the attention of even such careful theoretical investigators as Patinkin[11] and, following him, Peter Newman.[12] Donald A. Walker stands notably apart in interpreting §42 as a statement that "disequilibrium transactions do not occur in exchange markets."[13] Newman, however, is so oblivious of L. W.'s insertions that he goes so far as to affirm without qualifications that "there is no evidence that Walras considered the problem of 'false trading' serious for exchange. This is shown by his detailed discussion (*Eléments* [*E.P.E.*], pp. 84–86, [§42]) of his original example of exchange where he explicitly states that trading does take place at false prices." Not even in the first edition is there any such explicit statement, though there it may reasonably be inferred; but in the second and all subsequent editions, L. W., as we have just seen, explicitly excluded trading at 'false prices.' I had no excuse for following Newman's mistaken example after I had myself called attention, alas all too mechanically, to the insertion of L. W.'s crucial sentences in my Collation Notes [a] to Lesson 5.[14] *Mea culpa!*

No less mistaken was my complaint "that Walras missed perceiving the relevance of his 'theorem of equivalent redistributions of commodity holdings [§§140–144]' to his theory of tâtonnement."[15] Since the only

---

[11] Patinkin (1965), p. 533 n. 5.

[12] Newman (1965), p. 102.

[13] Walker (1972, pp. 347–48), nevertheless, chides L. W. for contenting himself with a mere assertion without "introducing a rule to the effect that such [disequilibrium] transactions are not allowed." Furthermore, Walker (1970, p. 693) insists "that it is not analytically defensible just to assume that disequilibrium transactions do not occur." In mitigation of this reproach, Walker might have found, on consulting L. W.'s article on "La bourse, la spéculation et l'agiotage" (L. W. 1880, etc.), that L. W. was persuaded by informed studies of the actual operation of the Paris Stock Exchange that disequilibrium transactions actually did not occur there. This, apparently, was the rule, which L. W. took for a fact, and which made the Stock Exchange an example drawn from reality for describing the mechanism of an ideal competitive market. See Walras (1898–1936), pp. 408–9 and also p. 432, where L. W. reemphasized the point as follows: "Le marché des titres doit être un marché type, et le marché type, nous l'avons dit, est celui où les ventes et achats se font par l'intermédiare d'agents que reçoivent les ordres des vendeurs et des acheteurs en n'opèrent qu'après avoir déterminé, comme prix courant, le prix pour lequel l'offre effective et la demande effective sont égales."

[14] *E.P.E.*, p. 566. Having fallen into this blunder, I wrongly took L. W. to task for overlooking the alleged trading at 'false prices' in §42 when he came to his theoretical analysis of *tâtonnement* in §§124–130. Now I see that my faultfinding was unfounded, since he had actually disallowed such trading in his preliminary concrete example of stock-market trading.

[15] Jaffé (1967), p.3.

redistribution taken into consideration in this 'theorem' was that resulting from trading at equilibrium prices, the several commodity holdings necessarily had the same market value in numéraire after trading as before trading; and similarly L. W.'s *tâtonnement,* from which trading at 'false prices' was excluded *de facto* or *ex hypothesi,* was bound to culminate in the same set of prices as that given by the algebraic solution of his systems of equations. The market solution he wanted was not reached by groping at all, but was predestined at the start by the exclusion of trading at 'false prices' from his hypothetical competitive market mechanism. It is no wonder that Robert Solow called L. W.'s "famous *tâtonnements* . . . a swindle,"[16] and so they must appear from Solow's standpoint; but not from L. W.'s standpoint, once that standpoint is taken, sympathetically or unsympathetically, into account.

In §127 of the fourth edition of the *Eléments,* L. W. began his definitive formal analysis of the *tâtonnement* process by assuming p'_b, a randomly chosen price of commodity (B), to be out of equilibrium, while the price of commodity (A), his numéraire, is set identically equal to unity and the prices of the remaining commodities (C), (D) . . . are supposed to be "determined" ["étant supposés déterminés"] at p'_c, p'_d . . . and consequently to admit of disjunction from the analysis—at least, for the time being. Thus the stage was set for a study of the market for (B) in isolation, where the positive or negative excess demand for (B), symbolized in the *Eléments* by $F_b(p'_b, p'_c, p'_d) \lesseqgtr 0$, is shown to vanish as competitive bidding of buyers or sellers raises or lowers p'_b until p''_b is reached which renders the excess demand, $F_b (p''_b, p'_c, p'_d$ . . .), equal to zero.

Before reaching this point in his step-by-step analysis of the *tâtonnement* process, L. W. paused in §128 and part of §129 to consider the question of the existence of an equilibrium solution in the market for (B) under the assumed conditions. He recognized at once that for positive prices of (B) in terms of (A), (C), (D) . . . to exist at all, the aggregate gross demand[17] for (B) when its several prices in terms of the other commodities were all zero would have to be greater than the total existing quantity of (B). Otherwise (B) would be what we call a 'free good' and not an item of the 'social wealth' with which L. W. was concerned. Taking (B) to be, as we would say, an 'economic good,' he then assumed, presumably for analytic simplicity, that the several prices of (B) in terms of (A), (C), (D) . . . would all rise (or fall) in the same

[16] Solow (1956), p. 88.
[17] I define 'gross demand' as the quantity of a good traders desire to possess at a given price of the good, in contradistinction to 'net demand,' which I define as the quantity of a good traders want to acquire at a given price in addition to what they already possess of it.

proportion ["proportionnellement"] so long as the excess demand for
(*B*) remained positive (or negative). This, as we have since learned from
Hicks,[18] is tantamount to reducing the collection (*A*), (*C*), (*D*)... to a
single composite commodity, which I shall call (*J*). Having thus, for the
moment, simplified his problem, L. W. was in a position to invoke his
theory of price determination in the two-commodity case, where he had
shown that an equilibrium might, under well-defined circumstances, be
either nonexistent or multiple.[19] For example, if, as we are now supposing, the two commodities are (*B*) and (*J*) and the market demand curve
for each of them is, as L. W. had it, continuous, negatively inclined
throughout its whole length with intercepts on both the price and
quantity axes, thus typifying in substance Alfred Marshall's "general
law of variation in the elasticity of demand,"[20] then the derived offer
curve of the other commodity would in each case be 'backward bend-
ing,' i.e. negatively inclined at higher prices, so that both the demand
curve and the offer curve of each of the two commodities would both
have negatively inclined segments and could, under certain circumstances, either not meet at all or meet at several points within the
positive quadrant. L. W. left it for later, in §156, to declare multiple
equilibria highly unlikely in the case of multi-commodity exchange,
which is, after all, the case here under consideration despite L. W.'s
provisional reduction of all commodities other than (*B*) virtually to a
single composite commodity. In §129, L. W. simply denied the possibility of a failure of an equilibrium solution "as long as there are any
parties to the exchange who are holders of more than one commodity"
["quand parmi les échangeurs il y en a qui sont porteurs de plusieurs
marchandises"]—a thought that had not struck him until the fourth
edition of the *Eléments*.[21] Having thus satisfied himself that in the
multicommodity case an equilibrium solution would exist in each
market taken separately, he proceeded from the isolated adjustment in
the price of (*B*) to an analysis of the *tâtonnement* process in the context of a
network of markets.

In order to follow the exact course of L. W.'s argument from his first
step to the next, it is necessary to clarify a detail which L. W. left

[18] Hicks (1946), pp. 33–34.
[19] Walras (1874, etc.), §§62–68 of the 4th and subsequent editions. See Translator's
Notes [1]–[4] and Collation Notes [a]–[g] to Lesson 7, p. 502, and pp. 566–67 of the
E.P.E.
[20] These elasticity properties of the demand curve, no less implicit in L. W.'s analysis
of demand since the first instalment of the first edition of the *Eléments* than they had been
in Cournot's differently directed analysis (1838), remained nameless until the appearance
of the first edition of Alfred Marshall's *Principles of Economics* in 1890, p. 163; cf. Marshall
(1920), p. 103. L. W. persistently ignored this innovation in nomenclature.
[21] See Collation Note [m] to Lesson 12, p. 576, of the *E.P.E.*

obscure. When we read in §127 that he was starting from the supposition that p_c, p_d . . . had already been "determined," leaving p_b alone to be "determined" ["Faisons abstraction de p_c, p_d . . . et cherchons, ces prix étant déterminés, et p_b restant seul à déterminer, comment il faut faire varier p_b entre 0 et l'infini pour que la demande de (B) soit égale à l'offre"], it looks very much as if he meant the arguments p'_c, p'_d . . . of his initial excess demand function to be adjusted equilibrium prices in their respective markets, though p'_b was out of equilibrium. This would imply that the whole brunt of any disequilibrium in the market for (B) would have to be borne by the market for (A), since, according to L. W.'s own version of the so-called 'Walras' Law,' there can be no positive (or negative) excess demand in the market for (B) without entailing a corresponding negative (or positive) excess demand in at least one other market.[22] But in §129, where L. W. undertook in his next step to probe the effect of the adjustment of p'_b to p''_b on other markets, he wrote the initial excess demand function for (C) as

$$F_c(p'_b, \ p'_c, \ p'_d \ . \ . \ .) \gtreqless 0.$$

Hence the p'_c, though described, along with p'_d . . . , as "determined," was clearly not an equilibrium price, but simply a parameter or variable to be provisionally considered given and fixed while adjustments in the market for (B) are traced within the confines of a temporarily assumed partial equilibrium model. That, in fact, is how L. W. explained his assumptions in a letter to Maffeo Pantaleoni dated September 2, 1889: " . . . *for the moment* I am supposing p_c, p_d . . . determined and constant, which allows me to consider the total demand and total offer of (B) [in exchange for the other commodities] as *functions of a single variable* p_b. Thus I determine [i.e. solve for] p_b *provisionally* as in the case of exchange of two commodities."[23] The stress laid in this letter on the provisional and interim character of the assumption of "determined" prices of commodities other than (B) makes it unmistakably clear that he intended this assumption to be understood as an analytical device and *not* as a description of the first of a succession of events occurring in a chronological sequence of *tâtonnement* adjustments. It is, indeed, disconcerting to find L. W.'s verb "déterminer" used in two different senses in the same sentence in §127 of the *Eléments* and in the same passage of his letter to Pantaleoni: first in the sense of designating p_c, p_d . . . as given and constant at unspecified levels, and the second in the sense of solving

[22] Cf. Walras (1874 etc.), §§123–126 of the *E.P.E.*

[23] Reading in the original, " . . . je suppose, *pour un moment*, p_c, p_d . . . déterminés et constants, ce qui me permet de considérer la demande et l'offre générales de (B) comme des *fonctions d'une seule variable* p_b. Et je détermine *provisoirement* p_b comme dans le cas de l'échange de deux marchandises." Jaffé (1965), 2:345, Letter 913; L. W.'s emphasis.

for p_b at its equilibrium level. Of one thing we may be sure, and that is the complete absence of any implication of a temporal ordering in L. W.'s sequential analysis: the adjustment in the price of (B) came first solely as a matter of expositional convenience, because the letter B comes alphabetically before letters C, D....

Having brought p_b to its equilibrium level in its own market, L. W. relaxed his partial equilibrium assumption in order to investigate seriatim and quasi-cumulatively: first, the effect of the change in p_b from p'_b to p''_b on the initial excess demand for (C), which thus becomes

$$F_c(p''_b, p'_c, p'_d \ldots) \gtreqless 0,$$

with $p''_b, p'_d \ldots$ as a new set of parameters for the separate adjustment in p_c from p'_c to a p''_c such that

$$F_c(p''_b, p''_c, p'_d \ldots) = 0;$$

then the effect of the preceding changes on the initial excess demand for (D) which, having become

$$F_d(p''_b, p''_c, p'_d \ldots) \gtreqless 0.$$

is ready-made for the separate adjustment in p_d from p'_d to a p''_d such that

$$F_d(p''_b, p''_c, p''_d \ldots) = 0;$$

and so forth until the excess demand of the last commodity in the system is reduced to zero, again separately and again involving in each case the preceding separately adjusted prices as parameters.

L. W. perceived perfectly that his sequence of adjustments carried out in each of the markets considered provisionally in isolation did not solve the problem. He acknowledged in §130 that the p''_b arrived at in his first step which culminated in $F_b(p''_b, p'_c, p'_d \ldots) = 0$ would not remain an equilibrium price after the successive adjustments of p'_c to p''_c, p'_d to p''_d ... had found their way into the excess demand function for (B), but he held that the resulting new inequality,

$$F_b(p''_b, p''_c, p''_d \ldots) \gtreqless 0,$$

would probably be closer to zero than the initially assumed inequality,

$$F_b(p'_b, p'_c, p'_d \ldots) \gtreqless 0.$$

The reason he gave for this probable outcome ran as follows: "This [approach to zero excess demand] will appear probable if we remember that the change from p'_b to p''_b which reduced the above [initial] inequality to an equality [i.e. $F_b(p''_b, p'_c, p'_d \ldots) = 0$], produced direct effects that were all in the same direction, at least so far as the [excess] demand for (B) was concerned, while the changes from p'_c to p''_c, p'_d to p''_d, ..., which moved the preceding inequality further off from equality [to zero], gave rise to indirect effects, some in the direction of equality and some in the opposite direction, at least so far as the [excess] demand for (B) was concerned, thus up to a certain point cancelling one another out. Hence," L. W. concluded, "the new system of prices p''_b, p''_c, p''_d ... is closer to equilibrium than the old system of prices p'_b, p'_c, p'_d ...; and it is only necessary to continue this process along the same lines for the system to move closer and closer to equilibrium."[24]

Seen now as a whole, L. W.'s definitive theory of *tâtonnement* in exchange proves to be a theory of virtually timeless, simultaneous and mechanical adjustment operation which L. W. broke down into its constituent parts for purposes of exposition and analysis. In the first stage of construction of his mechanical *tâtonnement* model, L. W. assembled in advance, as it were, a complete array of partial equilibrium solutions for each market, so ordered that, whatever its starting point, each successive solution in the array cumulatively incorporated the results of the preceding solutions. As he could not, however, integrate these separate parts into a comprehensive, unified over-all model without allowing for mutual feedback effects and as he really had no clear-cut theory for analyzing these repercussions at all rigorously, he fell back uncharacteristically on a probabilistic conjecture. It was worse than uncharacteristic, because, as it turned out, the conjecture violated a basic assumption of his theory of value and price. His whole theory of general equilibrium was founded on the assumption of independent cardinal utility functions, thus rendering all the commodities of his system gross substitutes for one another. This precluded interrelated demands for either close substitutes or complements. It, therefore, ruled out the mutually compensatory indirect feedback effects L. W. needed in order that his *tâtonnement* process might converge on general equilibrium. Under L. W.'s assumptions, a rise or a fall for example in the price of (C) would necessarily affect the prices of *all* the other commodities in the same direction,[25] so that there could be no accomodating

[24] Reading in the original (§130 of the 4th and subsequent editions of the *Eléments*), "Or cela paraîtra probable, si l'on songe que le changement de p'$_b$ en p''$_b$ qui a ramené cette dernière inégalité à l'égalité a eu des effets indirects et, au moins en ce qui concerne la demande de (B), en sens contraire et se compensant jusqu'à un certain point les uns les autres. Par ce motif, le système des nouveaux prix p''_b, p''_c, p''_d ... est plus voisin de l'équilibre que le système des anciens prix p'_b, p'_c, p'_d ... et il n'y a qu'à continuer suivant la même méthod pour l'en rapprocher de plus en plus." The same passage appears in §128 of the 2d and 3d editions. In §131 of the 1st edition, the same reasons for convergence of the market system on equilibrium are given, though the model is not quite the same (cf. Collation Note [i] to Lesson 12, p. 576 of the E.P.E.).
[25] See Hicks (1956), pp. 11–15.

compensations and, if the direction were perverse, there would, in general, be no convergence on equilibrium.

The attribution of a virtually timeless, mechanical property to L. W.'s *tâtonnement* model is no invention of mine; it is the way L. W. wanted it to be understood. So, indeed, he wrote to Pantaleoni in the aforementioned letter of September 2, 1889, in which, after emphatically characterizing as *provisional* each of the equilibrium prices separately and successively "determined" in its own market, and after calling attention to the disturbance of precedingly "determined" equilibria by the succeeding adjustments in other prices [e.g. " . . . Et je détermine provisoirement p_d (en dérangeant ainsi les déterminations précédentes de p_b, p_c.)"], he enjoined Pantaleoni now to view the separate *tâtonnements,* which, for convenience of analysis, he had set forth *in an ordered succession,* as, in fact, taking place *simultaneously* within the network of markets; and he asked, rhetorically to be sure, whether that was not exactly the way in which prices, when taken all together, are in fact determined by the market system in a multi-commodity economy operating under the rule of free competition.[26] L. W.'s contemporary Philip H. Wicksteed also perceived the process in this way in a note on the *tâtonnements* he sent to L. W. on April 8, 1889, suggesting, "Regard all the prices moving at the same time. Then for every equation

$$F_b(p_b,\ p_c,\ p_d \text{ etc.}) \lesseqgtr 0$$

the movement of p_b must, and the collective movements of p_c, p_d etc. *may* tend towards equality. . . ."[27]

However much clock or calendar time may be required for the working out of L. W.'s *tâtonnement* process, the process can still be regarded as theoretically instantaneous, since clock or calendar time is not an argument of L. W.'s excess demand functions. Given the postulated mechanism of L. W.'s competitive market system, given the exclusion, *ex hypothesi,* of non-equilibrium transactions in the operation of the *tâtonnement* process, given the assumed constancy of the data (i.e. of the resources or original endowments; of the tastes or utility functions of each of the traders; of the population or number of traders in the

[26] See note 23, above. The original I am paraphrasing reads in part, "Reprenez encore les tâtonnements que je vous présente ainsi *successivement* pour les besoins de l'analyse comme s'opérant simultanément sur le marché, n'avez-vous pas exactement dans son ensemble le fait de la détermination des prix de plusieurs marchandises sous l'empire de la libre concurrence?"

[27] Jaffé (1965), 2: 203, Enclosure appended to Letter 875. This 'suggestion,' referring to a passage on p. 152 of the 2d edition of the *Eléments* which corresponds almost exactly to §130 of 4th and definitive editions, is found in a long list of suggestions Wicksteed submitted to L. W. in response to a request for comments when the 2d edition was still in page-proof stage.

market system; of the market structure; and, in the case of production, of the technology), L. W.'s *tâtonnement* process takes place as if it were timeless, irrespective of the actual passage of clock or calendar time which is a built-in feature of the model. Hence it is clear that if, in such a context, time is to be considered at all, it is only to specify the *form* of the pre-assigned excess demand functions. Wicksteed apparently perceived that the disparity of time required for the separate adjustments of the several components of L. W.'s *tâtonnement* process is nothing more than a measure of differences in the mechanical potency of the components that contribute positively or negatively to the over-all movement toward equilibrium. This is seen in the following continuation of his aforementioned note to L. W.:

If p_c, p_d etc. tend towards producing equality, the movement of p_b need not be so rapid. If they tend towards producing inequality, the movement of p_b must be more rapid. But it can always counteract them, for whatever p_c, p_d etc. may be, p_b can always make D_b and O_b [i.e. the quantity demanded and the quantity offered at (B)] vary all the way from 0 to O_b, whereas it is not true that, whatever p_b may be, changes in p_c, p_d etc. can produce the like effect. Hence the effect of a movement in p_b either is or becomes at a certain point more potent in approximating $F_b(p_b, p_c \ . \ . \ .)$ to 0 than in separating all the other quantities $F_c(p_b, p_c \ . \ . \ .)$ etc. from 0.[28]

When L. W. passed from his theory of exchange, first to his theory of production and then to his theories of capital formation and money which incorporated his theories of exchange and production, it was precisely in order to avoid injecting an active time element into his corresponding enlarged model of *tâtonnement* that he introduced the device of fictitious "tickets"[29] into his account of the adjustment process. He had not done so in the context of his pure exchange theory only because he regarded the interval between a binding commitment to an exchange contract and its execution as negligible in comparison with the passage of time from the moment a product is ordered to the moment the production is completed and the delivery is actually made.[30] In any

[28] See note 27, above.

[29] For a definition of L. W.'s "tickets" ["bons"], see Translator's Note [6] to Lesson 20, pp. 528–29 of the *E.P.E.*

[30] Patinkin (1965, pp. 533–35) questions the logicality of L. W.'s omission of the use of 'tickets' from the theory of *tâtonnement* in a pure exchange economy, because, as Patinkin apparently sees it, the absence of 'tickets' (or some similar 'recontract' device) opens the door to trading at 'false prices' as much in an exchange economy as in a production economy. I retract, with apologies, my acidulous rejection, in n. 13 of my 1967 article (p. 5), of Peter Newman's surmise—Newman (1965), p. 102—which he based on §61 of the *E.P.E.* that L. W. neglected trading at 'false prices' in exchange because of the rapidity with which the market mechanism converges on equilibrium prices in a pure exchange economy. All I should say now is that this surmise was not wrong, but unnecessary, since, as has been seen in the above discussion, L. W., from the 2d ed. of the *Eléments* on, explicitly excluded trading at 'false prices' from the operations of a truly competitive exchange market—a point Newman completely missed.

appreciable time interval, 'complications' would more than likely set in[31] and disturb the structural features which L. W. assumed constant in his model. As long as he insisted on retaining his strictly static assumptions in his analysis of the emergence of an equilibrium set of prices via the competitive market process, he had somehow to render his *tâtonnement* in production as timeless as his *tâtonnement* in pure exchange. In the Preface to the fourth edition of the *Eléments* he announced that he "no longer represented the preliminary *tâtonnements* toward the establishment of equilibrium as actually taking place, but assumed instead that these *tâtonnements* are effected *by means of tickets*,"[32] i.e. by means of provisional contracts subject to mandatory cancellation until an equilibrium set of prices is reached in all markets of the system at once. There would then be no chance for changes in the data of the problem to occur. Thus L. W.'s *tâtonnement* in production was reduced essentially to a replica of his virtually timeless *tâtonnement* in pure exchange, as unrealistic in one case as in the other.

L. W. knew how unrealistic his *tâtonnement* model was, for, as he pointed out in §322 of the *Eléments,* while the tendency to general equilibrium is always present in competitive market systems of the real world, no full convergence to equilibrium is ever attained there, because in real life it takes time for market adjustments to work themselves out and "before the goal is reached . . . all the basic data of the problem, e.g. the initial quantities possessed, the utilities of goods and services, the technical coefficients, the excess of income over consumption, the working capital requirements, etc." will keep changing incessantly, and thus create at every moment a new form and structure for determining the behavior of the system.[33] This acknowledgment, it should be noted, is found in those closing Lessons of the *Eléments* which I call its coda,

[31] Walras (1874, etc.), §207 of the 4th and subsequent editions. See Collation Notes [g]–[i] to Lesson 20, pp. 582–83 of the *E.P.E.*

[32] Walras (1874, etc.), p. viii of the 4th and subsequent editions. The prefatory announcement reads, "En ce qui concerne la production, j'ai supposé les tâtonnements préliminaires pour l'établissement de l'équilibre faits non plus effectivement, mais *sur bons*, et j'ai maintenu cette hypothèse dans la suite."

[33] The relevant passage in §322 as it appears in the definitive edition of the *Eléments* reads: " . . . pour nous rapprocher de plus en plus de la réalité des choses, nous devons encore passer. . . de l'état statique à l'état dynamique. Pour cela, représentons-nous maintenant la production et la consommation . . . comme variant à chaque instant. . . . A toute heure, à toute minute, une fraction [des] diverses parties du fonds de roulement disparaît et reparaît. Les capitaux personnels, les capitaux proprement dits et la monnaie disparaissent et reparaissent aussi d'une manière analogue, mais beaucoup plus lentement. Les capitaux fonciers échappent seuls à ce renouvellement. Tel est le marché permanent, tendant toujours à l'équilibre sans y arriver jamais par la raison qu'il ne s'y achemine que par tâtonnements et qu'avant même que ces tâtonnements soient achevés, ils sont à recommencer sur nouveaux frais, toutes les données du problème telles que quantités possédées, utilités des produits et des services, coefficients de fabrication, excédent du revenu sur la consommation, exigences de fonds de roulement, etc., ayant changé."

because the Lessons from Lesson 35 on, constituting Parts VII and VIII of the *Eléments,* are structurally separate from, though not incongruous with, the preceding self-contained pure theory of a perfectly competitive economy. Dealing as Parts VII and VIII do with distinctly dynamic phenomena, with non-competitive price determination, and with intrusions of the State in the market economy, the final Lessons of the *Eléments* were designed by L. W., not as an integral part of his pure theory, but as a bridge to his projected applied theory and theory of the distribution of social wealth.[34]

The above interpretation when contrasted with Professor Morishima's interpretation illustrates how differently L. W.'s theory of *tâtonnement* appears to an historian of economics and to a mathematical economist *pur sang.* The latter, as I see it, is bent on exploiting to the full the mathematical implications he reads into the theory with a view to developing it further along his own lines; while the former has for his sole purpose to record in fastidious detail what was originally written, with no other view than to reconstruct, in the light of all the evidence that can be marshalled, the original author's meaning, however unpalatable that may seem to latter-day economists. The historian's compulsive microscopic scrutiny of texts is a tiresome business, but unless someone keeps doing it, myths, however unintentional or well-intentioned they may be, risk taking the place of history. It may be that myths are more attractive than history—at least in the eyes of those who look upon the austere historian as the French child looks upon his stern *papa* in the old song:

> Papa veut que je raisonne
> Comme une grande personne;
> Moi, je dis que les bonbons
> Valent mieux que la raison.

Who can gainsay the child?

Morishima, after reformulating L. W.'s theory of *tâtonnements* in highly sophisticated logico-mathematical terms so as to make it consistent with the modern econometric approach to the problem, does not hesitate to declare his reformulation also consistent with L. W.'s version as it was originally written.[35] If the portrayal of L. W.'s *tâtonnement* I have given above is correct, then the allegation of consistency of Morishima's *tâtonnement* process with that of L. W. is as wrong as any myth paraded as a fact of life.

[34] These projects were eventually realized in the form of two collections of papers (Walras 1898–1936) and (1896–1936) rather than systematically organized treaties.
[35] Morishima (1977), ch. 2, "The Tâtonnement."

The myth itself is not of Morishima's making. It goes back to Edgeworth's review of the second edition of the *Eléments*.[36] With nothing in 1889 but an early version of L. W.'s account of *tâtonnements*[37] before him, Edgeworth was quite understandably misled by L. W.'s propensity to waver between outright reality and abstract theory infused with enough reality to furnish a rational foundation for his cherished policy proposals. Edgeworth took L. W.'s theory for a stylized *description* of real market tendencies to equilibrium. This is clear from his statement, "He [L. W.] describes *a* way rather than *the* way by which economic equilibrium is reached."[38] If we add to this Edgeworth's immediate objection to L. W.'s way, "For we have no general *dynamical* theory determining the path of the economic system from any point assigned at random to a position of equilibrium," it becomes doubly clear that he thought that L. W.'s *tâtonnements,* instead of metaphorically representing elements of a quasi-instantaneous operation, were meant to depict an

[36] Edgeworth (1889). This was Edgeworth's opening salvo; his critical comments on L. W.'s early *tâtonnement* model continued unabated thereafter. To start with, he dismissed "what is called the 'tâtonnement' of the market" as "after all not a very good idea," and he explained this dismissal as follows: "What the author professes to demonstrate is the course which the higgling of the market takes—the path, as it were, by which the economic system works down to equilibrium. Now, as Jevons points out [see note 40, below], the equations of exchange are of a statical, not a dynamical, character. They define a position of equilibrium, but they afford no information as to the path by which that point is reached. Professor Walras's laboured lessons indicate *a* way, not *the* way, of descent to equilibrium" (op. cit., p. 435). Next, on September 12, 1889, in the course of his Presidential Address delivered to Section F of the British Association, republished in Edgeworth (1925, vol. 2, pp. 273-310), he argued, evidently apropos of L. W.'s *tâtonnement:* "when we advance from the simplest type of market to the complexities introduced by division of labour, it is seen to be no longer a straightforward problem in algebra or geometry, given the natures of all the parties, to find the terms to which they will come. Here, even if we imagine ourselves in possession of numerical data for the motives acting on each individual, we could hardly conceive it possible to deduce *a priori* the position of equilibrium towards which a system so complicated tends" (op. cit., p. 281). Then, in the *Revue d'Economie politique,* Edgeworth (1891) responded at length to "Bortkévitch's" defense of L. W. against his criticisms (see note 40, below). Here Edgeworth elaborated upon what he had already said in his Presidential Address and added, significantly apropos of the *tâtonnement,* that the market adjustment path depended very much upon the structure of the market—as if L. W. had not explicitly confined his analysis to one specifically defined market structure. Finally, in a "Note referring to p. 281 of the [republished] Presidential Address" (Edgeworth, 1925, vol. 2, pp. 310-12), he reverted to Bortkiewicz's (1890) denial of Edgeworth's allegation that L. W.'s *tâtonnement* described a dynamical approach to equilibrium and insisted that in default of a "general *dynamical* theory determining the path of the economic system . . . to a position of equilibrium, . . . Walras's laboured description of prices set up or 'cried' in the market is calculated to divert attention from a sort of higgling which may be regarded as more fundamental than his conception, the process of *recontract* . . ." (op. cit., p. 311). Cf. Jaffé (1965), vol. 2, p. 368, Note (5) to Letter 930; pp. 377-78, Note (3) to Letter 943; and pp. 431-33, Note (2) to Letter 998.
[37] For a summary of L. W.'s version of *tâtonnement* in the 2d edition of the *Eléments,* see Jaffé (1967), pp. 10-11.
[38] Edgeworth (1925), vol. 2, p. 311, Edgeworth's emphasis.

actual process that would require time to work itself out. From the standpoint of reality, Edgeworth's recontract theory made a far better job of dealing with time-consuming market tendencies. Each of the alternative paths guided by his *"curves of constant satisfaction* or *curves of indifference"* to a point on his Contract Curve is made up of segments in a temporal sequence.[39] But, as was seen above, no idea of a temporal sequence was implied in L. W.'s *tâtonnements*. In fact, L. W.'s analysis, being consciously and deliberately confined within a strictly statical framework, described no path at all. When seen in this light, L. W.'s theory of *tâtonnement* cannot be regarded simply as a less satisfactory variant of Edgeworth's recontract theory. The two are entirely different and must be judged by different standards.

Edgeworth's misapprehension lay in his inference that L. W. meant his *tâtonnements* to be market events in a dynamic sequence which L. W. nonetheless tried to elucidate on the basis of static assumptions from which no dynamic consequences can be drawn. The first to detect this misapprehension was a twenty-one-year-old Russian-Polish student Ladislaus von Bortkiewicz, who was destined to become a world renowned economist-statistician. Young "Bortkévitch" (as his name appeared in French), already in correspondence with L. W., leaped to the defense of his epistolary master in the *Revue d'Economie politique*.[40] He declared it was a mistake on Edgeworth's part to regard L. W.'s *tâtonnements* as any more dynamic than the price movements that are an accepted feature of static analysis. Thus ninety years ago, "Bortkévitch" put his finger on the very point at issue between my reading of L. W. and Morishima's— a difference that has cropped up again and again in the intervening years. If there were nothing else in favor of my reading, L. W.'s letters to "Bortkévitch" approving in advance and without qualification

---

[39] Ibid., vol. 2, pp. 315–317; and Edgeworth (1891), pp. 19–20. Cf. Walker (1973), p. 143.

[40] Bortkiewicz ["Bortkévitch"] (1890). As "Bortkévitch" stated his case, "... le critique anglais [Edgeworth] a eu tort en reprochant à M. Walras d'avoir passé du point de vue statique au point de vue dynamique, du moins si on emploie ces termes dans l'acception de Jevons. Et, en fin de compte, il est difficile de comprendre pour quelle raison M. Edgeworth trouve ... qu'après tout 'ce n'est pas une très bonne idée' que celle qui fait du mécanisme de la hausse et de la baisse des prix le mode de résolution des équations d'équilibre" (op. cit., p. 86). He had already cited Jevons's remarkably pertinent conception of statics and dynamics, which reads, "We must carefully distinguish ... between the Statics and Dynamics of this subject. The real condition of industry is one of perpetual motion and change. Commodities are continually manufactured and exchanged and consumed. If we wished to have a complete solution of the problem in all its natural complexity, we should have to treat it as a problem of motion—a problem of dynamics. But it would surely be absurd to attempt the more difficult question when the more easy one is yet so imperfectly within our power. It is only as a purely statical problem that I can venture to treat the action of exchange" (Jevons 1871, etc., p. 93 of the 4th ed.). Cf. Walras (1874, etc.), §322 of the 4th and subsequent editions.

"Bortkévitch's" confutation of Edgeworth's criticisms[41] ought, it seems to me, to settle the question once and for all.

Despite "Bortkévitch's" valiant effort to nip in the bud any attribution of a dynamic character to L. W.'s *tâtonnements,* Edgeworth's myth proved too hardy to die. Pareto, for example, in §§59, 101, and 135 of his *Cours d'économie politique* (1896)[42] praised L. W. for having shown that the bargaining process under free competition constitutes a trial and error method ("par tentatives") for solving the equations of exchange. In answer to Edgeworth's objection that it was nothing more than *a* method, Pareto replied that he agreed, but insisted that L. W.'s method was the principal one employed in the real world[43]—thus conceding, by implication, Edgeworth's view of L. W.'s *tâtonnement* as a dynamic phenomenon. In the same vein, Oscar Lange in 1945 described L. W.'s "traditional method of treating the stability of equilibrium [when 'excess demand for good makes its price rise and excess supply makes it fall']" as "an implicit (and therefore imperfect) form of dynamic analysis."[44] To purge the theory of its alleged imperfection, Lange introduced "a normal system of differential equations which has the solutions $p_r(t)(r = 1, 2, \ldots n),$" where t stands for time, r designates any one of the n commodities of the system, and "the functions $p_r(t)$ are the adjustment paths of the prices"[45]—surely more reminiscent of Edgeworth's "recontract" scheme than of L. W.'s *tâtonnements.* The successive prices of the r-th commodity which may be written as $p_r(t)$, $p_r(t + 1) \ldots$ would appear, accordingly, as functions of time measured in discrete units; and, if the temporal succession of these prices converges to equilibrium by progressively eliminating the positive or negative excess demands for all n commodities, the dynamic system is said to be stable. All this is offered in the name of L. W., with merely a technical improvement added! And Patinkin, whose detailed exposition of "Walras' Theory of *Tâtonnement*"[46] is widely accepted as authoritative, is no less oblivious of "Bortkévitch's" originally authorized interpretation of L. W.'s *tâtonnement* as an essentially static (and therefore timeless) adjustment process. In the manner of Pareto, Patinkin brings it under the heading of "The Method of Successive Approximation"[47] and calls it "Walras' dynamic theory of *tâtonnement.* "[48] He goes so far as to reject "as

---

[41]   Jaffé (1965), vol. 2, pp. 24–25; 45–47; and 59–61.

[42]   Pareto (1896–97), vol. 1, pp. 24–25; 45–47; and 59–61.

[43]   In Pareto's words, "M. Walras a fait voir que le marchandage qui s'établit avec la libre concurrence est le moyen de résoudre par tentatives les équations de l'échange. M. Edgeworth a objecté que ce n'était là qu'*un* moyen. Il a raison; mais le moyen indiqué par M. Walras est bien celui qui représente la partie principale du phénomène économique" (op. cit., pp. 24–25).

[44]   Lange (1945), p. 94.   [45]   Ibid., pp. 94–97.

[46]   Patinkin (1965), pp. 531–40.   [47]   Ibid., p. 38.   [48]   Ibid., p. 540.

a fundamental misinterpretation of Walras' conceptual framework" Richard M. Goodwin's (in my view, perfectly correct) assertion that L. W. "explicitly states that it [the *tâtonnement*] is only a mathematical method of solution and not the practical one exemplified in the behavior of real markets."[49] Presumably Patinkin would have been equally outraged by Kenneth Arrow's and F. H. Hahn's remark, if it had appeared in time for comment in the second edition of *Money, Interest and Prices*, that "Walras . . . first formulated the idea of a tâtonnement although in his more formal account of it he seemed to conceive of it as the Gauss-Seidel process" of solving a set of simultaneous equations, which being neither "a particularly attractive computational means" nor an imitation of the market "has rather little to recommend it."[50]

In his Chapter on "The Tâtonnement" already referred to,[51] Morishima tells us much about L. W.'s *tâtonnement* which is historiographically true, but then, following Edgeworth's precedent and Patinkin's example, he elaborates upon it as if L. W., in final analysis, meant his theory to be dynamic. It is, of course, true that "Walras assumed," as Morishima tells us, "that for each and every commodity there was a perfectly organized market."[52] It is no less true, again as Morishima tells us, that "under the pressure of competition" in L. W.'s well-organized markets, "prices cannot deviate far from equilibrium values."[53] Contact with historical record begins to fade, however, when Morishima goes on to distinguish in general between "two methods of competitive trading" in a perfectly organized market without reference to their respective conceptual authors.[54] According to the first of these methods, which Morishima calls "the usual one," "all trades are provisional and not effective as long as excess supply or demand remains in the market"; and according to the second, which Morishima simply calls "the second method," "agreement to trade may be made between any pair of traders at any point of time during the process of *tâtonnement*, even though" the total demand for each commodity does not equal its total supply. We are not told that the first is essentially L. W.'s method, and the second Edgeworth's. If we are prepared to pardon this as a mere sin of omission, the sins of commission which follow cannot be so easily condoned. When Morishima asserts that L. W. "unlike Hicks, arranged the markets in a definite order" and when he identifies L. W.'s "definite order" with a time sequence of interrelated adjustments and disturbances in the course of the *tâtonnement*,[55] then Morishima, like Lange

[49] Ibid., p. 532 n. 2, referring to p. 5 of Goodwin (1951).
[50] Arrow and Hahn (1971), pp. 306 and 322, "Notes." Cf. Nagatani (1978), p. 134 n. 2.
[51] Morishima (1977), ch. 2.   [52] Ibid., p.27.
[53] Ibid., p. 28.   [54] Ibid., pp. 28–29.
[55] Ibid., p. 36.

before him, clearly misrepresents L. W.'s *tâtonnement*.[56] As we have already seen, L. W.'s "definite order" of market adjustments to equilibrium is not an order of events in time, but simply an order of exposition of simultaneous aspects of a single, complex, virtually timeless event.[57] Moreover, when L. W.'s exposition is perceived as a translation into market language of the Gauss-Seidel algorithm for the solution of simultaneous equations by iteration,[58] then the solution does not depend in any way upon the order of progress to the solution. It is, therefore, a misreading of L. W. to claim, as Morishima does, that, for example, L. W.'s excess demand function,

$$F_c(p''_b, p''_c, p'_d, \ldots) = 0,$$

can be reformulated, without departing from its original significance, as

$$E_2[p_1(t + 1), p_2(t + 1), p_3(t), \ldots p_{n-1}(t), 1] = 0,$$

where t, $t + 1$ are successive "points in time."[59]

It must be admitted to Morishima's credit that he does not seem too sure of himself in assigning a dynamical character to L. W.'s *tâtonnement*. At one point he writes, "Walras was *apparently* [my italics] concerned with the dynamic movement of prices."[60] This concern, though only apparent, he sharply contrasts with Hicks's failure to derive stability conditions from an explicit model. He carries this contrast so far as to suggest, "If one does not like Walras' arrangement of markets in a definite order, one may follow Hicks and assume that when the price of commodity 1 changes from $p_1(t)$ to $p_1(t + 1)$, the prices of all the other commodities are adjusted so as to establish equilibrium in their markets simultaneously. . ."[61] This is unquestionably a correct interpretation of Hicks, who, in response to Samuelson's and Metzler's comments on the limitations of Hicks's stability conditions,[62] admits not only that his discussion of static stability was "deliberately and explicitly timeless," but also that, in passing to *his* dynamics, "the discussion of *stability* remained timeless." Moreover, Hicks leaves no room for doubt that this theory of "the mechanics of related markets" rested on his "hypothesis of essentially instantaneous adjustment." If my reading of L. W.'s theory of *tâtonnement* is right, nothing could be more similar than L. W.'s account of the *tâtonnement* and Hicks's stability analysis, Morishima's contention to the contrary notwithstanding.

Why is there so wide a difference between Morishima's and my own interpretation of the same Walrasian text which he gives every evidence

---

[56] Ibid., p. 27.   [57] Ibid., p. 28.
[58] Ibid., p. 28–29.   [59] Ibid., pp. 36–37.
[60] Ibid., p. 35.   [61] Ibid., p. 37 n. 13.
[62] Hicks (1946), pp. 335–37, "Additional Note C."

of having examined with at least as much care as I have given to it? Inasmuch as the issue I am raising is not mathematical, but historiographic, the fact that he applies to the problem much more mathematical skill than I could ever muster does not, I dare say, invalidate serious comparison between our two views. Mark Blaug calls Morishima's *Walras' Economics* a "profoundly ahistorical"[63] study; I go further and say that insofar as Morishima's book purports to be a contribution to the history of economics, it is replete with beguiling myths rather than history.

So far as the *tâtonnement* is concerned, I am not arguing that the mythological interpretation I complain of is pure invention. On the contrary, I grant that Morishima takes great pains to authenticate his interpretation by textual evidence always correctly cited and never out of immediate context. It is very much the same evidence I have listed above, in the fourth paragraph of this article, attesting to L. W.'s declared intention to give real life to his systems of general equilibrium equations. By adding to this L. W.'s §322 of the *Eléments*, Morishima justifies his attribution of an originally intended dynamical character to the *tâtonnement*. All this, however, leaves unanswered the nagging question why L. W., without renouncing his interest in the empirical relevance of his theory, nevertheless retreated, in the end, from his realistic conception of the *tâtonnement* and left us with a formal portrayal of the process which, as L. W. finally admitted, was neither empirical nor dynamical.

The inconsistency of L. W.'s declaration of purpose of his *tâtonnement* with his formal, mathematical discussion of the theory is reflected in Goodwin (1951). For Goodwin, whose primary interest lay in erecting "a useful dynamics," the same passage from §322 of the *Eléments* that I cite in note 33, above, constitutes a superb statement of the setting for his problem. The problem, as Goodwin sees it, is to investigate the similarity between "the traditional mathematical device of solving equations by trial and error" and economic dynamics regarded as "a series of iterated trial solutions which actually succeed one another at realistically great, regular intervals of time."[64] Though he finds it "a matter of considerable interest that Walras's conception of and term for dynamical [*sic!*] adjustment—tâtonner, to grope, to feel one's way—is literally the same as that of modern servo theory," Goodwin takes L. W. to task for having "unfortunately confused the matter by not being altogether clear as to whether he was talking about an iterative solution or about an actual temporal process."[65] In much the same manner,

---

[63] Blaug (1978). See also Jaffé (1978) and (1980), the latter being a companion piece to the above paper.
[64] Goodwin (1951), pp. 1-2.   [65] Ibid., p. 4.

Arrow and Hahn, as we have seen,[66] praise L. W. for having been the first to formulate "the idea of *tâtonnement*," but since it is clear from Arrow and Hahn's context that they mean by "a tâtonnement" a *dynamic* process that must take time to work itself out even "with recontract," they are apparently taken aback by L. W.'s "more formal account of it" which suggests to them the Gauss-Seidel method of solving essentially timeless simultaneous equations. Morishima neither cuts nor undoes the Gordian knot; he simply conjures it away.

The conceptual inconsistencies which troubled Goodwin and Arrow and Hahn vanish under Morishima's interpretation. He refuses to accept L. W.'s mathematical formulations as "self-contained," and sees in L. W.'s "verbal explanations and qualifications" a conjoined "supplement" designed to make up for what L. W. showed he was unable to express mathematically.[67] Hence, Morishima contends, we must look to the "supplement" for L. W.'s fully intended "economic reasoning"; and where the formal account proved inadequate to support the reasoning, a modern economist, like Morishima, who is not handicapped by L. W.'s "mathematical limitations," need only revise, correct and amend the original mathematics to furnish a true reconstruction of L. W.'s economics without deviating from L. W.'s "own spirit."[68] If by "own spirit" Morishima means L. W.'s original underlying (but imperfectly carried out) intention, then, in my opinion, an historian of economics must differ with Morishima. What he considers the "spirit" of L. W. turns out to be a myth.

The source of Morishima's misapprehension of the "spirit" of L. W.'s *tâtonnement,* as of L. W.'s whole general equilibrium theory, lies in Morishima's deliberately chosen limited perception of L. W.'s *œuvre.* On the very first page of the Preface to his book on *Walras' Economics,* Morishima, while admitting that "we can only judge the full value of his [L. W.'s] pure economics by considering it in the context of his original farsighted scheme [including L. W.'s *Etudes d'économie sociale* and his *Etudes d'économie politique appliquée*]," nevertheless makes no bones about restricting his view to the *Eléments* in the belief that "this will not have serious effects." As it happens, it does have serious effects and distorts his understanding of L. W.'s *tâtonnement* among other things. When examined in the light of "the full story of Walras' economics," then, L. W.'s formal account of his *tâtonnement* is revealed, not as a piece of deficiently formulated dynamics, but as an intentionally static exercise in stability analysis, subject to the same qualifications that govern his formal general equilibrium theory.

It is not easy for a non-historian to appreciate these qualifications. L.

---

[66] See note 50, above.   [67] Morishima (1977), p. 12.
[68] Ibid., p. 9.

W. himself, who suffered from a lack of recognition during his lifetime, consoled himself with the thought that his work would come into its own in the 20th century,[69] as indeed it has. But while the 20th century economists have, in fact, seized upon L. W.'s theoretical construct to elaborate highly interesting and useful variations upon the theme of his equational systems, they had no reason, given *their* aims, to investigate the special motivations that lay behind L. W.'s personal contribution. Though he felt he was writing for the 20th century, he did not live for long in that century, and was singularly influenced by the preoccupations of his time, not ours. As I have endeavored to demonstrate elsewhere,[70] L. W. formulated his general equilibrium theory with a distinctive normative bias colored by the prevailing ideologies and economic and social circumstances of his father's and his own day. It is because Morishima avowedly refrains from taking "the full story of Walras' economics" into account in order to review "the theoretical kernel" of L. W.'s contribution[71] that he missed perceiving that the "kernel" was meant to represent the formal rational design of his "social ideal." That is why I cannot agree with Morishima's opinion that "the ultimate aim of [L. W.'s *Eléments*] was to construct a model, by the use of which we can examine how the capitalist system works."[72] For the same reason, I cannot accept his view that Part VII of the *Eléments* (including §322) should be regarded as an integral part of the "kernel."[73] On the contrary I contend that the closing Parts VII and VIII were intended as a coda, which, although important, do not represent a completion of L. W.'s system, but an addition beyond the end of the formal composition. The *tâtonnements* discussed in Parts II–VI properly belong to the "kernel" and serve its static purpose well and consistently; the *tâtonnement* discussed in §322 of Part VII is an addendum that reaches beyond the "kernel" and serves quite a different purpose. The latter cannot be used to explain the former without violating the whole "spirit" of L. W.'s general equilibrium economics.

REFERENCES

Arrow, K. J., and F. H. Hahn (1971). *General Competitive Analysis*. San Francisco and Edinburgh.
Blaug, M. (1978). Review of Michio Morishima's *Walras' Economics: A Pure Theory of Capital and Money*, in *Economica* 45, no. 180 (Nov. 1978): 412–13.
Bortkiewicz ["Bortkévitch"], L. v. (1890). Review of Léon Walras's *Eléments d'économie pure;* 2d ed., 1889. *Revue d'Economie politique* 4, no. 1 (Jan.–Feb. 1890): 80–86.

[69] Jaffé (1965), vol. 1, p. 12, and Walras (1874, etc.), closing paragraph of Preface to the Fourth Edition.
[70] Jaffé (1975) and (1977).   [71] Morishima (1977), p. vii.
[72] Ibid., p. 4. · [73] Ibid., p. 5.

Edgeworth, F. Y. (1889). Review of Léon Walras's *Eléments d'économie politique pure*, 2d ed., 1889. *Nature* 40, no. 1036 (5 Sept. 1889): 434–36.
(1891). "Théorie mathématique de l'offre et de la demande et le coût de production." *Revue d'Economie politique* 5, no. 1 (Jan. 1891): 10–28.
(1925). *Papers Relating to Political Economy*, 3 vols. London.
Goodwin, R.M. (1951). "Iteration, Automatic Computers and Economic Dynamics." *Metroeconomica* 3, no. 1 (April 1951): 1–7.
Hicks, J. R. (1946). *Value and Capital*, 2d ed. Oxford: Clarendon Press.
(1956). *A Revision of Demand Theory*. Oxford.
Jaffé, W., ed. (1965). *Correspondence of Léon Walras and Related Papers*, 3 vols. Amsterdam.
(1967). "Walras's Theory of *Tâtonnement*: A Critique of Recent Interpretations." *Journal of Political Economy* 75 (Feb. 1967): 1–19.
(1974). "Edgeworth's Contract Curve: Part 1. A Propaedeutic Essay in Clarification." *History of Political Economy* 6 (Fall 1974): 343–59.
(1975). "Léon Walras: An Economic Adviser *Manqué*." *Economic Journal* 85, no. 340 (Dec. 1975): 812–23.
(1977). "The Normative Bias of the Walrasian Model: Walras versus Gossen." *Quarterly Journal of Economics* 91, no. 364 (Aug. 1977): 371–87.
(1978). Review of Michio Morishima's *Walras' Economics: A Pure Theory of Capital and Money*, in the *Economic Journal* 88, no. 351 (Sept. 1978): 574–76.
(1980). "Walras's Economics as Others See It." *Journal of Economic Literature* 18, no. 2 (June 1980): 528–58.
Jevons, W. S. (1871, etc.). *The Theory of Political Economy*, 4th ed. (1911), edited by H. Stanley Jevons. London.
Lange, O. (1945). *Price Flexibility and Employment*. Bloomington, Ind.
Marshall, A. (1920). *Principles of Economics*, 8th ed. London.
Morishima, M. (1977). *Walras' Economics: A Pure Theory of Capital and Money*. Cambridge.
Nagatani, K. (1978). *Monetary Theory*. Amsterdam.
Newman, P. (1965). *The Theory of Exchange*. Englewood Cliffs, N.J.
Pareto, V. (1896–97). *Cours d'économie politique*, 2 vols. Lausanne.
Patinkin, D. (1965). *Money, Interest and Prices*, 2d ed. New York.
Solow, R. (1956). Review of the *Elements of Pure Economics* [E.P.E.]. *Econometrica*, 24, no. 1 (Jan. 1956): 87–89.
Walker, D. A. (1970). "Léon Walras in the Light of his Correspondence and Related Papers." *Journal of Political Economy* 78 (July–Aug. 1970): 685–701.
(1972). "Competitive Tâtonnement Exchange Markets." *Kyklos* 25, no. 2 (1972): 345–63.
(1973). "Edgeworth's Theory of Recontract." *Economic Journal* 83, no. 329 (March 1973): 138–47.
Walras, L. (1874, etc.). *Eléments d'économie politique pure*, 1st ed. (in two instalments), Lausanne, 1874–77; 2d ed., Lausanne, 1889; 3d ed., Lausanne, 1896; 4th ed., Lausanne, 1900; definitive ed. (published posthumously), Lausanne, 1926. Reprinted, Paris, 1952. English translation, *Elements of Pure Economics*, translated from the definitive edition by William Jaffé, London and Homewood, Ill.; reprints of Economics Classics, New York, 1969.
(1880, etc.). "La bourse—la spéculation et l'agiotage." *Bibliothéque universelle*

et Revue suisse, 3d Period, 5 (March 1880): 452–72, and 6 (April 1880): 66–94; republished in Walras (1898–1936), pp. 401–45.

(1896–1936). *Etudes d'économie sociale (Théorie de la répartition de la richesse social).* Lausanne, 1896; 2d ed., edited by G. Leduc, Lausanne, 1936.

(1898–1936). *Etudes d'économie politique appliquée (Théorie de la production de la richesse sociale).* Lausanne, 1898; 2d ed., edited by G. Leduc, Lausanne and Paris, 1936.

PART V

WALRAS'S PLACE IN THE HISTORY OF ECONOMIC THOUGHT

15

REFLECTIONS ON THE IMPORTANCE OF
LEON WALRAS

Several years ago, when I went abroad on a Guggenheim grant leavened with funds from the Rockefeller Foundation for research assistance, I looked in England for a competent person to help me in something more than a clerical capacity. A young lady, apparently in her early twenties, came to see me about the job. She had a degree in economics from an English university. After I had briefly sketched the work I was proposing to do on Léon Walras, she loftily asked me, 'Who was Léon Walras? I've never heard of him. He wasn't important, was he?' The young lady did not get the job, but her question left me shattered and continues to haunt me.

Even at the risk of presenting my problem in a more personal way than is seemly, I must allude to the particular source of my interest in Walras and to the antecedents of my puzzlement about his importance.

It all began with a conversation I had with Henry Schultz at the University of Chicago soon after I arrived at Northwestern University in the closing years of the 1920s.

This was at a time when Schultz was writing his article on 'Marginal Productivity and the General Pricing Process,' which was to appear in the *Journal of Political Economy* in October 1929. That article contained a closing section on 'Errors and Changes in Walras' Marginal Productivity Theory'; and so we fell to talking about Léon Walras. Schultz, having been a student of Henry Ludwell Moore, was, of course, well acquainted with Walras' *Eléments,* while I knew only what I had read about it in Gide and Rist's *Histoire des doctrines économiques.* [1] To hold my own in these conversations, I began reading Walras's *Eléments d'économie politique pure.* [2]

This paper was read in earlier versions before faculty-graduate seminars at the University of British Columbia, Rice University and York University (Toronto). The underlying research was supported by Grants GS-1516 and GS-1997 to Northwestern University from the National Science Foundation to which the author wishes to express his gratitude.

[1] Charles Gide and Charles Rist, *Histoire des doctrines économiques,* ed. 1, Paris 1909; English translation: *History of Economic Doctrines,* trans. from ed. 2 by R. Richards, New York 1948, pp. 503–505.

[2] Léon Walras, *Eléments d'économie politique pure,* ed. 1, 2 vols. Lausanne and Paris 1874–77; ed. définitive (5th), Lausanne and Paris 1926; English translation: *Elements of*

Since I was then in charge of a graduate course on the economics of Alfred Marshall, I was struck by the contrast between the sheer formal architectonic beauty of Walras's pure theory and Marshall's muddling blend of theory and miscellaneous reflections and opinions. In Marshall's *Principles of Economics*,[3] we find, besides theory, a multitude of observations which shed more light on the mentality of the observer than on the conditions observed; we find broad, intuitive generalizations on human nature; also sketches of teleological economic history designed to demonstrate that all the travail of the human past from time immemorial had for its supreme purpose to produce that paragon of chivalrous and pragmatic virtue which was made incarnate in the person of the English business man of the late 19th Century;[4] and not only that, we are treated, in addition, to moralizing homilies with exemplary illustrations drawn from the way of life of the English middle class of Marshall's day, where 'a woman may display wealth, but she may not display only her wealth, by her dress,' where she is exhorted to abjure 'the evil dominion of the wanton vagaries of fashion'[5] and where 'those drinks which stimulate mental activities, ['tea'], are largely displacing ['the grosser and more immediately stupifying forms of alcohol'] which merely gratify the senses.'[6]

Alfred Marshall, who was certainly a consummate theorist, was nevertheless, in his heart of hearts, a little ashamed of it. Lest his private vice be too obvious, he consigned his analytical apparatus to furtive footnotes and secluded appendices. He even went so far as to deprecate any intensive mathematical treatment of economics. Marshall's 'Pure Theory of Foreign Trade' published for private circulation as far back as 1879, contained the following caveat: '... the use of mathematical analysis has been found to tempt men to expend their energy on the elaboration of minute and complex hypotheses, which have indeed some distant analogy to economic conditions, but which cannot properly be said to represent in any way economic laws.'[7] I suspect he had Léon

Pure Economics, trans. from the ed. définitive by William Jaffé, London and Homewood, Illinois, 1954. The following references are to the English translation.

[3] Alfred Marshall, *Principles of Economics*, ed. 1, London 1890; ed. 8, 1920. The following references are to ed. 8 of the *Principles*.

[4] A. Marshall, *op. cit.*, Appendix A, The Growth of Free Industry and Enterprise, pp. 723–753. *Cf.* Alfred Marshall, Social Possibilities of Economic Chivalry (1907), reprinted in A. C. Pigou, Ed., *Memorials of Alfred Marshall*, London 1925, pp. 327–346, where we read, 'I want to suggest that there is much latent chivalry in business life, and that there would be a great deal more of it if we sought it out and honoured it as men honoured the mediæval chivalry of war' (p. 330).

[5] A. Marshall, *Principles*, p. 88, *n*. 1.   [6] *Ibid.* p. 89, *n*. 1.

[7] L.S.E. Reprint No. 1, London 1930, p. 25, *n*. 1. In a letter to A. L. Bowley, dated February 27, 1906 Marshall wrote: '... I had a growing feeling in the later years of my work that a good mathematical theorem dealing with economic hypotheses was very

Walras in mind when he wrote that, for I know from the copy of the two-volume first edition of Walras's *Eléments* (1874–77) which I found in the Marshall Library in Cambridge, that his marginal annotations stop at p. 65 of vol. I, after which he appears to have given up in disgust. In fact, he declared in a letter to Walras dated September 19, 1889, 'I have not myself retired from the conclusion . . . that the right place for mathematics in a treatise on economics is the background.'[8]

I suspect that ever since Marshall's father, the author of a tract entitled *Man's Rights and Woman's Duties,* compelled little Alfred, when he was a boy, to suppress his passion for chess because life must be taken seriously, Alfred Marshall was tormented by a guilty conscience whenever he yielded to his penchant for pure theory, because it was too much like play and too remote from the serious goal of creating a humane Science of Social Perfectability. 'We are not at liberty', wrote Alfred Marshall, 'to play chess games, or exercise ourselves upon subtleties that lead nowhere.'[9] He was determined that his own lapses into the subtleties of pure theory should lead somewhere; and so he wrote on the 24th of March 1908 to John Bates Clark, 'My whole life has been and will be given to presenting in realistic form as much as I can of my Note XXI.'[10] It turns out that this Note XXI in the Mathematical Appendix, along with the preceding Notes starting with Note XIV, was a sketch of a general equilibrium model, working out the inter-relationship of markets in multi-equational form, and ending oddly enough with a Walrasian-like false statement, 'Thus, however complex the problem may become, we can see that it is theoretically determinate, because the number of unknowns is always exactly equal to the number of the equations which we obtain.'[11]

Alfred Marshall's attitude toward Léon Walras reminds me of John Stuart Mill's characterization of Saint-Simon. Mill wrote in a letter dated the 11th of April 1833, 'Saint Simon really for a Frenchman was a great man.'[12] So I think Marshall felt about Léon Walras: for a Frenchman he was a great economist; but, of course, being a Frenchman, he

unlikely to be good economics; and I went more and more on the rules — (1) Use mathematics as a shorthand language, rather than as an engine of inquiry. (2) Keep to them until you have done. (3) Translate into English. (4) Then illustrate by examples that are important in real life. (5) Burn the mathematics. (6) If you can't suceed in 4, burn 3. This last I did often' (Pigou, *Memorials,* p. 427).

[8] William Jaffé, Ed., *Correspondence of Léon Walras and Related Papers,* (henceforward referred to as *Correspondence*), 3 vols., Amsterdam 1965, vol. II, p. 355, Letter 922.

[9] J. M. Keynes, Alfred Marshall, 1842–1924, in Pigou, *Memorials,* p. 2.

[10] Pigou, *op. cit.,* p. 417.

[11] A. Marshall, *Principles,* p. 856. The note dates from ed. 1.

[12] Letter to Thomas Carlyle, April 11–12, 1833, published in Hugh S. R. Eliott, Ed., *The Letters of John Stuart Mill,* London 1910, vol. I, p. 44.

was frivolous and revealed his frivolity in an over-indulgence in mathematics.

Walras, on his side, was contemptuous of Marshall whom he denounced to Vilfredo Pareto on March 12th, 1892, as 'that great white elephant of political economy' *('ce grand éléphant blanc de l'économie politique').*[13]

Léon Walras's mentality was quite different from Marshall's—as different as the Caledonian mentality described by Charles Lamb was from the English mentality. As Lamb put it, 'The brain of a true Caledonian (if I am not mistaken) is constituted on quite a different plan. His Minerva is born in panoply. . . . He never hints or suggests anything, but unlades his stock of ideas in perfect order and completeness. He brings his total wealth into company and unlocks it. . . . Surmises, guesses, misgivings, half-intuitions, semi-consciousness, partial illuminations, dim instincts, embryo-conceptions, have no place in his brain or vocabulary. . . . Between the affirmative and the negative there is no borderland with him. You cannot hover with him upon the confines of truth, or wander in a maze of probable argument. You cannot make excursions with him—for he sets you right. . . . He cannot compromise, or understand middle actions. There can be but a right and a wrong.'[14]

What Lamb here says of the Caledonian can be said almost exactly of Léon Walras. Marshall was altogether different. As Enrico Barone so well brought out, Marshall contented himself with approximations and deliberately neglected subsidiary effects of the second order of smalls.[15] Both Walras and Pareto regarded this as seriously objectionable in general theoretical models. Like Lamb's Caledonians, they would not tolerate any departures from absolute rigor.[16]

Léon Walras did not suffer from any of Marshall's inhibitions. A glance at his *Eléments* reveals a brazen display of mathematical formulae

---

[13] *Correspondence,* vol. II, p. 486, Letter 1051. Writing earlier, on June 12, 1887, to an American correspondent, J. Laurence Laughlin, on whom he thought he could count to share his anglophobia, he gave full vent to his fury with Marshall for trying to steal his thunder. (W. Jaffé, Ed., *Correspondence,* vol. II, p. 210–211, Letter 799). Marshall, Walras alleged, had the impudence to claim that the object of *The Economics of Industry* (London 1879), which he had written in collaboration with his wife, Mary Paley Marshall, was to show, better than it had been done elsewhere, 'that there is a unity underlying all the different parts of the theory of prices, wages and profits.' As if Léon Walras had not done precisely that in 1874–77! On August 16th of that same year, Walras wrote to Charles Henri Vergé: 'M. Alfred Marshall . . . essaye en ce moment de s'approprier en Angleterre et en Amérique cette théorie que j'ai exposé complètement de 1874 à 1877 dans mes *Eléments d'économie politique pure'* (*Correspondence,* vol. II, p. 220, Letter 808).

[14] Charles Lamb's essay, "Imperfect Sympathies.'

[15] Enrico Barone, 'Sulla 'Consumers' Rent,' *Giornale degli economisti,* September 1894, pp. 211–224.

[16] *Cf. Correspondence,* vol. II, pp. 628–629, Letter 1200, Enclosure, Part I, where Walras contrasts his theory with that of Marshall. *Cf.* Gabriele de Rosa, Ed., *Vilfredo Pareto, Lettere a Maffeo Pantaleoni 1890–1923* (3 vols., Rome 1962), vol. II, pp. 60–63, Letter 561, where Pareto contrasts his work with that of Marshall.

on page after page of the text. The very title of his major treatise, *Eléments d'Economie Politique Pure,* announces unmistakably a study in the pure theory of economics, actually inspired by the pure theory of mechanics. Léon Walras did not address his work, as Alfred Marshall had done, to intelligent businessmen and literary scholars like Benjamin Jowett, as well as professional peers.[17] Walras addressed his *Eléments* to professional peers only—not only that, but quite consciously and deliberately to professional peers a generation or two after his time,[18] since his own contemporaries were, for the most part, too incompetent to appreciate his work. That is why he sank three quarters of his modest private patrimony in his publications and their free distribution, there being no profitable commercial outlet for such esoteric writings.[19]

Why all this zeal for pure theory and austere mathematical formulations which were far from fashionable in Walras's day? He was interested no less than Marshall in the amelioration of society.[20] Both his father, Auguste Walras, and he were initially impelled toward economics under the influence of the Saint-Simonists. Auguste and Léon Walras felt, however, that the Saint-Simonist approach to the problem of the regeneration of society was "unscientific,"[21] and in the manner of the 'doctrinaire' philosophers and politicians of the French Restoration—deriving their inspiration from Victor Cousin—they were addicted to abstract formulae on the ground that reason was an indispensable prerequisite for programs of viable political and economic reform. Throughout his life, Léon Walras declared himself a 'scientific socialist,' but, of course, a scientific socialist not of the Marxian variety, but of the petit-bourgeois stamp,[22] in favor only of limited state intervention where the conditions of pure atomistic competition were not fulfilled.

Petits bourgeois the Walrases certainly were, descended on the paternal side from tailors, small shop-keepers, and humble clerical employees in the city government. In fact, Léon Walras's paternal great-grandfather, who founded the Walras family in Montpellier around the middle of the 18th century, was an immigrant journeyman tailor from the village of Arcen in what is now the country of Limburg in the Netherlands. The name Walras was a French corruption of the Dutch

[17] Pigou, *Memorials,* pp. 17–18, 292–294.
[18] *Correspondence,* vol. I, p. 12, end of Walras's 'Notice autobiographique.'
[19] *Ibid,* vol. III, pp. 180–182, Letter 1508.
[20] Léon Walras, 'Recherche de l'idéal social,' 1868; reprinted in Léon Walras, *Etudes d'économie sociale,* Lausanne and Paris 1896; ed. définitive, 1936, pp. 1–202.
[21] Léon Walras, 'Ruchonnet et le socialisme scientifique,' *Revue socialiste,* July 1909, pp. 577–589; Auguste Walras, 'Lettres inédites de et à Léon Walras,' *Révolution de 1848, Bulletin de la Société de la Révolution de 1848,* November-December 1912, p. 377; and Léon Walras, *Etudes d'économie politique appliquée,* Lausanne and Paris 1892, ed. 2, Lausanne and Paris 1936, pp. 466–469.
[22] *Correspondence,* vol. I. p. 524, Letter 369; vol. II, pp. 696–697, Letter 1262; and p. 654, *n.* 3 to Letter 1322.

name Walravens. On Léon Walras's mother's side, the family was one of Norman solicitors, higher up in the bourgeois social hierarchy than the Walrases and though of noble descent—the name was *de* Saint Beuve—had long been read out of *noblesse* because of their ink-horn profession.

Auguste Walras was the first of the Walrases to rise out of virtual illiteracy and become an academic figure. He was a teacher of rhetoric and philosophy and a writer of books on economics as well as on literary subjects. Both father and son were *parvenus* in their station in life; and in an ancient country like France they felt and were made to feel their upstart position. Especially since they were engaged in a new-fangled science, political economy, which was viewed with great suspicion in France of their day, they had to be cautious, ever so cautious indeed, to survive at all. Theirs were days of strict censorship. First under the Restoration, then under Louis Philippe and Louis Napoleon, the public prosecutor pursued authors and publishers of books offensive to the government with ferocious assiduity. That is why Auguste Walras warned his son to be circumspect when he was writing his first book in economics, *L'économie politique et la justice; examen critique et réfutation des doctrines économiques de M.P.J. Proudhon* (1860)—a book, by the way, which contained nothing but ideas transmitted to him by his father.[23] Such were, in fact the influences which metamorphosed Léon Walras into a pure theorist.

At the start of his career, no one would have thought he had it in him to earn Schumpeter's encomium that 'so far as pure theory is concerned,' he was 'the greatest of all economists.'[24] All through his twenties in Paris Léon Walras appeared as a handsome, long-haired, bearded young man, looking for all the world like the hero in Puccini's *La Bohème*. In keeping with this role, he published a romantic novel[25] and a novelette[26] and lived for some ten years in secret quasi-conjugal bliss with a midinette whom he did not marry until the mantle of bourgeois-academic success in the form of a professorship at the Académie de Lausanne was finally about to descend upon him.

During the 1860s, he was a committed firebrand of sorts, engaged in mild, ever so mild, radical activities, such as the management of a bank for cooperatives and the advocacy of his father's pet scheme for regenerating society through the nationalization of land. This was enough, however, to cause the staid Swiss to hesitate to appoint him to the newly founded chair in political economy at Lausanne. Some actually regarded him as a *'communiste.'*[27] It was a narrow squeak, but he did get through

[23] A. Walras, 'Lettres inédites...,' *loc. cit.,* September-October, 1912, pp. 299–300.
[24] Joseph A. Schumpeter, *History of Economic Analysis,* New York 1954, p. 827.
[25] Léon Walras, *Francis Sauveur,* Paris 1585.
[26] Léon Walras, 'La lettre,' *Revue française,* 1859, pp. 193–206 and 275–285.
[27] *Correspondence,* vol. I, pp. 234–239, n. 2 to Letter 159.

and turned his initial provisional appointment into a tenure appointment by putting aside his earlier enthusiasms for social reform and taking safe refuge in the development of pure theory.

As it happened, the more he devoted himself to pure theory, the more he became enamored of it. Already in the 1860s, he had fiddled with it, as some surviving manuscripts reveal, but, for want of technical guidance and proficiency, he laboriously worked himself into a hopeless blind alley while trying to refute Cournot on value.[28] At Lausanne, however, he could, and did, buttonhole his mathematical colleagues, particularly Paul Piccard and Hermann Amstein. This was his take-off point; and then he soared to heights of pure theory hitherto unknown.

Léon Walras knew vaguely before he came to Lausanne that economics was essentially a mathematical science. His father had proclaimed it so in 1831, in his maiden treatise, *De la nature de la richesse et de l'origine de la valeur.*[29] Nevertheless, Auguste Walras did absolutely nothing himself to mathematize economics. Probably the first book in mathematical economics Léon Walras ever saw was Cournot's *Recherches sur les principles mathématiques de la théorie des richesses* (1838),[30] which, having been written by Auguste Walras's schoolmate, was known to the Walrases when practically no one among their contemporaries even noticed its existence. More important still was the fact that Léon, at the age of 19, was fired by the example of Louis Poinsot's *Eléments de statique,*[31] a text-book in pure mechanics, including celestial mechanics, which was presented in the form of simultaneous equation systems. It was Poinsot's model that Léon later imitated and adapted to his portrayal of general economic equilibrium. These were indeed the sources of Léon Walras's enthusiasm for mathematical economics.

Since he had little formal training in mathematics, his class-room studies having stopped short of the calculus, and since he had no formal training at all in economics apart from what he learned at his father's knee, it is not surprising that the working out of his general equilibrium model to the point where it embraced capital formation and money as well as exchange and production was long drawn out, beginning in the 1870s and not really completed until 1902.[32] When it was done, for all its faults, it was a beautiful thing to behold; and I fell in love with it at once.

[28]   *Ibid.* vol. I, pp. 216–221, *n.* 33 to Letter 148.
[29]   Auguste Walras, *De la nature de la richesse et de l'origine de la valeur,* Paris 1831; new ed., Gaston Leduc, Ed., Paris 1938, Chapter XVIII, of which the chapter heading reads, in part, 'L'économie politique est une science mathématique.'
[30]   Antoine-Augustin Cournot, *Recherches sur les principes de la théorie des richesses,* Paris 1838; new ed., Georges Lutfalla, Ed., Paris 1938; English translation: *Researches into Mathematical Principles of the Theory of Wealth,* trans. by Nathaniel Bacon, New York 1927.
[31]   Louis Poinsot, *Eléments de statique,* ed. 8, Paris 1842, *Cf. Correspondence,* vol. 3, pp. 148–150, Letter 1483 and *n.* 7 to that Letter.
[32]   Date of final manuscript revision of the *Eléments.*

As everyone knows, love at first sight does not always lead to a lasting alliance, but it did so in my case, for the charm of the Walrasian model improved upon further acquaintance and revealed itself to be more than skin deep. Moreover, the model had something intriguingly mysterious about it, which represented a challenge. Underneath the surface there lay many an enigma to which I was determined to find an answer. And then as time wore on and the blindness of infatuation wore off, I perceived that the model had blemishes, which only goes to show that it was born of man, or, in the words of Bernard Mandeville, that

> . . . *perfection here below*
> *Is more than gods can well bestow.*

Let there be no mistake: my devotion has been to the study of Walras and his works, not to the adulation of Walras or the glorification of his writings. Walras I simply find interesting as a human and social phenomenon, but not very attractive as a person. His character is best described in the words he wrote on the proof of a photograph of himself, 'un peu noir et de travers' ('a little askew and on the dark side'), for Léon Walras was pompous, pedantic, cantankerous, quarrelsome, megalomaniacal and hypochondriacal. His writings I find interesting and absorbing as an episode in intellectual history, by no means wholly satisfying, not merely because of certain defects in detail, but because their whole conception is so limited.

At the same time, my long familiarity with Walras's writings, both published and unpublished, has prompted me to leap to their defense against patent misunderstandings, denigrations or exaggerations. For example, when Patinkin, in one of his early articles,[33] overlooked the fact that Walras incorporated money, or rather the holding of money, into his utility functions, I called his attention to this oversight in the summary of a paper of mine, 'Walrasiana: The Eléments and its Critics,' which appeared in *Econometrica* in July, 1951.

Again in my Translator's Note 5 to Lesson 7 of the *Elements of Pure Economics,* I ventured to call attention to an historical-analytical error committed by Paul Samuelson, who, in an article published in *Econometrica* in 1941 and also in his *Foundations,*[34] credited Alfred Marshall with priority in establishing the Walrasian stability conditions. I pointed out that Marshall was indeed the first to lay down the stability condition of zero excess profits in the theory of production; but it was Walras who first discovered the stability condition of zero excess demand in the

---

[33] Don Patinkin, 'Relative Prices, Say's Law and the Demand for Money,' *Econometrica,* April 1948, pp. 135–154.

[34] Paul Samuelson, 'The Stability of Equilibrium: Comparative Statics and Dynamics,' *Econometrica,* April 1941, p. 103, *n.* 9; and *Foundations of Economic Analysis,* Cambridge 1947, p. 264, *n.* 9.

theory of pure exchange. In his review of the translation of the *Eléments,* Robert Solow made a special point of this note of mine and called it 'extraordinarily valuable.'[35]

On the other hand, in my article, 'New Light on an Old Quarrel,' published in the *Cahiers Vilfredo Pareto* in 1964,[36] my object was to show that it was incorrect to credit Walras with any rights to priority in the mathematical formulation of the marginal productivity theory. Invoking documentary evidence, I pointed out that the passages on marginal productivity which appeared in the later editions of the *Eléments* were really taken over from Enrico Barone. Walras had, indeed, for many years been in search of an analytical device which would permit him to introduce variable coefficients of production into his system. As far back as 1877, he had asked his mathematical colleague at Lausanne, Hermann Amstein, how this could be done; and Amstein actually showed him how in a very elegant way; but poor Walras, with his scanty mathematical equipment, could make neither head nor tail of the Lagrangean multiplier method Amstein employed.[37] Then in 1895, nearly 20 years later, an unpublished article of Enrico Barone, 'Sopra un recente libro del Wicksteed,'[38] came to Walras's attention; and there Barone formulated the marginal productivity theory in simpler mathematics. This Walras understood and immediately incorporated into the 3rd edition of the *Eléments* (1896). If the appropriate attribution to Barone was not made in the definitive edition (posthumously published in 1926), it was only because Barone would not answer Walras's repeated request for permission to name Barone in connection with his restatement of the theory. This may have been due, in part, to Barone's change of heart in 1901 about the theory, but I think it was mainly due to the fact that Barone did not want to have any part in Walras's ugly quarrel with Wicksteed over the question of priority in the mathematical formulation of marginal productivity.

Also, in order to rectify what I consider an overstatement of Walras's highly touted theory of *tâtonnement* , I argued in my 1967 article in the *Journal of Political Economy*[39] that the theory amounted, in final analysis, to

---

[35] *Econometrica,* January 1956, p. 87.

[36] William Jaffé, 'New Light on an Old Quarrel: Barone's Unpublished Review of Wicksteed's *Essay on the Coordination of the Laws of Distribution* and Related Documents,' *Cahiers Vilfredo Pareto,* 1964, No. 3, pp. 61–102.

[37] *Correspondence,* vol. II, pp. 516–520, Letter 364. For an English version of Amstein's letter of January 6, 1877, see William J. Baumol and Stephen M. Goldfeld, Eds., *Precursors in Mathematical Economics: an Anthology,* (L.S.E. Reprint No. 19), London 1968, pp. 309–312.

[38] The recent book was Philip Wicksteed's *Coordination of the Laws of Distribution,* London 1894 (L.S.E. Reprint No. 12, London 1932).

[39] William Jaffé, 'Walras' Theory of *Tâtonnement:* a Critique of Recent Interpretations,' *Journal of Political Economy,* February 1967, pp. 1–19.

an evasion of the problem of real adjustments of markets toward equilibrium. Latter-day commentators on the theory have been so intrigued by its mathematical implications as to forget that it was originally intended by Walras to clothe his model of general equilibrium with empirical relevance. Walras's invention of a process of recontracting by means of fictive tickets (provisional contracts) was little more than a clever artifice for circumventing the endowment effects of effective trading at 'false,' i.e. disequilibrium, prices in the course of the actual trial and error adjustments of the market. As a proof that real markets gravitate toward the self-same equilibrium which he defined in his multi-equational system, Walras's theory of *tâtonnement* turns out, therefore, to be a failure.

In the latest of my attempts[40] to arrive at just appreciation of Léon Walras, without overestimation as without underestimation, I tried to establish the limits of Walras's originality by adducing evidence of his unacknowledged indebtedness to an 18th Century French engineer, Achille-Nicolas Isnard, whose *Traité des richesses* (1781)[41] with which Walras was familiar, anticipated many of the structural features of the Walras model. This is a reflection not on the originality of Walras's work, but on the nature in general of the originality of any scientific contribution.

I said I do not find Léon Walras's writings wholly satisfactory, because, as I see it, their total import is too circumscribed. I think I can best convey what I mean by this in a comparison I should like to make between Léon Walras and Claude Henri de Rouvroy, Comte de Saint Simon, in short Saint Simon, whose ideas, I confess, fascinate me in some ways even more than those of Walras. This may sound strange, coming as it does from one notoriously preoccupied for years with an economist like Léon Walras.

The contrast between the two is striking. They stand at opposite poles.

Walras, who started life as a Bohemian turned into a stuffy, ambitious petit-bourgeois academic, a perfect 'square' in modern parlance; while Saint Simon, who started life as an authentic aristocrat of ancient lineage, became a 'hippy.' Léon Walras was a methodical and rigorous economic-analyst. Saint Simon was not an economic analyst at all and was certainly never methodical or rigorous. Léon Walras who liked to call himself a 'Socialist,' laid the foundations for the modern theory of

[40] William Jaffé, 'A.N. Isnard, Progenitor of the Walrasian General Equilibrium Model,' *History of Political Economy*, Spring 1969, pp. 19–43.

[41] Anon. [Achylle-Nicholas Isnard], *Traité des richesses*, 2 vols., London and Lausanne 1781.

free enterprise Saint Simon, who never called himself a Socialist, laid the foundations for some essential features of Karl Marx's doctrinal edifice. Léon Walras sought to systematize the economic forces that he regarded in *specie aeternitatis,* i.e. economic forces which he thought were independent of institutional constraints; and he thus developed a pure theory of the day-to-day operations of these forces. Saint Simon was concerned exclusively with the process of revolutionary change and with the effects of institutional upheavals on the economic structure of the modern era. Léon Walras, though he was born in 1843 and died in 1910, really envisaged the economic organization of society within a static framework; while Saint Simon, though born in 1760, nearly three quarters of a century earlier than Walras, and though he died in 1825, nine years before Walras was born, was struck quite early in life with the significance of the impending industrial transformations, and he bent all his thoughts in that direction. Léon Walras, of petit bourgeois origin, detested change and froze within his general equilibrium theory an idealized conception of the economic organization of society with which he had been familiar in his childhood in the 1830s and 40s in the sleepy town of Evreux in Normandy where he was born. This was an organization more characteristic of the artisan stage of production than of modern large scale factory production. Saint-Simon, on the other hand, a scion of ancient feudal aristocracy and a man of the world, welcomed change with a magnanimous indifference to its effects on his own personal fortunes, and he saw in the convulsions of his time the promise of a regeneration of humanity. To borrow a felicitous term from Professor Baumol, I should say that Walras's general equilibrium theory is a great pioneer work in magnificent statics, whereas Saint-Simon's grandiloquent lucubrations were the very essence of magnificent dynamics.

The shortcomings of the Walrasian general equilibrium model to which I allude were, so far as I know, first discussed nearly forty years ago in a little noticed article, entitled 'Marx's Analysis of Capitalism and the General Equilibrium Theory of the Lausanne School,' which appeared in the *Kyoto University Economic Review* of July, 1933.[42] The author, Professor K. Shibata, argued that the Walras-Pareto general equilibrium theory, for all its marvellous comprehensiveness, which Shibata evidently understood very well, is nevertheless "ineffectual in making clear systematically either the organization of present-day capitalistic society or the laws of its development.' In this article Shibata tried his hand at a heroic reconstruction of the Walrasian model in order

[42] K. Shibata, *op. cit.,* pp. 107–136.

to bring it explicitly into conformity with 'the organization of present-day capitalistic society,' but his reconstructed model failed to reveal any 'laws of development' and remained static.

Oscar Lange took his cue from Shibata when he wrote his article, 'Marxian Economics and Modern Economic Theory,' which appeared in the *Review of Economic Studies* in June 1935.[43] There Lange, while expressing agreement with Shibata on the gross inadequacies of the Lausanne model, nevertheless cautioned Marxists against turning their backs on it.

On the negative side, Lange criticized the Lausanne model for not giving the slightest hint of the steady increase in the scale of operation of capitalistic firms which has led to the transition from the competitive capitalism of the 19th century to present-day oligopolistic capitalism. This, it turns out, was no oversight on the part of Walras, who deliberately restricted the design of his model to a portrayal of the logical properties of pure atomistic competition operating within a perfect, self-adjusting system of interconnected markets. His purpose, as I have already indicated, was not that of a doctrinaire liberal who would exclude the state unconditionally from any active role in the economy, but rather to define as rigorously as possible the specific conditions and limits within which a market economy could work in the interests of constrained maximum welfare without the intervention of the state.[44] Thus we find in one of his rare allusions to the structure of the individual firm that in order to keep the dimension of such firms in strict conformity with the hypothesis of pure competition, he explicitly assumed away fixed plant and placed all fixed costs on the same footing as variable costs.[45] Dimly perceiving the consequent indeterminacy in the size of individual firms, Walras arbitrarily assumed, for simplicity, that they would be all equal in size. He went so far as to explain why the retention of fixed costs in his model would be inconsistent with the maintenance of perfect competition. He realized, as he said himself, that the elimination of fixed costs from his model coupled with the assumption that all firms are of equal size 'has no more objective reality than the assumption that profits and losses are zero, but,' he added, 'it is just as rational.' Then, to show what the retention of fixed costs might have led to, he wrote that 'if at a given moment . . . [we assume that fixed costs are present and that] a certain output corresponds to the absence of profit or loss, [then] those entrepreneurs who manufacture less than this

[43] Oscar Lange, *loc. cit.*, pp. 189–201.

[44] L. Walras, 'L'etat et les chemins de fer,' *Revue du droit public et de la science politique,* May-June 1897, pp. 417–436, and July-August 1897, pp. 42–54; reprinted in L. Walras, *Etudes d'économie politique appliquée,* pp. 193–232.

[45] L. Walras, *Elements of Pure Economics,* p. 474, *n.* 1 (Part II of Appendix I).

output will incur losses, cut down their production and finish by liquidating while those who manufacture more will make profits, expand output and draw to themselves the business of the unsuccessful entrepreneurs. Thus, in consequence of certain characteristic properties of fixed and variable costs, an industry which starts under free competition with a large number of small firms tends to be divided among a smaller number of firms of medium size, then among a still smaller number of large-scale firms, to end finally in a monopoly. . . .' Walras added significantly, 'This statement is confirmed by facts.' Thus Walras admitted in advance Shibata's and Lange's criticism that his model is 'ineffectual in making clear systematically. . . the laws of development' of the capitalist economy. I, for my part, think that the Walrasian general equilibrium theory is better suited to explain the operation of what Marx called a system 'einfache Warenproduktion' (i.e. a system of production by small, privately owned independent firms) than as an analytical tool for understanding the operation or development of the actual modern system of large-scale corporate enterprise.

Oscar Lange insisted, however, that precisely because the general equilibrium model of the Lausanne type is devoid of any specification of the institutional framework, precisely because it consists in nothing more than a pure theory of exchange, production and capital formation, positing only a freely competitive market of the atomistic variety, precisely because it is essentially non-historical, this sort of model provides a scientific base for understanding the day-to-day mechanics of any economy, be it a capitalist economy or a socialist economy, provided, of course, that in these economies freedom of choice in consumption and in occupation is preserved to any appreciable extent. Marxist though he was, Lange declared that 'there are some problems before which Marxian economics is quite powerless, while 'bourgeois' economics solves them easily.' 'What,' Lange asked, 'can Marxian economics say about monopoly prices? What has it to say on the fundamental problems of monetary and credit theory? . . . And (irony of fate) what can Marxian economics contribute to the problem of the optimum distribution of productive resources in a socialist economy?" Lange concluded, with the general equilibrium theory in mind, that ' . . . in providing a scientific basis for the current administration of the capitalist economy, 'bourgeois' economics had developed a theory of equilibrium which can also serve as a basis for the current administration of a socialist economy.'

This last point was by no means original with Lange. It had been made before by Vilfredo Pareto and Enrico Barone, neither of whom was by any stretch of the imagination a Marxist or a Socialist. As is well known, Barone, in his article, 'The Ministry of Production in a Collectivist State,' originally published in the *Giornale Degli Economisti* in September–October 1908 and first found in English in Hayek's *Collectivist Economic Planning* (1935),[46] actually constructed a mathematical model on the lines of the general equilibrium theory, to show how production and capital formation could work in a socialist economy. Barone's was a blueprint model designed to demonstrate that the problems of collectivist production can be pre-solved logically. We must bear in mind, however, that although that which reveals itself as faulty or impossible in a blueprint is bound to be faulty or impossible in practice, this is not the same thing as saying that everything which appears faultless or possible in a blueprint is *ipso facto* possible or desirable in practice.

Better still in support of Lange's thesis that general equilibrium economics has relevance for the economic administration of a socialist state is the present tendency in communist countries to assign increasing importance to input-output analysis, which is so useful a tool for economic planners whether on a national scale in collectivist economies or on a more restricted scale in mixed economies and in private enterprise. As Leontief never tires of pointing out, input-output analysis is an adaptation of the neoclassical theory of general equilibrium.[47]

There is another use for the general equilibrium theory, which I think has been insufficiently noticed. The Walrasian general-purpose model, when viewed in its entirety as an immense and highly complicated computer programmed simultaneously to allocate resources, to reward services and to distribute goods *via* a competitive price mechanism, is seen to contain a comprehensive inventory of rigorously coordinated relationships, all derived from the action of micro-economic forces. It is among these that the applied economist concerned with particular, limited problems of a practical nature, can pick and choose what parameters, variables and relations he needs for the construction of a suitable special-purpose model. If he formulates his *ad hoc* model with the general equilibrium theory in mind, he runs less risk of overlooking relations which may be far from negligible for his purpose, and since he is likely to deal in aggregates, he has a better chance of understanding what he is aggregating and of perceiving the difficulties which may be involved in the process of aggregation.

When Walras himself came to discuss particular aspects of the economic system, he recognized no less clearly than Alfred Marshall, that there is for each special problem a hierarchy of interrelationships

[46] F. A. von Hayek, *op. cit.,* pp. 245–290.
[47] *Cf.* Burgess Cameron, 'The Construction of the Leontief System,' *Review of Economic Studies,* 1951–1952, vol. 19, No. 48, pp. 19–27.

among economic variables, some sets being more closely interrelated than others in a given context. As he put it,

Theoretically all the unknowns of an economic problem depend on all the equations of economic equilibrium. Nevertheless, even from the viewpoint of static theory, it is permissible to consider some of these unknowns as especially dependent on those equations which were introduced into the system at the same time as the unknowns. It is all the more legitimate to do this when we pass from the static to the dynamic point of view, or, better still, when we pass from the realm of pure theory to that of applied theory or to actual practice, because the variations in the unknowns will be effects of either the first or second order, that is to say effects which need or need not be taken into consideration, according as they arise from variations in the special or the general data.[48]

It is, I should say, for want of attention to this passage that so much controversy has arisen over Walras's theory of money, which some (Patinkin among them) charge is vitiated by an invalid dichotomization between the real and monetary sectors, while others (Kuenne among these) steadfastly maintain that no such dichotomization is present in the Walrasian model.[49]

Walras exemplified the principle of concentration on selected, crucial variables, not only in his theory of money, but also in other studies in applied economics. In one of these studies, 'Economie appliquée et la défense des salaires,'[50] we find a maxim which I believe every economist ought to read, mark, learn and inwardly digest, or at least have framed over his desk: 'Mais l'économiste ne doit pas être la dupe de ses abstractions.'[51]

The most interesting of his applied studies is his 'Théorie mathématique du billet de banque' (1879).[52] This paper deserves especial attention for two reasons. First, with its emphasis on macro-economic relations, it helps dispel the impression that Léon Walras was nothing but a micro-economic analyst—an impression which is all the more unfounded because there is a substantial amount of macro-economics in the *Eléments d'économie politique pure*.[53] More important, however, is the opportunity which the 'Théorie mathématique du billet de banque'

---

[48] L. Walras, *Elements of Pure Economics,* pp. 307–308 (§266).

[49] Don Patinkin, *Money, Interest and Prices,* Evanston 1956, pp. 411–412 and *passim.*

[50] *Revue d'économie politique,* December 1897, pp. 108–1036; reprinted in L. Walras, *Etudes d'économie politique appliquée,* pp. 265–285.

[51] *Op. cit.,* p. 275.

[52] Paper read before the Société Vaudoise des Sciences Naturelles, November 19, 1897 and first published in the *Bulletin* of that society, May 1880, pp. 553–592; republished with revisions in L. Walras, *Etudes d'économie politique appliquée,* pp. 339–375.

[53] *E.g.* in Part V ('Theory of Capital Formation and Credit'), Part VI ('Theory of Circulation and Money') and especially in Lesson 35 ('The Continuous Market') of L. Walras, *Elements of Pure Economics.*

affords us to contrast Walras of the 19th Century with Keynes of the 20th. According to Keynes's analysis: given a liquidity preference schedule, any increase in the liquid assets in an economy makes people move along the liquidity preference schedule until they are willing to absorb the increased quantity of assets. This occurs at a lower rate of interest; and entrepreneurs then faced with a lower interest-rate increase their rate of investment.[54] According to Walras's analysis, on the other hand: when there is an increase in the amount of liquid assets, banks lend these additional assets to entrepreneurs, who are then in a position to increase their real capital. As real capital increases, the rate of net return on capital diminishes. Then the rate of interests adjusts itself to the rate of return on investments and remains lower. In Walras's view, bank note issues in particular, will have this effect, because they allow bankers to lend to entrepreneurs without borrowing from capitalist-savers. Walras, with an eye to his quantity theory of money, went to great pains to contrast the impact and long-run effects on prices of an increase in investment resulting from saving with the effects of an increase in investment resulting from the injection of new paper money, or for that matter, from the discovery of additional sources of metallic money.

I dare say that not all economists will grant that the Walrasian general equilibrium model lends itself fruitfully or with any discernable immediacy to applications. Milton Friedman, as he became increasingly aware of the trend among economists and econometricians to seek inspiration directly or indirectly from Walras, protested, 'We curtsy to Marshall, but we walk with Walras'[55] — obviously implying that it would have been better the other way round. Other economists (Boulding among them) looked upon the Walras-Pareto model as an over-elaborate statement of a platitude that everything depends on everything else, without noticing that really 'everything' is not included in the general model and that the model carefully defines the manner of the interdependencies included within it.

So little was known until recently of Léon Walras's contribution, that it was possible in 1929 for Othmar Spann to write a book entitled, *Die Haupttheorien der Volkswirtschaftslehre,* without once mentioning Walras's name. In several other histories of economic thought of the same vintage, in which Léon Walras's name did appear, it was only alluded to in passing or in a footnote with a condescending or denigratory remark

[54] John Maynard Keynes, *The General Theory of Employment, Interest and Money,* New York 1936.
[55] Milton Friedman, *Essays in Positive Economics,* Chicago 1953, p. 89.

that Walras was nothing more than a belated discoverer of the Austrian doctrine of value.

Had these text-book writers taken the trouble to read what one of the Austrians, Friedrich von Wieser, said of Walras's method, they might have discovered one of the profoundest appreciations of his theory. In von Wieser's words, 'It does not copy nature, but gives us a simplified representation of it, which is no misrepresentation, but such as to sharpen our vision in view of the complexities of reality—like the ideal picture which the geographer draws in his map, as a means, not to deception, but to more effective guidance, he meanwhile assuming that they who are to profit by the map will know how to read it, i.e. to interpret it in accordance with nature.[56]

In the light of these indubitable virtues of the Walrasian general equilibrium model, why, you may well ask, do I raise the question of Walras's importance? Certainly, as posed by the girl I interviewed in England, it was an incredibly silly question. Why should I take it seriously? In closing this paper, I should like to give two reasons why I do not dismiss the question out of hand.

In the first place, I feel about the question of the importance of Léon Walras as Henry Sidgwick did about the question of definitions of the cardinal terms used in economic theory. In his *Principles of Political Economy,* published in 1883, he said that economists 'underrate the importance of *seeking* for the best definition . . . and overrate the importance of *finding* it.' He pointed out that 'what we gain by discerning a definition is but slightly represented in the superior fitness of the formula we ultimately adopt'; what we really gain 'consists chiefly in the greater clearness and fulness in which the characteristics of the matter to which the formula refers have been brought before the mind in the process of seeking for it.[57] Likewise, it seems to me, that in taking seriously so childish and otiose a question as 'Is Walras important?,' it is not the answer that matters, but the search for an answer. In the course of speculating on the importance or unimportance of Léon Walras or any other figure in the history of economics, we are led to examine 'with greater clearness and fulness' the meaning and significance of that economist's contribution to our science.

When attempting to reevaluate Walras's contribution from a vantage point other than that prescribed by the 'general' equilibrium model, one is left with a feeling of uneasiness, not to say disappointment. The

[56] F. Wieser, 'The Austrian School and the Theory of Value,' *Economic Journal,* March 1891, pp. 108–121. Citation, p. 108.
[57] Henry Sidgwick, *The Principles of Political Economy,* London 1883, p. 52.

trouble lies not so much in the technical imperfections of the Walrasian analytical apparatus, which clever critics have, in time, shown themselves quite capable of overcoming,[58] as in the fundamental inadequacies of the whole conception, because of the narrowness of the range of problems the model was meant to elucidate. This was perhaps inevitable, since it was a static model, which by its nature excludes such differential or difference equations involving time as would generate an evolutionary transformation of the model itself. My view of the shortcomings of the grand design of Walras's theory of general equilibrium converges closely on that of Georgescu-Roegen in Part I of his *Analytical Economics*.[59]

Surely, the word importance, like the words value and relevance, can have only a relative meaning. Important for what? Value in relation to what? Relevant to what? Hence my original question, which I intend to be taken seriously, should be interpreted as meaning: Is Walras's contribution important as a help in clarifying the pressing economic problems which arise from the dominant economic and social trends of our time? I have already alluded to Oscar Lange's observation that the

[58] For example, it was Wilhem Lexis as far back as 1881 (and not Hans Neisser, H. von Stackelberg, and Frederick Zeuthen in 1932–1933, as we are repeatedly told, e.g. by Robert E. Kuenne, *The Theory of General Economic Equilibrium*, Princeton 1963, pp. 516–519), who first pointed out that the Walrasian system of production equations does not necessarily possess either real positive solutions or unique solutions. In Lexis's own words, '... aber hier könnte man einwenden, dass diese Gleichungen im allgemeinen nicht vom ersten Grade sein werden, dass wir überhaupt über ihre Natur nichts wissen, dass sie also möglicherweise gar keine reellen positiven Wurzeln, möglicherweise aber auch mehrere Systeme solcher Wurzeln haben können. Im ersteren Falle wären überhaupt keine Gleichgewichtspreise möglich, im letztern könnten mehrere Gleichgewichtszustände mit verschiedenen Preissystemen eintreten' (Lexis's comments, in the *Jahrbücher für Nationalökonomie und Statistik*, 1881, New Series, vol. 3, p. 431, on L. Walras's *Mathematische Theorie der Preisbestimmung*,, a German translation by Ludwig von Winterfeld). It remained for Zeuthen and Schlesinger to point the way out of this difficulty by substituting appropriate inequalities for Walras's (and Cassel's) equalities, thus placing necessary constraints on the system in order to render it solvable from the economic point of view (Frederick Zeuthen, 'Das Prinzip der Knappheit, Technische Kombination and ökonomische Qualität,' *Zeitschrift für Nationalökonomie*, 1932–1933, pp. 1–24; and Karl Schlesinger, 'Über die Produktionsgleichungen der ökonomischen Wertlehre,' *Ergebnisse eines mathematischen Kolloquiums*, Karl Menger, Ed., 1933–34, No. 6, Leipzig and Vienna 1935, pp. 10–11). *Cf*. Robert Dorfman, Paul A. Samuelson and Robert Solow, *Linear Programming and Economic Analysis*, New York 1958, pp. 360 ff..

[59] Nicholas Georgescu-Roegen, *Analytical Economics, Issues and Problems*, Cambridge 1966, pp. 104–107. *Cf*. R. E. Kuenne, *The Theory of General Economic Equilibrium*, pp. 34–37. At one point, where Georgescu-Roegen argues that ' ... in all societies the typical individual continually pursues ... an end ignored by the standard framework: the increase of what he can claim as his income according to his current position and distributive norms' (*op. cit.* p. 105), he appears to have forgotten that in at least one 'standard framework,' L. Walras's *Eléments*, the very book Georgescu-Roegen discusses in this context, the whole theory of capital formation rests precisely on the behavior of the typical individual in pursuit of an increase in income 'according to his current position.' Admittedly, Walras fell short of analyzing the macro-economic effects of such behavior on what Georgescu-Roegen calls 'the prevailing distributive relations' within the economy.

Walrasian model offers no clue to an understanding of the trend toward oligopolistic capitalism and its attendant problems. Nor, according to Lange, does it shed any light on the trend toward increasing state intervention in our private enterprise economy—a trend which, by the way, Walras alluded to in his *obiter dicta* and justified not so much on analytical, as on normative grounds.[60] Lange also taxed Walras with failure to make more than passing mention of the cyclical instabilities inherent in our system.[61] Moreover, Walras neglected the whole persistent problem of unemployment, as if unemployment were merely a cyclical aberration that would vanish under equilibrium conditions. The Walrasian model, formulated as it is in terms of equalities where inequalities alone would yield an admissible solution, conceals the possibility of a redundancy of labor services even when the system is in full equilibrium.[62] Walras himself was apparently unaware that this possibility was implicitly imbedded in his system and made no allusion to it; and Schumpeter supposed, mistakenly in my opinion, that Walras 'within his assumptions' and 'on so high a level of abstraction,' had furnished a proof that '*perfect* equilibrium in *perfect* competition would involve full employment.[63]

These are some of the characteristics of the Walrasian model, and there are others as well, which, I should say, quite legitimately elicit the question of the importance of Walras. I think I have said enough to show that I am far from denying or wishing to belittle what every economist knows to be Walras's contribution to the present day development of economic theory and econometrics. I ask, however, whether this is enough? Whether those economists, who look upon the question of Walras's importance as preposterous, have not yielded to the temptation of ranking economic problems in the order of the availability or ingenuity of techniques for solving them rather than in the order of their urgency in the 20th Century?

However far an inquiry of this kind is carried, it seems that, in the end, one is still left wondering, like the spectator at a Pirandello play, as to the significance of the principal protagonist—in our case, Walras.

[60] L. Walras, 'Esquisse d'une doctrine économique et sociale,' §V, *Etudes d'économie politique appliquée*, pp. 475–484.

[61] L. Walras, *Elements of Pure Economics*, pp. 380–381. (§322).

[62] Zeuthen's replacement of equalities by inequalities (see above, Note (58)), though intended as a correction of Cassel's rather than Walras's model, is equally pertinent to the latter. Walras's hypothesis that all productive services, including labor-services, can also be used for direct consumption only attenuates, but does not remove, the difficulty. There is nothing in the Walrasian model which precludes the possibility that the aggregate offer of labor services, even at a near-zero price (or wage), may exceed the combined aggregate demand for such services for consumption and production taken together, in which case labor-services must become a free good! Cf. R. E. Kuenne, *The Theory of General Economic Equilibrium*, p. 519.

[63] J. A. Schumpeter, *History of Economic Analysis*, p. 1026, n. 72.

16

LEON WALRAS'S ROLE IN THE "MARGINAL REVOLUTION" OF THE 1870s

I

On the occasion of a centenary, far from being a fault, it is particularly fitting to tell a twice-told tale . . . lest we forget, lest we forget. Although so much has already been written, and well written, by this time about the "marginal revolution"[1] that it is difficult to think of anything new to say, yet there is a danger that we may forget what transpired a hundred years ago in the history of economic theory, because that "revolution" has been so radically transformed and transmuted since its beginnings that all trace of its pristine character tends to fade away in our memories.

The successive and often contradictory reevaluations of the "marginal revolution" of the 1870s leave the historian of economics in the 1970s perplexed, wondering whether it is more appropriate dolefully to commemorate the "marginal revolution" as a disaster or joyfully to celebrate the event as heralding a great leap forward in the progress of economics. If the historian recalls his right role, however, he will do neither, but be guided in his judgment of a Jevons, a Menger, or a Walras by Shakespeare's sage comment, "So our virtues/Lie in the interpretation of the time" (*Coriolanus*, IV, vii).

The assessment of Léon Walras's "virtues" was, however, one thing at one time when the "marginal revolution" was simply interpreted as the overthrow of the labor or cost-of-production theory of value by the marginal utility theory; and it became quite another thing later on when the "marginal revolution" was interpreted as the commencement of model building on a grandiose scale, in which equilibrium is defined as a set of marginal equalities pervading the entire system of exhange,

[1] Perhaps better called "marginal revolt" or "marginal insurrection," since the "revolution" in standard economics was not an accomplished fact for several decades after the 1870s. Marginalism itself, considered as a mathematically expressed incremental concept, but applied to productivity rather than utility, had made its appearance earlier in von Thünen's *Isolierte Staat*, vol. 2 (1850); see Thünen (1930), pp. 584–87. I shall, nevertheless, continue using "marginal revolution" in this paper as a term consecrated by usage which is, after all, just as apposite as "Newtonian revolution" in the history of science. If I enclose the term in quotation marks, it is only to emphasize the obvious, that I am not responsible for the nomenclature.

production, capital formation, and money under ideal competitive conditions. The latter-day image being essentially mathematical, the revolution of the 1870s was viewed also as the turning point in the metamorphosis of economics from a branch of intuitively reasoned literary discourse into a rigorous mathematical discipline.

As there is no clear limit to the variety of interpretations that can be placed upon the "marginal revolution" after the event, let us turn to the event itself, viewed as a *marginal utility* innovation, and see how Léon Walras came to take part in it. Then, in the interpretation of *his* time, we may be better able to arrive at a reasonable appraisal of his "virtues."

II

Léon Walras first entered upon the scene as a revolutionary on August 16 and 23, 1873, when he read his paper, "Principe d'une théorie mathématique de l'échange,"[2] in Paris before the Académie des Sciences morales et politiques. It was from beginning to end a daring paper, a clarion call for a new approach to the theory of value and for the transformation of political economy into a mathematical science, issued, moreover, by a mere novice, an "outsider," making his debut as an economic theorist.[3] Loud and clear though the call was, it fell on hostile, uncomprehending ears. Walras left the meeting, enraged and defiant.

Little did he suspect at the time that he had fellow insurgents of the same ilk, who had, in fact, stolen a march upon him. When he learned shortly afterwards that he was not the very first to have issued a marginal utility manifesto, he was discountenanced; but he need not have been, for his "Principe d'une théorie mathématique de l'échange" possessed an extremely important feature, outlined in high relief, which had been barely hinted at in W. Stanley Jevons's *Theory of Political*

---

[2] Léon Walras [hereinafter referred to as L.W.] (1874a). In the republication of 1883, L.W.'s curves representing the marginal utility (i.e., *rareté*) functions were changed. They had originally been drawn as straight lines and appeared again as straight lines in the 1st ed. of the *Eléments* (Léon Walras, 1874b), but in the 1883 version and subsequent editions of the *Eléments*, they appear curvilinear in form. See Jaffé (1954), pp. 567–68, Collation Note [b] to Lesson 8; and Jaffé (1965a), 2:574, Letter 412, in which the change was announced.

[3] In the *Séances et travaux de l'Académie des Sciences morales et politiques* (L.W., 1874a), the paper was listed among the "Communications des savants étrangers," a bitter pill for L.W., who was as much a Frenchman as the academicians, though he did come from a foreign professorial post in Lausanne to deliver his paper. For an account of the reception of the paper by his audience, see Jaffé (1965a), 1:334–36, n. (7) to Letter 232, and for L.W.'s reactions, see ibid., pp. 332–34, Letter 232, and pp. 370–74, Letter 256. Cf. Jaffé (1954), p. 44.

Economy or in Carl Menger's *Grundsätze der Volkswirtschaftslehre,* both of 1871. It was this distinguishing feature which placed Léon Walras rather than Jevons or Menger in direct line of filiation with the modern development of economic analysis since the 1930s. What this feature was will appear in the course of the following sketch of Léon Walras's maiden analytical paper of 1873.

The paper opened with a statement of the relation of pure economics to applied economics, pointing out that before we can weigh the relative merits of *laisser-faire, laisser-passer* on grounds of efficiency or justice, we must first investigate "the natural and necessary" consequences of free competition in exchange and production. Given, to start with, certain predetermined quantities of productive services, it will inevitably follow from the free play of competition that, after a while, (i) certain definite quantities of various products will be turned out; (ii) each of the products will have a definite price at each instant of time; and (iii) each of the productive services will also have a definite price at each instant of time. The object of pure theory is then to inquire how these three natural effects of "free competition," i.e., the quantities of products, their prices, and the prices of the productive services, are determined. The answer to this inquiry is found by solving a system of equations in which the three effects of "free competition" appear as unknowns.

The problem seen in this way is, as Walras observed, "extremely vast and complicated," but it can be simplified by considering it in two stages. In the first stage, production is assumed away, so that the problem is reduced to one which Walras enunciated as follows: "Given certain quantities of commodities, to formulate a system of equations of which the prices of the commodities are the roots." This is what the mathematical theory of exchange is all about. Once the first stage has been completed, the way is open to the second stage. Now production is taken into account and the commodities whose quantities were given in advance in the theory of exchange are replaced by products resulting from purchases of productive services in suitable combinations. In the second stage, therefore, the problem becomes, in Walras's words: "Given certain quantities of productive services, to formulate a system of equations which has for its roots: (1) the quantities produced of the products; (2) the prices of these products; and (3) the prices of the productive services."

Thus, in Walras's hands, pure economics assumed the form of what he called a "physico-mathematical" science. He made no claim that this was anything really new. It had long been that sort of a science, as is seen in the writings of the Physiocrats and in the treatises of the English economists from Ricardo to John Stuart Mill. The trouble was that these economists did their mathematical thinking in everyday language, and hence cumbersomely and ineptly. Cournot, according to Walras, was the first to have undertaken to apply mathematics to economics explicitly and competently; and for having shown him the way, Walras expressed his profound gratitude to Cournot. At the same time Walras insisted that in his own work he had followed a line of his own, quite different from that of Cournot. His economics was different in that he took "free competition," which he considered the general case, as his starting point and studied monopoly only as a special case, whereas Cournot had taken monopoly as his starting point and proceeded from there by steps to an analysis of unlimited competition. Walras pointed out also that his mathematics was different in that he relied for his formal demonstrations mainly upon the elementary principles of analytical geometry, whereas Cournot had recourse exclusively to the infinitesimal calculus.

At this point Walras announced that in the remainder of his paper he would confine his attention to the theory of exchange in its simplest conceivable form, where only two commodities are traded for each other. Sections II to IV of the paper read before the Academy were little more than a crisp and crystal clear résumé of Lessons 9 to 13 inclusive of the first edition of the *Eléments*,[4] in which Walras dealt in analytical detail with the problem of price determination in a perfectly competitive market where only two commodities are traded. Though the first instalment of the first edition of the *Eléments* had not yet been published (it did not make its appearance until July 1874),[5] by June 1873 Walras already had in hand the proofs of sixty pages embodying his mathematical theory of exchange.[6] In at least one respect the résumé was superior to the *Eléments*: only in his 1873 paper did he explicitly undertake "to define with precision the mechanism of free competition by which we suppose our market to be regulated." It comes out more clearly in the résumé than in the *Eléments* that Walras meant by an ideally perfect competitive market one in which there is no friction or viscosity in the flow of bids and offers to a central point where positive or negative excess demand is eliminated prior to the closing of any contracts. Contracts are then executed at a unique current equilibrium price. The process of elimination of excess demand is normally entrusted in the best-organized markets to brokers, whose procedures are so mechanical

---

[4] Corresponding to Lessons 5, 6, and 7 of the definitive edition, L.W. (1874b).
[5] Jaffé (1965a), 1:410–11, Letter 284.
[6] Ibid., 1:319, n. (3) to Letter 218.

that a "calculateur" (a computer!) might have done just as well, though—Walras surmised in 1873—not as quickly.[7]

If that were all Léon Walras had to say in his first analytical paper, it might well have earned for him our praise for having perceived in Cournot's demand function the basis of an elegant reformulation of the old familiar theory of supply and demand, but it would hardly have earned for him a place among the initiators of the "marginal revolution" in our histories of economics. Fortunately, the paper did not end with a bare theory of the competitive market mechanism. It went on to two more sections in which Léon Walras expounded his theory of *rareté*, or, as we should call it, his theory of marginal utility. Section V was headed "How demand curves result from utility and the quantity possessed," and Section VI, "Analytical definition of the exchange of two commodities for each other. *Rareté*: the cause of value in exchange." *Rareté*, for Walras, constitutes the underlying motive force which furnishes the power to run the competitive market mechanism. As Sections V and VI of the paper simply resume Lessons 14 to 18 of the first edition of the *Eléments*,[8] there is no need to repeat the argument here.

There is need, however, to call attention both to the manner in which Léon Walras introduced his marginal utility principles and to the role he assigned to it in his "Principe d'une théorie mathématique de l'échange" and his *Eléments*. It is this, more than anything else, which distinguishes Léon Walras from his corevolutionaries and which made him, rather than Jevons or Menger, the favorite ancestor most frequently honored in the latest developments of economic theory since the 1930s. R. G. D. Allen wrote in 1956, "The analysis of equilibrium of exchange was left by Walras in a form to which only minor glosses need be added."[9]

[7] L.W.'s operational definition of the competitive market was further elucidated in a subsequent article, "La bourse, la spéculation et l'agiotage" (1880), and was slightly elaborated upon in an undated manuscript which came to light in 1966 when it was discovered in a forgotten cupboard of the Bibliothèque Cantonale et Universitaire de Lausanne, inside a folder containing L.W.'s long-lost translation of W. S. Jevons's *Theory of Political Economy* (see Jaffé, 1965a, 1:570–72, Letter 410; and pp. 644–48, Letter 465). The published article describes the operations of the Paris stock exchange as precluding not only nonuniformity of price but also any trading at "false prices." "Si la quantité demandée et la quantité offerte sont égales, il y a *prix courant* et l'échange a lieu à ce prix; les titres passent des mains des agents vendeurs à celles des agents acheteurs, ou du moins l'affaire est conclue, sinon réglée. Autrement, l'échange n'a pas lieu." It was because of this characteristic of the *modus operandi* of a well-organized market that L.W. saw no reason to introduce the use of "tickets" (provisional contracts) in his theory of pure exchange, and not because he overlooked trading at "false prices" in this theoretical analysis as I previously suggested (Jaffé, 1967). In the Walrasian perfect market, there is no such phenomenon to take into account. See L.W. (1898), pp. 407–9.
[8] Corresponding to Lessons 8, 9, and 10 of the definitive edition, L.W. (1874b).
[9] Allen (1956), p. 314.

From the very start, Léon Walras introduced his marginal utility theory immediately into his analysis of market price determination without considering it in any other context. His whole attention was focused on market phenomena and not on consumption. This is evident from the fact that in postulating diminishing marginal utility he said nothing more in his 1873 paper and in the first edition of the *Eléments* than "I submit" ("je pose en fait") or "It must be admitted" ("Il faut admettre")[10] that the intensity of want for an additional unit or fraction of a unit of a commodity decreases as the consumption of that commodity increases. Consumption, however, is only mentioned incidentally. While the driving force in the theory of exchange is, as Walras saw it, the endeavor of all traders to maximize their several satisfactions, it is marketplace satisfactions rather than dining-room satisfactions[11] which Walras had in mind. His passing allusions to consumption served only to reveal that he was perfectly aware that all trading is done with a view to ultimate consumption and that general experience in consumption influences the trader's market decisions. Walras went no further than this because, in effect, he defined the whole realm of economics in terms of catallactics.[12] He would have overstepped the bounds of a catallactic science had he done more than consider his *rareté* or marginal utility functions as exogenously determined parameters. The apparatus the economist has at his disposal no more fits him to derive these functions from consumption experience than to derive them from their presumed physiological, psychological, or sociological determinants.

This view is, I believe, borne out not only by the general tenor of Walras's argument throughout the *Eléments* in all its editions but also by certain subtleties in phrasing. For example, in his 1873 paper he defined *rareté* as the "intensity of the last want satisfied by the *quantity possessed* of a commodity."[13] In the first edition of the *Eléments* he defined *rareté* more technically as "the derivative of *effective* [i.e., total] *utility* with respect [again] to the *quantity possessed.*"[14] It is curious that in the second edition of the *Eléments* (1889), without offering any explanation and without changing anything else in the context, he changed *"quantity possessed"* to read *"quantity consumed"* in these definitions.[15] I suspect he did this more

[10] L.W. (1874*b*), §§74–75 of Lesson 14, corresponding to §§74–75 of Lesson 8 of the definitive edition.

[11] Cf. Stigler (1965), p. 124.

[12] Archbishop Richard Whately's term for the Science of Exchanges. Cf. Schumpeter (1954), p. 911.

[13] L.W. (1874*a*), §V, italics in original.

[14] L.W. (1874*b*), §75 of Lesson 14, italics in original.

[15] Ibid., §75 of the 2d ed. (1889). Cf. Jaffé (1954), p. 568, Collation Note [c] to Lesson 8.

as an accommodation than out of principle, in order to bring his
definition into conformity with those of Jevons and Menger with whose
writings he had become familiar in the interval between the appearance
of the first and second editions of his *Eléments*. In whatever edition we
consult the *Eléments,* we find that it is via exchange in the competitive
market and by no other process that Walras supposed his traders to
achieve the proportionality between *raretés* (or marginal utilities) and
prices, given only two sets of exogenously determined parameters: (i)
the marginal utility functions of the traders, and (ii) their initial
endowments (or initial "quantities possessed").

Locating his marginal utility theory where he did, as an integral part
of his theory of the determination of competitive market prices, Walras
succeeded far better than either Menger or Jevons in forging a clearly
defined analytical link between marginal utility and market price.
Analytically, Menger got no further than to demonstrate the relation
between given scales of "Bedürfnissbefriedigungen" and the quantities
exchanged in the case of two isolated barterers trading horses for cows.[16]
Though Menger clearly intended to extend his marginal utility theory
to explain price formation in a competitive market, when he finally
worked up to the case of "beiderseitiger Concurrenz," the connection
between the marginal utility scales and price formation lost its analytical
firmness.[17]

Whether Jevons's performance in this respect was superior to
Menger's depends upon the interpretation one places on the argument
from which Jevons derived his famous "equations of exchange."[18] So
vague was Jevons's method of harnessing his "final degree of utility"
theory to the determination of prices in a competitive market, that
Walras was left with the impression that no such harnessing took place
at all. In his famous letter of May 23, 1874, in which he acknowledged
Jevons's priority in formulating the concept of marginal utility with
mathematical precision, Walras declared that Jevons had missed the
opportunity to derive the "equation of effective demand" from considerations of maximum utility, a derivation essential, so Walras contended, to the solution of the problem of the determination of equilibrium price.[19]

[16] Menger (1871), pp. 163–67, corresponding to pp. 183–87 of Dingwall and Hoselitz
(1950).
[17] Ibid., pp. 201–5, corresponding to pp. 216–20 of Dingwall and Hoselitz (1950).
[18] Jevons (1871), p. 100 of the 4th ed., corresponding to p. 143 of the Pelican ed.
[19] Actually, as Professor Samuel Hollander pointed out to me, "Jevons took prices as
data during his analysis of exchange, so that he cannot be said to have dealt with price
determination at all, though he himself seems to think that he did." S. Hollander to W.
Jaffé, 27 July 1971.

If Walras did Jevons less than justice, Edgeworth was inclined to do him more than justice. How can one say, as Edgeworth did, that Jevons gave a lucid description of the working of a perfectly competitive or "open" market which results in the establishment of a uniform price?[20] Moreover, the illustration by which Jevons introduced his theorem of proportionality between "final degrees of utility" and prices in order to determine "the results of exchange," viz.,[21]

$$\frac{\phi_1 \, (a \, - \, x)}{\psi_1 y} = \frac{\phi_2 x}{\psi_2 \, (b \, - \, y)} = \frac{y}{x} = \frac{p_1}{p_2}$$

looks for all the world like an example of isolated barter, albeit between "trading bodies."[22] Edgeworth denied this, invoking Bishop Berkeley's "representative particular" in order to show that, though the trading Jevons described is done by a couple of individual dealers, "there is presupposed a class of competitors in the background." Edgeworth's erudite interpretation remains unconvincing. It is by no means evident that Jevons was aware of the implications Edgeworth later ascribed to his argument. All one can say is that Jevons juxtaposed his account of price determination in a perfectly competitive market with the theory of "final degree of utility."[23] It requires an excessively strained interpretation to see in this juxtaposition anything like the analytical integration which we find in Walras.

III

Of special interest to the historian of economic analysis is the question, How did Léon Walras arrive at his particular conception of marginal utility, the distinctive characteristic of which lay, as we have seen, rather in the employment of the idea than in its formulation? Fortunately, Léon Walras left to posterity a mass of documents revealing much of his private mental history.[24] These documents, besides shedding additional light on the genesis of the "marginal revolution," constitute excellent material for a case study of the process of scientific discovery.

The story thus unfolded does not, alas, possess high dramatic quali-

---

[20] Edgeworth (1881), p. 109. Rather than lucid, Professor Donald A. Walker regards Jevons's description as "confused, obscure and incomplete." D. A. Walker to W. Jaffé, 10 July 1971.

[21] Black (1970), pp. 22 and 204.

[22] Jevons (1871), pp. 88–90 of the 4th ed., corresponding to pp. 135–36 of the Pelican ed.

[23] Jevons (1871), pp. 114–18 of the 4th ed., corresponding to pp. 152–55 of the Pelican ed.

[24] For a description of the depositories of these documents, see Jaffé (1965a), 1:xii.

ties. We do not have here a case where a fundamentally novel theory occurred to the discoverer in a single illuminating flash nor one in which the discoverer appears congenitally endowed with serendipity in any extraordinary measure. On the contrary, Léon Walras's path toward his solution of the problem of exchange value was long and tedious. It had been first blazed ineffectually by his father, Auguste Walras, in 1831,[25] and was then trodden and retrodden by Léon, who began in 1859 and got nowhere until 1872. Léon Walras's contribution to the "marginal revolution" was, in fact, the fruit of efforts of two generations of Walrases.

Auguste Walras first turned his mind to the theory of value and to economics generally when, during a brief interval in his early career, he embarked in the late 1820s upon the study of law and became dissatisfied with the juristic conception of property as defined in the Civil Code.[26] Being of a philosophical frame of mind, and no doubt influenced by the attacks of the socialists of his day on the legitimacy of private property, he sought a more logically coherent basis than the socialists had to offer for drawing the line between public property and private property. He then consulted the principal economic treatises, both French and English; and again he was disappointed.[27] The trouble lay in their faulty theories of value, for without a satisfactory theory of value an adequate theory of property was impossible, since nothing is appropriated, whether for public or private use, unless it has value.[28] Neither the English labor or cost-of-production theory of value, nor the French utility theory would do. The true source of value, Auguste Walras argued, is not labor or cost of production or utility, but *rareté*, by which he meant literally scarcity. Only those things that are scarce, that is, limited in quantity as well as possessing utility, have value; and only to such things are property rights attached.[29]

In order to give an air of precision to the common-sense meaning of the term *rareté* or scarcity, he defined it as the ratio of the number of persons desiring the good, each person being presumed to want no more than a single unit of the good, to the total quantity of the good available.[30] In the course of time, Auguste Walras became aware of a

[25] Auguste Walras [hereinafter referred to as A.W.] (1938).

[26] L.W. (1908), pp. 2–3. For two excellent accounts in English of A.W.'s theory of property and value, see Gray (1931), pp. 333–36; and Howey (1960), pp. 28–32. See also "Avant-propos," A.W. (1831), pp. i–xxiv, corresponding to pp. 53–65 in Leduc (1958).

[27] The principal French economists A.W. consulted were J.B. Say, Destutt de Tracy, Charles Ganilh, Nicholas Massias, and Simonde de Sismondi; the English economists, Adam Smith, David Ricardo, James Mill, and John Ramsay McCulloch. See Leduc (1938), p. 303, n. 1; and pp. 308–9, n. 54.

[28] A.W. (1831), pp. x–xiii, corresponding to pp. 57–59 in Leduc (1938).

[29] Ibid., chap. 4, corresponding to pp. 99–112 in Leduc (1938).

[30] Ibid., p. 151, corresponding to p. 176 in Leduc (1938). Cf. Howey (1960), p. 31, where the ratio is inverted.

fundamental flaw in his mathematical definition of *rareté*. He wrote to his son Léon on May 18, 1861, that he was troubled by the fact that individuals frequently want more than one unit of a good, depending on their tastes, their age, their sex, their wealth, etc.[31] Since individuals differ from one another in so many respects, we cannot fall back upon the expedient of counting a person wanting, say, two units of a good as two persons and so forth. Auguste Walras now perceived that the first term of the ratio by which he first thought *rareté* could be defined and measured must be meaningless, made up as it is of a sum of incommensurable, non-additive entities. Since this "difficulty," as he called it, renders impossible the establishment of a standard unit of want (*unité de besoin*), Auguste Walras concluded that until such difficulties are surmounted, economics could not become a mathematical science like mechanics, physics, acoustics, and optics.

It was the challenge implicit in his father's conclusion which incited Léon to long labors that eventuated in his marginal utility theory. As Léon was the first to acknowledge, he owed much to his father for having adumbrated the problem,[32] but it is evident that he could not possibly have attained to any conception at all of marginal utility by pursuing Auguste Walras's line of reasoning. Even Auguste Walras's comparison of *rareté* to speed was spoiled as a potentially fruitful hint, where he added, "Just as speed is a ratio of distance covered to the time taken to cover it, so *rareté* is a ratio of the sum of wants to the total supply of goods available to gratify the wants.[33]

If it was not Auguste Walras who directly inspired Léon Walras's discovery of marginal utility, was it anyone else? Surely it was not Cournot, who deliberately backed away from any analysis of the relation of utility to demand.[34] Could it have been Jean Jacques Burlamaqui (1694-1748), a professor of law in Geneva, whose name Léon Walras coupled with that of his father as having furnished the correct solution of the problem of the origin of value?[35]

I cite the obscure Burlamaqui, who does not appear in Schumpeter's encyclopedic *History of Economic Analysis,* rather than a score of others whose names have been made familiar in studies of the prehistory of marginal utility, because Burlamaqui was one of the few early writers on the subject with whose work we may be sure Léon Walras was familiar in his formative years as an economist. Auguste Walras had quoted

---

[31] [A.W.] (1913), pp. 147-50. For fuller bibliographical information on A.W.'s published letters to L.W., see Jaffé (1965a), 1:19, n. (3) to Letter 1. Cf. Howey (1960), p. 31, and Leduc (1938), p. 306, n. 24.

[32] For example in L.W. (1908), p. 172.

[33] [A.W.] (1913), pp. 148-49.

[34] Cournot (1838), chap. 1, §3, and chap. 4, §21.

[35] L. W. (1874b), §155 of Lesson 27, corresponding to §157 of Lesson 16 of the definitive edition.

extensively from the *Elémens du droit naturel,* which was posthumously made up of Burlamaqui's lecture notes[36] and first published in the original Latin in 1754 and in French translation in 1820. The French version found its way into Léon Walras's private library,[37] presumably by inheritance in 1866.

The *Elémens du droit naturel* is of especial significance, not only because Auguste Walras had declared that Burlamaqui's doctrine of value was in every respect like his own[38] but more importantly, from the point of view of tracing the filiation of ideas, because Burlamaqui's chapter "On the Price of Things and Services Traded" (which followed his discussion of property),[39] was essentially a systematic restatement of Samuel von Pufendorf's theory of value enunciated in *De officio hominis et civis* in 1675.[40] Thus, Pufendorf's utility-cum-scarcity theory of value and price exerted via Burlamaqui very much the same influence on Auguste Walras as it did via Gershom Carmichael and Francis Hutcheson on Adam Smith, so far as we can judge from Adam Smith's *Lectures on Justice, Police, Revenue and Arms.*[41]

Apparently unaware of Pufendorf's still earlier anticipations of his doctrine of value and property, Auguste Walras looked upon Burlamaqui as his true forerunner. In the *Elémens du droit naturel* he found confirmation of his theory of *rareté* and was, therefore, all the more confident in using it to expose the errors he attributed to Adam Smith and Ricardo of the English school and to Condillac and J. B. Say of the French school.[42] Auguste Walras admitted that the English and French authors whom he attacked had occasionally brought *rareté* into the

[36] Burlamaqui (1821), Preface of anonymous editor, pp. xvii-xix.

[37] Burlamaqui (1821) is listed in an inventory of L.W.'s books drawn up by his daughter, Aline Walras, after his death. The list is contained in two copybooks which were bequeathed to Professor Gaston Leduc, who generously passed them on to me. See Jaffé (1965a), p. xii.

[38] "La doctrine de Burlamaqui . . . est la mienne." A.W. (1831), p. 212, corresponding to p. 220 in Leduc (1938).

[39] Burlamaqui (1821), part 3, chap. 11, pp. 209-19. Chaps. 8, 9, and 10 deal with property in a manner foreshadowing A.W.'s. How closely Burlamaqui anticipated A.W. on value is seen in the following passage: "Mais l'utilité seule . . . ne suffit pas pour mettre un prix aux choses, il faut encore considérer leur *rareté,* c'est-à-dire la difficulté qui l'on a de se procurer ces choses, et qui fait que chacun ne peut s'en procurer aisément autant qu'il en veut" (ibid., p. 212).

[40] The following passage from Pufendorf, quoted in W. L. Taylor (1965), p. 63, lies at the origin of Burlamaqui's doctrine (see above, n. 36): *"Hence an increase of value tends to be produced especially by scarcity . . . .* For articles in everyday use prices are raised especially when their *scarcity* is combined with *necessity or want."*

[41] Cf. Taylor (1965), chap. 2, pp. 63-72. In Adam Smith's brief discussion, "Of the Natural Wants of Mankind" found in his *Lectures,* he appears also to have apprehended the principle of diminishing utility, which he expressed as follows: "Nothing without variety pleases us. . . . Uniformity tires the mind." Smith (1896), p. 159. See below, n. 44, for Nassau Senior's similar expression of the idea.

[42] A.W. (1831), chaps. 12, 13, and 14; and A.W. (1849).

picture (true, above all, of Condillac),[43] but he contended that they did so only parenthetically or too unsystematically, which prevented them from perceiving unequivocally that value has its ultimate source in *rareté* and in nothing else.

For all their penetrating insight into the bearing of scarcity on value and price, neither Burlamaqui, nor Genovesi, nor Turgot, nor Condillac, nor Nassau Senior, all authors whom Léon Walras had apparently read at an early stage,[44] can be said to have offered a likely lead to anything like a rigorous formulation of the theory of marginal utility. They never sharpened their argument to a fine analytical point; their disquisitions on value were even more discursive than those of Auguste Walras. Little more can be claimed for the previous literature which we have reason to believe Léon Walras had consulted before 1874 than that it posed the problem. It did not contain any anticipatory suggestions of the way in which Léon Walras finally solved the problem. We are left, therefore, with no alternative but to search for such suggestions in Léon Walras's manuscripts and worksheets.

[43] A.W. was not entirely just to Condillac. Though at one point Condillac wrote, "La valeur des choses est donc fondée sur leur utilité" (Condillac, 1798, p. 10), he followed this up almost immediately with the corollary, "La valeur des choses croît dans la rareté, et diminue dans l'abondance" (p. 11), exactly A.W.'s thesis. Moreover, Condillac advanced the very argument A.W. later used to attack the English school, "Une chose n'a pas de valeur, parce qu'elle coûte, comme on le suppose, mais elle coûte parce qu'elle a une valeur" (p. 14). Condillac went further and discoursed upon the relationship of utility-cum-scarcity to trading behavior, first in the case of isolated two-party barter, and then in market exchange, where price is determined by demand and supply. Ibid., chap. 2. Though Condillac does not name Turgot in this context, his whole argument reads like an attempt to clarify Turgot's unfinished piece, "Valeurs et monnaies" (1769), where Turgot comes remarkably close to expressing in words the theory of proportionality between marginal utilities and ratios of exchange. See Turgot (1844), 1:85. As L.W.'s private library is known to have contained both Condillac's *Le Commerce et le gouvernement* and the *Œuvres de Turgot* (see above n. 37), these writings may well be regarded as direct sources of inspiration of the work of both Walrases. L.W., however, continued to reflect his father's view that Condillac, like J. B. Say, founded value on utility rather than scarcity. See L.W. (1874b), §155, corresponding to §157 of the definitive edition.

[44] L.W. named Nassau Senior along with Antonio Genovesi (1712-1769) as precursory exponents of the doctrine of scarcity. See L.W. (1847b), §159, corresponding to §161 of the definitive edition. Senior had written in 1836, "Of the three conditions of value, utility, transferableness and limitation in supply, the last is by far the most important. The chief sources of its influence on value are two of the most powerful principles of human nature, the love of variety [cf. n. 41 above] and the love of distinction [*pace* Veblen!]. . . . Not only are there limits to the pleasure which commodities of any class can afford, but the pleasure diminishes in a rapidly diminishing ratio long before those limits are reached." Senior (1938), pp. 9-10. As Professor Leduc informs us, A.W. published a review article in 1836 on a French version of Senior's writings which had appeared that year under the title, *Principes fondamentaux de l'économie politique, tirés des leçons édites et inédites de N. W. Senior* par le comte Jean Arrivabene. See Leduc (1938), p. 38 and pp. 309-10, n. 61. A.W.'s article was published in the *Revue Mensuelle d'Economie Politique*, 1836, pp. 359-68. In Genovesi the scarcity doctrine is more implicit than explicit, unsystematically developed and wanting in even a semblance of rigor. See Genovesi (1769), part 2, chap. 1.

IV

We begin with his manuscript entitled "Application des mathématiques à l'économie politique" and designated as "1ère Tentative, 1860."[45] It was a sorry performance which he had the good sense never to submit for publication. The whole effort centered around a labored attempt to assign meaning to the proposition that "the price of things is in inverse ratio to the quantity offered and in direct ratio to the quantity demanded," where quantity offered was defined as the total existing quantity in the possession of the several individuals in the world considered and the quantity demanded as the sum total of their wants or needs. He employed precisely drawn three-dimensional diagrams to illustrate his function, $V = F(q_d, q_0)$, and lost himself in a maze of simple algebra, all in an effort to confute Cournot. Auguste Walras's quasi-mathematical definition of *rareté* upon which his argument was founded led him completely astray. The "1ère Tentative" represented no advance at all toward the goal he was destined eventually to reach.

The next analytical manuscript, also entitled "Application des mathématiques à l'économie politique," but designated as "2ème Tentative, 1869–1870,"[46] is quite different and shows that in the interval, while he was engaged in a succession of occupations and enterprises that left him little leisure for theorizing, he had made considerable progress in shaping the structural pattern of his general equilibrium model. He formulated an equation of exchange[47] which he later used in his *Eléments*,[48] and then proceeded to develop his theory of the mechanism of exchange, first in the case of a two-commodity market, and then in the case of a multi-commodity market, again foreshadowing the *Eléments*.[49] This did not dampen his misconceived resolve, dating from the "1ère Tentative," to prove Cournot wrong in dismissing as meaningless the ratio of the quantity demanded of a commodity to the quantity offered.[50] Léon Walras still clung to his father's idea of *rareté*, which he expressed

[45] The manuscript, classified under the mark F.W. V, 1 in the Fonds Walras at the Bibliothèque Cantonale et Universitaire de Lausanne, is described and summarized in Jaffé (1965a), 1:216–17, n. (33) to Letter 148.

[46] The manuscript of the "2ème Tentative" is preserved along with that of the "1ère Tentative" under the same classification mark (see above, n. 45), and is described and summarized in Jaffé (1965a), 1:217–21, continuation of n. (33) to Letter 148. The second and third parts of the "2ème Tentative" reveal recognizable anticipations of the structural features of L.W.'s later theories of production, capital, money, economic progress, national income, and taxation, with which we are not here concerned.

[47] The equation, $mv_a = nv_b$, was probably derived from Isnard. See Jaffé (1969), pp. 25–28.

[48] L.W. (1874b), §44 in all editions.

[49] Ibid., §§44 and 108–14. See Jaffé (1965a), pp. 573–74, Collation Note [h] to Lesson 11.

[50] Cournot (1838), chap. 4, §20.

as the ratio of the utility of a commodity for all consumers taken together to the total quantity of that commodity in existence—though now with a shade less confidence. Reflecting his father's late misgivings, which had been disclosed to him, as we have seen, in 1861, Léon admitted that since the first term of the rato is a non-linear function of the second, a fixed standard of measure of relative *rareté* is impossible. His tortured algebra was of no avail.

It was this mixed bag of bungled mathematical economics and fruitful insights into a general equilibrium model that Léon Walras brought with him when he arrived in Lausanne in December 1870 to take up his post as professor of economics. There was certainly nothing in that bag which would point to his eventual role as a marginal revolutionist, except his dogged persistence in trying to make sense of his father's *rareté*.

The final manuscript of interest to us in studying Léon Walras's progress toward marginal utility consists of notes he prepared at Lausanne for a series of lectures he undertook to deliver in Geneva in January 1872.[51] Here we can see that even at that late date he still fell far short of the mark. For present purposes, we need only consider the notes for the third, fourth, and fifth lectures, which dealt with utility in the theory of exchange.

At a point where he discussed the demand curve for a given commodity, he enumerated the factors determining the curve as follows: (a) "l'utilité d'extension," which determines the intercept of the demand curve on the quantity axis; (b) "l'utilité d'intensité," which he said, determines the slope of the demand curve; (c) the total existing quantity among the holders of the commodity. He remarked that the second of these factors is imponderable.

Utility came again into his discussion in connection with what he called "price curves." These "price curves" represent demand price as the function of a fixed total quantity offered for sale in the market at whatever price it can fetch. As these fixed total quantities are assigned different values, i.e., as the quantity parameter is shifted, different prices ensue, and thus Walras obtained a special kind of demand curve which he called a "price curve." He subsequently introduced this concept into the *Eléments*,[52] but made very little of it there, whereas in his Geneva lecture notes of late 1871 he drew from it strange inferences concerning the relationship of utility to the "price function." He named

---

[51] This manuscript, entitled "Système des phénomènes économiques," is classified under the mark F.W. V, 1 in Lausanne and is summarized in Jaffé (1965a), 1:293–96, n. (2) to Letter 293.

[52] L.W. (1874b), §152, corresponding to §153 in the definitive edition.

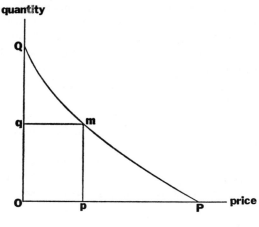

Figure 1

the total area (QOP in Fig. 1, drawn in the Walrasian manner, with
price measured on the horizontal axis) under such a curve "virtual
utility"; he described as "effective utility" the area of any rectangle
(qOpm) inscribed within the curve with one of its corners on the curve
and the diagonally opposite corner at the origin; he regarded the
mixtilinear triangle (mpP) outside the rectangle and bounded on one
side by the price axis as "the quantity of wealth which those who pay [a
certain price (Op)], would, if necessary, be willing to yield above and
beyond the wealth they actually do sacrifice."

What have we here but Dupuit's construction, including Dupuit's
consumers' surplus, without any mention of Dupuit's name! This is
indeed strange when we remember that in the 1877 instalment of the
first edition of the *Eléments,* Walras went to great lengths to demolish
Dupuit's theory and to denounce it as "one of the gravest of errors."[53] In
after years, Léon Walras and Pareto never tired of anathematizing
Dupuit, Alfred Marshall, and Auspitz and Lieben for allegedly identifying demand curves with utility curves.[54] In Walras's and Pareto's eyes,
this was *the* sin against the Holy Ghost. But, as we have just seen, Walras
in his unregenerate days, in 1871, prior to seeing the light, committed
the selfsame sin, identifying the utility curve not with an individual's
demand curve, but, worse than that, with a market demand curve. At
that time, he seemed totally oblivious of the fact that this implied
interpersonal comparisons of utility as well as the assumption of the

[53] Ibid., §§368–70, corresponding to §§385–87 of the definitive edition.
[54] Jaffé (1965a), 2:343–47, Letter 913; pp. 421–23, n. (3) to Letter 990; pp. 485–87,
Letter 1051; and pp. 488–89, Letter 1052. See also Pareto (1906), p. 585, §56 of the
Appendix; and Pareto (1960) 1:373. Letter 162, and 3:60–63, Letter 561.

constant marginal utility of whatever it was that was given in exchange for the commodity demanded. Neither of these implications had any place in Walras's definitive version of the marginal utility theory that was to make its first appearance quite soon in the paper he read before the Académie des Sciences morales et politiques in August of 1873. Certainly at the opening of 1872, Léon Walras was still floundering, though he had made progress in putting together a good part of the machinery of his general equilibrium model, including his mathematical theory of the aggregate market process by which equilibrium prices are determined.

Walras seems to have been painfully aware that he had not yet succeeded in integrating *rareté* into his model. Only when he managed to liberate himself from his father's conception of *rareté* and to redefine it in terms of a differential coefficient did a satisfactory integration prove possible. Then and then only could he be said to have made his entry into the "marginal revolution."

The turning point was reached some time in 1872. Walras, who was quite conscious of his mathematical inadequacies, was in the habit of buttonholing his mathematical colleagues and plying them with questions. Among these colleagues was a certain Paul Piccard (1844–1920?), then a professor of mechanics at the Academy of Lausanne. We do not know exactly how Léon Walras framed his question, but it appears from a letter he wrote to Piccard after the event[55] that the question had something to do with the derivation of demand curves from considerations of utility and quantity. That this was very probably the case is clear from an undated manuscript signed by Paul Piccard and found in a sheaf of Walras's papers all from the year 1872.[56] This manuscript contained an answer to just such a question.

What Piccard did was to furnish Léon Walras with the simplest analytical tools required for establishing the condition of maximum satisfaction for a trader. Piccard's exposition was on an extremely elementary level, probably in deference to Walras's limited mathematical attainments at this time. The demonstration was practically all geometrical; only the conclusions were translated into analytical symbols. Starting with two negatively inclined marginal utility curves, which Piccard called the "courbes de besoin" of a given trader for commodities (A) and (B) respectively, and assigning to the trader a certain quantity of (A) and no (B), he supposed a given price of (A) in terms of (B) to be current in the market and asked what our trader would do under the circumstances to improve his situation as measured

[55] Jaffé (1965a), 1:345–47, Letter 239.
[56] Ibid., 1:309–11, n. (4) to Letter 211, where the manuscript is described and the text published in full.

by the sum of bounded areas under the curves. Piccard pointed out that the sum of the bounded areas is maximized, subject to the condition now known as the budget constraint, when exchange is carried to the point where the last small increment of area under the trader's marginal utility curve of commodity (B) is equal to the corresponding last small decrement of area under the trader's marginal utility curve of commodity (A). Piccard, after translating into symbols the dimensions of the small areas relinquished and acquired at the critical point where maximization of the trader's satisfaction is achieved, then stated what was really a first-order condition of equilibrium for the trader, namely, equality between the marginal utility of the amount of (B) acquired and the marginal utility of the balance of (A) retained multiplied by the reciprocal of the price of (A) in terms of (B). In order to reduce the equation to one containing only two variables, the quantity of (B) acquired was expressed as the product of the quantity of (A) given up multiplied by its price in terms of (B), thus:[57]

$$\psi\,(A_0 p_a) = \frac{1}{p_a}\,\phi(Q_a - a_0)$$

So, at least, the equation appears inserted on the manuscript in Walras's hand, to correct a slip in Piccard's demonstration. Piccard concluded, "This equation is none other than that of the required curve, for the only variables it contains are p_a and A_0." Actually, he had derived an offer curve; but since in the two-commodity case, an offer curve of one commodity is derived from the demand curve for the other commodity, it doesn't make any essential difference.

Unquestionably it was from Piccard's mathematical demonstration that Léon Walras distilled his refined and analytically tractable conception of marginal utility. Piccard's method of deriving an individual's demand curve from marginal utility curves furnished Walras with the indispensable clue to his discovery of the fundamental theorem of proportionality of the *raretés* of commodities to their market prices,

$$r_a : r_b : r_c : \ldots \ldots :: p_a : p_b : p_c \ldots$$

Nevertheless it was truly Léon Walras's discovery,[58] for Piccard's note could hardly have helped him unless he had previously set himself the problem, first suggested by his father, of relating utility-cum-scarcity to the determination of market prices. It is no wonder Walras persisted in

[57] In this equation, Q_a is the trader's original endowment in (A), A_0 is the amount of (A) given up in exchange, p_a is the price of (A) in terms of (B), and ϕ and ψ are the marginal utility functions of commodities (A) and (B) respectively.

[58] Cf. Walker (1970), p. 688. In my judgment, Professor Walker is inclined to underestimate the credit due to L.W. for the discovery and to overestimate that due to Piccard.

calling marginal utility by the inherited term *rareté*, even after he learned of other terms in the literature—if only to mark the origins of the discovery.

How much Auguste Walras's drive was behind this discovery is seen in Léon's retention of his father's slogan, *"rareté* is the cause of value." Now Léon was able to endow the slogan with a semblance of cogency, for both Walrases envisaged the causal nexus in terms of two necessary, but admittedly not sufficient, conditions:[59] universal concomitance and exact proportionality. Walras's theorem established just such a nexus between *rareté* and market prices.

V

On reaching the end of the tale of Léon Walras's tortuous journey to marginal utility, one is left with the nagging question, Why did Léon Walras have to wait until Piccard, a professor of mechanics and not an economist at all, pointed the way? The answer, I believe, lies in Léon Walras's inadequate mathematical training. Though in his youth he had taken special mathematical courses in preparation for the entrance examinations of the famed Polytechnic School of Paris, and though, after twice failing these examinations, he was finally admitted upon examination to the Paris School of Mines, he still knew nothing about the extreme values of functions.[60] His secondary-school education had equipped him with a fair knowledge of algebra and analytical geometry, but only the vaguest notions of the calculus. After that, as he himself later acknowledged,[61] he spent his time reading about the history of the calculus instead of working out its problems. He could hardly have learned anything more at the School of Mines, where he was a student in name only—in order to give himself an acceptable status in the eyes of his parents while he dabbled in novel writing.

The fault, however, was not entirely his. In Léon Walras's youth the teaching of the calculus was in an underdeveloped stage. We know, for example that in the 1830's, when Cournot was asked to give a course of lectures on the differential calculus at Lyons, so novel did the subject appear that auditors flocked to the lecture hall in large numbers, only to dwindle to ten as the successive topics treated became too difficult for the untutored to follow.[62] No wonder, for the only pertinent books

---

[59] A.W. (1849), in Leduc (1938), p. 330. Cf. Jaffé (1954), p. 512, n. (3) to Lesson 10.

[60] This is evident from a manuscript dated "4 décembre 1853" which I have recently (1966) identified as L.W.'s, though it was misclassified in the Fonds Walras among A.W.'s paper under the mark F.W. VI. Written at the time he was studying for his entrance examinations, it was an elaborate exercise in "The Decomposition of Rational Functions into Partial Fractions," but shows no clear understanding of the theory of maxima and minima.

[61] See L.W.'s "Notice autobiographique" in Jaffé (1965a), p. 2.

[62] Cournot (1913), pp. 155–56.

available were advanced treatises on the differential and integral calculus which, being intended for specialists, slurred over demonstrations of the elementary principles. In the absence of textbooks designed for beginners, systematic teaching of the subject was quite impossible. It was not until 1860 that the first introductory calculus textbook[63] appeared in France for the benefit of students primarily interested in applications.

This suggests a hypothesis or, let us say, until further evidence is accumulated about the teaching of the calculus in countries other than France, a surmise which may help explain not only why it took so long for economic theorists to formulate the marginal utility principle but also why in the early 1870s three discoverers independently hit upon very much the same solution of the same age-old problem. Only then had Newton's and Leibnitz's inventions begun to trickle down to the classroom. When a knowledge of the calculus ceased to be an esoteric attribute of pure mathematicians and physicists, when it became generally one of the intellectual attainments of educated persons whose schooling was not exclusively literary, then economists within the wider circle of the mathematically cultivated, pondering upon the confused efforts of the past to relate utility to price, might quite spontaneously perceive the calculus way out of the confusion. At least, that was the way found by Jevons and Léon Walras.

We cannot be sure that Carl Menger furnishes a counterexample until we know something about his education, or at least whether he had been exposed to the calculus. Von Hayek assures us that "there is no reason to believe that he [Menger] lacked either the technical equipment or the inclination [toward mathematics]."[64] Unless we are prepared to dismiss out of hand the possibility of intellectual osmosis, we cannot ignore the fact that Carl Menger's brothers were intensely interested in mathematics. Consequently, it is not altogether unlikely that also in Menger's case the discovery of marginal utility may have been suggested by the calculus.

VI

What conclusions can be drawn from the above worm's-eye view of the "marginal revolution," disclosing but a small corner of the spectacle?

[63] Haton de la Goupillière (1860). See Jaffé (1965a), 1:528, n. (3) to Letter 372, for a quotation from Haton de la Goupillière's "Avant-propos."
[64] F. A. von Hayek, biographical introduction to Menger (1871), L.S.E. Reprint, p. ix. Carl Menger, however, objected in principle to the use of mathematics as a research tool or as a fundamental method in economics, though he granted that it might serve as a convenient mode of demonstration or exposition. See Jaffé (1965a), 1:768, Letter 566; and 2:2–6, Letter 602.

Does serious attention to the details of Walras's life here recounted distort rather than illuminate an understanding of his scientific work, as, it seems, Professor Stigler[65] would have us believe? Does it not rather throw a more penetrating light on the significance of Walras's contribution when it is seen how he fitted his newly found marginal utility principle into his slowly unfolding general equilibrium scheme? Does this not also make it more apparent that whatever the weaknesses and defects of the marginal utility principle may be, whether we have abiding faith in subjective motivation or abjure it in favor of its outward and visible signs, Léon Walras's role in the "marginal revolution" was clearly to delineate the need[66] and the place in a general equilibrium model for some such power-generating engine to activate the market mechanism? Does not the biographical narrative of Léon Walras's awesome voyage of discovery of marginal utility in terms of a differential coefficient reveal the voyage as an academic adventure, directed in large part by prevailing pedagogic winds? Does this not, at the same time, broaden the context of W. Stark's and Mark Blaug's relativist-absolutist dichotomy[67] by relating Léon Walras's discovery to contemporary intellectual conditions, including the contemporary memory of things past, as well as to external events? Does not the same narrative, starting with Auguste Walras's search for a passage leading from the stormy waters of

[65] Stigler (1970), p. 426. Professor Stigler asks the question, "What relevance have the details of a man's personal life to the nature of his scientific work?" He answers that "biography distorts rather than illuminates the understanding of scientific work," and, presumably alluding to my article on "Biography and Economic Analysis" (Jaffé 1965b), cites me as having recently given "the opposite answer." If Professor Stigler is inveighing against the fallacy of the *argumentum ad hominem*, he is undoubtedly right and there is no opposition between our views. Just as "the personal history of Gauss is entirely irrelevant to the question of the adequacy of his proof that every equation has a root" (Cohen and Nagel, 1934, p. 380), so also the personal views and actions of Knut Wicksell in matters of marriage, blasphemy, and national defense have nothing to do with the adequacy of his theory of capital and interest. It would be inadmissible to employ the biographical data of a discoverer to establish or negate the logical coherence of his novel theoretical model or its econometric correspondence with reality. But surely the historian of economics, *qua* historian, would be derelict in his duty if he confined himself to evaluating past theories on general analytical and empirical grounds, without investigating the *genesis* of these theories, thinking of the past in terms of the past and critically exploiting all the pertinent documentary evidence available. For an answer to the question of the relevance of biographical data to the performance of the specifically historical tasks of the historian of economics, Professor Stigler need not have gone far afield. His colleague, Professor Milton Friedman, provided a succinct and hardly contestable answer long before mine appeared when he wrote: "Progress in positive economics will require not only the testing and elaboration of existing hypotheses but also the construction of new hypotheses. On this problem there is little to say on a formal level. The construction of hypotheses is a creative act of inspiration, intuition, invention; its essence is the vision of something new in familiar material. The process must be discussed in psychological, not logical, categories; *studied in autobiographies and biographies,* not treatises on scientific method; and promoted by maxim and example, not syllogism or theorem." Friedman (1953), pp. 42–43; my italics.
[66] E. J. Mishan would say there is no such need. See Mishan (1961).
[67] Stark (1944), p. 1, and Blaug (1968), pp. 1–8.

the early socialist denunciations of property to some solid analytical
ground for socialist goals, dispose of the absurd myth that marginal
utility was expressly invented to refute the Marxian labor theory of
value? Does not a reexamination of Léon Walras's 1873 paper hinting at
an extension of the application of the marginal utility principle to the
theory of production, which he later carried out in the *Eléments* (along
with its extension, in the end, to capital formation and moneyholding)
help us perceive that a salient achievement, for better or worse, of the
"marginal revolution" was its shifting of emphasis away from production considered as a wealth-increasing process to production considered
as an aspect of exchange, away from a preoccupation with distributive
shares toward a preoccupation with the allocation of resources? Herein,
indeed, in the interpretation of the time, his time and ours, Léon
Walras's "virtues" lie. Whether such "virtues" are admirable or not is
another question.[68]

REFERENCES

Allen, R. G. D. *Mathematical Economics*. London: Macmillan, 1956.
Black, R. D. Collison, ed. *The Theory of Political Economy* by W. Stanley Jevons.
    Harmondsworth, Middlesex: Pelican Books, 1970.
Blaug, Mark. *Economic Theory in Retrospect*. 2d ed. Homewood, Ill.: Irwin, 1968.
Burlamaqui, Jean Jacques. *Elémens du droit naturel*. Nouvelle édition. Paris:
    Delestre-Boulage, 1821.
Cohen, Morris R., and Ernest Nagel. *Introduction to Logic and Scientific Method*.
    New York: Harcourt Brace, 1934.
Condillac, Etienne Bonnot de. *Le Commerce et le gouvernement. Œuvres de Condillac*,
    vol. 4. Paris: Ch. Houel, 1798.
Cournot, Augustin. *Recherches sur les principes mathématiques de la théorie des richesses*.
    Paris: Hachette, 1838. Reprint edited by Georges Lutfalla. Paris: Marcel
    Rivière, 1938. English translation by Nathaniel T. Bacon, edited by Irving
    Fisher. New York: Macmillan, 1927.
Cournot, Augustin. *Souvenirs (1760–1860)*. Edited by E. P. Bottinelli. Paris:
    Hachette, 1913.
Dingwall, James, and F. Bert Hoselitz, eds. and transs. *Principles of Economics* by
    Carl Menger. Glencoe, Ill.: Free Press, 1950.
Edgeworth, F. Y. *Mathematical Psychics*. London: Kegan Paul, 1881. Series of
    Reprints of Scarce Tracts, no. 10. London: London School of Economics,
    1932.
Friedman, Milton. *Essays in Positive Economics*. Chicago: University of Chicago
    Press, 1953.

    [68] For support of research leading to this paper, I am indebted to the National Science
Foundation under Grants GS-1516 and GS-1997 and to Northwestern University. I am
also indebted to my colleague, Professor Thomas T. Sekine, to Professor Samuel
Hollander, and to Professor Donald A. Walker, for valuable comments and suggestions.

Genovesi, Antonio. *Lezioni di commercio o sia d'economia civile* (1765). New Edition. Bassano, 1769.

Gray, Alexander. *The Development of Economic Doctrine*. London: Longmans, Green, 1931.

Haton de la Goupillière, J. N. *Eléments de calcul infinitésimal*. Paris: Mallet-Bachelier, 1860.

Howey, R. S. *The Rise of the Marginal Utility School; 1870-1889*. Lawrence: University of Kansas Press, 1960.

Jaffé, William, ed. and trans. *Elements of Pure Economics* by Léon Walras. Translated from the definitive edition (1926). London and Homewood, Ill.: Allen and Unwin, and Irwin, 1954. (Reprints of Economic Classics. New York: Augustus M. Kelley, 1969).

Jaffé, William, ed. *Correspondence of Léon Walras and Related Papers*. 3 vols. Amsterdam: North Holland (for Royal Netherlands Academy of Sciences and Letters), 1965. *(a)*.

Jaffé, William. "Biography and Economic Analysis." *Western Economic Journal 3* (Summer 1965): 223-32. *(b)*.

Jaffé, William. "Walras's Theory of *Tâtonnement:* A Critique of Recent Interpretations." *Journal of Political Economy* 75 (Feb. 1967): 1-19.

Jaffé, William. "A. N. Isnard, Progenitor of the Walrasian General Equilibrium Model." *History of Political Economy* 1 (Spring 1969): 19-43.

Jevons, W. Stanley. *The Theory of Political Economy*. London: Macmillan, 1871. 4th ed., edited by H. Stanley Jevons. London: Macmillan, 1924. For the Pelican edition, see Black (1970).

Leduc, Gaston, ed. *De la nature de la richesse et de l'origine de la valeur* by Auguste Walras. Paris: Alcan, 1938.

Menger, Carl. *Grundsätze der Volkswirtschaftslehre*. Vienna: Braumüller, 1871. Series of Reprints of Scarce Tracts, no. 17. London: London School of Economics, 1934. For the English translation, see Dingwall and Hoselitz (1950).

Mishan, E. J. "Theories of Consumer's Behavior: A Cynical View." *Economica*, n.s. 28 (Feb. 1961): 1-11.

Pareto, Vilfredo. *Manuel d'économie politique*. Paris: Giard [1909].

Pareto, Vilfredo. *Lettere a Maffeo Pantaleoni*. 3 vols. Edited by Gabriele de Rosa. Rome: Banca Nazionale del Lavoro, 1960.

Schumpeter, Joseph A. *History of Economic Analysis*. New York: Oxford University Press, 1954.

Smith, Adam. *Lectures on Justice, Police, Revenue and Arms*. Oxford: Clarendon Press, 1896.

Stark, W. *The History of Economics in Its Relation to Social Development*. New York: Oxford University Press, 1944.

Stigler, George. J. *Essays in the History of Economics*. Chicago and London: University of Chicago Press, 1965.

Stigler, George. J. Review of *The Evolution of Modern Economic Theory* by Lord Robbins. *Economica* 37 (Nov. 1970) : 425-26.

Taylor, W. L. *Francis Hutcheson and David Hume as Predecessors of Adam Smith*. Durham, N. C.: Duke University Press, 1965.

Thünen, Johann Heinrich von. *Der isolierte Staat*. Edited by Heinrich Waentig. Jena: Fischer, 1930.

Turgot, Anne Robert Jacques. "Valeurs et monnaies" (1769). *Œuvres de Turgot*. Edited by W. Eugène Daire, 1: 75–93. Paris: Guilaumin, 1844.

Walker, Donald A. "Léon Walras in the Light of His Correspondence and Related Papers." *Journal of Political Economy* 78 (July/Aug. 1970): 685–701.

Walras, Auguste. *De la nature de la richesse et de l'origine de la valeur*. Paris: Johanneau, 1831. For the Leduc edition, see Leduc (1938).

Walras, Auguste. *Mémoire sur l'origine de la valeur d'échange*. Paris: Typographie Panckoucke, 1849. Republished as appendix in Leduc (1938), pp. 316–43.

[Walras, Auguste]. "Lettres inédites de et à Léon Walras." *La Révolution de 1848* 10 (1913): 138–56.

Walras, Léon. "Principe d'une théorie mathématique de l'échange." *Séances et travaux de l'Académie des Sciences morales et politiques,* Jan. 1874, vol. 101 of the Collection, 33d Year of the New Series, part 1, pp. 97–116; first republished in the *Journal des Economistes*, April/June 1874, 3d ser. 34, no. 100:5–31; republished again with minor revisions in the *Théorie mathématique de la richesse sociale* (Lausanne: Corbaz, 1883), pp. 7–25. Italian version: "Principio d'una teoria matematica dello scambio," translated by Gerolamo Boccardo in the *Biblioteca dell'Economista*, 3d ser. 2:1293–1301. Turin: Unione tipografica, 1878. German version: "Prinzip einer mathematischen Theorie des Tausches," translated by Ludwig von Winterfeld, in *Mathematische Theorie der Preisbestimmung der wirtschaftlichen Güter: Vier Denkschriften*, pp. 1–17. Stuttgart: Enke, 1881. *(a).*

Walras, Léon *Eléments d'économie politique pure*. 1st ed. (in two instalments), Lausanne: Corbaz, 1874–77; 2d ed., Lausanne: Rouge, 1889; 3d ed., Lausanne: Rouge, 1896; 4th ed., Lausanne: Rouge, 1900: definitive ed. (published posthumously), 1926. Reprinted Paris: Pichon and Durand-Auzias, 1952. For English translation, see Jaffé (1954).

Walras, Léon. "La bourse, la spéculation et l'agiotage." *Bibliothèque Universelle et Revue Suisse*, 3d Period, 5 (March 1880): 452–76; and 6 (April 1880): 66–94. Republished in L.W. (1898), pp. 401–45.

Walras, Léon. *Théorie mathématique de la richesse sociale*. Lausanne: Corbaz, 1883.

Walras, Léon. *Etudes d'économie politique appliquée*, 1st ed., Lausanne: Rouge, 1898; 2d ed., Paris: Pichon and Durand-Auzias, 1936, edited by G. Leduc. The pagination is the same in both editions.

Walras, Léon. "Un initiateur en économie politique, A. A. Walras." *Revue du Mois* 6 (1908): 170–83.

17

MENGER, JEVONS AND WALRAS
DE-HOMOGENIZED

This is intended as an essay in historiography – to illustrate how the widely disseminated practice of lumping Menger, Jevons and Walras together under one caption has grossly distorted the history of their contributions to economic analysis. The usual caption is, of course, "The Marginal Revolution of the 1870s," a subject amply treated elsewhere.[1] The question I propose to raise here is not whether there ever was a "Marginal Revolution" in the proper sense of the term, but whether the use of any single appellation to designate the three "revolutionary" innovations of the 1870s obscures precisely those differences between them which the passage of time has revealed more important than anything they may have had in common.

Exactly when and where the name "Marginal Revolution" made its first appearance I do not know. For present purposes it suffices to take Schumpeter's *History of Economic Analysis* of 1954 as the starting point, for in that treatise the name was not merely used as a tag, but was discussed from the standpoint of its appropriateness.[2] Already in 1953, T. W. Hutchison had written apropos of Gossen and Jevons, "The playing up or playing down of the revolutionary newness of a writer's contribution is, of course, often largely a matter of temperament and intellectual vested interest."[3] Mark Blaug boldly headed Chapter 8 of his *Economic Theory in Retrospect* of 1962, "The Marginal Revolution," but added the caution, "To speak of a marginal *revolution* is in itself somewhat mislead-

Earlier versions of this paper, under a different title, were presented at the Birmingham History of Economic Thought Conference in September of 1972, and before the General Assembly of the Japanese Association of Theoretical Economics at Nagoya in 1974. The present revision is the result of welcome critical comments I received on these and other occasions. I am particularly indebted to Klaus H. Hennings of the University of Reading (England) for valuable insights into Menger's theory. Grateful acknowledgment is also due to the Canada Council for financial assistance in the preparation of this paper.
[1] Black *et al.* (1973): the papers in this collection having appeared both in the *History of Political Economy,* Fall 1972, 4, pp. 266–624, and in a separately published bound volume with a useful index added, the page references in the following notes to Black *et al.* (1973) will be to the volume, with corresponding pages in the journal placed immediately after in square brackets.
[2] Schumpeter (1954, pp. 909–920).   [3] Hutchison (1953, p. 15).

312   Walras's place in economic thought

ing."[4] And Lord Robbins in 1970 approached the term "Marginal Revolution" with characteristic reserve, admitting on the one hand, that "it became the starting point and the stimulus for much of the theoretical development since its day," while protesting, on the other hand, that "some of the innovators went much too far in regarding [their new discovery] as a substitute for Classical theory rather than as a valuable extension."[5] None of these historians of economics ever so much as hinted that there might be a question whether the contributions of Menger, Jevons and Walras were sufficiently akin to justify referring to them by the same family name and bringing them under one heading. No heed was paid to J. R. Hicks' admonition, conveyed timely enough in 1934, "But anyone who comes a little closer to these writers [Menger, Jevons and Walras] cannot help feeling a little resentment at the habit of classifying them together, even for the joint receipt of such an honourable title [as independent discoverers of the Marginal Utility principle]."[6]

The stress laid by historians of economics on the marginal utility tool as constituting the essential feature of the triple discoveries is in accord with Schumpeter's definition of science as "tooled knowledge."[7] This definition in the hands of historians of economics who construe it altogether too narrowly has tended to divert attention from the desired knowledge to the tools used in giving formal structure to the knowledge. That knowledge-structures are more important than the tools used in erecting them is seen in the fact that the theoretical edifices raised by Menger, Jevons and Walras, albeit with closely similar variants of the same tool, were markedly different and influenced the future course of theoretical model building in fundamentally different ways, the tool itself having in the meantime become obsolete.

Schumpeter himself called attention to the most important difference of all in the work of the three "revolutionaries," when he singled out Walras from the others as the sole architect of the general equilibrium structure. "This," he wrote, "was the achievement of Walras. So soon as we realize that *it is the general equilibrium system which is the really important thing, we discover that, in itself, the principle of marginal utility is not so important after all* as Jevons, the Austrians, and Walras himself believed."[8] True, but when Schumpeter went on to say that "analysis of Walras's schema discloses the fact that marginal utility was the ladder by

[4] Blaug (1968, p. 298).   [5] Robbins (1970, p. 16).

[6] Hicks (1934, p. 338). It was none other than Léon Walras who set the example in 1889 of classifying Jevons, Menger and himself together as co-discoverers of the modern marginal utility theory. See Walras (1874/ . . . , 2nd edition 1889: pp. VIII–IX and § 160, corresponding to pp. VI–VII and §§ 162–164 of the definitive edition and to pp. 36–37 and 204–207 of the English translation).

[7] Schumpeter (1954, p. 7).   [8] *Ibid.*, p. 918; italics added.

which Walras climbed to the level of his general equilibrium system," he drew an inference which, though plausible enough *a priori,* is contradicted by documentary evidence brought to light since Schumpeter's day.

Instead of climbing up from marginal utility to the level of his general equilibrium system, Walras actually climbed down from that level to marginal utility. This is abundantly attested by Walras's manuscript essays to which he privately confided his early analytical lucubrations[9] from 1860 until he ventured upon a full-dress public presentation of his "Principe d'une théorie mathématique de l'échange" before the Académie des sciences morales et politiques in Paris on the 16th and 23rd of August, 1873.[10] In this paper, after more than twelve years of unpublished efforts to piece together an analytical schema of interrelated competitive markets without ever once alluding to anything like a marginal utility theory, Walras suddenly brought forth, as fully accoutered as Pallas Athena from the head of Zeus, his new idea of *rareté,* which he defined mathematically as we do marginal utility. With the aid of this conceptual device Walras proceeded in the same paper to demonstrate the relation of his *rareté* (marginal utility) functions to individual demand functions in order to establish a logically "causal" link between *rareté* and value in exchange. All this is found toward the end of the "Principe d'une théorie mathématique de l'échange," the beginning of which is taken up with a theory of the competitive market mechanism for grinding out equilibrium relative prices in the simple two-commodity case.

The order of exposition followed in this article recapitulated exactly the order in which Walras had arrived at his ideas. Evidence I have adduced elsewhere[11] shows that Walras did not come into possession of his concept of marginal utility and his method of using it to derive a theoretical demand curve until after he had clearly outlined his mathematical theory of a network of interrelated markets.[12] For that the writings of Turgot, Quesnay, Adam Smith, Ricardo and J. B. Say had been his inspiration; and for the translation of the vision of general

---

[9] Jaffe (1965), cited hereafter as *Correspondence,* vol. I, pp. 216–221, n. (33) to Letter 148.

[10] Walras (1874/1883).

[11] Black *et al.,* (1973, pp. 113–139 [379–405], especially pp. 127–132 [392–398]).

[12] Toward the end of his life Walras described the sequence of his early progress in discovery as follows: " . . . en Octobre 1871, au moment ou je devenais professeur ordinaire, je tenais enfin la première des deux clefs de l'économie politique pure telle que je voulais la faire dans sa forme rigoureusement scientifique qui est la forme mathématique: savoir 'l'équation d'*échange.*' Et dans le courant de 1872, je trouvais la seconde: savoir 'l'équation de *satisfaction maximum*' que Jevons, je le sus bientôt, venait de trouver de son côté en Angleterre" [Walras (1909, p. 581)].

market equilibrium thus obtained into mathematical equations he found models in the works of A. N. Isnard,[13] Augustin Cournot[14] and Louis Poinsot.[15] From Isnard's *Traité des richesses* (1781), Léon Walras derived some of the main structural features of his theory of market exchange as well as suggestions for his theory of money and capital formation, though Isnard's mathematics took the form of running proportions rather than simultaneous equations.[16] From Cournot's *Recherches sur les principes mathématiques de la théorie des richesses* (1838), he learned to apply the technique of functional analysis to economics.[17] And in Poinsot's *Eléments de statique* (8th ed., 1842), which was a textbook on the theory of mechanics bristling with systems of simultaneous equations to represent, among other things, the mechanical equilibrium of the solar system, Walras found a pattern for representing the catallactic equilibrium of the market system.[18]

None of these sources of early inspiration, however, offered the slightest clue to a marginal utility theory of value or, indeed, to the need for such a theory to which Léon Walras was awakened, as will be seen below, by his father, Auguste Walras. As late as January 1872, when Léon Walras was called upon to draft an outline for a series of lectures to be delivered in Geneva, he was able to sketch a pure theory of interconnected markets though he still had no notion of how to relate utility to demand.[19] The best he could do at that stage was to identify the utility curve with the market (!) demand curve in the manner of Dupuit[20] and then take the slope of the same demand curve as an index of what he called "utilité d'intensité," the very term he later used in §74 of *Eléments* to describe marginal utility proper. So long as he had nothing but this paltry technical apparatus at his disposal, he wisely concluded that it was impossible to elucidate further the relationship between "absolute value" and demand, especially since the intensive dimension of utility seemed unmeasurable. That, indeed, was the state of confusion in which he found himself in trying to cope with the problem of utility and value until his colleague, Paul Piccard, a professor of mechanics at Lausanne, came to his rescue toward the end of 1872 by showing him how to construe utility and its derivative with respect to quantity mathemati-

[13] Isnard (1781).   [14] Cournot (1838/...).
[15] Poinsot (1842).   [16] See Jaffé (1969).
[17] Walras (1874/..., Preface to the 4th edition, p. VIII; p. 37 of the English translation).
[18] *Correspondence*, vol. III, pp. 149–150, n. (7) to Letter 1483.
[19] *Ibid.*, vol. I, pp. 293–296, n. (2) to Letter 198.
[20] Five years later, in § 370 of the second instalment (1877) of the first edition of the *Eléments*, Walras severely criticized Dupuit for having perpetrated the same identification to which he had himself previously subscribed. *Cf.* Walras (1874/..., § 387 of the definitive edition).

cally and how to apply the equi-marginal rule to the theory of value in exchange.[21]

The trail that led Walras finally to seek the help of Paul Piccard had been blazed at the start by his economist-father. Auguste Walras had wanted to prove that *rareté*, in the ordinary sense of scarcity, was "the cause of value," but ran into a snag.[22] The nearest he came to a definition of scarcity was to define it as a disproportion between the aggregate quantity of a good available and the sum total, over all individuals, of wants for the good. He himself eventually realized that this definition would not do, because one of the terms of the dispropor- tion, the sum total of wants felt by a multitude of persons of diverse tastes, conditions and means, did not admit of quantification even in principle. He then bequeathed the unsolved problem to his son, Léon.

Léon Walras was eager to solve the problem, not only out of filial piety, but because the conceptual machine he had already designed for the determination of equilibrium prices needed a motor to run it. What was lacking was something like Adam Smith's coupled motors made up of "a certain propensity in human nature . . . to truck, barter and exchange" and a universal "desire of bettering our condition." With Paul Piccard's technical assistance, Walras solved at one stroke both his father's problem of finding a cogent analytical definition for *rareté* and his problem of attaching a maximization motor to his all-comprehensive market machine.

It cannot be emphasized enough that what Walras was after was the completion of his competitive market model, and *not* the elaboration of a theory of subjective valuation in consumption. In the paper he pre- sented to the Académie des sciences morales et politiques in 1873 he defined his newly discovered *rareté* as "l'intensité du dernier besoin satisfait par une *quantité possédée* ("the intensity of the last want satisfied by a *quantity possessed*" [Walras's italics]), not a quantity consumed. Only in postulating diminishing marginal utility, did he allow the word "consumed" to slip in, inadvertently as it were. When in his later writings he occasionally used the expression "quantité consommée," he gave no indication that he meant by this anything else than "quantité possédée." It is as if he thought that the economist, *qua* economist interested in market behavior, had no more competence to derive utility functions from consumers' sensations than he had to derive these sensations from their presumed physiological, psychological and socio- logical determinants.[23] However that may be, his inattention to con-

---

[21] *Correspondence*, vol. I, pp. 308–311, *n.* (4) to Letter 211.
[22] See Black *et al.*, (1973, pp. 122–123 [388–389]).
[23] *Cf.* Mill (1844/1948, p. 132, *n.* *), where J. S. Mill contended "that Political Economy . . . has nothing to do with the consumption of wealth, further than as the

sumption can be confidently attributed to the fact that his gaze was fixed on the market place, and nowhere else. His pure theory was a catallactic "theory of the determination of prices under a hypothetical regime of perfectly free competition"; and it was strictly in that context that Walras invoked marginal utility.

What a far cry this was from the central concerns of Jevons or Menger. It is true that both Jevons and Menger, each in his own way, had caught glimpses of this or that salient aspect of general equilibrium analysis but never of the whole. Menger, in his theory of imputation[24] for example, had meditated deeply upon the same problem that Walras later treated with mathematical firmness and generality in his "Theorem of Maximum Utility of New Capital Goods Yielding Productive Services," as it appeared in the fourth (1900) and posthumously published definitive (1926) editions of the Eléments.[25] To Jevons we are indebted for a substantial mathematical argument functionally relating what we now call marginal productivity to marginal utility in Chapter V of his Theory of Political Economy, thereby broaching, if not solving, a significant general equilibrium problem. Jevons's "Preface to the Second Edition" of his Theory abounds in reflections of a general equilibrium character, but as he himself acknowledged in the same Preface, "Looking forward to the eventual results of the theory, I must beg the reader to bear in mind that this book was never put forward as containing a systematic view of economics."[26]

Premonitions of the whole, intuitive insights into the parts, programs for future investigation of general equilibrium are not enough. It remained for Walras alone among his "co-revolutionaries" of the 1870s to receive from his contemporaries, in a Jubilee Celebration at the end of his career, the honor of being proclaimed the first to have "established the general conditions of equilibrium."[27] And surely it is for that reason and for the the role he assigned in his grand system to marginal utility, rather than for the now outmoded theory of marginal utility itself, that

consideration of it is inseparable from that of production, or from that of distribution. We know not any of the *laws* of the *consumption* of wealth as the subject of a distinct science: they can be no other than the laws of human enjoyment. Political economists have never treated of consumption on its own account, but always for the purpose of the inquiry in what manner different kinds of consumption affect the production and distribution of wealth." I am indebted to Professor John Menefee of California State College, Bakersfield, whose unpublished working paper, "The Evolution of the Concept of Leisure in Economic Doctrines," called my attention to this passage.

[24] Menger (1871/..., pp. 67–70 and 123–126; pp. 106–109 and 149–152 of the English translation).

[25] Walras (1874/...), Lesson 27 of the 4th and definitive editions. Cf. second edition, §§259–261.

[26] Jevons (1871/..., pp. XLIII–XLIV of the 4th edition; p. 67 of the Pelican edition, where the Preface to the Second Edition is reprinted).

[27] Correspondence, vol. III, pp. 366–367, n. 5 to Letter 1696.

he is still honored or berated (as in Cambridge, England) by the foremost theorists of our day.

Jevons's accomplishment, though its impact on subsequent theory was not destined to be anything like as profound or far-reaching as that of Walras, was considerable. Certainly his "final degree of utility" is formally and analytically identical with Walras's *rareté*. Like Walras after him, Jevons looked upon his differential coefficient as a lethal weapon with which to strike down forever the classical theory of value. More-over, Jevons anticipated Walras in formulating the following two funda-mental propositions: (1) that *"the ratio of exchange of any two commodities will be the reciprocal of the ratios of the final degrees of utility of the quantities of commodity available after the exchange is completed,"*[28] a proposition which Jevons called the "keystone of the whole Theory of Exchange"; and (2) "that a person distributes his income in such a way as to equalize the utility of the final increments of all commodities consumed"[29] – Gossen's "second law," as he later learned.[30] When these propositions are reduced to symbolic form, they are found to have easily recognizable, but more precisely stated, counterparts in Walras.

There is, however, an important difference. In Walras, the theorem of proportionality of *raretés* to parametric market prices was used to derive individual demand and offer functions which, when aggregated over all individuals, served to determine equilibrium prices in a prespecified perfectly competitive market system. In Jevons, *per contra,* there is no analysis of the operations of the market mechanism by which his "consequent ratio of exchange" is arrived at. Jevons contented himself with describing his perfect market in quasi-institutional terms as a market in which "there must be no conspiracies for absorbing and holding supplies to produce unnatural ratios of exchange," and in which the "law of indifference" is in force, thus precluding effective transac-tions at other than equilibrium prices by virtue of a full and instantane-ous publication (compulsory, if necessary) of: (1) the stocks of commodi-ties available, (2) the "intentions of exchanging" (i.e., the individual demand and offer schedules) of all the dealers and (3) "the ratio of exchange [agreed upon] between any two persons."[31] It is, to be sure, a

[28] Jevons (1871/ . . . , p. 95 of the 4th edition; p. 139 of the Pelican editon; Jevon's italics).

[29] *Ibid.,* p. 140 of the 4th edition; p. 170 of the Pelican edition.

[30] *Ibid.,* p. XXXIV of the 4th edition; p. 61 of the Pelican edition.

[31] *Ibid.,* pp. 85–88 of the 4th edition; pp. 132–133 of the Pelican edition. Though Walras had less to say on the subject, he too saw the competitive market in a quasi-institutional light. He remarked in 1909 that he had assumed for his theoretical model "un régime hypothétique de *libre concurrence organisée* (ce qui est tout autre chose que le simple *laisser-faire)*" [Walras (1909), p. 581; Walras's italics]. Thus free competition in Walras's model was not spontaneous in origin, but something that had to be consciously *organized.*

perfect market not unlike that of Walras, but it is not one that could be seen to give rise to multiple equilibrium prices or, indeed, to any equilibrium price at all. Jevons, moreover, did not take systematically into consideration the interactions within a commercially interconnected network of markets.

Walras, while conceding Jevons's priority in the matter of marginal utility, was therefore justified in pointing out to Jevons: (1) that Jevons's ratio of exchange was nothing but a posited ruling price; (2) that Jevons had failed to derive "the equation of *effective demand* as a function of *price*, which could have been so easily deduced [from the 'final degree of utility function'] and which is so indispensable for the solution of the problem of the determination of equilibrium price;"[32] and (3) that Jevons had not produced "the theorem of general equilibrium and its corollary, viz. the laws of the emergence and variation of equilibrium prices."[33] In his Introduction to the Pelican edition of Jevons's *Theory of Political Economy*, R. D. Collison Black admitted that "Jevons's treatment of these matters cannot be regarded as satisfactory,"[34] and remarked elsewhere that Jevons's "economics would have been better. . . if he had dealt simply with the 'laws of demand' instead of trying to determine the 'laws of utility.'"[35]

Not only was Jevons's approach entirely different from that of Walras, but his point of departure also. Jevons started out from Bentham's felicific calculus;[36] I don't believe I have seen Bentham's name mentioned once in all of Walras's writings, published or unpublished, which is not surprising since he had always exhibited a strong antipathy to "utilitarisme."[37] Jevons focused his attention from the beginning on what Edgeworth called "Hedinometry"[38] and bestowed concentrated effort on an attempt to reduce utilitarian speculations to an exact science which would be useful as a foundation for the theory of value in exchange; while Walras peremptorily and nonchalantly – too nonchalantly some would say[39] – postulated a measurable marginal utility theory without more ado, for the sole purpose of rounding out his previously formulated catallactic theory of price determination.

Carl Menger clearly stands apart from the other two reputed founders of the modern marginal utility theory. Menger, of course, deserves to be celebrated no less than his two famous contemporaries as the discoverer

[32] *Correspondence*, vol. I, p. 397, Letter 275; my translation.
[33] *Ibid.*, vol. I, p. 414, Letter 286; my translation.   [34] *Op. cit.*, p. 21.
[35] Black *et al.*, (1973, p. 108 [p. 374]).
[36] Black (1972, pp. 122–127).
[37] Walras (1896/1936, pp. 194–196 in both editions); and Walras (1898/1936, pp. 457–459 in both editions).
[38] Edgeworth (1881, pp. 98–102).   [39] Georgescu-Roegen (1966, p. 18).

of a method of incorporating utility and scarcity into a novel, pathbreaking explanation of value. In fact, so impressive was Menger's performance that Stigler judges Menger's theory "greatly superior to that of Jevons"[40] and Georgescu-Roegen deplores the placing of Menger "by almost every historian on a lower level than either Walras or Jevons."[41] Von Hayek goes so far as to hold that Menger's *Grundsätze der Volkswirtschaftslehre* "provided a much more thorough account of the relations between utility, value and price, than is found in any of the works of Jevons and Walras."[42] No one familiar with the primary literature can doubt for a moment that Menger's treatment of the structure of wants in relation to *evaluation* was more profound and more penetrating not only than that of Walras who evinced no particular interest in such questions, but also than that of Jevons to whom the theory was, however, conceived on the analogy of a mechanical balance of physical forces, whereas Menger's theory was adorned with only one mechanical metaphor and that in the course of an argument purporting to prove that it is a mistake to regard "the magnitude of price as the essential feature of exchange."[43]

According to Menger, this "mistake" leads to "the further error of regarding the quantities of goods in an exchange as *equivalents*." Menger argued that quantities exchanged could only be *equivalents* "in the objective sense" if, *ceteris paribus*, exchanges were reversible; but since "experience tells us that in a case of this kind neither of the two participants would give his consent to such an arrangement [reversing the transaction], equality of the values of two quantities of goods (an equality in the objective sense) nowhere has any real existence."[44] As Georgescu-Roegen has observed, "Menger's theory cannot explain prices."[45]

Menger, however, did not mean to explain prices. If such an explanation had been his aim, surely he would have attempted to forge an analytical link between the "importance of satisfactions" and market prices. This he did not do. In his discussion of isolated two-party barter Menger never referred to rates of exchange while demonstrating the relation between given scales of "Bedürfnissbefriedigungen" and the quantities of horses and cows traded.[46] When he finally worked up to the case of "beiderseitiger Concurrenz," the connection between his scales of importance of want satisfactions and price formation found no place.[47]

[40] Stigler (1941, p. 135).   [41] Georgescu-Roegen (1966, p. 19).
[42] Hayek (1968, p. 125).
[43] Menger (1871/ . . . , pp. 172–173; p. 192 of the English translation).
[44] *Ibid.*, pp. 173–175, passages quoted from pp. 192–194 of the English translation.
[45] Georgescu-Roegen (1968, p. 251).
[46] Menger (1871/ . . . , pp. 163–167; pp. 183–187 of the English translation).
[47] *Ibid.*, pp. 175–179 and 201–206; pp. 194–197 and 216–220 of the English translation. *Cf.* Black *et al.*, (1973, p. 120 [386]).

Why should it, if market price is merely a superficial and incidental manifestation of much deeper forces at work in the exchange of goods and services?

The anomalous role of Menger in the "Marginal Revolution" was recently brought into high relief by Erich Streissler's question, "To What Extent was the Austrian School Marginalist?"[48] How could anyone ask such a question when everyone thinks of Carl Menger as one of the founding fathers, if not *the* founding father, of modern marginalism? Streissler, however, had good reason to raise this question, in view of the fact that Menger nowhere concerned himself with relative maximum or minimum values of a function, which Streissler rightly sees as embodying the essence of marginalism.[49] The issue does not hinge on Menger's eschewal of mathematics, for Menger could just as well have formulated a proper marginalist theory "in sentences of the common language,"[50] without any loss of precision, had he been so minded. But Menger kept too close to the real world for either the verbal or the symbolic formulation of the theory; and in the real world he saw no sharply defined points of equilibrium, but rather bounded indeterminancies not only in isolated bilateral barter but also in competitive market trading. To quote Streissler, "His [Menger's] economics in its substantive content was disequilibrium economics;"[51] it was also in a broad sense institutional economics.

It is not that Menger was unaware of tendencies to eventual equilibrium in the real world, but he was too conscious of the ubiquitous obstacles that, even *ceteris paribus,* impede the attainment of market equilibrium within anything less than secular delays. With his attention unswervingly fixed on reality, Menger could not, and did not, abstract from the difficulties traders face in any attempt to obtain all the information required for anything like a pinpoint equilibrium determination of market prices to emerge, nor did his approach permit him to abstract from the uncertainties that veil the future, even the near future in the conscious anticipation of which most present transactions take place. Neither did he exclude the existence of non-competing groups, or the omni-presence of monopolistic or monopoloid traders in the market.

Thorstein Veblen's strictures upon what he considered the Austrian preconception of human nature fit Jevons's or Walras's theory much better than they do Menger's. In Menger, man is not depicted as a

---

[48] Black *et al.,* (1973, p. 160 [426]).
[49] As G. L. S. Shackle expressed it, " . . . marginalism is (if I may be allowed to invent yet another word) simply maximalism or minimalism, when those are conceived in the formal mathematical sense" [Black *et al.* (1973, p. 325 [591])].
[50] Hicks and Weber, (1973, p. 38).
[51] Black *et al.,* (1973, pp. 172–173 [438–439]).

hedonistic "lightning calculator of pleasures and pains, who oscillates like a homogeneous globule of desire of happiness under the impulse of stimuli that shift about the area, but leave him intact."[52] Man, as Menger saw him, far from being a "lightning calculator," is a bumbling, erring, ill-informed creature, plagued with uncertainty, forever hovering between alluring hopes and haunting fears, and congenitally incapable of making finely calibrated decisions in pursuit of satisfactions. Hence Menger's scales of the declining importance of satisfactions are represented by discrete integers. In Menger's scheme of thought, positive first derivatives and negative second derivatives of utility with respect to quantity had no place; nothing is differentiable.

The absence of mathematical formulae and especially of applications of the classical calculus from Menger's work mark him off from Jevons and Walras in more than a formal sense. Carl Menger avoided the use of mathematics in his economics not because he did not know any better, but out of principle. When he wrote Walras on June 28, 1883 that he had been for some time thoroughly acquainted with Walras's writings,[53] he did not disclaim, as did other correspondents, sufficient knowledge of mathematics to follow these writings, which we may be sure he would have done if that had been the case.[54] Instead, Carl Menger declared his objection *in principle* to the use of mathematics as a method of advancing economic knowledge. He granted that mathematics has its uses as an expository device and as a subsidiary "Hilfsmittel," but genuine research or investigation, Menger insisted, should be directed toward the discovery of the underlying elementary causes of economic phenomena in all their manifold complexity. For the performance of this task what is required is not the mathematical method, but a method of process analysis tracing the complex phenomena of the social economy to the underlying atomistic forces at work. He called it the "analytic-compositive method."[55]

To understand what Menger meant by this, it may be useful to distinguish the type of *generative* casuality Menger had in mind from the *logical* causality on which Walras rested his case when he persisted in defending Auguste Walras's proposition, "La rareté est la cause de la valeur," as an analytically valid statement.[56] In Léon Walras's definitive general equilibrium model, proportionality between *raretés* and prices manifests itself everywhere: not only in exchange, but also in produc-

[52] Veblen (1919, p. 73).
[53] *Correspondence,* vol. 1, pp. 768, Letter 556.
[54] See Hicks and Weber, (1973, p. 44, especially *n.* 11).
[55] *Correspondence,* vol. 2, p. 4, Letter 602.
[56] Walras (1874/ . . . , §101 of the definitive edition; §98 of the 1st edition; §100 of the 2nd and 3rd editions).

322   Walras's place in economic thought

tion, capital formation and the holding of money. Having been taught by his father to regard universal concomitance and exact proportionality as the criteria of causality,[57] Walras felt that his construction of an overall system of simultaneous equations bound together by the marginal utility principle had proved that *rareté* is the cause of value. Menger, on the other hand, thought that the object of economic research was to discover those laws governing market phenomena which can be traced back to their ultimate genetic determinants in man's physiological, psychological and social nature. Mathematics cannot do this; the "analytical-compositive method" alone is appropriate.

The seeds of subsequent developments in economic theory found in Menger were very different from those found in Jevons and Walras. Several commentators on Menger have observed that Menger's non-calculus, numerical delineation of "scales of importance" of want satisfactions, being free from assumptions of continuity and differentiability, contained within it the germ of an ordinal, rather than a cardinal, conception of the measurement of utility.[58] Moreover, Menger's *Grundsätze*, with its stress on uncertainty in economic affairs and on the consequent search for information to mitigate the disadvantages of uncertainty,[59] foreshadowed present-day preoccupations with the stochastic and informational properties of economic systems. According to Carl Menger's son Karl Menger, a professional mathematician and an economist in his own right, the two eminent Austrians, Karl Schlesinger and Abraham Wald, who initiated crucial emendations of the Walrasian model, particularly on the side of the theory of production, drew their inspiration at least psychologically from the tradition in economics inaugurated by Carl Menger.[60]

What more need be said, after this, as to the folly of sticking a single label, whether it be "Marginal Revolution" or anything else, on the contributions of Jevons, Menger and Walras respectively – as if they could be homogenized! Indeed, outside the stereotype textbooks c. the history of economic thought, our three authors have been kept separate in the ordinary course of theoretical events. The leading theorists of our day do not even nod to Jevons or Menger; they talk with Walras, as Milton Friedman would say. Almost universally present-day writers on orthodox value theory refer to Walras alone as the founding father of their theoretical faith.[61]

[57] Auguste Walras (1831/1938, Chapter XVI, especially p. 234; pp. 235–236 of the Leduc edition); see also Auguste Walras (1849/1938, p. 317 in the Leduc edition).

[58] See, for example, Georgescu-Roegen (1968, p. 250).

[59] Black *et al.,* (1973, pp. 166–168 [432–434]); and Hicks and Weber, (1973, pp. 61–74 and 164–189).

[60] Hicks and Weber (1973, pp. 47–52).

[61] In a recent statistical study on the citation practices of doctorates in economics who received the degree between 1950 and 1955 from six major American universities, Stigler

Perhaps the time has come to question that faith, as G. L. S. Schackle has done in a paper entitled "Marginalism: The Harvest."[62] It is a harvest of doubts and difficulties profoundly considered and resolved so far as may be, not in the rejection of marginalism, but in the recognition of its limitations as a "frame of relevance and coherence" for a systematic explanation of how our economic universe works. Perhaps, too, a direct and close re-examination of the original texts of the 1870s may shed further light on the same troubling problem.

REFERENCES

Black, R. D. Collison (1972), "Jevons, Bentham and De Morgan," *Economica,* May 1972, 39, 119–134.
Black, R. D., Coats, A. W., and Goodwin, D. W. Craufurd, eds. (1973), *The Marginal Revolution, Interpretation and Evaluation.* Durham, North Carolina, Duke University Press, 1973.
Blaug, Mark (1968), *Economic Theory in Retrospect,* 2nd ed., Homewood, Illinois, Irwin, 1968.
Correspondence, see below Jaffé, William, ed., (1965).
Cournot, Antoine Augustin (1838/ . . .), *Recherches sur les principes mathématiques de la théorie des richesses,* Paris, Hachette, 1838. Reprint edited by George Lutfalla, Paris, Rivière, 1938. English Translation by Nathaniel T. Bacon, *Researches into the mathematical principles of the theory of wealth, edited by Irving Fisher, New York, Macmillan, 1927.*
Edgeworth, F. Y. (1881), *Mathematical Physics,* London, Kegan Paul, 1881. Series of Reprints of Scarce Tracts, No. 10, London, London School of Economics, 1932.
Georgescu-Roegen, Nicholas (1966), *Analytical Economics/Issues and Problems,* Cambridge, Mass., Harvard University Press, 1966.
   (1968), "Utility," *International Encyclopedia of the Social Sciences,* vol. 16, pp. 236–267, Macmillan Co. and Free Press, 1968.
Hayek, Friedrich A. von (1968), "Carl Menger," *International Encyclopedia of the Social Sciences,* vol. 10, pp. 124–126, Macmillan Co. and Free Press, 1968.
Hicks, J. R. (1934), "Léon Walras," *Econometrica,* October 1934, 2, 338–348.
Hicks, J. R. and Weber, W., eds. (1973), *Carl Menger and the Austrian School of Economics,* Oxford, Clarendon Press, 1973.
Hutchison, T. W. (1953), *A Review of Economic Doctrines, 1870–1929,* Oxford, Clarendon Press, 1953.
[Isnard, Achylle-Nicholas] Anon. (1781), *Traité des richesses,* 2 vols., London and Lausanne, Grasset, 1781.

and Claire Friedland (1975, pp. 486–488) found that in the subsequent articles in value theory published by these doctorates in the period from 1950 to 1968, Walras stood third, after Hicks and Samuelson, in the total number of citations, with Menger and Jevons nowhere in the running.
   [62] Black *et al.,* (1973, pp. 321–336 [587–602]).

Jaffé, William, ed. (1965), Correspondence of Léon Walras and Related Papers, 3 vols., Amsterdam, North Holland (for Royal Netherlands Academy of Sciences and Letters), 1965.

(1969), "A. N. Isnard, Progenitor of the Walrasian General Equilibrium Model," History of Political Economy, Spring 1969, 1, 19–43.

Jevons, W. Stanley (1871/ . . .), The Theory of Political Economy, London, Macmillan, 1871; 2nd ed. 1879; 4th ed. 1924. Pelican edition, R. D. Collison Black, ed., Harmondsworth, Middlesex, Penguin Books Ltd., 1970.

Menger, Carl (1871/ . . .), Grundsätze der Volkswirtschaftslehre, Vienna, Braumüller, 1871. Series of Reprints of Scarce Tracts, No. 17, London, London School of Economics, 1934. English translation, Principles of Economics translated by James Dingwall and Bert F. Hoselitz, Glencoe, Illinois, Free Press, 1950.

Mill, John Stuart (1844/1948), Essays on Some Unsettled Questions of Political Economy, London, John W. Parker, 1844. Series of Reprints of Scarce Works, No. 7, London, London School of Economics, 1948.

Poinsot, Louis (1842), Eléments de statique, 8th ed., Paris, Bachelier, 1842.

Robbins, Lord (Lionel) (1970), The Evolution of Modern Economic Theory, London, Macmillan, 1970,

Schumpeter, Joseph A. (1954), History of Economic Analysis, New York, Oxford University Press, 1954.

Stigler, George J. (1941), Production and Distribution Theories, The Formative Period, New York, Macmillan, 1941.

Stigler, George J. and Friedland, Claire (1975). "The Citation Practices of Doctorates in Economics," Journal of Political Economy, June 1975, 83, 477–507.

Veblen, Thorstein (1919), The Place of Science in Modern Civilization and Other Essays, New York: Huebsch, 1919.

Walras, Auguste (1831/1938), De la nature de la richesse et de l'origine de la valeur, Paris: Johanneau, 1831, 2nd ed., edited by Gaston Leduc, Paris, Alcan, 1938.

Mémoire sur l'orgine de la valeur d'échange, Paris, Typographie Panckoucke, 1849. Republished as appendix in Auguste Walras (1831/1938, Leduc edition, 1938, 316–343).

Walras, Léon (1874/1883), "Principe d'une théorie mathématique de l'échange," Séances et travaux de l'Académie des Sciences morales et politiques, January 1874, vol. 101 of the Collection, 33rd Year of New Series, Part I, 97–116; republished with minor revisions in Léon Walras (1883, 7–25).

(1874/ . . .), Eléments d'économie politique pure, 1st ed. (in two instalments), Lausanne, Corbaz, 1874–77; 2nd ed., Lausanne, Rouge, 1889; 3rd ed., Lausanne, Rouge, 1896; 4th ed., Lausanne, Rouge, 1900; definitive ed. (published posthumously), Lausanne, Rouge, 1926. Reprinted, Paris, Pichon and Durand-Auzias, 1952. English translation, Elements of Pure Economics, translated from the definitive edition by William Jaffé, London, Allen & Unwin, and Homewood, Illinois, Irwin, 1954. (Reprint of Economics Classics, New York, Augustus M. Kelley, 1969).

(1883), Théorie mathématique de la richesse sociale, Lausanne, Corbaz, 1883.

(1896/1936), Etudes d'économie sociale (Théorie de la répartition de la richesse sociale),

Lausanne, Rouge, 1896; 2nd edition, edited by G. Leduc, Lausanne, Rouge; and Paris, Pichon, 1936.

(1898/1936). *Etudes d'économie politique appliquée (Theorie de la production de la richesse sociale)* Lausanne, Rouge, 1898; 2nd edition, edited by G. Leduc, Lausanne, Rouge; and Paris, Pichon, 1936.

(1909). "Ruchonnet el le socialisme scientifique," *Revue socialiste,* July 1909, 50, 577–589.

18

THE NORMATIVE BIAS OF THE WALRASIAN MODEL: WALRAS VERSUS GOSSEN

Though Walras's *Eléments d'économie politique pure* is couched in the language of pure theory and appears, on the surface, as a completely *wert-frei* synoptic view of the interdependent operations of an economic system under a hypothetical regime of perfectly free competition, nevertheless the implicit moral convictions that inform the model occasionally show through—nowhere better than in Walras's theorem of maximum social satisfaction. I propose, therefore, to concentrate my attention on that theorem: showing in the first part how, for want of proper attention to Walras's moral bias, the theorem came to be misunderstood by Walras's most eminent critics, and, in the second part, how this bias was brought out into the open in Walras's analysis of Gossen's theory of maximum subjective gain from trade.

I

A common complaint against Léon Walras is that he misconceived the maximization of social satisfaction. A good example of this complaint appears in William Baumol's *Welfare Economics and the Theory of the State,* where we are told:

One of the most unfortunate bits of circular reasoning in the history of the discussion of our problem is found throughout Léon Walras's otherwise invaluable works. . . . [His] argument is the standard one, that given the price of any two commodities, the best any consumer can do for himself is to buy these commodities in such proportion that the ratio between their marginal utilities to him is equal to the ratio of their prices. Up to this point, no doubt, the argument is quite valid. But when one tries to argue further that in these circumstances

I am indebted to my colleagues, John Buttrick and Rasesh B. Thakkar, for assistance in the preparation of this paper. An earlier version was presented in 1974 at a Seminar on Walras in Tokyo under the joint auspices of Keio University and the Japanese Section of the History of Economics Society, and also at the Economics Seminar of the University of British Columbia. On both occasions I benefited from comments and criticism, and since then from helpful suggestions of the referee. Research support from the Canada Council and a Killam Senior Research Scholarship (1975–1977) is gratefully acknowledged.

consumers are as well off as human design and activity can make them, subject to the current state of technique and resources, that is an entirely different matter. . . . The price system, and the particular market price of each commodity, is a product of human activity, and, indeed, may be partly the result of exactly that type of consumer decision just considered. While it may be true that consumers are doing as well as possible for themselves given the level of various prices, it does not follow that they could not do still better for themselves, for example, by altering some of these prices from what they happen to be, or do better for others (in some sense in greater degree than they harm themselves) by e.g. paying higher prices or paying more than this role would require.

It is noteworthy that chary Wicksell . . . clearly saw the difficulties in the Walrasian argument. . . .[1]

I start with Wicksell's discussion, which Baumol considered "masterly," and which J. R. Hicks, more than thirty years earlier, had already declared definitive.[2] Though Wicksell held Walras's theory of exchange and production in the highest regard, he nevertheless took strong exception to Walras's theorem of maximum social gain under free competition, calling it "wrong or at least misleading" in one place,[3] 'undoubtedly wrong" in another,[4] and "quite untenable" in still another.[5] The criticism received its most ample development in the *Lectures on Political Economy*, where Wicksell showed himself, as Baumol put it, "chary," for he was careful to emphasize the specific constraint that Walras placed upon his theorem in its first enunciation in the *Eléments*. The theorem there reads:

The exchange of two commodities for each other in a perfectly competitive market is an operation by which all holders of either one, or of both of the two commodities [obtain, changed in second edition to] *can obtain the greatest possible satisfaction of their wants consistent with the condition that the two commodities are bought and sold at one and the same rate of exchange throughout the market.*[6]

Wicksell quite rightly understood Walras's conditioning clause to mean that Walras was speaking of a relative social maximum of utility subject to the constraint of uniformity of price; and Wicksell further

---

[1] Baumol (1965), pp. 60–62.

[2] Hicks (1934). Toward the close of his essay published on the occasion of the hundredth anniversary of the birth of Léon Walras (hereinafter referred to as L.W.), Sir John wrote: "Even he [L.W.] did not emancipate himself entirely from that sham utilitarianism which was the bane of his contemporaries, and which led them to suppose that the working of the free market 'maximized utility' for the community as a whole" (p. 348). Wicksell's inspiration was acknowledged in a footnote to this sentence, reading, "Cf. Wicksell's final exposure of this fallacy (*Lectures,* I, pp. 73 ff.)."

[3] Wicksell (1893/1954), p. 19. Here, as elsewhere in these notes, the page references are to the English translations of Wicksell's writings.

[4] Wicksell (1901/1934), Vol. I, p. 75. [5] Wicksell (1913/1958), p. 167.

[6] Walras (1874/ . . .), §99 of the 4th and subsequent eds. of the *Eléments d'économie politique pure,* Walras's italics.

perceived that implicitly the maximum is delimited by "existing proprietary rights."[7] Wicksell, however, did not make clear all that Walras meant by uniformity of price, nor did he indicate that Walras intended the condition of uniformity of price to assure the invariance of the existing distribution of wealth (or property, as he called it) under market trading. According to Walras, it is not by violating the principle of "justice in exchange" that the injustices of the existing distribution of property are corrected, but by applying another set of principles, those of "distributive justice."[8]

For a fuller explanation of what Walras meant, we must go to his article, "Théorie de la propriété," which was first published in the *Revue socialiste* in 1896.[9] Only in this article did Walras specify the particular type of uniformity of price he had in mind as a constraint on the social maximum. It was none other than the uniformity that emerges spontaneously and automatically in a perfect market, i.e., a market so organized that there is no viscosity in the flow of buyers and sellers toward what each conceived to be his best bargain, nor any impediment to the flow. As Walras stated it, uniformity of price is a condition such that,

if, at any given moment, there were several different prices quoted [in the same market] for the same commodity, sellers would be free to move from a point where the price was lower to a point where the price was higher and buyers would be free to take the opposite course, so that, in consequence of these moments, price would find the same level [throughout the market].[10]

It should not be overlooked that in the "Théorie de la propriété" Walras designated the uniformity of price thus attained "as a condition of justice."

Another of Walras's requirements for "justice in exchange" was that the price to be held uniform be a real price, not a nominal or money price.[11] After all, in Walras's theories of exchange, production and

[7] Wicksell (1901/1934), Vol. I. pp. 72–83.
[8] See footnotes 15, 27, and 28. Cf. Jaffé (1975), pp. 812–13, 816, and 819–21.
[9] Walras (1896), pp. 212–13. The page references both here and in the following notes are to the republished version of the "Théorie de la propriété" in Walras (1896/1936).
[10] *Ibid.*, p. 212; my translation. Cf. Cournot (1838/ . . .), Chapter IV, §23, note 1: "On sait que les économistes entendent par *marché*, non pas un lieu déterminé où se consomment les achats et les ventes, mais tout un territoire dont les parties sont unies par des rapports de libre commerce, en sorte que les prix s'y nivellent avec facilité et promptitude."
[11] See Walras (1896), p. 212: "*L'intervention de la monnaie* ne trouble pas non plus les conditions de justice de l'échange, si la monnaie ne change pas de valeur entre le moment où on la reçoit et le moment où on la donne. La fixité ou la régularité de variation de la valeur de la monnaie d'un point à un autre au même moment, et surtout d'un moment à un autre sur un même point, est donc essentielle à l'exercice du droit de propriété" (Walras's italics).

capital formation, in which money plays no role as a store of value, the utility to be maximized, whether on the individual scale or the social scale, relates to real goods and not to a mere medium of exchange. That, it seems to me, is the reason why Walras included in his condition of uniformity of price the stipulation that when money does intervene purely and simply as a medium of exchange, its purchasing power not only be the same at every point in the market at a given moment of time, but also remain the same in the course of receiving money and paying it out to effect a desired exchange of real goods. Walras's express purpose in specifying this requirement of his condition of uniform price was to eliminate any fortuitous redistributional backwash from exchange that might otherwise result when money intervenes in the process.

All this is in the *Eléments,* though not in so many words. We need only consider Walras's "equations of exchange" representing the budget constraint in his multi-equational model of general equilibrium.[12] These "equations of exchange" assert that at uniform prices expressed in terms of a given *numéraire, every* trader ends up with a vector of assets having the same *numéraire* value as his initial vector of assets. However much a trader may benefit subjectively by an exchange yielding him maximum satisfaction within the limits prescribed by competitively determined uniform prices, the *numéraire* value of his assets remains unchanged, so that he is no richer or poorer after the exchange than he was before. In Walras's theoretical model, the only way an individual can become richer is by capital formation through saving, and the only way he can become poorer is by consuming more than his income, but never richer or poorer by exchange at equilibrium prices in a perfect market operating under the rule of free (atomistic) competition. Thus, from the standpoint of the market as a whole, exchange by itself has no distributional effects, provided always that prices are determined by free competition and are uniform.

Obviously this does not preclude an individual from becoming richer or poorer from one period to the next in consequence of social changes in tastes, technology, resources, capital, etc. in the interval. In the *Eléments d'économie politique pure,* however, Walras assumed more or less tacitly that all such variables remain constant within the period in which the static equilibrium he defined is established. Even his theory of capital formation is confined to the determination of equilibrium at the moment decisions to invest are made on the basis of pre-existing data. This is as far as Walras could go in his heroic effort to squeeze capital formation into his static model. In his pure economics, therefore, he left out of account the economic consequences of investment once carried

[12] Walras (1874/ . . .), §§118, 210, and 244 of the 4th and subsequent eds.

out.[13] Only in a paper in applied economics, "La bourse, la spéculation et l'agiotage,"[14] did he discuss the sequential effects of new investment and other changes in the data. These effects, he argued, could be held to a minimum, if the practice of stock market speculation, which he defended in principle as socially beneficial, were closed by law to all but well-informed specialists, with the public in general excluded from the stock market and restricted to spot trading in reputedly established securities of "blue-chip" quality at a retail counter.

Uniformity of competitively determined price represented for Walras not only an analytic ideal, but an ethical ideal as well, constituting an indispensable pillar of social justice.[15] In the "Théorie de la propriété," Walras defined justice in exchange (or "commutative justice") in terms of two conditions: first, the complete freedom of every trader to pursue his own advantage in the market; and second, the complete elimination from the market of any chance for a trader to profit by exchange at the expense of his counterpart or anyone else.[16] The first condition is satisfied by the assumed perfection of the market mechanism, and the second by the stipulated universality of the budget restraint from which no trader is exempt in the Walrasian general equilibrium schema. Walras's multi-equational system of general equilibrium thus appears profoundly moralistic, at least in terms of the individualistic, bourgeois moral outlook characteristic of nineteenth-century European culture.

It was on moral grounds rather than on grounds of economic efficiency that Walras momentarily dropped his pure theory mask in §§222 and 223 of the Eléments to interject a strong plea for the removal of all obstacles (such as restraints of trade and monopoly practices) that stand in the way of absolutely free competition and freedom of production. This was not because he was under any illusion that free competition in

---

[13] See Walras (1874/ . . .), §274 of the 4th and subsequent eds. The telling phrase L.W. used in his theory of capital formation was "quantités à fabriquer de capitaux neufs" (op. cit., §252 and passim, my italics).

[14] Walras (1880/ . . .).

[15] See Walras (1860), pp. 44–45: "En tant qu'êtres libres et personnels, tous les hommes sont égaux. Les personnes s'opposent aux choses; mais toute personne, en tant que personne, en vaut une autre. Ce principe sert de base à une première forme de justice, la justice commutative, qui a pour attribut une balance.

"En tant qu'ils accomplissent librement leur destinée d'une manière plus ou moins heureuse ou plus ou moins méritoire, il se révèle chez les hommes des différences d'aptitudes, de talent, d'application, de perservérance, de succès qui les font inégaux; et cette inégalité est le fait sur qui se fonde la justice distributive, laquelle a pour symbole une couronne.

"Egalité des conditions; inégalité des positions, telle est alors la véritable formule sociale...."

[16] See Walras (1896), p. 212: "Il s'agit à présent de passer du troc à l'échange économique en introduisant sur le marché plusieurs échangeurs concurrents, avec la condition qu'il n'y aura pour tous qu'un prix unique . . . et de savoir si les conditions ne favorisent ni les acheteurs ni les vendeurs au détriment les uns des autres."

a perfect market stood supreme in generating the highest possible sum total of satisfactions for society, but because it was a system superlatively designed to eliminate profit both from exchange and from production. He was far from condemning the pursuit of profit, which, in fact, he regarded as necessary for the working of his system, since profits and losses serve as indicators to direct the movement of entrepreneurs from branches of production yielding less utility to branches yielding more. He counted, however, on free competition in an ideally perfect market to perform automatically the moral function of stamping out profits[17] that are something for nothing, unearned, the fruit of guile and antisocial conspiracy, and therefore unjust.

The constraint of zero profits (and zero losses) is implicit in Walras's second formulation of his theorem of maximum social utility, now amplified to read:

Production in a market ruled by free competition is an operation by which services can be combined and converted into products of such a nature and in such quantities as will give the greatest possible satisfaction of wants within the limits of the double condition: [1] that each service and each product have only one price in the market, namely the price at which the quantity supplied equals the quantity demanded, and [2] that the selling price of the products be equal to the cost of the services employed in making them.[18]

Here the first condition, requiring the uniform price to be the equilibrium price, was designed to obviate untoward distributional effects. If any transaction or partial transaction were allowed to take place at other than the equilibrium price, let us say in the course of a realistic *tâtonnement* process via firm contracts, i.e., without the use of Walras's imaginary "tickets" *("bons")*, then one of the parties to the contract might find himself richer in terms of *numéraire* than he would have been had the price been the equilibrium price, and the other party poorer,[19] in neither case as a result of saving or dissaving. The second condition, equating selling price to cost, is obviously synonymous with zero profit zero loss. In that case also, production is followed by no distributional effects either in favor of or against any entrepreneur.

I believe Walras had the same elimination of distributional effects in mind in his discussion of the theory of two-person, two-commodity barter, which he attributed to Jevons.[20] Walras envisaged the encounter of two prospective "Jevonsian" barterers as starting out with a proposal by one of them of a trial price and then turning into a haggling contest,

[17] Walras (1874/ . . .), §188 of the 4th and subsequent eds.
[18] *Ibid.*, §221.   [19] Jaffé (1967), pp. 2–3.
[20] Walras (1896), pp. 207–9. L.W. interpreted Jevons's theory of exchange between two "trading bodies" as a theory of barter between two individuals. See Jevons (1871/ . . .), pp. 95–101, corresponding to pp. 139–44 of the 1970 ed.

if, at the price first proposed, the quantities reciprocally offered and demanded of the two commodities did not match, but without any actual exchange of commodities intervening until the quantities demanded and offered became equal. "Alors le troc s'effectue," which means that only then does any effective exchange take place.

Walras was convinced of the theoretical possibility of the same sort of suppression of distributional effects in multiperson market trading, provided that the markets are appropriately organized. In §42 of the *Eléments,* he took the stock market as the closest approximation in the real world to his theoretically perfect market in order to illustrate how equilibrium price is established in reality. He described how the price of a given security is bid up or down in case of excess demand or excess offer until the excess is wiped out. In the second edition of the *Eléments* he added that on the appearance of excess demand, "Theoretically, trading should be suspended" ("Théoriquement l'échange doit être suspendu"); and on the appearance of excess offer, "Suspension of trading" ("Suspension de l'échange").[21] If no trading is allowed at "false prices" in real markets, there too the possibility of distributional effects is eliminated.

When these clarifications of Walras's constraint on his theorem of maximum social utility are taken into account, Wicksell's critique of the theorem loses much of its force. The critique, which Hicks and Baumol echoed, assumed that Walras intended his theorem to state that, subject to uniformity of price, free competition yields a higher social maximum of satisfaction than any other system of price determination could achieve. I can find no evidence of this either in the *Eléments* or in any other of Walras's writings.

To be sure, at the threshold of his career as a theorist, Walras believed that the prices and quantities of goods produced under free competition are the best possible—until he was persuaded by Lambert Bey, a highly respected Saint-Simonist and engineer, that no economist had ever furnished proof of such a proposition. Wicksell, who cited Walras's account of the incident to set the tone of his critique, unfortunately misread the issue.[22] He thought that Lambert Bey had made an "onslaught on the foundations of free trade theory" viewed as a system for procuring the best possible "exchange values." This, however, is not what Walras reported. According to Walras, Lambert Bey had merely argued that the case for free competition had not been made. Walras,

[21] Walras (1874/ . . .), §42 of the 4th and subsequent eds. See also p. 566 of the English translation, Collation Note [a] to Lesson 5.

[22] Wicksell (1901/1934), Vol. I, pp. 73–74. For L.W.'s account of the Lambert Bey incident, see Walras (1898/1936), pp. 466–67.

though forced to agree, then and there conceived the youthful ambition to furnish the missing proof himself—only to encounter soon afterwards an insurmountable obstacle. His father, Auguste Walras, who had wrestled with the same sort of problem in his own way, pointed out to Léon that the satisfactions enjoyed by different persons are incommensurable and therefore cannot be aggregated.[23] Walras's mature formulation of his theorem of maximum social utility under free competition shows how well he learned his father's lesson.

Wicksell, failing to see this, got off on the wrong foot and misdirected his critique. At the outset, he properly chided Walras for not perceiving that in the case of multiple equilibria, the several equilibrium positions could not "simultaneously represent positions of maximum satisfaction,"[24] but made more of this oversight than it deserved. According to Walras's "remarque" at the end of §156 of his *Eléments*, " ... multiple current equilibrium prices, which, as we have seen ... , were perfectly possible in the case of exchange of two commodities, are, in general, not possible, in the case of exchange of several commodities one for another." As Walras's treatment of the two-commodity case appears to be little more than a preliminary exercise to prepare the way for his theory of the multicommodity case, which Walras imagined did not admit of "multiple equilibrium prices," his failure to probe the utility implications of multiple equilibria in the two-commodity case, though an analytical fault, is of trivial significance.

After this sally, Wicksell brought up his really heavy analytical artillery to complete the demolition of Walras's theorem; and he succeeded perfectly in demolishing a theorem that was not Walras's at all. The attack was misdirected because Walras had not assumed that the subjective advantages and disadvantages to different persons are commensurable or addable. Hence it was beside the point for Wicksell to argue, in opposition to Walras's theorem, that since uniform monopoly or administered prices could certainly procure for favored individuals more satisfaction than they could have obtained from competitive equilibrium prices, though everyone else might be worse off, a system of prices can always be found at which exchanges will produce a larger sum of utility for all individuals taken together than can be produced at competitive prices.[25] *Quis negavit?* Certainly Walras never denied this. On the contrary, when we come to Walras's analytical discussion of Gossen, we shall see that Walras affirmed it; but for other than economic reasons, he refused to consider Gossen's maximum as beneficial to society.

[23] Jaffé (1972), p. 389.   [24] Wicksell (1901/1934), Vol. I, p. 75.
[25] *Ibid.*, pp. 79–80.

Baumol was even more severe than Wicksell in his criticism. We have seen that he denounced Walras's theorem as "one of the most unfortunate bits of circular reasoning in the history of the discussion of our problem." Circular, yes; unfortunate, no. I do not think Walras intended it to be other than circular, for the simple reason that his propositions bearing on maximization of social satisfaction subject to specified constraints are, I should say, essentially definitional, like Pareto's concept of optimality for that matter. In my view, Walras's relative maximum of social satisfaction is nothing more and nothing less than an anticipation of Pareto optimality, with the same virtues and the same defects. The mathematical prelude to Walras's propositions simply demonstrate the internal consistency of the definition—and this demonstration has never been challenged, not even by Walras's severest critics.

The merits of any definition depend not only on its internal consistency, but also on its usefulness for solving a given problem or set of problems. Once we identify Walras's problem as, in essence, a conceptual problem, then his "stipulative definition"[26] of a relative maximum of social satisfaction falls into place, however unsuitable the definition may be for other purposes. Walras's aim, even in his "pure economics," was prescriptive or normative rather than positive or descriptive. His object was to formulate an economic system in conformity with an ideal of social justice[27] compatible with the inexorable exigencies of man's sentient nature and his environment.[28] We may quarrel with the para-economic purpose Walras had in mind and disagree with his natural law philosophy of social justice. That, however, is another story, which has nothing to do with the formal properties of Walras's ideologically directed argument.

Wicksell's and Baumol's criticisms leave one with the impression that Walras fell into a "wrong or at least misleading" theory of maximum social satisfaction because he did not know any better. As far back as

[26] Hanson (1969, pp. 27–28) distinguished between *"historical-authoritative"* definitions that are factual reports of usage, and *"stipulative-prescriptive"* definitions that are arbitrary inventions specially designed for use in a proposed context.

[27] L.W. expounded his ideal of social justice in his "Recherche de l'idéal social," a series of public lectures he delivered in Paris in 1867–1868 (Walras 1896/1936), pp. 25–202). These lectures attest to L.W.'s indebtedness to his father, Auguste Walras, for his social philosophy.

[28] For L.W.'s views on the relation between social ethics and natural necessity, see Walras (1860), where we read, for example, "Ainsi, la théorie très ingénieuse de l'application de l'algèbre à la géometrie et les deux exemples cités ci-dessus, auxquelles on en pourrait ajouter mille autres, démontrent assez que c'est à la morale qu'il appartient de se subordonner aux sciences naturelles, sinon dans son principe, au moins dans ses applications, et que toute morale qui se permettrait de contredire la théorie du carré de l'hypoténuse, les lois de la réfraction, le fait de la circulation du sang, ou les résultats de la théorie de la valeur d'échange, serait une morale ridicule et caduque" (p. 32).

1885, Wilhelm Laundhardt held the same poor opinion of Walras's performance on that score. He called it a "serious error" for Walras to hold that, as Laundhardt put it, "what is generally the best is most surely achieved by the natural operation of the force of free competition, by 'laissez faire, laissez passer.' "[29] When this passage was translated from the German for Walras, he wrote immediately to Launhardt, on May 20, 1885, protesting in the following terms:

I stated that free competition procures maximum effective utility *within the limits of the condition of uniformity of price,* in other words a relative, not an absolute, maximum. It is perfectly clear that if one supposes commodities to be sold at a high price to the rich and at a low price to the poor, all that the rich will be compelled to forego are luxuries, while the poor will be able to afford necessities, and [consequently] there will be a considerable increase in effective utility. . . . It remains, however, to be seen whether uniformity of price is required by justice. This is a question which falls outside the purview of pure economics, but which I shall be very careful to examine in that part of our science which deals with the distribution of wealth and in which considerations of social ethics must enter. All I can say for the present, and I think you will agree, is that the object is not an absolute maximum of economic welfare, but a maximum economic welfare *compatible with justice.*[30]

Pareto, unlike Launhardt, saw perfectly clearly what Walras was driving at and did not like it. He wrote to Pantaleoni, on December 19, 1908, apropos of Walras's theoretical aims, " . . . I do not agree that pure economics *demonstrates* how events ought to occur. . . ; I find it inadmissible to study what *ought* to be rather than what is. . . ."[31]

II

More important than Walras's own declarations of purpose or the acute observations of others on the normative character of his "pure economics" is his analysis of Gossen's theory of maximum social gain from

---

[29] Launhardt (1885/1963), p. 30; my translation. Paradoxical as it may seem in view of his own criticism of L.W.'s theorem of maximum social satisfaction, Wicksell rejected Launhardt's interpretation and correction of the theorem (Wicksell (1893/1954), p. 76, note 2).

[30] Jaffé (1965), Vol. 2, pp. 49–51, Letter 652; my translation of the excerpts cited; Walras's emphasis.

[31] De Rosa (1960), Vol. III, p. 121, Letter 590; my translation of passages from the following sentence: "Per riguardi personali non ho mai detto che dal Walras ho solo preso il concetto dell'equilibrio economico *in un caso particolare;* che non accetto in nessun modo il suo modo metafisico di trattare la scienza; che non posso trovare buono che adoperi il termine *rareté* ora in un senso ora in un altro, traendo in inganno il lettore; che non ammetto che ci sia, come dice lui, un metodo razionale superiore al metodo sperimentale; che non ammetto che l'economia pura *dimostri* come debbono seguire i fatti, mentre è l'inverso; che non accetto di studiare ciò che *deve* essere, ma che invece studio ciò che è; che è da bambini figurarsi che si dimostra colle formole dell'economia pura la convenienze per lo Stato di ricomprare le terre, di stabilire il bimetallismo, ecc. ecc. ecc."

exchange. This analysis first appeared in §160 of the second edition of Walras's *Eléments*[32] and was later expanded in his "Théorie de la propriété" already alluded to above.

In both places Walras directed his attention to Gossen's proposition that in two-person, two-commodity barter the greatest sum total of "happiness" (*"Genuss,"* as Gossen called it) is achieved when the "value" (*"Werth,"* in the sense of utility) of the last atom of each commodity exchanged is the same for one barterer as for the other.[33] This proposition is, like Walras's definition, essentially "stipulative," but in Gossen's case it is the definition of a maximum maximorum subject only to the real social budget constraint, that is, subject to the limitation in the quantities of goods available as compared with the quantities wanted for perfect bliss in the whole economic system. Walras translated Gossen's verbal statement into a mathematical proposition that can be derived and generalized as follows with the aid of a simpler notation than Walras employed.

Consider, as Gossen does, a universe of two commodities, *(A)* and *(B)*, and two barterers, Messrs. 1 and 2. Let the initial endowments of commodities *(A)* and *(B)*, which are designated by the first subscript, be

$$\bar{x}_{a1}, \bar{x}_{b1} \quad \text{(for Mr. 1)}$$
$$\bar{x}_{a2}, \bar{x}_{b2} \quad \text{(for Mr. 2)}.$$

Let the corresponding (unknown) amounts of *(A)* and *(B)* to be held on completion of Gossen's ideal barter be

$$x_{a1}, x_{b1} \quad \text{(for Mr. 1)}$$
$$x_{a2}, x_{b2} \quad \text{(for Mr. 2)}.$$

Now, assuming with Gossen as with Walras that the utilities of the two commodities are independent, we may write the utility function of the *j*th individual ($j = 1,2$) as

$$U_j(x_{aj}, x_{bj}) = \Phi_{aj}(x_{aj}) + \Phi_{bj}(x_{bj}). \qquad (1)$$

Since these functions are twice differentiable, separable, and addable not only in the intercommodity sense but also (for Gossen, though not

[32] It was only in the interval between the first and second eds. of the *Eléments* that L.W. learned of the existence of Gossen's *Entwicklung*. See Walras (1874/ . . .), p. 580 of the English translation, Collation Note [c] to Lesson 16.
[33] See Gossen (1854/1927), p. 85. *"Es muss jeder der beiden Gegenstände nach dem Tausche unter A und B der Art sich vertheilt finden, dass das letzte Atom, welches jeder von einem jeden erhält, beiden gleich grossen Werth schafft. Es ergiebt dieses die einfache Betrachtung, dass bei jeder andern Vertheilung die Uebertragung des Atoms, welches bei dem einen geringern Werth schafft, auf den andern, bei diesem grössern Werth, also in Summa mehr Werth hervorbringen würde, und es folgt denn hieraus, dass, um dieses Grösste zu erreichen, in der Regel ungleiche Quantitäten gegen einander zu vertauschen sind."*

for Walras) in the interpersonal sense, we may write Gossen's social utility function of the two persons together as

$$U = U_1 + U_2 = \sum_{i=a}^{b} \Phi_{i1}(x_{i1}) + \sum_{i=a}^{b} \Phi_{i2}(x_{i2}). \tag{2}$$

Function (2) is a mathematical representation of the "happiness" that Gossen wanted to maximize. The maximization is, however, subject to the constraint that the respective total quantities of *(A)* and *(B)* remain constant. Without production (or destruction) of either commodity, Gossen's maximization of (2) is thus subject to the social budget constraint, which may be written as

$$x_{a1} + x_{a2} = \overline{x}_{a1} + \overline{x}_{a2} \tag{3}$$
$$x_{b1} + x_{b2} = \overline{x}_{b1} + \overline{x}_{b2}.$$

To prove Gossen's theorem of maximum social "happiness," we need only form the Lagrangean function

$$
\begin{aligned}
L(x_{a1}, x_{a2}, x_{b1}, x_{b2}, \lambda_a, \lambda_b) = &\sum_{i=a}^{b} \Phi_{i1}(x_{i1}) + \sum_{i=a}^{b} \Phi_{i2}(x_{i2}) \\
&+ \lambda_a(x_{a1} + x_{a2} - \overline{x}_{a1} - \overline{x}_{a2}) \\
&+ \lambda_b(x_{b1} + x_{b2} - \overline{x}_{b1} - \overline{x}_{b2}),
\end{aligned} \tag{4}
$$

and set the first-order partial derivatives of the function with respect to the x's and the indeterminate multipliers, λ_a and λ_b, equal to zero. Among the six resulting equations, we have

$$d\Phi_{a1}/dx_{a1} = d\Phi_{a2}/dx_{a2} \tag{5.1}$$
$$d\Phi_{b1}/dx_{b1} = d\Phi_{b2}/dx_{b2}. \tag{5.2}$$

It should be noticed that the solution given by equations (5.1) and (5.2) is much stronger than the usual (Walrasian) solution given below in (6), which merely asserts the *ratio* of the marginal utilities of the two commodities is the same for the two individuals. Such as it is, Gossen's solution was restated by Walras in terms, but for the notation, of the above equations (5.1) and (5.2), in order to contrast it with his own solution. In the fourth and definitive editions of the *Eléments,* Walras concluded significantly:

It is obvious that the maximum utility arrived at in this [Gossen's] way is not the relative maximum of free competition, nor is it compatible with the condition that all traders voluntarily exchange the two commodities at a common and uniform ratio. It is rather an absolute maximum which disregards the [two-fold]

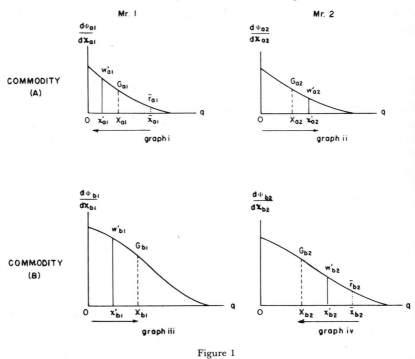

Figure 1

condition of uniformity of price and equality between effective offer and effective demand at that price, *thus abolishing* [private] property.[34]

Walras's inference that Gossen's solution is incompatible with the right to private property was elucidated geometrically in the "Théorie de la propriété."[35] There, with the aid of four graphs based on Gossen's Figure 20,[36] Walras graphically juxtaposed his own (as well as Jevons's)[37] theorem of maximum satisfaction in two-person, two-commodity barter with that of Gossen in order to bring out the difference in their respective distributional effects. Walras's diagram is here reproduced as Figure 1 with the original axes transposed and the lettering changed to conform to the analytical notation used above. The four curves depict the independent marginal utility functions of commodity *(A)* and com-

[34] Walras (1874/ . . .), §162 of the 4th and subsequent eds.; my italics. For changes in this statement from ed. 2 to ed. 4 of the *Eléments,* see English translation, p. 580, Collation Note [d] to Lesson 16. My translation here is slightly more literal than the version found in the *Elements of Pure Economics.* In ed. 4, L.W. inserted a footnote to this passage, reading: "Voyez Etudes d'économie sociale. Théorie de la propriété."
[35] Walras (1896), pp. 210–11.   [36] Gossen (1854/1927), p. 83.
[37] See footnote 20.

modity *(B)* for Messrs. 1 and 2 between whom there is an exchange of
the two commodities. Walras assumed that Mr. 1's endowment consists
of the $\overline{0x}_{a1}$ units of *(A)* shown in graph i and none of *(B)* as the absence of
an $\overline{0x}_{b1}$ segment in graph iii attests; while Mr. 2's original endowment
consists of the $\overline{0x}_{b2}$ units of *(B)* shown in graph iv and none of *(A)*, whence
the absence of an $\overline{0x}_{a2}$ segment in graph ii.

In the Walras (and Jevons) schema, the barterers are supposed to
haggle, without, however, effecting any exchange until they finally agree
upon a mutually acceptable ratio of exchange or price of *(B)* in terms of
(A), $p_{b,a}$, say 2. Then the whole exchange takes place in a single act in
conformity with Jevons's "law of indifference." Thus at $p_{b,a} = 2$, Mr. 1
trades $\overline{x}_{a1}x'_{a1}$ of *(A)* for $\overline{0x'_{b1}}$ of *(B)*, and Mr. 2 trades $\overline{x}_{b2}x'_{b2}$ of *(B)* for $\overline{0x'_{a2}}$ of
(A). The price $p_{b,a}$ is the "market" equilibrium price determined by
equality between the quantities offered and demanded, which are in
turn determined by the utility maximization drive of each barterer,
separately subject to his original endowment. As is well-known, this
simultaneous maximization result is defined analytically by

$$\frac{d\Phi_{b1}/dx_{b1}}{d\Phi_{a1}/dx_{a1}} = \frac{d\Phi_{b2}/dx_{b2}}{d\Phi_{a2}/dx_{a2}} = \frac{e_a}{e_b} = p_{b,a} = 2, \tag{6}$$

where e_a and e_b are, respectively, the quantities of *(A)* and *(B)* exchanging
hands. These quantities are defined in Figure 1 as

$$e_a \equiv \overline{x}_{a1}x'_{a1} \equiv 0x'_{a2}$$

and

$$e_b \equiv \overline{x}_{b2}x'_{b2} \equiv 0x'_{b1}.$$

Graphically, then, the Walras-Jevons condition of constrained maximum, stated in equations (6), appears as

$$\frac{x'_{b1}w'_{b1}}{x'_{a1}w'_{a1}} = \frac{x'_{b2}w'_{b2}}{x'_{a2}w'_{a2}} = \frac{\overline{x}_{a1}x'_{a1}}{\overline{x}_{b2}x'_{b2}} = p_{b,a} = 2,$$

where

$$x'_{b1}w'_{b1} \neq x'_{b2}w'_{b2} \text{ and } x'_{a1}w'_{a1} \neq x'_{a2}w'_{a2},$$

except by chance.

In Gossen's schema, though the two individuals have the same initial
endowments and the same marginal utility functions as in the Walras
schema, they do not haggle nor do they really barter. They behave as
though they threw their initial endowments into a common pool either
voluntarily or under command in order that these endowments might be
divided between them in such a manner as to maximize *the sum total of*

their utilities added together. As we have seen analytically in equations (5.1) and (5.2), this entails a division of *(A)* and *(B)* between Mr. 1 and Mr. 2 such that, graphically now, $\overline{X_{a1}G_{a1}} = \overline{X_{a2}G_{a2}}$ and $\overline{X_{b2}G_{b2}} = \overline{X_{b1}G_{b1}}$, these marginal utilities being, for Gossen, interpersonally commensurable. Out of their respective initial endowments, Mr. 1 gives up $\overline{x_{a1}X_{a1}}$ $(=\overline{OX_{a2}})$ to Mr. 2; and Mr. 2 gives up $\overline{x_{b2}X_{b2}}$ $(=\overline{OX_{b1}})$ to Mr. 1. Since the final outcome is independent of the distribution of initial endowments between the two individuals, Walras saw in the Gossen division a total disregard of individual property rights.

It is evident that with both $\overline{OX_{a2}} < \overline{Ox'_{a2}}$ and $\overline{OX_{b2}} < \overline{Ox'_{b2}}$ Mr. 2 is worse off than he would have been had he traded freely at the assumed "market" equilibrium price of 2 of *(A)* for one of *(B)*; and Mr. 1 with both $\overline{OX_{a1}} > \overline{Ox'_{a1}}$ and $\overline{OX_{b1}} > \overline{Ox'_{b1}}$ is better off. Moreover, in the particular example under consideration, Mr. 2's assets after the Gossen division are less than they would have been after a Walras-Jevons barter exchange, the final assets in the two situations being valued in *numéraire* at the same equilibrium "market" price $p_{b,a} = 2$:

$$\overline{OX_{a2}} + 2\,\overline{OX_{b2}} < \overline{Ox'_{a2}} + 2\,\overline{Ox'_{b2}} \; ;$$

and Mr. 1's assets are greater:

$$\overline{OX_{a1}} + 2\,\overline{OX_{b1}} > \overline{Ox'_{a1}} + 2\,\overline{Ox'_{b1}} \; .$$

This amounts to a transfer of assets from Mr. 2 to Mr. 1, which Walras denounced as incompatible not only with justice in exchange, but also with property rights, especially if the Gossen division is mandatory.

In conclusion, it is worth remembering that from his very first book on economics, *L'économie politique et la justice* published in 1860, to his last utterance on the subject at his jubilee in 1909,[38] Léon Walras's dominant preoccupation was with the problem of social justice. By osmosis, as it were, this paramount preoccupation passed through the partition Walras himself erected to separate his normative economics ("économie sociale") from his pure economics.[39] Thus Walras's pure economics became imbued with a distinctive moral content and was given a normative direction. Walras's latent purpose in contriving his general equilibrium model was not to describe or analyze the working of the economic system as it existed, nor was it primarily to portray the purely economic relations within a network of markets under the assumption of a theoretically perfect regime of free competition. It was, as Pareto perceived, rather to demonstrate the possibility of formulating axiomati-

[38] Walras (1909).   [39] Jaffé (1965), Vol. I, pp. 208–12, Letter 148.

cally a rationally consistent economic system that would satisfy the demands of social justice without overstepping the bounds imposed by the natural exigencies of the real world. It is to the great credit of Walras as an economic analyst that in formulating this system, he invented a model that proved to be eminently serviceable to later economists who were more positivistic in their approach than Walras or who were inspired by different social goals. While it is undeniable, even when due account is taken of Walras's underlying purpose, that his model can still be shown to exhibit flaws and serious limitations that are open to criticism, it is not justifiable, in my opinion, to impugn as technical defects the inadequacies of the model for dealing with other problems than those it was originally designed to solve.

REFERENCES

Baumol, W. J., *Welfare Economics and the Theory of the State, with a New Introduction, Welfare and the State Revisited* (Cambridge, Massachusetts: Harvard University Press, 1965).

Cournot, A., *Recherches sur les principes mathématiques de la théorie des richesses* (Paris: Hachette, 1838); reprint edited by Georges Lutfalla (Paris: Marcel Rivière, 1938); English translation by Nathaniel T. Bacon, *Researches into the mathematical principles of the theory of wealth*, Irving Fisher, ed. (New York: Macmillan, 1927).

De Rosa, G., ed., *Vilfredo Pareto, Lettere a Maffeo Pantaleoni*. 3 volumes (Rome: Banca Nazionale del Lavoro, 1960).

Gossen, H. H., *Entwicklung der Gesetze des menschliches Verkehrs und der daraus fliessenden Regeln für menschliches Handeln* (Brunswick: Fr. Wieweg & Sohn, 1854); 3rd ed. (Berlin: Prager, 1927).

Hanson, N. R., *Perception and Discovery. An Introduction to Scientific Inquiry* (San Francisco: Freeman, Cooper & Co., 1969).

Hicks, J. R., "Léon Walras," *Econometrica*, II, No. 4 (Oct. 1934), 338–48.

Jaffé, W., ed., *Correspondence of Léon Walras and Related Papers*. 3 volumes (Amsterdam: North-Holland, for the Royal Netherlands Academy of Sciences and Letters, 1965).

Jaffé, W., "Walras's Theory of *Tâtonnement:* a Critique of Recent Interpretations," *Journal of Political Economy*, LXXV, No. 1 (Feb. 1967), 1–19.

Jaffé, W., "Léon Walras's Role in the Marginal Revolution of the 1870s," *History of Political Economy*, IV, No. 2 (Fall 1972), 379–405.

Jaffé, W., "Léon Walras, an Economic Adviser Manqué," *Economic Journal*, LXXXV, No. 340 (Dec. 1975), 810–23.

Jevons, W. S., *The Theory of Political Economy* (London: Macmillan, 1871); 4th ed., H. Stanley Jevons, ed. (London: Macmillan, 1924); Pelican ed., R. D. Collison Black, ed. (Harmondsworth, Middlesex: Penguin Books, 1970).

Launhardt, W., *Mathematische Begründung der Volkswirtschaftslehre* (Leipzig: Engelmann, 1885); photographically reproduced (Aalen: Scientia Verlag, 1963).

Walras, L., *L'économie politique et la justice. Examen critique et réfutation des doctrines. économiques de M. P.-J. Proudhon* (Paris: Guillaumin, 1860).

Walras, L., *Eléments d'économie politique pure ou Théorie de la richesse sociale,* 1st ed. (in two installments) (Lausanne: Corbaz, 1874–1877); 2nd ed. (Lausanne: Rouge, 1889); 3rd ed. (Lausanne: Rouge, 1896); 4th ed. (Lausanne: Rouge, 1900); definitive ed. (published posthumously), 1926; reprinted (Paris: Pichon and Durand-Auzias, 1952); English translation by William Jaffé, *Elements of Pure Economics* (London: Allen and Unwin, 1954); Reprints of Economic Classics (New York: Augustus Kelley, 1969).

Walras, L., "La bourse, la spéculation et l'agiotage," *Bibliothèque universelle et Revue suisse,* 3rd period, V (March 1880), 452–76; and VI (April 1880), 66–94; republished in Walras (1898/1936), pp. 401–45.

Walras, L., "Théorie de la propriété," *Revue socialiste,* XXIII, No. 138 (June 1896), 668–81; and XXIV, No. 139 (July 1896), 23–35; republished with minor changes in Walras (1896/1936), pp. 205–39.

Walras, L., *Etudes d'économie sociale (Théorie de la répartition de la richesse sociale),* first ed. (Lausanne: Rouge, 1896); second ed., G. Leduc, ed. (Paris: Pichon and Durand-Auzias, 1936).

Walras, L., *Etudes d'économie politique appliquée (Théorie de la production de la richesse sociale),* first ed. (Lausanne: Rouge, 1898); second ed., G. Leduc, ed. (Paris: Pichon and Durand-Auzias, 1936).

Walras, L., "Ruchonnet et le socialisme scientifique," *Revue socialiste,* L, No. 295 (July 1909), 577–89.

Wicksell, K., Über Wert, Kapital und Rente nach den neueren nationalökonomischen Theorien (Jena: Fisher, 1893); Series of Reprints of Scarce Tracts, No. 15 (London: 1933); English translation by S. H. Frowein, *Value, Capital and Rent* (London: Allen & Unwin, 1954).

Wicksell, K., Föreläsningar i Nationalekonomi; Första delen: Teoretisk Nationalekonomi, Vol. 1 (Lund: 1901); English translation by E. Classen, Lionel Robbins, ed. *Lectures on Political Economy,* Vol. I (London: Routledge, 1934).

Wicksell, K., Review of Vilfredo Pareto's *Manuel d'économie politique* in the *Zeitschrift für Volkswirtschaft, Sozialpolitik und Verwaltung,* XXII (1913), 132–51; English translation in *Selected Papers on Economic Theory* by Knut Wicksell, Erik Lindahl, ed. (London: Allen and Unwin, 1958), pp. 159–75.

19

WALRAS'S ECONOMICS
AS OTHERS SEE IT

Così è (se vi pare)

– Luigi Pirandello

In this article, as in my brief review of Michio Morishima's *Walras'
Economics: A Pure Theory of Capital and Money*[1] for the *Economic Journal,* the
question is whether Morishima's interpretation of Walras's model is
correct or whether his extensions, emendations, and corrections of the
original model, designed to bring it in line with modern theoretical
interests, distort the historical record. Let me say at once that Morishima's argument is by no means valueless for being flawed from the
historian's point of view. On the contrary, such is the brilliance and
analytical penetration of his misinterpretations that their very contrast
with the original brings into sharp relief important but hitherto neglected aspects of Walras's theoretical writings.

At the outset of his preface to *Walras' Economics* (p. VII),[2] Morishima
expresses the hope that he "will not . . . give the reader a distorted view
of Walras" by focusing attention exclusively on the *Eléments* (1874 . . .),
without reference to Walras's other writings. A hope, however, is not a
demonstration. The fact, which Morishima notes, that Léon Walras left
his studies *(Études)* in applied and "social" economics in the form of two
volumes of collected papers (1898; 1896) instead of systematically
organized treatises is no proof of their irrelevance to an understanding
of Walras's "theoretical kernel," as Morishima calls it. Morishima
makes no mention of several other writings of Walras or of the recent
publication of his private economic letters and papers (Bousquet, 1964;

I owe particular thanks to my colleague, John Buttrick, for editorial guidance and for
insights into analytical subtleties that had escaped me. I am no less grateful to Samuel
Hollander, Robert Clower, Claude Ménard, Stephen Ferris, Charles Plourde, and John
Worland, who commented helpfully on earlier versions of this article. To the Social
Sciences and Humanities Research Council of Canada I am deeply indebted for
continuing research grants.

[1] Morishima (1977). My critique is restricted to a discussion of Morishima's reading
of Walras and does not extend to an evaluation of his own theory of capital and money for
which Walras is taken as the point of departure.

[2] The page numbers in parentheses (p. . . .) refer to Morishima (1977).

343

Jaffé, 1965) as potential sources of illumination of the "kernel" in question.

Morishima's decision to look no further than the *Elements of Pure Economics* in order to capture the essence of what is worth preserving of Walras's contributions has a long tradition. Vilfredo Pareto, who acknowledged Walras's formal pure theory as his principal source of inspiration, repeatedly denounced everything else in Walras's work as futile metaphysics.[3] Sir John Hicks, in his *Econometrica* article of 1934 on "Léon Walras," dismissed Walras's writings in applied economics, including, odd as it may seem, the theory of money, as "relatively uninteresting" (1934, p. 347). According to Hicks, "it was in pure economics that his [Walras's] real interest lay, and the discovery of the conditions of static equilibrium under perfect competition was his central achievement." Hicks did not deign to mention the "social economics." And Joseph Schumpeter, in his deeply moving obituary on the death of Walras in 1910, maintained a discreet and complete silence on everything Walras had ever written apart from pure theory. What Schumpeter really thought of Walras's *political,* rather than *pure,* economics came out later, in the *History of Economic Analysis,* where he wrote: "Unfortunately, Walras himself attached as much importance to his questionable philosophies about social justice, his land-nationalization scheme, his projects of monetary management, and other things that have nothing to do with his superb achievement in pure theory. They have cost him the goodwill of many a competent critic, and must, I imagine, try the patience of many of his readers" (1954, pp. 827–28).

It is surprising that Morishima should have fallen in with the tradition established by Pareto, Hicks, and Schumpeter. In his other books, especially in *The Economic Theory of Modern Society* (1976), Morishima displays a sensitive awareness of the broader historical, sociological, and ideological setting of the formal economic theories considered. The nearest he comes to taking so broad a view in his *Walras' Economics* is to allege that Walras's general equilibrium model was founded on a "four-class view of society" (pp. viii and 125), the four classes being workers, landowners, capitalists and entrepreneurs—with entrepreneurs playing an important decision-making role as Morishima sees it (p. 7). Unfortunately this attribution to Walras of a four-class conception of society with entrepreneurs in a decision-making role is sheer invention and a distortion of the record.

If Morishima had availed himself of what he calls "the full story of Walras' economics," he would have learned that instead of a four-class

[3] *E.g.:* Guido Sensini (1948), p. 61; G. De Rosa (1960), vol. III, p. 121; and Vilfredo Pareto (1935), § 1732, *n.* 2 and § 2129, *n.* 1.

view of society, which Morishima regards as "more advanced than Marx's two-class view" (p.9), the Walrases, father (Auguste Walras) and son, also held a two-class view, but an altogether different one from that of Marx. Though the Walrases, like Marx, envisaged their two classes in conflict, their idea of the composition of the classes and of the nature of the struggle was far removed from that of Marx. They saw the class struggle as a conflict between landowners and private proprietors of natural monopolies on the one side and all the rest of society, *including entrepreneurs and capitalists,* on the other.[4] As for the role of the entrepreneur in Walras's analytical model, the *Eléments* restricted it to that of arbitrageur, and nothing else. But of this more anon.

Where, in my estimation, Morishima got off on the wrong foot was in supposing that "the ultimate aim [of Walras's *Eléments*] was to construct a model, by the use of which we can examine how the capitalist system works" (p. 4). That, I contend, was not the aim of the *Eléments,* either ultimate or immediate. In my recent article, "The Normative Bias of the Walrasian Model: Walras versus Gossen" (1977), textual evidence is presented to show that the *Eléments,* instead of aiming to delineate a theory of the working of any real capitalistic system, was designed to portray how an imaginary system *might* work in conformity with principles of "justice" rooted in traditional natural law philosophy,[5] though the system remained subject to the same forces, the same "passions and interests," and the same material and technological constraints that govern the real world. The *Eléments* was intended to be and is, in all but the name, a realistic utopia, i.e., a delineation of a state of affairs nowhere to be found in the actual world, independent of time and place, ideally perfect in certain respects, and yet composed of realistic psychological and material ingredients.[6]

This view of the *Eléments* is diametrically opposed to that of Morishima and indeed to that of all twentieth century commentators on

---

[4] This view of class conflict was rooted in a distinctively French tradition of which an excellent account is found in E. Allix (1913).

[5] For a full-dress account of Walras's social philosophy, see Marcel Boson (1951) and for further bibliographical references on the subject, see Jaffé (1975), p. 813, n. 1.

[6] In an early paper, "Méthode de conciliation ou de synthèse," written in 1868 and repeatedly echoed in later writings, Walras plainly stated, "In science, our domain is that of ideas, of the ideal, of perfection. Nothing prevents us from defining, i.e. sifting out of experience by abstraction, the idea of social wealth, of capital and income, of productive services and products, of landowners, workers and capitalists, of entrepreneurs, of the market and prices..." (Walras, [1896] 1936, p. 187; my translation). And again, under a significant subheading, "Synthèse de l'utilitarisme et du moralisme," in the same paper, Walras went on to say, "... if the relative or perfectibility pure and simple is the hallmark of politics, the absolute or rigorous perfection is the hallmark of science. We are now in the domain of science; and therefore, in this domain, we look for the absolute or perfection. Semi-utility or near justice will not do; we must have complete utility or justice entire and full" (Walras, [1896] 1936, p. 188; my translation).

Walras's economics I am aware of. Since Walras was not always consistent or explicit in his approach, appeal against my view can be made by citing such passages in the *Eléments* as, for example, "my [Walras's] theory of capital formation . . . is indeed the abstract expression and rational explanation of facts of the real world."[7] This sentence is a translation of a passage in the fourth edition of the *Eléments* (1874 . . . , pp. xvii–xviii), which Walras claimed he was quoting without any change from the preface to a second edition. It so happens that that was not the case. In the second edition, the excerpted words read in fuller context: " . . . ma théorie de la capitalisation . . . est bien [ce qui doit être une théorie de cette nature:] l'expression fidèle et l'explication exacte des phénomènes de la réalité" (1874 . . . , p. xxii). This, in fact, was not what he reproduced in the fourth edition, but rather a revision of the sentence made for the third edition, the revision reading, "ma théorie de la capitalisation . . . est bien [ce qui doit être une théorie de cette nature:] l'expression abstraite [in place of 'fidèle' of the second edition] et l'explication rationnelle [in place of 'exacte' of the second edition] des phénomènes de la réalité." This was clearly more than a bit of stylistic polishing: the change makes a world of difference—all the more so because his idealization of reality was dictated not only by a desire "for simplicity" or analytical convenience but also by Walras's aim to depict his "idéal social" as a "synthèse de l'utilitarisme et du moralisme."

Of course, the words "l'expression . . . et l'explication . . . des phénomènes de la réalité" occur in both versions; but this only confirms Walras's constant preoccupation with creating a model of a terrestrial utopia in contrast with the otherworldly utopias of the early French socialists.[8] In repeatedly calling attention to the realism of the ingredients of his model, Walras meant to furnish a theoretical foundation for a rationally conceived program of remedial measures, which he called (or miscalled) "scientific socialism." From edition to edition, the *Eléments* reflected Walras's purpose in ever purer form: to devise "an *abstract* expression and *rational* explanation of facts of the real world," rather than "a *faithful* expression and *exact* explanation" of these facts [italics added]. When in the course of the successive distillations of his pure theory, Walras kept recalling the real-world source of his distillate, it was not to return to the real world for the sake of explaining how it works, but to show that the world of his ideal model, in its mathematical formulation, was still made up of perfectly real components after unwanted or unneeded impurities had been left behind in the retort.

Morishima mistakes Walras's verbal specification of unwanted resi-

[7] Walras (1874/ . . .), p. 46 of the English translation (1954).
[8] Cf., Walras ([1896] 1936), p. 5 and A. Duvillier (1956).

dues for aspects of reality that Walras left out of his equations only because he did not have sufficient mathematical skill to incorporate them into his formal schema of general equilibrium (p. 10). There is no doubt that Walras's mathematical prowess was quite limited, as he himself admitted.[9] It is, however, one thing to refine, correct, and modernize Walras's prolix, intuitive, and relatively primitive mathematics or to introduce needed emendations in analytical detail (such as the substitution of a composite commodity in the place of Walras's unsatisfactory *numéraire*) (Morishima, 1977, pp. 32–33), but it is quite another thing so to exploit the resources of latter-day mathematics as to give a different direction to Walras's theory than the one originally intended.

The question, therefore, is how to find out what Walras intended by his *Eléments*. On this point the *Eléments* itself is not clear; indeed it is ambiguous and ambivalent enough to furnish some support for Morishima's contention that Walras's "ultimate aim" was "to construct a model by the use of which we can examine how the capitalist system works." As George Stigler has taught us, when quotations and inconsistent counter-quotations abound, "textual interpretation must uncover the main concepts in the man's work, and the major functional relationships among them. . . . This rule of consistency with the main conclusions may be called the principle of scientific exegesis" (1965, p. 448). I should go further and consult not only "the man's work," but also the *Zeitgeist* in which "the man's work" was conceived.

When Walras declared in one of his last utterances that he had, from the beginning, considered it the purpose of pure economics to present a rigorously rational solution of "la question sociale" as an indispensable preliminary to the prescription of policy measures (1909, p. 587), he was not only rejecting the crude empiricism of which he accused the socialists of his day, but was faithfully following a tradition established by the "philosophes" of eighteenth-century France who were, above all, believers in the sovereign efficacy of systematized reason in coping with social and political problems. From his first full-length publication in economics (1860) to his closing reflections on his life work (1909), Walras posed "la question sociale" in terms of social schemes for correcting the flagrantly unjust distribution of property that reduced the laboring masses to life-long desperate poverty.[10] Repelled by the philosophical and scientific shortcomings of the "socialists" in coping with this problem, Walras's father had turned to conventional political

[9] See Jaffé (1965), vol. 2, p. 450, Letter 1010.
[10] Professor Claude Ménard of Paris reminds me that in nineteenth-century France, "la question sociale" embraced a whole gamut of social, political, and ideological, as well as economic, instabilities and conflicts generated by the "industrial revolution." *Cf.*, A. A. Cournot (1877), pp. 278–325.

economy, which he found equally disappointing; and so did Léon Walras after him. Father and son sought to transform classical political economy into a science that could serve as an intellectual basis for the needed reform of society. The *Eléments* was, consequently, designed, not as a "study of men as they live and move and think in the ordinary business of life" (Marshall, 1920, Book 1, chap. 2, §1), but as a theoretical representation of a just economy from the standpoint of "commutative justice"; "distributive justice" called for separate treatment in the *Études d'économie sociale*. [11]

When Walras defined his *pure economics* as, "in essence, the theory of the determination of prices under a hypothetical regime of perfectly free competition," [12] i.e., under a regime of strictly atomistic competition unexampled at any time in history, he chose a hypothesis that, in effect, precluded all gains (or losses) from trade in terms of *numéraire*. Under his assumption of perfectly free competition, "commutative justice," which would contribute to the welfare of the laboring poor, could be achieved—at least in principle. The market system, if perfectly competitive, could be shown to work automatically in the desired direction, though by itself it achieved only half of justice, the other half, "distributive justice," requiring appropriate and deliberate institutional reform in the distribution of property.

It is clear that Walras had no liking for realism as such. In fact, he vehemently denounced it in all its manifestations: in art and in literature as well as in philosophy, science, and economics. [13] At the same time, he recoiled from pure idealism. He preferred to take the position of a "synthesist," with the object of reconciling what is best in opposing schools, thereby creating a new entity. This passion for reconciling polar opposites permeated Walras's pure economics as it did virtually every subject he touched on in his writings. [14] His point of view, as he once

[11] Walras (1896). The disassociation of pure economics from normative considerations, which Walras enunciated in § 4 and § 223 of the *Eléments*, turns out, when read in the total context of part I and §223, to be a disassociation solely from issues of "distributive justice" inherent in the distribution of property, and not of "commutative justice" latent in any particular organization of market trading. "Commutative justice" in the traditional Aristotelian-Thomistic sense relates to acts of voluntary exchange in which the market value received is equal to the market value given up, thus excluding money gains to any party from trading; whereas "distributive justice," applied, say, to the award of prizes, is characterized by proportionality to superior performance, without any connotation of equivalence.

[12] Walras (1874...), p. XII of the second edition and repeated in all subsequent editions, see also §§ 221-22 of the definitive edition and p. 585 of the English translation, Collation Notes [a]-[d] to Lesson 22.

[13] Walras (1896), pp. 24-171. "Théorie générale de la société"; and pp. 175-202, "Méthode de conciliation ou de synthèse."

[14] Nowhere is this point of view more succinctly advocated by Walras than in his "Chroniques de la quinzaine" that he contributed to the *Gazette de Lausanne* from 12 January 1878 to 18 May 1878 over the pseudonym "Paul." See Jaffé (1965), vol. I, pp. 559-60, notes (4) and (5) to Letter 401.

described it,[15] was that while it is true that theoretical systems unrelated to observation and experience are bound to be as empty, shallow, and false as are representations in art completely devoid of reality, it is no less true that reality, observation, and experience, however indispensable to science as to art, serve only as a point of departure, or rather a foundation on which to mount creations of abstraction and imaginative invention. This position, which impressed upon Walras's *Eléments* the character of what I have called a realistic utopia, is not simple, but riddled with complexities inherent in the intellectual controversies that raged in Walras's day. From the historical standpoint, it is within this setting of the intellectual life of nineteenth-century France that the *Eléments* needs to be interpreted. To interpret it in a later setting (say, of a twentieth-century London School of Economics) is to commit a flagrant anachronism.

Walras's method of molding reality into an ideal fiction of "commutative justice" subject to economic efficiency is nicely illustrated by the role he assigned to his entrepreneur within the play of market forces under perfect competition. As Morishima sees it, Walras was guilty of an inconsistency in identifying the entrepreneur with the capitalist-investor in his mathematical model while holding, at the same time, a "four-class view of society" in which entrepreneurs constitute a class

---

If we may judge from an undated manuscript in Walras's hand, which Professor Gaston Leduc, who had inherited it from Walras's daughter, passed on to me, Walras, in his early youth, to which I attribute the manuscript, leaned toward idealism and was certainly skeptical then, as he remained through his life, of the value of accumulations of descriptive statistics so much in vogue in his day. The manuscript reads:

I am an idealist. I believe that ideas reshape the world after their own image and that the ideal a man conceives for his century commands the attention of all humanity. I believe that the world has striven without success for eighteen centuries to realize the ideal of Jesus and the first of the Apostles. I believe that the world will take another eighteen, or perhaps twenty, centuries, in trying, without better success, to realize the ideals of 1789, which we now perceive more clearly and which our successors will illuminate. How happy would I be if I could imagine that I had shed one ray of light, however small, on this vision. In this respect, I am swimming against the current of my century. Facts are now in fashion: the observation of facts, the investigation of facts, the acceptance of facts as laws. In stormy times, political power falls into the hands of the ignorant masses. Art, science, philosophy are swept away. Facts become masters; empiricism triumphant reigns supreme. Analytical minds closely study the explosion and wait for chaos gradually to take over as an object of fond description and serene glorification. As for me, I will have no part in this. It is possible that my ideal is narrowly conceived. But it is less so than my halting expression of it would lead one to believe. However that may be, I take comfort in my ideal—it is my refuge against the avalanche of brute facts; and if my century crushes me, as the universe Pascal's reed [Pascal had referred to man, though weak and miserable, as a thinking reed, still thinking despite being crushed by the universe], at least I shall have been spared being part of the century. I shall have lived in the past and in the future. [My translation with the assistance of my colleague, Professor C. Edward Rathé.]

[15] *Gazette de Lausanne*, January 12, 1878: "Chronique de la quinzaine."

apart, one of whose functions it is to make investment decisions (p. 7). Actually, Walras did neither. We have already seen that he held no "four-class view of society." It remains to show that his mathematical model neither expressed nor implied any identification of the entrepreneur, *qua* entrepreneur, with the capitalist-saver, and could not do so without destroying the essential character of the model.

The source of Morishima's misinterpretation lies, I suspect, in his failure to take due account of Walras's special use of the French term *profits* to designate the capital-services *in kind* yielded by capital goods (§§ 172 and 232),[16] not the value of these services in money or *numéraire*, and certainly not what is usually meant by *profits* in French or by "profit" in English.[17] For gain in the form of a positive difference between selling price and cost, Walras used the word *bénéfice*, a synonym of *profits* in everyday French and generally translatable as "profit" in English. When, therefore, Walras defined *his* entrepreneur as "a fourth person, entirely distinct from ... [the landowner, the worker and the capitalist], whose role it is to lease land from the landowner, hire personal faculties from the labourer, and borrow capital from the capitalist, in order to combine the three productive services in agriculture, industry and trade" (§ 184), and when he said that "in a state of equilibrium, *les entrepreneurs ne font ni bénéfices ni pertes*" ("entrepreneurs make neither profit nor loss," § 188),[18] he did not mean that there are no returns to capital in a state of equilibrium, but only that there is nothing left over for the entrepreneur, *qua* entrepreneur, when selling price equals *all* costs of production including the cost of capital-services for which payment is made to capitalists. It should be noted that in Walras's formal theory, capitalists alone decide, by virtue of their right of ownership, in what physical form their savings are embodied.

Of course, Walras's entrepreneur is not precluded from simultaneously assuming other roles. As Walras put it: "It is undoubtedly true that, in real life, the same person may assume two, three, or even all four of the above-defined roles. In fact, the different ways in which these roles may be combined give rise to different types of enterprise. However that may be, the roles themselves, even when performed by the same individual, remain distinct. From the scientific point of view, we must keep these roles separate and avoid both the error of the English economists who identify the entrepreneur with the capitalist and the error of a certain number of French economists who look upon the

[16] Unless otherwise indicated, both in the text and in these notes, the section numbers preceded by the symbol § are those of the definitive edition of the *Eléments* or the English translation.

[17] See Walras (1874), English translation, p. 525: Translator's Note [2] to Lesson 17.

[18] See also Walras (1874...), English translation, p. 526, Translator's Note [6] to Lesson 8; and Oulès, ed. (1950), p. 161, *n*. (35).

entrepreneur as a worker charged with the special task of managing a firm" (§ 184). It is solely in his role as entrepreneur that he is destined in equilibrium to "make neither profit [i.e. *bénéfices*] nor loss."

Why, then, should anyone want to be an entrepreneur if he is denied any reward or share in the national income for the trouble he takes in buying productive services and selling products? Walras's answer was that in the real world, which is rarely, if ever, in full economic equilibrium, one stands a fair chance of making a *bénéfice* by what amounts to arbitrage transactions (§§ 188 and 273).[19] In Walras's model, his "fourth person" acts like a catalytic agent, taking no part in the conversion of productive services into products, but merely standing by to prevent the reaction from going awry. Neither the entrepreneur's services (strictly interpreted) nor the price of these services find any place in Walras's "solution of the equations of production." Only when deviations from equilibrium are signalled by differences between selling price and cost of production does Walras's entrepreneur spring into action. Like an arbitrageur, he siezes the occasion to make a *bénéfice* and in so doing quickly chokes off the source of the *bénéfice*. Walras perceived perfectly clearly that in the state of full equilibrium defined by his mathematical model, "we may even go so far as to abstract from entrepreneurs and simply consider the productive services as being, in a certain sense, exchanged directly for one another, instead of being exchanged first against products, and then against productive services" (§ 188). This, indeed, is what his mathematical model comes to. There the entrepreneur is not identified with the capitalist, as Morishima mistakenly supposes; the entrepreneur is simply eliminated.[20]

In Walras's eyes, theory required that the role of the entrepreneur, *qua* entrepreneur, be narrowly construed (§§ 366 and 369).[21] To be sure, Say was right in describing "entrepreneurs" of the real world as often performing simultaneously the functions of management, investment, and risk-taking (or better, uncertainty-bearing). It was, however, only in so far as the "entrepreneur" is an ultimate private risk-taker, and only in so far as his positive or negative earnings are "bénéfices

[19] *Cf.,* Paul H. Cootner (1968), p. 117.

[20] That the entrepreneur has no place in the static distillate is gradually receiving recognition in the literature. See the *American Economic Review,* vol. 58, no. 2 (May 1968), pp. 60–98: especially the testimony of William J. Baumol, p. 64, and Harvey Leibenstein, p. 72. See also Israel M. Kirzner (1973) and (1978, p. 31), who attributes the absence of the entrepreneurial role from modern microeconomics to "its decisive absorption of Walrasian influence," without, however, tracing this influence to its source.

[21] In § 366, Walras criticized the English School for failing to distinguish between the role of the capitalist as recipient of "l'intérêt du capital" (the interest yield on invested capital) and the role of the entrepreneur as recipient of "le *bénéfice* de l'entreprise" (Walras's italics). In § 369, where Walras acknowledged his indebtedness to J. B. Say for drawing this and other distinctions, he found Say nevertheless wanting in a proper perception of their full theoretical implications.

d'entreprise," which depend, as Walras observed, "upon exceptional and not upon normal circumstances" (§ 366), that these earnings were excluded from Walras's equilibrium equations. Thus in his whole theoretical construct, Walras deliberately abstracted from uncertainty. This explains the absence of the entrepreneur, *qua* entrepreneur, from the Walrasian model in its "normal" operation.

As a practicing consulting actuary for an important insurance company, "La Suisse," Walras probably thought the distinction that F. H. Knight later drew between "measurable risks and unmeasurable uncertainty" (1921, pp. 19–20 and chap. 7) too self-evident to call for explicit definition. The ν_k, $\nu_{k\prime}$, $\nu_{k\prime\prime}$ ... in Walras's equations of capital formation show that he admitted *insurable risks* into his static system (§ 232, penultimate paragraph). Measurable risks are not incompatible with static assumptions when the insurance of these risks relieves the insured, on payment of a "technologically" determined premium, not only of the burden of bearing them but also of the burden of holding money he would otherwise need to hold against any "casual and stochastic demands" occasioned by these risks. So long as an individual is insured, he incurs no risk at all; he only incurs the expense of a premium, which can be reckoned as a normal item of cost of production. The ν_k, $\nu_{k\prime}$, $\nu_{k\prime\prime}$ ... in Walras's equations, far from symbolizing the presence of uncertainty in Walras's model, turn out to be a device for eliminating any vestige of uncertainty.

Of course, Walras's insurance premiums have an unexpressed time dimension. So do Walras's quantities demanded, quantities offered, quantities produced, and quantities saved and invested, which are all reckoned per unit of time, like the rate of gross or net return on capital and the rate of interest on money loans. While it is perfectly true that time in this sense inheres in Walras's model, that does not prevent the model from being essentially "timeless." It should be noted that the "unit of time" in terms of which the rates are calculated may be of any length as measured by clock or calendar, provided that in the interval considered no "changes in the data of the problem" can take place to affect anyone's state of expectations and give rise to unmeasurable uncertainties.

I trace the difference between Morishima's and my own interpretation of Walras's theory of *tâtonnement* (which I am reserving for detailed treatment elsewhere[22]) to Morishima's persistent disregard of the distinction between barren time and time productive of "changes in the data of the problem." Walras's theory of *tâtonnement* is a theory of the mechanics,

---

[22] In "Another Look at Léon Walras's Theory of *Tâtonnement.*"

not the history, of the emergence and maintenance of general equilibrium. To stress the connection between his ideal model and reality, Walras initially undertook to demonstrate how forces at work in the real world must, given perfect competition, generate (or restore) general equilibrium when it does not exist (or is disturbed). Here, however, Walras ran against a snag, which he had not taken into account in the first three editions of the *Eléments*.[23] As *tâtonnement* is described in the earlier editions,[24] if Walras had allowed the adjustment process to take time, the process itself might well have given rise to "changes in the data," in which case time would not be sterile, and a whole Pandora's box of theoretically intractable dynamic phenomena would fly open. To elude a snag of this sort, he introduced into the fourth edition his device of "tickets" ("bons," § 207), by means of which he could eliminate time in the unwanted sense. Whether or not *tâtonnement* by means of tickets must take appreciable time is, as I see it, a moot question; but even if it did, the time taken would, by hypothesis, be sterile and hence the whole mechanical adjustment would be as good as "timeless." Hence the time profile of *tâtonnement* described on pages 41–45 of Morishima's *Walras' Economics* neither corrects nor amends Walras's theory of *tâtonnement;* it refers to something else, which may be important enough, but which Walras neither had nor wanted to have in his static model.

With the elimination of the entrepreneur, the firm too was *ipso facto* eliminated. In Walras's theory of production, the adjustment of the supplies of both productive services and products to their respective demands (§§ 200–206) was conceived to take place entirely automatically by means of the market mechanism (§ 221). No room was left for firms privately to supersede the market in the direction and coordination of productive resources.[25] In Walras's "equations of production," which depict a state of equilibrium, we look in vain for the mainspring of the firm's activities, namely profits in the sense of *bénéfices*. As we have seen, *bénéfices* can arise only in the course of the emergence *(établissement)* of equilibrium via a *tâtonnement* process (§§ 208–20); but once a self-sustaining state of equilibrium has been reached, all *bénéfices* vanish. That a state of equilibrium arrived at in this way implied the absence of

[23] See Walras (1874 . . .), p. VIII of the fourth and subsequent editions; p. 37 of the English translation.
[24] Walras (1874 . . .), pp. 582–83 of the English translation: Collation Note [8] to Lesson 20.
[25] *Cf.,* Ronald H. Coase (1937). It should be noted in this connection that Walras assumed away all total fixed costs from his formal theory of production, leaving only total variable costs as alone compatible with his assumption of sustainable perfect (i.e., atomistic) competition. See Walras (1874 . . .), third edition, p. 473, *n.* 1 (in *Appendice I*) repeated in subsequent editions and on p. 474, *n.* 1 of the English translation. *Cf.,* G. L. S. Shackle (1977), pp. 25–26.

uninsurable risk, Walras was perfectly aware; but he does not appear to have perceived that he was ignoring the transaction costs that would be entailed in the absence of firms—unless the services of land, labor, and capital "technologically" required in the operation of the market mechanism were meant to figure among the "coefficients of production" in the calculation of costs (§ 203).

As the following quotation from Morishima shows, he rightly understands Walras's *bénéfices* (which he calls "excess" or "supernormal profit") to originate in the *tâtonnement* process, but he then assigns to these *bénéfices* a destination that does not fit Walras's model at all. According to Morishima, "In Walras' own model, it is implicitly assumed that the aggregate excess profit (or supernormal profit) which may accrue in a positive or negative amount in the process of establishing an equilibrium is not distributed among individuals, so that the same amount is saved or dissaved by firms" (p. 49). In conformity with this alleged implication and "in order to correct Walras' model so as to fulfil Walras' Law," Morishima enlarges Walras's model to include "the budget equation of the firms" in which the "aggregate excess profit" appear as their savings. Such an enlargement constitutes a misinterpretation rather than a correction of Walras, whose model admitted of no savings other than those made by utility-maximizing individuals.

It would have been a betrayal of the underlying intent of his general equilibrium model for Walras to admit into any part of it a normal distributive share consisting of *bénéfices* or other income that is not obtained in exchange for the productive services of either land or labor or capital on terms established in a perfectly competitive market. Surely it was Walras's intent, which he emphasized in a letter to Launhardt in 1885, that compatibility with "justice" be an overriding requirement of his general equilibrium system,[26] and this, given his philosophy of "justice," would preclude from his system the presence of any income that is not a functional return. The system portrayed by Walras's mathematical model of general equilibrium is rigorously static, with resources, population, tastes, and technology all invariant.

Just as there was no room in Walras's general equilibrium equations for the entrepreneur, the firm, profits (in the sense of *bénéfices*), uninsurable risk, and exogenous transaction costs, so, notwithstanding Morishima's opinion to the contrary, there was no room for growth either. Having mistaken Walras's theory of capital formation (*théorie de la capitalisation*) for a theory of capital accumulation or, as he calls it, "a real growth theory" (pp. 72–74), Morishima feels that the original version is in need of reformulation to make it more realistic and thereby provide

[26] Jaffé (1965), vol. 2, pp. 49–51, Letter 652 of which a pertinent excerpt is cited in English translation in Jaffé (1977), p. 380.

the entrepreneur with a normal participatory function,[27] which had been denied him in Walras's formal theory of production. Morishima claims that his reformulation retains "the essentials of Walras' theory, without any significant revision" and is, consequently, "harmless." Did not Walras himself agree that there was no essential difference between, on the one hand, his formal mathematical model in which it was assumed for theoretical simplicity that capitalists do their saving, not in liquid funds, but in physical capital goods which they hire out in kind on terms arrived at by competitive bidding in the market and, on the other hand, the real world in which entrepreneurs purchase physical capital goods as they see fit with funds borrowed from capitalists who accumulate their savings in money (§ 235)? Morishima is convinced that a model, constructed by use of more advanced analytical techniques than Walras had at his command, in which investment decisions are separated from saving decisions, entails no substantive misrepresentations of Walras's original conception. Once revised in this way, Walras's model can be brought historically within hailing distance of Keynes's model (p. 82).

When one reads the *Eléments* with "the full story of Walras' economics" in mind, Morishima's attempt to harmonize Walras's theoretical construct with reality can only lead to a distortion of the original general equilibrium model. Walras conceived all economic activities, including capital formation, solely as exchange phenomena,[28] all governed by the same fundamental laws of exchange and all motivated by the pursuit of maximum psychological satisfaction subject to budget and, where relevant, technological constraints. The whole system is everywhere pervaded by Walras's utility theory of exchange, which is not, as Morishima likes to think, a mere "hors d'oeuvre" served only to whet the appetite for such "main dishes: [as] the theory of capital formation and credit and the theory of circulation and money" (p. 70).

[27] The participatory entrepreneur is not the only gratuitous invention in Morishima's exposition of Walras's general equilibrium theory. Another is that of the "auctioneer" (p. 19). In fact, there is no "auctioneer" anywhere in the *Eléments*. It is an invention after the fact made in later expositions and extrapolations of the original model. When done with extreme caution, the introduction of a "Walrasian auctioneer" may be harmless enough in an exposition of Walras's theory of *tâtonnement*, but only if the role of the "auctioneer" is restricted to that of a pre-programmed mechanical device, which does nothing more than raise or lower initially quoted prices until positive or negative excess demands vanish everywhere. In the *Eléments* prices are said to be "cried," but Walras did not specify by whom they are "cried." It seems reasonable, therefore, to render Walras's *"crié"* by "quoted" or "called," the quoting or calling being done by anyone: the prospective seller, the prospective buyer, or third parties, say brokers or an "auctioneer." It may well be an "auctioneer," but as Walras conceived the adjustment process, it is the collective response to price by all the market participants, in other words, by the market acting like a vast computer, that does the adjusting automatically. *Cf.*, Walras (1874), p. 16 of the 1883 version, where Walras himself likened the equilibrating mechanism of the market to that of a *calculateur*, literally a computer, albeit pre-electronic.

[28] See Walras (1874...), pp. XIV–XV of the fourth and subsequent editions, pp. 43–44 of the English translation.

The constrained utility maximization principle is as vital to Walras's theories of capital and money (Lessons 26, 27, and 29 of the *Eléments*), as to his theories of pure exchange and production. The consistency of the entire system was then so defined by Walras as to render all exchange decisions not only internally compatible one with another, but also externally compatible with his ideal of "commutative justice"—a far cry from the actual world.

To avoid misapprehending the intended significance of Walras's theories of capital and money, it is not sufficient to view these theories as integral parts of the general equilibrium model (p. 4); it is no less important to take careful account of the juncture at which Walras introduced each of these theories in the course of constructing the comprehensive model. The construction of the rising edifice proceeded methodically by stages: first the stage of pure exchange theory, then that of production theory, then that of the theory of capital formation and credit, and finally that of monetary theory including circulation. Each stage after the first started from structures (solutions) completed in the previous stage or stages and at no point was allowed to incorporate features of a subsequent stage.

Thus at the third stage labeled "capital formation and credit," as at the two previous stages, all prices were reckoned in *numéraire*, since money was not to be introduced until the fourth stage. To remain in strict conformity with the statical assumption underlying his general equilibrium model, Walras continued to postulate constant technical coefficients of production and, more importantly, invariant stocks of capital goods even at the capital formation stage. The new feature he added to the edifice at the third stage was the theory of the determination of the prices of "capital goods proper," i.e., of capital other than landed and human capital, which either cannot be produced at all or are not wholly produced in consideration of price and cost of production. Only "capital goods proper" (hereafter called simply capital goods) were treated as a potentially variable factor in the equations of capital formation.

The whole purpose of acquiring and maintaining a capital good, which has no utility of its own, is to enjoy the net income it yields. With current techniques of production assumed constant, no allowance need be made for obsolescence. On the other hand, the normal susceptibility of capital goods to wear and tear and to accidental destruction cannot be ignored. To maintain a given stock of capital goods in a state of uninterrupted efficiency, provision for depreciation and insurance, which depends on the durability and exposure to accident of each capital item, is usually included in the gross price charged for the service of the item. The net price per unit of capital service is thus calculated by deducting from the gross price the share of the depreciation charge and insurance premium imputable to the corresponding unit of service. The price, then, which a buyer is willing to pay for a capital good depends upon the net income it yields and may yield in perpetuity if fully maintained and insured.[29] The ratio of the net income to the price of a capital good constitutes its rate of net income. In view of the inherent relationship between the prices of capital goods and their net incomes, the determination of equilibrium prices of capital goods is contingent on the determination of the equilibrium rate of net income. Hence Walras's conditions of equilibrium in perfectly competitive markets for capital goods included: not only (1) equality between the quantity demanded and the quantity supplied of each and every capital good, and (2) equality between the price per unit of each capital good and its cost of production; but also (3) uniformity in the rate of net income derived from all capital goods of every kind.

This, however, was not all. Walras contended that in an established static economy where all services are readily marketable, there is no incentive to trade in the capital goods themselves and consequently there is no possibility of establishing an equilibrium market price for such goods so long as the economy remains stationary (§§ 234 and 269). It is only when decisions are taken that are destined to result in an increase in the total quantity of capital goods, i.e., only in a progressively oriented economy, that a market for new capital goods can be envisaged to determine their prices in *numéraire*. An economy on the verge of expansion implies that some, if not all, individuals in the economy, besides providing for the maintenance of the capital goods they already have, are considering a sufficient reduction in their current expenditures on consumers' goods to have enough savings left over for a

---

[29] Walras's assumptions underlying the depreciation charges included in his equations of capital formation are far from clear. He wrote textually: " . . . we need only suppose that a sum proportional to the price of a capital good is deducted from its annual income as required either in order to maintain the capital good continuously as it was when new or [alternatively] to replace the capital good when it becomes useless" (§ 232; my translation). Robert Kuenne and apparently Morishima too (p. 75) interpret the second alternative to imply "the building up of reserve balances for future replacement" (Kuenne, 1954, p. 343; *cf.* Kuenne, 1963, pp. 227–28). True, but only if the above passage is taken out of context. Walras's definition and description of the depreciation of capital appeared in his theory of capital formation, which preceded his theory of money and therefore could not, at that juncture, refer to "the building up of reserve balances," since money was still out of the picture. In its own context the above quoted passage can only mean that Walras supposed either that the repair and replacement of parts of a capital good take place continuously without interruption of its operation at prime efficiency throughout the year, or alternatively, that a given capital good is such that it completely collapses at one fell stroke on turning out its annual product and is then immediately replaced from an existing actuarially determined stock of capital goods kept at the needed level out of gross proceeds from the sale of the product.

desired acquisition of additional capital goods in order to increase their aggregate net incomes. Consequently, besides the three conditions of equilibrium in capital formation above enumerated, there is the further condition (on a macroeconomic scale) that the value in *numéraire* of aggregate net savings (i.e., the value of the goods and services that would otherwise be directly consumed) be equal to the aggregate value in *numéraire* of the additional new capital goods to be produced.

From stage to stage, Walras's model reveals its austerely abstract character ever more starkly. This was undoubtedly deliberate, in line with Hicks's recent remark that "effective theories . . . cannot afford to bother about difficulties which are not important for the problem at hand" (1976, p. 140). But to judge the effectiveness of a theory it is necessary to identify "the problem at hand," which, in the case of Walras's *Eléments*, was to formulate a static model of "commutative justice" within a system of interdependent market decisions rather than construct a model of the operation of real markets.

As it did not serve Walras's purpose, he deliberately and explicitly left the flow of time out of account (assuming, for example, all production to be instantaneous), and, with time, he quite intentionally dismissed from his model considerations of uncertainty, expectation, changes in technological data, changes in resources, changes in population, and cyclical fluctuations. Since capital formation, once carried out, entails dynamic changes in the data, Walras confined his attention to decisions made at a given moment of time, without following up the consequences of the decisions. In his own words found at the close of § 251 of the *Eléments:* "Thus equilibrium in capital formation will first be established in principle. Then it will be established effectively by the reciprocal exchange between savings to be accumulated and new capital goods to be supplied *within a given period of time,* during which *no change in the date is allowed.* Although the economy is becoming *progressive,* it remains [for the time being] *static* because of the fact that the new capital goods play no part in the economy until later in a period subsequent to the one under consideration" (Walras's italics).

The crux of the matter is revealed in the words, "to be accumulated" (*à amasser*) and "to be supplied" (*à livrer*) in the above passage. These expressions and the definition of the symbols D_k', $D_{k'}'$, $D_{k''}'$ . . . Walras used in his "solution of the equations of capital formation" to designate quantities of new capital goods "to be manufactured" (*quantités à fabriquer*) (§ 252) clearly mark off Walras's theory of capital formation from theories of capital accumulation or growth. It is, therefore, not "harmless" or consistent with "the spirit of Walras" to regard Walras's *théorie de la capitalisation* as a "real growth theory," which is only in need of reformulation to make it work, as Morishima supposes Walras intended (p. 82).[30]

Walras was very much aware of the degree of abstraction from the real world that he allowed himself in his theory of capital formation. This is clear from the following: "In reality, only land and personal faculties are always hired in kind; capital proper is usually hired in the form of money in the market for services. The capitalist accumulates his savings in money and lends his money to the entrepreneur who, at the expiration of the loan, repays the money. This operation is known as *credit*. Hence, the demand for new capital goods comes from entrepreneurs who manufacture products and not from capitalists who create savings. Clearly, from the theoretical point of view it is immaterial to the capitalist and to the entrepreneur whether what the one lends and the other borrows is the capital good itself, new or old, or the price of this capital good in the form of money. It is only from the point of view of practical convenience that the latter arrangement is distinctly preferable to the former" (§ 235).

Actually the capital formation feature of Walras's general equilibrium model was designed entirely in real terms;[31] and though Part V of the *Eléments* was entitled, "Theory of Capital Formation and Credit," financial credit played a very insubstantial role in the theory—as insubstantial as the grin of the Cheshire Cat. Along with credit, securities (including bonds) and all the documentary paraphernalia of the businessman's "financial market" were explained away for theoretical purposes in a passage in § 255 of the *Eléments,* which ends as follows: " . . . It is clearly seen now that the key to the whole theory of capital is to be found in thus eliminating capital loans *in the form of numéraire* so that attention is directed exclusively to the lending of capital *in kind* [Walras's italics]. The market for *numéraire*-capital, however useful in practice, being nothing but a superfoetation in theory, we shall leave it on one side and return to the market for capital goods in order to find out how the equilibrium price of new capital goods is determined."

In the light of this passage, it is surprising that Morishima (p. 72) and other eminent general equilibrium economists, Don D. Patinkin (1965, p. 554, n. 52) and Kuenne (1963, p. 318, n. 53), for example, insist on interpreting Walras's pure theory of capital formation as if it included

---

[30] *Cf.,* William D. Montgomery (1971), in which the author's announced purpose was to *re*interpret Walras in order to "show that the Walrasian system and contemporary models of economic growth . . . share a family resemblance" (p. 378), which is not the same thing as saying, *à la* Morishima, that the Walrasian system constituted an imperfect growth model.

[31] Money being absent at the third stage, there can be no accumulation or borrowing and lending of money, so that saving, though evaluated in *numéraire,* can only take place in *real terms* and is necessarily identical with investment.

bondholding and contemplated bond acquisition as an alternative to holding and acquiring real assets in the form of durable goods. If, indeed, bonds can be allowed to have any place at all in Walras's theory of capital formation, it is only as paper representing the *numéraire* value of loaned income-yielding physical assets.[32] Morishima himself apparently perceives this at one point (pp. 137–38 *cf.*, p. 152), though just before reaching that point he contradicts this correct impression by telling us that "in Walras' system . . . individuals can [sic] save in the form of physical goods, as well"—i.e., as well as saving in the form of bonds (p. 136, *n.* 2). Walras's own words cited above show that he considered representative securities a supererogatory element *(une superfétation théorique)*, which may as well be left aside in any theoretical investigation of the ultimate determinants of the equilibrium prices of capital goods.

Even in § 242 of the *Eléments*, where, in order to round out the rational framework of his "théorie de la capitalisation," Walras introduced a commodity *(E)*, which looks for all the world like a consol, he explicitly defined it as a figment of the theorist's imagination ("il nous suffira d'imaginer une marchandise *(E)* consistant en *revenu net perpétuel . . .*"). If this is overlooked, a misreading of the entire theory results. Commodity *(E)* was not meant to be anything other than a pure abstraction serving to reduce the whole complex of heterogenous capital assets to a homogeneous net-income yielding entity.[33] With a unit of *(E)* virtually defined as a perpetuity yielding the equivalent of one unit of *numéraire* per annum

[32] The "promissory notes" that Kuenne (1959, pp. 121–23, and 1961, pp. 98–99) regards as virtually contained in Walras's monetary equations could only be there if they fell, implicitly or explicitly, into the category of paper representatives of income-yielding physical assets rather than of the money in terms of which the notes are denominated. Kuenne, however, argues that the presence of $o_u p_u$, on the income side of Walras's budget equation in § 275 must be construed to imply the presence of "promissory notes" for which a separate market is bound to exist in the system. At the same time, when due consideration is given to the fact that in the same § 275 and in Walras's "solution of the equations of circulation and money" (Lesson 30) each and every unit of money held in cash balances is assumed to be earmarked in lieu of a monetary unit's worth of a specified type of circulating or fixed capital, then it is seen that the "promissory notes" that Kuenne reads into Walras's model could hardly be anything else than representatives of non-monetary assets. Only if Walras had allowed money itself to be an autonomous type of circulating or fixed capital independent of other types, would trading in "promissory notes" have the place Kuenne assigns to it in Walras's model as an alternative to trading in real assets. While fully acknowledging the practice of independent trading in commercial paper and securities in the real world, Walras deliberately kept it out of his theoretical model in an effort to probe the deeper reality in economic relationships that, as he saw it, underlies appearances (§ 255).

[33] As Kuenne so well describes it: "By means of these constructions relating to commodity *(E)*, Walras was able under stationary conditions to reduce all capital goods to varying amounts of a homogeneous good on the basis of their earning power, since only this last quality is of importance in the consumer's decisions to invest or disinvest in them" (1963, p. 207).

forever,[34] Walras equated the *number, q_e,* of such imaginary perpetuities which an individual theoretically possesses to the *numéraire* measure of his *total* net income derived annually not only from his "capital goods proper," but from his landed-capital and human capital as well, as in his equation:

$$q_e = q_i p_i + \ldots + q_p \pi_p + \ldots + q_k \pi_k$$
$$+ q_{k'} \pi_{k'} + q_{k''} \pi_{k''} + \ldots,$$

where the right hand side is the sum in *numéraire* of the individual's net incomes derived from his several assets symbolized type by type. The *numéraire* price of a unit of *(E)* being defined as the reciprocal of the rate of net income, the equilibrium rate is such as to equate the *numéraire* value of the aggregate net quantity of perpetual annuity shares demanded in the economy to the *numéraire* value of all net savings, whether in the form of marketable or nonmarketable assets, aggregated over all individuals in the economy.[35] Obviously, it is a mistake to consider Walras's perpetuities as negotiable instruments in the usual realistic sense. In Walras's static model from which all transfer payments are excluded, securities, if they have any place at all, cannot be viewed as anything but a veil.

Money, however, was more than a veil in the Walras general equilibrium model, as is seen in the fourth stage where the overall theoretical edifice was completed.

Walras's aim in designing his pure theory of circulation and money was to construct a capstone that would fit neatly onto his still unfinished edifice without destroying its essential character. At this culminating stage, he explicitly declared his intention to introduce circulating capital and money "without abandoning the *static* point of view while taking a position as close as possible to the *dynamic* point of view" (§272, Walras's italics). This can only mean that he intended to complete the building of his general equilibrium model on unmitigated static principles. No changes that are inherent in the passage of time, none of the uncertainties and unpredictable fluctuations, and none of the speculative expectations growing out of irremediable ignorance of the future are admissible within the bounds of "the static point of view." In that case, what place could Walras possibly find for money considered as furnishing not only a unit of account and a medium of exchange but also a store of value against unforeseeable eventualities? Money without a store of

---

[34] *Cf.,* Walras (1874 . . .), English translation, p. 531: Translator's Note (9) to Lesson 23.

[35] Walras (1874 . . .), English translation, p. 531: Translator's Note (11) to Lesson 23.

value function to perform would be emasculated and deprived of its *raison d'être.*[36]

Walras, to be sure, understood the difficulty of his undertaking and perceived the need for a device, if one could be found, to overcome it. In the preface to the fourth edition of the *Eléments,* he wrote: "We shall see in this fourth edition how the inclusion of 'the desired cash balance' [*l'encaisse désirée'*] made it possible for me to state and solve the problem [of circulation and money] *within this static framework* [my italics] on exactly the same terms and in precisely the same way as I solved the preceding problems [of exchange, production and capital formation.]"[37]

How, exactly, did Walras go about making a place for money in a model characterized by decision-taking under certainty? Indeed, it has been pointed out, for example by J. Hirshleifer, that in a model without uncertainty where "market-clearing prices [are established at no transaction cost and] exist for all commodities..., all commodities are equally and perfectly 'liquid'" (1972, p. 136). Walras's way out of the difficulty was to assimilate money with "circulating capital," i.e., capital that is immediately used up or alienated when it is used at all, except in the performance of a technologically indispensable stand-by function. It is in this guise that money appears in his overall system of equations; but his verbal explanation was so sparse that it has still left many an acute analyst puzzled and wondering, "Why money?" To answer this question in terms of Walras's theory, I propose to flesh out his skeletal exposition while sticking as closely as possible to his fundamental assumption of a sustainable static state from which all uncertainty is absent in the large and in the small.

To that end, I turn to what I have called the technologically indispensable stand-by function of circulating capital. If, in the production process, the inflow of raw materials and intermediate products could be perfectly synchronized with the outflow of final output, there would be no need for a stand-by function of circulating capital. If, on the other hand, the best technology practicable makes such synchronization impossible, then in order to adjust the rate of output of final products to presumably foreknown market requirements, somewhere along the

[36] No one need hold money in significant quantity to perform its other functions, since any thing or combination of things having positive value in exchange could serve just as well as *numéraire* and an appropriately devised check-off system could take care of current transactions; but to perform the store-of-value function, money under normal circumstances (as long as its own purchasing power remains fairly stable) serves better than anything else either to cope with unfavorable contingencies or to take full and immediate advantage of favorable contingencies that may arise in the unforeseeable future. For a fuller discussion of the place of money in a stationary economy and for a survey of the literature on the issue, see Kuenne (1963, pp. 291–305); Robert W. Clower and Peter W. Howitt (1978, pp. 453 and 457–64); and Paul Davidson (1977, pp. 542–43 and 560). *Cf.,* Walras (1874 . . .), English translation, p. 542, Translator's Note [2] to Lesson 29.

[37] Walras (1874 . . .), p. 42 of the English translation.

various pipelines feeding the production process, there must be bins, tanks, refrigerators, etc. holding some of the raw materials and intermediate products that come in more lumpily until trickling ingredients catch up. These technologically determined stand-by stores perform what Walras called a "service d'approvisionnement," which I have translated as "service of availability"—not against uncertainty, but in conformity with a perfectly known and perfectly predictable production function. Analogously, in the consumption process, for intractable physiological and technological reasons, the flow of products to the consumer's hands is rarely synchronized with the flow of these products from hand to mouth, so to speak. Hence consumers' goods, even nondurable consumers goods, have to be accommodated in larders, freezers, cupboards, wardrobes, etc. in quantities that the assumed perfectly known and perfectly predictable time pattern of consumption makes necessary. Now since all the circulating capital performing services of availability represents an investment that cannot be undertaken except at an opportunity cost, services of availability are not free goods. Decisions to invest in technologically necessary stores of circulating capital are made in direct and indirect competition with decisions to invest in other sorts of capital, so that at equilibrium, in an ideally perfect market system, the rate of net yield is the same for the above defined necessary stores of circulating capital as for fixed capital. Within the all-comprehensive model, each particular service of availability, measured in one of its dimensions by the time during which it must be used, enters as a technical coefficient in the production function, and its price appears among the items in the cost of production equations. Moreover, at equilibrium the prices of the several services of availability are such as to equate the quantity demanded of each of them to the quantity offered.[38]

What has this to do with money? As it turns out, it has everything to do with money in Walras's scheme of things because there money was taken to be a form of circulating capital, having the same *raison d'être* and governed by the same principles as circulating capital.

To see how this can be so, we need only suppose the economy to be an exclusively spot economy, where everything is paid for, cash-on-delivery.[39] For technological reasons already described above, incoming deliveries to a person or firm cannot always be synchronized with

---

[38] Even under the assumption that all technical coefficients are fixed, equilibration can be effected by changes in the product mix as demand shifts from products requiring more (or less) than open "services of availability" to those requiring less (or more) of these services in their fabrication.

[39] Kuenne also perceives that " . . . in Walras' models all delivery dates and quantities are contract certain, and payments for all goods and services are made at the time of delivery" (1963, p. 316).

outgoing deliveries by the same person or firm, though the exact dates of these deliveries in each direction are specified and precisely known in advance. How then can everyone always be ready to pay cash-on-delivery even where every prospect is sure? Some, whose receipts antedate expenditures, will have cash balances not immediately required, while others, whose expenditures antedate their receipts, can only fulfill their obligations by borrowing cash balances from those who have a temporary surplus of cash. However that may be, under our assumptions cash balances will always have a role to play in the normal course of even perfectly predictable transactions. They are, indeed, necessary for the smooth running of the postulated static economy.

Like stores of circulating capital and for the selfsame reasons, stores of cash are required and have to be decided upon. It is to the *ex ante* quantity demanded of cash that Walras gave the name of *l'encaisse désirée*. It is generally overlooked that the adjective *désirée* in this term is no less important than the noun *encaisse* for an understanding of Walras's theory of money. The adjunct *désirée* differentiates Walras's *desired* cash balance theory from cash balance theories pure and simple. It preserved Walras's "timeless" model from dynamic intrusions that would have been alien to his static conception of general equilibrium. It made it possible for Walras fully to integrate the monetary complement of his general equilibrium edifice with the rest. By deriving the demand for cash balances from the same principles that he invoked in deriving the demand for everything else, he avoided dichotomizing his system.

Yet nowhere in Morishima (1977), not even in chapter 9 entitled "General Equilibrium with *encaisse désirée*," have I discerned any hint of the *ex ante* implications lurking in the adjective *désirée*. Where chapter 9 mentions the "high degree of substitutability" implicit in Walras's theory of inventory in money (p. 143), the obvious reason for this inherent property, namely that Walras's theory was confined to the decision stage, escapes notice. Morishima interprets Walras's theory of money as a cash balance theory *tout court*, and not surprisingly finds it "impossible or absurd . . . to reproduce it in its original form" (p. 125). Morishima's corrections and alterations of the theory in chapter 9 render it incontestably superior to Walras's as a realistic cash balance theory; but the reconstruction is not "in the spirit of [Walras's] *encaisse désirée*" as Morishima claims.

Walras conceived each unit of the desired cash balance to be earmarked and held in lieu of a monetary unit's worth of the specified item of circulating or fixed capital it was destined to purchase. While held until a prearranged date of delivery of the capital, each unit of the desired cash balance was regarded by Walras as rendering the type of service of availability peculiar to the item of capital to be purchased with it. This enabled Walras both to enlarge his set of utility maximization equations by adding to it the utility functions of the several services of availability of the consumers' goods demanded in the form of suitably earmarked money (§ 274), and to count among the productive services demanded the specific services of availability of money rendered in production (§ 276).[40] From these enlarged sets Walras then derived each individual's gross demand for money-to-be-held in exactly the same way he derived the gross demand for any commodity or productive service in his system.[41] Simple aggregation yields the total gross quantity demanded of cash balances which, when confronted with the total gross supply of cash (a supply that would be exogenously given in the case of fiat money), tells us what price (expressed in a *numéraire* other than money) is the equilibrium price of the service of availability of money. Once that price has been determined, the equilibrium price in *numéraire* of money itself can be determined on the assumption of an invariant one-to-one relation between a unit of money and a unit of its service of availability.

The definition of monetary equilibrium is especially tricky because it calls *both* for a price of the service of availability of money at which the quantity of money demanded is equal to the quantity offered or supplied *and* for the compatibility of that price with the market-clearing prices of everything else. Furthermore, equilibrium requires that the rate of interest, i.e., the ratio of the price of the service of availability of a store of money to the amount of money stored, be exactly equal to the rate of net return on capital generally (§ 277).[42]

Walras's strict adherence to the statical hypothesis on which the whole general equilibrium edifice rested led him to relegate his discussion of the "Conditions and Consequences of Economic Progress" to Part VII, toward the end of the *Eléments,* where it was tacked on, along with Part VIII, as a *coda* structurally separate from the preceding self-contained

[40] Walras might have introduced banking and credit operations into his model without either violating its "spirit" or impairing its structure simply by assuming that the services rendered by these operations are required by the technology of production. In such a revised model these services would find a place as input coefficients along with other technical coefficients; and the costs of credit and banking transactions would be considered on the same footing as other costs, including the cost of holding cash balances, in the cost of production equation. *Cf.,* S. C. Tsiang (1966, p. 331) and Lloyd S. Shapley and Martin Shubick (1977, pp. 942–43).

[41] I define "gross demand" as the quantity of a good or service traders desire to possess at a given price of the good or service, in contradistinction to "net demand" designating the quantity of the good or service traders want to acquire, at a given price, in addition to what they happen already to possess of it.

[42] See Walras (1874 . . .), English translation: pp. 545–46, Translator's Notes [15] and [16] to Lesson 29.

pure theory. That Walras meant the preceding Part VI to top off his all-encompassing model of general equilibrium is shown at the very outset of that part by his declaration that he intended his theory of circulation and money "to *complete* the general problem of economic equilibrium [my italics]"—so, at least, I understand his sentence, "Le moment est venu d'introduire ces éléments [the monetary elements] dans le problème général et complet de l'équilibre économique" (§ 272). When he came to the first Lesson of the next Part VII, Walras pointed out in the following passage how fundamentally the "continuous market" he was now introducing departed from his previous model: "Finally, in order to draw closer and closer to reality, we must go so far as to replace our hypothesis of a periodic annual market by that of a continuous market; in other words, we must pass from the static to the dynamic state. . . . [The continuous market] is perpetually tending toward equilibrium without ever actually attaining it because the market has no other way of approaching equilibrium than by groping [*par tâtonnement*] and before the goal is reached, it has to start groping afresh, all the basic data of the problem, such as the initial quantities possessed, the utilities of goods and services, the technical coefficients, the excess of income over consumption, the working capital requirements, etc., having changed in the meantime" (§ 322; my revised translation).[43] Yet Morishima deplores the failure of expositors of Walras's general equilibrium model to incorporate Part VII of the *Eléments* into their account of the model (p. 5). Why should they have done so, since Walras himself furnished a very good reason for not doing it, viz., the abandonment of the statical hypothesis it would entail?

Walras did not insist on keeping his general equilibrium theory static and stringently abstract out of indifference to the real world, just to construct a pretty axiomatic model for the fun of it.[44] On the contrary, as the *obiter dicta* in his other writings and in the *Eléments* (especially in Part I) attest, he was ardently interested in improving the real world. To cope with *his* problems, Walras indulged in a brinkmanship that might well have excited the envy of John Foster Dulles. Up to Part VII of the fourth

[43] In the dynamic context of Part VII, unlike the statical context within which he had analyzed the mechanism of *tâtonnement* (§§ 127–30) as a process analogous to the Gauss-Seidel procedure for solving simultaneous equation systems, Walras now alluded, without analysis, to a very different market adjustment process, which is bound realistically to take time entailing "changes in the data."

[44] It may be noted, in passing, that if Walras's general equilibrium theory was couched in terms of mathematical equalities instead of inequalities such as we find them in modern reformulations of the theory, it was, as Morishima has very well shown (pp. 13–14), not because Walras was unaware of inequalities yielding corner solutions (Walras [1874 . . .] §§ 80 and 89 of fourth and subsequent editions), but it was rather, as I see it, because the admission of inequality solutions would be incompatible with the rest of the model from which profits and losses, i.e., positive and negative receipts not representing a *quid pro quo* in conformity with "justice," were excluded as a matter of principle.

and subsequent editions of the *Eléments,* Walras's formal analysis brought him to the very brink of economic dynamics where, without ever overstepping the brink, he stood tiptoe to report, in digressions that Morishima takes for a "literary model," what he glimpsed beyond. The changes in the structure and organization of the *Eléments* from the first to the last edition[45] bear witness to a long and difficult struggle to achieve formal unification of his comprehensive system, while still keeping his vestigial nontheoretical interests before him and yet within proper bounds. The "purification" of his theory was progressive over the years, but never complete, so that his definitive version reads like a palimpsest with earlier inscriptions imperfectly rubbed out.

Whatever Morishima may say, Parts VII and VIII of the *Eléments* were not meant to be considered an integral part of Walras's general equilibrium edifice. The *coda* was meant rather to serve as a link between his pure statical theory and his applied and "social" theories, which are intrinsically dynamic. It was to show, as it were in anticipation of the later charges of sterility of his general equilibrium model, how the relations analyzed in the static theory could be used to elucidate such dynamic tendencies as the rise in land-rent and the fall in the rate of profit in an expanding economy (§§ 332–34). That is what makes it so irresistably tempting to extrapolate Walras's model and to imagine that the original model itself contained dynamic analyses. The formal model, however, remained strictly a model of mutually compatible decisions without any exploration in depth of the consequences of these decisions once carried out.

It is because our contemporary critics of Walras, our Patinkins, our Kuennes, our Garegnanis, our Morishimas, proceed blissfully unmindful of Walras's primary aim in creating his general equilibrium model that I suspect they misunderstand it and subject it to reformulations, emendations, and corrections that are beside the point—I mean, of course, the point the historian of economics is obliged by his craft to make.

REFERENCES

Allix, E. "La rivalité entre la propriété foncière et la fortune mobilière sous la Révolution," *Revue d'histoire économique et sociale,* 1913, *6,* pp. 297–348.
Baumol, William J. "Entrepreneurship in Economic Theory," *Amer. Econ. Rev.,* May 1968, *58*(2), pp. 64–71.

[45] See, for example, Walras (1874 . . .), English translation: pp. 573–74, Collation Note [h] to Lesson 11; pp. 574–75, Collation Note [a] to Lesson 12; p. 581, Collation Note [a] to Lesson 17; p. 586, Collation Note [a] to Part V; p. 587, Collation Note [h] to Lesson 23; p. 589, Collation Note [a] to Lesson 24; pp. 590–93, Collation Note [a] to Lesson 25; pp. 595–96, Collation Note [a] to Lesson 26; pp. 600–602, Collation Note [a] to Part VI; and p. 605, Collation Note [a] to Lesson 35.

Boson, Marcel. *Léon Walras, Fondateur de la Politique Economique Scientifique.* Paris: Librairie générale de droit et de jurisprudence, 1951.

Bousquet, G.-H. "L'autobibliographie inédite de Léon Walras," *Rev. Economique,* March 1964, *15*(2), pp. 295–304.

Clower, Robert W. and Howitt, Peter W. "The Transactions Theory of the Demand for Money: A Reconsideration," *J. Polit. Econ.,* June 1978, *86*(3), pp. 449–66.

Coase, Ronald H. "The Nature of the Firm," *Economica, N.S.,* Nov. 1937, *4,* pp. 386–405; reprinted in *Readings in price theory,* Homewood, Ill.: Irwin for the American Economic Association, 1952, pp. 331–51.

Cootner, Paul H. "Speculation, Hedging and Arbitrage," in *International Encyclopedia of the Social Sciences.* Vol. 15. Edited by DAVID S. SILLS. New York: Macmillan, Free Press, 1968, pp. 117–21.

Cournot, A. A. *Revue sommaire des doctrines économiques.* Paris: Hachette, 1877; reprinted, New York: Kelley, 1968.

Davidson, Paul. "Money and General Equilibrium," *Econ. Appl.,* 1977, *30*(4), pp. 541–63.

De Rosa, G., ed. *Vilfredo Pareto, Lettere a Maffeo Pantaleoni.* 3 vols. Rome: Banca Nazionale del Lavoro, 1960.

Duvillier, A. *Hommes et idéologies de 1840.* Paris: Rivière, 1956.

Hicks, J.R. "Léon Walras," *Econometrica,* Oct. 1934, *2,* pp. 338–48.

Hicks, J.R. "Some Questions of Time in Economics," in *Evolution, welfare and time in economics: Essays in honor of Nicholas Georgescu-Roegen.* Edited by ANTHONY M. TANG, FRED M. WESTFIELD, AND JAMES S. WORLEY. Lexington, Mass.: Heath, Lexington Books, 1976, pp. 135–51.

Hirshleifer, Jack. "Liquidity, Uncertainty, and the Accumulation of Information," in *Uncertainty and expectations in economics: Essays in honour of G. L. S. Shackle.* Edited by C. F. CARTER AND J. L. FORD. Oxford: Blackwell, 1972, pp. 136–47.

Jaffé, William, ed. *Correspondence of Léon Walras and related papers.* 3 vols. Amsterdam: North-Holland for Royal Netherlands Academy of Sciences and Letters, 1965.

Jaffé, William. "Léon Walras: An Economic Adviser *manqué," Econ. J.,* Dec. 1975, *85*(340), pp. 810–23.

Jaffé, William. "The Normative Bias of the Walrasian Model: Walras versus Gossen," *Quart. J. Econ.,* August 1977, *91*(364), pp. 371–87.

Jaffé, William. "Review of Michio Morishima's *Walras' Economics: A Pure Theory of Capital and Money," Econ. J.,* Sept. 1978, *88*(351), pp. 574–76.

Kirzner, Israel M. *Competition and entrepreneurship.* Chicago: Chicago University Press, 1973.

Kirzner, Israel M. "The Entrepreneurial Role in Menger's System," *Atlantic Econ. J.,* Sept. 1978, *6*(3), pp. 31–45.

Knight, Frank H. *Risk, uncertainty and profit.* Boston: Houghton Mifflin, 1921; reprinted by the London School of Economics and Political Science, No. 16 in Series of Reprints of Scarce Tracts in Economic and Political Science, 1933.

Kuenne, Robert E. "Walras, Leontief, and the Interdependence of Economic Activities," *Quart. J. Econ.,* August 1954, *68*(272), pp. 323–54.

Kuenne, Robert E. "Patinkin on Neo-classical Monetary Theory: A Critique in

Walrasian Specifics," *Southern Econ. J.*, Oct. 1959, *26*, pp. 119–24.

Kuenne, Robert E. "The Walrasian Theory of Money: An Interpretation and a Reconstruction," *Metroeconomica*, August 1961, *13*, pp. 94–105.

Kuenne, Robert E. *The theory of general economic equilibrium.* Princeton: Princeton University Press, 1963.

Leibenstein, Harvey. "Entrepreneurship and Development," *Amer. Econ. Rev.*, May 1968, *58*(2), pp. 72–83.

Marshall, Alfred. *Principles of economics.* Eighth edition. London: Macmillan, 1920.

Montgomery, William D. "An Interpretation of Walras' Theory of Capital as a Model of Economic Growth," *Hist. Polit. Econ.*, Fall 1971, *3*(2), pp. 278–97.

Morishima, Michio. *The economic theory of modern society.* Translated by D. W. Anthony. Cambridge and New York: Cambridge University Press, 1976.

Morishima, Michio. *Walras' economics: A pure theory of capital and money.* Cambridge and New York: Cambridge University Press, 1977.

Oulès, F., ed. *L'Ecole de Lausanne: Textes Choisis de L. Walras et V. Pareto.* Paris: Dalloz, 1950.

Pareto, Vilfredo. *The mind and society, A treatise on general sociology.* 4 vols. Edited by Arthur Livingston. Translation of *Trattato di sociologia generale* (1916), by Andrew Bongiorno and Arthur Livingston. New York: Harcourt, Brace, 1935.

Patinkin, Don. *Money, interest and prices.* Second edition. New York: Harper & Row, 1965.

"Paul." See below, Walras, L. ["Paul," pseud.] (1878).

Schumpeter, Joseph A. "Marie Ésprit Léon Walras 1834–1910," *Z. Volkswirtschaft, Sozialpolitik, Verwaltung,* 1910, *19*, pp. 397–402; republished in English translation in *Ten great economists from Marx to Keynes.* By Joseph A. Schumpeter. New York: Oxford University Press, 1951, pp. 74–79.

Schumpeter, Joseph A. *History of economic analysis.* New York: Oxford University Press, 1954.

Sensini, Guido, ed. *Correspondenza di Vilfredo Pareto.* Padua: Cedam, 1948.

Shackle, G. L. S. "New Tracks for Economic Theory 1926–1939," in *Modern economic thought.* Edited by Sidney Weintraub. Philadelphia: University of Pennsylvania Press, 1977, pp. 23–37.

Shapley, Lloyd S. and Shubik, Martin. "Trade Using One Commodity as a Means of Payment," *J. Polit. Econ.*, Oct. 1977, *85* (5), pp. 937–68.

Stigler, George J. "Textual Exegesis as a Scientific Problem," *Economica, N.S.*, Nov. 1965, *32*(128), pp. 447–50.

Tsiang, S. C. "Walras' Law, Say's Law and Liquidity Preference in General Equilibrium Analysis," *Inter. Econ. Rev.*, Sept. 1966, *7*, pp. 329–45.

Walras, Léon. *L'économie politique et la justice.* Paris: Librairie de Guillaumin, 1860.

Walras, Léon. "Principe d'une théorie mathématique de l'échange." *Séances et travaux de l'Académie des Sciences morales et politiques,* vol. 101 of the Collection, 33rd Year of New Series, Part I (Jan. 1874), pp. 97–116; republished with minor revisions in *Théorie mathématique de la richesse sociale,* Lausanne: Corbaz, 1883, pp. 7–25.

Walras, Léon. *Eléments d'économie politique pure.* First edition (in two installments). Lausanne: Corbaz, 1874–77; Second edition, Lausanne: Rouge, 1889; Third edition, Lausanne: Rouge, 1896; Fourth edition, Lausanne: Rouge, 1900; Definitive edition (published posthumously), Lausanne: Rouge, 1926; reprinted, Paris: Pichon and Durand-Auzias, 1952; English translation, *Elements of pure economics,* translated from the definitive edition by William Jaffé, London: Allen & Unwin; Homewood, Ill.: Irwin, 1954. (Reprint of Economics Classics, New York: Kelley, 1969).

Walras, Léon. ["Paul," pseud.] "Chroniques de la quinzaine," *Gazette de Lausanne,* Jan. 18, 1878–May 18, 1878.

Walras, Léon. *Etudes d'économie sociale (Théorie de la répartition de la richesse sociale).* Lausanne: Rouge, 1896; Second edition, edited by G. Leduc, Lausanne: Rouge; Paris: Pichon and Durand-Auzias, 1936.

Walras, Léon. *Etudes d'économie politique appliquée (Théorie de la production de la richesse sociale).* Lausanne: Rouge; Paris: Pichon, 1898; Second edition, edited by G. Leduc, Lausanne: Rouge, Pichon, 1936.

Walras, Léon. "Ruchonnet et le socialisme scientifique," *Revue socialiste,* July 1909, *50*(295), pp. 577–89.

INDEX

Alembert, J. le Rond d', 102
Allen, R. G. D., 292
American Economic Association, 112
Amstein, Hermann, 76, 83, 90, 118, 275, 277
  marginal productivity and, 204–6
anglophobia, 105–6, 272
annuity shares, perpetual, 146–7, 163–5, 360–1
Antonelli, Etienne, 17 n2, 27, 123, 135
Antonelli, G. B., 88
Aristotle, 104
Arrow, Kenneth, 91
  tâtonnement and, 260
Aulnis de Bourouill, J. d', 26, 79, 81, 106
Aupetit, Albert, 123
Auspitz, Rudolf, 30, 35 n43, 117

Bagiotti, Tullio, 178–9 n7
Barbon, Nicholas, 131
Barone, Enrico, 21, 33, 117, 127, 131, 177–80, 178 n6, 179 n10, 186–204, 187 n16, 189 n20, 192 n27, 195 n33, 195 n34, 196 n36, 197 n41, 200 n45, 201 n48, 202 n51, 207, 208–10, 272, 277
  coefficients of production and, 190
  marginal productivity and, 182–6, 189, 195–6
  socialism and, 282
Baumol, William J., 77 n57, 279, 326, 327
  maximum social utility and, 334
Bentham, Jeremy, 318
Berkeley, George, 295
Berney, Jacques, 194
Bertrand, Joseph, 87–8

Bey, Lambert, 332
bias, normative, 105
bimetallism, 112, 134
Black, R. D. Collison, 318
Bladen, Vincent, 93–4, 98
Blaug, Mark, 307, 311
  marginal revolution and, 311
Boccardo, Gerolamo, 88–9
Böhm-Bawerk, Eugen von, 32, 89–90, 145, 163
Boisguilbert, Pierre le Pesant, Sieur de, 105, 131
Bompaire, F., 123
Bonaparte, Napoleon, 59
bonds, 359–60
Bonnet, Victor, 113–14
Bortkiewicz, Ladislaus von, 28, 30, 34 n43, 89, 106, 122, 170, 192, 192 n26, 208, 208 n68, 214 n8, 215–16, 257 n36
  tâtonnement and, 258–9
Bory-Hollard, E., 24 n23
Boulding, Kenneth, 284
Bourouill, d'Aulnis de, 26, 79–81, 106
Bousquet, Georges, 123
Bowley, Arthur Lyon, 270 n7
Bryan, Jennings, 112
Burlamaqui, Jean Jacques, 103
  value and, 297–8
Buttrick, John, 93, 213

Canard, Nicolas François, 86
Cantillon, Richard, 105, 131
capital
  accumulation of, 148–50
  circulating, 360n, 363–4
  fixed, 360n
  formation of, 7–9, 134, 354–5, 356–7, 359

capital *(cont.)*
  personal, 166-7
capital goods, 31-2
  cost to consumer, 169, 172
  demand for, 143, 144, 153, 161,
    162, 165
  maximum utility of, 159
  net income from, 161, 170, 173
  prices of, 143
capitalist, 350, 359
Carlyle, Thomas, 271 n12
Carmichael, Gershom, 103, 298
Cartesian philosophy, 102-3
Carver, Thomas N., 182, 204
cash balance, 362
Cassel, Gustav, 286 n58, 287 n62
Castelot, E., 57
Chait, Bernard, 176 n1
Chevalier, Michel, 21 n15, 121
Chevreux, Henri, 110
Clark, John Bates, 117, 177 n4, 179,
    182, 196-7, 201, 202-3 n54,
    204, 207-8, 271
classes, social, 344-5
Clower, Robert W., 77 n58
Cohen, Stephen B., 77 n58
complementary goods, 116
Condorcet, Marquis de, 101 n15
Condillac, Etienne Bonnot de, 298,
    299n
Copeland, Michael D. G., 213
Corbaz, Louis, 84
cost
  average, 239
  average, minimized, 188
  fixed, 280-1
Cournot, Antoine A., 18, 20, 22
    n24, 25, 31 n31, 81, 86-7, 117,
    122, 124, 127, 132, 275, 291,
    292, 297, 300
Cousin, Victor, 273

Darimon, Alfred, 111
Darwin, George H., 91
Delaporte, Canon Ives, 108, 124
demand theory, 5-6, 25, 303-4, 314
depreciation, 357n
Descartes, René, 28, 102-3
Destutt de Tracy, A., 42 n23, 296
    n27

Di Marchi, Neil, 79
disequilibrium transactions, 223-4,
    246-7, 332
distribution, 179, 210-11
distributional effects, 331-2
Dobb, Marcel, 99
Dubois, Auguste, 55
Du Mesnil-Marigny, Jules, 23, 80
Dupriez, Léon H., 176 n1
Dupuit, Arsène J. E. J., 82-3, 86,
    302
dynamics, 361, 366-7

Eatwell, John L., 77 n58
economics
  applied, 128
  classification, 5, 23, 96
  conception of, 127-9
  mathematics and, *see* mathematics
  normative, 13-14, 43, 113, 114,
    292n, 330-1, 326, 334, 345,
    348
  positive, 273
  social, 128-9; *see also* economics,
    normative
  statistics and, 28-9
Edgeworth, Francis Y., 4, 27, 30-1,
    32 n38, 34 n43, 83 n21, 170,
    177, 177 n3, 186-7, 189 n20,
    192, 198, 235, 237, 259
  Jevons and, 295
  marginal productivity and, 193,
    194-5
  tâtonnement and, 257-8
Einaudi, Liugi, 200
Einstein, Albert, 129
entrepreneur, 116, 186-8, 180 n10,
    228, 232, 284, 349-52, 354-5
equilibrium
  existence of, 226
  monetary, 365-6
  multiple, 237, 249
  multiple markets, 248-9
equilibrium, general, analysis of, 25,
    131-2
  importance, 285
  purpose, 347
  shortcomings, 279-80, 286-7
  value of, 12-13, 281-2

exchange
 equation of, 62–3, 295, 329
 justice in, 328–9, 330
 theory of, 63–4, 68–72, 228, 290–
  1, 331–2

Ferry, Jules, 50, 122, 133
firm, 353
Fisher, Irving, 33–4, 116–17, 123,
  208 n66
 independent utilities and, 237
Francis Sauveur, 19, 46–7
Frenkel, Angele, 176 n1
Friedman, Milton, 110, 135, 284,
  307 n65
Fourier, François, 27

Ganilh, Charles, 296 n27
Gårdlund, Torsten, 189 n20
Garnier, Germain, 21 n15, 97 n8,
  100
Genovesi, Antonio, 299 n44
Georgescu-Roegen, N., 286, 286
  n59, 319
Giacalone-Monaco, Tommaso, 178–9
  n7
Gide, Charles, 1
Goodwin, Richard M., 175
 tâtonnement and, 260, 262
Gossen, Hermann-Heinrich, 25–6,
  41 n20, 82, 87 n39, 122, 219
  n19, 317
 maximum social utility and, 336–
  40
government
 economic functions of, 49
Grotius, Hugo, 103
Guilbaud, G. T., 165
Guillaumin, Melle F., 79, 81 n12, 97
  n8

Hahn, F. H., *tâtonnement* and, 260
Hayek, Friedrich August von, 29
  n29, 306, 319
Helmholtz, H. von, 103
Hicks, Sir John R., 91, 110, 152,
  211, 219, 237 n32, 249, 261,
  312, 327, 327 n2, 344, 358
 marginal productivity and, 200
Hirschleifer, Jack, 362

Hobson, John A., 117, 182, 201
Hollander, Samuel, 93–4, 294 n19
Horton, S. Dana, 112–13
Hoselitz, Bert, 294 n16
Hutcheson, Francis, 103, 298

income
 net, demand for, 163
 net, perpetual, 360–1
 net, rate of, 143
individualism, 39–41
insurance, 352
interest, 32, 365
Isnard, Achylle-Nicolas, 3, 55, 69–
  74, 132, 278, 300 n47
 biography, 58–9
 capital and interest and, 74–5
 exchange, equation of, 62
 exchange, theory of, 65–7
 Jevons and, 60
 money, 75–6
 numéraire, 75–6
 production theory, 72–3
 Walras's knowledge of, 60–1

Jaffé, William
 biography, 2–3
 essays, contents of, 2–14
Janet, Paul, 50 n46, 62 n4
Jevons, William Stanley, 25–6, 29–
  31, 31 n31, 33, 60–1, 64, 81,
  82, 86–9, 115, 122, 131, 177
  n4, 179, 182, 196 n36, 201, 201
  n48, 257 n36, 288, 289–90,
  292, 294–5, 316, 331
 on exchange, 317–18
 maximum social utility and, 339
Johnson, Harry, 40 n16, 54 n3
Jowett, Benjamin, 273
justice, 39, 43–4, 340, 354
 commutative, 348, 349, 356, 358
 distributive, 348
 philosophy of, 39–40

Keynes, John Maynard, 156, 284
Kornai, Jànos, 91
Knight, Frank H., 352
Kuenne, Robert, 236, 283, 286 n58,
  357 n29, 359, 360 n32, 360
  n33, 363 n39

Lamb, Charles, 272
land
    nationalization of, 38, 40-1, 49,
        113
    single tax on, 42
Lange, Oscar, 139, 159, 286
    socialiam and, 281-2
    tâtonnement and, 259
Langel, Auguste, 87
Laughlin, J. Laurence, 113, 115,
    272 n13
Launhardt, Wilhelm, 91
    maximum social utility and, 335
Laurent, Henri, 18 n3
Laurent, Hermann, 214, 217
Lave, Lester B., 221
law, natural, 43-4, 48, 49-50, 105,
    345
Lebrun, M. Pierre, 176 n1
Leduc, Gaston, 84 n25, 298 n37,
    299 n44
Leontief, Wassily, 123, 282
Leroy-Beaulieu, Paul, 237
Letort, Charles, 86
Levasseur, Emile, 214
Lexis, Wilhelm, 89-90, 286 n58
Lieben, Richard, 30, 35 n43, 117
Louis Philippe, 274

McCulloch, John Ramsey, 296 n27
Mahaim, Ernest, 194
Mailly, Léonide Désirée, 133
Malthus, Thomas R., 21
Mandeville, Bernard, 276
Marget, Arthur, 133, 135, 139
marginalism, 110
    see also productivity, marginal; rev-
        olution, marginal; utility, mar-
        ginal
market, continuous, 366
Marshall, Alfred, 26, 30-1, 78, 110,
    115, 117, 132, 177 n4, 179,
    182, 187, 189 n20, 193-6, 195
    n33, 196 n36, 202-3 n54, 223
    n6, 241-2, 270, 270 n7, 271,
    272, 272 n13, 276, 282 n47,
    284
Marshall, Mary Paley, 95 n5, 272
    n13
Marx, Karl, 47-8, 98, 279, 281, 345

Massias, Nicholas, 296 n27
mathematics, economics and, 27-8,
    29-30, 127 n15, 290-1
Maugin, Gustave, 104
Maxwell, J. C., 103
Meek, Ronald, 99
Ménard, Claude, 347 n10
Menger, Carl, 25, 29, 131, 288, 290,
    292, 294, 306, 316
    disequilibrium and, 320
    exchange and, 319
    mathematics and, 321-2
    value and, 318-22
methodology, 346-7
Metzler, Lloyd A., 237-8
Mill, James, 41 n20
Mill, John Stuart, 20, 34 n43, 79,
    211, 271, 291, 296 n27
Mini, Piero V., 102
Mishan, E. J., 307 n66
monetary policy, 45, 50
    United States and, 111
monetary theory, 133, 283, 284, 361,
    362-5
money, demand for, 365
monopoly, 281
Montemartini, G., 201
Montgomery, W. David, 77 n58
Moore, Henry Ludwell, 18, 20, 33,
    116, 117, 123, 269
Moret, Jacques, 56
Morishima, Michio, 91, 244, 258,
    264, 343-7, 350-2, 357 n29,
    359-60, 364, 366-7
    entrepreneur and, 354-5
    firms and, 354
    four-class society and, 349-50
    investment decisions and, 355
    tâtonnement and, 256, 260-3

Napoleon, Louis, 274
Negishi, Takashi, 235-6, 238
Neisser, Hans, 286 n58
Newman, Peter, 223, 224, 225 n13,
    236, 237 n31, 247
Newton, Isaac, 27, 93, 102, 129
non-*tâtonnement*, 236
numéraire, 21, 139-40, 157, 230-1,
    329, 357, 359
numéraire-capital, 158

Ocagne, P. M. d', 30

Pantaleoni, Maffeo, 26, 180, 196
    n36, 250, 253
Pareto, Vilfredo, 24, 33, 64, 88, 109,
    116–17, 123, 126, 134, 177 n3,
    178–82, 178–9 n7, 179 n8, 186,
    187, 191, 193, 194, 197 n41,
    198–9, 201–3, 202 n51, 237,
    237 n32, 259, 259 n43, 272,
    281, 284, 340, 344
  economics, normative and, 335
  Walras's contribution and, 79
Pascal, B., 349 n14
Patinkin, Don, 123, 221, 226, 239–
    41, 247, 276, 283, 359
  tâtonnement and, 259–60
Perozzo, L., 30
Perroux, François, 123
Petersen, Aleksis, 88
Petty, Sir William, 131
Pfeiffer, Edward, 27
Phelps Brown, E. H., 51
philosophy, social, 43–50
Piccard, Auguste, 206 n62
Piccard, Jean Félix, 206 n62
Piccard, Paul, 77, 81–3, 90, 118,
    206–7 n62, 207 n63, 275, 314–
    15
  demand and, 303–4
Pijadière, Louis Lacour de la, 122
Pirou, Gaëtan, 123
Plato, 39
Poincaré, Henri, 129, 213–19
Poinsot, Louis, 3, 132, 275, 314
price curves, 301
price, uniformity of, 328, 329, 330,
    331
production
  coefficients of, 83, 140, 190–1,
    192
  equations of, 353
  theory of, 9, 83, 140–2, 227–9,
    240–1
  tickets, in theory of, 9, 231–2,
    234–5
productivity, marginal, 7, 117, 140,
    182–6, 188, 277
profits, 21, 116, 331, 350, 354
property, 40

Proudhon, Pierre Joseph, 48 n40,
    114
Pufendorf, Samuel, 103, 298

Quesnay, François, 55, 131

rareté, 21, 100, 296–9, 315
  see also utility, marginal
realism, 346, 348–9
recontracting, 226
Reiter, Stanley, 77 n58
Renard, Georges, 104, 122
Renevier, Louis, 55–6, 58
Renouvier, Charles Bernard, 86
revolution, marginal, 288–9, 311–12
Ricardo, David, 76, 79, 132, 191,
    192 n27, 193, 195, 201 n48,
    291, 296 n27, 298
risk, 352
Rist, Charles, 1, 35, 38 n12
Robbins, Lionel, Lord, 94, 177 n4,
    190, 312
  marginal revolution and, 312
  Smith and, 94
Roth, Charles M., 176 n1
Rouvroy, Claude Henri de, 278
Ruchonnet, Louis, 50, 80, 118

Saint-Simon, Claude-Henri, 128,
    271, 273, 278–9
Sainte-Beuve, Charles Augustin, 124
Sainte-Beuve, Louise Aline de, 124
Samuelson, Paul, 91, 110, 123, 165,
    211, 276
satisfaction, maximum, 326–7
  see also utility, maximum social
savings, 145–6, 148–9, 154–5, 156–
    7, 160, 169–70, 174, 360
Say, Jean Baptiste, 48 n40, 96, 132,
    296 n27, 298, 351, 351 n21
Schlesinger, Karl, 91, 286 n58, 322
Schultz, Henry, 123, 159, 198 n42,
    269
Schumpeter, Joseph, 50, 60, 91, 98,
    109, 131, 177 n4, 213 n1, 274,
    287, 297, 344
  general equilibrium and, 312–13
  Isnard and, 56–8
  utility, marginal and, 312
Secrétan, M. Charles, 81 n15, 118

Senior, Nassau, 299 n44
Shakespeare, William, 288
Shibata, K., 279–81
Sidgwick, Henry, 285
Sismondi, Simonde de, 296 n27
Smith, Adam, 48, 79, 93–4, 95–106,
    132, 146, 241, 296 n27, 298,
    315
  compared to Walras, 103–5
  criticized by Walras, 95
  general equilibrium and, 94
  philosophy of, 101–2
  value theory, 96–9
socialism, scientific, 273
Solow, Robert, 226 n14, 248, 277
Spann, Othmar, 284
Spinedi, Francesco, 178 n5
Sraffa, Piero, 79
stability conditions, 276–7
Stackelberg, H. von, 286 n58
Stark, W., 307
statics, 329, 358, 361, 362, 366
statics and dynamics, 152–3, 160
statistics, and economics, 28–9
Stigler, George J., 177 n4, 200, 202,
    209, 221, 319, 347
  biography, 307
suffrage, universal, 125
Swift, Jonathan, 242

tâtonnement, 9–11, 87–8, 131, 140,
    159, 175, 188, 229, 232, 244,
    252–3, 260, 263, 264, 352–5,
    366
  Adam Smith and, 241–2
  disequilibrium transactions and,
    9–10, 223–6
  emergence of equilibrium, 156,
    353
  endowment effects and, 239
  exchange and, 9–10, 222–6, 245,
    246–54
  failure of theory of, 277–8
  income effects and, 239
  misinterpretations, 221
  as normative scheme, 11, 246
  as process of solving equations,
    11, 250–3
  production and, 9, 227–35, 240,
    245–6, 254–5

  purpose of, 222, 226, 234, 245–6
  real exchange markets and, 247
  realistic, 292n
  received view of, 10
  stability and, 238
  tickets in, 240–1, 255, 353
  timeless, 252–5
  unrealistic, 255
tax, single, 37–8
taxation, 37–8, 40, 42–3
Thakkar, Rasesh B., 213
Theocharis, Rheginos D., 56–7, 76
Thompson, Francis, 129
Thompson, Herbert F., 102
Thünen, Johann, Heinrick von, 86,
    179, 182
time, 116, 358
Turgot, Anne R. J., 57, 131

utility
  cardinal, 217–18
  independent, 237
  marginal, 12, 21–2, 100, 159,
    214, 215–18, 219n, 292, 293–4,
    300–1, 305, 306, 307–8, 312,
    313, 315, 355
  maximization, 356
  maximum social, 333, 334, 335
Uzawa, H., 224 n8, 238, 238 n35,
    238–9

Vacherot, Etienne, 38
Vandendorpe, Adolf, 77 n58
Vaud, Council of State of, 36–7
Vergé, Charles Henri, 272 n13
Viner, Jacob, 94 n1, 99
Volterra, Vito, 103

Wald, Abraham, 91, 322
Walker, Donald A.
  demand theory and, 6, 295n, 304
  disequilibrium transactions and,
    10, 247
  tâtonnement and, 247
Walker, Francis Amasa, 113, 115
Walras, Aline, 17 n2, 84 n25, 108,
    110, 134, 194 n30, 198 n42,
    298 n37
Walras, Auguste, 19–21, 36, 38–40,
    42 n22, 42 n24, 43 n26, 47, 53–

4, 56 n1, 56 n3, 57 n1, 58 n15,
60-2, 76 n50, 99, 103, 124,
125, 127, 132, 273-5, 300, 314,
321, 333, 345
rareté and, 21, 100, 296-9, 315
Smith and, 99
value and, 100, 296-7, 298-9
Walras, Léon, 278
biography, 18-24, 33-5, 108-9,
124-6, 133-5, 273-5
concern with theory, 112, 114,
125-6
contrasted with Marshall, 272-3
influence of, 109-10
productivity, marginal and, 180-1,
198-9, 201-4, 208-10
personality, 276
search for chair, 121-2
value, early work on, 300-1
Whately, Richard, 293 n12
Wicksell, Knut, 145, 189 n10, 208-
10, 209 n69, 328, 332, 334

maximum satisfaction and, 327
maximum social utility and, 327,
333
Wicksteed, Philip H., 31, 116, 117,
177, 177 n3, 177 n4, 179-80,
180 n10, 180 n12, 182 n13,
189-94, 195 n33, 200 n45, 202,
202 n51, 202 n53, 204-5, 206-
11, 208 n66, 209 n69, 253, 253
n27, 254, 277
productivity, marginal and, 178-9
Wieser, Friedrich von, 202-3 n54,
285
Winiarski, Léon, 201 n48
Winterfeld, Ludwig von, 113
Wood, Stuart, 117, 182, 201, 204
Wundt, Wilhelm, 91

Yasui, Takuma, 91

Zeuthen, Frederick, 286 n58, 287
n62